Handbook of
Business Strategy

Editor

WILLIAM D. GUTH

Chairman, Management/Organizational Behavior Area
Graduate School of Business Administration
New York University

Editorial Advisory Board

GEORGE BAKER

Vice-President, Communications
Booz, Allen & Hamilton

IAN MacMILLAN

Professor of Management and Director of Center for
Entrepreneurial Studies, Graduate School of Business
Columbia University

JOHN L. NEUMAN

Managing Director and Manager
Professional Resources Group, Investment Banking
Dean Witter Reynolds, Inc.

WARREN, GORHAM & LAMONT
Boston • New York

Contributing Authors

H. Igor Ansoff
Professor, European Institute for Advanced Studies in Management, Brussels; Professor, Stockholm School of Economics, Stockholm; Distinguished Professor of Management, U.S. International University, San Diego

Karl D. Bays
Chairman and Chief Executive Officer, American Hospital Supply Corporation

Peter Carroll
Vice-President, Hayes-Hill, Inc.

Patrick F. Dolan
Senior Consultant, Peat, Marwick, Mitchell & Co.

James W. Down
Senior Associate, Temple, Barker & Sloane, Inc.

Lionel Fray
Vice-President, Temple, Barker & Sloane, Inc.

Richard A. Furniss, Jr.
Vice-President, Towers, Perrin, Forster & Crosby

David Gaylin
Temple, Barker & Sloane, Inc.

Thomas N. Gladwin
Associate Professor of Management and International Business, Graduate School of Business Administration, New York University

Gus Grammas
Director of Technology and Company Programs, Graduate School of Business, Columbia University

William D. Guth
Chairman, Management/Organizational Behavior Area, Graduate School of Business Administration, New York University

Donald C. Hambrick
Professor, Columbia University

H. Michael Hayes

*Former Manager, Executive Education Operations, General Electric
Company; Professor of Business Policy and Marketing, Graduate School of
Business Administration, University of Colorado at Denver*

Mark R. Hurwich

Principal, Towers, Perrin, Forster & Crosby

S. K. Johnson

Senior Management Consultant, Arthur D. Little, Inc.

Abraham Katz

Director, Planning Systems, IBM Corporation

A. Duncan Kidd

Vice-President, Corporate Development, Amstar Corporation

John C. Kirby, Jr.

*Chairman and Chief Executive Officer, Plant and Field Service
Corporation*

Milton C. Lauenstein

Lauenstein & Associates, Inc.

Peter Lorange

*Professor of Management and Chairman, Department of Management,
The Wharton School, University of Pennsylvania*

Henry C. Lucas, Jr.

*Professor, Graduate School of Business Administration, New York
University*

Sharon Lyster

Senior Manager, Peat, Marwick, Mitchell & Company

Ian C. MacMillan

*Professor of Management and Director of Center for Entrepreneurial
Studies, Graduate School of Business, Columbia University*

James K. Malernee, Jr.

Vice-President, Management Analysis Center, Inc.

Michael A. Moses

*Professor, Graduate School of Business Administration, New York
University*

Ronald G. Quintero

*Senior Manager, Management Consulting Department, Peat, Marwick,
Mitchell & Company; Adjunct Professor, Corporate Finance, New School
for Social Research*

Charles H. Roush, Jr.

Vice-President, Management Analysis Center, Inc.

Sidney Schoeffler
> *Founding Director, The Strategic Planning Institute*

David C. Shanks
> *Arthur D. Little, Inc.*

Howard H. Stevenson
> *Sarofin-Rock Professor of Business Administration, Harvard University;
> Former Vice-President for Finance and Administration, Pretco Corporation*

Jon A. Turner
> *Assistant Professor, Computer Applications and Information Systems Area,
> Graduate School of Business Administration, New York University*

Ian Wilson
> *Senior Management Consultant, SRI International*

Robert G. Wilson
> *Arthur D. Little, Inc.*

Preface

THE FIELD OF STRATEGIC MANAGEMENT has developed rapidly in the past decade and a half. In this period, strategic planning—the central element of strategic management—has been installed as a formal management process in most large companies and in many medium-size and smaller companies. Experience with these formal strategic planning processes has led to increased managerial interest in the development of analytic tools and knowledge to help in the formulation of sound plans. In addition, experience with these formal processes has led to increased managerial interest in understanding how to manage other elements of the organization in relation to them. This increased interest stems from a recognition that quality in both the formulation and implementation of strategic plans is significantly influenced by the structure, compensation and incentive systems, information systems, management development systems, culture, and leadership styles of key managers in the organization.

The management consulting community and the academic community in major business schools throughout the world have both stimulated and responded to this increased managerial interest in the field of strategic management. The management consulting community has developed both new knowledge in the field from its own research efforts and reflections on its experience in helping managers adapt their organizations to changing environments, and new techniques in the field from its experience in translating existing knowledge into practical application. The academic community in the major business schools has developed new knowledge from research on the key variables and the relationships between them that affect the short-run and longer-run performance of the company, and from research leading to the development of new and more powerful analytic tools to help in the formulation and evaluation of strategic alternatives.

Managers committed to effective strategic management of their firms also have developed, of course, knowledge of what works and does not work for them in strategic management from their own unique experience. The degree to which this knowledge can be generalized and adapted by other managers in other companies is always something of a problem, but certainly much of the knowledge is indeed useful in widely different circumstances.

The purpose of this handbook is to provide a comprehensive reference on the state of the knowledge and practice of strategic management. To achieve comprehensiveness, given that developments in the field have come from the academic, management consulting, and management communities, the book is organized around an overall framework comprising seven major sections that capture the contributions of these communities. Contributing authors represent all three communities. They were recruited on the basis of our knowledge of their current research and experience in the field, and thus of their particular potential to contribute to a specific part of the overall framework.

To achieve greater usability, we asked each author to write a "stand alone" chapter—that is, a chapter that does not require that the reader who is generally familiar with the field consult previous or succeeding chapters. This allows better access to the current state of knowledge and practice in particular subject areas of the field of strategic management. For users who are unfamiliar with the field, the overall framework presents the material in a cumulative sequence, in which earlier chapters should be read before later chapters.

The handbook comprises twenty-eight chapters in seven part divisions:

- *Part I* provides an overview of central objectives and concepts in the field.

- *Part II* develops knowledge, techniques, and experience useful in analyzing business unit strategies.

- *Part III* presents knowledge, techniques, and experience useful in analyzing corporate strategies.

- *Part IV* discusses different types of generic strategies at both the business unit and corporate levels and the different conditions and requirements under which they work.

- *Part V* presents analytic tools useful in making strategic decisions and formulating strategic plans.

- *Part VI* covers formal strategic planning systems, their design, and their effective implementation.

- *Part VII* describes the requirements for effective and efficient implementation of strategic plans.

Given the speed of development in the field, one of our concerns was how to keep such comprehensive work current. The usual process of periodic republication inevitably would mean that prior to the next republication date, the handbook would become increasingly outdated. Accordingly, we plan an annual update in the form of supplements that will focus on new developments in the field.

Many people are involved in a project of this scope. Special thanks are in order, of course, to the contributing authors who lived through several revisions of their chapters, always in the face of very busy and successful consulting, academic, and managerial careers. Special thanks are also in order to the editors from Warren, Gorham & Lamont—Naomi Weinberg, who started the project with me, lending her wit and good spirits as well as her editorial competence, and particularly to Arthur J. Morgan, who completed the project with me, contributing much wisdom and good sense along with exceptionally disciplined and competent management of the editorial process. I am deeply grateful to all.

WILLIAM D. GUTH

New York, N.Y.
July 1984

Contents

ix

Overview

PART 1

Overview

1

Central Concepts of Business Unit and Corporate Strategy

WILLIAM D. GUTH

Chairman, Management/Organizational Behavior Area,
Graduate School of Business Administration, New York University

STRATEGIC MANAGEMENT AS A DISCIPLINE

The objective of strategic management in private businesses is to achieve at least above average performance measured by growth in earnings, return on equity and assets, and shareholder value. The time frame of strategic management analysis extends from the short term (one year) to the longer term (5 to 10 years, and sometimes beyond), frequently forcing consideration of trade-offs between short-term and longer-term performance.

The discipline of strategic management focuses, however, on the longer-term performance potentials and problems facing the company. It was developed and became widely supported in practice out of recognition that traditional management systems, principally designed to improve efficiency of current operations, often failed to identify and respond to opportunities and threats facing the company as a result of changing market and competitive conditions.

The discipline of strategic management is implemented through management analysis, planning, and decision making. Most large companies today have formalized strategic planning systems that require managers at various levels in the organization to develop, present, and integrate analyses of changing market and competitive conditions and plans for commitment of the company's resources in light of evolving longer-term performance opportunities and threats. Managers are also expected to formulate plans for the shaping of internal management systems and behavior to aid in the monitoring, adjustment, and implementation of decisions to commit resources based on forecasts of longer-term market and competitive conditions.

This chapter attempts to define, in operational terms, the central concepts in the discipline of strategic management.

THE TWO BASIC LEVELS OF STRATEGIC MANAGEMENT ANALYSIS

Companies compete in markets against other companies with their products and services. Thus, managers need to develop strategies for competing in each product-market area, in light of evolving market and competitive conditions. These strategies are called competitive strategies, or strategic business unit (SBU) strategies in diversified companies that compete in multiple product-market areas.

There are three types of generic competitive, or SBU, strategies:

1 Cost leadership, in which managers attempt to achieve and maintain competitive advantage through lower unit cost of production and/or distribution, which then can be translated into market effectiveness through competitive pricing;

2 Product differentiation, in which managers attempt to achieve and maintain competitive advantage through providing product-service features valued by the market that competitors cannot duplicate; and

3 Market segment focus, in which managers attempt to achieve and maintain competitive advantage by differentiating the product-service to better serve a segment of the total market, while at the same time attaining cost-competitiveness if not cost leadership.

For companies competing in more than one product-market area, managers must also develop a strategy for the overall firm, often referred to as "corporate strategy." The ofjective of corporate strategy analysis, planning, and decision making is the development of a portfolio of SBU strategies that will lead to high corporate performance in terms of growth in earnings, return on equity and assets, and shareholder value. Managers who address corporate strategy are concerned with three major functions:

1 Ensuring that the competitive strategy of each SBU is appropriate to its evolving market and competitive conditions;

2 Allocating corporate resources among current SBUs to maximize the performance potential of the total firm; and

3 Filling the gap between the performance potential of current SBUs and the desired performance level by adding new SBUs and/or divesting one or more current SBUs.

AN APPROACH TO FORMULATING STRATEGIC BUSINESS UNIT AND CORPORATE STRATEGIES

As a way of defining operationally the central concepts in the discipline of strategic management, Figures 1-1 and 1-2 offer a methodology for thinking through, in step-by-step fashion, performance objectives, a strategy for an SBU in relation to these performance objectives, and a strategy for the corporation as a whole.

Preliminary Performance Objectives

A principal step in the approaches outlined in Figures 1-1 and 1-2 requires the formulation of preliminary performance objectives for the strategic planning time horizon. An early articulation of performance objectives lends analytic sharpness to the remainder of the approach. In each succeeding step, forecasts of performance are required after considering conditions and trends, the present strategy, and strategy alternatives. Since the desired performance objectives have been articulated it is possible to check each forecast in each step against the objectives. If a gap exists between the desired performance objectives and what is forecast to be achieved with the present strategy and with the strategy alternatives being considered, additional alternatives must be developed.

The approach forces development of alternatives within the present product-market commitment of the SBUs (for the sake of clarity in terminology, these alternatives are referred to as "tactical"). The approach also forces development of alternatives outside the present product-market commitment of the SBUs that are still related to their present resource capabilities. In addition, the approach leads to a consideration of unrelated diversification in products and markets as part of the overall corporate-level methodology.

Thus, by starting with the articulation of desired performance objectives, the approach becomes a problem-solving methodology. The problem is how to meet the goals,and,in very general terms, the approach looks first at alternatives close to what is presently being done, and then, if these will not solve the problem, at more "distant" (and hence more risky) alternatives.

Key Concepts for Strategy Analysis

The methodologies in Figures 1-1 and 1-2 embody, in step-by-step fashion, the key concepts and theories in strategy analysis: the product life cycle, market segmentation, barriers to competitor response and mobility, product portfolio, experience curve, related and unrelated diversification, strategic investment, and risk. It is important that managers who use these methodologies be thoroughly familiar with these concepts, the research underlying them, and their limitations in application to specific corporate situations.

1. Assess how well the unit has been doing, and why, in relation to key measures of performance (market-competitive conditions and trends, resources, and competitive strengths and weaknesses).

2. Formulate preliminary performance objectives for one year, three years, and five years in the future. (Appropriate planning time horizons will vary depending on the degree of stability in environmental conditions and trends.)

3. Determine overall potential in present product-market areas, assuming no changes in strategy.

   a. Determine meaningful segments of markets for present products.

   b. Position each product on industry attractiveness/competitive position matrix.

   c. Forecast total demand for each product (at least three-point forecast).

   d. Determine present market share position and apparent competitor strategies in each segment.

   e. Forecast future market share position in each segment of the market for each product, assuming no changes in strategy.

4. Assess tactical alternatives for increasing profitability through increasing market share within segments of the markets for present products (e.g., price reduction, price increase, product modification, increased advertising and promotion, improved or enlarged distribution capability, increased inventory levels).

   a. Analyze volume, margin, and investment relationships.

   b. Assess probable competitor responses.

5. Assess tactical alternatives for increasing return on invested capital through reduction in share of total market (segment concentration).

   a. Determine competitive strength by segments of the market.

   b. Analyze "systematic" contributions of resources allocated to weak positions in different segments of the market.

6. Assess tactical alternatives for lowering unit costs of production.

   a. Evaluate rationalization proposals (risk-return-investment relationships).

   b. Evaluate cost-reduction proposals (competitor response, payoff, risk investment relationships).

7. Assess tactical alternatives for lowering the cost of capital employed in present products/markets.

   a. Determine potential for reducing capital employed for present and projected volumes of business (e.g., reduce working capital needs).

   b. Assess potential for greater use of "cheaper" capital.

8. Determine cash requirements of tactical moves and potential sources of supply of required funds (cash flow either from operations-current profits or external).

9. Select tactical moves and forecast performance for relevant time periods in relation to performance objectives.

(continued)

FIG. 1-1 An Approach to Formulating Performance Objectives and Strategy at the Strategy Business Unit Level

10. Determine gap between preliminary performance objectives and opportunity for achievement in present product-market areas.

11. Determine degree of resource utilization in present product-market areas; identify type and magnitude of resources available, by time period, to pursue opportunities in new product-market areas.

12. Identify new product-market areas to which excess resources might be committed.

13. Evaluate amount of opportunity, and additional resource requirements, in these "excess" resource-related areas.

14. Synthesize assessments and determinations into statement of objectives and strategy for presentation to corporate management. (Clearly identify investment capital and short-term profit requirements of strategy.)

FIG. 1-1   An Approach to Formulating Performance Objectives and Strategy at the Strategy Business Unit Level (cont'd)

1. Formulate preliminary performance objectives for one year, three years, and five years in the future.

2. Forecast performance in relation to objectives of existing SBUs following present investment and market strategies.

3. Determine gap between objectives and forecast performance.

4. Identify *alternative* investment strategies in each SBU and forecast their performance.

5. Identify broad *alternative* competitive position strategies (with existing level of resources) for each SBU and forecast their performance.

6. Discuss investment and competitive strategy alternatives for each SBU with SBU managers early in planning cycle.

7. Arrive at negotiated synthesis of corporate and SBU perspectives on objectives and strategy for each SBU.

8. Determine gap between preliminary performance objectives and forecast performance of all SBUs.

9. Specify the required characteristics of possible portfolio additions.

10. Determine the resources required to make such addition(s) and the impact (if any) on existing SBU objectives and strategies of these resource requirements.

11. Revise, if necessary, existing SBU objectives and strategies to provide necessary resources for portfolio additions (discuss with SBU managers).

12. Synthesize determinations into final statement of objectives and strategy.

FIG. 1-2   An Approach to Formulating Performance Objectives and Strategy at the Corporate Level

Uncertainty in Forecasts

The methodologies require systematic effort to identify the magnitude of uncertainty in the various forecasts and assess the downside risk as well as the upside potential associated with each alternative considered. The technique for dealing with uncertainty in the methodologies is relatively primitive, simply the use involving of three-point forecasts (pessimistic, most likely, optimistic). Managers often find that more sophisticated techniques, such as expected-value analysis and Monte Carlo simulation are useful in certain situations.

Short-Run Vs. Longer-Run Performance

The methodologies structure a year-by-year analysis of the impact of tactical and strategic alternatives on the performance measures. Thus, issues of short-run vs. long-run performance trade-offs are clearly indentified for evaluation as part of the overall strategy formulation process.

Many managers are acutely aware of the potential to improve current period profits by cutting current expenses or to increase revenues through price increases. The temptation may be strong to do either or both when a manager perceives himself or herself to be under pressure from the board of directors, his or her boss, or the shareholders to increase short-term profit performance. Either action, or both, may be justifiable, provided that a cut in current expenses does not inhibit the longer-term performance development of the organization or that the price increase does not result in a longer-term reduction in the competitive strength and profit potential of the firm.

It is precisely this potential to damage or inhibit the longer-term performance potential of the corporation through expense cutting and price-policy tactics that necessitates consideration of these alternatives as part of the overall strategy formulation process. Decisions not to employ such tactics are then translated into the annual budgeting process. Deviations from these decisions should not be allowed under short-term performance pressures without at least reconsidering the strategic implications.

An even greater impact on longer-term performance potential often is made by the level of investment in productive and distributive capacity. Under-investment in the capacity of the company to produce and distribute its products can result in high short-term returns on investment, but can lead to longer-term cost and product availability weaknesses in relation to competitors. Alternative levels of strategic investment are generated by the methodologies and evaluation of the projected impact of these alternative levels on short-term and longer-term return on investment is forced.

Integration of Strategic Business Unit and Corporate Strategies

Integration of SBU-level objectives, corporate-level objectives, and the strategy to implement them is accomplished in the methodologies by requiring managers at all levels to communicate their initial positions on the appropriate SBU strategy early in the planning cycle. While this approach does not always result in agreement between corporate-level managers and SBU managers, it does clarify early in the process those strategic issues that require the major amount of analysis, discussion, and exchange of views between the two levels of the organization.

FROM STRATEGIC PLANNING TO STRATEGIC MANAGEMENT

Managers in many companies have experienced some level of frustration in their strategic analysis, planning, and decision-making efforts. This frustration has stemmed from the observation that the strategic plans they formulated often were not implemented, or were implemented inefficiently. This observation, in turn, has led to increasing concern with what needs to be done within the organization to translate the intellectual outcomes of strategic analysis, planning, and decision making into organizational commitment and action—in other words, to go beyond simply thinking strategically to managing strategically.

Figure 1-3 presents a concept of strategic management that attempts to connect strategy formulation to organizational policies and procedures that will ensure strategy implementation. The form of presentation highlights the continuous nature of strategic management, in contrast with the periodic nature of formal strategic planning efforts. In this conception, strategic management requires continuous thought about how to connect strategy to organization structure, management processes, and personnel. Strategic management requires that managers view much of their own daily behavior as significant in the effective formulation and implementation of strategy.

The direction of the arrows in Figure 1-3 indicates the logical, or deductive, relationship among the elements of strategic management. The development of operational measures of performance for each organizational subunit, for example, cannot be accomplished deductively without having completed the tasks preceding it. Since problems and issues within the organization do not present themselves on a daily basis in logical, deductive order, it is up to the manager who wishes to manage strategically to discipline his or her own response, and the response of his or her organization, to these problems and issues in a manner that results in effective strategy formulation and implementation.

At the center of this conception is the articulation of, and demonstration of commitment to, fundamental organizational values. These values define what the organization stands for: what the people in it should see as its overriding or "superordinate" beliefs as to what is important for the organization to do well. These values are almost always stated in qualitative terms. They are most effectively articulated when they have the potential to inspire motivation from the people at all organization levels. The basic purpose of articulating these values is to infuse the day-to-day behavior of individuals in the organization with meaning and purpose.

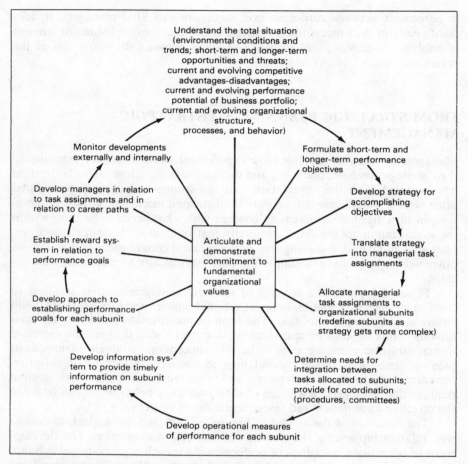

Understand the total situation
(environmental conditions and
trends; short-term and longer-term
opportunities and threats;
current and evolving competitive
advantages-disadvantages;
current and evolving performance
potential of business portfolio;
current and evolving organizational
structure,
processes, and behavior)

Monitor developments
externally and internally

Formulate short-term and
longer-term performance
objectives

Develop managers in relation
to task assignments and in
relation to career paths

Develop strategy for
accomplishing
objectives

Establish reward sys-
tem in relation to
performance goals

Articulate and
demonstrate
commitment to
fundamental
organizational
values

Translate strategy
into managerial task
assignments

Develop approach to
establishing performance-
goals for each subunit

Allocate managerial
task assignments to
organizational subunits
(redefine subunits as
strategy gets more complex)

Develop information sys-
tem to provide timely
information on subunit
performance

Determine needs for
integration between
tasks allocated to subunits;
provide for coordination
(procedures, committees)

Develop operational measures
of performance for each subunit

FIG. 1-3   A Deductive Concept of Strategic Management

According to Peters and Waterman,[1] managers of excellent performing companies tend to share commitment to the following fundamental organization values:

1 It is important to try to be the "best."
2 It is important to do any job well.
3 People are important as individuals.
4 It is important to try to innovate.
5 It is important to deliver superior quality and service to customers.

---

[1] Thomas J. Peters and Robert H. Waterman, Jr., *In Search of Excellence* (New York, N.Y.: Harper & Row Publishers, 1982), p. 285.

6 It is important to be informal to enhance communication.

7 It is important to strive for economic growth and profits.

CONCLUSIONS

This chapter develops, in operational terms, the central concepts in the discipline of strategic management. The chapters that follow attempt to define the state of the art, practice, science, and theory in each of the major elements of these central concepts.

In the design of this *Handbook*, it was anticipated that many users would turn directly to individual chapters for information relevant to specific issues or concerns they are experiencing in the strategic management of their firms. Accordingly, each chapter attempts to be comprehensive and independent in its treatment of its focal element of the strategic management process. Users of the *Handbook* might, however, find occasional reference to this chapter useful in placing specific issues or concerns into an overall, integrated perspective on strategic management.

Analyzing Business Unit Strategy

PART 2

Analyzing Business Unit
Strategy

2

Evaluating the Environment: Economic and Technological Factors

ABRAHAM KATZ

Director, Planning Systems, IBM Corporation

FRAMEWORK FOR ANALYSIS

Strategy and Environment

Firms grow and prosper only if their customers see continuing advantage in the use of their products and services over those of their competitors. Such advantage, however, is transitory—always in danger of erosion due to actions of competitors or to changes in other factors in the dynamic business environment. Accordingly, management must periodically evaluate its business environment, identify problems and opportunities, assess the firm's strengths and weaknesses, and devise corporate and business strategies that exploit existing competitive advantages or establish new advantages.

A Systems View of the Business Environment

Management needs timely and insightful forecasts of the trends and events likely to affect the firm's strategies and operations. Such forecasts, however, are extremely difficult to make:

- The environment at any given time is a result of the interplay of many complex and continually changing forces: economic, social, political, and technological. At best, these forces are interpreted in unduly different ways, and only afford the pundits a partial understanding of a complex picture. Forecasts based on any such modest degree of understanding are likely to be in serious error. For multinational firms, the problem is compounded. The direction and strength of these forces vary significantly from country to country because of inherent differences in social and economic development. While management may understand the business environment in its home country, it generally has a poorer understanding of the environment in the host countries in which the firm operates.

- The pace and volatility of changes in these environmental factors have increased markedly in recent decades. This is due in part to technological advances in transportation, communications, and computation, and in part to the social and political forces unleashed after World War II.

Whatever the difficulties in making forecasts, management must build its plans on some view of the future and accept the associated risks and uncertainties. This chapter focuses on evaluating the economic and technological factors in the environment, leaving to a later chapter (Chapter 3) the social and political factors.

The business environment is a complex system of interacting forces that can be partitioned into three subsystems:

- Industries and their suppliers and customers
- The government and associated interest groups
- Corporate and governmental funders and performers of research and development

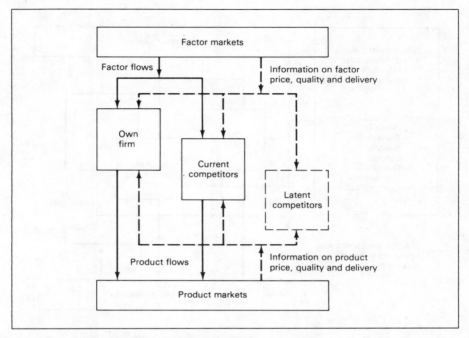

FIG. 2-1 Operations of Firms in a Market Economy

It is useful to study the interactions both within and among the three subsystems. Some business problems may be solved by analyzing only one of these subsystems; others may require analysis of all three.

The first subsystem is composed of the competing firms within an industry together with their networks of suppliers and customers (see Figure 2-1). In a market economy, each firm buys resources from its markets, adds value by creating products and/or services, and then sells these to its customers; there is little or no involvement by government. Although few countries operate in a pure market economy, the concept provides a useful simplification for understanding the rivalrous interactions within the industry.

Associated with the flows of resources and products are flows of information on price, quality, performance, delivery, and so on. These guide the decisions not only of the firms, suppliers, and customers of the industry, but also of the latent competitors: a supplier thinking of integrating forward; a customer integrating backward; a foreign firm producing the same product tapping into a new market; or a firm in an entirely different industry exploiting a new technical development. Systematic scanning of the environment coupled with careful analysis of the changing nature of competition is management's first line of defense against strategic surprise.

The second subsystem includes government and the various interest groups (e.g., unions, environmentalists, consumers, farmers, industry groups) that try to influence governmental policies. In mixed economies as in the

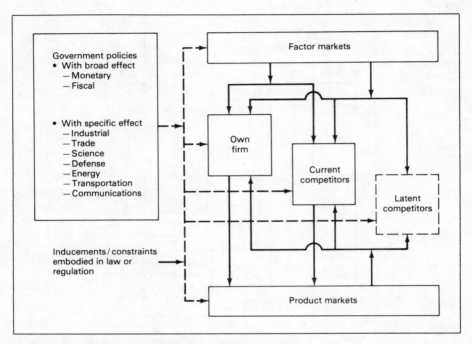

FIG. 2-2 Operations of Firms in a Mixed Economy

United States or in command economies as in the Soviet bloc, governments create the framework within which firms compete (see Figure 2-2). Certain governmental policies, like monetary and fiscal policies, have a broad and pervasive effect on a nation's entire economy and, indeed, on the world (e.g., tight monetary policies in the United States in the early 1980s have adversely affected many other economies). Other policies, such as science or industrial policies, tend to have a specific and differential impact on one industry or region, or another.

Governments themselves are seldom monolithic in their positions on any policy. Differences in values or ideology may exist among the branches of government, among the agencies in the executive branch, or among the legislators. These differences provide a fertile field within which alliances may form among various interest groups, agency officials, and legislators to advocate or oppose some change in public policy. Economic analysis can help the manager anticipate and understand changes in monetary or fiscal policies. For policies with more specific effect, however, one must couple economic analysis with social, political, and possibly technological analyses to gain the understanding needed.

The third subsystem centers on the research and development of industry and governments. Research and development, a key area of rivalry among firms, is now widely performed. It has its own inherent dynamics driven primarily by the quality of the scientific and technical people engaged and the nature and level of their support.

Advances in science and technology may be seen as environmental forces that firms and governments may anticipate, unleash, and influence, but ultimately not control with great precision. In varying degree, every industry and government may be affected by advances in science and technology. The products of a high technology industry (e.g., semiconductor components or computers) clearly incorporate continuing rapid advances. Users of these products often must restructure their own work processes and/or modify their own products to exploit the new advances.

Even when the products of an industry are quite stable in form and function (as in men's suits), firms use new technology to reduce costs in their work processes. Technological forecasting can help management to assess the rate and direction of technical change, whether of products or work processes.

Since economics and technology can seldom be far removed from politics, the patterns of these several factors will differ from country to country. Accordingly, this chapter presents a framework for analyzing changes in these patterns and concludes with some observations on forecasting, uncertainty, and management decision making.

ANALYSIS OF COMPETITION

Key Considerations in Competitive Analysis

In major team sports, it is common practice for coaches to scout their opponents' teams regularly to learn the other teams' strengths and weaknesses, identify the plays they execute well or poorly, and analyze the personalities, philosophies, and styles of the coaches and key players. In this way, the coaches can better prepare for a meeting of their teams on the playing field. Much of the raw material for the intelligence they need (i.e., information that has been processed so as to be relevant to strategy) lies in the public domain, but in fragmentary and often biased form. Some of it is deliberately deceptive, because that is the intent of the opposing coach. Recognizing the importance of good intelligence, however, owners and coaches willingly pay the cost of acquiring it.

As many industries become global in scope, competition intensifies. Business managements, like sports team owners, are faced with the same critical choice: They must pay the costs of improved intelligence about competitors or suffer the consequences of strategic surprise.

It is not enough to know in a general way what the capabilities and strategies of a competitor are. A military analogy is useful. The grand strategy of the United States and its allies during World War II could have been expressed in only two words: Europe first! This strategy clearly set the direction and priorities for the vast flows of resources necessary to conduct a global war. Although immediately evident to the Axis Powers, this knowledge was not of great value to them. Far more valuable would have been the specific and operational content of this grand strategy as applied to each theater of combat: the South Pacific, the beaches of Normandy, and the approaches to Moscow and Stalingrad. It was that specific and operational content that the Axis military intelligence actively sought to ferret out!

Some level of detail is required to understand a competitor's strategy, detail that the competitor will make every effort to deny. The task then becomes one of business intelligence: collecting fragments of publicly available information about competitors from many sources and with varying degrees of currency and accuracy; processing and interpreting that information rapidly in order to fill in the gaps in understanding and to cast it into forms suited to the diverse needs of the many users; and finally communicating it to these users on a timely basis.

The information need not be voluminous to be useful; it must, however, illuminate the overall direction and priorities of competitors. Moreover, information may be useful even if not current, since the organizational momentum any competitor needs to achieve past objectives prevents it from quickly changing its future direction. Organizations can not easily or quickly change such inherent properties as their culture, labor productivity, or capital intensity.

Industry Analysis (Industry/Suppliers/Customers)

An industry is a group of producers and sellers of close-substitute outputs who supply a common group of buyers; hence, it is defined in terms of both product (or service) and customer. Automobiles produced by General Motors are close substitutes for those of Ford or Toyota. Moreover, since these automobiles appeal to customers worldwide, General Motors, Ford, and Toyota are competitors within the same industry. On the other hand, bakeries in New York and Chicago may produce French breads that are identical in all respects. However, each serves a different set of customers whose numbers are limited by the costs of transporting the product and specific consumer concerns, such as the potential loss of flavor and freshness. An industry may be regional, national, or global in scope; one must therefore be careful to identify the appropriate groups of buyers and sellers in analyzing industry structure.

Structural analysis deals with the relations of sellers to each other, of buyers to each other, of sellers to buyers, and of existing sellers to latent sellers of the same products. These structural characteristics influence strategically the nature of competition within any industry.

Economists link the basic conditions of supply and demand in an industry to its structure. Among the principal factors that affect supply are: (1) the nature of the raw materials input; (2) the rate and direction of advances in technology; and (3) the degree of unionization and the value/weight relationship of products. Principal factors that affect demand include: (1) price elasticity; (2) the rate of growth; (3) the cyclic characteristics of demand; and (4) the method of purchase.

The interaction of these factors over time produces an industry structure whose key stratetic aspects are:

- The number and size distribution of sellers and of buyers
- The degree of product differentiation (i.e., the extent to which the sellers' products are seen as nonidentical by the buyers)

- The conditions of entry into the industry by a new seller, and of movement within the industry by an existing seller to improve its position or to leave the industry
- The structure of costs, particularly the relationship of fixed costs to variable costs
- The degree of vertical integration of the sellers moving upstream toward suppliers or downstream toward customers

The structure may change over the industry life cycle. When the automobile industry, for example, was born in the late nineteenth century, conditions of entry were easy; thus, there were many sellers. Products were highly differentiated and production volumes were low. With levels of plant mechanization quite low, variable costs tended to dominate fixed costs. There was little vertical integration. Today the industry structure is radically different: There exists a small number of global competitors, a lesser degree of product differentiation, very high levels of plant mechanization, fixed costs that dominate variable costs, and a considerable degree of vertical integration of sellers.

Since each industry has its own dynamics of change, a corporate strategy appropriate at one time may be inappropriate later. An example from the computer industry illustrates the point. The electronic computers of the early 1950s were based on vacuum tube technology. Firms such as General Electric, RCA, and Sylvania enjoyed great advantages as tube suppliers, so no computer manufacturer integrated backward toward components. With the advent of commercially available transistors in the mid-1950s and integrated circuits in the early 1960s, several computer manufacturers developed or acquired a capability for building some of their own components. Thus, an advance in electronic technology dramatically eased the conditions of entry into the component industry, enabling computer manufacturers to integrate backward toward supply.

A more current example of entrepreneurs capitalizing on eased conditions of entry is the birth of the personal computer industry. The idea of a personal computer for home or office use is at least 20 years old. Someone, however, was alert to two significant trends in supply and demand. On the supply side, the continuing rapid decline in semiconductor circuit cost (25 to 30 percent per year) made it clear that a personal computer would eventually be built at a price affordable by the consumer or small businessman. On the demand side, the increase in computer literacy was gradually creating a base of potential customers large enough to attract would-be entrepreneurs. It was only a matter of time before a latent competitor would see that the conditions for entry into that industry were extremely favorable.

Since the purpose of a corporate strategy is to provide a strong position for the firm relative to the competition and the market environment, the conditions of entry to an industry, and of movement to improve one's position within or to exit from the industry, are important to study. An alert management capitalizes on shifts in access to raw materials or production techniques, advances in technology, and shifts in customer demand. It also scales the size of its plans to gain economies in production, but with due regard to total industry capacity.

Careful analysis of industry structure can provide useful inputs to corporate strategy formulation.

Data Sources

Information about competitors can provide evidence of their capabilities and strategies, which can then enable a company to formulate strategy for competition. To satisfy its business intelligence needs, the firm may choose to set up formal organizations to deal with certain kinds of information and to rely on informal arrangements for other kinds. The trade-off is simply one of cost versus the value of more, better, or faster intelligence in a specific area of the business.

However the effort is organized, the company should structure the data bases for easy access and quick response to management questions. The volume of publicly available information on competitors is large and growing, as is the number of sources available for this information. Included among these sources are the following:

- *Company reports.* Quarterly and annual reports to stockholders and 10K reports to the Securities and Exchange Commission (SEC) provide valuable financial data in analyzing competition. The narratives in these reports often indicate the broad priorities and goals of management. Study of these reports over a period of years provides insight about management responses to problems and opportunities, and the results of these responses.

- *Speeches and articles by key executives.* Executives often meet with financial analysts or make keynote speeches at business and technical conferences. Their remarks and responses to questions provide information about their self-images and about their firm and its position within the industry. Such information also reveals the quality of their thinking.

- *Trade associations.* Much information can be obtained from association reports and meetings. The reports may, for example, provide data on trends in industry volumes and profits, or the changing nature of the market and work force. Some associations also solicit confidential reports from its members in order to be able to publish industry averages for key financial ratios.

- *Trade shows and conventions.* These offer opportunities for comparative analysis of competitors' products as seen from the perspective of potential customers. Brochures on competitors' products or capabilities often provide insights about a company's corporate image.

- *Scientific and technical meetings.* These can provide an understanding of the status, direction, and quality of the competitors' research and development. To retain the fleeting advantage that flows from its research and development, the competitor will not permit disclosure of important pending work until some time has elapsed and/or patents have been applied for. When management judges that the work does not have an important long-term effect on the future of the company, it may permit more prompt disclosure of research and development work. Clues pertaining to strategy are provided both by what the competitor feels important enough to have patented and by what it feels is relatively unimportant.

● *Government reports.* Agencies like the U.S. Department of Energy and the Department of the Interior publish reports that are useful to specific industries. The Department of Commerce, the Federal Reserve Board, and the Internal Revenue Service (among other departments and agencies) provide data or analyses by industry and across industries. Also, information provided by companies to regulatory agencies (e.g., the SEC, the Environmental Protection Agency) can sometimes be obtained under the Freedom of Information Act.

Information thus gleaned by the firm can be supplemented with privately commissioned studies from public sources by consultants, so as to gain a fresh perspective on the industry as a whole.

EVALUATING ECONOMIC FACTORS

Key Economic Indicators

When planning future operations, management must assess the general economic environment and forecast its probable behavior. Such forecasts are especially important when current decisions have significant implications over an extended period. Although our ability to forecast accurately the behavior of the economy is quite modest, decisions made while formulating the plan may prove better or worse depending on the quality of the underlying assumptions and forecasts. Later, as the plan is executed, management monitors the firm's performance and the economic changes to determine the causes of plan variances and any corrective actions to be taken.

A number of indicators are useful in measuring the general strength and vitality of the national economy. These include several interrelated factors that may be affected by political developments and by advances in science and technology:

● *Economic growth.* The rate of economic growth is normally defined as the rate of increase in real gross national product (GNP). GNP is a dollar measure of the value of all goods and services produced by the economy.

● *Productivity.* Total factor productivity is defined in terms of the ratio of value added to value of all input resources. Labor productivity is defined in terms of value added per man-hour worked.

● *Inflation.* This is a sustained tendency for the general level of prices to rise over time. One measure frequently used is the Consumer Price Index, which is the price today of a market basket of selected goods and services in relation to its price in a base period.

● *Employment.* Among the measures used here are the number of people employed, the hours worked per week, and the percentage of unemployed people who are seeking employment.

- *Balance of payments.* This is an annual account of all economic transactions between one country and the rest of the world. It provides a measure of the competitiveness of that country in world markets, and, hence, a guide to governmental policies that are likely to maintain a trade balance or to protect its industries.

In addition to these general indicators of economic health, management often monitors indicators relating to its specific industry (e.g., for a capital equipment manufacturer, business expenditures for machinery and equipment or the index of industrial production). Indicators, both general and specific, are published as time series by many governments, thus providing the historical basis for forecasting many economic trends.

FORECASTING

A wide variety of quantitative and qualitative forecasting methods has been developed. These methods generally rest on an assumption of constancy, that is, an assumption that the patterns and/or relationships discovered in past data will remain constant over the forecast period. This assumption may be explicit when the forecasting equations are based on statistical analysis; or it may be only implicit when the forecast is based on opinion or expert judgment.

Both quantitative and qualitative methods range from the very simple to the complex. The simpler methods generally produce forecasts more quickly and at lower cost than the more complex; they should be used unless the more complex methods will materially improve the accuracy of the forecasts.

QUANTITATIVE FORECASTING METHODS

Quantitative methods fall into two classes: extrapolative and causal.

Extrapolative Models

These are models in which the forecasts of a variable are based solely on historical values of the same variable. With no explicit connection between the forecasted variable and any other variable, these models simply assume that whatever pattern of forces drove the forecasted variable in the past will continue to drive it in the future. The more commonly used models are discussed here.

Simple Extrapolation. A company might find that its sales tend to follow a relatively stable trend. It might then choose to forecast monthly sales in the next time period in terms of a weighted combination of actual sales over some past period (e.g., for each of the past three months). The weights to be used for actual sales in each of the prior months might be obtained through statistical analysis.

Time Series Analysis. A somewhat more sophisticated extrapolative model may be derived by time series analysis. The historical values of the time series to be forecast are first separated into four basic components: (1) the seasonal variations within the year; (2) the secular trends over the longer term; (3) the fluctuations due to the business cycle; and (4) a residual component caused by random events. Knowing these several components and the most recent value of the time series, the forecaster can then project future values.

Exponential Smoothing. Random fluctuations in past economic data may be reduced through the use of moving averages or exponential smoothing. The exponential method is preferable because it gives greater weight to recent time series data than to data from the more distant past. It also requires less computer storage for data. An example of exponential smoothing is seen when the monthly sales forecast for the next time period is derived from a weighted combination of the sales forecast in the most recent prior period plus the difference between that forecast and the actual sales.

Because exponential smoothing is easy to use and provides some degree of control over the weights that are chosen, it has been widely applied in forecasting economic data. However, two problems remain with its use. There is no easy way to determine the proper value of the weights; also, whatever those weights, they normally will be changed from time to time since past economic trends and patterns may not continue.

Adaptive Filtering. Adaptive filtering enables the forecaster to handle a wide range of basic patterns in a time series by adjusting the weights. Simply stated, adaptive filtering tells how the weights should be adjusted after the forecast error has been computed. Because of its greater complexity, a program of adaptive filtering must be implemented on a computer system.

Causal Models

In causal models, the forecasts of a variable are based on historical values of some causal or explanatory variables. Causal methods, therefore, make explicit our understanding and assumptions about the forces that drive the variable being forecast.

Econometric Modeling. An econometric model is simply a set of relationships among economic variables, many of which are interdependent. If put in algebraic form, the model appears as a system of simultaneous equations displaying the various relationships among the several variables.

An unlimited number of models differing in the nature of and relationships among the variables can account for any given pattern of past economic trends. For example, the U.S. economy can be represented by fewer than 10 equations or by well over 300. The selection of the weights for the variables enables the model builder to mold the model's output to fit the historical data quite closely.

Econometric models are frequently used in government for evaluating alternative policies (e.g., fiscal or monetary policy). They are used for the same purposes in larger firms, as well as for sales forecasting. For example, a manufacturer of pumps and compressors might forecast its sales in terms of the following model:

- Future sales depend on sales effort and the level of producer durables expenditures.
- Sales effort depends on unit price and advertising expenditures.
- Producer durables expenditures depend on recent profits in the industrial sectors served by the firm and on the average hourly labor wage rates for those sectors.
- Advertising expenditures depend on desired future sales.
- Unit price depends on product cost, selling and other expenses, and profit.
- Product cost depends on the cumulative sales volume achieved.

Note that this model links variables relating to several different levels of the economy: macroeconomic, such as producer durables' expenditures; sectoral, such as industry profits; and corporate, such as sales effort.

Firms may develop or buy their econometric forecasts. Many of the larger firms have staffs of economists equipped with their own data bases and models. Multinational firms may also have economic models for the larger countries in which they operate (e.g., Germany and Japan, as well as the United States). Smaller firms may buy forecasts from an economic forecasting service or secure economic advice from their local banks or universities.

Corporate models of national economies can play an important role in the planning process of a multinational firm. Thus, forecasts of a country's GNP or of its investments in machinery and equipment can help set the business volumes for the company's plan. Similarly, forecasts of price trends in a country can help set prices for the company's products or compensation for its employees. Finally, forecasts of currency exchange rates can help in estimating earnings from abroad.

Input-Output Models. An input-output model describes an economy in terms of the relationship between the output of any given industry and the sizes of the inputs it receives. At a given time, such a model captures the entire range of technologies, scale of production, and materials inputs for the economy. Because the usefulness of the model depends on the persistence through time of this specific pattern of relationships, the model must be periodically revised to reflect any changes.

Input-output models are most frequently used at a governmental level— national, regional, or state. Again, the use is concerned with evaluating policy alternatives (e.g., testing for potential bottlenecks in an expanded national defense effort). One of the uses at the corporate level has been in forecasting sales potential by industry.

QUALITATIVE FORECASTING METHODS

Three basic qualitative methods are used widely: indicator-based forecasts, surveys of intentions, and subjective assessments.

Indicator-Based Forecasts

The behavior of the business cycle has long been studied and its associated indicators used for forecasting. The business cycle approach assumes that cycles are to be expected, that these are but temporary deviations about an equilibrium (which may, of course, exhibit a secular trend), and that some degree of regularity in behavior is discernible.

Two organizations prominent in the development of business cycle data and analytic techniques are the National Bureau of Economic Research (a private organization) and the Bureau of the Census of the U.S. Department of Commerce. On a monthly basis, the Bureau of the Census publishes a large number of indicator time series in the *Business Conditions Digest*. Some of these series tend to lead the business cycle (e.g., average work week for production workers in manufacturing); others are coincident with the cycle (e.g., personal income); and still others tend to lag behind the cycle (e.g., labor cost per unit of output in manufacturing).

Based on experience and judgment, the forecaster first selects the time series relevant to his or her purpose. Although the various series selected may give mixed signals, he or she uses the data to forecast the direction of changes and the turning point in the business cycle. These can be useful to management in determining the appropriate levels of inventories or the rate of expansion of capital facilities.

Surveys of Intentions

One way to find out what people think they will do in the future is simply to ask them. While this technique is widely applicable, the best-known surveys relate to expenditures for consumer durables and for business plant and equipment.

Consumer Durables. The Survey Research Center of the University of Michigan conducts regular surveys to measure consumer intentions to buy goods such as cars and major appliances. To check the validity of the responses, information is simultaneously gathered on consumer asset positions and savings plans. Allowing for all the difficulties of surveying (e.g., bias in the phrasing of questions, misunderstanding of questions, or competence to make judgments about the future), these regular surveys do help identify trends and turning points in consumer attitudes toward the future.

Business Plant and Equipment. Two widely used surveys of business capital expenditures programs are those prepared by the McGraw-Hill Company and by the Office of Business Economics (U.S. Department of Commerce) acting jointly with the SEC. As in the consumer surveys noted previously, additional questions are asked of business to check on the validity of the responses.

Judgmental Forecasts

The differences between the surveys just discussed and judgmental forecasts lie in the degree of structure in the questions asked and in the nature and size of the sample surveyed. From these factors arise differences in the cost, speed, and accuracy of the forecasts obtained. Among the methods for securing judgmental forecasts are Delphi techniques and scenario writing. Both seek to make more effective use of expert capabilities for dealing with very complex problems.

Delphi Techniques. These techniques seek a reliable consensus as to future trends or events from a group of experts. Delphi involves a program of sequential questionnaires addressed to individual experts, interspersed with feedback to them of results from prior surveys. Questions are not debated by the group as a whole, reducing the influence of group pressure or individual differences in persuasive skills. These techniques entail difficulties similar to those connected with consumer surveys.

Scenario Writing. The scenario writing method generally involves a group of experts working together to develop a well-defined set of key assumptions. Those assumptions are used to create a concept of the future. Normally the group creates a number of alternative futures, each based on some variations in the initial set of assumptions. Such scenarios have been written to explore a variety of geopolitical, social, and economic questions.

EVALUATING TECHNOLOGICAL FACTORS

Technological forecasting may be defined as the prediction of the following factors:

- The degree of change in some technical parameter or attribute;
- The characteristics or performance of materials, products, systems, or processes; and
- The timing of an invention or of its diffusion into widespread use.

Technological forecasting has been practiced at least as far back as the dawn of the Industrial Revolution. Designers of the early steam engine extrapolated the technical characteristics desired in new engines from their experience with prior designs. Despite this long history of usage, technological forecasting has remained a judgmental art for reasons that are discussed subsequently.

Tools for Forecasting Technological Factors

The tools for forecasting fit readily into the framework used earlier for evaluating economic factors: tools for extrapolating from some time series and tools for using expert judgment.

Extrapolative Models. Extrapolative models forecast a variable solely on the basis of historical values of the same variable. An example is the forecasting of future sales in terms of a weighted combination of actual sales over a three-month period. By contrast, in extrapolating technological trends, the time horizons are generally longer and the number of data points fewer. The underlying phenomena are not understood as well and the assumptions are more tenuous. The technological forecaster therefore must apply considerable judgment in interpreting the data and the forecast results.

Figure 2-3 illustrates some of the key ideas. This figure, which is from an unpublished study by Robert N. Noyce (Intel Corporation), shows an extrapolation of the trend in cost per bit of random access memory. Using cost data from the product generations prior to 1977, he projected a continued cost improvement of 28 percent per year through 1983. These improvements, of course, would not come automatically with the passage of time. Rather, Noyce anticipated that new lithography systems would be developed, a greater understanding of the physics and chemistry of surface phenomena would be achieved, and the topological problems of laying out and testing memory chips would be solved. Furthermore, Noyce anticipated that demand for memory bits would continue to grow at a rate enough faster than 28 percent per year to provide the profit motivation for continuing product development. The great difficulties in technological forecasting are demonstrated here. The forecaster must have an appreciation of the several scientific and engineering disciplines involved, as well as an understanding both of the uses of the product and the competitive dynamics of the industry.

Continuing with the Noyce example, the 28 percent compound rate of cost improvement represents the long-term trend. Within any product generation, there is a learning curve in which unit costs are initially higher than those of the prior generation and later are lower. Eventually, the improvement possible in that generation is exhausted.

While many different shapes of curves have been used in fitting technological data, the most frequently used is the S-shaped curve. For any given technology, the improvement over time in some technical parameter (e.g., unit cost per memory bit, speed of commercial air transport) is often characterized by a slow start, followed by a period of rapid growth, and then a plateau. Among the various equations used for fitting S-shaped curves are those by Pearl (the logistic curve), Gompertz, and Von Bertalanffy. These can produce very different forecasts as to when the period of rapid growth occurs or when the plateau in performance is achieved; judgment is required in selecting the appropriate equation.

Morphological Analysis. Morphology is the study of form. For a given product (e.g., the jet engine), a matrix of all possible technological approaches

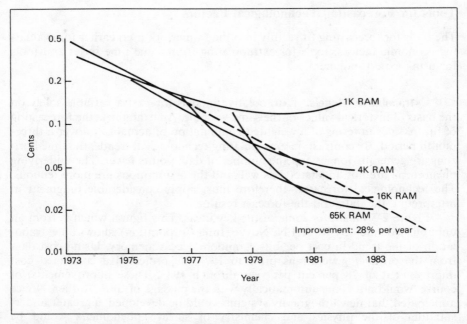

FIG. 2-3 Improvement in Cost per Bit of Random Access Memory

and product configurations can be created. Known products are first identified within the matrix. Following this, the matrix can be inspected for untried yet desirable possibilities. Morphological analysis can thus stimulate technical creativity, but cannot forecast the properties of a new product or its time of entry into the market.

Delphi Techniques. As discussed previously, Delphi techniques seek a reliable consensus from a group of experts concerning future trends or events. The questions asked are frequently more than purely technological questions. A statement provided to a group of experts such as "Holography will permit three-dimensional movies in the home by the year 19XX" requires that the group include not only technologists but also people who understand consumer behavior.

Cross-Impact Analysis. Cross-impact analysis also involves the use of experts and can be used together with Delphi techniques. A list of future developments of interest is established by the experts. These are then arranged in a matrix, listing the various developments as headings of both the rows and columns. The experts then address the question: "If any one event occurs, what will be its impact on each of the others?" Their conclusions are then entered in the cells of the matrix. Thus occurrence of a given event may delay or accelerate the timing of a second event, or it may intensify or moderate societal resistance to that second event.

FORECASTING, UNCERTAINTY, AND MANAGEMENT DECISION MAKING

In any country, the business environment is an extremely complex system whose behavior must be evaluated by management in order to arrive at sound strategies. The state of that system depends on the joint evolution of the firms making up the country's economic base, on the rate and direction of technological change, on the wisdom and timeliness of the government's policies, and on how effectively all have made use of resources available to them.

Forecasting is a difficult art because our understanding of the factors at work and their interrelationships is so limited. While continuing to press for improvement in the forecasting art, management should plan with the clear understanding that the forecasts presented to it may be reasonable but are likely to be in error (and sometimes in serious error!). Since uncertainty and risk are unavoidable, management must raise appropriate questions when presented with forecasts. Among these questions are the following:

- What are the core assumptions underlying the forecasts? Which are likely to be in error? What are the implications of error for the plan? How will we learn of any errors, and how soon?
- What risks do we know that we are taking? When, where, and in what form will they arise? How do we plan to manage them?

For example, suppose the development and marketing functions in a high-technology firm have agreed on the customer requirements to be met in the next-generation product. If development then bases its new product designs on a semiconductor technology that is extremely advanced, the risks taken will tend to be technical rather than marketing risks. Problems will appear sooner rather than later and may require additional resources in development to solve them. On the other hand, if development takes too conservative an approach in technology, the primary risks will be in marketing because of product shortcomings. Problems will appear later rather than sooner and may require greater sales effort and advertising expenditures to deal with them, or may even become irremediable. Hence, risk is unavoidable. By its decisions, however, management can sometimes determine the form, extent, and timing of the risks it is willing to take.

There has been enough experience with and study of forecasting to provide some indication of the conditions for improving forecasts:

- Forecasts over a shorter time horizon are more likely to be accurate than those over a longer horizon.
- Forecasts are strongly influenced by the current business climate: in good times, they tend to be overly optimistic; the converse is true in bad times.

- Forecasts are also strongly influenced by the position of the forecasting group in the organization. If, for example, the product forecasting group is placed under the product manager, the forecasts may tend to be more optimistic and self-serving than if placed at a higher level in the organization.
- The choice of forecasting methodology is less important than the considerations just noted. More complex and sophisticated forecasting technology may cost more than the increment in accuracy is worth. Accordingly, it is preferable to take a more eclectic approach, using a number of different forecasting methods so as to gain the benefits of multiple insights.

In closing, it should be noted that the firm is a purposive organization. If management understands the business environment moderately well, the firm can often achieve its objectives whatever the shortcomings in its forecasting methodology.

3

Evaluating the Environment: Social and Political Factors

IAN WILSON
SRI International

ENVIRONMENTAL ANALYSIS AND STRATEGIC MANAGEMENT

Environmental analysis must now surely be considered an integral part of strategic management, if for no other reason than that there is no escape from the turbulence and uncertainty of the business environment. Yet, this was not always so. As difficult as it may now be to remember the more stable conditions of the 1950s and early 1960s, there was a time when—as managerial rule of thumb had it—planners could count on 80 percent of major business factors being in some measure controllable, and on only 20 percent being noncontrollable. Competition and markets, as major external factors, could not literally be considered controlled. Yet even they were, in some sense, controllable in many industries where industry structure and patterns of consumption were well established and slow to change.

Now all that has changed. The new managerial calculus suggests that only 20 percent of business factors are, in any sense, controllable, and that 80 percent are noncontrollable. What is beyond business' control is its environment—that "buzzing, blooming confusion" (to many managers) of global, national, and business events. This environment is the source of the shocks, surprises, and discontinuities that batter traditional business performance and make mincemeat of strategies that are inadequately attuned to the new externalities.

Evaluation of the environment—systematic and continuous scanning, monitoring, and analysis of the trends and events that shape the environment in which a business lives, moves, and has its being—is the logical, businesslike response to these changes. It is the starting point for strategic thinking, and it sets the context for strategy development. Evaluation of the environment is premised on the notion that although the trends may not be controllable, they can, to some extent, be known; and that if they are well analyzed, their consequences can be more manageable.

IMPORTANCE OF THE SOCIOPOLITICAL ENVIRONMENT

Nowhere has business' lack of control (and, one might add, understanding) been more apparent than in the domain of social and political trends and events. In the 15 years between 1965 and 1980, corporations were repeatedly blind-sided by a succession of social movements (consumer, minorities, women, environmental), by the politics of oil and nationalist sentiment against multinational corporations, by shifts in consumer taste and behavior (natural foods, smaller cars, conservation), and by new work-life values (participation, employee rights, individualism). Time after time, changes in social values found their way into the agenda of new pressure groups, into legislation and regulation, and into the courts.

Observing this rapidly developing phenomenon in 1972, the Business Environment Studies component in General Electric encapsulated it in the dictum: "Without a proper business response, the societal expectations of today become the political issues of tomorrow, legislated requirements the next day, and litigation the day after." The table at the top of Figure 3-1 illustrates this sequence with a simple example taken from the women's movement. It also suggests how an issue, after completing this cycle, can be redefined and start the cycle all over again in a new form.

However, the significance of the sociopolitical environment and its impact on corporations extends far beyond such legislative and public policy issues. It is not simply a matter, as some suggest, of corporate social responsibility; it is a question of markets, of work-force availability and productivity, of costs and profitability, and of corporate credibility and legitimacy. It is also a matter of strategy and freedom to maneuver, as the lower portion of Figure 3-1 shows. The stronger the trend or the issue becomes, and the further it develops, the fewer the available corporate options and the narrower the space for maneuvering. It is thus much more advantageous to develop proactive strategy and move

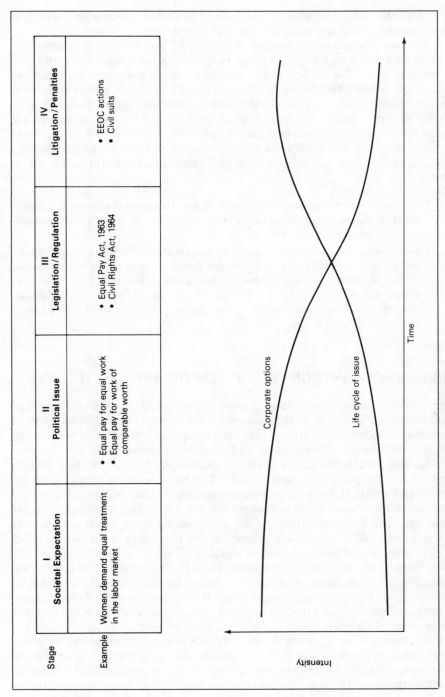

FIG. 3-1 The Corporate Impact of Evolving Societal Expectations

early in the formative stage of a trend than to be forced into reacting, with few if any options, when the trend or issue has crystallized.

The impacts and consequences of social and political developments are so great and affect so many aspects of business that they *must* be considered an integral part of a corporation's overall strategic management. To side-track responsibility for dealing with these factors to public affairs or human resource staffs is to deny their centrality in the business environment. This is not to say, of course, that components such as public affairs, marketing research, or human resource planning do not have a part to play in monitoring and analyzing the sociopolitical environment; of course they do. But the strategic planning component should play the central role for at least two reasons:

1 Successful business strategy, i.e., one that is in tune with the times that anticipates the future, is dependent on a systemic and systematic analysis of the business environment.

2 Since sociopolitical analysis needs to be integrated into the planning of virtually every function (certainly of the marketing, financial, legal, public affairs, human resources, production, and engineering functions), some component must coordinate and provide the holistic perspective and the common set of planning assumptions. Corporate or business unit planning would seem to be the logical candidate for such a role.

NEED FOR AN INTEGRATED, HOLISTIC APPROACH

This chapter is concerned with evaluation of the social and political environment; Chapter 2 deals with the economic environment. This dichotomy is in many ways artificial; to carry it over into the actual operation of a planning system would be highly misleading and counterproductive.

Social ... economic ... political ... technological ... all of these factors (and others) are parts of a single whole. The business environment must be viewed and analyzed, for planning purposes, as a unified entity—as Figure 3-2 attempts to illustrate—for the simple reason that everything is related to everything else. The interconnections of all of the elements in the environmental puzzle are virtually limitless, and are far beyond the ability of the human mind or of our most sophisticated models to track. (This is, of course, one of the main reasons why attempts at forecasting fail.) To deny this fact by attempting to analyze trends or classes of trends in isolation may be a logical expression of scientific reductionism, but it is scarcely a tribute to our powers of observation. History, the present, and the future simply do not work in this way; they are the product of interactions, not of discrete channeling.

For example, consumer and voter attitudes and expectations clearly affect the outcome of elections and, by extension, the course of public policy. Legislative changes in fiscal and monetary policy are an important determinant of economic growth. The structure and cyclical state of the economy have a bear-

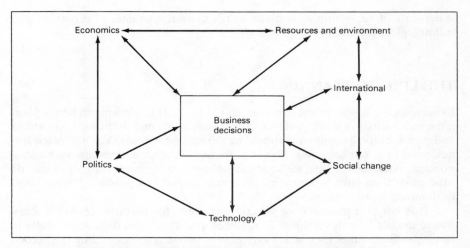

FIG. 3-2 The Complexity of Interconnections in the Business Environment

ing on research expenditures, which then affect the rate of technological development and diffusion. Technology, in turn, helps shape social values and consumer attitudes, as has been seen with automation, nuclear power, and microelectronics. It is possible to start at any point on this social-economic-political-technological chain and trace a circular pattern of linkages, to the point where the distinction between cause and effect is blurred. In this age of increasing complexity, dependent and independent variables are coming to merge into a unified set of interdependent variables.

Social and political trends thus affect, and are affected by, economic and technological trends. These four factors cannot be adequately analyzed except in a holistic context, that is, a comprehensive environmental assessment system that sees the business environment as a whole rather than piecemeal.[1]

The fact that environmental analysis requires an integrated, holistic approach is yet another reason for suggesting that it is ultimately a planning unit responsibility, not one that should be fragmented among a half-dozen functions. It also points strongly toward the utility of employing scenarios as an integrative mechanism (see the following discussion) to relate the qualitative

---

[1] In fact, a truly comprehensive environmental analysis should be comprised of four interlocking segments:

1. "Macro": the broad sweep of social, economic, political, and technological trends, both domestic and international
2. Industry: the structure, products, pricing, technology, government regulation, international position, and so forth of the industry or industries in which the company is engaged
3. Competitive: the history, strengths, weaknesses, goals, and strategies of major competitors (increasingly, with technological diversification, these are not necessarily found within neat classifications of discrete industries or particular countries)
4. Company: changes in the performance, resource quality and availability, corporate culture, stakeholder values, and competitive position of the company

statements of sociopolitical analysis to the quantitative data of economic and technological forecasting.

THE LINK TO PLANNING

Evaluating the environment is not an end in itself. It is a means to better planning, more sensitive strategy development and, in the end, improved operations and profitability. This linkage should be strong and explicit. Yet, too often it is neglected or is not achieved. This is particularly the case, it seems, with sociopolitical assessments. But, without this linkage, environmental analysis can do little more than stretch minds, raise consciousness, and produce "interesting" (a damning word) studies.

It is not that planners—or general managers, for that matter—are insensitive to the need for this linkage. It is, rather, that they seem to have difficulty in forging it. Sometimes they lack a systematic approach to assembling the needed business intelligence about their environment. Sometimes they have problems in distilling the resulting mass of data. Above all, they fail to maximize what might be termed the "planning utility" of their efforts.

Designing an effective system and forging this link between environmental analysis and planning defies easy prescription, in large part because every system must be designed to fit the corporate planning culture it must serve. In theory, however, there are a number of essential elements in this linkage. These are illustrated in Figure 3-3, and they are described in some detail in the remainder of this chapter. It is important to keep in mind that the focal point— the true link in the system—is the identification, analysis, and prioritizing of strategic issues.

"Issues" are the common language of environmental analysis and strategic planning. One broad but useful definition of a strategic issue, as the term is used here, is that it is a curent or prospective threat or opportunity arising out of some internal or external trend or development that would have a major impact on some aspect of the business (e.g., on its basic strategies, policies, growth, profitability, or survival), the course or impact of which can, to some extent, be influenced by corporate action.

This definition distinguishes an issue from a trend. For example, from a corporate point of view, inflation is not an issue but a trend, the course of which cannot be influenced by the corporation alone. However, the impact of inflation on business *does* affect corporate issues and *can* be dealt with by corporate action.

DESIGNING THE "FRONT END" OF THE SYSTEM

The front end of the environmental analysis system is, as shown in Figure 3-3, made up of three interlocking parts: scenarios, scanning, and monitoring. Each of these is described subsequently. Here it is necessary to stress their complementary purposes and their interrelationships.

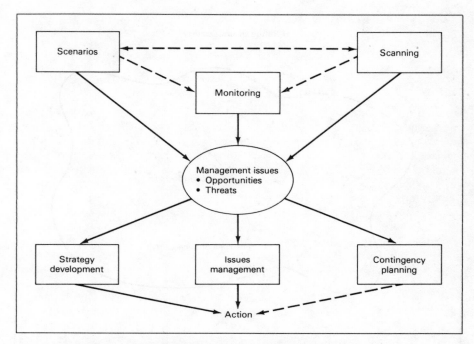

FIG. 3-3   Linking Environmental Analysis to Planning (and Action)

The purpose of scenarios is to provide managers and planners with what Pierre Wack (formerly with Royal Dutch/Shell Group) calls "mental maps of the future." Monitoring enables businesses to keep track of developments in trends of known importance. Scanning alerts businesses to new or previously unknown trends, and allows them to guard against surprises. These three elements constitute the corporate radar, the mechanism by which the corporation senses and makes sense of changes in its external environment.

Each front-end element interacts with and supports the other two. Scenarios, for instance, provide a frame of reference for both scanning and monitoring, which makes the analysis and interpretation of new data easier and more complete. Continuous feedback from the monitoring of actual events is required so that periodic adjustments or revisions can be made. Scanning, with its "wide-angle lens" and continuous coverage of the environmental horizon, picks up the new and the relevant trends and developments that need to be factored into both scenarios and the monitoring system.

In such a system, the macro and the micro, the future and the present, are mutually reinforcing parts of the environmental analysis whole.

The Nature and Role of Scenarios

There are two basic problems in most of the environmental analysis systems that are currently in operation in corporations:

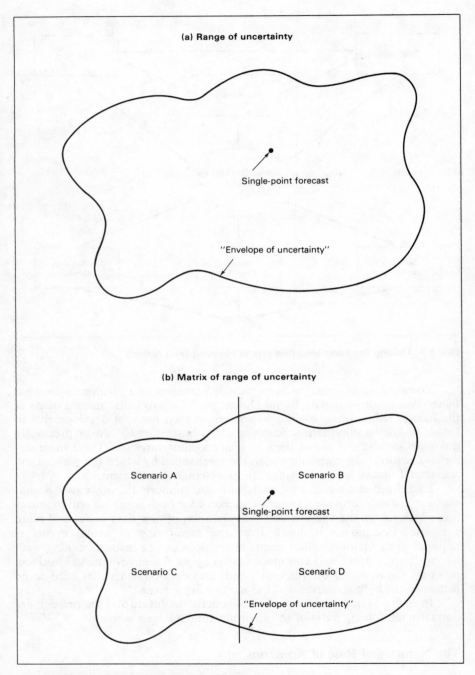

FIG. 3-4   Single-Point Forecasting Vs. Scenarios:
(a) Range of Uncertainty;   (b) Matrix of Range of Uncertainty

1 They focus on a single-point view of the future that excludes from planning consideration the inevitable uncertainty that is perhaps the single most distinguishing characteristic of our times.

2 They tend to analyze trends discretely, thereby ignoring the impacts and interactions of an interconnected world (see Figure 3-2).

Scenarios are an attempt to remedy both of these defects.

Consider, first, the uncertainty factor. Our current planning culture has a love/hate relationship with forecasting. On the one hand, there has been an openly acknowledged breakdown in forecasting in recent years; on the other hand, there is a persistent drive toward greater accuracy in forecasting and a continuing belief in a single-point view of the future. Despite all the evidence to the contrary, planning systems are, for the most part, predicated on a denial of uncertainty.[2] The basic premise seems to be, "Give me one prediction of the future, and I can plan for it; give me three or four alternatives, and you have been no help to me."

Yet, if any single forecast or set of environmental planning assumptions is analyzed, it quickly becomes apparent that there is much more uncertainty built into it than the single set of figures it gives rise to would seem to indicate. This is particularly true in the sociopolitical arena; but even economic and technological forecasting are not immune from the uncertainty syndrome, if for no other reason than their interconnections with social and political factors, as previously noted. It is not that we know nothing or that we are totally uncertain. Within tolerable limits we can, for example, predict five- to ten-year demographic trends, such as changes in the size and composition of the labor force or consumer markets. But beyond these quantitative measures, we encounter much greater uncertainty in the qualitative domain of consumer values and behavior, employee expectations, and political attitudes. These variables tend to be a major impetus in the business environment at both the macro and micro (or industry) levels.

Confronting the uncertainty factor in each of the elements contained in single-point forecast, one finds that what is really being (or should be) planned for is better described as an envelope of plausible (but usually unacknowledged) uncertainty, as shown in Figure 3-4. Although this is only a schematic representation, the magnitude of difference between the single-point forecast and the total envelope of uncertainty is probably not unreasonable. The envelope is intended to contain not every conceivable future possibility, but only what a planning team considers plausible and relevant. Plausibility depends on the judgment of the team (e.g., is the range of uncertainty regarding the future U.S. fertility rate 1.7 to 1.9? Or, does it range from 1.6 to 2.1?). Relevance is defined in terms of what the planners need to know about the future (e.g., the future fertility rate is of major importance to a baby foods producer, but it is irrelevant to a defense contractor).

---

[2] An important reason for this denial of uncertainty lies in our definition of managerial competence. Because competence is defined in terms of "knowing," any admission of uncertainty becomes unacceptable: It appears to imply *in*competence!

A well-constructed set of scenarios should structure and describe the range of uncertainty that planning should address (see Figure 3-4). Individually, each scenario is not a prediction or a single-point forecast, but a narrative of a plausible future. Collectively, the scenarios should define the boundaries of the envelope of uncertainty in a way that allows planning to identify the full range of threats and opportunities that the future may hold.

Scenarios attempt to remedy the second defect of most environmental analysis systems—their tendency to analyze the environment piecemeal rather than as a unit—by developing a logical structure that integrates all of the needed variables into a set of coherent and consistent patterns. A scenario is structured in dynamic terms because it is, after all, an evolving narrative, not a description of an endpoint. Scenarios describe how, in a given market or industry, social and political trends might interact with economic and technological factors to create a plausible restructure of that market.

Planners must develop the capacity to see things "whole"; for example, they must see not merely the economics of the future, be it recession or boom, but also the social values and political actions that go along with those conditions. In the euphoria of the early to mid-1960s, most companies, in effect, "hoped for the best" with respect to sociopolitical factors. They assumed that along with boom times there would be pro-business public attitudes and a relatively benign (though perhaps interfering) government. After the rude shocks of the late 1960s and early 1970s, there has been a tendency to overreact and to expect the worst from public attitudes and the government. Neither of these approaches is rational or businesslike. Possible alternative futures and the conditions that might create, and then flow from, them have to be thought through in a logical fashion.

Development and Use of Scenarios

Perhaps the best way to describe the uses of scenarios in planning and to demonstrate their relevance to analyzing the sociopolitical environment is to show the processes by which a set of scenarios is developed (see Figure 3-5).

The major steps include the folowing:

1 Clarify corporate decision or decisions regarding scenarios to be used;
2 Identify key decision factors;
3 Identify and analyze key macroenvironmental forces;
4 Define scenario logics;
5 Elaborate on the scenario descriptions; and
6 Analyze implications for strategic decisions.

These steps are described in detail in the following sections. They demonstrate the role and value of strategic planning and, more importantly, they point the way toward a viable methodology for assessing the social and political forces in the corporate environment. Executives and planners have traditionally been skeptical not so much about the importance of these forces but about the feasibility of factoring them into the mainstream of corporate planning. Scenarios

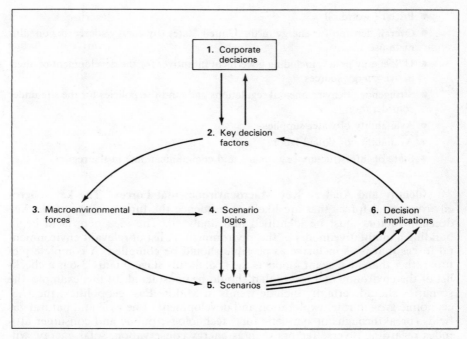

Fig. 3-5 Six Steps in Scenario Development

are discussed in this chapter primarily because they are perhaps the best means of showing social and political trends and events as part of the "seamless web" of the current and future planning environment.

Clarify Corporate Decisions Regarding Scenarios to Be Used. Scenarios for the purpose of planning are decision-focused. While scenarios can, of course, be developed for a broad topic, such as the future of the workplace or the global trading system, in planning they must focus on some point of corporate relevance. Since planning is intended to result in decision making, the focal point of scenarios should be a corporate decision or set of decisions. The basic aim of scenarios is to improve the quality of a decision by organizing perceptions about alternative future environments in which the decision might be played out. For purposes of illustration, assume the focus to be on a decision as to whether or not to proceed with a shale oil development project.

Identify Key Decision Factors. Having established a given decision as the basis of the scenarios, the next step is to answer the question, "What must be known about the future in order to make this decision?" Key decision factors are the macroenvironmental and microenvironmental factors that establish the future context for the playing-out of the decision. In this example, these factors might include the following:

- Price of world oil
- Overall demand for energy in the United States (by energy source/region/ultimate user)
- U.S. energy policy, including goverment incentives for the development of alternative energy sources
- Stringency of environmental regulations and land-use policies for the site under consideration
- Availability of water supplies
- Availability of skilled labor
- State of infrastructure (e.g., roads and communications) in the region

Identify and Analyze Key Macroenvironmental Forces. The key macroenvironmental forces that are likely to influence the future course of the key decision factors must be identified and analyzed. The idea here is to begin building a qualitative model of the environment. A list of relevant environmental forces that is as inclusive as possible should be compiled. A complete picture rather than an elegant model is the goal at this stage. Figure 3-6 is a checklist of the environmental forces that should be considered. In this example, the scenarios should certainly include trends in Middle East geopolitics; the U.S. economic growth rate; exploration and development of new oil and natural gas fields; breakthroughs in synthetic fuels technology; public and consumer attitudes regarding diverse factors such as energy conservation, solar energy, wilderness preservation, and work environment; cost and availability of capital; regional population growth and migration; and federal and state legislative power balance.

Following the identification of key macroenvironmental forces, they must be analyzed in order to:

- Establish their current trajectory and possible future branching points.
- Determine the range of uncertainty surrounding these future possibilities. (As noted previously in the discussion of plausibility, this is a matter of judgment and will vary from team to team; one team may find plausible a downside trend toward a global depression, while another may place the lower level of uncertainty at only zero to one percent annual growth rate for gross world product.)
- Assess the impacts of one trend upon another in order to avoid the pitfalls of discrete analysis and to lay the foundation for developing coherent, internally consistent scenarios.

The purpose of such an analysis is not to delay the scenario process for the sake of engaging in large-scale research programs, but rather to produce a limited number of "focus papers" that bring together currently available data and ideas in a form that is readily usable by the scenario team.[3]

---

[3] The scenario process is, or should be, an iterative one, and the first pass should proceed as rapidly as possible to produce a final product. Any trends or potential events that could be critical but that are too uncertain to warrant more detailed research in subsequent refinements and amplification of the scenarios should simply be noted.

Category	Examples
Demographics	• Age, family, household, and ethnic structures and trends • Regional and national migration • Labor force structure and trends
Social and lifestyle factors	• Consumer values, needs, and wants • Psychographic profiles • Education • Employee concerns • Special interest groups
Economic conditions	• Macroeconomic trends (GNP, trade, inflation, and so on) • Microeconomic trends (wages, consumer expenditures) • Regional and national variations • Economic structures
Natural resources	• Energy prices and availability • Raw materials • Land resources
Physical environment (ecosystems)	• Effluents and toxic wastes • Environmental quality
Political and regulatory forces	• Political attitudes and groups • National and local governments • Specific regulations and government policy
Technological forces	• Emerging technologies • Basic research trends • Technological infrastructure
International conditions	• International monetary system • Regional tensions • Protectionism

Source: SRI International

FIG. 3-6 Checklist for Identifying Macroenvironmental Forces

Define Scenario Logics. Scenario logics, or outcomes, are the heart of the scenario process. They give the set of scenarios a structure, an organizing principle, and a means of clear differentiation, and they enable planners to limit the set to a manageable number. Clearly, taking all of the possible permutations and combinations of outcomes to the macroeconomic forces identified and analyzed in Step 3 would be an indiscriminate way of proceeding, and would result in an impossibly large number of scenarios.

What is needed is the smallest number of scenarios that define the boundaries of the envelope of planning uncertainty (see Figure 3-4). This can be achieved by the following:

- Focusing on those key factors and forces that represent the maximum degree of criticality (i.e., those factors that are the real "drivers" of the future to be described) *and* uncertainty; and
- Defining alternate logics that explain why and how the key forces might take different trajectories.

The simplest structure is represented by two drivers, each with two alternate logics, which yields a matrix of four possibilities, as follows:

		Driver A	
		Logic 1	*Logic 2*
Driver B	*Logic 1*	Scenario 1	Scenario 2
	Logic 2	Scenario 3	Scenario 4

However, there is nothing inherent in the process that limits the structure either to two drivers or to two logics. Another structure, for instance, could be represented by the following schematic:

Driver A	*Driver B*	*Driver C*
Logic 1	Logic 1	Logic 1
Logic 2	Logic 2	Logic 2
Logic 3		Logic 3

One trouble with such a structure is that it yields 18 different scenarios, which are too many for most planning systems to manage. Some criteria for selecting a more manageable number would have to be developed (see Step 5, following).

If the scenario team in this example used the simplest structure of drivers and logics, they might decide that the envelope of uncertainty could best be covered by focusing on economic/energy growth and sociopolitical policies:

DRIVER A: ECONOMIC/ENERGY GROWTH RATES

Logic 1: The energy crises and recessions of the 1970s represented merely perturbations (albeit severe ones) of post-World War II growth rates and, following a period of adjustment, a resumption of economic growth near 1960–1973 levels should be expected, with a corresponding growth in energy demand.

Logic 2: The U.S. and global economies are in a period of radical restructuring that will result in different growth rates and patterns, with the U.S. economy growing more slowly through the 1980s as it restructures and more rapidly in the 1990s, but in less energy-intensive areas. Simultaneously, the energy conservation programs initiated in the 1970s will continue to work their way through the capital stock, effectively uncoupling energy growth from economic growth.

DRIVER B: SOCIOPOLITICAL POLICIES

Logic 1: The election of Ronald Reagan as President represented a genuine break in post-World War II social and political thinking, with the result that the United States will be moving toward a redefinition of public and private sector roles and toward increasing reliance on market forces rather than on federal policies and programs for our economic direction.

Logic 2: The U.S. economy is now so complex, with so many social and environmental effects beyond private-sector control, and is so locked in global competition with other nations whose goverments play an active role in promoting economic growth and exports, that the United States has no option but to increase the role of the federal government in shaping the company's economic direction (perhaps through some form of indicative planning).

In matrix form, this combination of drivers and logics is represented as follows:

Sociopolitical Policies

		Market-driven	*Government-directed*
	Resumed trajectory	Scenario 1	Scenario 2
Economic/Energy Growth Rate			
	Restructured growth	Scenario 3	Scenario 4

It is important at this stage of the process to avoid "false logics" that are actually, for example, assumptions of high growth and low growth. Logics must represent different theories as to how the world works or may work; and they must explain the why and how of the presumed outcomes.

Elaborate on Scenario Descriptions. Depending on the scenario structure developed in Step 4, all or just some of the scenarios produced by the interplay of alternate logics should now be described in detail. There is no golden rule as to the number of scenarios to be elaborated on for planning use. However, when just two scenarios are selected, it is too easy to perceive one as "good" and the other as "bad," and three are interpreted as "high," "middle," and "low." Much can be said in favor of a set of four, which is the product, for example, of a two by two matrix structure. If it is decided to elaborate on fewer than the total number of scenarios implied by the structure, those selected should:

- Be the ones with the highest degree of internal consistency;
- Be judged to be the most plausible (not necessarily the most probable);
- Best define the boundaries of the envelope of uncertainty; and

- Form the most useful alternative frames of reference for evaluating the strategic decision in question.

Scenarios are elaborated on not simply in terms of their drivers and logics but in terms of *all* of the decision factors and macroenvironmental forces identified in Steps 2 and 3. Normally, this involves anywhere from 15 to 30 major descriptors covering the full range of social, economic, political, and technological forces at the macroenvironmental level, and possibly a similar number at the microenvironmental (relevant industry/market) level. The elaboration of the differences in each descriptor across the set of scenarios can be most simply and clearly displayed in tabular form. However, separate treatment of the story line for each scenario is useful, if not essential, to bring out the basic character and thrust of each. Although the scenario elaboration will probably be predominantly qualitative, particularly at the macroenvironmental level, quantification should be introduced whenever possible and plausible. In this connection, the focus papers developed in Step 3 should be a useful source of both ideas and data.

Analyze Implications for Strategic Decisions. The bottom line in the scenario process is the usefulness of the scenarios in strategic planning and decision making. Scenarios are, after all, not an end in themselves, but a means—a way of improving the probable robustness and resilience of decisions made under conditions of great uncertainty. Scenarios do not make or dictate the decision, but they can provide useful "test beds" for assessing how a given decision or strategy might play out in different future environments.

Analysis of the implications of a set of scenarios should focus on answering the following questions:

- How is each scenario likely to affect the key decision factors identified in Step 2? (In this example, in Scenario 1 the world oil price might be driven up to $50 a barrel (in 1980 dollars) by the year 2000, while in Scenario 4 the price could fluctuate within a $25–$35 range over this period.)
- What are the major threats and opportunities posed for the business in each scenario? In the scenarios collectively?
- What should be done in any scenario? What should not be done?
- What seems to be the best strategy or decision to meet the conditions of the "planning focus" scenario?[4]
- How resilient or vulnerable would this strategy or decision be under the conditions of the other scenarios?

---

[4] Opinion is divided on the question of whether just one scenario (presumably, that judged to be "most probable") should be selected. Scenario purists would say "No, never." Certainly when, as in our example, the scenarios are focused on a single decision, all of the scenarios should be used and a "go" decision should be played out in each. However, when scenarios are used as an ongoing part of a continuing strategic planning process, pragmatism suggests the approach of designating one scenario as the "planning focus," provided that the remaining scenarios are still used as "test beds" and the basis for contingency planning.

/

- What modifications in this strategy or decision are suggested by this testing of it against the other scenarios?
- What contingency planning should be undertaken to deal with the major threats and opportunities posed by the other scenarios?

Designing the Scanning System

Scanning is the second leg of the three-legged stool of environmental analysis (see Figure 3-3). Like scenarios, scanning is a tool for dealing with uncertainty and alerting managers to signs of change. However, unlike scenarios, which describe the future as it might be, scanning deals with the present as it is or as it seems to be evolving. Scanning is a systematic attempt to detect what Igor Ansoff once termed the "weak signals" of new trends, and to do so sufficiently early (and accurately) that the business has lead time in which to develop an anticipatory strategy—if it so chooses.

The principal elements of an environmental scanning system are the creation of a network of scanners and a reliance on the media, principally the print media, for initial reporting of the symptoms of change.[5] A pioneering system is Weiner, Edrich, Brown's Trend Evaluation and Monitoring (TEAM), originally designed as the Trend Analysis Program in the life insurance industry (Figure 3-7). Like most good scanning systems, the development and operation of TEAM involves five steps.

1 Formation of the scanning network;
2 Development of guidelines;
3 Determination of resources;
4 Establishment of a synthesis/analysis process; and
5 Link to action; feedback.

These steps are discussed in the following sections.

Formation of the Scanning Network. Intelligence-gathering systems such as scanning operate best on the network principle. Increasing the number of scanning points within an organization and linking them up with external networks obviously increases the chances of detecting "weak signals." It also has the secondary advantage of diffusing a needed environmental sensitivity throughout the organization. In selecting the required number of "intelligence agents" a premium is put on those with an openness of mind, a sensitivity to change, a knowledge of the business, and on developing a broad multifunctional, multidisciplinary representation among the network's membership. Responsibility must also be assigned for overall management of the network because, while decentralization is an essential virtue, some central point must be designated to coordinate the gathering, synthesis, and analysis of the intelligence collected.

---

[5] As scanners gain experience and confidence, they frequently start noting changes before they are reported in the media.

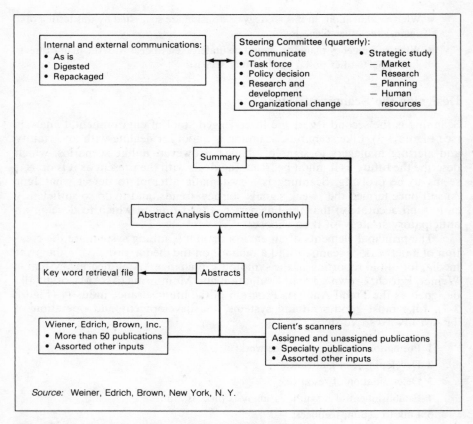

FIG. 3-7 The Trend Evaluation and Monitoring System

Development of Guidelines. Although the purpose of scanning is to turn a wide-angle lens on the business environment, and prevailing attitude of scanners should be to expect the unexpected, some frame of reference is needed both by the individual scanners and by the central analysis component. Two broad guidelines are suggested:

1 Business relevance: There should be some evidence that the detected change will have some impact on the current or future strategies and policies of the business. Therefore, scanners must be adequately briefed on these matters so that they can filter out the weak signals that may be interesting but that are irrelevant in this context.

2 Environmental perspective: As noted previously, one purpose of scenarios is to provide a frame of reference for the interpretation and analysis of scanning data. Whether or not scenarios are used, the current set of planning assumptions about the future should be communicated to the scanners so that they share a common perspective as to the corporation's view of the future.

The danger in providing any such guidelines is that they may "select out" from the scanners' horizons the very things that they should observe and report. This danger can be avoided only by making the guidelines as open and flexible as possible, while still providing a common and useful frame of reference within which the scanning network should operate.

Determination of Sources. If the print media are going to be the primary source of intelligence, then a first order of business is to identify and ensure coverage of the most important (and diverse) selection. The sources may include the following:

- General, business, and scholarly publications (Weiner, Edrich, Brown includes in its own coverage publications as diverse as *The New York Times, The Wall Street Journal, Mother Jones, Daedalus, National Review,* and *Science*)
- Government reports
- Trade association publications
- Clipping services
- Research organizations (e.g., John Naisbitt's *Trend Report,* with its content analysis of over 200 daily papers in the United States)

However, a thorough survey should also be made of potential sources *inside* the company. Reports from sales representatives, lobbyists, scientists, and community relations specialists can be important inputs for the scanning system.

Establishment of a Synthesis/Analysis Process. The intelligence that flows in from the scanning network may be likened to pieces of a jigsaw puzzle, or, more accurately, several puzzles. Individually, they may be meaningless or of little significance; joined with other pieces, they may provide an illuminating insight into a new trend. Pattern recognition is thus an essential talent for members of the central body within the organization (generally an analysis committee) that is responsible for the collation and interpretation of data. In periodic meetings (usually on a monthly basis), this group reviews scanners' abstracts and reports, discusses patterns and assesses their significance, identifies potential new issues, and decides which issues merit more detailed analysis.

Link to Action; Feedback. Summaries of analysis committee meetings should be given to the scanners and should be fed, directly or indirectly, into the planning system. It is vital that scanners receive this sort of feedback in order to assure them that their work is being used and to improve the effectiveness of the scanning by sharing the accumulated intelligence. The linkage to the planning system is equally important. The information can either be disseminated through a senior-level steering committee or given directly to those in the planning system who are responsible for scenario development, environmental assessment, and issue identification.

Monitoring: Focus on the Known

Monitoring is, in many ways, the most pedestrian of the environmental assessment tasks, entailing as it does the detailed, day-by-day tracking of trends and developments of known importance. Compared with scenarios and scanning, monitoring is concerned more with the immediate and the known than with the far future and uncertainty (although in this day and age, "known" must be considered a relative term).

The content of the monitoring system is defined by the results of scenario development, by the input from scanning, and by the needs of the business. That is, there is a finite and relatively limited number[6] of external trends of known importance to the success of the business that must be carefully tracked. The results of the tracking must be fed into the systems for current operations as well as for future planning. In the social and political arenas alone, trends that are monitored are likely to include:

- Population size and characteristics (e.g., birth rate, age mix, marital status, educational attainment)
- Regional migration and mobility
- Household formation (e.g., number of new homes, size of household, two-income families, single-person households)
- Values and life-styles (e.g., leisure patterns, shopping habits, consumption versus conservation, "entitlements")
- Public attitudes toward government, corporations, unions, and issues of the day
- Public-interest groups
- Political trends (e.g., shifts in party affiliation, federal-state relations, executive, legislative, judicial balance)
- Government spending (e.g., social versus defense expenditures, deficits, public debt) and taxation policies
- Legislation and regulation (e.g., antitrust, employment, environmental protection, product safety)

For monitoring purposes, the selection of trends must be much more focused than a generic listing such as that given above suggests. For example, a high-technology firm that is dependent for the success of its strategy on its ability to tap a labor pool with highly specialized skills will want to monitor enrollments and graduations in particular graduate and undergraduate fields. A consumer goods company will concentrate its political monitoring on product safety and protection legislation and regulation and on the activities of consumer activist groups. An aerospace/defense contractor will tend to follow more closely than those in other industries the federal budgetary processes and

---

[6] One of the most extensive and sophisticated monitoring systems, developed by Sears, Roebuck & Company in the mid-1970s, covered 150 trends in demographics, employment, income, housing, values and life-styles, technology, public attitudes, government, economics, and international issues.

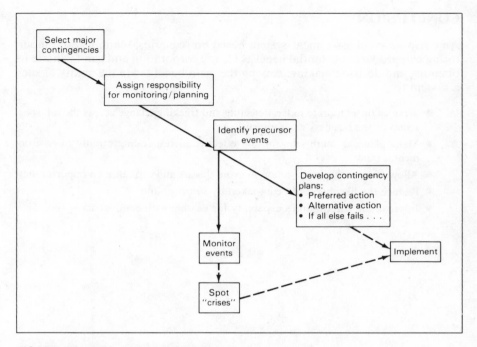

FIG. 3-8 Flow of Contingency Planning

congressional debates over defense spending. In each of these examples, monitoring focuses on an identified business need.

The information that is derived from monitoring activities serves at least three purposes:

1 It indicates the need for mid-course corrections in current action plans;
2 It serves as feedback into the scenario development process for fine-tuning and modifying initial scenarios; and
3 Where necessary it triggers the implementation of contingency plans (see Figure 3-8).

This last point is worth a note of explanation. It is axiomatic that in uncertain times, standby plans should be developed to deal with contingencies, that is, deviations from one or more of the assumptions on which current corporate strategy is based. It follows, therefore, that monitoring should pay special attention to the identification of:

• Precursor events (those events or developments that foreshadow the occurrence of a contingency)
• Trigger points (those points at which contingency plans should be put into action)

CONCLUSION

An environmental assessment system based on scenarios, scanning, and monitoring can produce substantial benefits for the corporation and can facilitate its planning and decision making. Among the main benefits are the ability of such a system to:

- Serve as the corporate radar, detecting and tracking change across the full spectrum of the business environment;
- Make planning more relevant and effective in responding rapidly to environmental trends;
- Allow more anticipatory action to avoid threats and capitalize on opportunities;
- Reduce the likelihood of being taken by surprise; and
- Improve the corporation's capability for dealing with contingencies.

4

Strategic Response
in a Turbulent Environment

H. Igor Ansoff

Professor, European Institute for Advanced Studies in Management, Brussels
Professor, Stockholm School of Economics, Stockholm
Distinguished Professor of Management, U.S. International University,
San Diego

INTRODUCTION

Experience, supported by extensive historical research,[1] suggests that at a given time there is an optimal level of strategic aggressiveness that brings success to the firm. Companies that attack their environment with optimal aggressiveness have the best chances of success, but success still depends on how responsive their competitive strategies are to the competitive conditions in the marketplace.

On the other hand, if a firm's aggressiveness lags or leads the optimal level, even the best conceived competitive strategy will not produce high profits. Thus the aggressiveness of a company's strategy can be thought of as a meta-strategy within which the specific competitive strategy is determined.

The annals of business history are full of "dead heros": managers who introduced innovations to markets that were not ready for them. One of these is

---

[1] A.D. Chandler, Jr., *Strategy and Structure* (Cambridge, Mass.: MIT Press, 1972), p. 54.

Henry J. Kaiser, who introduced the compact car 20 years before its time and paid dearly for his entrepreneurial aggressiveness. And the annals of history are also full of laggards: managers who were not aggressive enough in responding to major shifts in competition, nature of demand, or technology. In the early 1930s, Henry Ford's failure to recognize the shift in orientation from production to marketing cost the Ford Motor Company its dominant position in the automotive market.

During the first half of the twentieth century, changes in the optimal level of aggressiveness (such as the shift in orientation from production to marketing) occurred infrequently and slowly enough to permit many laggards to catch up and those ahead of their time to "hang tough" until the demand caught up with their innovations. For example, Robert Sarnoff, who introduced color television some 10 years before its time, held on long enough to make RCA one of the early dominant competitors in the market shift from black-and-white to color television.

In the second half of the century, the range of tolerance for nonoptimal strategic response has become progressively narrower because of the more frequent occurrence and the accelerating speed of discontinuous shifts in customer demands, competitive behavior, technology, and the sociopolitical environment. The laggards are in danger of being unable to catch up with the shifts, and the innovators are in danger of becoming obsolete by succeeding developments before the market is ready for their innovations.

Thus, in strategy formulation, not only must competitive strategy correspond to key success factors, but also the timeliness and aggressiveness of a company's strategic behavior must be in tune with the environment.

Two complementary but distinctive approaches to ensuring effective strategic responses to turbulent shifts in the market environment are strategic issue management and strategic business planning. Each is discussed in this chapter, along with a simple method by which management can select the approach appropriate to its own company.

HISTORICAL STRATEGIC RESPONSES IN TURBULENT ENVIRONMENTS

Strategic response means the process by which a company adjusts its position and approach to the environment: the way it changes its market focus and the products/services it offers to these markets; its product and process technology; and its approach to customers, competition, and powerful pressure groups.

During the first half of the twentieth century, the strategic response of a majority of companies was evolutionary and incremental. The acceleration of growth in most industries made it attractive for management to minimize investment in innovation and concentrate on making profits from the strategic positions they established at the start of the century.

But some firms responded discontinuously. On one hand, these were restless, entrepreneurial firms that continuously sought to expand their horizons through diversification and/or development of new technologies. These firms caused their own discontinuities. On the other hand, some firms were forced into discontinuities in their environments. For example, early in the century the DuPont Company was forced to change its strategic position when the invention of dynamite made obsolete DuPont's traditional and only competence, the manufacture and sales of black powder. A pervasive strategic discontinuity, which first occurred in the 1930s in consumer industries and some 25 years later spread to producer industries, was the transition from production orientation (firms offered undifferented products and competed through pricing) to marketing orientation (the key success variables became product differentiation and responsiveness to consumer wishes and needs).

Many historical studies have been made of forced strategic responses. Most of them show that the typical response was unplanned and reactive, that firms persisted in their historical strategic behavior long past the time when it was effective. Some, like Henry Ford, procrastinated so long they permanently lost their historical competitive dominance. But others, like DuPont, managed to catch up and regain or even enhance their previous position in the market. Such delay and recovery were possible because the speed of change was slow enough to permit delayed recovery and the frequency of novel discontinuities was low enough so that the company could deal with one discontinuity at a time.

The 1980s will not be as kind. It will be a decade of rapid change, and frequent and novel discontinuities. As a result, many thoughtful managements have already concluded that the response to potentially surprising discontinuities must be managed. Determining which method of managing strategic response is most appropriate to a particular company requires an understanding of the environment in which the company operates.

Turbulence level means the extent to which the environment has undergone observable change from the past. Figure 4-1, for example, depicts the various turbulence levels in the United States during the twentieth century. The environment is assessed in terms of five factors that determine the overall turbulence level:

- Market scope, which grew from national to regional to global.
- Success variables, which were economic in nature during the first 50 years of the century and technological since the 1950s, with sociopolitical factors joining the equation in the 1960s.
- Challenges faced by management as results of the changes in market scope and success. In a world of familiar challenges, responses were based on precedent and experience. By the 1930s it became necessary to extrapolate historical trends. In the mid-1950s, extrapolation became increasingly dangerous because new technological and competitive factors produced discontinuities in the historical trends. In the 1970s, the challenges frequently became not only discontinuous but also novel, in the sense that prior experience was of little help in developing responses. The key source of novelty was the sociopolitical variables that forced management to devise innovative responses and approaches.
- Speed of change, which is a ratio of the speed at which challenges develop in the environment to the speed at which a company responds to these challenges. As Figure 4-1 shows, between 1900 and 1930 change was slow enough to permit companies to catch up after the impact of change was felt. In this environment, great companies like Sears, DuPont, and General Motors could take 10 to 20

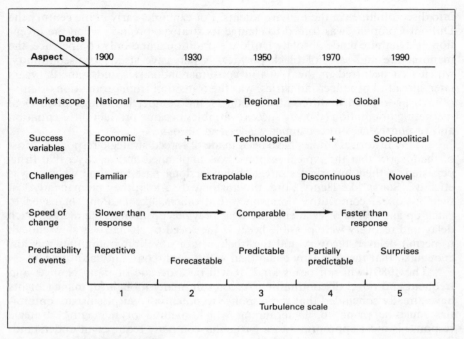

FIG. 4-1　Evolving Turbulence

years to respond to major environmental challenges and still remain leaders in their respective fields. As the rate of change accelerated as the century progressed, corporate response time shortened in absolute terms, but not in relation to the rate of change. Today, significant changes such as the formation of an oil supply cartel like the Organization for Petroleum Exporting Countries can occur virtually overnight, catching a great majority of petroleum-dependent companies flat-footed and surprised.

- Predictability of events. In the last 80 years, events have become increasingly difficult to predict. The serene world in which events were repeated and responses to those events could be based on historical precedents and experience became only a fading memory by the end of the 1920s. The future could be forecast, however, by extrapolating past trends; when smooth extrapolation could no longer be trusted, the future was predicted through analysis of discontinuous threats and opportunities. By the 1970s, the combination of complexity, novelty, and speed began to limit the ability to predict the future accurately. For an increasing number of environmental discontinuities, only partial and imprecise information could be obtained by the time a company had to formulate its response. The world is now full of surprises that arrive virtually unannounced.

Few managers would disagree, then, with the conclusions reached by 500 senior managers from various developed countries who attended a strategic management seminar in 1982. In their view, the 1980s will be highly turbulent, characterized by numerous, frequent, rapidly developing events that are discontinuous from the past, difficult to anticipate, and difficult to respond to. In such times and conditions, well-planned management of the strategic responses to these challenges is absolutely essential to survival. Two such management approaches are strategic issue management and strategic business planning.

STRATEGIC ISSUE MANAGEMENT

One systematic approach to responding to discontinuities that has attracted much attention is strategic issue management. In this context, "issue" means a trend, threat, or opportunity that has a potentially major (positive or negative) impact on future corporate performance. Issue management starts with a systematic identification of developments that potentially can affect the company's strategic performance. This is accomplished by scanning the external environment, comparing historical performance with current and future goals, and monitoring the company's internal environment.

The second step in issue management is issue evaluation, in which the effect of each issue on the future performance of the company, as well as the probable timing of these effects, is estimated. By evaluating issues in this way, companies can assign priorities, thereby reducing the number of critical issues that must be dealt with on a short-term basis. Issues are sorted into four categories. From lowest to highest priority, they are:

1 False-alarm issues, which have limited impact on the company and which are dropped from further corporate consideration;

2 Issues with some potential impact, which are monitored over time as they evolve;

3 Issues of moderate urgency, which are accumulated in anticipation of the next annual planning cycle, at which time they are addressed along with other annually planned programs; and

4 Urgent issues, whose resolution cannot be delayed, which receive special attention and resources.

Issues of moderate or great urgency are analyzed further, approximate response strategies are developed, and attendant programs and budgets are prepared and implemented.

An issue is considered resolved only when a threat has been averted or an opportunity has been converted into new sales and profits for the company. Three levels of management are involved in strategic issue management: (1) a staff group charged with issue identification and evaluation; (2) a group of line managers, which sets priorities; and (3) ad hoc groups, who address and resolve the issues.

Not all approaches to managing issues are this comprehensive. Some companies formalize only issue identification, and depend on line managers to resolve those issues that fall within their areas of responsibility. Other compa-

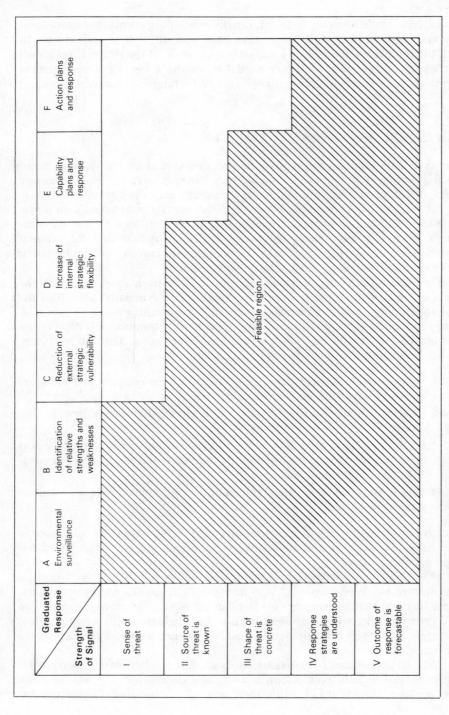

FIG. 4-2 Weak Signals and Graduated Responses

nies appoint issue managers who are responsible for coordinating resolution of the issue within the organization.

Effective issue management requires two kinds of feedback: operating feedback, in which actual performance (i.e., progress in resolving the issues) is compared with the plan, and strategic feedback, in which the nature, the potential impact, and the urgency of the issue are periodically evaluated. Operating feedback results in changing, reorienting, or strengthening efforts to resolve issues. Strategic feedback can result in changing issue priorities and the resources allocated to their resolution.

The extent of the need for and the sophistication of an issue management system depends on the environment in which the company operates. If the amount of turbulence is minimal or moderate, there is no need for a system in which issues are reworked frequently. However, when the environment is highly volatile, an issue management system must encompass not only issues of current interest but also those with longer-term implications and less precisely known impacts. When reliable estimates of their probable impacts on company performance—such as profit loss or gain—can be made, numerical values can be assigned according to the extent of the impact. An issue management system that uses such a numerical form provides strong signals to the system participants about which issues are most important to the strategic success of the company.

When the environment is highly turbulent, several issues arise whose impacts cannot be predicted easily, necessitating a series of weak rather than strong signals to company participants. Weak signals are warnings of external or internal events and developments that are still too incomplete to permit an accurate estimate of their impact and/or to determine full-fledged responses.

Almost every issue evolves from a point at which it is felt to be a vague threat, through realization of the reality of the threat, to the point at which the impact of the threat can be predicted (see Figure 4-2). The field of electronics provides an example of this progression.

In the 1930s, it was becoming increasingly evident that electronics was undergoing change, but few were aware of the specific areas in which the next significant discoveries would be made. By the 1940s, everyone in the field knew that solid-state conduction of electricity was the source of the challenge. Toward the end of the 1950s, the shape of the challenge became concrete in the form of the prototype transistor developed by Bell Labs, but it was not until several years later in the 1960s that entreprenurial firms like Texas Instruments developed response strategies by perfecting the manufacturing technology, identifying the potential markets, and developing commercially marketable transistors. This initial response was based on faith in the transistor, not on exact profit-and-loss estimates, which became possible only after the commercial technology was developed.

Signals of change can be detected early in the life of a discontinuity, and companies can respond to these signals accordingly. That is, they can keep their options flexible until the weak signals become strong enough to warrant specific strategic response. For example, a strong sense of threat is sufficient to justify intensified environmental surveillance and identification of the company's strengths and weaknesses in relation to the changes that are occurring.

When the source of the threat is identified, the company can reduce its external vulnerability by reducing its dependence on business areas that may be affected, or it can improve its internal flexibility by strengthening its relative weaknesses. When the threat becomes a reality, the company can develop specific response strategies: for example, matching the competition with a comparable product, ignoring the development and pursuing other avenues of competition, or developing a second-generation entry in the marketplace.

The advantage of a system that includes the use of early-warning signals is that it enables the company to move through a series of progressively stronger, more costly, more irrevocable responses. The disadvantage is that the costs incurred in the early responses are wasted if a threat turns out to be a false alarm or if it develops differently from original forecasts.

STRATEGIC BUSINESS PLANNING

Strategic issue management is similar to the radar-based early warning and response system used by the military. Like its military counterpart, issue management enables a company to respond to singular, fast-moving threats. But neither system prepares the organization for a broad-scale, comprehensive, and coordinated attack on the environment. For this battle, business and industry, like the armed forces, needs a comprehensive, systematic method for deploying available forces. That is, they need strategic planning that includes setting the company's goals and objectives; analyzing the company's strengths and weaknesses; identifying threats and opportunities; matching strengths/weaknesses with threats/opportunities; and choosing a comprehensive future strategy. This process, which is known as strategic business planning, is different from issue management. It is comprehensive, encompassing most of the threats/opportunities in all business areas of the company; it is coordinated, developing the various parts of the company simultaneously and in harmony; and it is highly complex and costly.

The concept of business strategy is complex and elusive, described by some as a basic decision rule that guides an organization in adapting to a changing environment, and by others as the pattern that underlies a series of strategic moves, such as the development of new products or expansion into new markets.

A strategy can be implicit; that is, it is the underlying leitmotif of a company's strategic behavior. Strategy also can be evolutionary and reactive. For example, some companies follow a consistent, step-by-step adaptation of their products and markets until the point at which environmental discontinuity forces a basic change in direction.

Implicit, evolutionary, and reactive strategies were typical of U.S. companies and corporations during the first half of this century. With the emergence of systematic strategic planning in the 1960s, however, strategy became prescriptive, emphasizing what companies should do in the future (e.g., diversify by entering new business areas). Strategic planning forces strategy to be explicit and anticipatory.

Some academic researchers who have focused on understanding historical strategies have been suspicious of and even hostile to the idea of explicit strategic planning. Some have argued that planning encounters organizational resistance, and that planned strategies produce unplanned results, and that a highly unpredictable and turbulent environment makes planning impossible. Their advice is to do long-range planning, as long as the environment is predictable, and to return to adaptive strategic behavior, based on intuition and experience, when the environment becomes unpredictable.

Strategic planning *has* frequently encountered organizational resistance. However, the question is: Should strategic planning be abandoned on those grounds or should ways be found to minimize the resistance? The evidence strongly suggests the latter, a position that will be explored more fully later in this chapter.

On theoretical grounds, a return to intuition and experience is a difficult position to defend because, as Figure 4-1 shows, unpredictable challenges do not lend themselves to response based exclusively or even largely on intuition. On practical grounds, surveys have shown a growing use and acceptance of strategic planning techniques as the means of dealing with complex environments. For example, one recent comprehensive survey in the United States of the use of strategic portfolio balance[2] showed that a majority of the surveyed companies used some form of portfolio analysis to assist management in positioning the company. And although strategic planning is still not universal, numerous corporations (e.g., General Electric and IBM) have a rather long history of using it. That history, however, is not a single continuum.

During the 1970s, many changes occurred in management's perception of strategic planning. The causes of slowed growth and decline were better understood: The former occurs because of market saturation and the latter because of technology substitution, which enables new firms to supersede traditional competitors in the market. In addition, the concept of demand life cycle was articulated and generally accepted. Therefore, the saturation observed in some businesses in the 1950s was a precursor of eventual saturation of markets in many other so-called first-generation industries born during the second half of the nineteenth century. Further, research showed that technological fertility, improved transportation, more sophisticated communications, and skillful management were shortening the demand life cycles of technological processes and products. Finally, management determined that as the demand curve passed from one growth stage to another, the critical factors that determined success in the marketplace changed, necessitating modifications in their strategic planning.

These new perceptions changed management's approach to strategic planning. Specifically, instead of reviewing strategic planning as a "once-in-a-lifetime" repositioning, it was now perceived as a continual activity concerned with maintaining a balanced business unit and profit portfolio for the com-

---

[2] Strategic portfolio balance can be used to determine the competitive position a company wants to occupy in a strategic business unit (SBU), decide on future resource commitments to different SBUs, ensure both near- and long-term growth profitability of the company, and reduce strategic vulnerability.

pany. An important criterion in creating this balanced portfolio was the vulnerability of its contents to unexpected events. In addition, management reevaluated the rate of diversification in strategy, especially the importance of divesting the company of products or businesses no longer economically attractive. At the same time, investment, once considered a sign of failure, became a positive act on the part of insightful management.

Maintenance of viable competitive strategies in the firm's strategic business areas became a major concern. "Where there is growth, there is profit" was replaced by a realization that companies cannot profit unless their competitive strategies are periodically updated in response to shifting customer needs and to their competition.

Clearly, during the 1970s, strategic planning evolved into an ongoing process of managing a company's overall portfolio of products and businesses in response to changing internal and external events and circumstances. But the very nature of the evolutionary process implies further change—and, indeed, the events of the 1980s have begun to act as catalysts for such changes in strategic planning.

STRATEGIC POSTURE PLANNING

Matching Strategic Agressiveness to Turbulence

Strategic planning originally was based on an implicit assumption of strategic continuity. That is, future threats and opportunities could be met without making fundamental changes in "what business we're in." Organizational strengths were expected to remain strengths, and weaknesses, if left unchanged, were expected to remain weaknesses. New strategies could be determined by selecting those areas in which the company maintained a position of competitive strength.

In the future, either in search of growth or in response to threats, companies will increasingly make discontinuous shifts to new technologies, new markets, new competitive strategies, and new societal responses. Thus, strategic planning in the 1980s must be based on an expectation of strategic discontinuity. That is, companies must *expect* change to be the norm, and therefore must periodically reevaluate their strategic aggressiveness in light of this expected turbulence in the environment.

Strategic Aggressiveness

The first step in evaluating strategic aggressiveness is diagnosing probable future turbulence in the respective business areas of the company: turbulence caused by product and technology innovation and turbulence caused by competitive changes in the market. For example, today in the synthetic fibers industry, product-innovation possibilities have pretty much been exhausted. Hence the extent of innovation turbulence is moderate. On the other hand, because of global overcapacity, market turbulence is high.

| | | Product-Technology Innovation | | | | |
		Stable	Incremental Evolution	Anticipatory Evolution	Novel Departure	Creativity
	Turbulence Level	1	2	3	4	5
Grow with market	1					
Defend market	2					
Enlarge position	3					
Attain novel position	4					
Create market	5					

Market Position (label on left vertical axis)

FIG. 4-3 Strategic Aggressiveness and Turbulence Matrix

The aggressiveness of the responsible strategies depends on the extent of the anticipated innovation and market turbulence. For example, as shown in Figure 4-3, when innovation turbulence is repetitive (level 1), the optimum innovation aggressiveness is stable. The optimum strategy in this instance is to leave products virtually unchanged. This was the case of the Ford Model T between 1910 and 1930. As the extent of innovation turbulence increases, strategy becomes evolutionary, then anticipatory, then incremental. At the extreme—that is, under highly volatile innovation and market turbulence (level 5)—successful companies become creators of new products and technologies.

A similar progression occurs with respect to a company's market aggressiveness as market turbulence increases.

The second step in evaluating strategic aggressiveness is assessing the current level of strategic aggressiveness the company has chosen. The gap between the degree of aggressiveness needed and the current aggressiveness policy of the company must be closed to ensure a competitive position in the market. If the implication of the comparison is that the current aggressiveness is sufficient and will remain so in the near term, there may still be a need to adjust competitive strategy to take advantage of technological and market changes. However, there is no need to rethink the basic strategic thrust of the company.

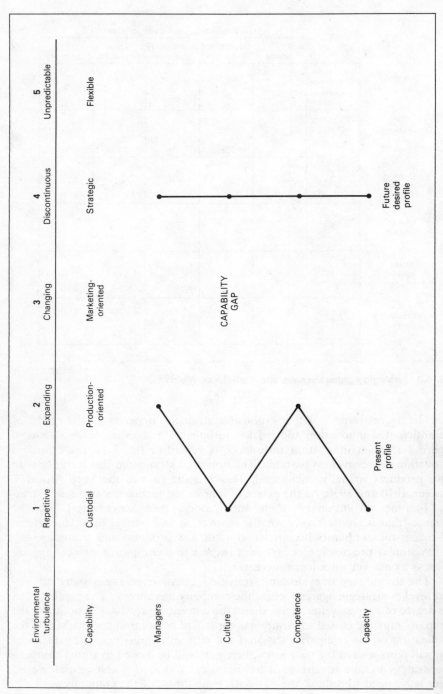

FIG. 4-4 General Management Capability Planning

General Management Capabilities

A shift in strategy is followed quickly by a realignment in the various functions of a company, such as production, research and development, and marketing. However, general management usually fails to follow suit quickly. In changing times, general management frequently becomes the major obstacle to timely, smooth shifts in strategy and adaptations to environmental turbulence.

The reason is that general management skills are often thought to be universal, transferable from one industry to another, regardless of differences in environments. Obviously, this is not the case. Companies must be as concerned with adapting their management capabilities to fit new strategies as they are with adapting their strategies to changing environments.

General management capability has four components:

- The qualifications of the managers
- The characteristics of organizational climate
- The problem-resolving capability of general management
- The through-put capacity of general management

The qualifications of managers are determined, in part, by their talents, their personalities, their knowledge, and their skills. In addition, a manager's contribution depends on the influence he or she can exert on the organization (power position) and his or her propensity to use this influence (power drive). It also depends on the manager's awareness of the internal and external environment; his or her relative reliance on historical results vs. future possibilities; his or her propensity for risk; the way he or she perceives the critical factors for success (the model of the world); and the values and goals that motivate him or her. These variables determine the manager's acceptance, support, or rejection of discontinuous strategic responses by the company.

The organizational climate reflects the prevailing corporate structure, including the rewards and incentives scheme for strategic activity.

Management capability is also determined by its problem-solving competence, in particular the ability to use the systems and processes by which the organization operates. For example, long-range planning systems are incapable of recognizing the need for and responding to strategic challenges, but strategic planning is capable of handling such challenges.

A combination of managers' mentality and corporate culture or climate determines how aggressive the company's strategic behavior will be. The ability to act effectively is determined by the talents, skills, and knowledge of managers together with the structure, systems, and capacity of the organization.

To determine whether a company has the necessary management capability, one need only compare what is available with what is needed, as shown in Figure 4-4. The future desired profile line is the capability the company will need to deal with expected turbulence; the present profile line indicates the present capability of the company. The capability gap in the various components must be eliminated if the company is to be prepared to deal with future turbulence.

Environmental turbulence	Repetitive	Expanding	Changing	Discontinuous	Unpredictable
	Repetitive	• Slow • Incremental	• Fast • Incremental	• Discontinuous • Predictable	• Discontinuous • Partially predictable
Strategic aggressiveness	Stable	Reactive	Anticipatory	Exploring	Creative
	Stable, based on precedents	Reactive, based on experience	Anticipatory, based on extrapolation	New, based on observable alternatives	Novel, based on creativity
Management capability	Custodial	Production	Marketing	Strategic	Flexible
	• Rejects change • Seeks efficiency	• Adapts to change • Seeks efficiency	• Seeks familiar change • Synergistic	• Seeks related change • Global	• Seeks novel change • Creative

FIG. 4-5 Levels of Environmental Turbulence, Strategic Aggressiveness, and General Management Capability

As Figure 4-4 shows, companies can determine their future capability needs directly from the environment without knowledge of the details of their future strategy. This facilitates simultaneous development of the strategy and the necessary capabilities. This feature is particularly important in highly turbulent environments, in which the detailed strategy may not become clear until a threat or an opportunity is well developed. In such cases, a flexible capability can be developed ahead of the strategy, thus preparing the company to respond rapidly to fast developing threats and opportunities.

Planning Capability

The basic assumption in strategic posture planning is that a company's success depends on the matches between the amount of environmental turbulence and the strategic aggressiveness in response to that turbulence, and between strategic aggressiveness and general management capability (see Figure 4-5).

When the firm's strategic aggressiveness and capability match the anticipated level of turbulence, the company's potential for success is greatest. The potential decreases to the extent the strategy or the capability, or both, deviate from the optimum.

For practical purposes, capability planning should be done in two parts: one for the respective functional areas and the other for general management capability. The reason is that functional capabilities are determined by the critical competitive success factors in a strategic business unit (SBU), whereas general management is determined by the SBU turbulence.

Strategic Posture Management

When companies undergo fundamental changes in their strategies because of market and innovation turbulence, management often encounters significant resistance to change—an unwillingness or inability to support a new strategic thrust—within the organization. A brief summary of the implications this common but poorly understood phenomenon has for managers should prove helpful.

The size of the capability gap illustrated in Figure 4-4 suggests how much resistance can be expected in an organization facing a changing environment. Resistance is directly proportional to the capability gap and inversely proportional to the time period needed to close the gap.

Resistance can be behavioral or systemic. Behavioral resistance is opposition to change by groups and individuals, and usually is proportional to the perceived impact the change will have on the culture and the power structure. (Interestingly, perceptions tend to exaggerate negative impacts.) Groups and individuals whose power is increased can be expected to support rather than resist the change. Behavioral resistance can be triggered when a direct attack is made on the culture or the power structure, when capability or capacity changes threaten consequent changes in the culture and the power structure, and when changes in strategic behavior threaten the culture and the power structure.

Systemic resistance is opposition from individuals and the managerial infrastructure. It stems from a sense of self-perception that finds it impossible to plan and implement the change. Systemic resistance occurs when a change in strategic behavior imposes a load on competence or capacity when the individual or managerial structure is ill-equipped to handle the change.

Resistance depends on the sequence in which strategy, culture/power, and competence/capacity are changed. The maximum resistance occurs when all three occur simultaneously. When the change is made sequentially, the highest resistance is encountered by the following sequence:

$$\text{Strategy} \rightarrow \text{Competence / Capacity} \rightarrow \text{Culture / Power}$$

But this sequence is the quickest way to change strategic behavior. The lowest resistance, but also the slowest, sequence is

$$\text{Culture / Power} \rightarrow \text{Competence / Capacity} \rightarrow \text{Strategy}$$

In most situations, the rapidity of environmental change makes it impractical to use the low-resistance sequence. Therefore, the challenge to management is to organize the change process in a way that minimizes resistance. But whatever sequence is chosen, sufficient power and influence have to be mustered in support of the change to overcome the resistance.

Management has a number of variables it can use to reduce resistance:

● The length of time allotted to effect the change
● The perception of change held by the affected groups and individuals
● The involvement of those affected by the changes
● The choice of the sequence of change

Management must fundamentally reorient itself to managing the *total* change process, a responsibility that can be called strategic posture management.

In strategic posture management, management must design an approach that takes into consideration not only what has to be changed or implemented but also how those changes can be effected with the least resistance and who will be affected in what ways by the planned changes in culture, operations, power structure, and the like.

As a first step in carrying out these responsibilities, management must identify the sources and probable levels of support of and resistance to the proposed changes. Once these individuals and groups are identified, efforts can begin to include those who are supportive and, when possible, exclude opponents from the process. In addition, behavioral resistance can be minimized by making clear to all affected individuals the intent and consequences of the proposed change. A further means of defusing a potentially explosive reaction is to disseminate a master plan that lays out the details of the change process and a schedule for accomplishing it.

The change process itself must be carefully orchestrated and closely monitored. Strategy and capability changes are planned and sequentially phased in. After the strategy has been implemented, the capability changes continue to ensure that the change is institutionalized: That is, that capability matches the new strategy. Institutionalization is necessary in most cases because changes in culture and mentality take a long time to accomplish.

COMPARISON OF STRATEGIC ISSUE MANAGEMENT AND STRATEGIC POSTURE MANAGEMENT

Issue management treats environmental challenges one at a time, responding through a planned positioning of the company as a whole in a complex and turbulent environment. Issue management enables a company to react to novel developments arising from unfamiliar sources, to ensure real time response without delays normally caused by organizational complexity, and to prepare the company to respond to early signals of impending developments.

This planned positioning helps management anticipate the future environment and develop a coordinated strategic thrust, explain the growing complexity of the environment, balance and relate the contributions made by the company's different business units to help optimize allocation of strategic resources, enhance the company's flexibility and reduce its strategic vulnerability, and enable management to take the strategic initiative in shaping the company's future.

Planned positioning is a much more comprehensive and powerful tool than strategic issue management, which basically consists of loosely coordinated responses. But it is relatively slow and may not capture the turbulent environmental developments captured in strategic issue management. Thus, planned positioning and issue management can be viewed as complementary responses to turbulence. The preferred choice of a combination of positioning and issue management is determined by the turbulence characteristics of the company's environment.

5

Resource Assessment: Identifying Corporate Strengths and Weaknesses

HOWARD H. STEVENSON

Sarofin-Rock Professor of Business Administration, Harvard University
Former Vice President for Finance and Administration, Pretco Corporation

INTRODUCTION

Strategic planning requires management to set goals, to define the distance between goals and current position, and to plan the strategy and tactics for bridging the gap. In a sophisticated planning system, goals are no longer one-dimensional. The days of a five-year plan consisting solely of budget expectations have passed as senior management has come to recognize the need for coordinating resources such as people, machinery, plant, and dollars. The process of evaluating resources becomes even more complicated if one considers intangible factors such as innovation, morale, customer loyalty, financial credibility, and product quality. Resources must be assessed in a way that contributes to managerial decision-making.

Great importance has been placed upon resource assessment by authors in the field. The need for unflinching self-examination is taken as requirement by authors with as diverse backgrounds as Leavitt, Drucker, Simon, Cordiner, and Ansoff.[1] One text on corporate strategy stated the importance of self-examination succinctly:

> The first step in validating a tentative choice among several opportunities is to determine whether the organization has the capacity to prosecute it successfully. The capability of an organization is its demonstrated and potential ability to accomplish against the opposition of circumstances or competition, whatever it sets out to do. Every organization has an actual and potential strength and weakness. Since it is prudent in formulating strategy to extend or maximize the one and contain or minimize the other, it is important to try to determine what they are and to distinguish one from another.[2]

The fact that strengths and weaknesses should be defined is hardly in dispute. Increasing evidence shows that companies grow best by identifying core strengths and building in a systematic way on those strengths. Failures often occur because the strengths and weaknesses of an organization were not properly assessed. Examples of poor assessments include:

- Failing to assess properly the strength of competition relative to a new market entry;

- Attempting to stretch resources that are adequate for current activities to areas where they prove to be inadequate; and

- Attempting to correct noncritical weaknesses in a way that is not cost-effective.

Internal and external factors are causing corporations to focus on analyzing their resources and their strengths and weaknesses on a periodic basis. This chapter analyzes some of those factors. It then focuses upon the practical problems of resource assessment, defines the current state of the art in assessing strengths and weaknesses, and discusses the problems of both identifying excess resources and specifying resource limitations. Finally, it discusses strategies for acquiring resources.

---

[1] Theodore Leavitt, *Innovations in Marketing* (New York: McGraw-Hill Book Co., Inc., 1965), p. 176, Peter Drucker, *Managing for Results* (New York: Harper & Row, 1964), pp. 313 et seq.; H.A. Simon, D.W. Smithburg, and V.A Thompson, *Public Administration* (New York: Alfred A. Knopf, Inc.; 1950), p. 24; Ralph J. Cordiner, *New Frontiers for Professional Managers* (New York: McGraw-Hill Book Co., Inc., 1956), pp. 95–98; H. Igor Ansoff, *Corporate Strategy* (New York: McGraw-Hill Book Co., 1965), p. 92.

[2] E.P. Learned, C.R. Christensen, K.R. Andrews, and W.D. Guth, *Business Policy: Text and Cases* (Homewood, Ill.: Richard D. Irwin, 1965), p. 21.

FACTORS THAT MAKE RESOURCE ASSESSMENT CRITICAL

The internal and external environments in which planning takes place require a comprehensive understanding of an organization's strengths and weaknesses. The rate of change in today's business environment means that the organization must be capable of doing a rapid, accurate, and dispassionate analysis of its own capability to capitalize upon an unexpected opportunity or to respond effectively to an unforeseen risk.

External Environment

Since 1974, corporations of all sizes have faced recurring periods during which financial resources were essentially limited to those that were generated internally. Even though many capital-intensive industries have been able to marshal considerable debt to finance capital requirements, the equity markets generally have been unattractive, and the major constraint upon growth has been lack of capital. Many managers have been faced with more opportunities than they have had the resources to pursue. In such situations, growth can occur only if management assesses internal operations in order to decide where to invest and where to disinvest, either through outright sale or through attrition.

Formulating strategy in an environment in which resources are limited means that the strategist must understand the assumptions with which the organization is dealing. Higher requirements for return on investment are brought about in the face of higher debt costs, lower price earnings ratios, and longer time periods for realizing returns. Managers at all levels are seeking a competitive edge in order to succeed.

Need to Capitalize Upon Strengths

Business is deemed by many observers to be faced with the probability of a slow or no-growth economy. In addition, the competitive threat has increased with transnational competition, uneven regulatory impact, rapidly changing costs, and rapid advances in technology. The game of business is perceived by many to be zero sum in that gains by one competitor come largely at the expense of another. In this situation, the model of business as warfare is often used.

Using the warfare analogy, the purpose of defining strengths and measuring resources is clear. Management must answer three questions for which a knowledge of the corporation's strengths are paramount. These questions are:

1 What is an acceptable competitive position?

2 What are the aggressive strategies that a company can intelligently pursue?

3 What are the critical defensive requirements of the company?

In order to determine an acceptable competitive position, management must determine whether the company's product, market, and technological bases are stable and will continue to be stable over time. Mounting evidence shows that dominance of a defensible market is the single most important corporate strength.[3] Companies require cost competitiveness, product differentiation, customer recognition, and acceptable technological achievement. All of these requirements are analyzable through a careful process of defining the corporation's strengths and weaknesses. Analysis of the opportunities that arise from a stable competitive position and threats to that stability require the analysis of both offense and defense.

Strengths and the Business Strategy Offense

Offensive business strategy is like warfare in that the attacker is often able to choose the battlegrounds, the enemy, and the timing. As in warfare, the competition will be fought in different geographic places, with different classes of weapons, and with the outcomes being worth more or less in terms of future strategic advantage. Both at the corporate level and for the individual manager's career, the key question is the choice of which battles to fight against whom.

Applied to business, the "principle of mass" holds that superior combat power must be concentrated at a critical time and place for a decisive purpose.[4] In order to apply that principle, aggressive questions must be asked. These questions include the following:

- Which facets of the competitive field do we dominate currently?
  a. Price or manufacturing cost
  b. Distribution or marketing
  c. Product value to the consumer: quality, service
  d. Technology
  e. Financial resources
- Which current resource bases can be expanded most cost-effectively?
- What will the effect of an aggressive campaign be on our resources?
  a. People
  b. Finances and financial relationships
  c. Profits margins
  d. Manufacturing experience
- Can we define the proper battleground and limit the battle to that ground?

Most of the serious failures of analysis occur because the resources required for a proper attack are underestimated. The computer industry of the seventies, the watch industry, and the real estate field are littered with the wounded and dead firms that underestimated the resources required for a successful aggressive move.

---

[3] Michael E. Porter, *Competitive Strategy* (New York: Macmillan Publishing Co., 1980), p. 52.
[4] Sun Tzu, *The Art of War* (New York: Oxford University Press, 1963).

RESOURCES FOR DEFENSE

Military experts have always known that an attacking force will generally require vastly superior resources in order to succeed in a frontal assault on a well-fortified position. Military campaigns give the defender a much greater advantage than does business warfare. War is usually declared openly. Even if not publicized, only a limited number of sneak attacks can occur before the state is alerted to the danger. Clear frontiers, a sound system of border guards, and general access to the diplomatic communication network makes warfare different from business.

Firms in the automobile, semiconductor, textile, shoe, and numerous other industries have had their positions seriously eroded before they recognized the dangers arising from new competitors.

The defense in business must answer three basic questions:

1 Am I being attacked?
2 What are the attacker's weapons, and where will the crucial battles be fought?
3 How much of my territory can I successfully defend?

These questions can only be answered by a thorough understanding of the strengths and weaknesses of the business unit under study. Such a study cannot be a one-time effort. In order to know when it is under attack, a firm must periodically assess its own competitive strengths and weaknesses. It must compare its current position with that of its known competitors and with estimates of competitors' future strategies and strengths. Detailed and time-phased assessments are required because of the variety of attacking strategies available to competitors. Subtle measures are required in order to determine the nature of competitive thrusts and to counterattack effectively.

Few managers would fail to notice a frontal assault that is announced by advertising and promotion. In such an assault, management must examine its strengths in two primary areas: customer loyalty and responsive resources. First, the company must determine if the distribution, quality, and features of its product are less than the customer expects. Second, the company must assess if its resources are adequate to respond by touting its own fine qualities. The question of customer loyalty is often not asked by the complacent firm that is used to a position of dominance. Leaders often do not assess fully their own vulnerability. Brands and the perception of brands among relatively undifferentiated products often are subject to the frontal assault. The decline of Scott Paper's dominance in the tissue market when Proctor and Gamble entered is an example of failure to assess customer loyalty. Proctor and Gamble brought new product characteristics into a stable market and developed more marketing resources than Scott could fight. Even though Scott was aware of the attack, it had to retreat to defend its market share. The defense was too costly for Scott to maintain its dominance. Proctor and Gamble has repeated this thrust in toothpaste and diapers, and may do so in the future with soft drinks. Even companies delivering a good product to well-satisfied customers may not have adequate resources. IBM will get a major share of the personal computer market for the same reasons.

There are more subtle attacks in the business world. Schlitz was knocked from a favorable position in the brewing business when Miller attained dominance first in the light-beer sector and then used the distribution and resources acquired there to attack traditional product lines. It takes an intelligent and wary competitor to be aware of a serious assault in a related but undominated field. The task is to decide which of the many feints poses a serious threat. Feints can come against new and relatively unimportant product lines or geographic markets. Such threats cannot all be met with the full weight of business unit resources. However, competitive analysis can assist in determining which attacks pose a threat to organizational survival. Many successful Japanese businesses have followed this offensive pattern.

The greatest military generals are characterized by their capacity to distinguish between real threats and low-resource guerrilla assaults. Misjudgments as to the seriousness of the threats have allowed the IBM electric typewriter and the Japanese automakers to succeed. Coca-Cola's energetic response to Dr. Pepper's early success and the subsequent market behavior shows a good defense.

In business and in warfare, the advantage goes to the defense only if it is mobilized in time and if it makes effective use of its territory and weapons. In order for the strategic manager to plot the defense, he or she must understand the mode of attack, estimate the size and depth of the attacking force, and be able to assess accurately the range and potency of the weapons available. (The pitfalls involved in such an assessment are discussed later.) The primary advantage to the defense in business is the subtle nature of many attacks. The attack often can be detected by a clear and careful monitoring of internal conditions and by comparison of those conditions with those of competitors and potential competitors.

INTERNAL ROLE OF DEFINING CORPORATE STRENGTHS AND WEAKNESSES

In addition to defining corporate strengths and weaknesses in relation to those of competitors, it is critical to examine those factors that contribute to the smooth functioning of the internal operations. This entails two primary requirements: defining organizational voids and formulating and communicating objectives relating to internal improvements. Operating managers must then analyze the vulnerabilities of their subunits. Both of these objectives requires a specific approach.

Defining Organizational Voids

History has shown that many corporate disasters occur because of changes in areas where responsibility and authority overlap. There are many examples of failure to see the interaction between technology and marketing, the effect of changing costs on customer acceptance, or the effect of the changes in financial markets on the growth plans of a company. Sophisticated management views the planning and review process as a means to explore the interactions among functional activities and as an activity that allows periodic assessment of the effectiveness of interdepartmental interaction and coordination.

Voids, or areas where voids could occur, must be monitored. In order for the monitoring to be effective, management either must assign individuals to supervise the overlapping areas or must identify those overlaps or organizational voids that need to be monitored. It is often impossible to have prior knowledge of all of the critical interactions. Formal task forces can be set up for this purpose, but this can lead to an unproductive checklist approach. The territories and fiefdoms of existing management structures make it hard, if not impossible, to assess voids between groups whose self-interest requires defending their prerogatives and their "turf." In companies where top management believes that a serious assessment of potential organizational voids is needed, ad hoc task forces or outside consultants are often used in order to be certain that old habits and territorial divisions are not perpetuated in the review.

Formulating and Communicating Objectives

Perhaps the most critical aspect of resource definition is identifying the gap between what should be and what is. The process of examining resources can create perceptions of both the existing condition and the desired result. The most productive effort of the resource definition process comes in the process of defining the required resources, answering the rationalizations and excuses regarding the status quo, and then getting commitment to create change at the levels where the action occurs.

As discussed later, there is a great danger in "yes, but" analysis, where weaknesses are defended as inevitable or insignificant. The formality of a process that brings weaknesses under public scrutiny can often overcome the defenses of managers who prefer the status quo. This process of analysis can get the right individuals involved in both defining the problem and implementing a solution. One of the primary problems in defining corporate strengths and weaknesses is determining the relevant resource definition. Definition of the problem often determines the solution.

Much of the planning literature has cited the importance of involving the line manager in the analysis, because the process of the planning activity is crucial to the results. In defining corporate strengths and weaknesses, involvement of the line managers is a requirement if meaningful work is going to be accomplished. A budget, product forecast, and technology reviews can be developed and can have meaningful impact even if handled by staff groups. The involvement of line managers in this process is not essential. But in the process of resource assessment, line managers must be involved.

EVIDENCE OF SUCCESS

Many business executives have voted with their corporate funds on the importance of defining corporate strengths and weaknesses. It has met the market test; it is not merely an academic theory. Most of the top strategic consulting firms, such as PIMS, Boston Consulting Group, Bain Associates, and McKinsey, all developed consulting tools that emphasize analysis of the corporation's competitive strengths and weaknesses by market sector. The emergency of the strategic business unit concept is, in large measure, a response to the need to perform meaningful analysis of strengths and weaknesses on the terrain where battles will be fought and won or lost.

The managements of successful firms in the 1970s retreated from the concept of the financially managed conglomerate in order to do the kind of analysis discussed here. Interaction of strategic strengths seems to create and sustain growth and profitability. The long-term future of a business unit cannot be forecast solely from the perspective of financial criteria measured on an annual basis. It is clear that in-depth understanding of relative strengths has caused top managements to reassess the desirability of "numbers only" evaluation. They seek planning and decision-making approaches that allow them to make use of their own insight and experience. The organization must be structured in such a way as to ensure that general management can bring to bear experience and market expertise in the critique of plans, budgets, programs, and analysis of strategic strengths and weaknesses.

Although causality was not established, Rumelt showed that performance was strongly associated with strategic choices that group businesses in closely related market-based units. Such groupings were defined by Rumelt as congeneric. The congeneric strategy's power seems to be associated with the ability of top management to judge competitive strategies and to evaluate subordinates in an objective, market-related way.

Both general management and warfare are arts. The skill is in attaining a balance between defense and offense. It is critical to understand one's own position relative to the enemy and then to shore up weaknesses while attacking with massed forces at points of local dominance.

As Robert Frost said, "No number ever caught the whole thing."

PROBLEMS IN RESOURCE ASSESSMENT

Successful competition in formularized games such as weight lifting is relatively easy to predict. The judge can look to the past to determine evidence of strength and to the present to see the evidence of conditioning. More complex games such as football are more difficult to predict since the bettor must trade off speed, brawn, guile, intelligence, preparation, momentum, and all the other subjective elements that crowd the pregame talk shows. Still, the problem is relatively easy since the objectives are known, the rules are written, and the same number of players are allowed for each team both on and off the field.

In warfare, the outcome of a battle is difficult to predict. The commander must assess the troops, the terrain, the materials, the physical barriers, the weather conditions, the physical condition and morale of the groops, the tactics of the opposing commanders, and the strategies of their generals. Even when the strengths and weaknesses of both sides are known, the outcome of a long war is hard to predict. Other conditions come into play, including the depth of the reserves, the commitment of the populace, the industrial base, the technological base, and allies. The trade-offs are rarely clear in advance, and are often only marginally so in hindsight. In spite of the problems, however, nations commit immense resources to evaluating their own strengths and those of their adversaries. The CIA and the KGB, for example, consume immense quantities of national resources in order to determine more accurately national strengths and weaknesses.

This section examines competitive intelligence activity in the context of corporate warfare, where many of the problems are the same as in actual warfare. It is imperative to define relevant resources, gather information systematically, and decide upon the nature and scope of the output.

Defining a Resource

A manager attempting to define the organization's strengths and weaknesses must answer five fundamental questions:

- What resources are to be examined?
- How are they to be characterized in the measurement process?
- What criteria will be used to judge resources as either strengths or weaknesses?
- What is the time frame for assessing the resources?
- Who is going to do the job?

Managers who address these questions should be aware of the pitfalls involved.

Historical research by this author shows that the resources defined as strengths and weaknesses did not represent a census of the company's resources. In 1967, the author interviewed 50 managers of six companies in an effort to distinguish practice from theoretical construct within organizations. Managers were chosen from a variety of functions and they had widely varied responsibilities within their organizations. The strengths and weaknesses identified in this study are shown in Table 5-1.

Resource appraisal can and should also be expanded to include the following categories:

- Financial
- Productive
- Marketing and distribution
- Buying

- Research and development
- Employees
- Management
- Position in the industry

Within these categories are further potential areas for examination. For example, finance includes subcategories such as cyclical nature of profitability, debt-to-equity ratios, dividend policy, article of association, property values, inventory levels, special tax advantages, selling terms, long-term contracts, and leasing arrangements.

TABLE 5-1 The Relative Importance of Attributes Identified as Strengths and Weaknesses (All Managers)

General Category	Percentage of Response	Particular Attribute	Percentage of Response	Number of Responses
Organizational	22.0	● Organizational form and structure	5.8	11
		● Top management interest and skill	4.2	8
		● Standard operating procedures	4.2	8
		● Control system	5.8	11
		● Planning system	2.1	4
Personnel	21.5	● Attitudes	11.0	21
		● Technical skills	7.3	14
		● Experience	2.6	5
		● Number	0.5	1
Marketing	26.7	● Sales force	4.7	9
		● Knowing the needs of the customer	3.7	7
		● Breadth of product line	8.9	17
		● Product quality	2.1	4
		● Reputation	3.7	7
		● Customer	3.7	7
Technical	22.0	● Facilities	6.3	12
		● Production techniques	6.8	13
		● Product development	6.8	13
		● Basic research	2.1	4
Financial	7.9	● Financial size	3.1	6
		● Price-earnings ratio	1.6	3
		● Growth pattern	3.1	6
Total responses	100.0		100.1*	191

* Error due to rounding

Porter provides a useful list of areas of competitor strengths and weaknesses for managers in *Competitive Strategy*,[5] This list, although not exhaustive, does provide a point of departure for analysis:

- *Products*
  a. Standing of products, from the user's point of view, in each market segment
  b. Breadth and depth of the product line
- *Dealer/distribution*
  a. Channel coverage and quality
  b. Strength of channel relationships
  c. Ability to service the channels
- *Marketing and selling*
  a. Skills in each aspect of the marketing mix
  b. Skills in market research and new product development
  c. Training and skills of the sales force
- *Operations*
  a. Manufacturing cost position—for example, economies of scale, learning curve, newness of equipment
  b. Technological sophistication of facilities and equipment
  c. Flexibility of facilities and equipment
  d. Proprietary know-how and unique patent or cost advantages
  e. Skills such as capacity addition, quality control, and tooling
  f. Location, including labor and transportation cost
  g. Labor-force climate; unionization situation
  h. Access to and cost of raw materials
  i. Degree of vertical integration
- *Research and engineering*
  a. Patents and copyrights
  b. In-house capability in the research and development process (for example, product research, process research, basic research, development, imitation)
  c. R&D staff skills in terms of creativity, simplicity, quality, and reliability
  d. Access to outside sources of research and engineering, such as suppliers, customers, and contractors
- *Overall cost*
  a. Overall relative costs
  b. Shared costs or activities with other business units
  c. Where the competitor is generating the scale or other factors that are key to its cost position

---

[5] Porter, op. cit., p. 64.

- *Financial strength*
    a. Cash flow
    b. Short-term and long-term borrowing capacity (relative debt/equity ratio)
    c. New equity capacity over the forseeable future
    d. Financial management ability, including negotiation, raising capital, credit, inventories, and accounts receivable
- *Organization*
    a. Unity of values and clarity of purpose in the organization
    b. Organizational fatigue based on recent requirements placed on it
    c. Consistency of organizational arrangements with strategy
- *General managerial ability*
    a. Leadership qualities of CEO; ability of CEO to motivate
    b. Ability to coordinate particular functions or groups of functions, such as manufacturing with research coordination
    c. Age, training, and functional orientation of management
    d. Depth of management
    e. Flexibility and adaptability of management
- *Corporate portfolio*
    a. Ability of corporation to support planned changes in all business units in terms of financial and other resources
    b. Ability of corporation to supplement or reinforce business unit strengths
- *Other*
    a. Special treatment by or access to government bodies
    b. Personnel turnover

Porter asks some critical questions regarding priorities for analysis. Although his context is the analysis of competitors, the same questions are relevant to the analysis of the company's own strengths and weaknesses. Some of the useful diagnostic tests that Porter develops are the following[6]:

- *Growth*
    a. Will the capabilities increase or diminish with growth?
    b. What is the capacity for growth in terms of people, skills, and plant?
    c. What is the sustainable growth level in financial terms?
- *Response time*
    a. Are there available reserves in terms of:
        —Uncommited cash?
        —Reserve debt capacity?
        —Unintroduced products?
        —Excess plant capacity?

---

[6] Ibid, p. 68.

● *Adaptability to change*

a. What is the organization's functional capacity to adapt to
   —Cost cutting?
   —Managing broader and more complex product line?
   —Escalation in marketing activity?
   —Competing on service?

b. How well can the organization respond to exogenous events such as
   —Sustained inflation?
   —Rapid deflation?
   —Recession?
   —Technological change?
   —Government regulation?

Characterizing Resources

The list of possible strengths and weaknesses is almost infinite. The problem of identifying the resources to be measured is often further complicated by considerations as to the level of abstraction. For any significant set of resources, it is possible to develop a ladder of generalization which will have utility to different members of the organization who must make judgments. The problem of marketing strength is an example of the complexity of this task. The analyst could ask any of the following questions and could ultimately have to answer them all in different contexts:

1. Does the company have a strong presence in its major market?
2. Is it well balanced in its marketing mix?
3. Do its sales force and distribution network service the broadest base of potential customers?
4. Does its sales management adequately consider both the short-term and long-term requirements of its customer?
5. Does the sales force have adequate technical training?
6. Is Joe X, the sales representative in Hickory, N.C., aggressive enough to be effective?

The level of abstraction and the resources examined vary according to the level of the individual within the organization who is asking the question. As will be shown next, the very existence of different evaluative standards regarding the same attribute raises serious issues regarding how data should be collected, analyzed, and discussed. An attribute may be both a strength and a weakness depending on the criteria on which it is judged and on corporate strategy.

Criteria for Judgment

One of the most serious problems in determining whether an attribute is a strength or a weakness is in ensuring that proper criteria are used. There are three primary types of criteria:

- *Historical*
    - a. Historical experience of the company
    - b. Intracompany comparisons
    - c. Budget
- *Competitive*
    - a. Direct competitors
    - b. Indirect competitors
    - c. Noncompetitive companies
- *Normative*
    - a. Consultant's opinions
    - b. Rules of thumb
    - c. Normative management literature
    - d. Opinion

In the author's survey of management practice, the impact of the use of differing criteria was striking. Attributes judged to be strengths were judged by different sets of criteria than weaknesses. The results are summarized as follows:

Criterion Used	Strengths	Weaknesses
Historical	90%	10%
Competitive	67	33
Normative	21	79

It would seem that historical criteria are associated with strengths because managers are constantly searching for improvements in problem areas that they have previously identified; the base from which these improvements have been made becomes the standard by which the current attributes of the organization are judged. The converse is true with respect to weaknesses. The organization's current position is only on the way to where the managers wish it to be. The gap between the current position and the goal reflects a normative judgment of what ought to be. This is illustrated below:

Strength   *Weakness*

Past accomplishment ↔ Present attainment ↔ Future goals

The criteria for judging attributes must be decided upon before the manager considers questions such as the time frame and the techniques for gathering of data. These can only be resolved by a clear understanding of the purpose for which the analysis of strengths and weaknesses is being undertaken.

Some guidelines for resolving these questions have emerged from practice. These guidelines are in the form of yet more questions, but the questions should help managers to define strengths and weaknesses. The questions are:

1 For what purpose are we defining our strengths and weaknesses?
2 To whom will the answer be relevant?
3 Have we developed an adequately encompassing definition of the resource to be measured?

These questions emphasize the necessity for clearly understanding both the strategy and the organization structure of the business unit under study.

Since strategy is dependent on assessing corporate strengths and weaknesses, and assessing strengths and weaknesses is dependent on the identification of corporate strategy, it seems that we are examining a circle without an end. However, a resource is a strength or weakness only in relationship to a strategy and to a competitive environment in which the strategy is to be executed. The business unit's plan of action depends as much upon the assessment of the adequacy of its resources as the general's strategy depends upon relative strengths of troops in order of battle.

Strategies succeed or fail based often upon their strength or coherence. So, too, must the manager examine the interrelatedness of the strengths and weaknesses. Again, the military concept of a balanced attack with mutually reinforcing armaments and tactics is relevant. Weaknesses alongside pinnacles of strength may mean that the whole is only as effective as its weakest resource. Just as heavy fortifications often can be breached by an effective attack at a single weak point, so, too, can the corporate strategy be brought to naught if there is a critical missing link in the chain from research to after sale service to customers.

Gathering the Information

One of the difficult problems in defining resources is gathering timely, unbiased, and relevant data. Initial efforts in defining corporate strengths and weaknesses often rely on a budgetary model of the process. Subunits are required to assess strengths and weaknesses, and from their assessments higher-level assessments and generalizations are drawn. There are two flaws in using the budgetary model to define strengths and weaknesses:

- Strengths and weaknesses are not additive. A strong production department plus a weak procurement department cannot be the only basis of evaluation of the organizational unit responsible for both. The relationship of the resources to the unit's mission must also be taken into account.
- The resource to be examined varies depending upon the levels of the managers in the organization.

Thus, a model depending upon a bottom-up identification of strengths and weaknesses often will not bring to the attention of top management critical problems such as those in coordination among subunits and strategic planning. Each organizational level must make its own assessment of the factors and the resources relevant to the success of its own mission.

Clear statements of mission for individual managers enables them to analyze the strengths and weaknesses of the organizational unit. The model of management by objectives (MBO) is more useful than the budgetary model in this respect. Under the MBO model, the manager assesses only those strengths and weaknesses of subordinates that are relevant to the manager's goals. The manager defines only those resources that are required for the tasks for which his or her unit has responsibility.

The definition of strengths and weaknesses cannot be done in the abstract. The purpose determines the strategy and the time frame for data collection and analysis. Examples of purposes for which resource assessment might be undertaken include the following:

- Go/no-go decisions
- Iterative planning
- Long-term planning
- Competitive monitoring
- Developing a reward system for internal management

Each of these tasks requires analysis of strengths and weaknesses. Each also requires the development of separate resource definitions, different criteria for measurement, and, ultimately, different processes of information gathering.

ANALYSIS OF COMPARATIVE STRENGTHS AND WEAKNESSES

Ultimately, analysis of strengths and weaknesses can be useful only if it involves a comparison of the business unit and its relevant competitors. As Sun Tzu said 24 centuries ago[7]:

> There are five ways by which one can win victories
>
> He who knows when to fight and when not to fight will win
>
> He who knows how to match a large force with a small force will win
>
> He who has the wholehearted support of all rank and file will win
>
> He who is well prepared to seize favourable opportunities will win
>
> He who possesses generalship and at the same time is free from interference by his sovereign will win
>
> These are the five roads to sure victory.
>
> Therefore, it may be said: He who has a thorough knowledge of his own conditions as well of the conditions of the enemy is sure to win in all battles. He who has a thorough knowledge of his own conditions but not the conditions of the enemy has an even chance of winning and losing a battle. He who has neither a thorough knowledge of his own conditions nor of the enemy's is sure to lose in every battle.

---

[7] Sun Tzu, op. cit., p. 82.

The business world resembles warfare in many dimensions. General management earns its highest rewards in making and implementing the critical strategic decisions that determine victories over the long run. These decisions depend upon developing clear definitions of the weapons with which the battles will be fought and then deciding which weapons will be the most efficient and effective.

The first step in such an analysis is a clearly stated definition of the strategic business unit (SBU). Weapons must be analyzed in the context of a particular battlefield, battlefield conditions, and opponents. The SBU is that context. Management must set goals and policies and identify them by function. Then, standards of comparison must be developed. Finally, the manager must determine the scope of the monitoring activity in order to make plans either to accomplish an ad hoc examination or to develop the systems necessary to make continuing assessments of the resources.

Sources of Information

Each business unit must develop its own system for monitoring competitors' strengths and weaknesses. These systems do not have to be formal or structured, but they should be reviewed periodically to ensure that they are comprehensive. Acquiring market and financial intelligence is a normal part of most successful managers' activities. However, managers must also make comparisons of the internal assessment and the external competitive data.

The primary task in developing information sources for management action is training internal subordinate managers to analyze their relevant sources and to report the results of their analyses. Operating managers should be required to review published sources of information relating to their business units. Someone should have responsibility to review and develop synopses of all published financial reports of actual and potential competitors. These often assess coming changes in competitive stances. Many government publications provide convenient benchmarks for the analysis of comparative results. Technological and market forecasts prepared for antitrust studies often replicate expensive and time-consuming studies prepared in the private sector. Careful analysis of 10-K reports can give insights into capacity decisions and geographic commitments.

All internal analysis must be done in a systemic way so that the decision maker can review the existing policies and resources. More important, however, is that the absence of a policy or the unavailability of critical resource is brought to management's attention. Reviewing competitive data often enables managers to become aware of gaps in their own resources, skills, or policies. Hiring announcements can give clues about new areas on which competitors are focusing.

These sources of information can provide a basis for judging the results of the internal assessments. They also provide a check on any lists that purport to show the configuration of critical resources in the company. Occasionally, go/no-go decisions and other managerial activities will require specifically commissioned studies and assessments. Many firms are developing resources within their industries that will give them access to large data bases and compilations of publicly available information. The electronics industry, for example, is covered by Venture Development Company in Wellesley, Mass., with a multimillion-item data base. Many narrowly defined industries such as disk drives and paper products have source publications that are continuously updated, for example, Predicasts and Funk and Scotts. New on-line computer banks can also provide information.

Common Traps

There is never certainty that avoiding common traps will ensure success for a business, but falling into them will increase the probability of failure. The traps are:

- Quantification
- Timeliness
- Telegraphing
- Answering the wrong question

The urge to quantify is most often expressed by the development of a questionnaire and rating system. Although these systems can be useful to ensure coverage of all of the important areas, they will ultimately fail to capture most critical subtleties. Only rarely can the adequacy of a resource be defined in quantitative terms. Qualitative judgments, noncommensurable trade-offs, and nonadditive resources give quantitative techniques an illusion of precision that at best is misleading and at worst is dangerous. Quantitative data must be captured and analyzed in the process of defining strengths and weaknesses, but the resource appraisal process is ultimately an input to the creative but subjective process of strategy setting.

The urge for completeness and formality often creates problems of timeliness. Processes are cascaded, and managers probe in depth only a small part of potential analytical paths. The system must therefore contain certain elements, such as:

- Early warning completeness to signal competitive challenges
- Evaluation of priorities for probe relating to strategic consequences
- Tools for in-depth comparison of identified competitive resources
- A rigorous "so what" test

Failure to identify large numbers of potential strengths and weaknesses too often leads to expending time, money, and effort on analysis that in hindsight fail the "so what" test. Timing is critical for those strengths and weaknesses that merit in-depth analysis to be identified. Once they are identified, critical resources and weaknesses can be evaluated in time for effective decisions to be made.

Many successful companies telegraph coming decisions to their competitors as part of their market strategy. Often, these organizations put forth claims to market territory before their technical, productive, and sales troops arrive. Products announcements by small companies in the electronics industry are rife with false information. The intelligent businessperson learns to rely more upon multiple information sources rather than upon a single source for the evaluation of strategic information. He or she must determine whether statements of "what is" are in reality an expression of future expectation. During World War II, Winston Churchill honed his "misinformation" skills to a high degree. He claimed that the best protector of the truth was "a bodyguard of lies."

Strategies within the same market often are built on competitive strengths that are not strictly comparable. One computer may compete on cost, another on product differentiation. Subordinates must be encouraged to let managers know when they are not asking the right questions.

Successful comparative analysis of strengths and weaknesses hinges ultimately on the ability of company management to understand their own decision processes, to evaluate the competitor's value systems, and to understand the competitive strategies that they are going to face. Managers must understand that intermingling of the strategic evaluation of strengths and weaknesses with any internal reward mechanisms will bias the data. They must understand their own key policies and the links among them.

The strengths and weaknesses that must be analyzed first are those that are affected by changes in the market or in the technological or financial environment. Analysis must also be undertaken when there is unusual competitive activity and evaluation of key strategic policies. Market, technological, or financial change may convert old strengths to new weaknesses. Policy changes by competitors may mean that the stakes are changing, and the adequacy of current resources may be in question. Signs of change signal both opportunity and danger.

Identifying Excess Resources

Every manager is faced with the challenge of running "lean and mean," although there are disagreements over what that connotes. At the operatonal level, the literature is replete with discussions about the trade-off between adequacy of service and excess of inventory. This kind of analysis can also be applied to other elements of the working capital equation. Managers have a tendency to accumulate resources that are on the "nice to have" list but that are not critical to their success. Techniques such as economic order quantities analysis, receivables management, warehouse location analysis, and buy-lease analysis help to control this tendency.

Diligence to excess operational assets is perhaps easier for the general manager than diligence with respect to excess strategic assets. The high cost of capital, the relative unavailability of new equity, and the disappearance of long-term debt may have increased the importance of the monitoring task for each business manager. It is critical to pay attention to the resource mobilization opportunities that can be generated through liquidating assets. Strategic consulting firms such as Boston Consulting Group, Bain and Company, and McKinsey have built upon techniques developed both by themselves and by major diversified companies to address the issues regarding excess strategic assets.

The literature on management has increasingly focused on the general management role of portfolio evaluator. The manager is seen as investing and disinvesting in a portfolio of business opportunities. Based upon that model, managers have sought techniques to facilitate the comparison of business commitments. Portfolio managers of liquid investments often state that the "essence of investment decision making is comparison." New techniques of business portfolio analysis use methods of comparison that are based upon estimates of future prospects.

The fundamental precept underlying this model is that investment for the future will depend upon the ability of the corporation to generate cash. Where sustainable growth and profitability in existing business is insufficient, the task of top management is to disinvest systematically from its less attractive businesses in order to augment investment in businesses with rapid growth and high market share. Each business is analyzed according to the techniques shown in Table 5-2. The corporation's overall portfolio is then in a form that identifies relative prospects for future success. An example of such a portfolio array is shown in Figure 5-1.

Under a technique identified with McKinsey and General Electric, individual business units are arrayed in a matrix as shown in Figure 5-2.

There are some fundamental questions to be asked regarding excess resources:

- To what purpose will the company put cash generated from the harvesting of excess assets?
  a. What is the relative return?
  b. What is the relative risk?
  c. What is the projected time for the persistence of the stream of earnings?
- What is the cause of the lackluster performance for the assets identified as excess?
  a. Has the business unit achieved critical mass?
  b. Has it received adequate managerial attention?
  c. Has it been kept modern?
- Is the economic unit to be harvested truly independent?
  a. Are the supplier relationships of other units independent of the company's activities in this field?
  b. Are there critical joint production economies?
  c. Are there critical marketing economies?
  d. Does it provide a technological window?
  e. Is it necessary to a corporate exporting strategy?
  f. Is it part of a marketing migration pattern for the customers?
- Will the prospective purchaser become an effective competitor in the closely allied fields in which we maintain an interest?
- What will be the impact on personnel?

TABLE 5-2 The BCG Growth/Share Matrix

Variable	Ideal Measuring Stick	Acceptable Measuring Sticks or Reasonable Proxies	What Does It Tell Us?
Market segment growth (vertical axis)	Compounded annual growth rate in units for the next 5 to 10 years	Historical growth rate in units Historical growth rate in dollars Projected growth rate in units Projected growth rate in dollars	How fast is the market growing?
Firm's relative market share (horizontal axis)	Actual unit production for current year If firm is largest in industry, divide units by units of second largest If not, divide by units of largest firm	Annual sales in units Annual sales in dollars Annual capacity in units Annual profits in dollars	Firm's relative position on experience curve Firm's cost position Firm's profitability
Division's size (bubbles)	Annual units produced should be equated with the area of the circle	Annual sales in units Annual sales in dollars Annual capacity in units Annual profits in dollars	How important is this division to the firm?

Note: The middle of the market growth axis can be set to reflect a number of different things. It could reflect the inflation rate, the firm's cost of capital, the targeted rate of growth for the firm, or the historical real growth of GNP. While the middle of the market share axis is almost always set at 1.0, sometimes it is set at 1.25 to show that only business segments that are more than the same size as the competition should be considered high-share divisions.

Caveats:
1. Data is never uniform, consistent, complete, or readily available.
2. Forecasts may not come true.
3. This matrix is most useful for looking at a company's portfolio of business units. Its application for industries is less useful.
4. This chart would be just one slide in a BCG presentation; a total presentation is usually more than 200 slides. Keep it in perspective.

Sources: F&S Predicasts and Worldcasts, trade journals, industry analysts, annual reports, government documents

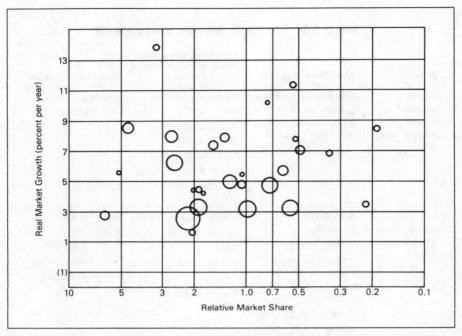

FIG. 5-1   Portfolio of Businesses on Growth Share Matrix (Balloon Areas Proportional to Sales)

Executives should reevaluate proposed excess resources in light of these questions.

Other elements of analysis are also required in order for managers to be certain that the disposition of assets will be successfully accomplished: First, the manager must define the time horizon; and second, the manager must develop a strategy for disposition.

Defining the Time Horizon

Increasing theoretical criticism is arising about the shortsightedness of current planning and capital budgeting techniques. Abernathy and Hayes caused considerable media attention with their article entitled "Managing Our Way to Economic Decline" in 1980.[8] The logical consequence of increased use of discounted cash-flow analysis in the face of rising interest rates is a foreshortening of the time horizon of relevance.

Two problems are evident when the time frame of analysis is foreshortened by analytical techniques. The manager must be certain that analysis covers and is sensitive to the needs for a continuing stream and for future opportunities. The manager must recognize the requirement to bring upon the defense of the corporaton's basic strength as many resources as are necessary.

_____
[8] *Harvard Business Review* (July 1980).

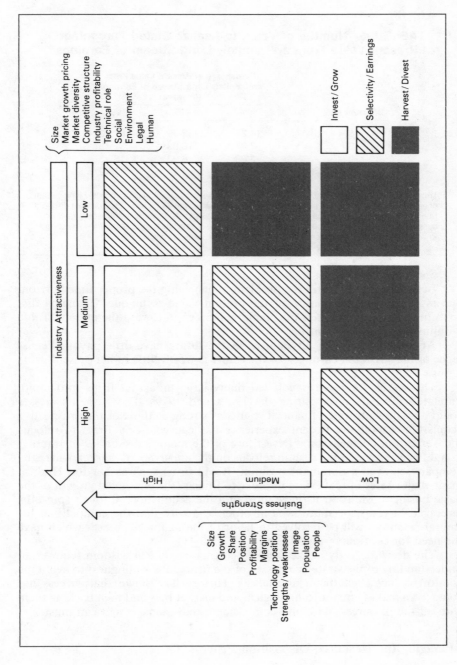

FIG. 5-2 GE/McKinsey Screen

TABLE 5-3   Number of Years to Realize Stated Percentage of Present Value From an Infinitely Long Stream of Earnings*

Discount Rate	Percentage of Present Value From an Infinitely Long Stream of Earnings (in years)		
	50%	80%	95%
5%	14.21	32.99	61.40
10	7.27	16.89	31.43
20	3.80	8.83	16.43
30	2.64	6.13	11.42

* Thus, at a 30 percent discount rate, 50 percent of the total present value of an infinitely long stream of earnings is achieved in the first 2.64 years. This compares with 14.2 years at a 5 percent discount rate. Ninety-five percent of the present value is achieved in 11.42 years at a 30 percent rate, compared with 61.4 years at a 5 percent rate. Thus, a change in rate has a serious impact on the degree to which the future is considered in any form in present value analysis.

In order to understand the problem of achieving the proper time horizon, one must examine the nature of the present value technique. Changing discounting assumptions brings the planning horizon in toward the present. Table 5-3 illustrates this phenomena.

At high hurdle rates, investment in the future have little payoff. Persistence of the stream of earnings for the future is worth little in net present value terms.

The search for rapid payoff led many large industrial firms into rapid, unrelated diversification during the 1960s and 1970s. The basic businesses could not show projected financial results as strong as those of the prospective acquisition candidate. Recent experience has caused many firms to refocus their attention on their stars. Divestiture of the major subsidiaries of International Paper provided the cash to refocus on the linear-board market, where the company enjoyed a dominant position. Retail firms such as Dayton Hudson made major sales of real estate in order to finance the continued growth of the basic business. Many firms have unwound the acquisitions through spin-offs, leveraged buyouts, or shutdowns in order to assure that the competition for capital resources will be resolved in favor of the major businesses which have the need for continuing investment.

The decision to fly in the face of accepted analytical wisdom requires an understanding of the strategic mission of the firm and a willingness to avoid the comfort of detached financial analysis. History has shown that success has come from making major technological and market bets and then backing them with all the resources, skill, and commitment that management can muster.

Managing the Resource-Disposition Process

Managing a successful disposition program requires emotional commitment and a high level of strategic and tactical skill. The advantage of disposition harvesting comes from the ability to generate either a large single source of cash or a continuing cash flow from ongoing operation of the business. Either goal requires the development of soundly conceived and executed strategy. Setting up a lump-sum sale is one of the most rigorous managerial tests. It entails the process of finding a buyer, setting a price, and negotiating the bundle of rights to be sold and continuing obligations. Many choices must be made early on in planning the strategy, often before adequate information is known. Among the choices are:

- *How will the business be marketed?*
  a. Breadth of exposure
  b. Use of an agency
  c. Sequential or coincidental offerings
  d. Public or private acknowledgement of the desire to sell
- *What pricing techniques will be adopted?*
  a. Bidding
  b. Confirmed non-negotiable floor
  c. Independent appraisal
  d. Comparable market sales
- *What continuing roles will be accepted?*
  a. Financing
  b. Supplier
  c. Customer
  d. Licensee/licensor
- *To whom will the opportunity be exposed?*
  a. Competitors
  b. Customers
  c. Suppliers
  d. Financial backers
  e. Employees

Once these decisions are made, the tactical skill becomes paramount. Obviously, the competitive reaction can be expected to be intense. A decision of a competitor to withdraw signals an opportunity for a major and permanent realignment of market share and profitability. Distributors, key employees, and key customers will hear claims by competitors about the firm's rapidity of change and its lack of continuing responsibility. Mismanagement will result in a failure to achieve the goals set in the divestiture decision. The critical decisions are in the information management area. Among the issues that must be addressed are:

- Who to inform;
- When to inform them;

- What to say;
- What not to say; and
- How to combat competitive misinformation.

The internal problems of harvesting a business rather than disposing of it are more complex. The assignment to harvest a business over a protracted period of time is a difficult one. Few managers would care to have their mission defined as spending five years losing market share by keeping prices high, investment low, and innovation nonexistent for a dwindling number of customers served at the lowest acceptable level of service. Even if management can agree in advance on a reasonable set of goals and measures for the activity, the manager must always face the morale problems created within the organization, which cannot be fully informed, and the ethical dilemmas that will arise in hiring, promotion, and staff evaluation. The manager must knowingly withhold the resources that would allow subordinates to achieve success along conventionally measured dimensions.

From a career perspective, the manager cannot look for public plaudits based upon a successful harvesting strategy. The strategy dictates that the goals be secret, the results hidden, and the tactics invisible. The single key factor for success is trust between the individual responsible for harvesting and the corporate management. They must agree that the rules and the measurements are different but the rewards will be the same, if not greater. The issue of added reward is likely to arise because success will not lead to external visibility and marketability; the individual is casting his or her lot with the present organization. Successful management of the careers of individuals assigned to the harvesting task is a prerequisite to successful harvesting.

BRIDGING THE RESOURCE GAP

Businesses risk failure in mismatching resources and opportunities. Most business problems can be overcome by pouring on resources. Identification of organizational strengths and weaknesses is fundamentally an analysis of the adequacy of managerial, economic, technical, and financial resources in light of those required to prosecute a desired set of opportunities. There is no such thing as an absolute determination regarding the adequacy of the resources; there is only an acknowledgment that the resources are or may be inadequate with respect to those required to safely pursue the corporate goals. The art of management often consists of both minimizing the resources required for a given task and then acquiring control over the resources at a minimum cost in time, money, control, and loss of future options. The skill in dealing with the resource constraint is to make the appropriate trade-offs.

The general manager/strategist is faced with conflicting goals. The lesson of management is that generally you can have anything you want; you just cannot have everything you want. Among possible trade-offs are those listed here:

Long-term success	*or*	Short-term success
Analysis		Action
Developing people		Judging people
Directing		Listening
Control equity		Capital adequacy
Motivating employees		Structuring jobs
Leadership		Friendship
Ambiguity for information		Consensus for action
Negotiation		Direction
Focus		Diversification
Quality		Cost
Innovation		Experience
Growth		Personal control
Fast change		Slow change

Both columns are desirable in certain contexts. Management must decide which to select in the situation at hand.

Andrews identifies four components of corporate strategy as follows: (1) market opportunity, (2) corporate competence and resources, (3) personal values and aspirations, and (4) acknowledged obligations to segments of society other than stockholders.[9] Although one of the four fundamental parts of the strategy model requires the identification of resources, the critical decisions by management are "how much," "how soon," and "at what cost." Many companies have expanded rapidly by adding to their capital base. Such expansion generally comes at the cost of management control. Debt allows capital equipment purchases, but it also increases earnings volatility.

Total elimination of weaknesses is an illusion. As noted above, the question of weakness is relative to competition and environment. American car manufacturers are weak in the competitive market of the early 1980s as now defined. This weakness is a direct outgrowth of their strength in the large-car market in the mid-1970s. Homelite Chain Saws' servicing dealer network was its strength for distribution to professional and farm users. When the casual firewood user of chainsaws emerged in response to the energy crisis, the company's rural and suburban dealers were poorly located to serve the new market of price-oriented users. The Baierd Poulan Division of Emerson Electric has no established network and was better able to expand through mass merchandisers. Baierd's strength later became a weakness in the face of market saturation.

One of the most difficult challenges for the manager is to adjust the scope of analysis in order to be able to compete both in the current environment and in the future. The trade-off between concentration of resources to ensure suc-

---

[9] Kenneth R. Andrews, *The Concept of Corporate Strategy* (Homewood, Ill.: Richard D. Irwin, Inc., 1980), p. 28.

cess in the battle of today and the preservation of future options is the skill in both offensive and defensive strategy.

Acquiring Resources

Throughout the discussion of resources, there has been an underlying theme of control rather than ownership. More and more, managers are feeling resource constraints. The response is to do more with less. Nevertheless, particular resources may be an absolute requirement for particular goals rather than simply something that facilitates reaching the goal. The managerial skill needed in this situation is that of deciding when to acquire use and control of a resource and when to acquire ownership.

Every piece of property relates to a bundle of rights. Management must decide the "level of acquisition." A new business owner often believes that a typewriter is a necessary accoutrement to a business office. It is possible, however, to perceive the problem differently. Some options are as follows:

Equipment	Personnel
Own	Hire full-time
Lease with option to buy	Hire part-time
Lease	Use a temporary manpower service
Rent with option to buy	
Rent	
Arrange time-sharing with a secretarial service	
Pay a secretarial service on a piecework basis	
Get spouse to handwrite the required material	

A larger firm would tend to look at the first option as the one giving it the required level of control of the typing/letter-writing resource. Other businesses have exercised other options depending upon their needs, resources, and relative priorities. Deciding that all resources must be owned or employed will tax capital resources and limit flexibility. In the letter-writing example, the decision may not have serious consequences. Other committments may be more seriously wasteful of the corporate resources as firms become overly capital and labor-intensive.

Every manager should stop to think about three elements with respect to a particular resource:

- How much control is required?
- How much cost is affordable?
- How much risk is there in not having it?

All decisions will be based upon the trade-offs arising out of the answers to these questions.

Table 5-4 Range of Control in Real Estate Ownership

	Use	Time Frame	Cost per Unit Time	Capital Value of Position	Flexibility
Ownership in fee	Yes	At discretion			
Ownership on a ground lease	Yes	For stated period Usually long			
Long-term lease	Yes	Stated period long	Increasing	Increasing	Increasing
Short-term lease	Yes	Short			
Short-term rental	Yes	Short			
Tenant at will	Yes	Uncertain			

Almost every resource can be acquired at more or less cost and on the basis of more or less control. There is, therefore, more or less risk that it will be responsive to the particular needs of the possessor.

The bundle of rights in any resource involves decisions regarding control, commitment, and future usage. Real estate is an example of where even major corporations must decide upon the level of ownership. The range of control in real estate ownership is shown in Table 5-4.

Many times real estate, equipment, and even current assets can be used without full ownership. The tax attributes, the cash-flow implications, and the capital-appreciation potential often are valued differently by the corporation and by independent investors. Splitting up the rights and burdens of ownership therefore can be attractive to many separate entities. The degree of attraction depends on a firm's time horizons, perceptions of risk, and perceptions of the market for the future usages.

Each manager must examine the reasons underlying the acquisition of the resource in question and acquire only so much of the bundle of rights associated with the resource as is required to achieve the corporate goals that gave rise to the need. The decision is time-based. It must consider risk, availability of alternative, and relative priorities.

SUMMARY

The resource assessment process is as critical to the success of a business as it is to a military commander. The assessment process requires analysis of both internal and external conditions. This chapter outlines several guidelines for the process. These include the following:

- Resource assessment can be successful only if the decision maker is involved. The process outweighs the final output.

- Resource assessment must be carried out in light of a clear perception of perceived opportunities and a dispassionate analysis of the competitors.
- A budgetary model is not successful in the resource assessment process because the strengths and weaknesses of a company are not additive.
- The level of ownership and control needed over resources must be defined.

Most critical analysis depends upon meeting three tests:

- *Completeness:* Does the analysis cover all of the critical areas?
- *Connections:* Does the analysis comprehend the interrelated nature of the resources and make explicit the ways in which changes will rebound throughout the system?
- *Consequences:* Does the analysis aid the decision maker in understanding the effect of changes upon the business unit, its competitive position, and the corporation as a whole.

A systematic review of the corporate resources that is complete, that identifies connections, and that aids in predicting consequences of change is the foundation of the managerial trusteeship of corporate resources.

PART III

Analyzing Corporate Strategy

6

Evaluating the Corporate Portfolio

S. K. JOHNSON

Senior Management Consultant, Arthur D. Little, Inc.

PORTFOLIO ANALYSIS AND STRATEGIC PLANNING

In the 1960s, U.S. corporations went through a period of buying independent companies which made the idea of a "mergers and acquisitions" function part of the commonly held notion of what constitutes the process of managing a corporation. Most Fortune 500 companies and many smaller ones developed an acquisition department whose task was to identify attractive companies to buy. However, determining which acquisition targets were attractive to a particular acquirer required organizational agreement on a set of criteria about what constitutes an appropriate acquisition. The need for a means of explaining why acquisitions were being made was one of the driving forces behind the rapid acceptance of portfolio analysis as a standard part of strategic planning.

Just as an analysis of the collection portfolio or of parts of a corporation may reveal the need to add certain types of companies to balance the current mix, it also may point out that previously acquired or developed businesses are no longer necessary to the performance of the corporation. This kind of analysis seems to be behind the wave of company divestitures which have become commonplace in the 1980s.

There is an important difference between the corporation as a central director of activities and the activity of business units that serve particular customers with specific products or services in the expectation of earning a profit. As outlined in Chapter 1, and implicit in the material in Part 2 on analyzing the strategy of a business unit, the distinction between competing in the marketplace and governing the resources that implement the competition is a broadly accepted way of looking at the complexity of modern business activity.

Although most younger managers accept this model of the corporation without challenge, older managers recall that the concept was not explicitly recognized before the mid-1960s. Prior to that time, the prevailing view was that corporations should be thought of as a collection of functional activities which could be aggregated as divisions and which were deployed to achieve customer satisfaction. This view placed great focus on "operating" effectively. Thus, in setting out to evaluate the corporate portfolio today, the manager should remember that business unit strategy is a fairly recent concept and that there still is considerable debate about what should be evaluated as well as the appropriate way to do it. New analytic techniques continue to appear in the business literature. This chapter examines those techniques that have best stood the test of time and experience.

THE PORTFOLIO CONCEPT AND ITS EVOLUTION IN PRACTICE

During the period of economic expansion in the mid-1950s, corporate management was confronted with two problems that presented increasing challenges. Corporations were becoming increasingly diverse in their activities, not merely larger manifestations of a single activity. At the same time, management was faced with choosing among many growth opportunities in an environment of business expansion and cash constraints. The top managers of some of the largest U.S.-based firms were experiencing frustration with the inability of available methodologies to address these issues convincingly.

By coincidence, the latter part of the 1950s coincided with the development of a major new concept for determining how to understand and construct a desirable collection of stock market investments. These collections had long been referred to in the financial community as "portfolios" of stocks. By the mid-1960s, portfolio selection it was broadly accepted as a major advance in the ability of portfolio managers to measure diversity and to determine how much diversity was desirable in a collection of stocks. The book is considered the foundation of modern "portfolio theory," the phrase used in the financial community to describe the most popular set of guidelines for managing multiple stock ownership.

At the same time, a major effort was underway at the General Electric Company to bring greater management focus to bear on the natural businesses inherent in the diversity of activities within the various divisions of the corporation. Given the prevailing wisdom about the nature of management as a shepherd or caretaker of assets on behalf of the stockholders, there was ready accep-

tance of the dual concepts that a corporate management was charged with the
ownership and governance of a series of entities (strategic business units) and
that each corporation's collection of such entities constituted a portfolio, in the
same sense that an investor might own a portfolio of stocks. By 1967, several
pioneering companies (Mead, General Electric, Olin, etc.) had developed the
concept of dividing the entire corporation into business units and referring to
the entire group as a portfolio whose quality could be determined by analysis
and changed by managerial action.

     As the management consulting firms that were working with these compa-
nies began to apply the business unit concept with other clients, the portfolio
term gained greater exposure. Today, like the safety pin, it seems so obvious
that it is taken for granted. This acceptance is partially due to the aggressive
publicity efforts of several small specialty consulting companies, particularly
the Boston Consulting Group. Bruce Henderson, the founder, and his employees constantly advanced the theme (in direct mail to key executives, in seminars, and in speeches) that the important task of corporate management was to
build a good portfolio for the corporation. The Boston Consulting Group
argued that the quality of individual businesses was evidenced by (1) the
growth rate of their market and (2) their share of that market, relative to that of
the largest competitors.

EVALUATION APPROACHES

Portfolio evaluation is the presentation of a series of analyses which clarify the
role of individual components of the corporation within the entity and their
contribution to overall corporate performance. For example, the projected
annual sales of each product group within the corporation for the next five
years are listed, and then it is determined which product groups are expected to
contribute the bulk of the sales and which product groups are expected to contribute specific proportions of the incremental sales during the period. This
kind of analysis can also be carried out for geographic markets or classes of
customers. To plan for the orderly financing of a corporation's capital needs, it
is necessary to anticipate the capital requirements of the individual plants as
well as the working capital needs of the various sales entities. Companies have
found that one way to bring some continuity to this type of analysis is to use
the "natural business unit" as the logical base on which to organize the presentation of these data.

     There are long checklists of topics that can be analyzed individually in
order to determine the relationships, contribution, or absolute needs of component parts of the corporation. However, one of the most important developments in the evaluation of portions of the corporation was the introduction of
two-dimensional matrices which are used to display the relationship among
components in visual terms. By selecting factors that are critical in management's decision processes, these matrices can be used to crystallize key issues
for management. The first of these matrices to gain wide exposure is known as
the growth/share matrix (Figure 6-1). While there is some debate as to who

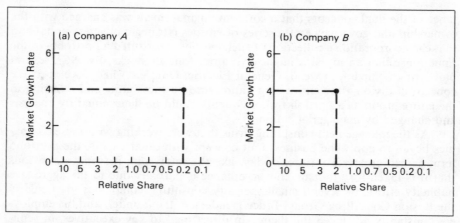

FIG. 6-1 Growth Share Matrix

first popularized this concept, it was widely adopted among management consultants in the late 1960s as a technique for summarizing these key issues to top management.

The growth/share matrix is prepared by plotting the expected (or historical) growth rate of the entity or its market in one dimension (usually vertically) and the market share of the entity in the other dimension. Most analysts believe that absolute market share is less important than the relationship between a company's share and that of its competitors. Consequently, most analysts using the growth/share matrix use a "relative share" figure, which is variously defined as the unit's market share divided by the share of (1) its largest competitor or (2) the three (or four) largest competitors in that market.

For example, if the market for laboratory instruments is growing at 4 percent per year (in real terms), then the height of the business unit on the vertical axis would be set at the 4 percent level. If the business unit of company *A* has an 8 percent market share while company *B*, the industry leader, has a 32 percent market share, then the *relative* share of market assigned to company *A*'s unit is 25 percent (8 is one-fourth of 32). (If the company *B* division were analyzing its position and the second largest competitor in the industry had a 16 percent market share, company *B* would assign itself a relative market share of 2, which represents 32 percent divided by 16 percent.) The horizontal scale is normally set up as a logarithmic scale to condense the chart.

An analysis of a corporation using this technique provides a sense of the natural growth and likely profitability of the various businesses. The growth/share matrix takes on importance when it is used to portray a sense of how many "winners" (leading market share businesses) a corporation has and whether there is some apparent balance between the amount of business in high-growth markets (which theoretically need steady capital infusions to build further capacity or expand working capital) and those in slower growth markets (which should be producing a net cash throw off from the profitability that a market leader should enjoy).

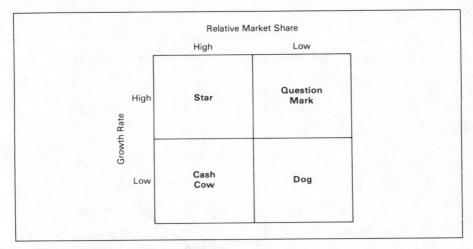

FIG. 6-2 Boston Consulting Group Matrix

The growth/share matrix can be used as a proxy for the cash needs and cash generation potential of the mix businesses and provides insight into whether the corporation appears to face cash shortages or high sales growth. The generally accepted rule of thumb is that high-growth businesses are likely to be cash users, that low market share businesses are likely to have low profitability over time, and that a corporation needs to balance its portfolio to have cash users providing significant growth and cash generators that grow more slowly but provide the cash for sustaining growth businesses.

On the Boston Consulting Group matrix (Figure 6-2), the growth businesses are referred to as stars while the high-share, slow-growth businesses are called cash cows. When it was first advanced, this simplification was enormously appealing. However, many analysts now go to a second level of assessment of the growth/share matrix which involves some subjective integration of multiple factors in order to provide a more thoughtful assessment of industry structure.

The Arthur D. Little, Inc. approach uses the concept of industry maturity as a shorthand for industry structural characteristics that are likely to affect overall growth and profitability of participants, and the concept of relative competitive position as a measure of a business' ability to achieve above average growth and/or profitability within the industry in which it competes. Maturity is determined by, and has impact on, certain observable business actions; therefore, it can be "tracked" by noting the level and rate of change in such things as technology, breadth of product line, rate of industry growth compared to gross national product, degree of market concentration, and conditions of exit and entry. (See Figures 6-3 and 6-4.)

Industries can conveniently be grouped into four stages of maturity. An embryonic industry (for example, veterinary diagnostic tests or home video-text services) is normally characterized by rapid growth, changes in technology, great pursuit of new customers, and fragmented and changing shares of market.

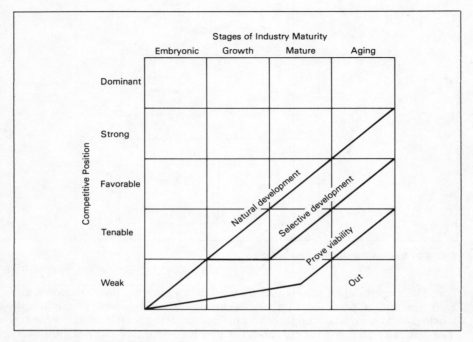

FIG. 6-3 Arthur D. Little, Inc. Matrix

A growth industry is one that is still expanding rapidly, but customers, shares, and technology are better known and entry into the industry is more difficult (as illustrated by RCA's unsuccessful attempt to enter the mainframe computer business in the 1970s). A mature industry (like automobiles or paper) is characterized by stability in known customers, known technology, and shares of market, although the industry may still be market-competitive and have segments with high growth rates. Aging industries (such as monorail track) are usually characterized by falling demand, a declining number of competitors, and, in many cases, a narrowing of the product line. In some instances, national industries fragment into regional businesses whose effective radius of competition is determined by shipping costs.

The value of this analytic approach is that it tries to look beyond market share in evaluating the strategic options available to a business unit and to determine likely industry volatility based on factors other than the change in unit sales from year to year. The weakness of all these matrix approaches is that they oversimplify a situation. For example, General Motors's large market share was considered an adequate shield against the impact of foreign competition in the late 1970s. It would have required extraordinary insight to recognize in the early 1970s the vulnerability of U.S. automobile manufacturers to Japanese competitors.

The General Electric Company and the McKinsey Company have used a matrix that focuses attention on a concept called industry attractiveness, which

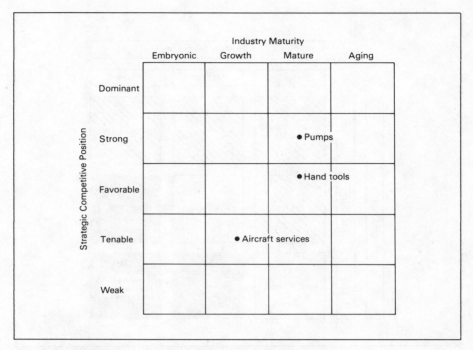

FIG. 6-4 Arthur D. Little, Inc. Matrix for Cooper Industries, 1978

replaces the industry growth rate concept of the growth/share matrices. (See Figures 6-5, 6-6, and 6-7.) Like that of Arthur D. Little, Inc., the General Electric/McKinsey approach also measures a vaguely defined concept called business strength in place of the original relative market share measure. Since the formal definition of these terms is not clear or simple, the analysis is difficult for outsiders to reproduce. There are minor differences in the recommended factors to consider (see Figure 6-8). However, a thorough competitive analysis (as discussed in Chapter 5) provides a basis for ranking relative strength of business units in their particular environment. The intent of the matrix is to highlight those components of the corporation that should be supported, abandoned, watched carefully, or used to suport other parts of the company. Thus, the cells are coded to correspond with "instructions" to the user.

A very formal treatment of the same topic is provided by the Strategic Planning Institute, an organization based in Cambridge, Massachusetts that is best known as PIMS, the acronym for Profit Impact of Market Stragtegy, its largest program. The staff of this nonprofit association carries out extensive mathematical analyses of a common data base comprising detailed financial information for business units of member companies. The hope of this program is that with sufficient information from a variety of businesses, it will be possible to uncover basic laws of business behavior. Participant companies are provided with extensive mathematical analyses of the apparent trends and patterns

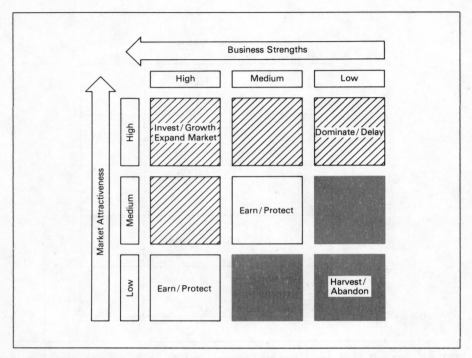

FIG. 6-5 McKinsey Matrix

in their own data as demonstrated by the experience of many different companies.

Participants in the program with access to the data base can use PIMS to rank the computer-predicted strength of position (which is shown as a percentile score based on the relative market share of a business compared to all businesses in the data base); industry attractiveness can be determined (again using percentile ranking) based on the computer-predicted return on investment likely in a business as suggested by the comparison of the unit's industry economic structure, value added, capital requirements, and so forth to the pattern shown by the data base as a whole. Now, analyses can be based on the performance of *all* the businesses in the data base or on a selected subgroup. Data on specific competitors is not available.

After an initial period of enthusiasm in the 1970s, planners have become less optimistic that PIMS will be a major tool in portfolio analysis. The logic behind PIMS is that relationships among variables in business hold true, regardless of the business. There was great curiosity about what these rules of thumb might be, but planners have not been able to rely on PIMS predictions without including some assessment of the context of their individual businesses. PIMS continues to have an active membership and to develop additional models, but few people are optimistic that the approach will supplant more traditional approaches to strategy formulation.

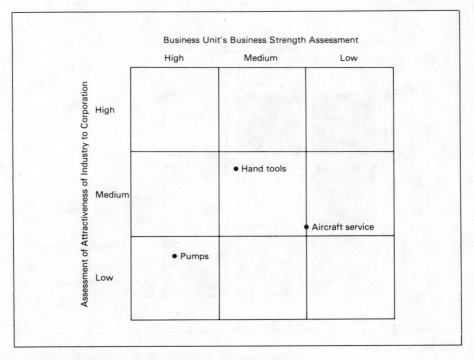

FIG. 6-6 McKinsey Matrix for Cooper Industries, 1978

THE PORTFOLIO CONCEPT TODAY

The members of top management of virtually all major U.S.-based corporations have at least discussed their corporation in portfolio terms, if only with investment analysts, bankers, and management consultants. An extensive survey of Fortune 1,000 companies in 1979 indicated that almost half of the Fortune 500 companies had installed formal portfolio planning systems and that about one fourth of the second 500 companies had done so. These numbers were rising by about five percentage points per year. However, two thirds of portfolio planning systems were fairly unsophisticated, and it required five or more years to establish portfolio planning in an organization.

From the initial crude efforts at balancing cash flow among expanding and stable businesses, the portfolio approach to corporate planning has evolved to provide three significant contributions to thoughtful consideration of corporate direction. First, it encourages (and most analyses require) a thorough analysis of the competitive effectiveness of each of the corporation's business units. The approach was not common prior to the mid 1970s. Second, it offers corporate management a rationale for differentiating among the competing needs of the parts of the corporation in the resource allocation process. The rationale used

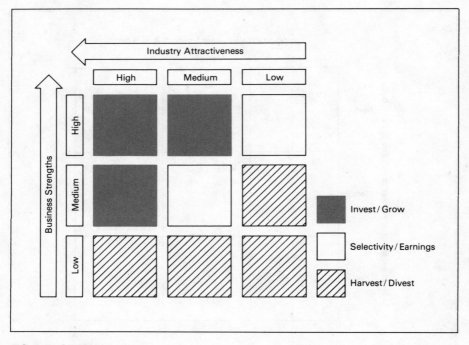

FIG. 6-7 GE Matrix

may be simple (e.g., market growth rate) or quite sophisticated. However, the business units are ranked by criteria in considering their worthiness to be funded or their ability to deliver predicted results. Corporate management can make much more informed decisions in the context of business unit intentions and corporate constraints or desires.

The third major contribution of the portfolio approach to corporate strategy is that it provides a vehicle for identifying the opportunity for shared resources or themes among units. The trend toward explicitly recognizing that specific resources are shared (and will require management in the context of intra-organizational competition) is the focus of intense attention today. A good example is the rise of strategic technology management methodologies.

Simultaneously, many of the original advocates of particular matrices as the appropriate vehicles for interpreting corporate portfolios are trying to disassociate themselves from their earlier advocacy. For example, the Boston Consulting Group has recently been referring to a new matrix that considers interrelatedness among units and degree of market fragmentation as appropriate to the 1980s, in contrast to growth/share, which was appropriate to the 1970s.

Industry Attractiveness
- Size
- Market growth, pricing
- Market diversity
- Competitive structure change
- Industry profitability
- Inflation vulnerability
- Technical role
- Social
- Environment
- Legal
- Human

Business Strengths
- Size
- Growth
- Share
- Position
- Profitability
- Margins
- Technology position
- Strengths/weaknesses
- Image
- Pollution
- People

FIG. 6-8 Elements of Matrix Coordinates

MATCHING THE CORPORATE PORTFOLIO TO CORPORATE OBJECTIVES

Evaluating the corporate portfolio involves analyzing what the portfolio currently contains and matching that against a concept of something "better" for achieving corporate objectives.

The setting of specific corporate objectives is a very situational problem which has been subject to extensive debate. The variety of objectives that management may set is limited only by imagination. Objectives can range from specific performance targets for various financial parameters of the corporation, such as annual earnings or return on shareholders' equity, to more qualitative characteristics, such as deciding what kind of culture is desired. In the early 1980s, there is widespread consensus among U.S. management that the primary objective of corporations should be to increase shareholders' wealth (which is seen as increasing the stock price and the dividend stream). Other objectives are viewed as subordinate to this overriding one and are often portrayed as a means toward the larger end.

Portfolio evaluation is the primary action that supports making changes in the mix of pieces or business units constituting the corporate portfolio. Changes may be made through acquisitions, divestitures, or resource allocations to various units in support of specific strategies. Since the evaluation is in the context of assessing the support for corporate objectives, it is important to achieve as much clarity as possible about the initial objectives.

It is usually helpful to group corporate goals and objectives into five generic categories:

1 *Growth and renewal*—the intended accomplishments that will provide for the sustained existence of the organization;

2 *Financial dimension*—the specific performance measures that must be achieved consistent with management's planned sources and uses of capital;

3 *Corporate entity*—the degree to which the organization is committed to remaining an autonomous entity, and the intended ownership structure;

4 *Managerial system*—the type of organization to be created; and

5 *External relationships*—the goals that go beyond the internal organization to create the desired environment or social context for the organization.

While the composition of the corporation's portfolio affects all of these categories, its primary impact is in the areas of providing for the final, integrated growth and renewal of the corporation. It goes without saying that this is in the nature of the corporation's achieved financial performance. No single set of corporate objectives can be established for all corporations and no single portfolio configuration can meet the needs of all possible sets of corporate objectives. Most corporations set their explicit corporate objectives and goals with some recognition of the current portfolio. They recognize that restructuring the portfolio may be the most effective way (perhaps the only way) to achieve desired goals. Thus, manufacturing-based companies such as American Can and Xerox are acquiring major positions in the financial industries sector and, in the case of American Can, selling off traditional divisions such as their Dixie brand paper cup business.

In evaluating plans for future performance, management must consider both the magnitude of the performance (and related resource demands) and the uncertainty associated with those plans. This duality is what prompted management's interest in the early matrices which offered the measures of inherent market growth and security of market position (relative share) as surrogates for the predictability of growth and profitability. Other risk dimensions that normally receive some assessment in the process of portfolio evaluation are political risk, economic cycle vulnerability, and those exposures that are not limited to the particular business units.

Political risk assessment involves arraying the corporation's activities and resources by country and assessing the likelihood that the resources associated with each country (located or dependent on activity in the country) will become less valuable or useful to the corporation. Loss of value or usefulness may be the result of specific national government action (e.g., expropriation or capital repatriation restrictions) or the collapse of the commercial infrastructure, as happened in Lebanon and Iran. Many large multinational corporations routinely assess the political stability of their operating areas and may choose to rebalance their exposure to potential political instability.

Individual businesses can be strongly influenced by forces outside the business area. For example, sales of cattlefeed supplements are sharply influenced by the weather as it is reflected in the price of corn. The price of corn, in turn, affects the economics of feeding cattle rather than slaughtering them earlier than usual or leaving them on pasture longer than usual. A company with several divisions that were strongly affected by weather patterns might find that this introduced an unacceptable level of uncertainty in future performance. The company might choose to restructure itself in order to have fewer weather-dependent businesses and perhaps some counter-cyclical businesses. Corporations with portfolios that contain a high proportion of business units dependent on capital spending (e.g., lift trucks, automotive tooling manufacturing, cranes) might try to diversify into more predictable consumer products industries. A case in point is Cooper Industries.

Cooper Industries is a Houston-based company whose primary businesses in the 1960s were focused around providing Cooper-Bessemer pumps to the oil and gas production industry. These activities were supplemented by several brand franchises in the hand tool markets. Following a near collapse in the early 1970s during a disastrous downturn in the gas production business, Cooper set out to develop a diversified portfolio of businesses which would not be subject to the violent swings in annual demand in the oil and gas transmission equipment business. The company's management sought to develop sustained earnings growth, and over a period of five years, it acquired a series of slow-growth, established hand tool companies, each of which had a very strong name in a particular category (such as Crescent brand adjustable wrenches).

By consolidating the manufacturing facilities and marketing capabilities of the various small companies that were acquired, Cooper was able to achieve manufacturing economies and greater marketing leverage with trade channels. The result was a sustained pace of corporate sales growth and even faster earnings growth reflected by a rising stock price-earnings ratio in the face of a declining market trend in price-earnings ratios. During the latter half of the 1970s, Cooper achieved a very attractive corporate performance with a portfolio that, on the surface, might have looked remarkably undistinguished—an old pump company, a handful of consumer hand tool companies, and a regional aircraft servicing operation. However, this portfolio was consistent with Cooper's objectives of offsetting the volatility of the pump business with simple, easily understood businesses that could be acquired at low cost and that presented little risk to the organization.

Cooper's situation demonstrates that improved corporate performance can be achieved without resorting to flamboyance in the portfolio. The appropriate descriptors for evaluating this portfolio, consistent with the pattern of management objectives, are those that address operating characteristics of the individual businesses. The corporation must also be willing to divest otherwise unattractive operating units that have been "fixed" when the opportunities for margin improvement have been achieved. In Cooper's case, after steadily improving the performance of the aircraft service company for five years, the company sold it and applied the funds to other acquisition opportunities.

A frequent solution proposed to improve the performance of a corporate portfolio is to acquire a high-technology growth company. The corporate bidding war for so-called growth companies has pushed the prices of those companies to heights that are difficult to justify. For example, in 1982 Warner-Lambert paid *$465 million* for Imed, a *$100 million* per year manufacturer of intravenous therapy equipment and some promising new pump products. While this investment may ultimately be justified, it will require extraordinary performance by this new addition to Warner-Lambert's portfolio. Thoughtful consideration of the many dimensions of business performance and the development of portfolio assessment criteria that illuminate opportunities for change in a corporation's portfolio may reveal potentially lower cost paths to improved aggregate performance and investor perception.

By way of contrast to the normal perception of business practices in the U.S. environment, the descriptors appropriate to the assessment of a portfolio of businesses in developing nations introduces some unusual dimensions. Companies that are committed to achieving growth and profitabililty performance through participation in the unusually high natural economic growth rates associated with developing nations often are very concerned with the quality of the economic sectors in which the company competes. In countries where there are relatively high rates of growth, substantial absolute size (in terms of wealth and population), and little industrialization, the corporation normally faces an unusually wide, but volatile, range of opportunities. Here the attractiveness of an industry as a candidate for portfolio inclusion may depend on the likelihood that the sector will be inflation resistant, will receive preferential tax treatment by the local government, will be permitted to remain in private hands despite changes of government, and will not be overpopulated by new entrants. Other considerations are whether the industry has export potential or may suffer from skilled labor shortages. Structuring ways to explain the quality and distribution of the portfolio elements along each of these dimensions thus becomes very important to addressing the corporate strategic choices in these countries. Portfolio evaluation considerations in developing nations differ from the conventional criteria used in the assessment of business activity in developed nations.

INTERRELATEDNESS IN THE PORTFOLIO

Most of the criteria or dimensions discussed here for the evaluation of corporate portfolios tend to treat the individual units of activity as discrete, unrelated entities. During the 1980s, there has been renewed attention to corporate portfolios as they reflect threads of continuity or interrelatedness among the individual elements. The specific objectives of the corporation should include overt recognition of these unifying themes, although the pattern of corporate objectives will probably be unique to each situation. Tregoe and Zimmerman argue, in *Top Management Strategy*, that the pattern of objectives should reflect some concept of the *driving force* of organization in the corporation.[1] They argue that these driving forces serve as organizing and unifying themes within the portfolio of the corporation and the strategies of its management, and that they can best be addressed within nine general topics:

1 *The products offered by the businesses*—their similarity to each other

2 *Market needs*—the diversity of needs within an identifiable customer group

3 *Technology*—continuity of technology across business areas

4 *Production capability*—continuity of processes and skills in product creation

5 *Method of sale*—continuity of marketing

6 *Method of distribution*—continuity of how products reach the customer

---

[1] Benjamin B. Tregoe and John W. Zimmerman, *Top Management Strategy* (New York, N.Y.: Simon & Schuster, 1980).

7 *Natural resources*—shared basic ingredients

8 *Size/growth*—standards of achievement

9 *Return/profit*—performance hurdles

When this perspective is applied, the role of portfolio evaluation is to help clarify the driving forces of the corporation and the relationship of the individual business units to those forces. Specific analyses should involve identification of the amount of continuity and diversity that exists among the businesses along each of the unifying themes and of the extent to which the individual businesses do (or could) benefit from that unity (e.g., competitive advantage in unrelated products through shared distribution to a common customer).

BUSINESS STRATEGIES IN THE PORTFOLIO CONTEXT

The setting of business unit strategy in the context of corporate portfolio considerations represents a trade-off between what operating management might desire and the greater priority of the corporation's needs. To help the corporate management group appreciate the appropriateness of the operating management's desired course, the unit plan normally reviews where the business unit stands within its industry as well as how the unit has performed within the industry over time in response to various management actions and competitor initiatives. The plan then defines where operating management would like to take the business over some future time frame, and the resources required to do this. The intent is translated into so-called strategies and the more specific actions designed to achieve the desired result. The results are laid out in financial and other performance characteristics.

Corporate management normally can decide whether the desired resources will be made available to the unit and whether the expected performance is an acceptable return on those resources. Alternately, management can define a desired strategic position that it wishes the unit to attain and request information on what resources are required to achieve this goal. It may also identify the resources that can be made available to the unit and solicit information about the kind of performance that can be achieved with those resources. No matter which course is taken, the intent is to achieve a contract between the nonoperating, corporate management and the operating managers. The expectation is that both sides will abide by the contract or renegotiate it.

The process of linking overall portfolio strategy to business unit strategy requires three major characteristics to exist in the corporation in order for successful results to be achieved. First, for purposes of evaluation and direction setting, the corporation must conceptually assign all of its resources to the individual strategic business units. Second, operating management and corporate management must be prepared to enter into an *iterative* process designed to achieve a strategy (planned pattern of resource commitments and behavior) that is acceptable to both interests, that can be implemented by actions which can be taken (not just luck), and that is consistent with the corporation's needs. Third, once it has entered into an agreement, the corporation cannot arbitrarily change the resources available to the business unit without renegotiating the expected performance. This last condition is probably one of the most frequently violated within corporations as relationships between corporate management and operating management take on an adversarial tone, particularly in the context of unexpected developments of either group.

In well-managed companies such as Johnson & Johnson, Inc., business unit strategies are set in the context of previously approved corporate mission statements. These tend to define broadly the charter of the business unit (its legitimate turf relative to the corporation's portfolio considerations) and the overall thrust of the direction of effort for the unit. The role of the mission is to set general directional guidelines, not performance targets which will be quickly achieved. To provide the business unit with a sense of the immediate, but perhaps temporary, necessities for conformance with the corporation's near-term needs, the corporation typically provides business units with a statement of corporate constraints or introduces explicit hurdle rates and targets in order to clarify short-term performance goals. All parties learn that these are more flexible than long-term direction and may be driven by year-to-year accounting trade-offs.

A strategy directs resource investment to a series or program of related actions which together constitute a selected path to a certain objective. Setting the unit mission and confirming that the actual strategy is consistent with the mission is the primary interface between portfolio strategy and business unit strategy. Business unit strategies are normally designed to create and exploit a competitive advantage in the marketplace. Indeed, business unit strategy is about competing.

There are times, however, when a corporation may find that the desired strategy is precluded by internal trade-offs (or external competitive moves). When a corporation's long-term objectives conflict with the exploitation of the business unit's competitive advantage, or when the corporation simply cannot afford to fund the unit's desired strategy, then the unit may be assigned a set of resources that will permit only a "suboptimal" strategy. This is normally done in the context of corporate good, although individual business units may suffer as a consequence. Specific competitive business strategies are addressed more completely in Chapter 8.

IDENTIFYING SPECIFIC PORTFOLIO BALANCING NEEDS

The decision as to what constitutes a need in a specific portfolio is one of the major contributions of the portfolio evaluation process. The first test is to determine whether the existing businesses collectively can provide the desired performance (as identified in the corporate objectives) over the planning horizon and the likelihood that they will do so beyond the planning time frame. The first objectives identified are usually magnitude and growth rates for sales and income (with the expectation that these will be reflected in the stock price performance of public companies). The second step is usually to check the cash flows against desired financing and dividend characteristics. The last step typically involves assessing the risk and vulnerability of the planned performance. If all components of this evaluation are acceptable, then there is usually little perception of a need to "balance," and the evaluation process is considered complete.

Needless to say, the expected overall performance and that of all the individual pieces is rarely acceptable on the first iteration. The portfolio evaluation process is a continuous one which can never be exhaustive of all possibilities. Because the environment of the corporation is constantly changing and the make-up of the portfolio is dynamic, portfolio evaluation requires constantly changing analysis parameters. At times it runs the risk of becoming a seemingly endless exercise, but at such moments it is appropriate to review why the evaluation is being conducted in the first place. The purpose of portfolio evaluation is to make clear to management the opportunities for strategic decisions, direction, and action in a business environment characterized by complexity and diversity.

7

Assessing the Multinational Environment for Corporate Opportunity

THOMAS N. GLADWIN

Associate Professor of Management and International Business,
Graduate School of Business Administration, New York University

SEARCHING FOR INTERNATIONAL BUSINESS OPPORTUNITIES

The Process as Courtship

The process of searching for corporate opportunities has much in common with courtship leading to matrimony. The quest often begins with the corporate suitor fishing for an opportunity, but it usually ends with the opportunity making the catch. The expedition involves an ocean of emotions, surrounded by a sea of expenses, and it requires audacity, tenacity, and—occasionally—mendacity. In reality, accident accounts for much, because the search is a high sea for which no compass has yet been invented. The main challenge is that one can never tell whether the opportunity is the real thing until it is too late. Yet, as with a future spouse, an opportunity assessed or exploited "in haste seldom proveth well."

What is really different about the assessment and exploitation of opportunities in a multinational setting as compared to a domestic setting? According to Richard D. Robinson of the Massachusetts Institute of Technology, international business is different "because it involves operating effectively within different national sovereignties; under widely disparate economic conditions; with peoples living within different value systems and institutions; as part of an industrial revolution set in the contemporary world; often over greater geographical distance; and in national markets varying greatly in population and area."[1] The multinational corporation (MNC) thus has to contend with some differences in kind, i.e., new institutions, forces, and problems that require new policies, approaches, and techniques. But, most of the differences are of degree, and they flow from the challenge of dealing simultaneously and effectively with:

- *Environmental variability:* Some nations that are changing relatively slowly and/or predictably and others that are changing rapidly and/or unpredictably;

- *Environmental complexity:* Some nations that rely heavily on covert silent language and hidden dimensions in the transmission of information and interpersonal relations, and others where human behavior and communication tends to be more overt and explicit;

- *Environmental hostility:* Some nations where the goals of private enterprise tend to be viewed as legitimate and acceptable, and others where MNCs find themselves at odds with the interests of elite groups and politicians;

- *Environmental diversity:* Some nations that share much in common in terms of culture, economics, and politics, and others that are very different, e.g., preindustrial versus postindustrial societies; and

- *Environmental interdependence:* Some nations that are tightly linked via flows of communication, goods and services, people, and intergovernmental policies such that a change induced or emitted in one nation tends to affect many nations, and other nations that have no such connections between them.

---

[1] Richard D. Robinson, *International Business Management: A Guide to Decision-Making* (New York: John Wiley and Sons, 1978), p. 80.

Increased variability generates uncertainty and demands flexibility on the part of the multinational firm. Higher complexity raises the difficulty of understanding, and it necessitates considerable education about and experience with complex cultures. Increased hostility threatens the firm's goal attainment and demands skills of external relations and conflict management. Greater diversity burdens centralized decision-making with information overload and demands decentralization. And, higher interdependence calls for system-wide coordination and reduced autonomy for individual subsidiaries. For the task of opportunity assessment in particular, greater variability demands more continuous scanning, contingency logic, and multiple scenario analysis; complexity requires deep "contexting" in order to attain true cultural and market understanding; hostility calls for astute forecasting and analysis of political and economic risks; diversity necessitates skills of comparative analysis; and interdependence mandates an integrative or systems perspective.

The Nature of Opportunity

Another up-front question is, What is meant by the word "opportunity"? Webster's New World Dictionary defines it as "a combination of circumstances favorable for the purpose." The purpose addressed in this chapter is that of multinational corporate growth, profitability, and survival. Three circumstances will be examined in relation to this purpose: market attractiveness, competitive advantage, and risk exposure. The first two largely shape expected returns, and the latter affect variance in those returns. The task of opportunity analysis will be viewed as a two-stage process, with the first involving the appraisal and measurement of product/project/country situations in terms of the three circumstances and the second involving the making of judgments as to the favorableness of the combined market/competitive/risk profiles which emerge. A portfolio approach is needed in this second stage, because the favorableness of a given situation can be determined only in relation to a firm's specific risk/return preferences and overall portfolio of existing and prospective businesses.

This chapter is thus organized into four major sections. The first deals with global market analysis, which includes a statistical snapshot of the international marketplace and surveys methods useful in screening and estimating sales potential in various national markets. The second focuses on global competitive analysis and examines the growing globalization of competition and offers frameworks for gauging corporate competitiveness and analyzing competitive forces on a global basis. The third deals with global risk analysis, focusing primarily on analytical methods for dealing with risks of a political nature. The final section integrates the first three and offers a portfolio approach to identifying international business opportunities. Building upon existing portfolio grid technologies, a three-dimensional (market attractiveness/competitive advantage/risk exposure) matrix is developed and explored with regard to its potential for improving the quality of multinational corporate opportunity assessment and, as a result, the strategic allocation of resources on a global basis.

GLOBAL MARKET ANALYSIS

A Statistical Snapshot of the Global Marketplace

A good way to begin this discussion of global market analysis is by taking a quick statistical tour of the varied nature of country markets around the world. Some development indicators, growth projections, and business opportunity ratings are discussed for this purpose. Table 7-1, for example, provides some social and economic indicators for various country groupings compiled by the World Bank. A survey of the table quickly reveals tremendous diversity in the world economy. Fifty-three percent of the world's population is found in low-income countries where, on a weighted average, gross national product (GNP) per capita in 1979 was 230 dollars. In contrast, 15.6 percent of the globe's population resides in the industrial market economies where GNP per capita averaged $9,440, 41 times the low-income country average on an exchange rate conversion basis (the figure would probably be half as much if allowance was made for large differences in purchasing power between countries). GNP per capita is only a very crude indicator of living standards, but the difference between, for example, $90 for Bangladesh and $13,920 for Switzerland in 1979 is both startling and sobering. Similarly dramatic differences can be found in the table with regard to adult literacy, life expectancy, energy consumption, urbanization, and merchandise trade.

Table 7-2 provides World Bank projections of average annual percentage growth in GNP per capita for different country groups over the 1980s. Projections are offered under two scenarios: a high case, in which industrial countries are assumed to be relatively successful in making structural adjustments so as to boost productivity growth, economize on energy, and stimulate production; and a low case, in which the important "locomotive" nations in the world economy fail to make the needed adjustments. Under the high case, average per-capita incomes are expected to grow at the rate of only 1.8 percent a year in the low-income oil importers, while rates of 3.4 percent and 3.1 percent are forecast respectively for middle-income oil importers and industrial countries. The lowest rates of growth over the next decade, under either scenario, are expected for the sub-Saharan African nations that have to import oil (excluding South Africa). The fastest rates of growth, on the other hand, are expected to be achieved by middle-income oil importers in East Asia and the Pacific, China, and oil-exporting countries. As the World Bank has noted,[2] "both the relative and the absolute gaps between the richest and poorest countries will widen in the years ahead, including the gap between middle- and low-income developing countries."

Per-capita income projections tell only a small part of the story as to where market or business prospects may be the brightest in the years to come. A broader picture of comparative business potential among nations can be gleaned from the composite country opportunity ratings produced by Business International's Country Assessment Service (BI/CAS). This service (which is

[2] World Bank, *World Development Report 1981* (New York: Oxford University Press, 1981), p. 3.

TABLE 7-1 Some World Development Indicators

	Population, Mid-1979 (millions)	GNP per Capita Dollars, 1979	Adult Literacy Rate, 1976 (percent)	Life Expectancy at Birth, 1979 (years)	Energy Consumption per Capita, 1979 (kilograms of coal equivalent)	Urban Population as a Percentage of Total Population, 1980	Merchandise Trade, 1979 (millions of dollars) Exports	Imports
Low-income countries	2,260.2 t	230 w	51 w	57 w	463 w	17 w	47,194 t	49,699 t
China and India	1,623.7 t	230 w	54 w	59 w	594 w	17 w	20,985 t	26,307 t
Other low-income	636.5 t	240 w	43 w	50 w	129 w	19 w	26,209 t	23,392 t
Middle-income countries	985.0 t	1,420 w	72 w	61 w	1,225 w	50 w	272,496 t	304,700 t
Oil exporters	324.8 t	1,120 w	64 w	57 w	893 w	45 w	94,803 t	77,204 t
Oil importers	660.2 t	1,550 w	76 w	63 w	1,388 w	52 w	177,693 t	227,504 t
Industrial market economies	671.2 t	9,440 w	99 w	74 w	7,892 w	77 w	1,028,279 t	1,106,534 t
Capital-surplus oil exporters	25.4 t	5,470 w	N.A.	56 w	1,458 w	69 w	118,417 t	44,700 t
Nonmarket industrial economies	351.2 t	4,230 w	N.A.	72 w	6,161 w	64 w	126,079 t	122,992 t

t = total
w = weighted average

Source: The World Bank, World Development Report 1981 (New York: Oxford University Press, 1981), World Development Indicators Annex

TABLE 7-2 Growth of GNP Per Person by Region, 1960–1990

Country Group	Population, 1980 (millions)	GNP per Person (1980 current dollars)	1960–1970	1970–1980	Low Case 1980–1990	High Case 1980–1990
			Average Annual Percentage Growth			
Low-income oil importers	1,166	220	1.8	0.8	0.7	1.8
Africa (sub-Saharan)	175	260	1.7	−0.4	−1.0	0.1
Asia	991	210	1.8	1.1	1.0	2.1
Middle-income oil importers	735	1,710	3.9	3.1	2.1	3.4
East Asia and Pacific	183	1,242	4.9	5.7	4.3	6.0
Latin America and Caribbean	249	1,820	2.7	3.4	2.3	3.2
North Africa and Middle East	34	850	2.4	2.7	0.0	0.9
Africa (sub-Saharan) (a)	87	520	1.7	0.4	0.0	0.3
Southern Europe	152	3,070	5.7	2.9	1.7	3.3
Oil importers	1,901	790	3.4	2.7	1.8	3.1
Oil exporters	482	1,060	3.8	2.7	2.9	4.0
All developing countries	2,383	850	3.5	2.7	2.2	3.3
Low-income	1,307	250	1.8	1.6	1.5	2.6
Middle-income	1,075	1,580	3.9	2.8	2.2	3.4
China (b)	977	260	–	4.1	2.9	4.1
Capital-surplus oil exporters	27	7,390	–	4.2	2.1	2.8
Industrial countries	674	10,660	4.1	2.5	2.3	3.1
Nonmarket industrial economies	356	3,720	–	3.9	2.8	3.0

(a) Not including South Africa
(b) GNP for China refers to 1979; growth rate is for 1970–1979.

Source: World Bank, World Development Report 1981 (New York: Oxford University Press, 1981), p. 3.

described in greater detail in the risk analysis section below) regularly analyzes 56 environmental factors affecting business operations in 70 countries and provides numerical ratings for risk, opportunity, and operating conditions under different scenarios for a five-year forecast period.

The environmental factors are assessed by Business International specialists who reside in each of the countries. Factors that enter into the BI/CAS opportunity rating for each country include: desire of the nation for foreign investment; attitudes toward the private sector; size/influence of middle class; market size/GNP; real GNP growth rate; market wealth-GNP per capita; real growth of GNP per capita; industrialization; regional market intensity;

regional market size; regional market growth; level of foreign direct investment; growth of foreign direct investment; fixed capital formation; and foreign investment profitability. Composite ratings produced by BI/CAS in mid-1981 projected that the greatest opportunities for corporations in 1985 would be found in nations such as Japan, the United States, Australia, Singapore, Hong Kong, and Korea, while the fewest would be offered by nations such as Zaire, Iran, Nicaragua, Ghana, and Liberia.[3] From a regional standpoint, the greatest opportunities for business were expected to be in North America, Europe, and the Pacific Rim. With the exceptions of Mexico, Venezuela, Brazil, Saudi Arabia, and South Africa, no other Latin American, Middle Eastern, or African nations were projected to be among the top 25 nations from the standpoint of business opportunity in 1985.

The notion of macrolevel or general opportunity in a nation may not possess a great deal of meaning. Opportunity, like risk, is something that is largely specific to an industry, a firm, or even a project. What is important is micro market opportunity, not macro market opportunity, and this will depend on a whole host of factors, including industrial sector, type of technology, mode of entry, competitive intensity, corporate strategy. Opportunity assessment must be, in the final analysis, a custom-tailored affair. But, as discussed below, general country ratings are still useful from the standpoint of broad environmental monitoring, first-cut screening, and red flagging the attention of corporate planners and senior managers.

A Filter Approach to Global Market Analysis

The ultimate goal of global market analysis is to identify country markets with high sales potential for candidate products of the firm. Finding these high-priority target markets is not an easy task, given the bewildering array of countries, decision factors, information problems, and uncertainties involved. And, many levels of research and analysis must be traversed prior to arriving at company-specific estimates of sales potential. According to Robinson,[4] country markets need to be screened through a number of filters or levels of analysis in this sequence:

1) *potential need* (which is a constant over the relevant time horizon and is physically determined); 2) *felt need* (which is culturally determined and may be stimulated if the potential need is there, albeit slowly); 3) *potential demand* (which is economically determined); 4) *effective demand* (which may be equated with potential demand modified by political considerations); 5) *market demand* (which is commercially determined, such as by cost of selling); and 6) *sales* (which is determined by competitive conditions).

As one proceeds down through the filters, the cost of market research tends to rise for the needed data shifts from secondary to primary (or field-

---

[3] Business International, *Country Assessment Service: Country Ratings—August 1981* (New York: Business International, 1981).

[4] Robinson, op. cit. pp. 52-53.

gathered) in kind and required analysis grows more demanding and time consuming. It would obviously be prohibitive for an MNC to attempt to examine all the markets of the world in the in-depth fashion required to produce company sales potential estimates. What is needed then is a phased approach to market analysis that efficiently and inexpensively weeds out poor prospects early in the game and reserves full-fledged in-depth investigation only for high-probability target market prospects. A three-phase approach, based on Root,[5] is recommended. This approach (1) begins with preliminary market screening, in order to identify potential target market countries that warrant further investigation; (2) then turns to the estimation of market potential, using extrapolation techniques to develop more precise and quantified estimates of market size and growth for these high-priority candidate markets; and (3) ends with the in-depth estimation of company sales potential for those markets deemed to possess high potential as determined in phase two.

Preliminary Market Screening

The purpose of preliminary market screening, according to Root,[6] is to minimize two errors:

> "(1) ignoring countries that offer good prospects for a company's product type, and (2) spending too much time investigating countries that are poor prospects. To minimize the first error, which is by far the more common, preliminary screening should be applied to *all* countries ... to minimize the second error, preliminary screening should be quick and economical, using quantitative data that are readily available from public sources."

Sources of secondary data relating to country markets are numerous and diverse. General economic, financial, social and demographic data for most nations are gathered and published by organizations such as the World Bank, the United Nations, Business International, and Euromonitor. Figure 7-1 shows the broad range of data included in Euromonitor's "International Marketing Statistics." More specific product-market and industry data is readily available from sources such as the Global Surveys of the U.S. Department of Commerce, special reports of the Economist Intelligence Unit, and "Worldcasts," produced by Predicasts. In using data from these sources, the analyst has to be aware of problems in data accuracy, equivalence, and interpretation.

Such aggregate macroindicators can be utilized in a variety of ways with regard to preliminary market screening. Business International, for example, as part of its Country Assessment Service, mentioned above, uses such indicators to produce multiple-factor indexes of (1) market growth, (2) market intensity, and (3) market size for most countries each year. These indicators have also been employed to classify and cluster countries according to their characteristics. The system is based on the concept that countries with similar characteristics may also possess similar market potential. But, as argued above, the notion of an opportunity or an attractive market is a micro-level phenomenon, not a

---

[5] Franklin R. Root, Foreign Market Entry Strategies (New York: Amacom, 1982), Chapter 2.
[6] Ibid., p. 44.

Population
- Total population
- Area, population distribution, and density
- Population growth and forecasts
- Vital statistics
- Household population
- Demographic breakdowns by age and sex

Employment
- Labor force by age
- Unemployment
- Average working week
- Industrial disputes
- Accidents at work
- Female working population
- Economically active population
- Employment by activity

Production
- Land use and irrigation
- Indices of agricultural and food production
- Livestock
- Meat production
- Animal and fishery products
- Fruit and vegetables
- Cereals
- Forestry products
- Other crops
- Manufactured foods
- Beverages and tobacco
- Natural resources
- Refined metals
- Building materials
- Energy resources and production
- Electrical energy
- Chemical products
- Automotives
- Consumer durables
- Clothing and textiles

Trade
- Balance of trade
- Direction of trade (imports and exports)
- Imports of selected manufactured goods

Economy
- Economic indicators
- Gross national product
- Productivity
- State budget
- Gross domestic product (origin and distribution)
- Money reserves and supply
- Exchange rates

Standard of Living
- Comparative wages and earnings
- Consumer prices
- Comparative costs
- Radios and televisions in use
- Car ownership
- Ownership levels for consumer durables
- Household expenditure
- Retail trade

Consumption
- Industrial products
- Energy
- Agricultural requisites
- Food
- Beverages
- Tobacco
- Sales of durables

Housing, Health, Education
- Dwelling stock
- Size of dwellings
- Facilities in dwellings
- Hospital establishment
- Health personnel
- Primary education
- Secondary education
- Higher education
- Expenditure on education
- Illiteracy level

Communications
- Cultural indicators
- Libraries, museums
- Communication services
- Telephones, telegrams
- Transport statistics
- Roads, railways, air traffic, shipping
- Tourist statistics

Source: Euromonitor Publications Ltd., *International Marketing Data and Statistics* (London: Euromonitor, 1977–1978)

FIG. 7-1 Euromonitor International Marketing Data

macro-level phenomenon. The same indicators are not likely to be relevant for all product markets and firms. A customized approach to preliminary market screening is thus called for.

A custom-tailored approach would involve the following steps. The analyst would first need to identify the basic needs served by the candidate product and the characteristics of potential customers. The key here is to pinpoint the major factors that determine demand for the product. This consumer/use profile then can be used to select indicators (of a macro-country and/or specific product market kind) that are closely correlated with, or predictive of, the market potential for the product. Since a single variable will seldom be an adequate indicator of relative market potential, a multiple variable index will generally need to be constructed. Weights thus have to be assigned to the different indicators selected according to estimates of their relative influence on the sales of the product or service in question and the strategic market objectives of the company. The index can then be calculated for each country and the national markets thereby ranked in priority. Country markets that do not meet the company's minimum requirements for market potential can be eliminated at this stage. Those that do meet the requirements then can be subjected to deeper and more precise analysis in phase two of the market analysis program, estimating market potential.

Estimating Market Potential

After preliminary screening has yielded a working set of prospective target countries, the next step in the filtering process is that of estimating industry market potential within these countries. Root defines industry market potential as "the most probable total sales of a product by all sellers in a designated country over a strategic planning period."[7] Two dimensions of potential will typically be of concern: (1) absolute size of the current market, and (2) projected growth of the market over a specified period, for example, three to five years. Different MNCs will give greater or lesser emphasis to each dimension in accordance with their particular product lines and strategies. But, accept/reject decisions at this stage of market opportunity searching will depend on the establishment of explicit growth/size tradeoffs.

There are many tools and techniques available for use in estimating foreign demand and market potential. These are extensively treated in the international marketing literature,[8] and they need to be only briefly reviewed here. All market-demand forecasting represents some blend of the following approaches. It "can be based either on past experience in the country being studied or on analogous experience in another country. Forecasts can be made directly by

---

[7] Ibid., p. 50.

[8] Scott J. Armstrong, "An Application of Econometric Models of International Marketing," *Journal of Marketing Research* (No. 2, 1970), pp. 190-198; Susan P. Douglas and C. Samuel Craig, "Information for International Marketing Decisions," Section 29 in Ingo Walter and Tracey Murray, eds., *Handbook of International Business* (New York: John Wiley and Sons: 1982); Warren J. Keegan, *Multinational Marketing Management* (Englewood Cliffs, N.J.: Prentice-Hall, Inc., 1980); and Reed Moyer, "International Market Analysis," *Journal of Marketing Research* (Nov. 1968), pp. 353-360.

extending actual sales data into the future, or indirectly on the basis of an established relationship between demand for the product or service and independent variables such as economic or demographic characteristics of the country."[9] Great ingenuity and caution will be required when sales or production experience in the nations under study is limited and data on other variables is unavailable.

Douglas and Craig's provided an excellent review of low-cost data extrapolation techniques for use in estimating future market size and growth is summarized here.[10] Using these techniques requires a number of assumptions regarding the relevance of data collected in one country to another, equivalence of measurement units, similarity of relationships between sales and demand determinants among countries, and comparability of product classes. The simplest method is probably lead-lag analysis, which assumes that demand patterns in a leading country are predictive of those that will occur in a country under study. Time series data from one nation are used to predict sales trends in another country with a lag of a specified number of years. Empirical evidence regarding television sets and automobiles does support the hypothesis that regional lead-lags exist,[11] but difficulties in identifying precise time lags and the restrictive assumption that countries are identical with respect to everything except time tends to reduce the utility of this technique.

Barometric analysis, which is done on the basis of either an entire market or a specific segment of a market, is a much more valuable approach to forecasting market potential. As noted by Douglas and Craig,[12] this technique (1) relies on the use of cross-sectional data; (2) assumes that if there is a relationship between the demand for product and a gross economic or other indicator in one country, then the same relationship will hold in other countries and from one time to another; and (3) can employ a variety of mathematical methods to develop model parameters (e.g., linear regression, logarithms, exponential smoothing). Even if elegant multiple linear regression techniques are used, however, extreme caution is needed in making the assumption that roughly the same relationship holds from one country to another and from one time to another. This will often not be the case.

Barometric analysis to estimate market potential can also be done on a segment basis rather than on an aggregate basis. This is needed, according to Douglas and Craig,[13] when there are different market segments for a given product (e.g., pleasure and fishing boat markets for small diesel boat engines) that have different underlying demand determinants and when different market segments have different levels or rates of market penetration. The first case naturally requires the development of different indicators for each market segment. The second calls for an approach as follows:[14]

---

[9] Stefan H. Robock, Kenneth Simmonds, and Jack Zwick, *International Business and Multinational Enterprise* (Homewood, Ill.: Richard D. Irwin, 1977), p. 379.

[10] Douglas and Craig, op. cit.

[11] Keegan, op. cit.

[12] Douglas and Craig, op. cit., p. 18.

[13] Ibid., p. 20.

[14] Ibid., p. 21.

"different user industries can be identified, and rates of penetration in each of these industries determined for one country. The number of companies in each of these industries in another country can then be assessed and multiplied by the relevant penetration rate in order to determine potential market size. In the case of minicomputers, for example, the key user industries might be financial institutions or commercial data-processing and market-research companies."

Econometric forecasting models, which typically require both cross-sectional and time series data, can also be useful in estimating foreign market potential. Armstrong, for example, developed a model for projecting camera sales in 19 countries that attempted to specify the factors that determined demand rather than that that were merely associated with demand.[15] Such efforts can produce high-quality predictions, but they generally take considerable time to develop and they involve problems in constructing indices and estimating the most appropriate coefficients. Before turning to the next step in the target market selection process, note that a variety of other techniques may also be of assistance in producing market potential estimates. These include multiple factor indexes, macro surveys, demand pattern analysis, income elasticity measurements, comparative and cluster analysis, and input/output analysis.

Estimating Company Sales Potential

Given a pool of countries identified by the methods above as possessing high market potential, the next step in the chain of market research is that of estimating specific demand or company sales potential so as to identify truly attractive target markets. Root defines company sales potential as "the most probable sales of a company's product in a designated country over a strategic planning period, given assumptions with respect to entry mode and marketing effort."[16] Alternatively, this can be thought of in terms of most probable market share (i.e., share of market potential). The basic question at this stage is whether the MNC can meet or better the terms (in regard to product or service quality, design, sizing, packaging, pricing, credit, delivery, service, and warranties) offered by its competitors.

Sales potential will largely be determined by competitive conditions, a subject explored extensively in the next section. The firm's ability to compete will depend on its foreign market entry strategy (e.g., exporting vs. investment vs. licensing) and the level of its marketing effort.[17] As such, MNCs need to evaluate and compare carefully their selected high market potential countries with regard to export and nonexport entry barriers, market structure, competitor products and marketing programs, availability of distribution channels, marketing effort required, and so on.[18] Sales potential profiles can be developed for each country on this basis and then ranked so as to produce a prioritized list of target countries for the specific product in question. Entry into target

---

[15] Armstrong, op. cit.

[16] Root, op. cit., p. 53.

[17] Ibid.

[18] Ibid., pp. 54-58.

countries would not be automatic, of course, since other aspects of the situation, such as risk exposure, would also need to be considered. But, designation as a target country would tend to justify test marketing, on-the-spot consumer surveys, sampling programs, and other in-depth market research.

If the MNC is already selling the product in the nation, then a useful exercise is that of comparing actual sales to sales potential via gap analysis. When actual sales are below potential sales, there may be a gap in usage, competition, product line, or distribution, which if closed could potentially result in increased sales. Nestle and Interfood have used this tool to decide which country markets to emphasize and to differentiate their marketing programs among nations.[19]

GLOBAL COMPETITIVE ANALYSIS

The Globalization of Competition

The globalization of competition has become a fact of life for U.S. companies in a wide variety of industries: steel, automobiles, minicomputers, commercial aircraft, consumer electronics, semiconductors, textile machinery, and machine tools, to name just a few. And, this fact is radically altering the old competitive dynamics in these industries and is changing the rules of the game. This internationalization of competition is reflected in a variety of trade, investment, sales, and foreign content data. International trade of manufactured products, for example, grew in real terms on an average of 8.8 percent from 1963 to 1978, while total real manufacturing production grew only at the rate of 5.5 percent, with the result that exports and imports have dramatically grown as a percentage of total industrial production in most major industrial countries. As has been noted,[20] "In 1960, the U.S. imported only 8.5 percent and exported only 11.5 percent of total production. By 1978, imports had risen to 29.0 percent and exports to 22.4 percent."

Globalization is also indicated by the rapid development of international direct investment over the past two decades, both in absolute terms and relative to the growth of other economic aggregates such as visible trade, domestic investment, and GNP. The stock of direct investment grew from $105.3 billion at the end of 1967 to $287.2 billion at the end of 1976. It also changed dramatically in its composition over time, as shown in the flow data provided in Table 7-3. As a percentage of outward direct investment of 13 countries, the share of the United States decreased from a peak of 61.1 percent during the period 1961 to 1967 to 29.3 percent during the period 1974 to 1979; Germany's share, on the other hand, jumped from 7.2 percent to 17.0 percent, while Japan's went from 2.4 percent to 13.0 percent. Table 7-3 also shows a dramatic change in the

---

[19] Anonymous, "Chocolate Makers in Switzerland Try to Melt Resistance," *Wall Street Journal* (Jan. 5, 1981), p. 14.

[20] Thomas M. Hout, Michael E. Porter, Eileen Rudden, and Eric Vogt, "Global Industries: New Rules for the Competitive Game," Graduate School of Business Administration, Division of Research, Harvard University, Working Paper No. 1980-53.

TABLE 7-3 Outward and Inward Direct Investment Flows (Percentage Distribution Among 13 Countries)

	Outward Flows			Inward Flows		
	1961–1967	1968–1973	1974–1979	1961–1967	1968–1973	1974–1979
Canada	2.3	4.5	6.2	16.2	12.1	3.2
United States	61.1	45.8	29.3	2.6	11.4	26.7
Japan	2.4	6.7	13.0	2.0	1.7	1.2
Australia	0.7	1.4	1.6 (a)	15.6	12.9	9.5 (a)
Belgium	0.3 (b)	1.4	2.5	4.5 (b)	6.1	9.4
France	6.9	5.2	7.8	8.2	8.2	15.2
Germany	7.2	12.5	17.0	21.3	16.4	14.7
Italy	3.6	3.3	2.0	11.5	8.3	5.0
Netherlands	4.4	6.8	9.6 (c)	4.7	8.5	6.0 (c)
Sweden	2.0	2.4	3.7 (d)	2.4	1.7	0.5 (d)
United Kingdom	8.7	9.1	9.2	9.7	7.4	6.1
Spain	—	0.3	0.6	2.7	3.7	3.7
Norway	—	0.3	0.9	0.8	1.4	4.1

(a) From 1974 to 1976
(b) From 1965
(c) From 1974 to 1978
(d) From 1974 to 1977

Source: I.M.F.-O.E.C.D. Common Reporting System on Balance of Payments Statistics. The figures for the United Kingdom and the United States do not include reinvested earnings to place the data on a more comparable basis. Data for the United Kingdom do not include the petroleum sector. Reported in O.E.C.D., International Investment and Multinational Enterprises: Recent International Direct Investment Trends 40–41 (Paris: O.E.C.D., 1981).

destination of direct investment. The United States received only 2.6 percent of foreign investment during the period 1961 to 1967, but the figure for the years 1974 to 1978 was 26.7 percent. The result was that by 1980, European and Japanese firms had achieved significant U.S. market shares in a variety of industries through their investments in, and exports to, the United States. The competitive dynamics changed considerably, in part due to this reason: "Because many of these foreign competitors are either nationalized, quasinationalized or highly salient in their own countries, they are frequently willing to accept lower returns in U.S. markets, offsetting these lower returns against unemployment, balance of payments, and capital gains at home."[21]

Changes in the nature of global competition are also indicated by changes in the relative size of firms based in different countries. Data from the *Fortune* list of leading industrial companies (on the basis of sales revenues) reveals the rise of non-U.S. companies on the world scene. In 1962, for example, 292 (60.5 percent) of the largest 483 industrial companies in the world were U.S.-owned, 51 (10.6 percent) were U.K.-owned, 91 (18.8 percent) were owned by other European countries, 29 (6 percent) were Japanese, and 3 (0.6 percent) were owned from developing countries. The corresponding figures for 1977 were 240 (49.7 percent) for the United States, 40 (8.3 percent) United Kingdom, 104 (21.2 percent) other European, 64 (13.3 percent) Japanese, and 18 (3.7 percent) developing countries.[22] These figures indicate the growth in size and technical and financial capabilities of non-U.S.-based corporations.

Another perspective on the globalization of competition is provided by data on the sheer importance, and increasing importance, of the multinational corporation in the modern world economy. Firms engaging in foreign direct investment have been growing at the rate of 10 to 12 percent per annum, nearly twice the growth of world output. As reported by Dunning and Pearce,[23] in 1977, some 27 percent of the sales of 866 of the world's largest industrial enterprises was derived from their foreign affiliates; of 381 enterprises with sales of more than $1 billion, 153 had a foreign content ratio (i.e., percentages of all sales, assets, or employment accounted for by their foreign-based activities) of more than 25 percent, and 52 had a foreign content ratio of more than one-half. Table 8-4 provides some details regarding these foreign content ratios. As shown in the table, the ratios vary considerably both between industry and home country. The variance is highest within the research-intensive sectors and among European nations. The five most global industries in 1977, on the basis of this index, considering all home countries, were petroleum; office equipment and computers; tobacco; rubber; and measurement, scientific, and photographic equipment. Seven of the industries based in the United States had foreign content ratios of greater than 25 percent. Note, however, that companies in a range of nonmanufacturing industries, and thus not included in Table 7-4,

[21] William K. Hall, "Survival Strategies in a Hostile Environment," *Harvard Business Review* (Sept./Oct. 1980), p. 76.

[22] John H. Dunning and R. D. Pearce, *The World's Largest Industrial Enterprises* (Farnborough: Gower, 1981).

[23] Dunning and Pearce, op. cit.

TABLE 7-4 The Foreign Content Ratio of 866 of the World's Largest Industrial Enterprises in 1977

	Home Country of Multinational Enterprises				
	United States	Europe	Japan	Other Countries	All Countries
High research intensity					
Aerospace	7.6	6.8	N.A.	N.A.	7.5
Office equipment and computers	42.2	39.3	10.0	N.A.	41.5
Petroleum	47.0	59.5	1.0	1.3	42.7
Measurement, scientific and photographic equipment	35.2	21.0	8.0	N.A.	33.1
Electronics and electrical appliances	21.3	26.6	4.5	45.8	20.5
Chemicals and pharmaceuticals	25.7	40.5	4.3	4.3	29.0
Total	35.8	44.0	3.6	5.2	33.5
Medium research intensity					
Industrial and farm equipment	28.1	26.9	2.8	48.5	22.9
Shipbuilding, railroad, and transportation equipment	5.0	1.6	7.1	31.7	8.8
Rubber	31.6	48.5	7.0	N.S.A.	34.2
Motor vehicles and components	21.4	20.5	17.4	N.A.	20.6
Metal manufacturing and products	13.7	16.8	3.3	15.2	13.5
Total	19.6	20.4	8.6	21.6	18.4
Low research intensity					
Building materials	21.7	38.7	3.0	2.0	27.9
Tobacco	29.0	52.1	N.A.	N.A.	40.8
Beverages	23.6	20.5	N.S.A.	3.7	17.4
Food	18.9	55.2	2.1	5.8	28.8
Paper and wood products	13.6	32.8	4.0	32.4	18.1
Textiles, apparel, leather goods	10.2	26.5	12.3	11.7	15.5
Publishing and printing	6.2	15.3	4.1	N.A.	9.2
Total	17.9	44.6	4.8	13.3	25.0
Other Manufacturing	11.0	0.9	5.0	2.0	5.8
Total	27.4	35.1	6.1	11.5	26.6

Note: Foreign content is defined as the percentage of sales of foreign affiliates of multinational enterprises (excluding goods imported from the parent companies for resale) to the worldwide sales of the enterprises.

N.A.: not applicable
N.S.A.: not separately available

Source: J.H. Dunning & R.D. Pearce, *The World's Largest Industrial Enterprises* (Farnborough, U.K.: Gower, 1981)

also have major and expanding interests outside their national boundaries; these would include the nonfuel mineral, agribusiness, and service sectors.

The facts on the dramatic growth and increasing importance of international trade, foreign market penetration, foreign direct investment, competitors based outside the United States, and multinational enterprise in general speak loud and clearly: The nature of the competitive game is growing increasingly global for more and more companies every day. Particularly for U.S. companies, the increased and more intense competition coming from Japanese and European firms in established markets, both at home and abroad, implies a large need for new ways of thinking about, preparing for, coping with, and marking out defensible positions against competition on a global basis. The global environmental analyst must therefore fully understand: (1) What factors promote and impede competition on a global basis; (2) the kinds of advantages that a firm must possess to be globally competitive; (3) the broad array of structural factors and market forces that determine the intensity of competition the firm will confront around the globe; and (4) the various means by which global competitive intelligence can be gathered and evaluated. These four issues are addressed in the sections that follow.

Global Competitive Facilitators and Impediments

The first task for the competitive analyst is to determine the extent to which his or her firm is in a global industry, or one that is becoming a global industry. A global industry is defined as "one in which the strategic positions of competitors in major geographic or national markets are fundamentally affected by their overall global positions . . . global industries require a firm to compete on a worldwide, coordinated basis or face strategic disadvantages."[24] In other words, to what extent can firms in a particular industry acquire advantages by competing on a global basis? Or, how threatened will a firm be by international competitors? The essential task for the analyst, according to Porter, is to understand clearly the evolving balance between the factors that promote or facilitate versus those that impede or block global competition as they pertain to a particular industry.[25] Some of the key factors in each group are listed in Figure 7-2, and are discussed below.

Facilitators of Global Competition. A variety of forces drive the globalization process.[26] The classic determinant, of course, is comparative advantage; i.e., differences among countries in the availability of factors in production such as land, skilled labor, and capital. These factors, in large measure, determine the location and concentration of production as well as the basis and patterns of trade among nations.

---

[24] Michael E. Porter, *Competitive Strategy: Techniques for Analyzing Industries and Competitors* (New York: Free Press, 1980), p. 275.

[25] Ibid., p. 278.

[26] Ibid., Chapter 13.

Facilitators	Impediments
• Comparative advantage	• Transportation and storage costs
• Production economies of scale	• Differing product needs
• Logistical economies of scale	• Established distribution channels
• Purchasing economies of scale	• Sensitivity to lead times
• Marketing economies of scale	• Lack of world demand
• Global experience	• Differing marketing tasks
• Amortization of research and development	• Rapidly changing technology
	• Perceptual impediments
• Proprietary product technology	• Governmental impediments
• Product differentiation	• Intensive local selling and service
• Mobility of production	

Source: Michael E. Porter, *Competitive Strategy: Techniques for Analyzing Industries and Competitors,* Ch. 13 (New York: The Free Press, 1980)

FIG. 7-2   Facilitators of and Impediments to Global Competition

Another inducement to centralized production and global competition is economies of scale that exceed national markets. These can take many forms. They may arise in production in some industries, whereby the lowest unit costs are likely to be achieved by the largest producers, and these producers are likely to export into smaller markets that cannot support producers of minimum efficient scale. Potential cost advantages can also be derived from scale economies in logistics. The fixed costs of a global logistics system can often be spread by involving many source and destination countries. The Japanese steel producers, for example, "have achieved significant cost savings in the use of specialized port facilities, carriers and loading procedures to transport raw materials and finished products."[27]

Still other cost savings due to scale economies may be achievable in the areas of purchasing and marketing, thereby stimulating globalization of an industry. Opportunities for sourcing economies may arise "as a result of bargaining power or lower suppliers' cost in producing long runs, which go beyond what is needed to compete in individual national markets ... for example, worldwide producers of television sets appear to be able to purchase transistors and diodes at lower costs."[28] In the marketing area, the global firm may achieve cost savings relative to purely local firms by spreading the fixed costs of a common sales force over, or standardizing its marketing activities among, many markets around the world. Pepsi-Cola, McDonalds, and Levi Strauss are among some of the many MNCs that have been able to achieve gains through the use of standardized and proprietary marketing techniques, such as advertising appeals on a worldwide basis.

[27] Hout, et. al., op. cit., p. 9.
[28] Porter, op. cit., p. 280.

Cost advantages for global producers versus national producers may also arise from the global firm's ability to move down the experience curve or learning curve more quickly through its sales of the same or similar product or service on a worldwide basis. The logic of the experience curve, of course, is that manufacturing costs for a product will tend to fall as the cumulative production volume increases. This is particularly the case in industries with high labor content (e.g., shipbuilding), complex assembly operations (e.g., aircraft), or high unit volumes of standardized products (e.g., semiconductors). "With more experience due to worldwide volume, a multinational firm can presumably learn how to make workers' methods more productive, to design plant layout and work flow more efficiently, to coax more production out of machinery, to develop specialized new processes as well as product design modifications that make manufacturing easier, and to institute better management control."[29]

Still other factors that promote globalization of competition, according to Porter, [30] are: (1) the global economies that can result from amortizing the cost of product development or proprietary process technology over sales in multiple national markets, a motive which has been very important in the research-intensive computer, semiconductor, aircraft, turbine and broadcasting equipment industries; (2) the potential edge in reputation and credibility (i.e., product differentiation) that may develop from maintaining a multinational presence; and (3) the gains that can accrue to global competitors in industries where the production of a product or service is mobile (e.g., heavy construction, oil rig operations, consulting) by being able to spread the fixed costs of skilled specialists and mobile equipment over operations in many locations.

Impediments to Global Competition. The analyst must also consider a variety of factors that may impede the transformation of national industries into global ones. These impediments range from economic to managerial to institutional; a listing of some of the more important ones, according to Porter,[31] appears in Figure 7-2.

A number of economic factors raise the direct cost of competing on a global basis. High transportation and storage costs, for example, serve to offset the economies of rationalized production and logistics systems; this explains, to a large extent, why production and competition in industries such as pre-stressed concrete, hazardous chemicals, and fertilizers has primarily remained a local rather than global affair. Global economies of scale or learning are also prevented by differing product needs from market to market that arise from cultural, economic, climatic, legal, and other variations among nations and thereby demand heterogeneous product offerings on the part of a firm.

Other mainly economic factors that raise barriers to global competition include difficulties in gaining access to fragmented and well-established distribution channels in national markets; requirements for intensive localized selling and service operations, where local firms may tend to be more responsive;

---

[29] Michael E. Porter, "Experience Curve," *Wall Street Journal* (Oct. 22, 1979), p. 30.

[30] Porter, *Competitive Strategy*, pp. 280-281.

[31] Ibid., pp. 281-287.

great sensitivities to lead times that are short, as in the fashion business, where the "distance between the national market and centralized production, product development, or marketing activities tends to create delays in responding to market needs that can be unacceptable";[32] and, of course, the lack of world demand for products that have emerged in very unique environments and are in very early stages of their international life cycles.

Other factors impede globalization by raising the complexity of management tasks involved.[33] Extreme cultural diversity, for example, reduces a firm's ability to transfer and exploit knowledge from one nation to another, burdens attempts at centralized decision-making and coordination of subsidiary behaviors, and demands differentiated management practices, particularly in "culture sensitive" areas such as marketing and human resource management.[34] MNCs have little to offer and will tend to be outcompeted by locals when extreme diversity compels the "when in Rome, do as the Romans" rule. Self-contained, national firms may also have the advantage when "rapidly changing technology requires frequent product and process redesign attuned to local markets."[35] Note that in this area of particular complexity there are many subjective or perceptual impediments to going global (e.g., uncertainty, perceived risks, home country preferences) which leads to "inertial resistance" and a tendency towards pessimism; managers often overestimate the risks and underestimate the expected returns of going abroad.[36]

Finally, the competitive analyst must carefully consider the broad range of impediments to global competition that are imposed by governments for reasons of protectionism and nationalism. These impediments generally constrain the strategic freedom of MNCs. They often demand local-for-local production, and they may make it impossible to compete at all in certain markets. Examples of such impediments include tariffs, quotas, voluntary export restraints, orderly marketing arrangements, discriminatory practices in government procurement, discriminatory effects of technical and legal standards, arbitrary customs valuations, and a variety of so-called operating and performance requirements related to ownership, research and development, exports, employment, and local content. These types of barriers arise most often in connection with strategic industries (e.g., telecommunications equipment, heavy electric-power generation, shipbuilding, nuclear engineering), but they are also often imposed by governments to protect salient local "exposed industries" (e.g., automobiles) and new "high-growth industries" (e.g., microelectronics and aerospace.)[37] These requirements impose constraining political imperatives on foreign MNCs and impede their ability to meet economic imperatives by preventing them

---

[32] Ibid., pp. 283-284.

[33] Ibid., p. 282.

[34] Geert Hofstede, *Culture's Consequences: International Differences in Work-Related Values* (Beverly Hills: SAGE, 1980).

[35] Porter, *Competitive Strategy,* p. 285.

[36] Yair Aharoni, *The Foreign Investment Decision Process* (Cambridge, Mass: Harvard Business School, 1966).

[37] Yves Doz, "Multinational Strategy and Structure in Government-Controlled Business," *Columbia Journal of World Business* (Fall 1980), pp. 14-25.

from rationalizing and integrating their activities in search of efficiency and lower costs. [38]

The Global Competitive Balance. Some of the many factors that either promote or impede competition on a global basis have now been examined. The job of the analyst is to analyze the relevance and significance of each of these factors to his or her industry in general and, more specifically, to different product segments within that industry. This is not an easy task, given the diverse, interactive, incommensurable, and dynamic nature of the factors involved. The key, however, is developing at least a rough feel for the balance between the most important facilitators and impediments at a particular time and for how that balance may evolve over the next 5 to 10 years. If the impediments significantly outweigh the facilitators for a given business, then competition within it is likely to be local in character, with national firms probably preeminent over foreign competitors. If the impediments and facilitators balance out, then it is probable that competition will entail aspects of both "localness" and "globalness," with local and global firms, however, operating in different strategic niches within that particular industry. But, finally, if the impediments are powerfully outweighed by the facilitators in a given industry, then it is likely that competition for market share will be global in character, with firms finding it essential to compete on a worldwide coordinated basis in order to avoid substantial strategic disadvantages. The balance of forces relevant to a particular product line or an entire industry, of course, will be changing constantly. The competitive analyst must, therefore, carefully monitor changes in the external environment and strategic innovations on the part of competitors that bear upon the global competitive balance in his or her industry. [39]

Auditing a Firm's Global Competitiveness

If a firm is part of a global industry, or an industry that is becoming global, the next essential task for a competitive analyst is to audit his or her firm's situation to determine whether it possesses or can acquire the resources or advantages needed for competing effectively on a global scale. What is required in order to be able to compete with local firms in foreign nations and with other multinationals based at home and abroad? What particular advantages are required in order to compete internationally in different ways (i.e., via exporting versus licensing versus direct investment abroad)? And, what is needed to compete in different locations around the world?

Some of the advantages that can potentially accrue to a firm that chooses to compete in a coordinated, worldwide fashion are surveyed in a general way and on a macro level. But, the task of assessing a particular firm's ability to compete internationally requires a more comprehensive and detailed micro level framework of analysis. For this, one should be aware of Dunning's pio-

---

[38] Ibid.

[39] Hout, et. al., op. cit., pp. 15-23.

neering "eclectic approach" to the explanation of international economic involvement.[40] Competitiveness in serving foreign or domestic markets, according to Dunning, depends on the possession, or acquisition on more favorable terms, of assets, or resource endowments, that are not available to, or are not utilized by, present or potential competitors. These assets can be tangible or intangible, and they can be internal or external to the enterprise. The why, where, and how of international production depends on three types of assets: (1) the why of international business activity on the part of an enterprise depends on the extent to which it possesses ownership-specific advantages, that is, assets or rights that are exclusive to the enterprise that owns them and are, at least in part, transferable (i.e., mobile) across national boundaries; (2) the where of international production is viewed as a function of location-specific advantages of countries, which are external to the enterprises that use them and are not transferable or mobile across national boundaries; and (3) the how of international involvement (e.g., direct investment and exporting versus contractual resources exchanges, such as licensing) depends on internalization incentive advantages, that is, gains to the enterprise that arise from replacing external mechanisms of resource allocation with internal administrative means of asset allocation.

From an auditing standpoint, it can be predicted that the better an enterprise is able to acquire and sustain these three types of advantages relative to other firms based both at home and abroad, the larger the net global competitive advantage of an enterprise will be. The origin and nature of each type of advantage is discussed below.

Ownership-Specific Advantages. The possession of ownership advantages is a necessary prerequisite for foreign involvement of any kind, whether it be exporting, direct investment, or contractual resource transfers. This is because an enterprise operating outside of its home environment faces certain "distance" costs, involving factors such as knowledge of the market, communication difficulties, and political risks, which are not borne by host country firms. The enterprise must thus have at its disposal certain proprietary assets, leading to net advantages vis-à-vis firms in these host countries; otherwise, the locals would possess overall cost advantages that would preclude the possibility of profitable foreign involvement.

Oligopoly-creating or ownership-specific advantages that reduce a firm's costs or raise its revenues relative to other competing firms may be tangible or intangible, and they may be internally generated or their proprietary right of use may be acquired from other institutions. Although their origin may be linked to a particular country or industry, they can be used anywhere. Dunning classifies such ownership-specific advantages into three categories. The first follows from Bain's classic work on the barriers to new competition,[41] and it includes the advantages that flow from size, monopoly power, and superior

---

[40] John H. Dunning, *International Production and the Multinational Enterprise* (London: George Allen & Unwin, 1981).

[41] J. S. Bain, *Barriers to New Competition* (Cambridge, Mass: Harvard University Press, 1956).

resource capability/usage that any firm may have over others producing in the same location. The second includes those advantages that a branch plant of an established enterprise may enjoy over de novo enterprises or those just breaking into the established firm's product area. Whereas the de novo firm will normally have to bear the full cost of factors such as research and development, market knowledge, administrative experience, the branch plant of the established firm, producing in the same location, typically will be able to benefit from the assets or endowments of its parent company at no cost or at a very low marginal cost. The third set of ownership-specific advantages arises because of the multinationality of a company; gains arise from wider opportunities, better knowledge, and risk diversification.

Internalization Incentive Advantages. This set of advantages is based on the theory of property rights and the economics of transaction costs. The basic proposition is that firms can achieve real competitive advantages if they can successfully avoid the disadvantages, or capitalize on the advantages, of imperfections or disequilibria in external mechanisms of resource allocation. These external mechanisms are of two types: the market system, in which structural and cognitive imperfections may be present; and the public intervention system, whereby governmental policy instruments create distortions in the allocation of resources that a firm may wish to circumvent, counteract, or take advantage of. In the absence of market-induced and government-induced imperfections and inefficiencies, no gains could be achieved by attempting to coordinate interdependent activities internally instead of relying on external mechanisms of resource allocation. But, as these external systems grow more imperfect, firms will be motivated increasingly to protect themselves against or to exploit the imperfections involved by internalizing the transactions in intangible assets or goods that otherwise would be externalized.

Dunning summarizes the reasons why a firm might wish to replace an external resource allocation mechanism by internal administrative fiat as follows: [42]

(1) [T]o avoid or reduce transaction and negotiating costs;

(2) the fact that, owing to the lack of knowledge or inefficiency on the part of the buying firm, it is unwilling or unable to pay the selling firm a price that will be sufficient to compensate it for not internalizing the transaction;

(3) to gain advantage over one's competitor through controlling the supply of inputs, product or production strategy and the access to markets;

(4) to exploit, or protect oneself against, the consequences of government intervention, for example, by taxation and other actions, which may otherwise place the firm in a less favorable position (the ability of a firm to engage in transfer pricing is one such example);

(5) to protect the property rights of the owning firm, *inter alia* by avoiding misrepresentation by the sellers of one's product, and/or ensuring product quality and after-sales maintenance and servicing;

---

[42] Dunning, op. cit., p. 96.

(6) to make better use of capacity or overheads to gain advantage of size, joint production, integration and/or diversification (one of the main reasons for takeovers and mergers).

The reasons and the propensities for internalization will vary among industries. A bauxite or copper firm, for example, may wish to ensure stability of supply at the right price and to control markets; a consumer electronics firm may wish to exploit the economies of vertical integration; an automobile firm may wish to maximize the gains from intedependent activities; and a computer firm may wish to exploit its technological advantages and overcome high transactions or information costs. In general, internalization advantages may tend to be the greatest for large, technologically intensive, widely diversified (across markets and products), and highly integrated (both vertically and horizontally) types of firms.

Location-Specific Advantages. With the "why" of multinational business activity explained by ownership advantages and the "how" explained by internalization advantages, the only question that remains is where this activity will be carried out. Drawing on theories of location and trade,[43] Dunning suggests that location-specific endowments will determine the industrial geography of multinational enterprise. Such location advantages are external to the enterprise that uses them, and thus they are available, on the same terms, to all enterprises, whatever their nationality or size. These advantages, however, are immobile across national boundaries, and they must therefore be used where they are located.

Location-specific advantages are of many types. They may take the form of low labor costs or governmental incentives for local production, which are vitally important to firms pursuing rationalized specialization of processes such as camera or consumer electronics firms. The availability, quality, and cost of raw materials, along with political risk considerations, would constitute key locational determinants in natural-resource-based industries. To a pharmaceutical or computer firm engaged in import substituting manufacturing the sources of locational advantage might arise from exploiting large markets and differential tariff and nontariff barriers, tax rates, investment incentives, and labor/material costs. Motor vehicle and electrical appliance firms, on the other hand, might attain locational gains in their rationalization efforts by optimizing cost factors such as production, transfer, communication, culture, and regulations so as to achieve the greatest economies of product specialization and concentration.

The Eclectic Approach in Summary. Dunning's eclectic approach provides the international competitive analyst with a useful framework for gauging whether his or her firm can compete, how it should compete, and where it should compete on a global basis. The key message is that of acquiring and

---

[43] Raymond Vernon, "The Location of Economic Activity" in John H. Dunning, ed., *Economic Analysis and the Multinational Enterprise* (London: George Allen & Unwin, 1974).

sustaining net advantages. As for the form of involvement, foreign direct investments will tend to make sense when the firm possesses substantial ownership and internalization advantages and when the overseas sites involved yield dividends of location. Exporting from home to overseas markets, on the other hand, will become the preferred route when the home country yields location endowment advantages over the importing countries. And, contractual resource transfers such as licensing will become attractive when the enterprise possesses ownership-specific advantages but is unable to derive any gains from internalization or foreign locational advantages.

As Dunning notes,[44] the three sets of advantages are not independent of each other, and this will naturally complicate the task of auditing a firm's situation. The level and structure of the resource endowments of a country, for example, will affect the form of ownership-specific advantages of its firms. The global competitive analyst must also realize that ownership, internalization, and location advantages are not static, but change over time. The falling outward/inward investment stake of the United States for example, probably reflects the falling ownership advantages of U.S. enterprises vis-à-vis those of other countries, as well as the rising location advantages on the part of the United States as a site for production.[45]

Analyzing Global Industries and Competitors

Frameworks for assessing the extent to which competitors within an industry will be global in nature have been examined, and the extent to which and the manner in which a firm can be competitive as a participant in that industry have been discussed. But, some key questions still remain. For example, what forces drive or shape competition in different global industries? What determines whether competition in a given global industry will be mild or intense? And, on what does the ultimate profit potential in a given global industry really depend?

Answering these questions requires a framework that views competition not simply as the direct struggle among rival firms, but rather more broadly as an extended rivalry. In Porter's structural framework for analyzing industries,[46] the nature and degree of competition in an industry is seen as hanging on five forces:

- *The threat of new entrants,* which will tend to be higher in a multinational industry when the barriers to entry are lower (e.g., scale economies, product differentiation, capital requirements) and/or when the retaliation that newcomers can expect from entrenched competitors is weaker;

- *The bargaining power of buyers,* since when they are powerful they "compete with the industry by forcing down prices, bargaining for higher quality and serv-

[44] Dunning, op. cit., Chapter 4.

[45] Ibid., Chapter 5.

[46] Porter, *Competitive Strategy*, Chapter 1.

ices, and playing competitors off against each other—all at the expense of industry profitability"[47];

- *The bargaining power of suppliers,* since when they are powerful they can squeeze profitability out of an industry (assuming the industry is unable to recover cost increases in its own prices) via raised prices or reduced quality of purchased goods and services;

- *The pressure from substitute products,* which "limits the potential returns of an industry by placing a ceiling on the prices firms in the industry can profitably charge"[48]; and

- *The rivalry among existing competitors,* via means such as price cutting, advertising battles, and new-product introductions; such rivalry is likely to be very intense in a global industry when the competitors are numerous or are roughly equal in size and power; when capacity is normally augmented in large increments; when exit barriers are high and thus keep companies in the business despite low returns on investment; and, when the rivals are diverse in strategies, origins, personalities, time horizons, and relationships to their parent companies, which is a fact of life in most global businesses.[49]

These five forces shape competition both in domestic and global industries. "Structural analysis in global industries," however, "must encompass foreign competitors, a wider pool of potential entrants, a broader scope of possible substitutes, and increased possibilities that firms' goals and personalities will differ as well as their perceptions of what is strategically important."[50] In addition, "to analyze competition in a global industry, it is necessary to examine industry economics and competitors in the various geographic or national markets jointly rather than individually."[51] Despite this additional complexity, an in-depth knowledge of these forces is absolutely essential if the firm is to identify its real strengths and weaknesses from a strategic standpoint in the global competitive arena. Only after these strengths and weaknesses are fully analyzed can a firm devise a plan of action that[52]

> "[M]ay include 1) positioning the company so that its capabilities provide the best defense against the competitive force; and/or 2) influencing the balance of forces through strategic moves, thereby improving the company's position; and/or 3) anticipating shifts in the factors underlying the forces and responding to them, with the hope of exploiting change by choosing a strategy appropriate for the new competitive balance before opponents recognize it."

---

[47] Ibid., p. 24.

[48] Ibid., p. 23.

[49] Ibid., pp. 142-143.

[50] Ibid., p. 276.

[51] Ibid., p. 275.

[52] Ibid., p. 143.

Toward a Global Competitive Intelligence System

Three analytical frameworks that should be useful to a MNC in analyzing its competitive environment and its role within that environment have been reviewed. The first dealt with the globalization of competition, the second with the advantages needed to compete effectively in a global fashion, and the third with the broad range of forces that collectively determine competitive intensity and, as a result, profit potential, within any domestic or global industry. Conducting a full-blown analysis along the lines of any of these three frameworks is a massive and difficult task. The factors in each of the frameworks are highly diverse, numerous, complex, interrelated, and dynamic. And, each framework requires a great deal of data; much of it, of course, will not be easy to come by. But, given current trends in the global environment, it is clear that the growth—even the survival—of MNCs will depend increasingly on the quality and quantity of their competitive analyses and astute use thereof in global strategy formulation and implementation.

This challenge implies that there is a need for global competitive intelligence systems within MNCs that are explicit, comprehensive, continuous, and systematic in nature. Such systems must encompass the collection of field data and published data, the compilation, cataloging, and analysis of this data, and communication of the results to the firm's strategists.[53] Systems designed for multinational analysis as opposed to purely domestic analysis will have to contend with a variety of special complications, including language differences; unavailability of data on foreign firms, given the absence of SEC-type full-disclosure laws in many other nations; difficulties in understanding how foreign institutions (e.g., codetermination in West Germany, business-government partnership in Japan, state-owned enterprises in Europe) really work; and analytical complexities introduced by connections among firms and among markets due to joint ventures, common markets, trade agreements, and global interdependence. A competitive intelligence system within a multinational firm will thus need to operate at all levels of the MNC—subsidiary, regional headquarters, and world headquarters—with data inputs and analytical outputs efficiently moving up and down those levels as needed. The system will also need to involve many functional parts of the organization, drawing, for example, on the expertise of the firm's market researchers, sales force, purchasing agents, engineering personnel, research and development personnel, and governmental relations specialists.

Sources of raw data for competitive analysis are both internal and external to the firm and are diverse in nature. Published data can be gathered by academics and consulting firms from newspapers, financial journals, trade journals, business magazines, corporate documents, corporate directories, government publications, and industry studies. Field data can be acquired via interviews and contacts with suppliers, customers, middlemen, agents, brokers, wholesalers, retailers, security analysts, stockbrokers, investment and commer-

---

[53] Ibid., Chapter 3 and Appendix B.

cial bankers, auditors, advertisers, consultants, and market researchers.[54] Note
that many other techniques are part of international business life. These range
from the continuous acquisition and evaluation of competitors products, to the
hiring of competitor's key employees, to undercover industrial espionage. The
FBI's "sting" operation, which caught employees of Hitachi paying hundreds
of thousands of dollars for stolen IBM documents in 1982, highlights the
importance to MNCs of taking elaborate precautions to protect their technological secrets and marketing strategies, which can spell success or failure in the
increasingly competitive international business arena.[55]

GLOBAL RISK ANALYSIS

The Fall of the Shah

The recent Iranian revolution clearly represents the most powerful political
shock to international business in modern times. Most multinationals and most
governments misread the political and socioeconomic signs in Iran during the
mid-1970s and thus failed to forecast the success and the effects of the Islamic
revolution against the Shah. Such signs included explosive urban growth, gal-
loping inflation, rapid industrialization, large and burdensome military
expenditures, a widening gap between rich and poor, a large and well-organized
group of unhappy dissidents living in exile, tensions imposed by new ways of
living in a tradition-bound society, and the growth of a new proletariat with a
growing number of college-educated young people willing to excite and lead a
opposition movement against an increasingly unpopular, unstable, and cruel
one-man regime. Failing to read the handwriting on the wall cost the multinational business community dearly, both during and after the turmoil, as a result
of strikes, reduced production, sabotage, terrorism, canceled contracts, sus-
pended projects, blocked imports and exports, nationalized assets (often, without compensation), defaulted loans, and massive civil litigation.

The Political Risk Assessment Surge

Most cases of politically induced corporate adversity are not as dramatic, cata-
clysmic, or catastrophic as that associated with the Iranian bloodbath. More
common, less visible, and perhaps even more crucial, is the erosion in corporate
profits that can be traced to more mundane shifts in government laws and regulations with regard to such things as tax rates, price controls, and local ownership requirements. As such, more than 60 percent of U.S. companies doing
business abroad have suffered politically inflicted damage over the past five

---

[54] Robert Hershey, "Commercial Intelligence on a Shoestring," *Harvard Business Review*
(Sept./Oct. 1980), pp. 22-30; Jerry L. Wall and Bong-gon P. Shin, "Seeking Competitive Informa-
tion" in William F. Glueck, ed., *Business Policy and Strategic Management*, 3rd ed. (New York:
McGraw-Hill Book Company, 1980).

[55] William M. Bulkeley, "Computer Analysts: IBM Watchers Process Data on the Big Firm
to Divine Its Program," *Wall Street Journal* (July 23, 1982), pp. 1, 18.

years, usually in the form of delayed payments or restrictions on profit repatriation.[56]

But, without a doubt, the unexpected fall of the Shah's regime in Iran, along with other recent events in such places as Nicaragua, Poland, Afghanistan, South Korea, Turkey, Angola, and Lebanon, produced a surge of interest in the field of political risk assessment (PRA). This interest is indicated, for example, by dozens of conferences on the topic; the recent formation of the Association of Political Risk Analysts; the outpouring of books, reports, and articles on the topic;[57] the spawning of as many as 30 PRA consulting firms; the creation of in-house PRA units in a broad spectrum of MNCs that have the tasks of monitoring, processing, analyzing, and evaluating data to provide senior managements with political assessments; and the recent scrambling of many MNCs to insure themselves against political risks (it is estimated that MNCs paid $600 million to $700 million in political risk premiums in 1980[58] As for the future, a survey of 401 top corporate executives[59] reveals that these leaders think as follows: 89 percent—U.S. corporate assets overseas will be subjected in the future to more terrorism and/or sabotage; 83 percent—there will be more political and economic instability; 82 percent—there will be more excessive foreign government regulation; 71 percent—there will be more nationalization and expropriation. Thus, is essential for the global environmental analyst to understand fully the role of PRA in the broader risk management process, to be aware of the different kinds of risks that his or her MNC may encounter, to comprehend the challenges and limitations involved in PRA, and to be knowledgeable about the range of analytical approaches that MNCs might find useful. These matters are considered in the sections below.

PRA and the Risk Management Process

PRA involves the assessment and evaluation of "current and potential impacts of the political environment" on a firm.[60] As such, its focus is on political events, both continuous and discontinuous, that give rise to policies or actions, both positive and negative, which affect the short-run and long-run returns of

---

[56] Ronald Alsop, "Foreign Ventures: More Firms Are Hiring Own Political Analysts to Limit Risks Abroad," *Wall Street Journal* (March 30, 1981), pp. 1, 17.

[57] Stephen Blank, John Basek, Stephen J. Kobrin, and Joseph LaPalombara, *Assessing the Political Environment: An Emerging Function in International Companies* (New York: The Conference Board, 1980); Business International, *Managing and Evaluating Country Risk* (New York: Business International, 1981); Dan Haendel, *Corporate Strategic Planning: The Political Dimension* (Beverly Hills: SAGE, 1981); Stephen J. Kobrin, *Managing Political Risk Assessment: Strategic Response to Environmental Change* (Berkeley, California: University of California Press, 1982); Louis Kraar, "The Multinationals Get Smarter About Political Risks," *Fortune* (March 24, 1980), pp. 86-100; Pancras Nagy, *Country Risk: How to Assess, Quantify, and Monitor It* (London: Euromoney Publications, 1979).

[58] Anonymous, "Insuring Against Risk Abroad," *Business Week* (Sept. 14, 1981), p. 62.

[59] Marsh & McLennan, "Risk in a Complex Society" (public opinion survey conducted by Louis Harris and Associates, Inc.) (New York: Marsh & McLennan, 1980).

[60] Stephen J. Kobrin, "Political Risk: A Review and Reconsideration," *Journal of International Business Studies* (Spring-Summer 1979), pp. 67-80.

the individual firm or project. As one writer notes, "What is of concern to firms is not political events and processes per se, but the managerial contingencies they may generate. Political events are of interest only to the extent that they produce impacts on the firm that affect either the security of assets or the viability of projects."[61]

PRA is relevant to both strategic planning and operational decision-making. Banks, for example, need inputs from PRA, or more broadly, "country risk assessment," as background for credit decisions, investment choices, and liability management. Business International, in a survey of 90 MNCs,[62] found four types of decisions generally being affected by risk assessments: status decisions (e.g., should the firm invest or divest in a given location), early-warning decisions (e.g., early identification of troublesome situations so that contingency plans may be prepared), exposure decisions (e.g., corporate portfolio decisions); and situation analysis/contingency decisions (e.g., hypothesizing alternative future conditions and preparing strategies to minimize their negative and maximize their potential impact).

In order to understand the role of PRA, it is useful to place it into the broader context of the full-risk management process, which consists of five steps: (1) identification of risks; (2) measurement of risks: (3) specification of risk-handling alternatives; (4) selection and implementation of alternatives; and (5) evaluation and monitoring of results.

In the first step of the process, the risk manager must painstakingly discover and identify the possibilities of loss (e.g., strike, expropriation, sabotage, contract repudiation) to which the firm or project is exposed. The next step is to measure these potential losses in terms of their frequency, severity, predictability, and probability in order to determine the relative importance of the potential losses and to determine the best risk-handling techniques. In the third step, the risk manager must gather or develop a set of risk-handling options that is appropriate to the identified and measured risks. Risk management techniques are of two major types, which are often used in combination: (1) risk control, i.e., minimizing, at the least possible cost, the risk of losses to which a firm is exposed; and (2) risk finance, i.e., financing risk management via corporate funding or through transfer to others such as insurance companies. Risk control encompasses risk or loss avoidance, risk prevention, risk reduction, and risk spreading. Risk finance, on the other hand, involves techniques of risk retention and transfer. Examples of techniques within all of these categories are shown in Figure 7-3.

With the firm's risks identified and measured, and with the full range of risk handling options specified, the next step in the risk management process is selecting and implementing the best techniques or combination of techniques for coping with the risks involved. Alternative strategies must be formulated for a given situation and then compared in terms of their benefits and costs in order to derive an estimated payoff for each strategy. Assuming that the overall objective is to minimize the cost of risk to the firm, the strategies can be compared with regard to the expected rate of return they will earn for the firm. For

---

[61] Kobrin, *Managing Political Risk Assessment*, op. cit., p. 26.

[62] Business International, *Managing and Evaluating Country Risk*, op. cit.

Risk Avoidance
- Exposure limits or ceilings
- Rejection of investments
- Divestments or withdrawals
- Short payback periods

Risk Prevention
- Plant security measures
- Employee protection measures
- Counterintelligence activity
- Harmonious government relations

Risk Reduction
- Joint ventures or consortia
- Local borrowing
- Transnational alliances
- Management contracts

Risk Spreading
- Geographic diversification
- Component interchange plans
- Product/process diversification
- Currency diversification

Risk Retention
- Operational/financial hedging
- Currency speculation
- Premiums for risk
- Loss absorption plans

Risk Transfer
- Expropriation insurance
- Contract repudiation insurance
- Kidnapping/terrorism insurance
- Currency inconvertibility insurance

FIG. 7-3 Examples of Risk Management Techniques

example, the choice of risk control or risk finance must be based in part on the grounds of loss severity, the finance option becoming more attractive as the severity of potential losses rises. And, choices must be made within each broad category. Within the category of risk finance, for example, retention may be appropriate when the losses are highly predictable, very frequent, and of low severity, while transfer would generally make sense when losses are unpredictable, infrequent, and severe.

The final phase of the risk management process is periodic monitoring and evaluation of the results of the firm's programs in order to provide for control, coordination, and improvement. Risks in international business are dynamic; their frequency, severity, predictability, and probability will vary according to changes both within the firm (e.g., different stages of a project's life cycle) and outside of the firm (e.g., changes in political regimes). The risk management cycle is thus a continuous one. It is important to note that the procedures of risk identification, measurement, and treatment can be improved only if results are fully, carefully, and periodically evaluated. With this in mind, the front end of the cycle is now discussed.

The Risk Assessment Challenge

The political risk analyst confronts a massive conceptual and operational challenge. In the first place, potentially significant managerial contingencies ranging from loss of remittance flexibility, to loss of operating profits, to loss of assets, to loss of opportunity can result from a wide variety of causes, including internal political turmoil (e.g., terrorism, armed rebellions, civilian revolutions); regime change (e.g., via assassinations, coups d'etat, elections, other extra-legal activities); foreign interaction (e.g., border tensions, foreign invasions or occupations, new international alliances); socioeconomic unrest (e.g., strikes, riots, demonstrations, and guerrilla activities due to tribal, religious,

ethnic, and class divisions); and governmental actions in response to nationalism, economic problems, or vested local interests (e.g., in the form of changes in
laws and regulations in equity, repatriation, local content, price control, and
taxes).

The analyst has to consider both macro and micro risks. Macro risks
encompass environmental events that affect all foreign firms in a country without regard to organizational characteristics (e.g., mass expropriations or non-
discriminatory changes in tax regimes). Micro risks are those that are specific
to an industry, firm, technology, and project. Kobrin has found that micro risks
are becoming increasingly significant.[63] The analyst must also evaluate both
host nation and home nations risks. For U.S. companies, the so-called Washington risk[64] has been growing more important. This risk results from the
uncertainty surrounding the role of the U.S. government in influencing world
events, maintaining order, and extending its regulatory purview overseas in the
form of laws regulating Arab boycott, anti-bribery, antitrust, taxation, and
trading with the enemy. Finally, the analyst also needs to consider both asset
protection/investment recovery and operational profitability/cash-flow risks.
The former affects security of assets, while the latter affects the viability of
operations. As Haendel has noted:[65] "Most forecasting efforts to date have
been aimed at asset protection and investment recovery risks, but corporate
interest in the future will increasingly focus on operating profitability and cash
flow risks."

In addition to diversity in sources and types of risks, the PRA analyst
confronts an even larger challenge of ignorance and uncertainty. The problem
is dramatized as follows: "Political analysis is like playing the stock market or
flipping a coin . . . you're right about 50% of the time."[66] The reasons for this
are both operational and conceptual. The essence of PRA has been captured as
follows:[67] "To assess the potential impact of political events on a firm one must
first forecast the nature of the political environment over the relevant time
period, and then given a specific prediction (or range of predictions), determine
how political events are likely to affect a project." Operational problems—such
as limitations of existing data, and of accuracy, validity, and comparability—
hamper the first of these tasks, while substantial problems in attempting to
model the process conceptually through which political-economic environments actually affect projects impedes the second. The reason, according to
Kobrin,[68] is that "We simply do not know a great deal about the nature of the
relationship between political environments abroad and impacts on firms."
Despite these challenges, the task of PRA, however imperfect, must be undertaken if MNCs wish to maximize their chances of survival in our increasingly

---

[63] Kobrin, *Managing Political Risk Assessment*, op. cit.

[64] P. Field, "Meet the New Breed of Banker: The Political Risk Expert," *Euromoney* (July
1980), p. 21.

[65] Haendel, op. cit., p. 48.

[66] Alsop, op. cit., p. 17.

[67] Kobrin, *Managing Political Risk Assessment*, op. cit., p. 254.

[68] Ibid., p. 23.

turbulent and hostile world. Some analytical approaches which MNCs can employ in this quest for survival are now presented.

Approaches to Political Risk Assessment

A wide variety of assessment methodologies exists in the PRA field. Some methodologies use observational (i.e., secondary source) data while others rely on expert-generated data; some are rather unstructured, while others are very structured; and some utilize a systematic methodology, while others rely more on intuition or on implicit forecasting.[69] Some examples in three broad categories are examined below: (1) political instability approaches, (2) country rating approaches, and (3) project-specific approaches.

Political Instability Approaches. A number of models exist that attempt to measure degrees of macro political risk in terms of political instability and political development using observational data. The Political System Stability Index (PSSI),[70] for example, rests on the assumption that political stability is related to a society's capacity to cope with new demands. Fifteen indirect measures formed into three indices (socioeconomic, societal conflict, and government processes) are used to gauge a political system's stability and adaptability. The Rummel and Heenan model[71] proposes an integrated approach to risk assessment based on projections of domestic instability, foreign conflict, political climate, and economic climate, using factor analysis and regression analysis. The Futures Group has proposed a third method for measuring and predicting political stability called "Political Stability Prospects."[72] An index of political instability potential is constructed and extrapolated by combining two subindices: (1) a time series on destabilizing events; and (2) a time series on economic deprivation, which has often been employed by political scientists as an important determinant of the potential for political conflict. A fourth quantitative model for forecasting political instability[73] is based on the assumption that macro country risk is related to the unevenness of the development process (defined in terms of difference in level of attainment of political development, social achievement, technical advancement, resource abundance, and domestic peace) and the strength of the country in terms of economic, military, and diplomatic power. Strong, unevenly developed countries are believed to represent the greatest potential for risk for MNCs.

---

[69] Kobrin *Managing Political Risk Assessment*, op. cit.; Blank, et. al., op. cit.; Haendel, op. cit.

[70] Dan Haendel, Gerald T. West, and Robert G. Meadow, eds., *Overseas Investment and Political Risk*, Foreign Policy Research Institute Monograph Series #21 (Lexington, Mass.: Lexington Books and D. C. Heath, 1975).

[71] R. J. Rummel and Davis A. Heenan, "How Multinationals Analyze Political Risk," *Harvard Business Review* (Jan./Feb. 1978), pp. 67-76.

[72] The Futures Group, "Political Stability Prospects" (Glastonbury, Conn.: The Futures Group, Jan. 1980).

[73] Howard C. Johnson, *Risk in Foreign Business Environments: A Framework for Thought and Management* (Cambridge, Mass.: Arthur D. Little, Inc., 1980).

All four of the formal quantitative approaches to forecasting political instability on the basis of observational data noted above are perhaps valuable for analytic purposes, but they are problematic from the point of view of prediction. They all assume that a universal set of variables exists that will predict cross-national political stability, but different variables may have more importance in different countries. As first-generation models, they suffer from the lack of validation, and, as Kobrin has concluded,[74] they are "somewhat dated in terms of theoretical constructs and/or analytical methodology."

The most serious weakness of these approaches, however, lies in their assumption that firm-specific political risk is caused by macro level political instability. Most PRA analysts have now concluded that internal stability is not, by itself, an adequate indicator of a favorable investment climate; they have also concluded that internal instability does not necessarily pose a serious risk to foreign investments. As one writer has noted, "You could sell ice cream today in Nicaragua, but if you're an oil company in Canada, where the government is relatively stable, you might want to run" (given the new national energy program designed to limit the activities of foreign-owned companies and reduce foreign ownership).[75] Another writer has stated more emphatically that "Stability per se is irrelevant . . . one-third of the world's governments change every year, often not by normal or democratic processes. The question for a corporation is whether it can identify the nascent scenarios and cope profitably—and ethically—with them."[76] Macro level forecasts of political instability thus tell a firm very little about specific impacts that it might experience. For all of the above reasons, Kobrin has concluded that methodologies based on observational data are currently of limited utility to managers.[77]

Country Rating Approaches. Another type of approach to PRA is that of generalized country rating systems, whereby risk indices or probabilities are constructed on the basis of expert-generated data. The Business Environment Risk Index (BERI),[78] for example, was one of the earliest in the country risk rating business. BERI's objective is to gauge the general business climate, in terms of the political environment and the degree to which nationals are given preferential treatment, in 45 countries. The index is reported on a quarterly basis and is accompanied by short narratives discussing each nation and by an in-depth qualitative analysis of two countries per quarter. A permanent panel of about 105 experts around the world (executives in companies, banks, governments, and institutions) judgmentally rate 15 criteria such as political stability, currency convertibility, and economic growth that shape the business climate in a country from zero (unacceptable conditions) to 4 (superior conditions). The panelists rarely rate their own countries, and typically each panelist rates 5 to

[74] Kobrin, *Managing Political Risk Assessment*, op. cit., pp. 258-259.

[75] Alsop, op. cit., p. 1.

[76] Kraar, op. cit., p. 99.

[77] Kobrin, *Managing Political Risk Assessment*, op. cit., p. 266.

[78] F. T. Haner, "Business Environment Risk Index," *Best's Review* (Property Liability Insurance Ed.) (July 1975).

10 countries for a period of 6 to 12 months in the future. The criteria are weighted to place emphasis on "critical success factors,"[79] so that the sum of the weighting equals 25. A rating of 4 on each criterion would indicate a perfect environment of 100. The BERI rating for each country is arrived at by averaging the forecasts of the experts that have rated that particular country via a version of the Delphi method. In addition to the overall rating, subindexes related to political, operations, financial, and nationalism dimensions are also provided.

BERI ratings in 1979, for example, ranged from a low of 24.1 (Ethiopia) to a high of 83.1 (Germany).[80] No countries were thus found in the 100–86 category which, according to Haner, would have indicated an "unusually stable and superior business environment for foreign companies."[81] Germany, Switzerland, Japan, and Singapore, however, fell into the 85–71 category, where any tendency toward nationalism was deemed to be "offset in varying degrees by the country's efficiency, market opportunities, financial entities, etc."[82] Nations such as France, Ireland, Norway, and Mexico scored in the 70–56 range, generally indicating moderate-risk countries with complications in day-to-day operations but sufficiently stable political structures to permit business without serious disruption.[83] The "high risk for foreign-owned business" category, i.e., scores of 55–41, included Egypt, Israel, Ecuador and Argentina where "profits must provide a high rate of return on resources invested. Otherwise, only special situations should be considered (e.g., scarce raw materials)."[84] Finally, scores below 41 were generally deemed to represent "unacceptable business conditions"; this category included, for example, Iran, Pakistan, Ghana, Ethiopia, and Tanzania.

Haner has also developed a Political Risk Index (PRI) that focuses wholly on political conditions in a country and relies on experts who have a political science, rather than a business orientation.[85] Ten variables are included in the PRI index, classified into eight causes and two symptoms of political instability. In late 1979, according to the PRI index, Germany, Japan, and the United States were deemed to represent "minimal risk" countries; Brazil, Canada, and France were rated "acceptable risk"; Indonesia, Nigeria, Portugal, and South Africa were rated "high risk"; and Iran and Pakistan were rated "prohibitive risk."[86]

A more comprehensive set of country ratings are provided by Business International's Country Assessment Service (BI/CAS). BI/CAS analyzes 55 factors in 70 countries, grouping them into categories related to country risk,

[79] F. T. Haner, *Global Business Strategies for the 1980s* (New York: Praeger Publishers, 1980), p. 197.

[80] Ibid., pp. 40-41.

[81] Ibid., p. 198.

[82] Ibid.

[83] Ibid.

[84] Ibid.

[85] Ibid., Chapter 8.

[86] Ibid., p. 135.

Political Factors
- Political stability—institutional
- Political stability—social
- Attitude major opposition groups
- Probability opposition group takeover
- Nationalization
- Expropriation
- Limits on foreign ownership
- Restrictions on imports
- Privileged environment for local competition
- Export requirements
- Stability of labor
- Relationship with the West
- Relationship with neighboring countries
- Terrorism
- Quality of government management

Economic Factors
- Balance of payments
- Reserves/imports ratio
- Export composition
- Energy vulnerability
- State of the economy
- Distribution of wealth

Financial Factors
- Strength of currency
- Convertibility to foreign currencies
- External debt
- Profit repatriation controls
- Price controls
- Availability and cost of local capital
- Inflation level

Source: Business International Country Assessment Service, *Country Ratings: August 1981* (New York: Business International Corporation)

FIG. 7-4   Factors Considered in Business International's Composite Country Risk Ratings

business opportunities, and operating conditions. A separate index number is computed for each of these three elements. This service, which replaced BI's Country Rating Service which it began in 1971, relies on BI country specialists who reside in each of the 70 countries. These specialists, using factor assessment report forms, evaluate each of the 55 factors in terms of one of five possible scenarios, ranging from extremely favorable for foreign companies to extremely unfavorable. Each factor and each scenario is forecast for the current year plus four. The assessment reports coming out of the 70 nations, which are updated semiannually, are checked at BI's regional level, as well as at BI's headquarters in New York, in order to ensure accuracy and consistency of the results. Subscribers receive individual country assessments as well as regional and global assessments on a multi-scenario basis twice yearly, presented in numerical, graphical, and narrative forms.

Figure 7-4 shows the political, economic, and financial factors that are considered in producing composite risk ratings for each country.[87] Each of the factors are weighted according to the results of a survey of 100 major corporations. The factor scores are multiplied by the factor weights, divided by the sum of the risk weights, and multiplied by 10 in order to derive composite ratings on a zero to 100 scale, with zero representing the worst possible rating and 100 the highest. The five safest nations on a "most likely scenario" basis in 1981 according to this rating system were Singapore, Hong Kong, Japan, Netherlands and Switzerland, while the five riskiest for MNCs, according to BI/CAS,

---

[87] Ratings of opportunity, operating conditions, etc. are not discussed here.

were Iran, Zaire, Yugoslavia, Ghana, and Angola.[88] In terms of trends over the next five years, BI saw risk increasing dramatically in such nations as Egypt and moderately in countries such as Saudi Arabia, Panama, Nigeria, and Kenya. Country risk was forecast to diminish significantly, however, in such nations as the Ivory Coast, Nicaragua, Korea, Iran, Yugoslavia, Liberia, and Ghana.

A very different type of country risk ratings is provided by Frost and Sullivan's World Political Risk Forecasts (WPRF). The model for WPRF quantitive forecasts on approximately 60 countries and more detailed, qualitative country reports is actor-based, and its assumption is that the political process is relatively pluralistic with the existence of influential groups participating in the determination of policy and other political events. The analysis for each country begins with the identification of an issue, such as repatriation restrictions, and the individuals and groups (e.g., labor, local industrialists), that are salient in the outcome process. Panelists—mostly academics selected on the basis of their expertise as measured by publications and recommendations—score each actor on a linear scale as to (1) its position on the issue, (2) its potential influence in the decision process, and, (3) the salience of the issue to the actor. Panelists also indicate their degree of confidence in their estimates. The three scores of each panelist for each issue in a particular nation are then multiplied (i.e., position × power × salience), and the sum for each issue is calculated for a total score. From these scores, raw probabilities are obtained and are combined with subjective estimates to derive "final probabilities" of an issue occurring.

Along with qualitative country reports that analyze country "power structures" and issues of relevance to foreign investors, monthly summary reports provide probabilistic information for each of the 60 countries. A subscriber is given the individual probabilities for each country that a "major loss will be sustained by foreign business in the next eighteen months as a result of regime change, political turmoil, equity restrictions and repatriation restrictions."[89] The World Summary also contains an 18-month political risk summary, which is a simple average of the four probabilities mentioned above. In addition, a 5-year probability of major loss is also provided, indicating the "likelihood that international business would suffer from a major upheaval or a significant shift in governmental policies toward international business."[90]

According to the summary 18-month and five-year probabilities reported by WPRF in June 1981, the highest probabilities of business losses for the 1981 to 1982 period were forecast to be present in El Salvador (64%), Iran (51%), Zaire (44%), Nicaragua (38%), Bolivia (35%), Libya (32%), and Turkey (31%). WPRF predicted, however, that the chances were less than one in 10 of sustaining loss in the same time period due to regime change, political turmoil, or equity or repatriation restrictions in nations such as Austria, Finland, Singapore, the United States, or West Germany. As for the forecast for the period

[88] Business International *Country Assessment Service*, op. cit.

[89] Frost & Sullivan, Inc., *World Political Risk Forecasts by Country* (New York: Frost & Sullivan, June 1981), p. 6.

[90] Ibid.

through June 1986, the probability of major loss was forecast as being greater than 50 percent in Bolivia, El Salvador, Iran, Libya, Nicaragua, Pakistan, the Philippines, Thailand, Turkey, Zaire, and Zambia. At the other end of the spectrum, it was projected to be less than 20 percent in Canada, Denmark, Finland, Japan, the Netherlands, Norway, the United Kingdom, the United States, and West Germany.

The numbers-oriented country risk rating systems reviewed above, such as BERI, BI/CAS, WPRF, and those provided for use by bankers in publications such as *Euromoney* and *Institutional Investor*, can be quite useful as one element in a firm's overall program of PRA. For a relatively small fee, a subscribing company on a regular and systematic basis can scan a large number of countries, obtain access to the collective thinking of many country assessment specialists, and—assuming consistency in the composition of the country panels—track changes over time and thereby "red flag" country situations of special relevance to the firm for more in-depth analysis. But, such risk indices are not without their critics.[91] Sources of concern include possible over-reliance on business people as panelists; the absence of an explicit model of either the political-economic environment or of its potential impact on the firm, in the case of BERI; the validity of the final probabilities, given the use of subjective estimates to derive them; and the applicability of a pluralistic model of policymaking developed in a liberal democracy to more autocratic and closed societies, in the case of WPRF.[92] The biggest drawback of risk indices, however, is their high level of superficiality and generality. As argued above, "both vulnerability to contingencies arising from the political environment and their potential cost generally varies across industries, firms, and projects. Once one moves away from macrorisk, vulnerability is clearly a function of factors such as industrial sector, level of technology, ownership structure, and managerial style."[93] Generalized, macro-level assessment of political risks may thus have little value to corporations beyond the first-cut monitoring and red-flag functions that they serve. The real need is for risk assessments that are custom-tailored to specific projects of specific MNCs in specific countries, an area to which we now turn.

Project-Specific Approaches. A wide variety of multinational firms, including American Can, Citibank, Continental Group, Dow Chemical, Exxon, General Electric, General Motors, Gulf Oil, ITT, Shell Oil and United Technologies, have gone beyond political instability and country rating approaches to PRA, and have developed custom-tailored in-house risk assessment systems for use in project analysis and strategic planning.[94] The general notion is that of constructing a coherent framework that identifies precise political issues, their particular implications for the firm's operations, and the information required

[91] Anonymous, "Foreign Investment: The Post-Shah Surge in Political Risk Studies," *Business Week* (Dec. 1, 1980), p. 69.

[92] Kobrin, *Managing Political Risk Assessment*, op. cit., p. 252.

[93] Ibid., p. 254.

[94] Haendel, *Corporate Strategic Planning*, op. cit.

to address these issues so that the resulting analysis can be effectively integrated into the firm's strategic actions and plans.

One such structured and systematic project-specific methodology is the ASPRO-SPAIR system developed by Shell Oil, which has been well documented,[95] adopted by another oil firm,[96] and extended to a broader range of industries by Risk Insights, Inc.[97] Shell's effort is aimed at "systematically assessing the probabilities of specific adverse political actions facing a prospective Shell venture in a particular country as a means of neutralizing senior management's biases, aiding in contract negotiations, making cross-country comparisons, and providing an early warning system."[98]

Political risk is defined in this approach as the probability of not maintaining a contract for the exploration, development, and production of oil that is perceived as equitable by both company and host country over a 10-year period in the face of changing political and economic conditions.[99] Two general categories of political risk are constructed: (1) political actions leading to a unilateral modification of the initial contract such that the return is inadequate; and (2) political actions that prevent the free repatriation of funds or oil entitlements out of the host country. These categories are further disaggregated into nine components, each cast as a proposition that a described undesirable political event will occur. These include production restrictions that prevent recovery of investment in a timely fashion, civil disorder losses resulting in the loss of opportunity to produce oil for at least one year, external war losses, taxation changes, domestic price controls, oil export restrictions, restrictions on remittances, sudden expropriation, and creeping expropriation. Under each proposition is listed a set of economic, political, and social factors that will tend to influence the truth of the proposition; the experts rank the factors for two five-year periods.

This method provides for a large panel of experts, consisting ideally of two representatives each from economics, political science, international relations, sociology, history, and business (especially the oil business); in addition, some nationals of the country under investigation are included in the panel. The panel members are personally interviewed and, with the aid of a questionnaire, they consider each influencing factor independently; the members also rank their confidence in their judgments. A higher weight is given to an assessment in which a panel member has "firm" confidence than one in which he or she only has "weak" confidence. Panel members are asked to make their judgments

---

[95] Christopher A. Gebelein, Conrad E. Pearson, and Michael Silbergh, "Assessing Political Risk to Foreign Oil Investment Ventures," Society of Petroleum Engineers Paper SPE 1665 (Dallas: 1977).

[96] D. W. Bunn and M. M. Mustafaoglu, "Forecasting Political Risk," *Management Science* (Nov. 1978), pp. 1557-1567.

[97] C. E. Pearson, "An Expert Panel Model for Assessing Political Risk" in T. H. Moran, ed., *International Political Risk Assessment: The State of the Art* (Washington, D.C.: Georgetown University Press, 1980).

[98] Gebelein, et. al., op. cit., p. 57.

[99] Ibid.

within the context of generalized global scenarios provided to them, one relatively optimistic and the other relatively pessimistic.[100]

A sophisticated computer program, using Baye's Theorem, combines the probability assessments into probability functions for each proposition, from which the "best estimate" (means of the distribution) and confidence intervals are derived. After the computer analysis, the panel members are contacted again in a variant of the Delphi approach. If the members think their probability estimates are reasonable, this is further validation of the estimates. In addition, an individual's reasons for making unusual judgments are communicated to the other panel members, which serves as an important source of information and insight.

The ASPRO/SPAIR approach to political risk assessment and variants of it[101] has been deemed by Kobrin[102] as one of the "most sophisticated and effective" approaches in existence, since it entails a well-specified model that is generally project-specific and solicits expert opinion within a framework that reduces bias and variability. As such, it overcomes the major drawbacks of the political instability and country rating approaches noted above, and it facilitates genuine integration of risk analysis into the corporate decision-making process. But, each assessment, of course, "involves a major and costly effort . . . that constrains frequency of application."[103]

The Future of Political Risk Assessment

The key to success with virtually every global corporate strategy is that of maximizing corporate returns while minimizing the exposure of the firm's cash, property, personnel, and technical resources. Accomplishing this requires a prudent and balanced evaluation of risks and opportunities in the context of all strategic business planning efforts and resource allocation decisions. Some of the methods by which the risk analysis portion of this task can be undertaken are surveyed above. It is important to note, however, that in MNCs at the present time, "the process of assessment and evaluation of nonmarket environments appears to be relatively unsophisticated and unstructured."[104] Although there is a great deal of variation in the structure and performance of PRA among large multinational firms, it seems in general that it tends to be a reactive rather than a proactive function. U.S.-based MNCs are relying mainly on ad hoc, unsystematic assessments and internal rather than external sources for information regarding external environments. Many MNCs, in addition, still confront the problem of integrating environmental and risk assessments into decision making in a more systematic and objective manner.

Risk management, particularly with regard to making decisions among risk management techniques (i.e., avoidance, prevention, reduction, spreading,

---

[100] Ibid., p. 58.

[101] Bunn and Mustafaoglu, op. cit.

[102] Kobrin, *Managing Political Risk Assessment*, op. cit., p. 265.

[103] Ibid.

[104] Ibid., p. 33.

retention, transfer) must be a line management responsibility. But, much improvement in the effectiveness of a firm's risk management function, according to Kobrin, [105] can come from having a "formally constituted political assessment unit within the firm." Such a staff unit can make real contributions both to the front end (i.e., assessment) and back end (i.e., evaluation) of the risk management process. A formal unit can facilitate better utilization of a wider range of information sources, can enable assessment specialists to fulfill a number of important educational roles, and can improve patterns of communication within the firm through the coordination and control of information flows.

Improvement in PRA in the final analysis, of course, will only come about from a better understanding of the political sources of risk and of how the firm and its projects are affected by political risks and events, particularly those of a micro and operational profitability/cash-flow nature. However, the PRA is bound to remain a "tauntingly imprecise science." [106] Given limits on human ability to understand, model, and forecast political and social developments, MNCs must accept the fact that a certain amount of environmental adversity can be neither predicted or avoided. This unpredictability demands flexibility and rapid response capabilities, which can come only from sensitive early-warning systems and the use of scenario building and contingency planning. The inability to avoid all political hostility, on the other hand, calls for sophisticated approaches in managing conflicts and host/home government interventions.

A PORTFOLIO APPROACH TO IDENTIFYING OPPORTUNITIES

Markets, Competitors, and Risks

This tour of three major types of global environmental analysis is now completed. All three types need to be conducted if a multinational corporation is to identify opportunities in a systematic, comprehensive, and balanced fashion. Using the frameworks and methodologies reviewed above, the MNC environmental analyst should be able to: (1) pinpoint markets that are likely to be attractive for the firm's present and prospective products in terms of growth, size, intensity, and untapped potential; (2) gauge the extent to which the firm possesses a competitive advantage relative to domestic and foreign rivals in various product and geographic areas; and (3) estimate the degree to which the firm is exposed to political and other types of risks on a project-specific and country-specific basis.

As defined at the beginning of this chapter, the existence of an opportunity depends on market attractiveness, competitive advantage, and risk exposure. Expected returns to the enterprise are largely determined by the first two

---

[105] Ibid., p. 27.
[106] Kraar, op. cit., p. 87.

factors. Market attractiveness basically shaping revenue and growth potential, and competitive advantage (i.e., possession of ownership-specific, location-specific, and internalization incentive advantages relative to other firms) largely determines the firm's ability to realize that potential profitably via cost leadership and/or differentiation. The third factor, exposure to political and economic risks that may affect both costs and returns, determines the variance in the returns that can be expected.

For a typical risk-averse MNC (i.e., one that prefers smaller risk or variance at comparable levels of return or greater return at the same level of risk), the extremes of the environmental opportunity continuum are easy to define. In product/project/country-specific terms, a tremendous opportunity would naturally exist given the combination of a dynamite market, strong competitive position, and highly predictable or safe political and economic environment; this is a high-return, low-risk proposition. At the other end of the spectrum, a moribund market, woeful competitive disadvantage, and highly uncertain and turbulent operating environment would imply very little opportunity, given its low-return/high-risk character. The analytical reality, of course, is that a MNC confronts an infinite variety of combinations of relative market attractiveness, competitive advantage, and risk exposure that lie between these two extremes. And, each such combination will differ in terms of the volume, rate, and certainty of cash use and generation it implies.

Searching for opportunities in international business must therefore deal with three facts of life. The first is that fabulous opportunities in terms of high return and low risk are likely to be a rather rare commodity; an assessment system is thus needed that will enable the firm to evaluate (and select for exploitation) opportunities on a relative and comparative basis. Another fact is that specific risk/return preferences are likely to differ among MNCs, with some being conservative (i.e., more interested in preserving their capital and earning a fairly consistent and predictable return) and others more aggressive (i.e., willing to absorb higher risk in exchange for the prospect of possibly earning higher but more variable and less certain returns). The implication is that opportunity scanning and selection must be custom-tailored to the specific risk/return objectives of the enterprise. The third fact is that MNCs can and do gain substantial benefits from product and geographical diversification. Opportunities therefore cannot be assessed or ranked properly in isolation; they must be judged in relation to the firm's entire business portfolio. Diversity in exploiting different combinations of market attractiveness, competitive advantage, and risk exposure may enable the firm, for example, to reduce overall risks, stabilize overall returns, and use cash flow generated by mature businesses to gain new leadership positions in others. What is needed is a portfolio approach to identifying international business opportunities.

Toward a Portfolio Approach to Opportunity Identification

Building upon the well-known portfolio grid technologies—The Boston Consulting Group growth/share matrix, the General Electric/McKinsey industry

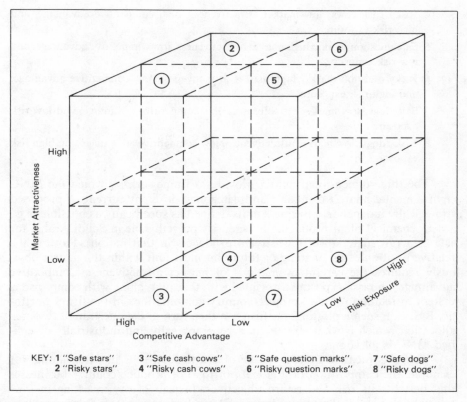

FIG. 7-5 A Three-Dimensional Opportunity Assessment Matrix

attractiveness/business position grid, the Arthur D. Little industry maturity/
competitive position grid, and the Shell Directional Policy matrix—the three
determinants of corporate opportunity discussed here can be displayed in the
form of a three-dimensional matrix, as shown in Figure 7-5. Although finer
distinctions are certainly possible, and probably are needed for planning purposes, for the sake of illustration here, market attractiveness is divided on the
vertical axis, competitive advantage on the horizontal axis, and risk exposure
on the third axis. Each is further divided into low and high categories. This
creates eight cells in the matrix, which can be labeled, by adapting the classic
descriptors of the Boston Consulting Group model, as follows:

1 Safe stars: high market attractiveness, high competitive advantage, and low risk
  exposure

2 Risky stars: high market attractiveness, high competitive advantage, and high
  risk exposure

3 Safe cash cows: low market attractiveness, high competitive advantage, and low
  risk exposure

4 Risky cash cows: low market attractiveness, high competitive advantage, and high risk exposure

5 Safe question marks: high market attractiveness, low competitive advantage, and low risk exposure

6 Risky question marks: high market attractiveness, low competitive advantage, and high risk exposure

7 Safe dogs: low market attractiveness, low competitive advantage, and low risk exposure

8 Risky dogs: low market attractiveness, low competitive advantage, and high risk exposure

The three-dimensional matrix provides a framework by which the MNC environmental analyst can chart and categorize different current or proposed strategically independent business units defined as specifically as possible (e.g., a petrochemical plant producing low-density polyethylene in Saudi Arabia for sale as a raw material to downstream producers in that nation). Plotting the relative position of an ongoing or future business unit within the matrix obviously requires the careful estimations of market attractiveness, competitive advantage, and risk exposure associated with that unit, along with comparisons thereof in relation to other project/country combinations in the firm's portfolio. Based on such a plotting, the firm can then turn to the question of resource allocation, which is what strategy in a geographically and industrially diversified MNC is all about.

This classification system can be of use to the MNC in determining, for example, the composition of a global portfolio of product/country businesses that best fits its risk and return objectives. Instead of overinvesting in low-return/high-risk businesses, underinvesting in high-return/low-risk businesses, subsidizing marginal businesses, or inadequately funding new growth opportunities, for example, a portfolio assessment system along the lines of the one proposed here could potentially better enable top management to allocate resources directly and selectively—both capital investment and strategic expenses such as R&D or market research—to existing and proposed businesses in accordance with their distinct contributions, in a portfolio sense, to overall corporate performance.

Specific resource allocation strategies would, of course, depend on a firm's risk/return preferences, but a typical MNC would probably give the green light to opportunities found in Cell 1 in Figure 7-5. These are the "safe stars," which do not come along very often and should receive absolute priority in resource allocation. It is here where the firm should aggressively enter, expand, and build market position to ensure long-term profitability. Existing or prospective situations falling in Cell 2, the "risky star" category, on the other hand, would call for a more cautionary approach. The high expected returns derived from a powerful position in a rapidly growing market would generally, however, still mandate investment and expansion, assuming the firm is willing to accept or contain the risks involved by such means as insurance and others reviewed in our risk management section above.

Situations falling in Cell 3, the "safe cash cow" zone would tend to call for a very different investment strategy. Given a current or attainable high relative share in a low-growth but safe market, the proper course of action would probably be that of minimizing investment, stressing efficiency, forgoing share for profit, and in general, "milking" the operation for maximum cash generation. As for "risky cash cow" situations found in Cell 4, the agony of high variance in expected cash generation may often not be worth the trouble. Selectivity is probably required here. One would hold on to some of the businesses and opportunistically dispose of others in this category. Entry into such a "hostile business environment" would tend to make sense only under extraordinary conditions. [107]

Business operations or prospects falling into the safe (Cell 5) and risky (Cell 6) "question mark" zones would tend to call for extremely careful analysis and conservatism from the standpoint of resource allocation. Operating in either cell implies high cash use to keep up with rapid growth, as well as to build market share, but it also implies weak cash generation because of the firm's poor competitive position. Selectivity is once again called for, with investments being made in some business, and harvesting for cash generation being attempted in certain particularly high-return segments. Phased withdrawals (or avoidance of investment in the first place) might be appropriate for those businesses in Cell 6, for example, that are likely to have a difficult time improving competitive position and that are also exposed to extremely high political and economic risk.

Avoidance and defensive modes will tend to make sense for the "dogs" in Cells 7 and 8. Harvesting for maximum short-term earnings or phased divestment is appropriate for "safe dog" situations, and complete avoidance or rapid running for daylight is the recommended course of action in the "risky dog" or death-trap zone.

As implied in the generalized resource allocation implications discussed above, the sequencing or scheduling of resource allocation (e.g., market entry, market exit) is also part of the balanced portfolio logic. Different strategic missions with respect to growth and financial objectives (i.e., cash use and generation) can be assigned to businesses in different categories so as to ensure the firm's future in terms of growth and profits. The classic logic, of course, is that of: (1) milking the cash cows, harvesting or divesting some of the question marks, and eliminating the cash-trap dogs; and (2) rechanneling the cash so generated generously into the stars that will earn big profits in the future and selectively into some of the fledgling and cash-devouring growth businesses of the question mark variety. In so doing, one hopes that some of the question marks will turn into stars as the businesses acquire competitive position, and that some of the stars will become cash cows as their markets mature and slow down.

Along with portfolio composition and sequencing, this approach to classifying business opportunities can also be employed as a guide to shaping management selection procedures, incentive compensation systems, investment appraisal processes, risk management approaches, and forms of involvement

---

[107] Hall, op. cit., p. 80.

that make sense for different types of businesses. Different types of managers, evaluated on different grounds, for example, may be appropriate for operations in different zones of the matrix. Risk-taking and ambitious entrepreneurs evaluated largely on the basis of market share would be most appropriate, for example, for star and question mark businesses, while penny-pinching hard-nosed operators evaluated on return and cash-flow grounds might be best suited for cash cow and dog harvesting or divesting operations. As for forms of involvement, wholly owned foreign investments would seem most appropriate for safe stars and cash cows, while risk-reducing or resource-contributing joint ventures could be most useful in the safe and risky question mark zones, and minimal forms of involvement such as licensing or exporting might be the best way of dealing with risky cash cows and dogs. Strategic influence and administrative process should be differentiated for different types of business opportunities in the firm's portfolio.

Translating this portfolio framework into practical reality will certainly not be an easy task. A multitude of obstacles and administrative hurdles must be overcome. MNCs will confront problems of market definition and segmentation; of accommodating interdependencies among strategic business units; of comparing prospects in different areas due to foreign exchange variation and, over time, due to inflation; of achieving strategic aggregation and disaggregation; of line management resistance; and of sheer complexity, given the tremendous diversity of most MNCs. But, international portfolio analysis and strategy is truly the challenge of the 1980s. As a major study of the Fortune 1000 companies recently discovered, the portfolio approach holds great promise for (1) promoting substantial progress in the quality of strategies developed at both the business and the corporate level; (2) producing selective resource allocation; (3) providing a framework for adapting the overall management process to the needs of each business; and (4) furnishing companies with a greatly improved capacity for strategic control. In sum, a well-developed portfolio approach to identifying and exploiting opportunities, based on sound market, competitive, and risk analysis, may be the key to success in playing the increasingly complex, diverse, and competitive global business game in the years ahead.

BIBLIOGRAPHY

Abell, D.F. and J.S. Hammond, *Strategic Market Planning: Problems and Analytical Approaches,* Englewood Cliffs, N.J.: Prentice-Hall, Inc., 1979.

Abernathy, William J., Kim B. Clark, and Alan M. Kantrow, "The New Industrial Competition," Harvard Business Review 68–81 (Sept./Oct. 1981).

Aharoni, Yair, *The Foreign Investment Decision Process,* Cambridge, Mass.: Harvard Business School, 1966.

Alsop, Ronald, "Foreign Ventures: More Firms Are Hiring Own Political Analysts to Limit Risks Abroad," Wall Street Journal 1, 17 (March 30, 1981).

Anonymous, "Foreign Investment: The Post-Shah Surge in Political Risk Studies," Business Week 69 (Dec. 1, 1980).

Anonymous, "Insuring Against Risk Abroad," Business Week 59–62 (Sept. 14, 1981).

Anonymous, "Chocolate Makers in Switzerland Try to Melt Resistance," Wall Street Journal 14 (Jan. 5, 1981).

Anonymous, "Shell's Multiple Scenario Planning: A Realistic Alternative to the Crystal Ball," World Business Weekly 14–15 (April 7, 1980).

Armstrong, J. Scott, "An Application of Econometric Models of International Marketing," 2 Journal of Marketing Research 190–198 (1970).

Armstrong, J. Scott, "Long-Run Sales Forecasting for a Consumer Durable in an International Market," Cambridge, Mass.: Unpublished Ph.D. dissertation, Sloan School of Management, M.I.T., 1968.

Baglini, Norman A., Risk Management in International Corporations, New York: Risk Studies Foundation, 1976.

Bain, J.S., Barriers to New Competition, Cambridge, Mass.: Harvard University Press, 1956.

Barkas, W.L., D.A. Ober, and J.L. Silak, "Country Risk Analysis: A Cross Impact Futures Model," Washington, D.C.: First International Political Risk Management Conference, May 7–8, 1981.

Blank, Stephen with John Basek, Stephen J. Kobrin, and Joseph LaPalombara, Assessing the Political Environment: An Emerging Function in International Companies, New York: The Conference Board, 1980.

Blauvelt, Euan and Jennifer Durlacher, eds., World Sources of Market Information (Vol. 1: Asia/Pacific, Vol. 2: Africa/Middle East, Vol. 3: Europe), Cambridge, Mass.: Ballinger Publishing Co., 1982.

Brenner, Lynn, "How to Insure Against Political Risk," Institutional Investor 212–220 (April 1981).

Brewer, Thomas L., "Political Risk Assessment for Foreign Direct Investment Decisions: Better Methods for Better Results," Columbia Journal of World Business 5–12 (Spring 1981).

Buckley, Peter J. and Mark Casson, The Future of the Multinational Enterprise, New York: Holmes & Meier, 1976.

Bulkeley, William M., "Computer Analysts: IBM Watchers Process Data on the Big Firm to Divine Its Program," Wall Street Journal 1, 18 (July 23, 1982).

Bunn, D.W. and M.M. Mustafaoglu, "Forecasting Political Risk," Management Science 1557–1567 (Nov. 1978).

Business International, Country Assessment Service: Country Ratings—August 1981, New York: Business International.

Business International, Managing and Evaluating Country Risk, New York: Business International, 1981.

Calvet, A.L., "Markets and Hierarchies: Towards a Theory of International Business," Cambridge, Mass: unpublished Ph.D. dissertation, Sloan School of Management, M.I.T., 1980.

Casson, Mark, Alternatives to the Multinational Enterprise, London: MacMillan, 1979.

Caves, Richard E., "International Corporations: The Industrial Economics of Foreign Investment," Economica 1–27 (Feb. 1971).

Channon, Derek F. and Michael Jalland, *Multinational Strategic Planning,* New York: Amacom, 1978.

Coplin, William D. and Michael K. O'Leary, *Everyman's Prince: A Guide to Understanding Your Political Problems* (rev. ed.), North Scituate, Mass: Duxbury Press, 1976.

Coplin, William D. and Michael K. O'Leary, "Policy Profiling: Judgmental Data for Analysis and Improvement of Policy Decision Making," Syracuse: Syracuse Research Corp., 1978.

De la Torre, Jose, "Product Life Cycle as a Determinant of Global Marketing Strategies," Atlanta Economic Review 9–14 (Sept./Oct. 1975).

Doyle, P. and Z. Gidengil, "A Strategic Approach to International Market Selection," *Proceedings of the European Academy for Advanced Research in Marketing,* Copenhagen, 1976.

Douglas, Susan P. and C. Samuel Craig, "Information for International Marketing Decisions," Section 29 in Ingo Walter and Tracy Murray, eds., *Handbook of International Business,* New York: John Wiley and Sons, 1982.

Doz, Yves, *Government Control and Multinational Strategic Management,* New York: Praeger Publishers, 1979.

Doz, Yves, "Multinational Strategy and Structure in Government Controlled Businesses," Columbia Journal of World Business 14–25 (Fall 1980).

Dunning, John H., *International Production and the Multinational Enterprise,* London: George Allen & Unwin, 1981.

Dunning, John H. and R.D. Pearce, *The World's Largest Industrial Enterprises,* Farnborough: Gower, 1981.

Field, P., "Meet the New Breed of Banker: The Political Risk Expert," Euromoney 21 (July 1980).

Frost & Sullivan, Inc., *World Political Risk Forecasts by Country,* New York: Frost & Sullivan, June 1981.

Futures Group, "Political Stability Prospects," Glastonbury, Conn: The Futures Group, Jan. 1980.

Gebelein, Christopher A., Conrad E. Pearson, and Michael Silbergh, "Assessing Political Risk to Foreign Oil Investment Ventures," Dallas: Society of Petroleum Engineers Paper SPE 6335, 1977 (also in Journal of Petroleum Technology 725–730 (May 1978).

Gladwin, Thomas N. and Vern Terpstra, "Introduction to the Cultural Environment," Preface in Vern Terpstra, ed., *The Cultural Environment of International Business,* Cincinnati, Ohio: South-Western Publishing Company, 1978.

Gladwin, Thomas N. and Ingo Walter, *Multinationals Under Fire: Lessons in the Management of Conflict,* New York: John Wiley and Sons, 1980.

Grosse, Robert, *The Theory of Foreign Direct Investment* (South Carolina Essay in International Business, No. 3), Columbia, S.C.: University of South Carolina, Dec. 1981.

Guzzardi, Jr., Walter, "The Great World Telephone War," Fortune 142–154 (Aug. 1977).

Haendel, Dan, *Corporate Strategic Planning: The Political Dimension* (The Washington Papers, Vol. XIV), Beverly Hills, Calif.: SAGE Publications, 1981.

Haendel, Dan, *Foreign Investments and the Management of Political Risk,* Boulder, Col.: Westview Press, 1979.

Haendel, Dan, Gerald T. West and Robert G. Meadow, eds., *Overseas Investment and Political Risk* (Foreign Policy Research Institute Monograph Series #21), Lexington, Mass: Lexington Books and D.C. Heath, 1975.

Hall, William K., "Survival Strategies in a Hostile Environment," Harvard Business Review 75–85 (Sept./Oct. 1980).

Haner, F.T., *Global Business Strategy for the 1980s,* New York: Praeger Publishers, 1980.

Haner, F.T., "Business Environment Risk Index," Best's Review (Property Liability Insurance Ed.) (July 1975).

Haner, F.T., "Rating Investment Risks Abroad," Business Horizons 18–23 (April 1979).

Haspeslagh, Philippe, "Portfolio Planning: Uses and Limits," Harvard Business Review 58–73 (Jan./Feb. 1982).

Hershey, Robert, "Commercial Intelligence on a Shoestring," Harvard Business Review 22–30 (Sept./Oct. 1980).

Hofer, Charles W. and Terry P. Haller, "GLOBESCAN: A Way to Better International Risk Assessment," The Journal of Business Strategy 41–55 (Fall 1980).

Hofstede, Geert, *Culture's Consequences: International Differences in Work Related Values,* Beverly Hills: SAGE, 1980.

Hout, Thomas M., Michael E. Porter, Eileen Rudden and Eric Vogt, "Global Industries: New Rules for the Competitive Game," Graduate School of Business Administration, Division of Research, Working Paper, Harvard University, 1980-53.

Hymer, Stephen, *The International Operations of National Firms: A Study of Direct Foreign Investment,* Cambridge, Mass.: The MIT Press, 1976 (originally published 1960).

Johnson, Harry, *Comparative Cost and Commercial Policy Theory for a Developing World Economy,* Stockholm: Almquist and Wiksell, 1968.

Johnson, Howard C., *Risk in Foreign Business Environments: A Framework for Thought and Management,* Cambridge, Mass.: Arthur D. Little, 1980.

Keegan, Warren J., *Multinational Marketing Management* (2nd ed.), Englewood Cliffs, N.J.: Prentice-Hall, Inc., 1980.

Kiechel III, Walter, "Playing the Global Game," Fortune 111–126 (Nov. 16, 1981).

Kobrin, Stephen J., "Assessing Political Risk Overseas," The Wharton Magazine 24–31 (Winter 1981–1982).

Kobrin, Stephen J., *Managing Political Risk Assessment: Strategic Response to Environmental Change,* University of California Press, 1982.

Kobrin, Stephen J., "Political Assessment by International Firms: Models or Methodologies?" 2 Journal of Policy Modeling 251–270 (1981).

Kobrin, Stephen J., "Political Risk: A Review and Reconsideration," Journal of International Business Studies 67–80 (Spring–Summer 1979).

Kobrin, Stephen J. with John Basek, Stephen Blank and Joseph LaPalombara, "The Assessment and Evaluation of Non-Economic Environments by American Firms: A Preliminary Report," Journal of International Business Studies 32–47 (Spring–Summer 1980).

Kraar, Louis, "The Multinationals Get Smarter About Political Risks," Fortune 86–100 (March 24, 1980).

Marsh & McLennan, *Risk in a Complex Society* (public opinion survey conducted by Louis Harris and Associates, Inc.), New York: Marsh & McLennan, 1980.

Mehr, Robert I. and Bob. A. Hedges, *Risk Management: Concepts and Applications,* Homewood, Ill.: Richard D. Irwin, 1974.

Moyer, Reed, "International Market Analysis," Journal of Marketing Research 353–360 (Nov. 1968).

Nagy, Pancras, J., *Country Risk: How to Assess, Quantify and Monitor It,* London: Euromoney Publications, 1979.

Organization for Economic Cooperation and Development, *International Investment and Multinational Enterprises: Recent International Direct Investment Trends,* Paris: O.E.C.D., 1981.

Pearson, C.E., "An Expert Panel Model for Assessing Political Risk," in T.H. Moran, ed., *International Political Risk Assessment: The State of the Art,* Washington, D.C.: Georgetown University Press, 1980.

Porter, Michael E., *Competitive Strategy: Techniques for Analyzing Industries and Competitors,* New York: The Free Press, 1980.

Porter, Michael E., "Experience Curve," Wall Street Journal 30 (Oct. 22, 1979).

Punnett, Betty Jane, "Sources of Information for International Business," Appendix B in Ingo Walter and Tracy Murray, eds., *Handbook of International Business,* New York: John Wiley and Sons, 1982.

Richardson, G. Frederick, "International Risk Management," Section 12 in Ingo Walter and Tracy Murray, eds., *Handbook of International Business,* New York: John Wiley and Sons, 1982.

Robinson, Richard D., *International Business Management: A Guide to Decision-Making* (2nd ed.), Hinsdale, Ill.: Dryden Press, 1978.

Robock, Stefan H., Kenneth Simmonds and Jack Zwick, *International Business and Multinational Enterprises,* Homewood, Ill.: Richard D. Irwin, 1977.

Root, Franklin R., *Foreign Market Entry Strategies,* New York: Amacom, 1982.

Rugman, Allan M., "Internationalization as a General Theory of Foreign Direct Investment: A Reappraisal of the Literature," *Weltwirtschaftliches Archiv,* No. 2., 1980.

Rummel, R.J. and David A. Heenan, "How Multinationals Analyze Political Risk," Harvard Business Review 67–76 (Jan./Feb. 1978).

Sethi, S. Prakash, "Comparative Cluster Analysis for World Markets," Journal of Marketing Research 348–354 (1971).

Teece, David J., "The Multinational Enterprise: Market Failure and Market Power Considerations," 3 Sloan Management Review (1981).

United Nations Economic and Social Council, *Transnational Corporations in World Development: A Reexamination* E. 78 II A5, New York: United Nations, 1978.

Vernon, Raymond, "The Location of Economic Activity," in John H. Dunning, ed., *Economic Analysis and the Multinational Enterprise,* London: Allen & Unwin, 1974.

Wall, Jerry L. and Bong-gon P. Shin, "Seeking Competitive Information," in William F. Glueck, ed., *Business Policy and Strategic Management* (3rd ed.), New York: McGraw-Hill Book Company, 1980.

Walter, Ingo, "Country Risk Assessment," Section 21 in Ingo Walter and Tracy Murray, eds., *Handbook of International Business,* New York: John Wiley and Sons, 1982.

Weber, J.A., "Comparing Growth Opportunities in the International Marketplace," 1 Management International Review 47–54 (1979).

Wells, Jr., Louis, ed., *The Product Life Cycle and International Trade,* Cambridge, Mass.: Harvard University Press, 1972.

Wind, Yoram and Susan Douglas "International Portfolio Analysis and Strategy: The Challenge of the 80s," Journal of International Business Studies 69–82 (Fall 1981).

World Bank, *World Development Report 1981,* New York: Oxford University Press, 1981.

PART IV

Formulating Business Unit and Corporate Strategies

8

Competitive Business Strategies

ROBERT G. WILSON
Arthur D. Little, Inc.

COMPETITIVE STRATEGY AS A MEANS OF SPURRING CORPORATE GROWTH

Over the last 15 years, there is strong evidence that the U.S. economy has changed from one of growth and innovation to one characterized by maturity. Many U.S. industries seem to struggle to maintain health and profitability. Many managers believe that there has been a fundamental and long-term shift in the maturity of the economy and its ability to foster the development of new growth industries.

Certainly some of that vision is true. The unmistakable signs of increasing maturity are evident. A great many domestic industries, especially in heavy manufacturing, exhibit all the classic signs of maturity. This should be neither surprising nor alarming.

Some of this "coming of age" in American industry has been brought about by the natural forces of economics at work. But, unfortunately, some evidence indicates that the maturity of certain industries is accelerated by the strategic activities of a few leading companies.

A major challenge faced by the business world today is how to manage and renew slow growing companies operating within mature industries. There is a constantly more vigorous quest for competitive strategies that not only improve a company's long-term position, but also generate growth above the industry average.

The quest for this mythical "fountain of youth" has gone on in business for centuries. Explorers have navigated the globe in the search, always believing the "fountain" for their business lay just beyond the horizon, in a territory they had yet to explore. Corporations have searched for renewal, sometimes by acquiring businesses in unfamiliar territories. Early concepts of strategic planning suggested that maturity in the industry could be traded or balanced by acquiring an infusion of growth from the mythical "fountain."

Evidence now suggests that many of the most successful companies have done the reverse: They invested selectively in mature industries to enhance positions against companies embarked on a "harvest" strategy.

The main theme of this chapter is how to uncover competitive strategies in maturing industries. The search for the fountain of youth need not lead a corporation into acquisitions of unrelated businesses in hopes of balancing maturity. Instead, exploring for growth should begin with a searching examination of the mature business that the corporation currently owns and understands.

A supplemental theme is the proposal of a systematic review of *all* strategies, even those originally conceived for use in growth and embryonic industries. Such a search, among the widest possible array of options, frequently uncovers unique opportunities. Too often companies have overlooked strategies intended for more vigorously growing situations because hidebound methodology has labeled them inappropriate. Many companies are blind to industry renewal or competitive opportunities because the organization has a stake in continuing to deal with its stable, unchanging environment.

STRATEGY DURING MATURITY

During the last decade, the conventional wisdom from a simplistic reading of portfolio management theory has been to "milk" businesses in mature, low-growth/high-share positions. Furthermore, the theory suggests that such funds be reinvested to support or acquire businesses in high-growth industries. However, Professor William K. Hall, in an article appearing in *The Harvard Business Review* for September-October 1980,[1] reported on the results of studies conducted among 64 companies in slow growing, mature industries. The results of his research indicate that those companies that actively reinvested in highly differentiated positions, low-cost operations, or defensible niches were significantly better off than others that attempted to "milk" their positions to provide

---

[1] William K. Hall, "Survival Strategies in a Hostile Environment," *Harvard Business Review* (September-October 1980), pp. 75–85.

diversification funds. In fact, Professor Hall's data suggest that the industry leaders in all eight mature industries produced *better* results than leading companies in rapidly growing, high-technology fields.

In a related examination, Professor Kathryn Rudie Harrigan of the University of Texas studied 60 companies in eight other industries[2] (none overlapping with Professor Hall) that were not merely mature, but actually declining. Her findings also suggest that even when there is convincing evidence that an entire industry may be starting an inexorable slide to oblivion, rapid and immediate abandonment may *not* be the best strategy. The data suggest ways in which alert companies can prosper as the industry slides downhill.

None of the recent scholarly explorations lead to the belief that the concept of industry maturity is invalid. On the contrary, the very framework for understanding the dynamics of these industry conditions enriches the range of strategies from which to choose.

The recent studies *do* support, however, the need for a critical examination of the simplistic conclusions drawn from matrix portfolio management theory. The proposition that a portfolio heavily weighted toward investments in mature industries must be balanced with investments in growth industries is often wrong. Furthermore, the proposition that competitive position in a mature-to-declining industry can be improved by striving for "differentiation" or "low-cost" is not, by itself, very helpful. Striving for "differentiation" is so broad an activity as to be meaningless without a set of related action programs. Some of the literature describing successful differentiation strategies from the past has all the earmarks of an "ex post facto strategy"—one that was invented to encompass the conditions observed substantially after the fact. An example of this is the widely used case of Timex and their struggles in the early 1960s with the wristwatch industry. It was only years later that scholars ascribed their success to their "brilliant strategic insight." At the time, the management of Timex was merely struggling to survive in a terribly hostile world.

To be sure, "low cost" and "differentiation" are valuable concepts, but they are too broad for most managers facing today's hostile world. To elaborate on these themes, the following discussion suggests several subsets of strategic recommendations.

Although the mnemonic acronym "SQIRM" suggests too much of wiggling one's way to success, it has the merit of keeping a few simple ideas in order. They are:

    S = segment
    Q = quality
    I   = invest selectively
    R = revitalize research
    M = management changes

---

[2] Kathryn Rudie Harrigan, "Strategies for Declining Industries," *J. Business Strategy* (Fall, 1980), pp. 20–34.

Segmentation Tactics

An important way to become specific about differentiation is through segmentation. Virtually no mature-to-declining industry is homogeneous. Some parts are subject to greater or lesser growth, more price warfare, more import competition, and less technological obsolescence. Those segments must be identified by standard market research, user surveys, multivariate analysis, or psychographic trending. In addition, the unusual strengths or weaknesses of present products must be located. One of the following segmentation tactics should be used to capitalize on what has been discovered.

Repositioning. Creating a new natural customer base for the product, especially one built on fast-growing market groups or population segments, can strengthen product position in the marketplace. Levi Strauss, an adept marketer in a mature industry, recognized that its huge rise in volume was built upon a surge in the population of postwar babies. As this group moved out of their twenties, they needed other types of garments. Levi Strauss was among the first big manufacturers of jeans to see this opportunity and reposition its product, organization, and brand to grow with the baby boomers into their thirties.

Warners, manufacturer of ladies' foundation garments, recognized that women perceived its brand as one intended for conservative, middle-aged women with fit and control problems. Warners had built its business on products and distribution that sold well in a fitting-room environment. In the early 1970s, research pointed the way to a new and fast-growing segment of the female population. Warners redesigned its product, and its promotion and packaging, and introduced the product to a new location in many stores. The emphasis was on light control and sexy designs. While some of Warners' older customers were scandalized, the company succeeded in repositioning its product for new, rapid, and profitable growth.

Multiple Branding. The tobacco industry frequently uses the tactic of establishing brand loyalty with one segment of the user population. It then locates a different user group, identified by benefit segmentation, feature, quality level, or life-style characteristic, and introduces a new brand that will appeal to that group. In the cigarette industry, although the product inside the pack may be largely the same from brand to brand, parallel promotion and distribution does little to cannibalize its corporate brother brands. R. J. Reynolds, makers of Camel, Winston, Vantage, Doral, Now, and other cigarette brands, has developed marketing for each brand to address its own fairly discrete target customer group.

This approach has ready application to other consumer goods as well as to many industrial product categories. It is also known as product line extension.

The "Warm Dark Cave." A company without enough industry-wide volume to be a low-cost producer, or without sufficient strength to survive in concentrated industries, may elect to become a "niche player." But beware the porous niche! For a company to succeed in a niche, three conditions must be met:

1. The niche must have a different basis of competition[3] from the industry at large;
2. The niche must be large enough to support profitable growth, but small enough to escape the interest of the full-line, full-industry competitors; and
3. The niche must be defensible.

Thus, the "quality niche" some companies boast about fails to meet the criteria. No wonder they find lots of competition in their "warm dark cave."

Other Strategies. A "distribution" strategy normally is not appropriate to positions in mature industries. (By "distribution" is meant the aggressive commitment of resources to adding new outlets and new sales channels.) Typically, by the time an industry matures, distribution has stabilized and the more appropriate activity is a rationalization or pruning out of marginal and unprofitable distribution.

In some late mature industries, however, the very fact that some producers are "rationalizing" or withdrawing from a segment opens an opportunity for others to consolidate the departed territory and *add* distributors of their own. For example, major oil companies are withdrawing from certain segments of the farm and rural fuels and lubricants business. Aggressive, well-financed rural cooperatives, already specialized in those arenas, are in hot pursuit. They are bringing uncharacteristic growth and competitive vigor to a market outsiders consider somnambulant.

Quality of Product or Service

The second major competitive strategy for mature industries centers on the concept of quality: How much? What kind? Relative to whom? How is it perceived?

Traditional axioms from strategy theory assert that mature industries compete largely on price, and that low-cost producers therefore have a great advantage. Nevertheless, it can be argued that many companies in mature industries, without commanding market shares, have succeeded without striving to become the lost-cost producer. Obvious examples include Mercedes Benz in automobiles and Paacar in trucks.

Without confronting that argument directly, certainly some companies have carried a low-cost strategy so far that quality has been sacrificed and a competitive vacuum has developed. Success stories abound of companies that have staunchly maintained a high-quality course in mature industries. Their products command a premium because customers are willing to pay for what

---

[3] The term "basis of conpetition," as used here, refers to a short list of attributes that provide distinctive advantage to one company versus another in the same industry.

they perceive to be a better value. One of the following tactics can open avenues to quality postion.

Market Position Defense. Barriers can be built to customer switching to make it unattractive to switch to a competitor's product. These barriers make it difficult for competitors to enhance the perception of their product. One method is through research to discover what customers really perceive as "quality." Fast-food operators offer meals that are at best commodities, with relatively little opportunity for meaningful differentiation. But what MacDonalds discovered very early was that the customer's perception of quality had more to do with reliable consistency, speed, and friendliness than with what was served between the buns. They have built a formidable wall of "quality" around their position by concentrating on *adding* to the perceived value of their offering through training mechanisms for their high-turnover staff.

Building-in a Service. Like the MacDonalds example, many products are in reality a complex package of physical goods and associated attributes. This is especially true in highly fragmented industries and in mature industries, where the products have been sold for a long while. In these environments, strategists can find new growth opportunities by adding to or replacing services in their product offering. This approach, too, should be based upon a careful assessment of what the customer is willing to pay for, what reduces his or her costs, increases his or her flexibility, and reduces his or her response time. A small U.S. manufacturer of specialty motors has built an almost unassailable position for high quality, not because the products are better built or more reliable, but because sales efforts are focused on pricing policies and production systems to assure rapid delivery of small order, "new" motor/control designs. This company has gained a reputation for quality in an industry whose products are becoming commodities. This strategy also can be described as creating a new product within the same market.

Image Enhancement. In most products, one or two components or characteristics carry a disproportionate share of the responsibility for the customers' perception of "quality." By correctly identifying those attributes and how they change over time, a strategist can gain unusual advantage. For example, in men's shirts the quality of make is difficult or impossible for the average customer to determine at the point of sale. Fabrics, however, can be seen and touched. Thus, for years Hathaway has built a reputation for high quality by seeking out exceptional fabrics and putting a disproportionate share of their promotion on fabrics. They create a romance for fabric origins, the care with which they are selected, and the loving attention given to their delivery to the discriminating buyer. At sales meetings and customer presentations, the fabrics are stroked tenderly and handled with reverence. The image projected is a far cry from the standard anonymity of the "rag business"!

Conventional wisdom suggests that the image of a mature industry is best projected by advertising aimed at brand name and feature identification. Promotion of generic products or primary demand development is usually left behind in embryonic or early growth situations. Conventional wisdom is not strategic thinking, however. The competitive strategist can turn the use of generic product promotion to unique advantage. For example, when everyone else was promoting wide-screen, big-image television sets, Sony talked about the many places a second set could be enjoyed. Then they advertised the one unique strength they had—small size. Their "tummy TV" carved out a niche by promoting generic product demand for the two-television household.

Aim toothpaste is another good example. By promoting the use of toothpaste among young children, they are on the side of parents in the battle against tooth decay. Not a bad place to be in a market dominated by Colgate and Crest!

Invest Selectively

As studies by William K. Hall suggest, a mature, slow growing industry sometimes "offers an excellent basic investment opportunity and reinvestment climate, at least for the industry leaders insightful enough to capitalize on their positions."[4] Aside from the kinds of reinvestment discussed previously (product line extension, market position defense, or new product/same market), there is a whole range of deployment activities that can solidify a position in a mature industry.

Acquire and Rationalize. The corporate quest for the fountain of youth may point toward acquisition in unrelated industries. Too often such a search has proven to be an illusion when fast growth and easy profits remain just beyond the horizon. But acquisition in the same or related industries often offers attractive possibilities unavailable in growth industries. For example, several corporations recognized the special needs of relatively small, late-mature/early-aging businesses. They watched them struggling with low margins, a need for capital, expert but unimaginative management, and small market shares. Often these businesses are in fragmented, low-technology, metal-bending and industrial product or component industries. By selectively acquiring such businesses, instilling a strategic concept, offering high rewards for cash flow, and then managing them without a heavy corporate overhead burden, they have often achieved great success. By giving the experienced management freedom, autonomy, and incentive, several of these corporations have developed steady, attractive profits from mature businesses with 15 to 18 percent gross margins.

Acquire and Consolidate. Many industries offer advantages from large-scale economics. In cases where the conditions squeeze our marginal producers, subscale competitors can sometimes be acquired and reassembled into effective competitors through consolidation. This has happened in the domestic news-

---

[4] Hall, *op. cit.*

paper, major appliance, and television industries. A plan of gradually acquiring and consolidating special situations sometimes offers the simultaneous advantage of picking up well-established brand names, which can be repositioned and revitalized with different products.

Widen the Horizons. By not taking a wide enough view of the industry structure, some strategists miss huge opportunities for growth. Many industries are mature in the United States. Conditions of development, trade, and competition, however, are changing throughout the world. Some multinational corporations gained new economic advantage in the domestic U.S. market by reinvesting as if the world market was in a growth phase. Thus, more modern plants, newer technology, and expanded capacity could be justified by a wider view of the horizons. While there are many reasons for their success, the Japanese have frequently taken this view of expanding world markets. Too often U.S. producers have been caught with their horizons down.

Invest in Capacity Expansion. Another strategic outgrowth of expanding horizons is "excess capacity." These key words describe a strategy of purposefully investing in major capacity expansion well beyond near-term needs. The purpose of this approach is to gain incremental cost advantages, which can be leveraged as competitors struggle to catch up. Taking this course is risky and very sensitive to correct timing. As total industry capacity nears saturation, an "excess capacity" strategy probably would not make sense.

Yet a company that makes an investment in expanding capacity as industry volume tops out or begins to decline sends a strong signal to its competitors: "We are here to stay. Join us if you wish, but bring lots of cash." Such signaling has often discouraged less committed participants and accelerated the consolidation of the market. The first new brewery added to Miller's capacity when they were acquired by Philip Morris in 1970 doubled production. By 1980, Miller's capacity had expanded more than eightfold from its 1970 level. It is not coincidence that the number of competitors dropped from 117 to 20 during the same decade, and that the share of the market of the top five beer brewers moved from 50 percent to over 80 percent. All this occurred in a very mature beer industry characterized by deeply entrenched local favorites.

The unnatural approach taken by GTE Sylvania in the declining vacuum tubes industry typifies this strategy. By increasing their investment in a business widely acknowledged to be on the decline, they encouraged their competition to cut their losses early and get out of the market gracefully. Sylvania soon found itself almost the only domestic source for many vacuum tubes. They have profited handsomely from that unique position for many years.

Revitalize Research

Usually, the role of technology in mature industries is largely oriented toward process development, cost reduction, and materials substitution— and correctly so. This overall strategy does not, however, automatically imply a reduction in technical expenditures or efforts. Technical tactics play an important role in competitive business strategies.

Develop and Promote New Features. If a company's overall strategic thrust is to differentiate its product from the competition, then product and market research must be an important part of the strategy implementation program. A user survey can help pinpoint the areas where customers are not completely happy with existing products, and thus point the way toward new features and benefits.

By regularly adding sensible "bells and whistles" to its line, a company can avoid a slide toward commodity price warfare and also gain a reputation for innovation. The new features need not represent a major scientific breakthrough. But in the home appliance industry, for example, the addition of automatic defrosting, icemakers, and washer minibaskets have selectively kept some manufacturers a step ahead of their competitors.

Look for New Key Technologies. One of the sad truths of recent years has been that most of the technical breakthroughs that have upset the basis of competition in U.S. industries have come from *outside* these industries. By not fully controlling their key technologies, or by failing to recognize when those technologies have become base technologies, too many companies have been caught unaware by new developments. A classic illustration is the way in which the medical imaging (x-ray) industry was dramatically restructured by the introduction of the CT scanner, a product based not on Roentgen ray technology, but on mass processing and display of digital electronic signals. The breakthrough introduction was not made by the leaders in the medical products industry, but by a British company in the audio recording industry. The millions of dollars spent on CT scanners are threatened by obsolesence as new technologies produce new techniques. Nuclear magnetic resonance (NMR) in medical imaging may well be today's pacing technology and tomorrow's key technology.

The moral is: Monitor developing technologies in all segments of the industry. Many companies overspend on base technologies and fail to spend enough (or anything at all) on pacing technologies. These are the technical arenas from which tomorrow's competitive advantage often comes.

Monitor Maturities. Just as products and industries go through life cycles, so do technologies. When developing competitive strategy, therefore, a corporation must monitor the maturity of its own industry and also the maturity of the technologies that support the products in its industry. Sometimes both the industry and its technologies are mature. But when the technologies are more mature or less mature than the industry, important strategic information can be gained.

For example, today the data terminals industry has most of the earmarks of maturity: relatively stable competitive positions, predictable growth and potential, and well-established customer/supplier relationships. But the technologies supporting these products are in great transition. The potentiality for flat-screen displays, voice-recognition inputs, and character-reading equipment are so great that tomorrow's competitive structure may become very different. Tomorrow's successful companies may well be those, inside or outside the industry, that make a significant breakthrough in one of these technical arenas.

The danger signals to watch for lie within the corporation's organization and management system. The company structure, reporting and control system, reward and measurement mechanisms, and human resources may be oriented toward the maturity of their generally stable *industry* conditions. At the same time, the research and development division should be operating with a very different kind of management environment, oriented toward embryonic or growth conditions. It should not be measured by cost/benefit analysis, governed by short-range planning, or controlled by rigid budgets. In such cases, it should be given great latitude to search, explore, and invent in the areas of promising new pacing technologies. Its management system should be very different from that of other divisions in the organization.

Managing the organizational implications of sharp difference between industry and technical maturity can be one of the most productive routes to finding the elusive corporate fountain of youth.

Management Changes

In the 1970s, strategic literature focused on developing strategies. The 1980s have already seen the beginnings of a new trend—making strategies. One of the most important implementation steps in a wide recognition that a new strategy may require changing management systems as well as changing individual managers. Successful companies are separated from unsuccessful companies by their skill in understanding how to manage particular strategies. While it may be true that a good manager can manage anything, it is becoming clearer and clearer that certain organizations and certain managers learn how to carry out certain strategies more effectively than others.

There is a growing body of knowledge on this fascinating topic. The following are a few appropriate ideas to spark new competitive spirit within a mature industry.

Revitalize Performance Measurements. By the time the industry is solidly mature, companies within it usually have very well established management systems. Through the normal course of events, performance is measured principally against budget or last year's results. Rewards are usually meted out to those with the best financial results or to those who show the greatest improvement in efficiency.

If management wants to change the thrust to encourage growth and renewal, however, the performance measurement and rewards system must be adjusted. To accomplish the revised objectives, performance must be redirected outward. Success must be measured against key competitors, selecting characteristics that are both reported and inimitable. Rewards must be shifted more heavily toward marketing and product development activities, even at the expense (and to the chagrin) of those who are providing the same strong financial performance they have in the past.

The result may well be a company that operates differently in two types of product-market segments. This is not only unavoidable, it is often desirable. The company needs to maintain the steady performance from its more stable segments while generating growth and excitement from the rapidly changing ones.

Relieve the Layers of Management. One of the ironies of developing strategy in mature industries involves decision making. Because competition is more severe and the marketing infrastructure more sophisticated, product introduction often occurs frequently and with quick success. Management information networks need to be clear and must allow rapid communication. But at that time in company history, hierarchical layers of management decision making are often at their peak. The need to respond is bogged down in bureaucracy.

This is the time when top management should try to shorten the lines of communication and widen their span of control. Decision making should be pushed to the lowest level.

Strip the Staff. Another element of overhead expense that sometimes slows the process toward change in mature industry companies is the corporate staff. Staff tends to improve the quality of decisions in businesses that perpetuate existing industry operations. Good staff officers examine issues, raise questions, challenge assumptions, and explore alternatives. But if the needs of the company are shifting toward rapid decision making or shifting toward more line management autonomy, then staff analysis can get in the way.

One way of skirting this obstacle is to specifically forbid analysis or decision-making challenge in the segment where growth and renewal is desired: Leave this zone "staff-free" for line management. This tends to keep lines of authority clean, short, and responsible for their own future.

This may shock and frighten the staff. But such an edict from the top sends a loud signal to the organization that renewal requires different strategies, not business as usual.

CONCLUSIONS

Operating a business in a maturing industry need not be a quick trip to quietus. Oversimplified, traditional approaches to business strategy have tended to overemphasize the "milking" strategy during maturity. In some cases, this has caused maturity to become a self-fulfilling prophecy. Many industries are thus highly vulnerable to aggressive attack, both from within and without. Careful selection of targets and strategies coupled with adroit investments can bring about renewal. Many mature industries represent unusual growth opportunities for tomorrow.

9

Preemptive Strategies

IAN C. MACMILLAN

Graduate School of Business, Columbia University

INTRODUCTION

The strategist seeks opportunities to upset industry equilibrium, pursuing strategies that will allow a business to disrupt the "normal" course of industry events and forge new industry conditions to the disadvantage of its competitors. The preemptive move is one weapon that the strategist can exploit to secure an advantage over competitors.

A preemptive move is defined here as a major move by a focal business, ahead of moves by its adversaries, that allows it to secure an advantageous position from which it will be difficult to dislodge because of the advantages it has captured by being the first mover. A common example of a preemptive move is to expand capacity well ahead of industry demand in the hope of gaining market share by discouraging competitors from expanding.

This chapter dicusses preemptive strategies. The first part reviews certain key characteristics of preemptive moves. This is followed by a section that suggests where to seek preemptive opportunities. Finally, some general guidelines for developing effective preemptive strategies are presented.

CHARACTERISTICS OF PREEMPTIVE STRATEGIES

A number of key issues are important to recognize in dealing with preemptive strategies: First, as in any business endeavor, preemptive actions have associated risks. Second, preemptive moves need not occupy *all* possible positions in a competitive arena, nor need all competition be preempted. Third, since preemptive moves are not permanently effective, it is necessary to recognize that competitors will eventually respond to the move. Last, for maximum effect, the preemptive move has certain ideal characteristics.

Preemptive Moves Are Neither Risk Free Nor Deterministic

Preemptive moves are made on the basis of the strategist's assumptions about the behavior of the market or of its competitors. The competitors or the market may not respond as anticipated, in which case the preemptor may regret the move. On the other hand, preemptive moves may be *too* successful and precipitate government intervention or competitive lawsuits. So preemptive moves are not risk-free, and the ideal preemptive move is one where the downside risk is low because the firm can reverse its decision, if it so desires, with a minimum of damage. While it must be recognized that preemptive moves are inherently risky, the strategist should seek to take only well judged, calculated risks, as

IBM did in spending $6 billion to preempt the dominant-product position in mainframe computers with the system 360. This was a large risk with huge stakes, but it *had* to be taken if IBM was to maintain its commanding position in the mainframe business. By ensuring that it was on top of technology and fully conversant with market needs, IBM succeeded in making the risk a *calculated* one, and preempted an entire generation of mainframe products.

This need to take calculated risks, with nondeterministic outcomes, is in direct conflict with those theorists who have an obsession with highly planned, unilateral, deterministic strategies. There is nothing wrong with "shaping one's luck" by capitalizing on a preemptive opportunity that emerges as a result of good fortune, particularly good fortune one has helped create by shaping the odds. For nearly a decade the business strategist has been portrayed as an analyst who deterministically plans every strategic move. This is about as accurate as portraying good generals as officers who precisely predict and deterministically conduct entire, complex campaigns. Good generals *make* their luck by shaping the odds in their favor and then being able to spot and rapidly capitalize on every emergent opportunity created by the mistakes of their opponents, or by the good fortune they have helped shape.

In the same way, the good strategist should be poised to spot, and vigorously exploit, any opportunities to preempt that expose themselves as the competitive game is played out. For instance, when the Red Lobster chain was first acquired by General Mills, the acquirer started by following the traditional strategy in the restaurant chain business: trying to preempt the geographic locations and the liquor licenses in each geographic area they entered. However, it transpired that the chain's early success was due to the fact that the previous owners of Red Lobster had secured access to the best seafood sources and seafood distribution system in the industry. And preferential access to a consistent and sustained, reliable, quality supply of seafood is critical to the seafood chains. Once this fact was recognized, General Mills "made their luck" by rapidly consolidating their supply advantage, and continued to preempt the best supply positions as they expanded their chain. As discussed in the next section, it is not necessary to have exclusive positions occupied, only the prime positions—and this is what General Mills capitalized on.

Preemptive Moves Need Not Occupy All Positions, Nor Preempt All Competitors

Preemptive moves, to be effective, need not occupy *all* possible preemptive positions, but only the best positions; nor need the move impact all rivals, as long as it impacts some. For instance, moves by International Nickel Company earlier this century to preempt deposits of nickel secured several *major* sources of supply, but *not* all of them; yet it created a competitive edge because this access made a material difference to the supply structure. De Beers did the same in diamonds. Similarly, Du Pont's capacity expansions in titanium dioxide have not discouraged *all* competitors from expanding, but have discouraged enough competitors to make a difference in titanium dioxide industry. What is important is the impact of preempting the "prime" positions: It is a common phenomenon that a relatively small proportion of customers, or suppliers, or distributors, or market segments, or key accounts, or geographic locations (and so on) account for a disproportionately large proportion of total revenues in a market. When a preemptor secures these highly concentrated (prime) positions in an industry, it creates a double advantage for itself: First, the preempted competitors must now compete for the lesser positions, with successively decreasing marginal return on effort for each additional position. In addition, as the competitors try to compete against the preemptor for the remaining, dispersed, lesser positions, the preemptor already has a large base of revenues from which it can recover fixed costs. This large base is denied to competitors, creating cost barriers for them.

So the object in preemption is not to preempt *all* positions, but enough of the prime positions to make a material difference.

Benefits of Preemptive Moves Are Not Permanent

In all but the most stagnant industries, the success of preemptive moves tends to have a limited lifespan, and the more dynamic the industry, the shorter the lifespan.

For instances, many private hospital systems from the 1950s through the mid-1970s were able to secure strong competitive positions by preempting the best locations and preempting support from the best physicians in a particular geographic region. This tactic was highly successful as long as the demand came *from* individual consumers and the demand was *for* acute medical care. Over time, the nature of the demand for medical services has changed radically; today major clients include government agencies or corporations, whose demand is for comprehensive health care systems that span employees' homes, hospitals, and nursing homes. Since the current health insurance systems merely pass on the costs to the corporations, there is every indication that a new dominant design will emerge, based on medical systems that position themselves as preferred health care providers to self-insuring organizations. This development will create new preemptive opportunities in the medical service industry and will make obsolete the old advantages created by preempting location and physician support. The irony is that the old health care systems may find themselves hamstrung by their original preemptive commitments to physicians and locations.

Since it is clearly unrealistic to expect permanent benefits from a preemptive move, the response lag (MacMillan & McCaffery, 1982) or time it takes competitors to overcome the first mover's advantage becomes an important factor to take into account when formulating a preemptive strategy.

Preemptive Opportunities Exist Along the Entire Industry Chain

It is important to note that preemptive strategies are not confined to direct moves against competitors. It is necessary to scan along the entire industry chain, from supply of basic raw materials through delivery of post-sales service, for opportunities to preempt.

The sources of preemptive opportunities are discussed later in this chapter.

Preemptive Moves Should Not Be Illegal or Quasilegal

In the ensuing discussion, it should become abundantly clear that there is sufficient opportunity for the imaginative strategist to generate preemptive moves without having to resort to illegal or quasilegal behavior.

Characteristics of an Ideal Preemptive Move

On the basis of the preceding discussion, an ideal preemptive move should have the following characteristics:

1 It should be possible to rapidly occupy "prime" positions at any advantageous point along the *entire* industry chain.
2 Once the move is made, it should be difficult for most of the adversaries to follow into these positions.
3 Conditions should exist that slow down the response rate of any competitors who can respond.
4 It should be relatively easy for the preempting business to reverse its move, if it so desires.

The problem is how to identify preemptive opportunities that have at least several, if not all, of these ideal characteristics. There are two classes of preemptive opportunities to seek:

1 Opportunities that exploit the rival's weakness or its lack of commitment;
2 Opportunities that exploit the rival's strengths or its strong commitments.

Preemptive Opportunities That Exploit a Rival's Weaknesses or Its Lack of Commitment

The most aggressive preemptive moves are those that exploit the fact that the rival has a vulnerable position, either because of a specific competitive weakness or because it has not made a commitment to that position. It is possible to identify preemptive opportunities by analyzing the length of the industry chain for four general sets of conditions:

1 Opportunities to reshape infrastructure;
2 Opportunities to occupy prime positions;
3 Opportunities to secure critical skills; and
4 Opportunities to preempt a psychological position.

Opportunities to Reshape Infrastructure. A rich source of preemptive opportunities lies in reshaping the industry "infrastructure," that is, the set of institutions required to ensure the smooth flow of product down the industry chain from raw materials to serviced, delivered goods (MacMillan 1982.) Supplies, sudstitute materials, technologies and customer demand are in a continual state of evolution throughout the chain. Under these evolutionary pressures, the ways of supplying, the status of supply sources, the viability of substitute materials or products, the changes in products and technologies of production, the status of distribution channels, the ways of distributing, the service and delivery systems, and the demands of the final consumers are all continually in flux. Aggressive businesses can preempt their competition by seizing opportunities to reshape the infrastructure: creating a new supply system or a radically different service system, occupying an emergent distribution system, and so on. This requires systematic scanning of changing conditions in the industry chain and skill at interpreting these trends as preemptive opportunities to reshape, develop, or enhance the infrastructure.

Opportunities to Occupy Prime Positions. Another general area for preemptive opportunities is the occupation of "prime" positions. While occupation of key geographic locations is the most obvious example, there are prime positions that can be preempted by securing key accounts, key suppliers, key distributors, key service organizations, or key government contracts. Here the chain must be analyzed to identify any future concentration of organizations that probably will be responsible for a large proportion of the commercial activity in a sector of the chain, and opportunities must be sought to move into these prime positions.

Opportunities to Secure Critical Skills. In an era when our educational systems are becoming steadily less effective and the needs for increasingly qualified staff are becoming more critical, there will be escalating opportunities to preempt pools of skills that are, or will be, critically needed in the chain. In fact, it will become progressively more important for business to develop forecasting techniques that can be used to anticipate emerging skill needs. Shortages of talent will create opportunities to preempt not only the skills needed to produce and sell the business' *own* goods, but also to preempt skills needed to assure adequate and reliable supply, adequate and reliable distribution, and adequate and reliable after-sales service of the product.

Opportunities to Preempt a Psychological Position. Another set of opportunities to preempt involves preempting a "psychological position" in the minds of the customers. With this preemptive strategy, the focal business uniquely positions itself in the minds of customers by developing an appeal (e.g., Avis: "We try harder"; Frito-Lay: "99.5 percent service") that is hard for competitors to refute or copy: Can Hertz credibly "try even harder than harder"? Can competitors of Frito-Lay credibly offer "more than 99.5 percent service" to their distributors? The key in positioning preemption is to develop and rapidly disseminate to customers a really *compelling* appeal with the effect of a rallying cry that firmly fixes the business' position in the mind of the customers.

It should be noted that opportunities for preemption of psychological position of the business in relation to the competition are not confined to customers, but also occur in situations where it is important to secure support from other critical organizations, such as distributors (Frito-Lay: "99.5 percent service to distributors"), suppliers (IBM: "fairness to vendors"), and even unions (Delta Airlines: "We are a family of professionals").

Further, psychological positioning need not be in relation to competitors. A company may consciously cultivate a general image; for example, as an effective innovator (3M, Citibank), which gives the business a preemptive advantage when untried new products are being offered; or as a tried and true, stable and reliable giant (Prudential: "piece of the rock"; IBM, "service is our business"; Holiday Inn: "No surprises"), which gives the business a preemptive advantage with customers who seek assurance of consistency and permanence.

Preemptive Conditions That Exploit a Rival's Strengths or Commitments

Preemptive opportunities are enhanced by selecting moves where the period of preemptive advantage is extended because the business' competitors are highly reluctant to respond because the move dilutes their strength, forces them to relinquish a major commitment, or precipitates antagonistic responses from powerful vested interest groups. This issue of response barriers, or lags in competitive reaction, is discussed in detail by MacMillan and McCaffery, (1982).

Evaluation of the industry in these terms can be used to anticipate which factors can delay responses from each competitor. If it appears that enough competitors will be delayed long enough to make a material difference in the competitive arena, then the preemptive move is justified.

Appropriate Response Cannibalizes Existing Strengths or Competitive Advantages. High reluctance to respond to a preemptive move occurs when the appropriate response by a competitor means that it must cannibalize an existing profitable product. If the existing product happens to be distributed by independent distributors, this resistance can be transferred to distributors if they also generate high profits from this product. The response can even be resisted by employees (or unions), if the competitor's remuneration system depends on the profits generated by the cannibalized product.

Appropriate Response Damages Competitor's Image, Tradition, or Strategy. Another factor that will slow down a competitor's response is when the competitor's image will be damaged (e.g., an "inexpensive Mercedes-Benz" is a contradiction in terms), company tradition will be overturned (e.g., Japanese shipbuilders cared less about the western traditions of ship building; the western builders clung to their traditions and were totally out-performed), or the competitor will have to abandon or divert from a major strategic direction (this is usually accomplished by a company that enters the industry with a substitute product; the industry ignores the substitute until the established companies are really hurting).

Appropriate Response Threatens a Major Investment. A third source of response lags occurs in any place in an industry chain where a major investment is threatened by the appropriate response to the preemptive move. This can be an investment in the competitor's production capacity, distribution system, or supply system.

Appropriate Response Antagonizes Powerful Third Parties. The final area to identify whether responses to the preemption will be delayed is whether the appropriate response will antagonize powerful third parties, such as governments, unions, or powerful suppliers or distributors.

PREEMPTIVE OPPORTUNITIES ALONG THE INDUSTRY CHAIN

The industry chain can be viewed in terms of five major areas of opportunities for preemption: Supply system opportunities, product opportunities, process and production opportunities, customer opportunities, and distribution and service system opportunities.

This section includes an exposition of preemptive opportunities in each of the five major areas of the industry chain. In addition, factors that influence competitors' responses are discussed. Each major opportunity area has several targets for preemption, which are described with supporting examples from actual cases. This necessarily calls for a lengthy discussion. Therefore, the section has been organized so that the reader may scan the first part of each subsection to identify key preemptive targets (also summarized in Table 9-1), then return to a detailed reading of those major areas where a detailed exposition is sought.

Supply System Opportunities

There are three targets for preemption in the supply system:

1 Secure access to raw materials and components
2 Preempting production equipment
3 Dominating supply logistics

Critical Raw Materials and Components. The supply of raw materials and components may be preempted: By securing the major sources of key raw materials (as International Nickel did), the preemptor can hamstring competition. Alternatively, preempting access to critical components in a time of high growth in demand can give the focal firm a major advantage. For instance, Atari was a major market share beneficiary because it had secure supply sources during the shortage of integrated circuit chips created when video games took off. In this period, even as large a company as General Electric, which was preparing to take advantage of a substantial demand for new micro-

TABLE 9-1   Sources of Preemptive Opportunities

Supply Systems
1. Secure access to raw materials or components
2. Preempting production equipment
3. Dominating supply logistics

Product
1. Introducing new product lines
2. Developing dominant design
3. Positioning
4. Securing accelerated approval from agencies
5. Securing product development and delivery skills
6. Expanding scope of the product

Production Systems
1. Proprietary processes
2. Aggressive capacity expansion
3. Vertical integration with key suppliers
4. Securing scarce and critical production skills

Customers
1. Segmentation
2. Building early brand awareness
3. Training customers in usage skills
4. Capturing key accounts

Distribution and Service Systems
1. Occupation of prime locations
2. Preferential access to key distributors
3. Dominance of distribution logistics
4. Access to superior service capabilities
5. Development of distributor skills

processor-based appliance products it had introduced, was seriously hampered in its expansion due to lack of access to computer chip supplies. Note that the preempted "supplies" need not be physical. For decades the ability to preempt a few critical data sources has secured particularly enduring niches for data services companies: Once one company has signed up the dozen or so most prestigious professional sources and/or publications, its competitors cannot develop a viable alternative service with those data sources that remain. The preempted component or supply need not be particularly exotic; on one occasion an overseas brewer was able to thwart an attack on its new product introduction by preempting a large part of its competitors supplies of returnable beer bottles. Lacking sufficient bottles to sell the increased volume of business it expected, the competitor retracted a massive advertising campaign that it had poised to swamp the brewer's new product introduction. On the other hand, a preempted material or component *can* be highly exotic; Cargill's recent development of a dramatically more productive hybrid wheat seed, supplied to the farmers who in turn supply Cargill with grain, will preempt sustained "loyalty" on the part of the farmers.

Production Equipment. Supply of production equipment may also be preempted: When double knit fabrics were first introduced in the United States, the equipment to produce such fabrics had to be secured from a single supplier, located in West Germany. One of the textile producers in the United States was able to preempt a dominant market position by placing sufficient orders with the German equipment supplier to tie up its production capacity for 18 months. (This is an example of a preemptive move that was not particularly successful: The U.S. public did not take to double knit fabrics and the expected growth in those fabrics did not materialize; however the preemptive move *did* limit the number of competitors that eventually entered the double knit market.)

Supply System Logistics. The third area where it is possible to preempt is in supply system logistics. For instance, a considerable advantage accrued to oil companies that preempted "pipeline space" in the pipelines that pumped crude oil from well sources to refineries in the Northeast, so much so that Justice Department intervention (another risk of preemptive actions) eventually occurred. "First-in-line" or priority access to railroad cars or shipping holds creates major advantages to the preemptor of that access, particularly if specialized carriers are needed (such as refrigerated or high pressure conveyances).

So, in scanning the supply system for opportunities to preempt, it is useful to look at supply of production equipment, supply of materials and components, and the logistical systems needed to deliver these materials and components to see if there is an existing, or an emerging, possibility of seizing a competitive advantage by securing access to a critical part of the supply system, and for some time denying it to the competitors.

Response Barriers Inhibiting Competitive Reactions. Clearly, the securing of supply access has its own risks, since access is usually secured via vertical integration or long-term contract. Not only does this carry the danger of locking the focal firm in to a commitment that may turn sour later, but it may also create problems for the focal firm itself, by making it slow in responding to preemptive moves by its adversaries: Many a backward integrated firm has been extremely reluctant to counter a preemptive strike by some brash new competitor with a substitute material (like plastic replacing wood or metal, or aluminum replacing steel or copper) because it has found itself either with long-term supply contracts or owned subsidiaries that lock it into the challenged material.

Conversely, a major way in which to screen for preemptive opportunities is to preferentially select any preemptive option that, if selected, would force the competitors to abandon existing contractual agreements or discontinue subsidiaries in order to respond. Situations like this are likely to make the preemptive move much more effective and enduring, because the competitors' responses will be delayed by their reluctance to pay the "adjustment cost" involved in canceling the contracts or divesting the subsidiary.

Product Opportunities

As far as the product/service itself is concerned, there appear to be six target areas in which to seek preemptive opportunities:

1 Via new product introductions;
2 By developing the dominant design of the product;
3 By skillful positioning of the product;
4 By preempting accelerated approval programs where regulatory approval is required;
5 By securing the major share of product development and delivery skills; and
6 By expanding the scope of the product.

New Product Introductions. The first, and most obvious, product preemption is the introduction of *innovative products* that have a proprietary position. Even for nonpatentable products and services, however, it may be possible to develop a proprietary position by virtue of the company's *credibility* or image as being a successful innovator: For years Citibank was able to preempt new product opportunities because it was known as an aggressive product innovator whose new products "worked." So its clients regarded it as credible and effective, and quickly embraced Citibank's new product introductions in preference to similar offerings by less credible competitors. In recent years this type of preemptive advantage has also accrued to Merrill Lynch and Shearson-American Express.

Dominant Design. A more challenging opportunity to preempt occurs when the object is to capture the next generation *dominant design* of a product. Interactions between producers and the market they serve can be viewed as experiments in which the most desired characteristics of the product are eventually articulated by market forces. Then, as Abernathy and Utterback (1978) point out, there emerges a "dominant design" that incorporates all these desired characteristics and features, and becomes the standard for industry. This dominant design persists until new needs in the market, or new technologies, reinitiate the articulation process. A company can attempt to preempt the next dominant design: This is a huge challenge that requires an in-depth understanding of both market and technology, and a willingness to invest large amounts of funds "placing the chips" on big bets. IBM is the epitome of this type of preemption; for decades it has preempted successive dominant designs, in mainframe computers (the system 360 being the most dramatic) and even in typewriters. Currently, IBM appears to be seeking the dominant design in personal computers (perhaps as a route to the microprocessor market). Similarly, Boeing has consistently preempted generations of dominant design commercial aircraft, the most recent being the 767. This type of preemption is not confined to "hard" goods: McDonalds developed a dominant design for fast food restaurants, while Pillsbury deliberately experiments (by continually changing decor, ambiance, and menus) to create dominant design restaurants.

Positioning of the Product. There are a multitude of opportunities for preempting via positioning, and many "positions" that could be occupied. Quality, service, size ("preferred second source"), price, geographic region, demographic group, product value and reliability are but a few that have been successful; the number of other options are limited only by the imagination of the strategist.

Accelerated Approval. A fourth opportunity for product/service preemption occurs in those highly regulated industries where the product or service requires a regulatory approval process that takes an extended period. Here it may be possible to preempt the market by persuading the agency involved to agree to an accelerated approval program with the company, so the product moves ahead of those of the competition. The first company to secure accelerated approval has virtual exclusivity, since logistics usually preclude the agency from handling more than one acceleration of approval. This happened with anti-ulcer drug therapy products, where one company's product got out of the regulatory pipeline well ahead of others due to an accelerated approval program.

Product Skills. A fifth possibility for preemption is securing the lion's share of the pool of product skills needed to develop and deliver the product to the market place. For years the degree to which companies were successful in electronics depended on their being "*the* place to work" for the best electronics engineers; the same is now happening in genetic engineering. In particular, the astute strategist may be able to anticipate what key new skills may be needed, and will be in short supply, in the future. For instance, it can be argued that in the 1980s, a determining factor in Third World sales of large complex capital equipment to governments will not be engineering skills as much as skills at developing and communicating (in Third World languages) creative financing deals that take into account fluctuation in currencies, international balances of payment, and the evolution of the relevant local economies, and then tying these deals in with international banks. The engineering and technical skills associated with the product are no longer sufficient conditions for a sale. Those companies that can secure the best experts from the limited pool of multi-lingual financing managers with international banking contacts may be able to preempt a number of initial goverment purchases. (Once the first sale of more complex capital goods are made it becomes inordinately costly in training, spares, and service to buy the second item from another supplier. These switching costs become barriers to subsequent sales by competitors.) Similarly, it is almost inevitable that commodities businesses are going to be able to preempt positions in many countries that are facing escalating foreign exchange problems if they can secure the dominant share of those few experts in the structuring of international *bartering* deals.

Expanding Scope of the Product. A final option involves preempting the opportunity to expand the scope of the product or service being offered. Merrill Lynch, for instance, created the cash management account, which offered "one stop" banking service to wealthy individual consumers who wanted checking, savings, securities, and trust services under one account. Their software to support this service has now been patented and they have effectively secured a dominant position in the most lucrative segment of the retail market. In a similar way, CTI, a container leasing service company, was the first to offer full container service leases (administration, loading, transportation, repairs, and positioning of empty containers, not just financial leases to finance the purchase of containers). They support this full service via suitable facilities at primary *and* secondary ports world wide, including the Union of Soviet Socialist Republics, India, and the People's Republic of China, and have thus preempted a major share of the entire international market (currently about 20 percent). Product expansion preemptions may be difficult to counter by traditional competitors, who often have neither the skills nor the inclination to expand their offering in turn. The extreme form of this preemption is when Kodak preempted part of the consumer camera market by producing film compatible only with Kodak cameras (once again this preemption was perhaps too effective—competitors brought suit).

Response Barriers That Inhibit Competitive Reactions. In screening preemptive options, it is important to preferentially select opportunities where an effective response from competitors may be delayed. As far as product preemptions are concerned, response lags occur primarily when an appropriate response requires that the competitor cannibalize an existing profitable product; for example, Savin's low price copier line vs. Xerox, NOW accounts vs. traditional savings accounts, or Pepsi's low calorie colas vs. Coke's traditional cola. Alternatively, the competitive response may be slowed because the appropriate response is damaging to the image of the competitor, as occurred when generic drugs attacked brand name drugs. Finally, commitments to powerful interest groups, or interference by these groups, may delay responses to preemptive product moves: World Airways was able, after deregulation, to preempt several low price but high density routes ahead of other low fare airlines. Meanwhile, the established airlines were locked into expensive union contracts with various professional employee unions and could not cut rates themselves.

Process and Production Opportunities

There are four major targets for preemptive action in the area of process and production:

1 Develop proprietary production processes.
2 Undertake aggressive capacity expansion.
3 Vertically integrate with key suppliers.
4 Secure scarce and critical production skills.

Production Innovation. The obvious preemptive opportunity is to develop innovative (preferably proprietary) production processes that dramatically reduce the cost of the product, particularly if learning curve benefits allow the product to be produced with high reliability and dependable quality at high volumes. A dramatic recent example is the successes of Japanese producers with the 64K RAM chip.

Aggressive Expansion of Capacity. Another obvious preemptive opportunity lies in the aggressive *expansion of capacity* ahead of demand, to discourage less aggressive opponents. Du Pont's success in titanium dioxide is notable here. Aggressive expansion is the classical preemptive move. Hambrick (1983), in his comprehensive analysis of industry settings and associated successful strategies, found evidence that entire industries may be held in a condition of orderly competition by what he terms a "gendarme" strategy—a strategy whereby a dominant competitor maintains order by keeping surplus capacity as a weapon for strong-arming any other competitor that steps out of line.

Vertical Integration. Being the first company to undertake vertical integration allows the preemptor to acquire, at a good price, the most reliable and lowest cost suppliers. This move also leaves competitors at the mercy of higher cost or less reliable suppliers.

Production Skills. Preemption of critical production skills needed to produce the product, such as die makers, precision machinists, or other skilled workers, has often given particular companies the competitive edge, especially in the construction or military contract business. At present there is a critical need for graphics programmers in the video games industry. The next generation of dominant manufacturers/assemblers will probably be those that have cornered the market in engineers and technicians skilled in robotics, and there will be distinct advantages to those foundries that can secure the few engineers who can redesign and manufacture products using modern casting technology.

Response Barriers That Slow Counterresponse. Preemption is virtually assured when competitors' major investments in processes or production capacity are threatened by the appropriate countermove, and the competition is reluctant to write off this investment. In the last decade huge market shares, or entire industries, have been preempted by foreign competition because of the (perfectly natural) reluctance of U.S. companies to write off enormous amounts of production capacity that would have been made obsolete by new technology (steel production), by changing demand (compact autos), or by substitution (electronics). If the appropriate response to a preemptive move forces the competition to write off a major investment in production capacity, then the probability of preemptive success is high and the option should receive high priority.

Customer Opportunities

The four key targets for preemptive opportunities with customers are:

1 Segmentation of the market;
2 Building brand awareness by capturing early usage via reduction of risk of trial;
3 Training customers in key skills; and
4 Capturing key accounts.

Segmentation of the Market. The obvious opportunities to preempt customers are by specifically focusing on, and serving very well, particular segments in which the firm specializes. Segmentation opportunities are once again limited by the imagination of the strategist.

Early Usage and Brand Awareness. It is important to note that with new (or substantially redesigned) products and services, the credibility and acceptance of the product poses a problem, and it may be possible to preempt a dominant position by rapidly building brand awareness with and product acceptance by opinion-leading initial customers. To accomplish this, it could be highly effective to reduce the "risk of first trial" for these initial customers, particularly if the product is a substitute for an existing product and there is some reluctance to take the risk of switching. For example, by guaranteeing performance, and agreeing not to bill the customer until the product had been proven, a synthetic cloth company was able to persuade an initial group of influential industrial customers to replace their cotton filter cloth applications with synthetics. With these influential orders in hand, it was easy to convince other customers to place orders. So by reducing the risk for the first few purchasing agents, the synthetic cloth producer was able to preempt the business from its other, less aggressive, competitors. The foothold thus created proved to be of lasting benefit. Reduction of risk strategies can be particularly powerful for preempting footholds in international markets, where customers may be leery of risking their resources (or their professional reputations) on an untried product from an unknown foreign supplier.

Customer preemption is particularly important if the switching costs are high. It may pay handsomely to preempt initial positions with customers by making the financing of the first deals as easy as possible, so as to secure the initial sale—a ploy popular with many equipment manufacturers. If the customers ever switch to another supplier, they face the problem of stocking two inventories of expensive spare parts.

Enhancing Customer Skills. A third area for preemptive opportunities is identification of key skills needed by the customer to use or sell the product effectively and providing training in those skills. For instance, long before computer programming courses were part of the curriculum for high schools, IBM recognized a need for programming capabilities for its customers and preempted staunch support on the part of programmers and companies alike with its extensive programming schools. Similar strategies are allowing word processing companies to preempt customer segments by conducting word processing training programs in special areas such as legal, government agencies, building or government contractors, architects, consultants.

Key Accounts. Finally, a major area of opportunity is identifying and preempting key accounts. This approach was used with success by the first insurance companies that decided to "invade" the group pension fund market and secured the "cream of the crop" in pension fund accounts, and by Citibank and Chase Manhattan when they moved into international markets and rapidly "occupied" all the major countries before the competition could do so.

Response Barriers That Slow Competitive Reactions. Long standing relations with powerful customers can act as a serious brake on competitors' responses to a preemptive move. In a study by Harrigan (1980), a number of companies in declining businesses were held in behind exit barriers by powerful customers that did not wish to see all competitors leave the industry after one or two had made preemptive exit moves.

Harrigan also found occasions where the focal company was able to exit the industry by preemptively selling the business to a supplier or customer, striking the best deal ahead of more tardy competitors who subsequently got less attractive deals or no deals at all.

Distribution and Service Options

For delivery and service systems, there are five key targets:

1 Occupation of prime locations
2 Preferential access to key distributors
3 Control of distribution logistics
4 Access to superior service systems
5 Development of distributor skills

Occupation of Prime Locations. First is the preemptive occupation of prime locations. To this day, John Deere is acknowledged as having the most effective distribution network in agricultural machinery and occupies the "prime distribution" position in many U.S. states. Sears has been able to occupy prime locations in retailing; McDonalds has built prime locations in fast food; and Holiday Inns has occupied prime locations in accommodation.

Key Distributors. A second opportunity is preemption of exclusive or dominant access to key distributors. Particular attention needs to be given to opportunities to preempt *new* distributors. Coca Cola's aggressive moves into the *major* fast food chains (like McDonalds) secured for them a lasting niche in this new distribution channel, while BIC (ball-point pens) and L'Eggs (pantyhose) preempted the originally "nontraditional" supermarket chains to lasting advantage. The efficacy of such preemptive moves into new distribution channels is particularly enhanced by the fact that the competitors are often hamstrung in their responses by their own very powerful *existing* distributors.

Distribution Logistics. Opportunity may lie in preempting the distribution logistics. Cargill, by building a huge modern infrastructure of grain terminals with unit train loading and off-loading facilities in key locations, and specialized fleets of railroad cars and export vessels, was able to forge a position as one of the five dominant grain dealers in the world; AT&T was able for decades to dominate the long distance call market with its long-lines network; the major soft drink producers were able to secure equally long lasting niches by the preemptive licensing of local bottlers; and major perishable food manufacturers such as Pillsbury preempted prime retail space by installation of freezers and coolers.

Service Systems. Another powerful source of preemptive opportunities lies in the area of service. Particularly in the United States, where labor costs of skilled workers are very high, there are emerging radically different service challenges. To name but one: Demographic trends towards families in which both partners work are creating new opportunities for packaging an appliance offering in which high reliability, utilizing diagnostics from installed microprocessors, minimize service needs. This could preempt important niches in the major appliance business. Sears is currently experimenting with "one stop" servicing of *all* appliances in a home with each visit, which could preempt a niche for that growing segment of families where nobody is at home during normal working hours.

Distributor Skills. A fifth opportunity lies in identifying key existing or emerging skill requirements among distributors and preempting distributor loyalty by providing such skills. Many a supplier has carved a relatively long-lived niche in the market by offering services, such as inventory or merchandising, or training schools to train managers and employees of these distributors. In a similar vein, First Bank of Minneapolis is gearing up for interstate banking by securing many of the best regional banks as franchisees of its First Interstate System, which provides complex software systems and support skills that regionals need to operate a modern bank.

Response Barriers That Affect Competitive Reactions. In screening preemptive options, it is important to investigate the extent to which the appropriate response by competitors to the preemptive move may antagonize a powerful distributor network, as Scripto did when attempting to follow BIC into the supermarkets or as some designer clothes manufacturers found when they wished to enter lower price distribution chains. Alternatively, the competition may find itself reluctant to scrap a major investment in its own distribution system (as will many commercial banks who have invested in "brick and mortar" branches, if they wish to match Citibank in electronic funds transfer.) Competitors with such problems are sure to be slowed down as they overcome their reluctance to make the countermove. This enhances the effectiveness of the preemptive move.

OPPORTUNITIES FOR DECISIVE PREEMPTION

One other factor that must be taken into account in assessing the competitive environment for preemption possibilities is the stage of development of the product. As the product moves through the stages of the life cycle, major strains are placed on different parts of the industry infrastructure. These pressures on the infrastructure create highly challenging opportunities for *decisive preemption*, where the company that is fortunate enough to grasp this opportunity can expect a period of sustained advantage over competitors. This type of preemptive move is not easy to pull off. If it *can* be pulled off, however, it is devastating because the destiny of an entire industry can be determined by it.

Decisive Preemption in the Introductory Stage

In the introductory stage of the product life cycle, the product is relatively unknown by users. The challenges are (1) to find a way to get the users to try and to accept the product and (2) to have the company emerge from this exposure to users as the reference by which all other companies' products are evaluated. Then, when the industry takes off into the growth stage, the company's product is firmly established as the dominant product in the minds of the customers. The essence of decisive preemption is what could be called *"denial of recognition"* to the competitors: Any preemptive move that denies competitors recognition in the introductory stage is decisive, for it leaves them still desperately trying to achieve acceptance of their product while the preemptor moves ahead into the growth phase.

A review of Table 9-1 for opportunities to accomplish denial of recognition reveals the following options:

- *Preempting brand awareness.* The most successful preemption of this type occurs when the company's name emerges as synonomous with the product (Kleenex, Xerox).

- *Preempting opinion leaders and early users* ensures early customer acceptance and builds the credibility of the business as a successful innovator for the business' products. Monsanto was able to preempt a dominant position in the herbicide business by capturing the attention of opinion-leading local farmers and agricultural colleges when it introduced its new Lasso herbicides.

- *Identifying and preempting key accounts,* where the dominant proportion of usage will occur. This not only ensures that maximum revenues are obtained for the minimum of the company's effort, but also denies the competitors a large base for recognition and the opportunity to articulate their product offering in the market place.

- *Preempting distribution channels,* particularly since there are usually few distributors who are prepared to carry the new product.

- *Preempting the dominant design* that emerges as the product moves into the take-off stage. The business' product then becomes the reference product in customers' minds, the yardstick by which customers compare, specify, and evaluate all other products in the market.

Decisive Preemption in the Growth Stage

In the high growth stage of the life cycle, those competitors that have managed to secure recognition now find that the demand for the product starts to take off exponentially. Thus major stresses are placed on logistical systems: the logistics of supply, production, and distribution. The essence of decisive preemption at this stage is via *denial of growth*: Preemption moves should be sought which will allow the company to develop a dominant position while denying growth opportunities to its competitors. This leaves the competitors still battling for viable positions when the full impact of direct competition hits them in the mature stage.

A review of Table, 9-1 reveals that the following are opportunities for decisive preemption in this stage.

- *Preemption of supply sources and supply logistics* is particularly important in this stage: It is vital that the business has access to supply, while the competitors suffer from supply shortages and disruptions.

- *Preemption of existing or emerging distribution logistics* assures that the product reaches the hands of the consumer, while those of the competitors do not.

- *Preemption of critical skills* in product and process design assures that the company is in a position to deliver the next generation of product and the services necessary to support it.

- *Preempting prime positions* is important. In particular, early identification of what the important segments of the future will be allows these positions to be occupied well ahead of the competition.

- *Preemption of the next generation product* is the key strategy for keeping the competition off balance and having to continually play catch up. When the competitors finally do catch up, yet another generation product is introduced.

Decisive Preemption in the Mature Stage

In the mature stage of the life cycle, it is no longer possible to "grow around" competition, so direct competition starts to heat up. The functions of the product have been clearly defined, and the need for those functions in the market have been clearly established. Customers understand the product well and increasingly start to demand value. Not only is there increased direct competition, but now that the product and its functions are well understood, major pressures from substitute products, which can also satisfy the needs, start to appear. In seeking decisive preemptive moves, the essence is in *denial of revenue* to the competition. Preemptive moves that deny revenue to competitors while enhancing revenue of the focal company leave the competitors weaker for each successive round of competition.

Scanning Table 9-1 reveals that the following opportunities can be sought for the mature stage:

- *Preemption of new production and distribution technologies* becomes decisive. Production technologies that allow the business to maintain low costs yet still deliver reliable products to increasingly fragmented demands of proliferating customer segments are critical. This tactic also requires innovative, low-cost distribution and service systems, which can efficiently deliver well-serviced products to those increasingly fragmented markets. These systems create cost advantages that enable the company to deliver the *value* that the increasingly discriminating customers start to demand.

- *Preemptive positioning* becomes a powerful weapon, especially for lower market share competitors. By now the customers are knowledgeable enough to embrace appeals that have the compelling characteristics discussed earlier.

- *Preemption of substitution* is often decisive in the mature stage. By substitution is meant much more than substitution of products; in the mature stage there are many opportunities for substituting. Besides product substitution, there are opportunities to preempt substitute activities in all of the following areas: supplies, components, raw materials, new methods of distribution and servicing, new supply channels, and new distribution channels. These areas are all vulnerable to substitution, and it is generally the mature industries that single-mindedly refuse to accept, let alone exploit, emerging alternatives. As a result, they find themselves preempted by businesses outside the traditional industry.

Decisive Preemption in the Decline Stage

Although the decisions are tough ones, the need to be able to make bold, preemptive moves is perhaps greater here than in any other stage of the life cycle. As Harrigan (1980) points out, the company has to face up to the fundamental strategic choices of exiting or staying and attempting to shape the consolidation of the industry.

The essence of decisive preemption lies in *denial of the best deal* to competitors. Regardless of whether the company elects to exit or stay on, the challenge is to be able to time the necessary exit or consolidation moves so that the firm, and not its competitors, gets the benefits of the best deal—generally a well-executed first deal which plays a decisive role in the subsesquent destiny of the industry.

Hence, if the company elects to exit, it should seek opportunities to:

- *Preempt the first sale* of the business to any key supplier or customer or other party (such as a government) who wishes to keep the industry "alive." This assures that a better price is obtained than when the last surviving businesses are attempting to sell out.

● *Preempt first exit* if intervention by any powerful third parties, such as suppliers, key customers, distributors, foreign governments, and unions, could prevent others from exiting. If the first out is likely to be the only one allowed out, it pays to preempt the exit.

On the other hand, if the business intends to stay on in the consolidated industry, then it needs to stay alert for the following preemptive imperatives:

● *Preempting the first consolidation move* secures the best of surviving businesses at a reasonable price. The remaining survivors then have fewer viable alternatives from which to choose.

● *Preemptive moves to shrink the business* ahead of others, as by trimming less profitable products, markets, and customers, creates cost advantages, which can then be used as weapons against more unwieldy competitors who have not yet shrunk their fixed cost base.

● *Preemptive sale of excess assets* assures that better prices are obtained for the assets because they precede the later flood of excess assets on the market.

● *Preemptive de-integration,* in a vertically integrated industry, frees the business from the difficulties of having to manage two stages of business in decline, while the competitors continue to do so.

In concluding this section on decisive preemption, it should be pointed out once again that preemptions are not risk-free. In fact decisive preemptions usually involve a level of risk that causes the more cautious competitors to balk: There are not too many competitors who will "place big chips" on a strategy that seeks to preempt a dominant design or a next generation product, a major new product, supply, or distribution system, or a major reduction in the company's scope and assets, for there is no guarantee that it will work well. However, if the business takes the calculated risk and succeeds, then a period of sustained competitive advantage is secured, and the payoff can be enormous.

PREEMPTIVE STRATEGY GUIDELINES

To summarize, there are five major steps to take in designing a preemptive move.

First, analyze the changing industry chain with the purpose of identifying emerging opportunities to exploit places in the chain where competitors are weak or have made little commitment. Key areas to identify are opportunities to reshape the infrastructure, opportunities to occupy prime positions, and opportunities to preempt psychological positions.

Second, recognize that to be effective, preemptive moves need not occupy *all* positions, nor need they preempt *all* competitors. It is sufficient to select any emerging opportunities that impact enough competitors, for long enough, to make a material difference in the industry. Sources of opportunities are listed in Table 9-1.

Third, there are some opportunities that are decisive, creating for the pre-emptor a period of sustained advantage. These decisive opportunities depend on the stage of the product's life cycle. In the introductory stage, moves that deny recognition to competition are decisive: Preempt user awareness and dominant design. In the growth stage, moves that deny growth to the competition are decisive: Preempt prime positions, next generation products, and supply, production, and distribution logistics. In the mature stage, moves that deny revenue to the competition are decisive: Preempt new production and distribution technologies and preempt substitutions. Low share businesses may preempt positioning. In the decline stage, moves that deny the best deal are decisive: Either preempt the best exit deal or preempt the best consolidation deals.

Fourth, recognize that preemptive moves cannot be undertaken without some risk. Therefore calculated risks are called for, and the extent to which a particular preemptive opportunity can be reversed later, if necessary, enhances its attractiveness.

Fifth, recognize that the benefits of preemptive moves are not permanent: Competitors will respond. Hence it is important to seek moves that can be implemented rapidly and to which competitors will respond slowly. Factors to consider in estimating the response of competitors are the extent to which an appropriate response by competitors will (1) cannibalize their existing products; (2) threaten a major investment they have made in supply, production, distribution, or service systems; (3) challenge the competitor's image, traditions, or major strategic thrust; or (4) antagonize powerful third parties with a vested interest in the competitor's response.

This chapter does not address the fact that preemptive moves can be made against parties *other* than competitors. In fact, preemptive moves are appropriate to secure an advantage over any institution, organization, or group whose behavior can have a substantive impact on the performance of a business: suppliers, distributors, unions, local or federal government agencies, public interest groups, and foreign organizations. For example, Northern States Power, under recent scrutiny by regulatory agencies and public interest groups who wanted to develop yet another set of regulations governing utility charges (this time to disadvantaged groups), preempted such regulation by offering discounts directly to the disadvantaged. The opportunities for preemption with groups other than competitors can be identified and developed by using the same approach described previously.

10

Turnaround Strategies

DONALD C. HAMBRICK

Columbia University

Today, with heated global competition, technological turbulence, high costs of capital, and maturing markets, situations requiring turnaround seem to be more common than ever. This chapter discusses the main issues and options confronting a turnaround manager, with some practical consideration of implementation. The perspective is that of a general manager responsible for a business unit, or of the chief executive of a single-business firm. A section on corporate-level issues regarding the turnaround of business units is also included.

OVERVIEW OF THE TURNAROUND SITUATION

Most firms would like to be performing better than they are, but only a fraction can be said to be in need of a "turnaround" as the word is meant here. A precise definition of a turnaround situation is not important, but it is useful to put rough boundaries on the terrain. As a starting point, a turnaround situation is defined as one in which business performance is persistently below some minimally acceptable level. So, a business whose mission is generating profits would be in a turnaround situation if it earned less than the firm's cost of capital. Excluded from the definition are businesses that are "moderate" performers and those whose poor performance is due to short-term industry cycles (such as cement and fertilizer companies.)

Distinguishing Features

For this chapter to be warranted, there must be something distinctive about turnaround situations. That is, turnarounds must call for a different way of thinking and different types of actions than do other strategic situations. Four factors serve to set apart turnaround situations from other strategic settings: limited resources, poor internal morale, skeptical stakeholders, and urgency.

- *Limited resources.* Almost by definition, a troubled firm has limited resources for improving its situation. Depending on how long the firm has been performing poorly, a turnaround manager can encounter a situation of high debt levels, overextended payables, and aged plant. Banks and the parent firm are usually reluctant to infuse more funds. For example, Herbert Sams took over the presidency of ailing Scripto in 1971, following three years of losses. Retained earnings were at a 10-year low, debt (most of it current) was at an all-time high, fixed assets were dated, and the bloated inventories were generally unsalable. This situation is not unusual for the turnaround manager. The challenge for such a manager is to work with what is available, find ways to stretch resources, and find terrain that somehow tolerates the firm's sharply restricted resources. Some of the strategies open to managers in other settings—aggressive pricing, heavy advertising, product development, and plant modernization—are effectively ruled out because of limited resources, at least in the short run.

- *Poor internal morale.* The turnaround manager usually confronts a dismal personnel situation. If the firm has been a long-time poor performer, there are probably few talented or aggressive people left. A general malaise will have set in, such that even if there are capable people who remain, they will feel sapped. Even in situations where a downturn has been recent, it is not unusual to find poor morale, bickering among units, and lack of confidence among employees at all levels. A common wag among turnaround specialists is "All the stars are circulating their résumés, while the deadwood is circulating the water cooler." It is not enough that the turnaround manager has limited financial resources. The people needed to apply those resources creatively are usually in short supply or in disarray.

- *Skeptical stakeholders.* An organization exists in a broader environment and is dependent on certain stakeholders in that environment. Examples of stakeholders are suppliers, creditors, distributors, franchisees, and unions. For the troubled firm, there is a natural tendency for these parties to withdraw support, especially if they feel that they have viable alternatives. For example, at its darkest hour in the late 1970s, Kentucky Fried Chicken's franchisees threatened class-action suits that would have allowed them all to go their own way. In fact, Hicks Waldron, the chief executive of parent company Heublein, who oversaw the Kentucky Fried Chicken turnaround, speaks of letters, phone calls, and meetings on almost a daily basis, in which key parties threatened to "pull the plug." The turnaround manager is not only in a position of having to work with limited resources. There is also the threat that even those resources will be taken away.

- *Urgency.* Taken together, the above factors clearly suggest the fourth distinguishing characteristic of turnaround situations: Time is of the essence. Unlike the manager of a more stable status quo operation, the turnaround manager must act promptly, since allies are getting restless, key employees are preparing to leave, and competitors typically are making rapid inroads. Poor corporate performance, gone unchecked, becomes a rapidly deteriorating spiral. This urgency has implications for the ways in which decisions must be made, for the substance of those decisions, and for the sequence of actions.

What is clear is that the turnaround manager basically only gets one round of moves. Everything attempted must work; there is no slack; there is no organizational resilience; patience is frayed. Therefore, the selection of moves must be sound, and the orchestration must be smooth.

For many writers, such a situation evokes colorful imagery for describing the turnaround manager: the swashbuckling Green Beret parachuted in with a knife in his teeth. In this chapter, a different theme emerges. The turnaround situation is one of awesome responsibility, where many jobs, careers, and financial and physical resources lie in the balance of a few key decisions. Analysis must be quick, but not cavalier. Turnaround managers have an important job, but they do not operate from on high. They must know the limitations of their data and their limitations in acting on the data.

Stages of the Turnaround

Most turnarounds can be thought of as having three stages: crisis, stabilization, and rebuilding.[1] In practice, these stages are blurred together and cannot possibly be conducted in strict sequence. But, knowing about them gives the turnaround manager some sense of the ground that needs to be covered.

---

[1] Charles H. Hofer, "Turnaround Strategies," *Journal of Business Strategy* (Spring 1980), pp. 19-31; Donald B. Bibeault, *Corporate Turnaround: How Managers Turn Losers Into Winners* (New York: McGraw Hill Book Co., Inc., 1982); Donald C. Hambrick and Steven M. Schecter, "Turnaround Strategies for Motive Industrial-Product Business Units," *Academy of Management Journal* (Fall 1983), pp. 45-57.

It is tempting to treat "evaluation" as the first discrete stage in a turn-around. After all, the manager needs a period—even a brief one—in which to gather data and deliberate on alternative courses of action. But, it is preferable to view evaluation as something that is done throughout a turnaround, not only at its start. The front-end planning needs to be done, but it cannot be exhaustive. All of the contingencies cannot be foreseen at the outset. Throughout the entire turnaround effort, the manager is re-evaluating and adjusting course. There is an incremental element to turnarounds, just as there is to any other strategic situation—possibly even more.[2]

The features of the three stages are as follows:

- *Crisis.* Depending on the severity of the situation, the manager's first task is to ensure the survival of the business. This primarily means arresting cash outflow, or what many turnaround specialists call "stopping the bleeding." This can involve small steps such as putting clamps on accounts payable or instituting restrictive travel and expense account policies. It can also mean major steps such as disposing of inventories, closing down or selling plants, and firing people.

- *Stabilization.* After the trauma of the crisis stage, the task is to stabilize the remaining operations. The company is no longer shrinking, but it is not growing, nor is it capable of growth. Attention is directed at improving margins, fine-tuning the product mix, targeting new high-return market segments, and seeking new efficiencies. New control and information systems are often put in place. At this point, these systems are not elaborate; they are only the minimum necessary to support the firm's quest for stability and breathing room.

- *Rebuilding.* Only after successfully dealing with the crisis and stabilizing the firm can the turnaround manager attempt once again to expand the business. In the rebuilding stage, several activities of an entrepreneurial quality can be started or accelerated: product development, aggressive marketing campaigns, and asset renewal/expansion. In addition, more ambitious programs can be started in the areas of human resource development, control, and information systems. In many respects, the rebuilding stage is like any other strategic situation, since many of the extraordinary features of the turnaround will have passed. If the firm is lucky, the lessons learned will remain.

There are no convenient rules of thumb to predict how long each of these stages will last or how long the whole process takes. Obviously, the time periods vary depending on the severity of the situation, the nature of the industry, the size of the firm, and other factors. However, available research generally supports the time frame elaborated by one author[3]:

The length of time necessary to perform each stage can vary dramatically. It takes anywhere from two weeks to six months to make value judgements about a business. A small company takes two weeks; a billion dollar company takes six months. If you are going to liquidate parts of the business, it takes ninety days

---

[2] James B. Quinn, *Strategies for Change: Logical Incrementalism* (Homewood, Ill.: Richard D. Irwin, 1980).

[3] Bibeault, op. cit., p. 93.

from the time you decide to liquidate until you actually clean out the warehouse. If you are selling off segments of the business, it's a six-month process from the time you decide to sell. The period of stabilization takes six months to a year. The return-to-growth phase takes at least another year. Altogether, we are talking about anywhere from one to three years, with a $20 million company taking one year, and a [billion-dollar company] taking three years.

SITUATION ASSESSMENT

The turnaround manager's first task is to gather and analyze facts about the firm's situation. Since resources and time are limited, this assessment of the situation must often be less thorough than would otherwise be ideal. The manager must be creative and astute in deciding what types of analyses are most important and where the underlying data will come from.

Diagnosis of Severity

Just how bad is the company's situation? This is the starting point for the turnaround manager. A host of factors will eventually be of interest: morale, product quality, equipment reliability, and so on. But, at the broad level, the interest is financial: How far is the firm from making money, and how much longer can the bills be paid? The classic techniques for answering these questions are break-even analysis and cash-flow analysis.

- *Break-even analysis.* The technique of break-even analysis is discussed in most managerial accounting books, but its relevance usually eludes executives in healthy businesses. For turnaround managers, however, break-even analysis is of central importance. So, a brief review here seems appropriate.

  A firm's break-even point, as seen in Figure 10-1, is that level of volume at which revenues equal total costs. Total costs consists of two components: fixed costs and variable costs. Fixed costs, as the name suggests, do not vary with output levels. Examples of fixed costs are depreciation, supervisory salaries, interest, and advertising. In reality, of course, these costs are fixed over some range of output, but they can be adjusted if volume rises or falls sharply. For example, network television advertising comes in blocks of $50,000 that can be added to or dropped as volume warrants. Thus, a more accurate portrayal of fixed costs would be as a series of steps—level over a small range and then increasing abruptly. The schematic is much easier to follow, however, if the portrayal is perfectly flat, since this implies that these costs will occur regardless of volume.

  Variable costs are those that vary directly with volume. Direct labor, direct material, power, and sales commissions are examples of variable costs. Thus, when volume is zero, variable costs are at zero. For schematic simplicity, variable costs are portrayed here as rising in a linear relationship with volume, even though nonlinear relationships (through quantity discounts, critical mass efficiencies, and so on) are possible.

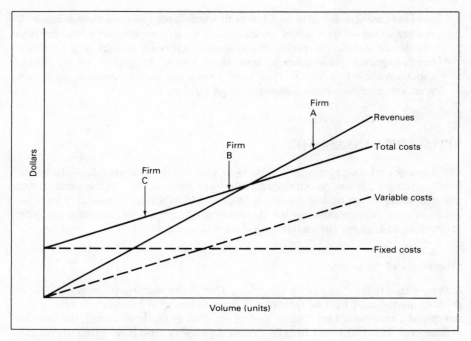

FIG. 10-1 Example of a Breakeven Chart

Strategic turnaround options are discussed in a later section. However, it is apparent at this point that the situations facing turnaround managers in Firms A, B, and C in Figure 10-1 are very different. Firm A is actually operating slightly above the break-even point. The firm has some leeway and may not have to pass through the crisis stage. To some extent, the managerial task in Firm A could be seen as fine tuning a generally viable enterprise. Firm B, operating slightly below the break-even point, is in a more serious situation, and will have to undertake more severe actions than Firm A. And, finally, Firm C, is far below the break-even point and faces the most radical reshaping of its volume/cost/capacity relationships. Firm C has to acknowledge that it is not going to be as large as its decision makers once thought that it would be.

• *Cash-flow analysis.* If break-even analysis gives an indication of the magnitude of the firm's problems, cash-flow analysis sheds light on the degree of urgency. There is nothing elaborate about preparing a cash forecast, and, in fact, it is more straightforward than preparing an earnings forecast. Usually, a cash forecast is broken out on a monthly basis. The starting point is today's cash on hand. To that is added the expected cash receipts for each month (accounts receivable stemming from earlier sales, less bad debts) and any special infusions of cash (e.g., from inventory liquidations and sale of assets). Then subtracted out are all expected cash outlays (such as wages, payables due, taxes due, and equipment purchases). The remaining figure is the expected cash balance at the end of the month.

It is not unusual for a healthy firm to develop projections in which cash flow for some months is negative. For the troubled business, there is the prospect of an unending procession of such months, and the turnaround manager needs to know how long it will be—under current conditions—until cash will be completely gone. Businesses that have a seasonal element—which most businesses do—need to do a particularly careful cash-flow analysis. Of course, businesses that are part of larger firms often have their parents' coffers to tide them through a severe period. But, even in such a case, a cash-flow analysis is important.

The use of break-even and cash-flow analysis provides opportunities for the turnaround manager to ask a variety of "What if" questions. For example, what would be the effect on cash flow if payables could be stretched out by another 30 days or obsolete inventories are disposed of? What would be the effect on the break-even point if a five-cent-an-hour concession is won from the union or if an underused facility is closed down? Asking these sorts of questions is a valuable way for the turnaround manager to grasp the dimensions of the situation. With the help of a qualified financial analyst who knows how to use any of the spreadsheet microcomputer software packages that are available today, the manager can profitably invest some portion of his or her time in the first six weeks on the job delving into these types of analyses. However, while analysis is crucial, it is just an adjunct to the data that the manager must gather from interaction with key managers, employees, customers, suppliers, and other sources. In fact, the turnaround manager who buries himself or herself only in sterile financial analysis will grasp only a small fraction of the situation.

Diagnosis of Cause

Decisions about how to turn around a business can be made intelligently only if there is an understanding of the key factors causing the poor performance. While it is true that no two turnaround situations are exactly the same, research on organizational failure has been strikingly consistent in identifying a limited number of common failure syndromes[4]:

- *Maladaptation.* A business is like any other organism embedded in an environment: It must adapt in order to survive and prosper. When a firm fails to revise its product to meet changing tastes, fails to change its way of competing to meet changes by competitors, and fails to differentiate itself from its competition, the firm is *maladapted.* The typical symptom of maladaptation is dwindling sales figures. If the turnaround manager plots sales and cost figures for the past few years and observes a drop-off in sales (either in absolute dollars or in market share), but no major changes in costs, the conclusion must be that the firm is maladapted (Figure 10-2a). Maladaptation means either that volume is down or prices are down, both of which indicate that the firm is not in attractive terrain or is not well-positioned within its terrain.

---

[4] John Argenti, *Corporate Collapse: The Causes and Symptoms* (New York: John Wiley and Sons, 1976), p. 40.

- *Poor controls.* Some firms are troubled primarily by poor internal controls. Their sales are relatively healthy, but they are lacking in their ability to monitor and manage their various cost and current asset categories. Poor controls are often especially a problem in firms that are growing rapidly and/or are growing by acquisition. A look at the recent sales and cost figures for a firm plagued by poor controls will reveal steady or even growing sales, rapidly increasing fixed costs (inventory carrying costs, general and administrative expenses), and ballooning variable costs (poor labor controls, inefficient purchasing, shipping and distribution, and bad-debt write-offs (Figure 10-2b).

- *Excessive risk-taking.* If the essence of management is risk-taking, then the essence of good management is prudent risk-taking. Many firms end up in trouble because of excessive risk-taking—expanding at a rate in excess of the resources that the business will have available in the near future. The most typical form of this is "the big project"—especially new plant and equipment installed in advance of sales at hand. The recent sales and cost figures for such a firm are portrayed in Figure 10-2c. Usually, there is a healthy sales trend which encourages the firm to make a major expansion, resulting in a sharp increase in fixed costs. Unfortunately, sales do not increase as steeply as the fixed costs. It could be said that this is a problem of maladaptation; but, frequently in this situation, sales are occurring at a respectable rate, and overoptimism is the real culprit. Variable costs per unit may actually diminish, since the new plant may result in somewhat greater efficiencies. The net effect, however, is usually substantial overcapacity, depleted cash, and a heavy debt burden. Other forms of excessive risk-taking are acquisitions, launching a new product, bulk purchase of materials, or any obligation that is large in relation to the resources of the firm.

    For the turnaround manager, there is a great irony in the excessive risk situation. Often, the situation is more severe than one brought on by maladaptation or poor controls. That is, the gulf between costs and sales can be very great. However, the source of the problem tends to be more isolated. It is not as likely that there is widespread malaise, chaos, or ineptitude throughout the firm, as there would tend to be in other turnaround situations. Thus, the manager may have more reliable resources in the form of people, organization, and processes with which to work.

- *"Uncontrollables."* This term is put in quotes because managers are prone to attribute their problems to forces outside their control. It is true that factors such as foreign competition, government actions, technological discontinuities, and natural disasters can play a major part in crippling a firm. But, only some subset of such circumstances—probably a small one—is totally unforeseen or unmanageable. Management needs to be vigilant about such possibilities; it must navigate so as to avoid their potential impact, and it must find creative ways to respond when they do occur.[5] The turnaround manager must decide whether the problem really has emanated from the outside or whether the problem is systemic, and resides in some fundamental internal weakness that needs to be dealt with.

---

[5] Michael P. Porter, *Competitive Strategy* (New York: Free Press, 1981).

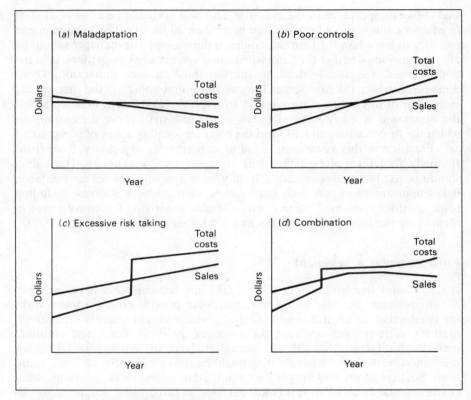

FIG. 10-2 Some Common Failure Patterns

- *Combinations.* Many turnaround situations, of course, stem from some combination of the problems described above. Often, one weakness brings on another: The firm encounters one form of trouble, and then acts in a way that brings on another type of problem. The financial symptoms of such a firm are portrayed in Figure 10-2d.

What should be clear from this discussion is that even though the details of turnaround situations occur in endless variety, there are some major commonly recurring classes of turnaround situations. As we shall see, strategic responses can also be grouped in ways to help managers find the most logical matches between sources of problems and avenues for recovery.

Internal Assessment

The turnaround manager should delve beyond financial indicators in order to determine the firm's strengths and weaknesses. He or she must conduct an internal analysis quickly and with generally sketchy information. Thus, the manager must target the inquiry. One way to proceed is to identify the dimensions of key importance in the industry. This will normally be a list of at least five factors, but it should not contain more than 20 factors. Then, the manager must try to learn how the firm rates on each dimension. The manager should be able to conclude whether the firm, when rated against key competitors, is in the bottom third, the middle third, or the top third on each dimension. Those dimensions where the firm scores low are those that either (1) the firm should steer clear of in crafting a turnaround strategy, or (2) the firm must correct if the dimension is a key survival factor in the industry. Those dimensions on which the firm is strong should form the basis for locating a way of competing.[6]

Precision in this assessment is not as important as objectivity, since firms routinely fool themselves as to their strengths and weaknesses. Hard data should be used whenever available. If only subjective impressions are available, it is important to obtain such impressions from multiple sources, including some outside "objective" parties, with the aim of striving for convergence in identifying the firm's real strengths and weaknesses.

Environmental Assessment

A turnaround attempt must, of course, take into account what is occurring in the environment. Strategy books and articles can provide excellent frameworks for conducting an environmental analysis, which should address technology, markets, competitors, suppliers, the economy, political scene, and cultural/demographic factors. As with an internal analysis, the environmental assessment must be done more hastily than might be the case in other strategic situations. So, here again, targeting is important. Some examples of questions about environmental factors that seem most germane in turnaround situations are the following:

1 How rigid are market shares? Can the firm realistically expect to increase its volume? As a product life cycle matures, customer loyalties become entrenched and competitors become more tenacious, such that certain turnaround avenues are effectively cut off.

2 What are the current pockets of market opportunity? For example, what segments are "hot" right now? In order to pull through the crisis era of turnaround, the firm may have to be opportunistic. Attention to long-term, secular trends can be postponed until the firm is ready for its rebuilding phase.

3 What are the firm's competitors doing? For example, are they leaving any vacuums that the firm can fill? Are they preempting some segments? Are there some inexpensive "me too" tactics that can be pursued?

4 What are the economics of this business? For instance, can some subassemblies be economically contracted out? Can goods be shipped from just one plant instead of three regional plants?

---

[6] Boris Yavitz and William H. Newman, *Strategy in Action* (New York: Free Press, 1982).

Sources of Information

A major frustration for the turnaround manager is that the information needed to do a situation assessment is often not at hand. After all, the company probably got into trouble because its management was not scanning the right information. Subordinates in the marketing and control functions, for example, may be completely in the dark on some important facts.

The turnaround manager must be creative and aggressive in pulling together the important facts. The first source is internal. It may be that the functional heads *do* have good data that the previous general manager had not asked for or had ignored. As discussed below, the turnaround manager must open up all information passageways, even if it means bypassing a functional head to tap into a subordinate's information base.

The firm has stakeholders who can be sources of good information. Suppliers and customers can be experts on the economics and competitive trends in the industry. Certainly, it is important to tap these sources regarding the firm's posture relative to competitors. Also, if the business is part of a larger corporation, it is likely that some line or staff units elsewhere in the firm are knowledgeable about key events and trends in the industry. Their expertise should be tapped, even though there is often a natural hesitance to go to the parent for advice or help.

In addition, there is an abundance of publicly available data on most industries. Trade journals, government statistics, industry yearbooks, and newsletters are good examples of data sources for the turnaround manager—especially one who is new to the industry. All of these sources, along with sparing use of consultants to help mold the data into a meaningful whole, can give the turnaround manager a reasonable picture of the firm's internal and external situation in as short a time as six weeks.

STRATEGIC COMPONENT OF TURNAROUND

At the heart of the decisions facing the general manager are those dealing with strategy: choices of where to compete (in terms of products and markets) and how to compete (e.g., asset structure, functional emphasis). Strategy is the topic of this section.

Generic Turnaround Strategies

Turnaround strategies, like the failure syndromes discussed above, can be concisely grouped: (1) revenue push, (2) cost cutting, (3) selective product/marketing pruning, (4) major retrenchment, and (5) combination strategies.[7] These options are listed roughly in ascending order of their degree of short-term unpleasantness, with revenue push being least traumatic and major retrenchment typically being the most traumatic for an organization. Each strategy con-

---

[7] Hofer, op. cit., pp. 19-31; Hambrick and Schecter, op. cit., p. 50.

sists of sub-moves that must "hang together" to allow it to succeed. As discussed below, the timing of turnaround strategies varies.

Revenue Push. In some turnaround situations, it is possible and appropriate to put the primary effort into increasing sales. Such a strategy can be successful only if market shares are not rigid and/or if niches exist where the firm can use some special advantage. A revenue push strategy, of course, requires that the firm have some underused competence in product development, sales, or marketing. If these functions are generally deficient, then a revenue push strategy will not succeed, at least not without first replacing or revitalizing the sales/marketing or product development staffs. At least one study has found that revenue push strategies are not often successful in mature industries.[8]

Since time and money are limited in a turnaround situation, a revenue push strategy must somehow be crafted so that large up-front outlays are not required. This usually rules out totally new products, where tooling, customer education, and sales force education are required. Instead, selective reintroductions of products earlier dropped, expansion to new geographic markets or to different types of users, and taking on subcontracting work to help fill capacity are among the relatively inexpensive and quick avenues open for expanding the revenue base.

Some mention should be made about the tactic of price cutting to build sales. In general, this is a flawed move in a turnaround situation. Usually, the turnaround firm does not have the financial resources to wage any sort of price war. And, as often as not, the turnaround firm—as part of its broader symptoms—does not have the efficiency edge that will allow it to have the lowest unit costs in the industry. Price cuts will only provoke retaliatory moves by stronger competitors who can generally afford even lower prices and who can sustain those prices for a longer period of time than the troubled firm. A wise revenue push strategy will involve differentiating and niche-seeking behavior and will avoid price cutting. The key seems to be in locating new markets based on competitors' weak spots.

Cost Cutting. Some turnaround situations are best dealt with by various forms of belt tightening, or cost cutting. Sometimes, such moves require careful negotiations, as when wage or work rule concessions are sought from a union. Other such moves can be made more unilaterally. Examples are decisions to cut advertising, research and development, travel/entertainment, or managerial pay, or to centralize purchasing. Also part of a cost-cutting strategy—although not involving costs per se—are attempts to drive down inventory levels and to seek quicker collection of accounts receivable in order to free cash.

A cost-cutting strategy has the advantage of achieving its results quicker than the other strategies. But, the magnitude of those results is usually limited. That is, in many circumstances, cost cutting alone is insufficient to turn the firm around. It is also important to note that cost cutting sometimes so enfee-

---

[8] Hambrick and Schecter, op. cit., p. 51.

bles the firm that it is sent into an even deeper slide, thus further delaying (or even ruling out) the eventual stabilization process.

Selective Product/Market Pruning. This strategy is aimed at having the firm focus on those arenas that are most lucrative or in which the firm's position is most defensible. Sometimes, whole product lines are dropped, but often, there is careful pruning of each product line's breadth and depth to get rid of marginally profitable items that proliferated during earlier good times. Sometimes, pruning will be done around market considerations—scrapping lines where demand is dwindling or where competition is fierce. And, sometimes, pruning will be done around competence considerations—scrapping lines where the firm is at a competitive disadvantage or is just a "me too" player whipsawed by stronger competitors.

A look at the profile of a firm after it has executed a pruning strategy will reveal some or all of the following changes:

- Decrease in sales by 10–20 percent
- Decrease in capacity utilization—letting least-efficient plants sit idle (or, ideally, disposing of the assets)
- Increase in gross margin percentages—the firm is now in lines where prices are stronger and where it has relative efficiency
- Decrease in marketing expenses and inventories as a percent of sales—the firm has a more homogenous set of customers and products, allowing for improved efficiencies in these areas
- Reduced receivables as a percent of sales—the firm drops marginal customers or those who exert a great deal of power over credit terms.[9]

Major Retrenchment. The most traumatic turnaround strategy is one that involves a major retrenchment. This strategy differs from the pruning strategy in terms of the magnitude of the cutbacks. Here, major plant closings and consolidations are required, and the primary aim is to reduced fixed costs and the asset base. Selection of this strategy amounts to an awareness that the firm simply cannot be as large as earlier decision makers thought it could be.

With this strategy, as with pruning, selectivity should be exercised. But the selectivity here is not nearly as fine, since more of the business must be closed down. Generally, only assets that are certain to be used in the near term should be kept. The sale of assets should be done aggressively but with great deliberation, since the sale price of most fixed assets can vary within a wide range, depending on timing and careful identification of interested buyers. Unfortunately for the firm, newer facilities are those that bring the highest price, so there is an obvious trade-off between how much cash the business will get and the quality of the remaining assets.

---

[9] Ibid.

TABLE 10-1   Matches Between Turnaround Situations and Strategies

Source of Problem	Severity of Situation	
	Mild	Grave
Maladaptation	Revenue push	Product/market pruning or major retrenchment
Poor controls	Cost cutting	Cost cutting or product/ market pruning
Excessive risk taking	Revenue push	Major retrenchment
Combination	Combination, with emphasis on revenue push and cost cutting	Combination, with emphasis on major retrenchment and cost cutting

Combination Strategies. In practice, the four turnaround strategies discussed above are often used in various combinations. Sometimes, if time allows, they are employed in series, for example, first pruning and then cost-cutting. Other times, the strategies are used simultaneously in a balanced effort. Such an approach is very complex, and usually requires a nucleus of talented managers in addition to the general manager. Still, this approach can be necessary if the firm's situation is severe and stems from multiple weaknesses.

Matching the Strategy With the Situation

Different situations call for different turnaround strategies. In order to discuss this "matching" process, the earlier classification of problem sources must be considered: maladaptation, poor controls, excessive risk taking, and "uncontrollables." A classification of the severity of the firm's troubles must be added to the list. Severity means the amount of negative gap between sales and costs. A firm making modest profits or operating just below the break-even point would be in a situation of mild severity. A firm operating well below the break-even point would be in a position of grave severity. The two classification schemes yield the framework for Table 10-1.

If maladaptation is the source of the problem and the situation is of mild severity, a revenue push strategy is logical. The firm has some financial resources with which to engage in new product/market initiatives. Its costs and assets are not necessarily out of line; rather, it primarily needs to update its offerings and to be more aggressive in the marketplace. Often, key marketing, sales, or product development personnel will need to be replaced to execute this strategy. If a maladapted firm's situation is of great severity, it will not have the resources to embark on any immediate entrepreneurial initiatives. Instead, selective product/market pruning or major retrenchment will probably have to be undertaken in order to refocus the business around a viable core. After stabi'ization has been achieved, product/market initiatives can be undertaken.

For a firm suffering from poor controls and facing a situation that is not severe, a cost-cutting strategy is generally appropriate. The primary emphasis must be on getting costs under control. Since the situation is not severe, the generally limited impact of a cost-cutting strategy may be sufficient to move the firm to much better health. On the other hand, if the situation is severe, a firm plagued by poor controls must often go beyond cost cutting and also engage in some form of scaling down—usually pruning. This is needed to allow the firm to become more manageable and to free up resources to see the firm through the turnaround.

If a firm is suffering the aftermath of excessive risk taking, but the situation is of mild severity, a revenue push strategy is often called for. The task is to achieve enough volume to fill the unused capacity. Since the situation is of mild severity, resources will often be available to engage in product/market development activities. If an excessive risk situation is severe—that is, if assets are far underutilized—then the realistic strategy is major retrenchment. It would be quixotic to attempt to achieve enough revenues to close such a huge gap, and cost cutting would barely make a dent and would not address the problem at all.

If "uncontrollables" are the primary cause of the firm's troubles, the strategy must be selected to respond to the particular circumstances. So many types of "uncontrollables" can occur that it is not possible to narrow down to one or two likely strategies here. (Uncontrollables are not included in Table 10-1 for this reason.) For example, a strike would suggest very different actions than would import dumping. Turnaround managers should ask themselves candidly whether the underlying problem really has been "uncontrollable" or whether there might not be some notable deficiency in the organization that will impede an effective turnaround.

If a combination of problems plagues the firm, then, logically, some combination of strategic moves is probably necessary. In situations of mild severity, an emphasis on revenue push and cost-cutting measures will often be sufficient to stabilize the firm. In situations of greater severity, the more stringent strategies of pruning and retrenchment must likely play major roles in a turnaround.

In sum, there are three key patterns evident in Table 10-1:

1 The turnaround strategy must somehow respond to the real source of the problem, not the imagined source.

2 Situations of mild severity can often be dealt with by use of the less traumatic strategies such as revenue push and cost cutting, whereas situations of grave severity require pruning or major retrenchment.

3 Situations of mild severity can often be dealt with by use of a single strategic theme; situations of grave severity usually call for multiple themes.

Common Patterns in Unsuccessful Turnarounds

Far from all turnarounds are successful. Some turnaround failures are generally hopeless situations in which no one could possibly succeed. Other failures can be traced to managerial mistakes in the turnaround attempt. There are three broad classes of such errors: overkill, underkill, and inconsistency.

Overkill is the managerial error of excess. An obvious example is when the turnaround manager cuts costs to the bone, only to drive out all talented employees, strangle the marketing effort, and slash product quality. A more subtle example occurs when the manager retrenches far more than is necessary. For example, as a result of the turnaround effort at A&P, the supermarket chain is just one-third the size it was in the early 1970s. Was that much cutback necessary? Some would say "yes." But the turnaround manager can reach the point where he or she only relies on more and more surgery to achieve his or her aims. This is unimaginative management, and the resulting tiny firm—even if it is healthy—is not a turnaround; it is a new firm consisting of reassembled leftovers. A turnaround can easily be a "success" if the finished product is only one-third the size of the original.

Underkill is the more common error of not doing enough. Often, turnaround managers will make relatively minor adjustments in the hope that they will be adequate for a turnaround. The most common is to cut costs in only one or two areas, for example, research and development or advertising. By and large, such cuts are trivial, even though they may be painful and momentous in the eyes of the management. (As noted above, sometimes, minor cuts are all that is needed.) Another form of underkill occurs when a strategy is poorly balanced. A relatively common example is the firm that attempts to expand its revenue base while allowing its efficiency and controls to deteriorate further. Clearly, the turnaround manager can avoid the polar pitfalls of overkill and underkill only by conducting an early and accurate situation assessment.

A final type of turnaround failure arises because of inconsistencies. In such an instance, the various components of the strategy are not mutually reinforcing and may even be flatly incompatible. An example found with striking frequency in one study is the firm that introduces a wave of new products at the same time that it cuts marketing expenses across the board.[10] Not only must the strategy fit the situation, but the individual pieces of the strategy must fit one with the other.

POLITICAL COMPONENT OF TURNAROUND

All businesses rely on striking favorable relationships with outside parties: suppliers, distributors, unions, and so on. For troubled businesses, attention to these links is especially crucial. This is because, as noted earlier, some stakeholders become skeptical and want to reduce their support for the troubled firm, just at the same time the firm needs more generous support. The successful turnaround manager must be able to conceive and execute an effective political component to the turnaround.

---

[10] Ibid.

The starting place in a political analysis is to determine the amount and nature of the vested interest each major party holds in the turnaround firm.[11] To the extent that a party is (1) very dependent on the firm, and (2) has few alternatives, there is the basis for political maneuvering, i.e., negotiation. At one extreme is a party who is barely dependent on the firm and who has many alternatives. For example, if a supplier provides a firm with only a small portion of its output, and/or if there are ample alternative buyers for that output, then there is not much of a basis for negotiation. And, in fact, this will be the type of external party who will most promptly sever ties with a troubled firm. At the other extreme is the case of the supplier who sells 50 percent of its output to a firm; and all of the firm's major competitors are vertically integrated backward and so have no interest in the supplier's output. Such a situation is fertile ground for political maneuvering by the turnaround firm.

The turnaround manager needs to look beyond simply financial considerations in determining how dependent an ally is on the firm and the nature of that dependence. The key factor to bear in mind is that decisions by allies—like decisions by all organizations—are made by people, not by a black-box profit maximizer. These people have values, career aims, and political battles peculiar to their own organizations. Examples of these varied types of vested interests are provided below. At this point, it is important to understand that the turnaround manager will often find it worthwhile to learn something about the inner workings of a stakeholder organization and the values and perceptions of its key decision makers.[12]

The turnaround manager should be imaginative and comprehensive in identifying potential allies. Suppliers, distributors, franchisees, unions, trade associations, government agencies, and even competitors are among the numerous groups who might have an important stake in the survival of the firm. Discussed below are political maneuvers involving these types of allies. That is followed by a discussion of political moves with a much more obvious constituency: creditors.

Arousing Support of Stakeholders

There are basically two ways to arouse support from stakeholders.[13] The first is to alter the substance of the situation so that the stakeholder is even more dependent on the firm and its survival. This usually takes time, resources, and a naive stakeholder—all of which are usually in short supply for a turnaround firm. The second approach is to alter the stakeholder's perception of the situation. This usually amounts to extending graphic reminders of how dependent the ally is on the firm and providing some clear picture of the consequences—short-term and long-term—if the ally does not make concessions. Since this basically involves making threats, which often evoke personal antagonism and hence stubbornness, it is sometimes necessary to communicate with an ally

---

[11] Ian C. Macmillan, *Strategy Formulation: Political Concepts* (St. Paul, Minn.: West Publishing Co., 1978).

[12] Ibid.

[13] Ibid.

through a third party—for example, a board member, trade association executive, or even the press.

Some examples of extracting concessions from allies are in order:

- A troubled manufacturing firm convinced a local union leader to support its bid to revise the labor contract by presenting a detailed analysis of the cost makeup of their product and of their most direct Asian competitor's product. The company went on to stress that they would be prepared to provide the press with these figures. The national union had recently been the object of negative publicity regarding its intransigence in the face of inexpensive, high-quality imports and was eager to appear more flexible in negotiations. Since the local leader aspired to office in the national union, his cooperation was secured, and the contract negotiation was successful.

- Harley Davidson, the only maker of motorcycles in the United States, was able to obtain strict quotas on competing imports. Because it is a small company, its appeal could not possibly be on the grounds of overall economic impact. Instead, it sought out key parties in Washington and built a subtle, emotional appeal about the uniquely American "Harley," and how this instance of David and Goliath was a precursor of future such problems.

- Troubled Hudepohl Brewing Company, which serves primarily its hometown of Cincinnati, is able to get preferential shelf space and retailer support because it constantly reminds the dealers—sometimes explicitly, sometimes subtly—of the uncomfortable squeeze they will feel if Hudepohl (with about 25 percent of the Cincinnati market) were gone and only giants Miller and Anheuser Busch were left.

- Crown Cork and Seal, when severely troubled in the late 1960s, was able to get the major steel producers to undertake major product and process research on its behalf, since the big can makers, American and Continental, had switched to aluminum. Tinplate had been a major revenue producer for the steel companies, and so they had a vested interest in keeping Crown Cork—a major tinplate user—afloat.

- Kentucky Fried Chicken, in the midst of a turnaround attempt, faced the threat of mass defections and even lawsuits from its disgruntled franchisees. The company had nothing substantive it could offer, but its top managers worked to communicate the details of the turnaround plan, including its content and timetable to the franchisees. The threatened defections were forestalled by the candor and aggressiveness of this communications campaign.

These examples are far from exhaustive, but they illustrate the types of concessions a turnaround firm might seek, the array of parties from which it might attempt to gain concessions, and the basis on which the negotiations might occur.

Negotiating With Creditors

Usually, the most nagging problem for a turnaround manager is a shortage of cash with which to fund strategic moves or even to pay off existing obligations. Negotiating with creditors is, in concept, no different from negotiating with any other ally. However, since favorable negotiations with creditors are so crucial to a turnaround, some special considerations are worth noting.

Banks are most responsive to a request for leniency or for more funds if the troubled firm can present a realistic but creative plan for the turnaround, along with some indication that the turnaround is already underway. For example, a bank might be more comfortable about a troubled firm's prospects if a new general manager is in place, the firm's labor contract has been renegotiated, and key suppliers have extended the firm's payable dates. For this reason, it is important to carefully plot the sequence in which negotiations with stakeholders are conducted. In the same vein, banks can sometimes be influenced by contacts from the firm's key suppliers or customers, especially if they too are key clients of the bank.

Banks also like to see benchmark dates by which the firm will make certain progress. A firm may ask to pay off a loan in 18 months, but the bank will be far more comfortable if the firm can point to interim dates by which key steps will be achieved—sale of some equipment by a certain date, a new product launched by a certain date, and so on. This is basically what Pan American Airlines did in 1974, when it had enough cash to last only about three weeks. They formulated a detailed survival plan which, although not upbeat, was realistic and comprehensible. The banks, led by Citibank, concluded that they could keep a close pulse on progress, and so they agreed to provide the bridge financing for the survival plan.

A common mistake made by turnaround firms and their banks is that they set their sights on the crisis stage of the turnaround and fail to lay the groundwork for financing the stabilization and rebuilding stages. Some would-be turnarounds are stopped short because of overanxious creditors. The task for the turnaround firm is to have some idea of how much money will be needed, and when it will be needed, to complete the entire turnaround. The firm should either portray the full picture to the bankers up front or have a way in mind of unveiling and negotiating the increments as the turnaround progresses.

HUMAN AND ORGANIZATIONAL COMPONENTS OF TURNAROUND

A turnaround manager, like any other general manager, is dependent on the firm's people and organization to achieve his or her aims. Before turning to potential actions in these areas that turnaround managers may wish to consider, it is important to review some common human and organization pathologies found in troubled firms.

Research has consistently concluded that firms often get into severe trouble because of an ineffective top manager. The most common form of this problem is the long-term autocrat: the top manager who requires all information to flow to him or her and who, in turn, makes basically all decisions.[14]

---

[14] Argenti, op. cit., p. 40; Danny Miller, "Common Syndromes of Business Failure," *Business Horizons* (Fall 1980), pp. 43-53.

Such a "strong" chief executive can be the factor behind a firm's success as long as his or her biases and values are in line with what is required by the environment. But, as soon as there is a mismatch, severe trouble develops.

A turnaround manager who steps into the aftermath of this common situation generally finds that the upper-level and mid-level managerial talent is sparse, or at least atrophied. Talent could be sparse for two reasons: (1) the autocrat did not search for or select truly strong managers into the organization, and (2) over time, any capable and aggressive managers will have left the autocratic firm if they had alternatives. Generally, the longer the autocrat has been in place, the fewer the creative and aggressive managers there are to assist in the turnaround. A more generous, yet sometimes quite accurate, view is that substantial managerial talent may reside in the firm, but it is simply atrophied from lack of use. Obviously, an important early task for the turnaround manager is to evaluate key people—a subject to which we will turn in a moment.

Studies of organizations under crisis have identified some other common symptoms that a turnaround manager must address. First, people in troubled organizations tend to act erratically; they make genuinely bad decisions in the face of crisis.[15] They misperceive data, integrate data poorly, and engage in precipitous and harmful interpersonal and interunit bickering. There are two broad implications from this for the general manager. The first is that tasks, structures, and processes must be put together in a way that responds to these problems. The emphasis must be on simplicity, explicitness, and pinpointing of responsibilities. The second implication is that the turnaround manager needs to sort out whether seemingly weak performers are inherently weak or are basically capable people just revealing various stress behaviors. If the latter, they still might have to be released, or they might somehow be harbored or reassigned so that their real talents can be tapped.

Another major symptom in troubled organizations is that behavior tends to be very rigid.[16] People seem to restrict information flows by limiting their scanning, relying only on formal information channels, and communicating in abbreviated form (for example, yes/no, stop/go, buy/sell). People also try to tighten control during a crisis, by restricting information flows, attempting to concentrate power, and introducing complex systems of approvals for every action. To some extent, such control is called for in some turnaround situations, but its negative consequences should also be clear.

Evaluating Key Managers

Since the general manager probably cannot intelligently make all decisions alone (even though he or she might be tempted to try) and certainly cannot execute and monitor all those decisions, he or she must compose a suitable managerial team as quickly as possible. Thus, the evaluation of key managers is

---

[15] Carolyn Smart and Ian Vertinsky, "Designs for Crisis Decision Units," *Administrative Science Quarterly* (Summer 1977), pp. 640-657.

[16] Barry M. Staw, Lance E. Sandelands, and Jane E. Dutton, "Threat-Rigidity Effects in Organizational Behavior: A Multilevel Analysis," *Administrative Science Quarterly* (Autumn 1981), pp. 501-524.

one of the first and most important tasks to be conducted by the turnaround manager. As noted above, there is a distinct likelihood that some managers will have to be fired or reassigned.

In evaluating key subordinates, the turnaround manager should be interested in three qualities: knowledge, aptitude, and attitude. In this context, knowledge means the degree to which the manager "knows" his or her job and/or possesses information that is crucial to the organization. Sometimes, a manager is absolutely crucial to the turnaround effort because of some important knowledge he or she possesses. Examples would be the sales manager who possesses detailed but undocumented knowledge of key customers' buying patterns and processes, or the operations manager who has mastery over otherwise unruly and uncooperative equipment. However, sometimes subordinate managers have highly specialized knowledge but not any broader knowledge, such as of key trends in the industry, competitors' moves, or new technologies. In such a case, the choice is between the safe continuity available from the manager with specialized internal knowledge and the possibility of new insights/directions from a manager brought in from the outside with broader knowledge.

Aptitude refers to the abilities of the manager to do things—to analyze, to lead, to control, and so on. Sometimes, a manager can have tremendous knowledge but not the wherewithal to do much with it. For example, a manager may not be capable of complex reasoning, may not be decisive, or may not bring out the best in subordinates. Depending on the type of turnaround envisioned and the mix of talents within a management team, key people could have to be replaced because of limited aptitude.

Attitude is a third quality to look for in a subordinate in a turnaround situation. The turnaround manager needs people who do not feel defeated by the situation, who are capable of psychologically reinforcing each other, and who are supportive of the top person and the direction in which he or she wants to head. Subordinates who are not supportive are not only lackluster performers; they also tend to poison the atmosphere so that others' attitudes are affected as well.

The turnaround manager, of course, relies heavily on informal observation and his or her sense of people to conduct evaluations of subordinates. But, the astute manager, recognizing that time is of the essence, will devise tests to determine the capabilities of people in the three broad areas discussed above. The most common test is to request the subordinate to conduct an analysis of some limited part of his or her area within a fairly short deadline, such as two days. An example would be to ask the marketing manager to identify the three largest orders won and the three largest orders lost over the last year, and to analyze the factors underlying the outcomes. In doing this task, the marketing manager will have to demonstrate his knowledge (Can he even identify the orders? the competitors to whom we lost?) his aptitude (Does he demonstrate sound logic? Does he extract any reasonable common threads from his analyses?), and his attitude (How eager to please does he appear? Did he take the request seriously?).

For such tests to be genuinely useful, some caveats must be borne in mind. First, these tests should not be labeled as such. Savvy subordinates in a turnaround situation know they are always under careful scrutiny, and will only resent a single contrived exercise to put them on the spot. This raises the second caveat: No test like the one described should be used in isolation to evaluate a manager. Rather, several such tests over the first few weeks of a turnaround, in concert with informal observation and other data, provide the information to make a reasoned decision about the person. The third caveat is that these tests should never involve detours for the managers. That is, they should only involve asking the manager to do something that genuinely is needed to conduct the turnaround. Time and resources are too tight to be asking key subordinates to engage in academic side trips.

The turnaround manager should extend his or her evaluation of key people to at least two levels below, since there may be some very capable managers who are obscured by their bosses. Knowing what talents exist at multiple levels will be important in making all other moves—firings, reassignments, even choice of strategy. Another reason for opening communications with mid-level people is that they are often valuable repositories of information about markets, technologies, and their bosses' capabilities. The textbook nicety of always strictly observing the chain of command when communicating in the organization is probably poor procedure in most firms, and it is especially ill-suited for a turnaround firm.

At this point, it is useful to say a few words about firings—the logical aftermath of the managerial evaluation process in many turnaround firms. Actually, firings are not inevitable, and they should not be seen as such. However, if a major strategic retrenchment is needed, there is usually no choice.

Firings are always agonizing, but their harmful effects on individuals and on the organization are minimized if clear criteria exist. In contrast to across-the-board cuts, the usual starting criterion is to cut by product or function. Cuts are made in those areas that are losing the most money or that are grossly overstaffed. The most talented people in these areas should be considered for reassignment to continuing operations, since it makes little sense to get rid of strong people or to keep mediocre people just because of their departmental affiliations. In general, merit should be the guiding principle in firings (except, of course, in laying off unionized employees, where seniority usually must be observed).

Since managers at each level will be responsible for ranking their subordinates, a difficult dilemma arises: Should firings proceed from the top to bottom or from bottom to top? If done from the bottom to the top, it is possible that a subordinate will be rated (and either kept or fired) by an inept supervisor who in a few weeks will be fired himself or herself. If firings are done from the top to the bottom, there is the possibility that subordinates will be rated by a new supervisor who cannot accurately assess their performances. An additional consideration is that firings from the top down can carry great symbolic and negotiating power. There is no easy answer to this dilemma, but recognizing it may allow the manager to think through the factors involved.

Probably the most crippling thing a turnaround manager can do is to have waves of firings. If after one round people know that more firings are imminent, their productivity will be disastrous. It is far better for the manager to do all the firings at once and to pledge that there will be no further firings. Since an airtight pledge of this sort can be difficult to honor, a compromise position might be to stress that there will be no more firings, as long as certain turn-around goals are met. Such an approach supplants the employee's negative pre-occupation with a very positive, constructive goal.

Rewards and Motivation

The turnaround manager is usually short on resources with which to bestow rewards to key people. This means that motivation must center on intangibles and on the promise of later rewards, in addition to the obvious fear of being fired.

Fortunately, turnaround managers often encounter situations where intangible rewards are powerful motivators. Many troubled firms get into that condition because of an autocratic, dictatorial general manager. The turnaround manager who selects a team of managers with some raw talents, and then pushes them to start initiating improvements and to exercise discretion, will, after some initial skepticism on their part, often find those managers utterly exhilarated by the challenges of managing. They will be motivated by being part of an organization with renewed momentum and a sense of direction.

Now, this phenomenon only occurs if there is substantial progress. Achievement brings about motivation, just as much as motivation brings about achievement. This means that subordinates should be given challenging tasks that can be broken into discrete parts, so that they will have a series of short-term goals and can enjoy a steady stream of small but motivating victories. Managers, like other people, respond to reinforcement. Particularly in a turn-around, they need to be put in situations where progress is called—loudly called—"a win." [17]

Intangible motivators alone will not keep good people for long. Even though financial straits sometimes prevent it, every effort should be made to keep salaries at competitive levels. Turnaround managers sometimes cut sala-ries instead of cutting people, but this is generally a way to send the best people looking for jobs elsewhere. As the firm approaches stabilization, the turn-around manager should also consider announcing the point at which incentive compensation will again start, and maybe even give some indication of how the incentive compensation plan will be structured so as to bring the bright horizon into sharper focus for the managers.

Organizational Structure

The turnaround manager often will find a situation in which the organization's structure needs to be changed, due to confused roles and relationships and poor suitability of the structure to the turnaround strategy. To a great extent, the guidelines that are available in any good book or article on structure will apply. [18] But, there are two specific things that an organization's structure must

---

[17] Thomas J. Peters, "Symbols, Patterns, and Settings: An Optimistic Case for Getting Things Done," *Organization Dynamics* (1978), pp. 3-23.

[18] Jay R. Galbraith and Daniel A. Nathanson, *Strategy Implementation: The Role of Structure and Process* (St. Paul, Minn.: West Publishing Co., 1978).

accomplish in a turnaround situation: pinpoint accountability and eliminate information blockage.[19]

The assignment of responsibilities must be absolutely clear in a turnaround situation. This often means revising tasks so that each person has an identifiable domain and goals (with interim benchmarks). In general, structure must be simple in order to achieve this aim. Complex matrices and standing cross-functional teams usually run counter to the aim of pinpointing accountability. Effective turnaround managers will often set up talented subordinates as "champions" of discrete tasks or projects, even though the tasks could legitimately be woven together across departments to achieve so-called synergies or economies of scale. The key seems to be in assigning or instilling "problem ownership."

In a turnaround situation, organizational structure can be a key to eliminating information blockages. A typical move is to reduce the number of layers in the organization, so that information does not have to travel as far, either upward or downward. The greater the number of levels, the longer it takes for the information to flow, the less information gets through, and the more distorted the information becomes. Another way to open up information flows—this time laterally—is to convene two-person or three-person ad hoc task forces to deliberate on key policy issues. Often, these will consist of functional heads who have not been communicating with each other at all up until now. Such task forces must be temporary (with a rigid deadline—sometimes no more than two weeks), high-level (with the authority to implement), and focused on some issue with cross-functional implications (such as the marketing and production heads developing policy and tactics regarding product quality). The task forces should not have any lingering operating responsibilities, since, as noted above, operating accountability must reside with individuals.

Information and Decision Processes

The turnaround manager needs to make decisions about what information is needed, where it is needed, how it should flow, and, in general, how decisions should be made. Here again, the emphasis should be on simplicity and fluidity. The manager, possibly with the help of a consultant or inside aide, should draft some very simple forms for reports to track information about the key areas of the business. Ideally, each report will require only a handful of figures and will pertain to a crucial dimension of the business. The manager must resist asking for information on every possible facet of the business.

It is crucial to engage key subordinates in the process of refining these reports, since they will be providing the eventual data and since they often have important insight into what type of data is most necessary. In fact, it is useful to first establish a set of simple, highly focused reports that will flow from the functional heads to the general manager and then charge the functional heads with doing the same within their respective areas. The quality of the first set of reports will dramatically shape the quality of those developed at middle and lower levels of the organization.

---

[19] Smart and Vertinsky, op. cit., p. 650.

It is important that turnaround managers not rely only, or even primarily, on formal written information flows. In fact, many turnaround managers replace chief executives who had essentially cut off personal contact with subordinates. The effective turnaround manager will engage in face-to-face exchanges with subordinates, rather than relying on more detached and sterile media. Such meetings—especially when one-on-one (as opposed to larger groups)—promote fluid and subtle information flows. In a situation where rigidity, confusion, and lack of trust probably abound, achievement of these aims is essential.

SYMBOLIC COMPONENT OF TURNAROUND

A symbol can be defined as anything that has meaning beyond its inherent substance. A manager's formal language, informal language, decisions, use of time, and general demeanor convey far more than their substance might indicate. In fact, symbols are the very stuff of top management.[20] And, they take on particular importance in turnaround situations, since, as noted above, substantive resources for accomplishing goals are in short supply. When people's nerves are frayed, they are particularly sensitive to signals.

Managers do not really have a choice about using symbols. They emit them all the time. In fact, every substantive action—a statement, a meeting location, a walk through the plant—can be thought to have symbolic fallout. Managers mismanage their use of symbols in two ways.

The first is failing to understand that the symbolic fallout exists. A common example is the turnaround manager who holes up in his or her office, often with the door shut, at the same time he or she is asking people to step forward with ideas. The inconsistency is far from obvious to the general manager, but it is profound in its impact on subordinates.

The second way of mismanaging symbols is failing to use them to their fullest. Through careful staging, the potential symbolic fallout from an action can be greatly expanded. For example, a new turnaround manager came into a situation where the executive offices were located in a modern, fairly expensive office building a few blocks from the company's main plant. By happy coincidence, the office lease lapsed two months after his arrival. And, he knew that the prudent thing—both substantively and symbolically—was to move the executive offices back to the plant where there was older, unused office space. He decided to heighten the impact of the move by having the moving trucks start the unloading on a workday, just at the time employees were going to lunch down a long corridor where the moving was taking place. Everybody was made aware of the move, and they had the remainder of their lunch hour to talk about it and the general manager's personal commitment to cut costs.

Some will argue that such behavior is manipulative and slick, and is not going to "fool" anyone. But, truly great leaders through history have been separated from the merely good leaders by their astute and persistent use of sym-

---

[20] Peters, op. cit., p. 14.

bols. And, if these examples seem trivial, it is worth noting that the exceptional manager seeks every way imaginable to convey a point to the people whose acts and attitudes he or she is trying to influence. Sometimes, this will be through grand settings, but, more often, it will be through fairly mundane contexts.

When symbols are used consistently, and with appropriate frequency, they form a theme. Turnaround managers need such themes to provide clear direction and motivate people who are, in various degrees, confused, frightened and skeptical.

To a great extent, symbols represent the manner in which the turnaround manager uses all the other levers available—strategy, political initiative, structure, rewards, and people. Symbols, then, overlay the entire turnaround task.

CORPORATE-LEVEL TURNAROUND ISSUES

This chapter has focused primarily on the manager who has been charged with the turnaround of a business unit. But, there are also important issues that must be addressed at the corporate level of a diversified firm, often before the turnaround of one of its businesses can get under way. Chief among these issues are: whether to attempt the turnaround or to sell off the business, what kind of manager should head up the turnaround, and how much time should be allowed for the turnaround.

Turn Around or Sell?

A turnaround should be attempted only if there is a high probability that the going-concern value of the business is substantially greater than its liquidation value. To reach that determination, someone at the corporate level must do an analysis of the prospects for the industry and for the business within its industry. Often, this analysis must be done even more quickly and with less data than the eventual analysis conducted by the turnaround manager.

The corporate analysis must not rely only on the financial statements of the business, no matter how unequivocal they may seem. Rather, the analysis must extend to the overall health of the industry, and data—even if impressionistic—must be gathered from a variety of sources, including the business' suppliers, customers, key managers, and employees. If the prospects for the industry appear dismal or if the problems of the business are particularly deep-rooted or pervasive, selling the business or its assets may be more sensible than attempting the turnaround. Of course, sometimes firms are prevented from exiting, due to such factors as union severance agreements, long-term contracts with customers, and crucial synergies between the troubled business and other healthier businesses within the corporation.[21]

---

[21] Kathryn R. Harrigan, "Exit Decisions in Mature Industries," *Academy of Management Journal* (Fall 1982), pp. 707-731; Michael E. Porter, "Please Note Location of Nearest Exit: Exit Barriers and Strategic and Organizational Planning," *California Management Review* (1976), pp. 21-33.

In weighing the sale of a business (or of its assets), two key factors should be borne in mind. The first is that the business may well be worth much more to someone else than it is to its current management. That is, the business may fit particularly well with the strategy or competence of another firm, such that they would pay a reasonable price—perhaps even a premium—to acquire it. Second, the business will yield a much higher price if sold in an orderly, deliberate fashion than if it is sold under duress or crisis. Among other things, this means that assets are usually worth more before a turnaround attempt than after an *unsuccessful* turnaround attempt, when the firm is desperate and has only confirmed the poor health of the business in the eyes of potential buyers.

The corporate analysis of the liquidation value of the business must be communicated to the turnaround manager. Such a figure provides the turnaround manager a reference point against which all actions and timetables can be measured. It is especially important for the turnaround manager to know that he or she has a "walkaway" position in negotiating with stubborn stakeholders.

There are substantial costs and risks in attempting a turnaround rather than getting rid of the business. Some of these costs are obvious, but there are also hidden tolls in the amount of time, creativity, and emotional energy the troubled business diverts from other more promising operations within the firm's portfolio. Probably, far more turnarounds are undertaken than should be.

Selecting a Turnaround Manager

Once the company has decided a turnaround attempt is warranted, there is the decision as to who should lead the effort. Here, two questions are relevant: Should the present general manager be replaced? If so, by what kind of person?

Some authors feel strongly that replacement of the present top manager is crucial in a turnaround situation.[22] The rationale for such a view is that the present manager has already demonstrated ineptness by allowing the business to deteriorate; he or she is psychologically wedded to the present way of doing things, and so would be unable to generate and accurately weigh alternatives; and, because of his or her close ties to subordinates, customers, and other parties, he or she could not make the hard decisions that must be made in a turnaround situation. There is no systematic data as to whether or when this view is correct. However, it seems to be widely subscribed to, as judged by one finding that three-quarters of the executives heading up 81 turnaround attempts were new to the job.[23]

Not all such new managers are from outside the firm, and, in fact, the idea of picking a turnaround manager from among the present management team is

---

[22] Hofer, op. cit., p. 25.
[23] Bibeault, op. cit., p. 95.

an appropriate compromise in some situations. Such a person has the advantage over an outsider of knowing the business and its key players, and may have a relatively open mind about changes that need to be made. In larger companies, a subordinate is more likely to have held truly responsible general management experience yet still be psychologically detached from the incumbent executive's view of the firm. For example, at NCR, William Anderson was the extremely successful chairman of the firm's Japanese subsidiary. He was known for experimentation and deviation from the established NCR approach. He had the combined advantage of knowing NCR but not fully accepting it, and so he was an obvious (and eventually successful) choice by the board to head up the firm's turnaround.

Any further discussion of selecting a turnaround manager inevitably becomes a litany of "it all depends." It depends on what type of turnaround is most likely, for example, revenue building versus cost cutting. It depends on whether the person is being selected only to bring the business through the crisis or whether he or she will also engineer the rejuvenation. It depends on the mix of talents and attitudes of the key subordinates in the business. Additional contingent factors could be listed. In short, there are no clear guidelines. It is clear, however, that corporate decision makers need to become knowledgable enough about the troubled business so that they can identify intelligently the most appropriate type of turnaround manager.

How Much Time to Allow

A fitting—in fact, crucial—question for corporate managers to ask is, "How long will this turnaround take?" Here again, there are no rigid guidelines. Chrysler tried to turn around for 15 years. Other firms accomplish it in a year or two. Turnaround researchers have found fairly consistently that the *average* elapsed time from start of a turnaround to satisfactory profits is about three years. But the range is immense, as one could easily expect. The key determining factors are the health of the industry, the severity of the firm's condition, the strategic position of the firm (often indicated by market share), its capital intensity, and its middle management quality.[24]

Instead of trying to delineate exactly how long a turnaround might take, corporate-level executives should set benchmarks and a timetable for the business during the turnaround. A tentative timetable can be established based on the early analysis that is done to determine whether a turnaround is viable. Then, the timetable should be renegotiated after the turnaround manager has had a chance to develop his or her own estimates. Interim benchmarks should be set so that the parent firm is not in a "wait and see" situation. Progress must be continually visible, and there should be logical points in the timetable when bail-out can be reconsidered.

---

[24] Bibeault, op. cit., p. 98; Dan Schendel, G. R. Patton, and James Riggs, "Corporate Turnaround Strategies: A Study of Decline and Recovery," *Journal of General Management* (Fall 1976), pp. 3-11.

A CLASSIC TURNAROUND–THE CASE OF ARTHUR KELLER

This chapter has stressed that there are a vast array of components, or levers, that the turnaround manager can draw upon, and that the levers chosen must fit the situation. But, orchestration of these levers—appropriate balance, sequence, and pace—is also crucial to a successful turnaround. The best way to illustrate orchestration of a turnaround, and at the same time summarize how the various levers can be used, is through discussion of an actual turnaround. The example is from a case study that is widely used in university and corporate executive programs.[25]

The Situation

Arthur Keller became the general manager of a major Swedish dressmaker when it was acquired by the large Austrian yarn producer for which he worked. Keller knew before starting the job that the dressmaker, Hedblom, was in trouble, since he had been involved in the (often bitter) acquisition negotiations. But he scarcely could have known the real magnitude of the problems.

Sales had dropped by 50 percent over two years, due to delivery delays, poor merchandising, and increased competition. New machines were on order, despite the fact that the company was operating at 25 percent of capacity. With its present cost structure, the firm would have to double its sales just to break even.

Keller found that at the core of the company's problems was the owner-founder, Mr. Hedblom. It seemed he had exercised a very centralized, authoritarian management style. He personally processed all the company's mail, required all managers to punch a time-clock, and, needless to say, made all the key decisions for the firm. Unfortunately, he was slow and risk-averse in his decision making, which, in this seasonal industry, led to very peaked and costly production cycles, late deliveries, and poor channel relations.

The human resource situation that Keller encountered was in keeping with the rest of the picture. The six key managers were cold and skeptical. The marketing manager said he would probably leave. The controller still had obvious loyalties to the old Mr. Hedblom, and the production manager was demoralized because Mr. Hedblom had him reporting to a consulting engineer who was retained to install a production control system. The workforce complained openly about lack of work, while at the same time a substantial amount of work was subcontracted outside.

Controls and budgets were nonexistent. In fact, the only two reports generated were a daily report of the firm's bank balance and a daily report of sales orders (but only for those orders received by mail). Since Mr. Hedblom had been the funnel for all information, there was essentially no communication among the functional heads.

---

[25] L'Institute pour L'Etude des Methodes de Direction de l'Enterprise (IEMDE), "Hedblom (A)" and "Hedblom (B)," distributed by Harvard Case Services, 1968.

The Turnaround

The situation facing Arthur Keller sounds unappealing, but it is not unlike the turnaround conditions described throughout this chapter: urgency, skeptical stakeholders, poor morale, and a vacuum left by an autocratic chief executive. As will be seen, Keller measured up to the task. This discussion of Keller's various moves will be tied to the array of turnaround levers that provided the framework for this paper.

It is difficult to improve on Keller's own words for describing how he entered the organization and conducted his situation assessment:

> My main task at the beginning was to gather information and to get cooperation. I knew nothing about the dress business and little about Hedblom. I therefore conducted a detailed and systematic investigation of all aspects of company operations. Every time [I am in the plant] I walk around the building, meet the people, talk to them as best I can in my broken Swedish, and particularly ask questions, questions, questions. You simply take nothing for granted. By having people explain and justify what they have been doing for years as a matter of unquestioned routine you often discover what needs to be investigated and appraised. Also, in this way you learn a lot about your people. [26]

In terms of strategy, Keller faced the option of either a major retrenchment or pushing sales up past the break-even point. His assessment of the industry and his diagnosis of Hedblom's problems led him to conclude that a sales-push strategy was feasible. So, Keller sought ways to expand volume. These included the introduction of four off-season dress collections (in addition to the customary two peak-season collections), a line of separately branded dresses to be sold through chain stores, sale of fabrics to other dressmakers, and expanded sales in other Scandinavian countries. The off-season dress collections were an especially important move, since they were directly responsive to the growing uneasiness of retailers to make big semiannual inventory commitments, and they helped to even out Hedblom's own production cycles. This was a major innovation in the industry, and it was made possible by Keller's fresh view and persistent questioning.

Keller also introduced some important cost-cutting measures. By advancing the start of each season's production cycle, inefficient peaks and valleys were nearly eliminated. Changes in plant layout were made to facilitate product flow and reduce costs, and new fabric cutting processes were introduced to reduce waste. Keller's search for quick, creative ways to cut costs is perhaps best illustrated in his decision (recommended by someone in production) to use transparent thread in sewing, which permitted the use of just two threads (one light and one dark), thereby facilitating sewing operations and minimizing thread inventories. This decision and other cost-cutting moves reinforced the primary strategy of expanding revenues.

Only sketchy data is available on how Keller used political moves to aid in his turnaround attempt, but there is some indication that he was imaginative on

---

[26] "Hedblom (B)," p. 10.

this front as well. Using his parent company as a fulcrum, he was able to obtain a sizeable cooperative advertising budget from one of the parent's biggest fiber suppliers. Similarly, he was able to get credit on good terms by working through the parent company's lead bank.

Keller conducted his turnaround effort without replacing any of his managers. As badly as the firm had been performing, he concluded that the remaining managers were not to blame. Of course, they were not dynamos, but he sensed that they were generally competent and, in addition, they carried a great deal of information which, even if unwanted or unused by his predecessor, would be invaluable in the turnaround effort.

Naturally, the company could not afford financial incentives for the managers. Instead, Keller had to rely on—and accentuate—the degree to which the managers could be motivated by a sense of teamwork, vitality, and expanded discretion. On the heels of his predecessor, these were powerful motivators.

He modified the structure only slightly, by putting one manager in overall charge of the new dress line. And, after releasing the consulting engineer, he put the production manager in overall charge of the production function. Both of these changes were prompted by Keller's desire to give key managers clear and bounded areas of responsibililty.

Keller's attempts to introduce new controls and information flows centered on the themes of simplicity and timeliness. He concluded that a budgeting system could only be put together on an incremental basis, by starting with the information on hand and adding to its detail and quality in each successive month's budget. He set up three quality-control posts through the production process, so that problems could be caught before the whole production cycle was completed. He designed a set of four one-page weekly reports on crucial aspects of the business and encouraged his subordinates to develop similarly simple and straightforward reports in their own areas. Overall, Keller delegated many decisions, but he exercised control by maintaining close personal contact with each manager and persistently asking questions.

Finally, Keller was a master in the use of symbols. He engaged in numerous substantive actions which, when enhanced by appropriate staging and timing, greatly helped to reinforce the themes he was striking in the turnaround effort. Here are several of those actions and the themes he tried to accentuate with each:

- *Action:* He gave early, visible attention to the next year's line.
  Theme: "We're going to start making decisions and taking risks."

- *Action:* He moved the executive offices from across town to the unused top floor of the plant.
  Theme: "We're going to start talking with each other."

- *Action:* He eliminated almost all outside subcontracting.
  Theme: "We have a lot of talent and resources right here."

- *Action:* He fired the consulting engineer.
  Theme: "I want *you people* to start making the key decisions."

- *Action:* He held open houses for employees' families, press, and community.
  Theme: "We've got plenty to show off."

- *Action:* He made many personal tours of the plant.
  Theme: "I'm involved and interested."

- *Action:* He sent personal letters to customers, guaranteeing on-time delivery.
  Theme: "Things are changing here. I am personally involved in the changes."

In contrast to his predecessor, Keller used powerful themes, and he drove them home by the careful and persistent use of symbols.

Keller's turnaround of Hedblom was exceptionally successful. Within nine months, the business was breaking even; and, within 15 months, it was earning roughly 10 percent on sales.

Keller's turnaround effort is a snapshot of the key points of this paper. He conducted an early, quick, but in-depth analysis of his situation and players. He charted a course that was responsive to the nature and magnitude of the firm's problems. He creatively engaged all the components of an effective turnaround: strategic, political, human, organizational, and symbolic. And, he engaged them in a balanced fashion, so they were mutually reinforcing.

SUMMARY

A turnaround situation is a special general management situation, typified by limited resources, poor morale, skeptical allies, and urgency. The turnaround manager is under sharp pressure to do an early analysis and get on to key actions: strategic, political, human, organizational, and symbolic. Use of these various levers must be carefully orchestrated, since the turnaround manager basically is allowed only one round of moves.

This chapter draws on actual studies of troubled firms and turnaround efforts, in order to portray the key issues and options faced by turnaround managers. There are oversimplifications at many points, such as in the discussions of four recurring causes of downturn and five main types of turnaround strategies. This approach is necessary, since it is hardly useful to lay out a long stream of anecdotes along with the shallow wisdom that no two turnaround situations are the same. The goals of this chapter are to broaden the turnaround manager's vision of the kinds of analyses and actions that might be undertaken, and then to help the manager develop ways to narrow down to what is most pertinent in his own situation.

11

Diversification Strategies

JAMES K. MALERNEE, JR.

Vice President, Management Analysis Center, Inc.

JOHN C. KIRBY, JR.

Chairman and Chief Executive Officer, Plant & Field Service Corporation

Diversification—development of a new product or entry into a new market—is a strategic decision that must be based on solid strategic analysis, not on an intuitive feel for what might be appropriate. Raytheon is both a major supplier and a major user of electronic components. A superficial analysis of the situation might suggest that it would have made sense for Raytheon to be in the electronic components distribution business as well. However, a careful study of the electronic components business reveals a number of factors indicating that a company that supplies and uses electronic components would not necessarily succeed as a distributor of electronic components. For example, the field of electronic components distributors is very fragmented—a situation that is encouraged by suppliers and customers—which means that distributors have little bargaining power in their relations with customers and suppliers. In addition, pricing is extremely competitive. Despite conventional wisdom, hindsight suggests that Raytheon made the correct decision in not entering the distribution business.

This chapter presents state-of-the-art tools and techniques for developing a diversification strategy. The following topics are discussed:

- Identifying business opportunities
- Analyzing the implications of the diversification strategy
- Developing a systematic process

IDENTIFYING BUSINESS OPPORTUNITIES

The purpose of developing a corporate strategy is to identify businesses in which the company can best defend itself against competitive forces or in which it can influence competitive forces in its own favor. The key to successful strategy formulation, then, is to identify the structural characteristics of industries that determine their attractiveness and their level and degree of competition.

Three tools that are commonly used by planners in formulating strategy are discussed below: the business policy model, the portfolio model, and the industry/competition model. The decision as to mode of entry into a business—internal development or acquisition—should be subordinate to the decision about being in the business at all, and a discussion of entry options is therefore the final topic in this section.

The Business Policy Model

Business policy models examine the relationship between the company and its environment.[1] This analytical process attempts to match market opportunities with the resources and competencies of the firm. Opportunities may exist because of segments that are unrecognized by competitors. Or, a firm may have a superior product, superior technology, or superior financial resources. Managers using a business policy model examine the environment and the strengths and weaknesses of a firm. Then, they develop a set of choices, and list aspects of each choice such as capability, limitations, risks, and opportunities.

Managers who use the business policy model are encouraged to ask the following questions about their firm's diversification program:

- Are the diversification plans consistent with the desired direction of the firm?
- Do these plans exploit industry opportunities?
- Does the timing of the plans reflect the ability of the environment to absorb the firm's projected actions?
- Does the firm have the necessary resources available to pursue the diversification plans?
- Is there sufficient managerial capability to allow for effective implementation?

---

[1] Kenneth R. Andrews, *The Concept of Corporate Strategy* (Homewood, Ill.: Dow Jones-Irwin, Inc., 1971), pp. 59–102.

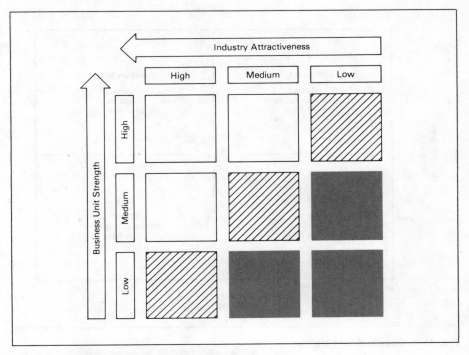

FIG. 11-1 The Strength/Attractiveness Grid

The Portfolio Model

A firm may be thought of as a portfolio of businesses that vary in their levels of attractiveness and competitive strength. The two most popular approaches to the portfolio model seem to be the strength/attractiveness model and the growth/share model.

Using the strength/attractiveness model, the firm attempts to characterize its businesses in terms of their attractiveness compared with their own competitive strength in that business, as shown in Figure 11-1.

Examples of measures of strength and attractiveness are listed below.

Strength	*Attractiveness*
Relative size	Size
Growth	Market growth
Share	Market diversity
Position	Pricing
Relative profitability	Competitive structure
Margin	Industry profitability
Technological position	Technical role
Image	Social
People	Environmental
	Legal constraints

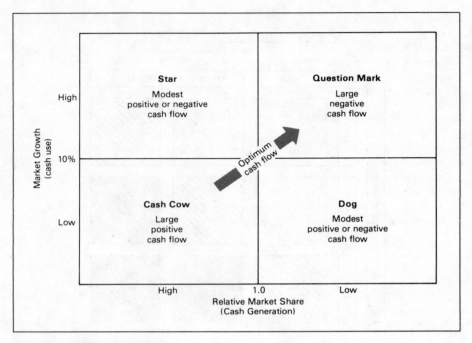

FIG. 11-2 Growth/Share Matrix

A firm using the portfolio model approach invests in businesses that are attractive and in which it has a competitive advantage. It will get out of, or not invest in, businesses that are unattractive and in which it is at a competitive disadvantage. Management must often make some tough decisions about the appropriate action to be taken for businesses that lie in the middle ground. In these cases, application of the industry/competition model (discussed below) can be very useful.

Detractors of the strength/attractiveness approach point to the subjectivity required in evaluating and weighting the underlying measures. However, the very process of working through an assessment of these factors can provide powerful strategic insights to managers in many cases.

A popular variant of the strength/attractiveness concept (actually, its antecedent) substitutes market growth for attractiveness, and market share (relative to that of the largest competitor) for strength. The growth/share model developed by the Boston Consulting Group is shown on the four-celled matrix in Figure 11-2.

This approach is based on an underlying assumption that the experience curve concept is operative and that the firm with the largest relative share will be the lowest cost producer. Because of these assumptions, this methodology has found its greatest success in commodity-type businesses.

Firms using the growth/share methodology try to build or maintain share in high-growth businesses, which requires investment in these businesses—

sometimes a very large investment. As growth declines with the product life cycle, high market share businesses become cash generators since there is little need for investment. The dynamics of the model suggest that this cash will be reinvested in low-share/high-growth opportunities or in high-share, high-growth opportunities.

Using either of these portfolio models, it is vital that the businesses be defined correctly; otherwise, strength and attractiveness may be improperly evaluated. For example, the actions of G.D. Heileman indicate that its management correctly defined the beer business as a regional business rather than a national business. On the basis of national market share, Heileman would be rated weak competitively, leading to improper strategic decisions. However, the company has diversified into a number of strong regional brands which have provided a foundation for their innovative regional strategies.

Using portfolio models to assist in formulating diversification strategies requires managers to ask the following questions[2]:

- What are the cash-flow characteristics of the new business?
- How will their attractiveness evolve over time in view of the competitive situation?
- What investment on our part will be required over time to make a success of this business?
- How does the cash flow pattern fit with our portfolio?

The Industry/Competition Model

In addition to viewing the firm's portfolio of businesses, it is useful to consider the dynamics of each individual business. A helpful model can be pulled from the large body of economic literature available. Porter has developed a framework for analyzing the major forces driving industry competition, as shown in Figure 11-3.[3]

This model goes beyond a simple consideration of the established players in the market, and considers five competitive forces: entry barriers, threat of substitution, bargaining power of buyers, bargaining power of suppliers, and rivalry among competitors. Using this model in formulating new diversification strategies, Porter points out that "If these market forces work perfectly . . . no entry decision can ever yield an above-average return on investment."[4] On the other hand, market forces rarely operate perfectly, and this model can help diversifiers to understand the opportunities and threats they face. Some of the questions posed to the diversifier using this approach are:

- What is the likely effect on the supply/demand balance of the industry by the entry of a new firm?

---

[2] Malcolm S. Salter and Wolf A. Weinhold, *Diversification Through Acquisition* (New York: Free Press, 1979), p. 76.

[3] Michael E. Porter, *Competitive Strategy,* (New York: Free Press, 1980), p. 4.

[4] Ibid.,p. 340.

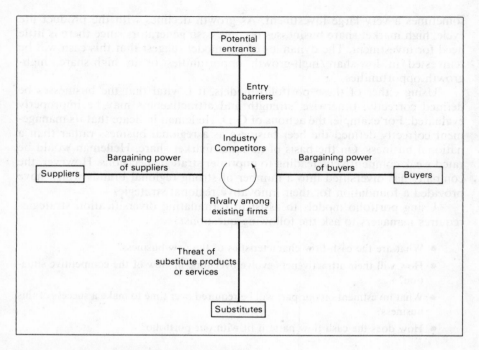

FIG. 11-3 Forces Driving Industry Competition

- What is the probable reaction of existing firms (e.g., regarding pricing, promotion, and change in products)?
- Does this firm have lower or higher entry costs than other potential entrants?
- Is it possible to construct entry or mobility barriers to the industry for subsequent potential entrants?
- Can entry into the new business provide a beneficial impact on the existing business (e.g., through shared costs)?

Entry Options

Internal development, acquisition, and joint venture represent the firm's entry options into new businesses. Since joint venture is a partial entry into a new business, this section deals only with the first two options.

Porter has pointed out that the feasibility analysis of internal development must confront the two sources of entry barriers: structural entry barriers and retaliation by existing firms. And, in the analysis, expected cash flows must be compared with the following[5]:

---

[5] Ibid., pp. 340–341.

1 The investment costs required to be in the new business, such as investment in manufacturing facilities and inventory

2 The additional investment required to overcome other structural entry barriers, such as brand identification and proprietary technology

3 The expected cost from incumbents' retaliation against the entry

Furthermore, internal development adds a new participant to the marketplace, resulting in increased capacity, and the likelihood of retaliation is greatest in industries that have high fixed costs (especially if they are combined with excess capacity), slow growth, and commodity-like products.

Generic approaches to internal entry including the following[6]:

- Reduce product costs
- Buy in with low cost
- Offer a superior product
- Discover a new niche
- Introduce a marketing innovation
- Use piggybacked distribution

Since entry by acquisition does not add a new competitor to the industry, this decision focuses on what it will cost to make the acquisition compared with the expected benefits to be derived. Such analysis would use some of the analytical tools discussed above. It should be noted, however, that a considerable body of research has been conducted on this subject, and, while there are notable examples to the contrary (e.g., P&G's acquisition of the Charmin Paper Company), the bulk of the research indicates that the sellers, not the buyers, are the real winners!

ANALYZING THE IMPLICATIONS OF THE DIVERSIFICATION STRATEGY

A careful formulation of the firm's strategy—and the place for diversification in that strategy—will lead to fruitful results only if the implications of the strategy are also considered. Three key areas that must be considered are: (1) the strategy/finance system, (2) the financial implications, and (3) the impact on shareholders.

The Strategy/Finance System

Strategy is often formulated in a vacuum; that is, little regard is given to the ability of the firm to implement the strategy in light of its financial or human resources. The strategy/finance system describes the relationship between the firm's objectives and its strategies and the financial realities of the firm. The elements of this system, which are shown in Figure 11-4, are as follows[7]:

---

[6] Ibid., p. 349.

[7] James K. Malernee and Gary Jaffe, "An Integrative Approach to Strategic and Financial Planning," *Managerial Planning* (Jan.-Feb. 1982).

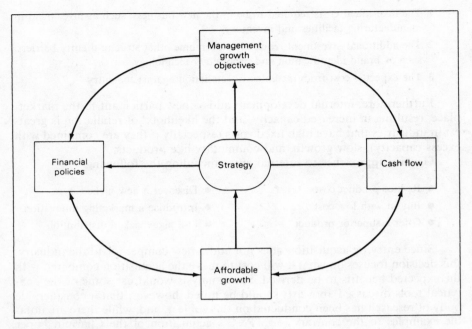

FIG. 11-4 The Strategic Finance System

- *Strategy:* Refers to the product/market decisions that have been made about the firm's businesses. If developed using one of the models discussed earlier, it will include a statement of the strategic thrust of each business unit (e.g., grow, maintain, harvest, or divest) and the expected cash use or generation of each business.

- *Management growth objectives:* Refers to both the qualitative ("be a high-quality producer of widgets") and quantitative ("provide a 15 percent ROI") expressions of the company's future performance goals.

- *Financial policies:* Reflects the dividend, financing (capital structure), and investment policies (especially those regarding risk) of the firm.

- *Cash flow:* Represents the required investment in capital and working capital to support a higher level of sales.

- *Affordable growth:* Estimates the annual percentage increase in sales that the firm can maintain, given its underlying financial policies and parameters.

Obviously, this is a complex system with substantial interaction among the elements. Management cannot arbitrarily approve capital expenditures or acquisitions without considering their implications for affordable growth. Moreover, management cannot undertake strategies that project a growth rate higher than the firm can sustain unless it is prepared to face the consequences (e.g., obtaining more equity).

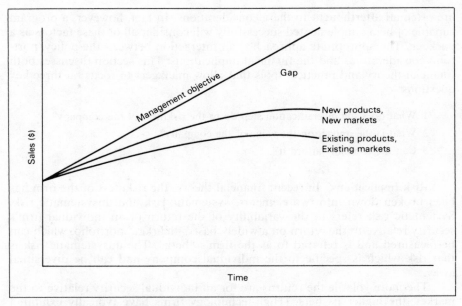

FIG. 11-5 Classification of Growth Opportunities

The interaction within the strategy/finance system may be described as follows: A preliminary strategy is formulated and is translated into or is compared with management's objectives. If the growth objective is higher than the growth implied by the preliminary plan, a planning gap may exist, as shown in Figure 11-5.[8] Indeed, this is frequently the point at which many companies decide to embark upon a diversification program. If internal diversification will not meet the firm's objectives, the "planning gap" may be filled with one or more acquisitions.

The decision to consider incorporating acquisitions as one of the alternatives enabling management to reach its growth objectives will enable management to play out the first of perhaps many acquisition scenarios. Evaluation of a number of these scenarios will permit the development and description of the financial policies and parameters consistent with the strategy and objectives.

Finally, the firm's affordable growth is calculated and compared with the growth rate projected by the plan. If the two are approximately the same, a refinement of the plan may be all that is required.

Financial Implications

Pursuit of a diversification program begins with considerations of business policy, the firm's portfolio of businesses, and an analysis of the industry competitive structure as described earlier. The financial consequences of the program

---

[8] Ibid.

are often an afterthought to these considerations. In fact, however, a program capable of being implemented successfully will consider all of these factors as a package. The appropriate approach is an interaction between the policy/portfolio considerations and the financial implications. This section discusses both financial theory and practical tools that allow managers to focus on three key questions:

1 What does the diversification step do to the riskiness of the company?
2 What is the impact on the value of the company?
3 Can the company afford it?

Risk Implications. In recent financial theory, the riskiness of the firm has been broken down into two elements: systematic risk and unsystematic risk. Systematic risk refers to the variability of the return of an individual firm's security relative to the return on a widely based "market" portfolio, which can be measured and is referred to as the firm's "beta." The unsystematic risk is that risk which is specific to the individual company and can be diversified away.

The more volatile the returns are for an individual security relative to the market, the higher its beta. (High-technology firms have typically exhibited betas of two and higher.) On the other hand, a beta of one indicates that the firm's returns tend to vary closely with the market. (IBM, for example, has had a beta of approximately one for a long time.)

The systematic and unsystematic components of risk have two important implications for a company that is diversifying through acquisition. First, if the selling company is in a narrow business line and has a good deal of unsystematic risk, the acquiring firm may be able to diversify this risk away. Second, the acquiring company must determine the beta of the combined companies that will result and decide whether that is acceptable. This is especially important if the selling company is large and its beta could significantly alter the beta of the combined entities.

Valuation. The valuation question can also be addressed through application of recent developments in financial theory. Capital market theory relates the expected return from investments to the riskiness of that investment.[9] While the underlying theory is beyond the scope of this chapter, a simplistic view of the relationship between risk and return is shown in Figure 11-6.

Figure 11-6 shows that as risk increases, the expected return from a security also increases. At zero risk, the expected return is shown as R_f (risk-free rate), which is sometimes thought of in terms of a U.S. Treasury security return. As securities increase in their riskiness, the required return also increases; that is, a risk premium is assigned. Theory, which is borne out by a rich body of empirical research, has shown that firms' securities tend to lie along this risk/return line. The implication of this relationship is that combin-

---

[9] Charles A. D'Ambrosio, *Principles of Modern Investments* (Chicago: SRA, 1976), p. 341.

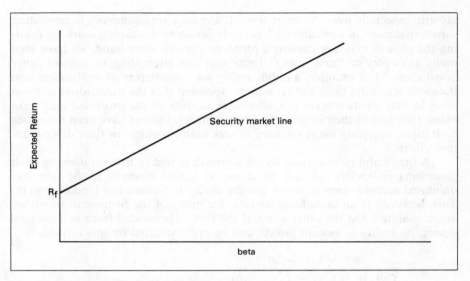

FIG. 11-6 The Risk/Return Relationship

ing two securities will simply result in a combination of securities along this line. Therefore, it has been argued that it is not in the best interest of shareholders that management undertake such combinations, since the shareholders could accomplish the same result if they so desired. A benefit can accrue to the shareholders, however, if an economic benefit to the business combination exists and if the selling company is not asking too high a price. Examples of economic benefits of the combination include plant scale (larger size resulting in lower unit costs) and marketing effectiveness (especially in sales, promotion, and distribution).

While a number of valuation tools are available, including the multiple of earnings and the premium relative to book value, the most widely acclaimed approach is the measurement of the present value of the future net cash flows less the investment cost, (i.e., the net cash flow or net cash benefit of the investment). Using this popular capital budgeting technique, a discount rate reflecting the riskiness of the investment is applied to the projected future cash flows to determine their present value. From that, the present value of the investment and any future outflows is subtracted to arrive at a net present value (NPV). If the correct discount rate is applied and the projected cash flows are accurate, the NPV theoretically represents value that is being added to (or subtracted from) the value of the firm.

Affordability. Too often, diversification plans are formulated without regard to the acquiring firm's ability to afford or sustain the projected growth. Using discounted cash flow techniques, valuation is a long-term perspective. It is generally accepted that this is the appropriate perspective; however, long-term growth and valuation is realistic only if the firm is capable of funding its growth, especially over the short term. If the acquiring company is generating substantial sums of cash and/or has ready access to the capital markets, funding the growth may not present a problem. On the other hand, we have seen many examples of "cash using" firms that are attempting to acquire other "cash users." For example, a public utility was considering diversification into the cable television field, until it became apparent that the tremendous start-up costs in that business were not affordable in spite of the projected long-term value. (Because of their large capital expenditures, utilities have been notorious cash users, requiring many of them to seek cash providers in their diversification efforts.)

A firm's ability to sustain its sales growth is tied to its cash using or cash generating characteristics and its access to capital markets. If the firm has unlimited access to new equity, it has the ability to finance any kind of growth. This, however, is an unrealistic scenario for many of the firms with which we are acquainted. On the other hand, if the firm is precluded from seeking new equity, its ability to sustain growth can be approximated by this formula[10]:

$$g = \frac{p(1 + L)(1 - d)}{C + W - (p(1 + L)(1 - d))}$$

where: p = after-tax return on sales

L = long-term debt-to-equity ratio

d = dividend payout ratio

C = portion of each new sales dollar required for capital expenditures

W = portion of each new sales dollar required for additional working capital needs

As the formula illustrates, the ability of a firm to sustain growth depends upon its cash using/cash generating characteristics. Large needs for capital investment, including needs for working capital, and high dividend payments can severely restrain a firm's growth. Conversely, improving profitability and the judicious use of financial leverage can enhance its ability to grow.

Since a firm's profitability and its ability to grow are really a compilation of these elements from the business unit level, it is often useful to consider the individual business units in the framework shown in Figure 11-7.

Using this methodology, the business units' ability to be profitable and to add value to the firm is contrasted with their ability to be self-sustaining. The four quadrants are described as follows[11]:

- *Upper right:* Business units in this quadrant are adding value to the company and are self-funding. That is, they are profitable and they generate cash. These businesses are often in mature industries.

[10] Robert C. Higgins, "How Much Growth Can a Firm Afford?" *Financial Management* (Fall 1977), pp.7–16.

[11] James K. Malernee, Jr., "Planning for Profitability in the Eighties," *Planning Review* (Jan. 1983).

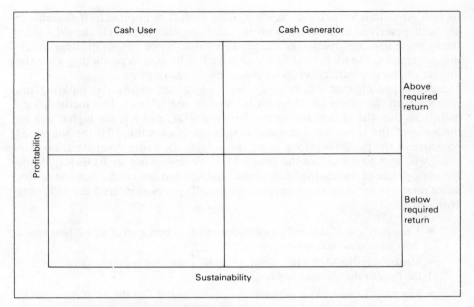

FIG. 11-7 Individual Business Unit Matrix

- *Upper left:* These businesses, while showing long-term value, require large investment. Growth industries are typified by these characteristics.

- *Lower left:* These are problem businesses or industries that require funding and are destroying company value. That is, they are cash users and are not profitable.

- *Lower right:* Businesses in this quadrant can stand alone on a financial basis, but they are not earning an acceptable return.

Both acquiring and divesting companies have found this to be a useful way to think of their businesses. It is an easy way to spot problem business units and to plan appropriate action. For example, Esmark's 1979 portfolio contained Swift Foods, a business known for its poor returns and high cash needs, and Vickers, a profitable oil company with high cash needs. Esmark announced the divestment of both in 1980.

A diversifying company should understand the value contribution/profitability role that the new business will play in its portfolio. If the business is on the lower left quadrant, why buy it? If it is in the lower right, how do they plan to improve it? If it is in the upper left, can they finance it? Finally, if it is in the upper right, is it priced correctly?

Impact on Shareholders

While there may be a number of motives influencing the diversification decision, improving value to shareholders is usually one key objective. The above section on valuation outlined the discounted cash flow approach. If shareholders both perceived and agreed with the analysis, this approach should reflect the increase in or destruction of shareholder value. Since neither of these conditions may exist, the usefulness of the approach is limited in predicting what the impact of the diversification move might be on share price.

An approach that has recently been advocated involves comparing the firm's return on equity (ROE) with its cost of equity (Ke). The methodology maintains that the greater the spread between ROE and Ke, the higher will be the ratio of the firm's market value (M) to its book value (B), the suggested objective of the firm. Therefore, using this model, the firm's diversification program will seek to maximize the firm's M/B by improving its ROE-Ke. While the importance of improving profitability is discussed above, application of this naive model is misleading for several reasons. Rappaport offered the following criticism[12]:

- The equity spread is based on an inappropriate subtraction of a cash-flow return from an accrual accounting return;
- Maximizing the M/B ratio is not a reliable proxy for maximizing the value of the firm to the shareholder; and
- The positive correlation between the equity spread and the M/B ratio can be significantly influenced by accounting capitalization versus expense rules that do not affect cash flow.

The correlation between the equity spread and the M/B ratio can be partially driven by an accounting tautology. The smaller the fraction of total investment capitalized on the books, the greater will be ROI or ROE and the smaller will be the book value. Thus, the same accounting policy that increases ROE, and thereby the equity spread, also decreases book value and thereby increases the M/B ratio. Business units, companies, and industries that expense a large fraction of investment will show higher ROIs and ROEs than their counterparts who invest at the same economic rate of return but capitalize a larger proportion of investment outlays. Thus, it comes as no surprise that companies in the pharmaceutical and cosmetic industries, which ordinarily invest relatively large amounts in noncapitalized assets such as research and development and advertising, report systematically higher book ROIs and ROEs than companies in other industries.

The Information Content of Share Prices. Another field of research might shed light on this problem. Professor William H. Beaver of Stanford University has devoted approximately 20 years of research to the subject of the information content of share price. Some of his findings that have a bearing on the problem posed above might be summarized as follows:

- The firm's share price reflects its expected future earning capability;

---

[12] Alfred Rappaport, "Corporate Performance Standards and Shareholder Value," *Journal of Business Strategy.* (Spring 1983), p. 33.

- Anticipated changes in the future earning power of the firm due to an acquisition or divestment will be reflected in a change in share price; and

- Dramatic share price movements in response to announcement of a possible acquisition or divestment signal shareholders' evaluation of that undertaking.

Using Beaver's methodology, recent research on other unrelated issues produced findings that had interesting implications for the field of acquisitions/divestments. Examples include the following:

- An announcement by an oil company of its merger discussions with another company met with extremely unfavorable response from its shareholders. The merger was completed anyway, and the stock price subsequently fell by about 40 percent.

- An announcement by a multi-business firm of its intent to divest its unprofitable meat subsidiary was met with shareholder approval, and share price climbed dramatically after the divestment.

These examples suggest an approach to analyzing the potential impact of an acquisition or divestment; i.e., evaluate the possible share price implications of the move *before* finalizing the deal.

While this approach is conceptually simple, there are some subtleties to the analysis that may not be readily apparent. For example, what standards are applied to determine what is "extremely unfavorable" or meets with "shareholder approval"? Moreover, what measurement process can discern the factors that are influencing share price movements?

Beaver's approach deals explicitly with these problems, using the following process:

1 A model is constructed that explains the forces driving the firm's share price and the extent of their influence. Those forces include market-wide and economic effects, industry effects, and firm-specific events. An appropriate control period is selected for construction of the model.

2 The model is applied to the period being analyzed, providing predicted returns for the firm's stock on a weekly basis.

3 Predicted returns for each week in the period are compared with the actual returns, producing a residual return.

4 Announcement dates of public information are compared with weeks that showed substantial (positive or negative) residual returns. (The determination of what is "substantial" can be done statistically using a confidence interval, or objectively using percentage changes on the returns.)

5 Announcements about possible acquisition or divestiture are evaluated on the basis of their impact on the residual return.

The major underlying assumption in this approach, other than that of market efficiency, is that the factors influencing share price in the control period have the same importance as in the period being analyzed. While this assumption might be criticized in specific isolated instances, they are usually self-evident cases and can be dealt with on an independent basis once the prob-

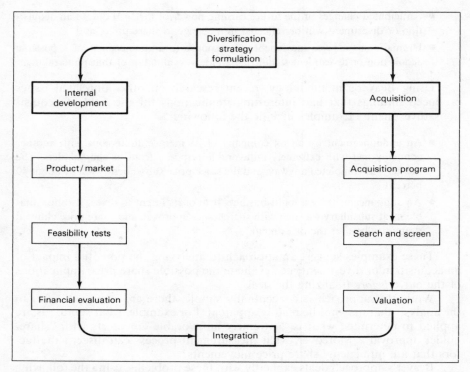

FIG. 11-8   A Systematic Process

lem is recognized. Certainly, this methodology is far superior to the approaches that have to make assumptions about what *should* be important to the firm's shareholders.

DEVELOPING A SYSTEMATIC PROCESS

Once the firm has undertaken a critical evaluation of where it is and where it is going in terms of diversification, as outlined above, a number of considerations remain. The precise considerations depend on whether internal development or acquisition is being pursued. Figure 11-8 illustrates a generic approach for dealing with the critical questions that should be addressed in either case.

Internal Development

The chief uncertainties in internal development are: Can a competitive product be developed; and can it be developed in time? Accordingly, three topics are discussed below: product/market decisions, feasibility tests, and financial evaluation.

Product/Market Decisions. Four combinations of old and new product/ market decisions are possible: old product/old market, old product/new market, new product/old market, and new product/new market. In addition to making an evaluation of the relative risk of each of these undertakings, managers should consider several questions, including the following:

- What is the competitive advantage of competing in an existing market segment with a "me, too" product?
- Does the firm have unique strengths (e.g., distribution) that will help it to take an existing product into new market segments?
- Does the firm have the skills to develop a new and better product for existing market segments?
- What factors indicate that the firm could be competitive with a new product in a new market?

Feasibility Tests. Two types of feasibility analyses should be conducted very early in the process. One type examines the economic benefits that might accrue and asks the questions, "What can happen if the firm succeeds? Is the potential market large enough to warrant an effort?"[13] These questions are similar to those asked in the internal formulation of the diversification strategy. They help to ensure consistency between the planners and those responsible for executing the plan.

The second type of feasibility analysis addresses the important questions of whether the task is technically feasible at all, and whether the firm has the internal capabilities to undertake the project successfully.

Financial Evaluation. Depending on the length of the time period dedicated to the development project, several interim evaluations might be desirable. These evaluations help to minimize the possibility of development projects being "grandfathered" into existence.

Two points at which financial evaluations should be conducted are: (1) the point at which the decision is being considered to go from product development to pilot production; and (2) the point at which the decision is being considered to proceed to full-scale production and commercialization.[14] Criteria mentioned earlier, such as marketability, profitability, and affordability, should be applied at these points.

Acquisition

The main uncertainty in the acquisition approach is whether the firm can locate and purchase a company or assets at a price that will yield an appropriate return. The environment for diversification through merger and acquisition in

[13] Eugene F. Finkin, "Developing and Managing New Products," *The Journal of Business Strategy,* (Spring 1983), p. 41.

[14] Ibid., p. 42.

the 1980s has changed dramatically from the late 1960s and mid-1970s. The odds have been stacked against successful acquisitions. Premiums have been high, pushing down returns. The hurdles of integration have been high, as proven by the inability of companies to do a successful job of merging two businesses and by the less than optimal results of many acquisitions.

Thus, the acquisition process has become a very selective one which requires special skills and industry knowledge that will permit management to examine cost reduction opportunities, redistribution of cash flow, or opportunities to leverage other assets in the combined organization in a way that will allow acceptable rates of return. Furthermore, an ability to consider management and cultural fit is required in those situations where the organizations will be completely integrated. Last, an ability to examine various transaction structures is required in order to "put the deal together."

Whether management decides to engage in a search for acquisition candidates or decides to be opportunistic and wait for situations to come over the transom, a structured process is required in order for managers to examine the issues identified above in a strategic, financial, and organizational context. This process will result in a logical methodical framework and screening system, and will permit the examination of a universe of potential targets, regardless of their source.

The process presented below is a comprehensive one that has been useful in the past. It addresses the three key steps in the acquisition process: acquisition program definition, search and screen, and candidate valuation and evaluation.

Acquisition Program Definition. Having determined the role of acquisitions in the firm's corporate strategy, the next step is to define a detailed framework for evaluating acquisitions by establishing acquisition criteria and specific timing responsibilities. For top management, the development of these criteria should clarify not only what managers want to achieve through acquisition, but how they plan to accomplish their goals. The framework can then serve as a comprehensive guide in identifying specific candidates.

An interactive approach to creating the acquisition framework is described below. This process requires a dedicated effort from top management. In essence, "straw men" are listed as potential takeover candidates. The parameters of the companies and their respective industries are defined in detail. A ranking process is developed according to which management ranks those aspects of each company and industry they find appealing and that fit with their company's objectives (which may be unstated). This process forces the management group to come to terms with different views on each of the variables, and frequently moves the group toward consensus on a set of diversification objectives.

The completion of this effort, regardless of the approach used, results in the type of output structure shown in Table 11-1.

Search and Screen. The search and screen process, which is based on the detailed criteria developed in the program definition phase, is a systematic

TABLE 11-1 Diversification Output Structures

Parameters	Industry	Firm
Financial	*Risk/reward* • Projected growth • Projected returns • Asset recoverability • Capital intensity	*Risk/reward* • Historic growth • Historic returns • Historic margins • Productive asset utilization • Hidden liabilities/bonuses • Work force/management profile • Unfunded pension liability
Fit	*Acquirer capability* • Financial • Customer base • Distribution channels • Manufacturing capabilities	*Acquirer capability* • Financial • Customer base • Distribution channels • Professional skills • Managerial skills • Location
Competition and portfolio	*Ease of entry* • Life cycle position • Requirements for achieving optimum scale • Product/service void	*Key products* • Life cycle position • Product/market portfolio composition • Potential competitors/competitive response • Raw material availability • Customer concentration
Miscellaneous	*Environment* • Legal/regulatory • Technological change • Industry structural change • Customer trends	*Organization* • Organization structure • Healthy competitor or turnaround situation • Culture

approach to seeking and identifying potential acquisition candidates. By applying the established criteria, the screening process enables management to select a few of the best candidates from as many as thousands of possibilities. While many publicly owned companies can be identified through computer data bases, information-gathering on both private and small publicly owned firms generally requires special research techniques.

Among the research sources that may be used are the following:

• Compustat and similar computer data bases
• Public data sources
• Client management interviews
• Industry expert interviews
• Supplier interviews
• Customer interviews

The output of search and screen phase is a ranking of potential target firms. For the most attractive of these, formal profiles are compiled covering known financial, operational, and managerial characteristics.

Candidate Valuation and Evaluation. Having isolated a select set of acquisition candidates, the potential of a consummated merger must be quantified. The correct approach to financial valuation focuses on discounted cash-flow analysis. Such an approach provides managers of the acquiring company with sufficient information both to make a go/no-go decision on the candidate and to formulate an effective negotiating strategy for acquisition. This process also forces management to reach the decision to pursue acquisitions (which is an investment of the firm's resources) with internally generated opportunities that the firm may have.

The go/no-go decision is based upon the value added by combining the candidate's future cash-flow stream with that of the acquiring company. These projections of cash-flow streams are prepared on both a stand-alone basis and a consolidated basis; the consolidation permits management to assess the value created by merging the acquisition candidate into current operations. Estimating the components of cash flow is critical to the valuation, and it depends heavily upon an understanding of industry economics, the candidate's competitive position, its strengths and weaknesses, and the integration plans of the acquiring company.

Various "deal structures" also need to be evaluated during this phase. The evaluations permit the examination of the impact on earnings per share and on the capital/financial structure.

There are a number of commercially available computer models that can handle the mechanical number-crunching parts of this process. Many companies have also developed their own in-house programs and models. Some of the questions typically addressed by most models are as follows:

- What is the maximum acceptable price, given a range of returns?
- What value is being created for the shareholders?
- What are the major areas of risk?
- What are the cash-flow implications of the acquisition?
- What are the earnings implications of completing the acquisition?
- What is the best financing package?

Complete evaluation, however, often consists of much more than a sophisticated financial analysis. Depending upon the specific situation, the amount of preplanning that has been done, and the interests of the acquiring company, an in-depth review of the anti-trust implications and risks may also be required. Such an analysis should be undertaken when:

- The parties involved sell similar or identical products or services in the same market;
- The parties involved either sell to or buy from one another; and

- Through acquisition, the acquiring firm brings unmatched financial or other resources to the industry.

There are three reasons for a thorough analysis. First, if problems are detected before the merger, a course of remedy may be open that will enable the merger to proceed. Second, if the problems seem insurmountable, an unnecessary tender or acquisition offer can be avoided. Third, in order to provide acquiring companies with preliminary indications of potential problems, the government provides for a formal, premerger conference known as the Hart, Scott, Rodino procedure. This permits the acquiring company to present a well-prepared position paper on the proposed merger and its impact on competition. In certain cases, this option, while requiring substantial preparation, may be recommended or required.

Integration

In 1968, Rockwell and North American pursued a merger based on the synergistic potential it could achieve. Rockwell, looking for new technologies and new products for commercial markets, saw North American as a place where "scientific longhairs" threw away ideas every day that could be useful. In turn, North American was attracted to Rockwell's potential ability to commercialize new technologies.[15] However, after more than a decade, Rockwell continued to have problems with its strategy of capitalizing on North American's scientific strengths to develop important new commercial businesses. The simple diagnosis is that the poor cultural fit of these two firms inhibited their ability to implement the most desirable strategy for the combined firms.[16]

When two firms are contemplating a merger, the resulting organization of the combined entities—beyond the question of who is going to be president—is usually considered only lightly, if at all. However, there are several critical questions that should be answered, as follows:

- *Organization structure*

    a. What will be the structure of the combined companies?

    b. Are there overlaps or redundancies in the new structure?

    c. Will the new entity require a significantly different structure?

- *Systems*

    a. How compatible are the existing management processes and systems (e.g., incentive compensation)?

    b. Does one firm contribute advanced systems to the other (e.g., information systems)?

    c. What are the formal and informal channels of communication in the firms and how will they fit?

---

[15] "Forget the Magic Mergers," *Forbes* (July 15, 1972), p. 28.

[16] *Organizational Diagnosis* (concept paper published by Management Analysis Center, Inc., 1981).

- *People*
  - a. How homogeneous are the expectations of the people in the two firms?
  - b. How much overlap is there? How many will stay and how many will go?
  - c. Are key people willing to stay?
  - d. What are their attitudes toward the merger?
- *Culture*
  - a. How is conflict resolved in each firm?
  - b. What is the management style in each firm? Are they compatible?
  - c. Are the guiding beliefs of the firms compatible?

Uncertain or negative answers to any of these questions may signal trouble ahead and suggest discussion topics that should be addressed during negotiations. If the diversification move is to be through internal development, these topics may still need to be considered. In this case, there is more time to reflect on the issues and plan accordingly than there is in the heat of merger negotiations.

SUMMARY

There are a number of reasons firms pursue corporate diversification, and the corporate development officer is subject to pressures from a variety of internal sources, often from individuals with preconceived ideas or vested interests. The only way to deal effectively with conventional wisdom is to apply a systematic framework for understanding and interpreting the facts.

The first step in such a framework is to develop the strategy. Using one or several analytical tools, the study identifies the key structural characteristics of businesses that determine their attractiveness and the nature of competition, by indicators of the new entrant's opportunity for success. The second step is to understand the implications of the diversification strategy. Considerations include the affordability and sustainability of the plan, the risk implications, and the probable impact on the share price of the firm. The final step is to develop a structural process, which includes a check list of issues that might be encountered on the formulation and implementation of the diversification strategy.

Once adopted, such a program will clearly highlight the problems that exist with the questionable ventures and, by contrast, showcase the several business ventures that make sense and will be of value to the company.

12

Acquisitions and Divestitures

LIONEL L. FRAY, JAMES W. DOWN, DAVID GAYLIN

Temple, Barker & Sloane, Inc.

ACQUISITION AS A STRATEGY

The word "acquisition" is used in this chapter to describe the addition of a business to a parent company through merger, consolidation, or takeover. Since the mid-1960s, acquisition activity has fluctuated widely. It peaked in 1969 with over 6,000 mergers, decreased during the early 1970s, and leveled off in the late 1970s and early 1980s at around 2,000 mergers per year (Table 12-1). The reduction in the number of mergers, however, has been more than offset by a significant increase in the size of mergers, many of which have been called megamergers in recent years. Table 12-2 illustrates the increase in the number of mergers in excess of $100 million from 1975 to 1983. In 1981 there were a record 12 mergers in excess of $1 billion, the largest being Du Pont's $8 billion acquisition of Conoco. (There were 11 such mergers in 1982 and 6 in 1983.)

Some of the most notable companies in U.S. industry were acquired during the early 1980s merger wave, including Conoco, Marathon Oil, Cities Service, Bendix, Salomon Brothers, Heublein, and Schlitz. F.M. Scherer states that the latest surge in merger activity "has only two quantitative equals in United States industrial history": the largely horizontal merger wave of 1898 to 1902, when the great industrial monopolies were formed, and the conglomerate wave of the 1960s, when large companies diversified by purchasing unrelated businesses.[1]

There are differing opinions on the long-term effects of the merger wave of the early 1980s. Some analysts believe that the mergers are, for the most part, a different type than those of the 1960s. In the 1960s, many companies pursued a corporate strategy, attempting to increase earnings per share and spread risk through investment in diverse enterprises. While this strategy worked for a time, the longer-term performance of the resulting conglomerates led the stock markets to accord them below-average price earnings (P/E) ratios. By contrast, in the late 1970s and early 1980s, the merger movement centered around the attempt to produce synergy between the companies.

Critics of the merger movement, however, cite concerns over the high premiums paid and the significant debt incurred to finance the deals, and they question whether the claimed synergies will materialize.

---

[1] "After Wave of Mergers, Analysts Debate Pluses," *New York Times*, May 31, 1982.

TABLE 12-1   Net Merger and Acquisition Announcements, 1969–1983

Year	Number	Year-to-Year Percentage Change
1969	6,107	+37%
1970	5,152	−16%
1971	4,608	−11%
1972	4,801	+ 4%
1973	4,040	−16%
1974	2,861	−29%
1975	2,297	−20%
1976	2,276	− 1%
1977	2,224	− 2%
1978	2,106	− 5%
1979	2,128	+ 1%
1980	1,889	−11%
1981	2,395	+27%
1982	2,346	− 2%
1983	2,533	+ 8%

Source: W.T. Grimm & Co.

TABLE 12-2   Increase in Value of Acquisitions

Year	Acquisitions in Excess of $100 Million	Total Dollar Value Paid (billions)
1975	14	$11.8
1976	39	20.0
1977	41	21.9
1978	80	34.2
1979	83	43.5
1980	94	44.3
1981	113	82.6
1982	116	53.8
1983	138	73.1

Source: W.T. Grimm & Co.

This chapter examines the motivation to acquire, the elements of the acquisition process, and some of the reasons for success and failure in acquisitions.

ACQUISITION PLANNING: MAKING THE ACQUISITION DECISION AND PLANNING STRATEGY

The overall objective of any acquisition is to maintain or increase profits. The pursuit of this broadly stated policy, however, is one of the major reasons that many acquisitions fail. To guard against failure, an acquisition program should be soundly based on specific objectives and strategies.

Acquisition Objectives

Acquisitions can be made for a variety of specific reasons. Some of the more common reasons are discussed below.

Strengthen or Protect the Base Business. The desire to acquire elements such as key personnel, assets, and purchasing power is often the driving force behind an acquisition. Many of the acquisitions of oil and gas holdings are examples of tactical purchases of assets. In 1981, Shell Oil purchased Belridge Oil for $3.6 billion in order to increase Shell's domestic U.S. oil holdings. Similarly, Sun Company purchased Seagram's oil and gas holdings, Texas Pacific Oil Company, for $2.3 billion.

Many acquisitions are made to adapt to competitive or environmental changes. In 1978, as the regulation of the railroad industry was beginning to ease, two connecting railroads, Chessie Systems and Seaboard Coast Line Industries (SCL), announced their plans to merge, creating a major southeastern railroad. In response to this structural change in the industry, the Chessie's major competitor, the Norfolk and Western, announced its plans to merge with the SCL's direct competitor, the Southern Railroad.

Diversify. Acquisition can be a means to gain entry into new markets or businesses. Baldwin-United, through its $329 million acquisition of Sperry and Hutchinson in 1981 and MGIC Investment in 1982, tried to transform itself from a staid piano manufacturer into a major financial services company, ultimately ending in bankruptcy. On the other hand, Sears, Roebuck & Company, the nation's number-one retailer, facing slow growth and depressed profits in its base business, made two major acquisitions in 1981 that have been highly successful. Sears added the stock brokerage firm, Dean Witter Reynolds, and the largest real estate broker in the United States, Coldwell Banker & Company, to its existing Allstate insurance business as part of its major effort to diversify into financial services.

Avoid a Takeover. Acquisition can be used to defend against an unfriendly takeover attempt. Frank B. Hall acquired Jartran in 1981 in a defensive move to fend off an acquisition attempt by Ryder Systems. Since Ryder and Jartran are direct competitors, Ryder could not acquire Frank B. Hall without violating antitrust statutes.

Improve Financial Returns. A company often makes an acquisition to improve its return on excess capital or to take advantage of tax benefits. For example, the Penn Central Corporation, following its bankruptcy and the subsequent divestiture of its railroad operations, emerged in 1979 as a conglomerate with substantial federal tax-loss carryforwards. To take advantage of this tax protection, Penn Central embarked on a series of acquisitions, including those of Marathon Manufacturing and GK Technologies. Gulf + Western, under Chairman Charles Bluhdorn, employed a policy of acquiring companies whose assets it believed were undervalued. (Since Bluhdorn's death, however, G + W's new management has reversed course, selling off some 25 businesses and a large stock portfolio.)

Corporate Evaluation

Before the goals of an acquisition program can be determined, a corporation must evaluate both its present and future position. It should evaluate the external environment, analyze the company's internal strengths and weaknesses to compete in this environment, and assess its corporate objectives and the company's ability to fulfill them. The external environment includes the economic, competitive, political, legal, social, and institutional pressures that bear upon any company. The internal environment includes corporate strengths and weaknesses, shareholder goals, management style, and corporate culture. Some of the key strategic questions to ask during the evaluation include the following:

- What are the long-term financial and nonfinancial corporate objectives?
- How mature are the corporation's present businesses, and what growth potential remains?
- What technological trends are taking place, and what threats or opportunities do they pose?
- What legal or regulatory changes are taking place, and how will they affect the corporation?
- What is the corporation's competitive position? How is it changing?
- Should the corporation deepen its penetration in existing businesses, or expand into new business areas?

The result of this evaluation is typically a set of long-term corporate objectives and an evaluation of the capability of the company's present business to satisfy these objectives. The evaluation should include the identification of any expansion or diversification needs.

Acquisition Alternatives

Before embarking on an acquisition program, a company should evaluate alternatives to acquisition as a means of achieving its long-term corporate objectives.

Joint ventures should be considered as an acquisition alternative, even though they can be difficult to manage. Over time, the goals of the joint venture partners may diverge, resulting in disputes, attempts by one partner to buy out the other, or, in some cases, protracted legal battles. For example, when Conoco decided not to fund $12 million for testing a new industrial boiler because of the poor economy, it left Stone & Webster, its partner in the project, with the prospect of funding part or all of the testing cost.

The internal start-up of new ventures should also be evaluated as an acquisition alternative. This strategy is probably most appropriate where a company has skills and resources it can apply to new areas and has significant time to develop the new venture. Ralph Biggadike determined in a 1978 study that new ventures typically suffer substantial losses and negative cash flows in their early years of operation, and, on average, they require eight years before they achieve profitability, and 10 to 12 years before their return on investment equals that of mature businesses.[2]

Acquisition Strategy

Once a determination has been made to embark on an acquisition program, an acquisition strategy must be developed to guide the program. This strategy addresses issues such as the strategic direction of the corporation, the size and type of the firm to be acquired, and the type of acquisition desired.

Strategic Direction. The corporation must decide whether to seek horizontal expansion (e.g., Nabisco-Standard Brands), vertical integration (e.g., Conagra-Banquet Foods), or diversification. If the corporation selects diversification, it must decide whether the new firm should be related to existing businesses (e.g., American Express-Shearson Loeb) or unrelated (e.g., ITT-Sheraton).

While there are no hard and fast rules on these issues, a review of prior experience with strategic development in U.S. industry is enlightening. For example, research by Richard Rumelt demonstrated that since World War II, there has been a strong trend for large U.S. corporations to diversify away from single businesses.[3] One of the more compelling points brought out in the

---

[2] Ralph Biggadike, "The Risky Business of Diversification," *Harvard Business Review* (May-June 1979).

[3] Richard P. Rumelt, *Strategy, Structure, and Economic Performance* (Cambridge, Mass.: Harvard University Press, 1974).

research is that the financial performance of diversifying companies is closely correlated with the way in which firms relate new business ventures to their old businesses, rather than with the magnitude or pace of diversification.

Most important is the finding that companies that exhibit the best financial performance (i.e., highest returns to capital and least variability in earnings relative to growth in earnings) are those that have tightly controlled and consistently focused their diversification efforts by building on a single core of existing skills, knowledge, or experience. In contrast, companies that have either disregarded their existing core of skills and knowledge or tried to build in various different directions, each new direction drawing on a different skill, knowledge, or experience, have not performed as well. Similarly, the authors of *In Search of Excellence* point out that all of the companies they identified as having particularly effective management have grown by building on their strengths.[4] Not one of their so-called excellent companies is an unrelated conglomerate.

Research by Salter and Weinhold[5] also indicates that related diversification can be divided into two types:

1 *Related-supplementary diversification* is accomplished by diversifying into new markets requiring functional skills identical to those already possessed by the company. The purest form of this strategy is horizontal integration with minimal departure from key functional activities.

2 *Related-complementary diversification* is accomplished by adding key functional activities in order to participate in the same market but in a broader fashion. The purest form of this strategy is vertical integration, i.e., adding new skills but making minimal change in market orientation.

The two major criteria for choosing between related-supplementary diversification and related-complementary diversification are the attractiveness of the market (e.g., rate of growth) and the company's competitive position within the market (e.g., market share). Salter and Weinhold conclude that (1) companies with strong positions in low-growth markets should pursue related-supplementary diversification, and (2) companies with limited positions in attractive industries should pursue related-complementary diversification.

Type of Company. The corporation must decide whether to seek a private company, a public company, or a division that is being divested. To a great extent, this decision is influenced by the availability of the various types of companies. Despite the fanfare surrounding many acquisitions of public corporations, the data from W.T. Grimm presented in Table 12-3 demonstrate that in recent years, the predominant activity in mergers and acquisitions has been acquiring divestitures and private companies.

---

[4] Thomas J. Peters and Robert H. Waterman, Jr., *In Search of Excellence* (New York: Harper & Row, 1982).

[5] Malcom S. Salter and Wolf A. Weinhold, *Diversification through Acquisition* (New York: The Free Press, 1979).

TABLE 12-3 Composition of Acquisition Announcements

Year	Divestitures	Acquisitions of Public Companies	Acquisitions of Private Companies	Total
1980	666	173	988	1,827
1981	830	168	1,330	2,328
1982	875	180	1,222	2,277
1983	932	190	1,316	2,438

Source: W.T. Grimm & Co.

Size of Company. Is the corporation looking for a $10 million company or a billion-dollar company? This usually depends on its objectives and resources. Alco-Standard follows a strategy of acquiring relatively small companies that can be operated on a decentralized basis but that can still benefit from being associated with a multi-billion-dollar corporation. Sears, on the other hand, had to acquire very large corporations (Dean Witter and Coldwell Banker) in order to succeed in diversifying from its $20 billion retailing business.

Type of Approach. Is the corporation looking for a "friendly" deal (e.g., Dart and Kraft)? Is it willing to be an "unfriendly" acquiror (e.g., Brown-Foreman and Lenox)? Does it want to play the role of the "white knight" (e.g., Allied opportunistically coming to the rescue of Bendix)?

Pursuing a friendly acquisition usually increases the chances of retaining the acquiree's management, but it limits the opportunities available since the managements of many companies are not interested in being part of a merger. Pursuing unfriendly acquisitions, however, has some serious risks, as evidenced by the notorious four-cornered battle among Bendix, Martin Marietta, United Technologies, and Allied Corporation.

In 1982, Bendix attempted to acquire Martin Marietta in what *Time* magazine referred to as "one of the dirtiest, sloppiest, most wasteful takeover battles in U.S. corporate history."[6] In a series of moves that resembled a game of checkers more than chess, Martin Marietta turned from prey to hunter by teaming with United Technologies and tendering an offer for Bendix at the same time that Bendix was tendering its offer for Martin Marietta. Bendix finally was forced to turn to Allied Corporation in a merger that kept it out of the hands of Martin Marietta, but it cost the initiator of this battle, Bendix Chairman William Agee, his job. W. Richard Bingham, managing director of Lehman Brothers, Kuhn Loeb, feels the Bendix-Martin Marietta dogfight could discourage future hostile takeovers. "Hostile transactions have become accepted strategy, but the Bendix affair had so many convoluted maneuvers that boards of directors are likely to be more cautious this year."[7] Similarly, in

---

[6] "White Knights and Black Eyes," *Time*, Feb. 14, 1983.

[7] "Deals of the Year," *Fortune*, Jan. 24, 1983.

a futile attempt to take over Conoco, Seagram's ended up owning 20 percent of Du Pont-Conoco, and shortly thereafter it incurred a $650 million paper loss as the price of Du Pont's stock tumbled.

The role of the white knight is not always clear. As Michael Marks puts it, "There is no such thing as a white knight, only shades of gray."[8] For example, shortly after Allegheny International came in as a white knight to rescue Sunbeam Corporation from IC Industries, it terminated several hundred Sunbeam managers ranging from high-level executives to middle managers. As one Sunbeam manager viewed it, "They went at us with a meat ax. If Allegheny is a white knight, God save us from white knights."[9] Similarly, Wheelabrator-Frye "rescued" Pullman, Inc., from McDermott, Inc., only to terminate more than 1,500 Pullman employees beginning the day after the merger was completed. There can also be significant risks for the white knights. They often enter as the battle is in progress, and they have little time to negotiate or do research. Chairman Robert Buckley of Allegheny commented that he discovered in Sunbeam "problems under the surface that were greater than they seemed."[10] Occidental Petroleum, for example, reached an agreement to acquire Cities Service for $4 billion in only nine days. As one Wall Street investment banker puts it, "How can anyone be expected to investigate all the ramifications of a $1 billion or $2 billion commitment in such a short time?"[11]

ACQUISITION PROCESS AND IMPLEMENTATION

Once a decision to make an acquisition has been made, an implementation plan should be developed. The plan's level of formality depends upon the time available and the management style of the corporation. Formal plans tend to be inflexible and stifling, while informal ones are usually inefficient and risky. The best plans incorporate both formal and informal elements, allow for speed and innovation, but take an organized approach that promotes efficiency and minimizes risk. The basic elements of an acquisition program are discussed below.

Development of Criteria

Acquisition criteria serve three purposes:

1 They ensure coherence with corporate strategy and objectives;

2 They guide personnel in evaluating and screening industries to enter and companies to acquire; and

---

[8] "Employees at Acquired Firms Find White Knights Often Unfriendly," *The Wall Street Journal*, July 7, 1982.

[9] Ibid.

[10] "White Knights and Black Eyes," *Time*, op. cit.

[11] Ibid.

3 They assist board members, management, bankers, attorneys, or brokers who can play a role in identifying and evaluating acquisition candidates.

Criteria should not be formulated so tightly that nothing passes through, nor so loosely that too much passes; they should be flexible and be allowed to change over time to reflect changing experience and priorities.

There are many types of acquisition criteria; the criteria discussed below are typically included in an implementation plan, either formally or informally.

Industry Focus. Is the corporation looking for a company involved in any manufacturing industry, or is it seeking a company involved in a specific area (e.g., the manufacture of specialized heavy truck equipment)?

Synergy With Acquiror. What type of synergy with its present operations is the corporation seeking? Conglomerates such as Gulf + Western do not necessarily require acquisitions to have any synergy with existing operations. Most companies, however, are in the acquisition market to strengthen existing operations. Examples of areas of synergy between the acquiror and acquiree include the following:

- *Functional* synergy, such as a strong marketing company acquiring a company with a solid product line but limited marketing expertise (e.g., Philip Morris acquiring Miller Beer and Seven-Up);

- *Financial* synergy, such as a cash-rich company acquiring a company whose growth is limited primarily by a shortage of capital (e.g., United Technologies acquiring Mostek); and

- *Distribution* synergy, such as a company with an existing distribution chain acquiring a company that is seeking to expand the distribution of its products (e.g., Sears acquiring Dean Witter or Cheseborough-Pond acquiring Bass Shoe).

Financial and Economic Criteria. Financial and economic criteria typically include the following:

- *Growth:* Is the corporation looking for a high-growth company or an average-growth company? Or, is growth unimportant?

- *Return on equity/return on total capital:* How should the returns compare to those of the existing operation, to those of U.S. industry on average, or to those of the candidate's competitors?

- *Financial leverage:* Is the corporation seeking a company with high or low leverage? How does the leverage compare with that of the corporation's existing operation, or with that of the candidate's competitors?

- *Operating leverage:* What should be the acquisition candidate's relative level of fixed and variable costs? What level of capital and labor intensity does the corporation want?

Competitive Posture. Is the corporation looking for a company that is a leader in its primary market and that could, therefore, command a premium price? Or, does it seek a troubled company that has the potential for turnaround and, therefore, the potential for a substantial increase in value? How important is potential competition, obsolescence, or substitution? The Pritzker family, owners of Hyatt Corporation, has successfully employed a strategy of acquiring troubled companies, usually at a price substantially below book value, and turning them around.

Management. Should the company have experienced, stable managers who will continue to run the operation, or will the corporation provide its own managers? Should the firm's management have the same style and culture as the corporation's own (e.g., the polished investment bankers of Salomon Brothers merging with the commodity traders at Phibro)?

Geography. Does the corporation want a company primarily with domestic revenues, or one with international revenues? Does it matter where the company is headquartered? Will it consolidate physically with the corporation?

Acquisition Search Process

There are several approaches to the acquisition search process. The choice of an approach depends on a company's objectives, time horizon, prior planning and analysis, resources available, and corporate culture. Jerold L. Freier identified three major types of approaches: opportunistic (starting from what is already for sale), research (starting from acquisition criteria), and combination (a blend of the first two approaches).[12] Each approach is discussed below.

- *The opportunistic approach.* This method first identifies companies available for sale and then determines which are attractive. It permits immediate movement into the flow of deals and consideration of a wide range of candidates, while not wasting time on companies that may not be for sale. Some disadvantages of this approach are that it requires a heavy reliance on third-party brokers, it can result in significant time and effort devoted to inappropriate candidates, and it may not support an overall strategic direction. The opportunistic approach is usually most appropriate for companies that have extensive acquisition experience and are bargain-hunting or pursuing a conglomerate strategy.

- *The research approach.* This entails performing detailed screening and research to determine which industries and companies fit the acquiror's strategy and criteria, selecting the companies that fit, and then determining what companies may be for sale. The advantages of this approach are that it is highly focused and is likely to yield candidates that "fit" with the acquiror. The major disadvantage is that it involves a significant commitment of research time and effort,

---

[12] Jerold L. Freier, "Acquisition Search Programs," *The Journal of Corporate Venture* (Summer 1981).

which requires patience and discipline. It is particularly effective for companies that do not have much acquisition experience or that are unsure of the industries they wish to enter.

- *The combination approach.* This approach to acquisition searches blends elements of both the opportunistic and research approaches. It is a flexible method that involves researching and identifying industries and companies that should be pursued while still being open to attractive deals that may become available. This method is not as structured as the research approach or as loose as the opportunistic approach. It appeals to companies that have a good sense of where their acquisition program is headed but that still could benefit from the additional research.

The first step in the research approach or combination approach is to screen potential industries by identifying all those that meet the company's criteria. This process could start with a broad criterion of seeking a consumer products company, for example. The next step is identifying all standard industrial codes (SICs) that fall into this category. After this initial screening, financial and secondary research is conducted (using on-line databases, such as Disclosure and Compustat, and trade journals) to provide a preliminary evaluation of each industry. The industries should then be ranked in terms of potential, and several of the highest ranked should be chosen for in-depth analysis. This analysis should be performed using (1) interviews with individuals and groups such as industry participants and trade associations; (2) secondary research (e.g., published industry reports, consultants, investment reports); and (3) a complete literature review aided by the on-line databases. The output of this process should be a comprehensive report on each industry containing the following information:

- Industry size
- Industry growth and projections
- Industry structure and dynamics
  - a. Number and market shares of participants
  - b. Profitability
  - c. Historical and projected changes
- Competitive profile of significant participants
  - a. Financial
  - b. Products
  - c. Organization
  - d. Management
  - e. Performance
- Criteria for long-term success
- Determination of interest in entering each of the industries analyzed and list of target companies for further analysis

Acquisition prospects can be generated from many sources, including industry analyses, directors, consultants, investment and commercial bankers, attorneys, accountants, and other brokers.

Initial Contact With Candidates. Once a prospect has been identified, a decision must be made to attempt a friendly or unfriendly takeover. If an unfriendly takeover is going to be undertaken, the company proceeds directly to the in-depth corporate analysis. If a friendly takeover will be attempted, contact with the candidate may be initiated in addition to the in-depth research. There are several ways to initiate this contact, including direct contact by letter or telephone and indirect contact through mutual friends or professional intermediaries. The initial contact with the candidate serves many purposes, including the following:

- Assessing potential management and cultural fit
- Assessing potential business fit and value added
- Determining the candidate's interest in merging
- Creating interest in merging

Detailed Company Investigation and Appraisal. If further interest exists after the initial contact, or if the contact stage was bypassed, the next phase is an intensive analysis and appraisal of the candidate. The following activities should be included:

- Conducting preliminary operations, legal, and financial audits (e.g., Are there any major lawsuits pending? What are the candidate's balance sheet strengths? What accounting policies have been used to govern reported earnings?)
- Performing an appraisal of the assets
- Commissioning special studies needed in areas such as pension funds or antitrust
- Developing detailed information (marketing, technical, management, manufacturing, and financial/economic)
- Consulting with experts on accounting, financing, legal, and regulatory issues (e.g., pooling versus purchase, tax-free options, antitrust)
- Determining the impact of merger on both parties under various scenarios
  - a. Purchase price
  - b. Merged business forecast
  - c. Financial plans (e.g., pricing, volume, cost)
  - d. Industry and other microeconomic outlooks

Negotiations. The form of negotiations varies with every transaction. Negotiations usually begin informally at the initial meeting, and they become more formal in subsequent discussions as the price, terms, and conditions are refined. However, it is important that the acquiror develop a negotiating strategy prior to serious discussions. This strategy should include a plan covering the following:

- *Price:* How much does the corporation want to pay? What is the maximum that will be paid?

- *Type and terms of financing:* Will cash, notes, stock, or another form of payment be used?

- *Employment contracts:* Will specific contracts or other incentives be provided? If so, what will be the general clauses?

- *Organization:* How will the candidate report to the acquiror? What flexibility and what constraints are envisioned? What cultural issues can be anticipated?

- *Employee benefits:* Will the candidate retain its present policies, or adopt those of the acquiror? Will the employees retain the perquisites to which they are accustomed (e.g., company cars, offices, travel arrangements, bonuses, vacations, sick days)?

Documentation, Confirmation, and Closing. Acquisition negotiations can often take a long time, during which many changes can take place within the candidate company. Prior to closing, all studies and analyses should be carefully reviewed and updated. This includes final legal and accounting audits, final forecast and scenario analyses, and analysis of any major changes that have occurred in the personnel, financial, marketing, or operational areas. In addition, the closing itself usually involves significant legal review for both parties to the transaction.

Implementation of Transition Plan. The closing of the deal does not end the acquisition process; instead, it begins the transition phase. The chances of a successful relationship are increased greatly if a detailed transition plan has been developed *prior* to the closing. The turnover of top management in an acquired company is extremely high in the first few years following acquisition. This turnover can often be attributed to the changing work environment that has occurred. Managers often cite the parent's information reporting requirements or a real or perceived loss of status as reasons for the high turnover. The transition plan should address the following:

- Integration with parent's systems (e.g., accounting, personnel)
- Level of autonomy
- Reporting relationships
- Reporting requirements (e.g., budgets, plans)
- Compensation and benefits
- Perquisites (e.g., company cars, travel arrangements, bonuses)
- Other policies and procedures

PARTICIPANTS AND RESOURCES IN THE ACQUISITION PROGRAM

As shown in Table 12-4, the acquisition process usually involves multiple participants, both internal and external, in almost every stage. Some participants, such as top management, are usually involved in every stage, while others, such as consultants or internal functional groups, are usually involved in very specific areas, such as evaluating one facet of the candidate's business.

The resources required to support an acquisition program depend upon the type of search process used and the number and size of acquisitions planned. For example, pursuing a research-based search process requires a more significant in-house staff than an opportunistic process that relies primarily on intermediaries to identify prospects. Similarly, the staffing required to consummate one acquisition will be less than that required to support multiple acquisitions. There is, however, some basic internal support that is required in almost all cases.

Internal Resources

There should be one person who is the recognized leader in planning and implementing acquisitions. This could be the chief executive officer, the chief financial officer, the corporate planner, or the head of the merger and acquisitions group. Large, active acquirors will usually have a staff dedicated to identifying and analyzing prospective deals. Smaller or less active acquirors often rely on a multidisciplinary internal task force to analyze opportunities as they are identified. Even companies with merger and acquisition staffs will usually make use of task forces, drawing, as needed, on internal resources in areas such as finance, taxation, labor, and operations.

In addition to internal personnel, the acquisition program should be supported by access to some of the many on-line informational databases that are available for screening and analysis (e.g., Disclosure, Compustat, Mergex), and access to financial valuation models (either internal or external).

External Resources

Almost all acquisitions involve external parties. The degree of their involvement depends upon the availability of internal resources and the complexity of the acquisition. The following is a brief description of the types of external support usually employed and the circumstances under which they are most effective. Note that while there are potential pitfalls in using any external resource, the well-respected firms providing merger and acquisition support have succeeded over the years by developing strong relationships with their clients based on competent guidance and trust.

Investment Banks. Supporters swear by the assistance they receive from investment bankers; detractors often refer to them as salesmen in pinstripe suits. Bankers can assist both the buyer and the seller in a variety of areas, including the following:

Table 12-4 Participation in the Acquisition Process

Acquisition Element	Top Management	Corporate Development	Finance/ Accounting	Legal	Other Functional Groups	Consultants	Investment Bankers
Criteria	XX	XX	X			X	X
Industry analysis and candidate identification	X	XX				X	X
Preliminary candidate analysis	X	XX	X			X	X
Candidate contact	XX	X				X	X
Detailed evaluation	X	XX	X	X	X	X	X
Negotiations	XX	X	X	X			X
Documentation, confirmation, and closing	X	X	XX	XX	X		
Transition	XX		X		X		

XX = Major participant

X = Participant

- Industry and company identification
- Initial contacts with prospects
- Financial valuation
- Negotiating the terms of the deal
- Financing arrangements
- Takeover defenses

In large acquisitions, it is common for both the buyer and seller to be represented by their own investment bank (see Table 12-5). This becomes even more complex when several companies are involved in an unfriendly takeover attempt. While the jury is still out on the success of the $1.9 billion Allied-Bendix merger, it is clear that several investment banks came out winners. Lehman Brothers served Allied for an estimated $5 million to $6 million fee; Salomon Brothers and First Boston each received about $3 million from Bendix; and Kidder Peabody, representing Martin Marietta, and Lazard Freres, representing United Technologies, each received about $1 million.

To make effective use of investment banks, it is important to determine what functions they can perform that cannot be handled by internal resources. For example, while investment banks will gladly perform industry and company analyses for a fee, they usually bring no more expertise to this undertaking than exists within many companies' planning staffs. However, in terms of entering the flow of deals or providing guidance on financing issues, the investment banks often can be of significant value.

Similarly, it is important to understand how the terms of payment might affect the actions of the investment bank. For example, investment banks are usually paid a percentage of the purchase price. This often involves the Lehman formula of 5 percent of the first million dollars, 4 percent of the second million, 3 percent of the third million, 2 percent of the fourth million, and 1 percent of all monies over $4 million. But this could also be a negotiated percentage, particularly in large deals, such as Allied-Bendix. Being paid a percentage of the purchase price provides incentive to the seller's investment bank to find a buyer and receive the highest price possible; however, it may result in a conflict of interest for the buyer's investment bank. It also can result in the investment banks on both sides placing more emphasis on finalizing the transaction than on determining whether it is the right transaction for either party from a strategic standpoint.

Consultants. Consultants are often used for many of the same functions that investment bankers perform, such as assisting in industry and company identification, making initial contacts, and assisting in valuation. Their primary role, however, is usually in the area of performing special studies, which could range from technical engineering studies to market research surveys to comprehensive industry or strategy studies.

Compensation for consultants is most likely to be on a per-diem or project basis, and is not tied to the acquisition itself. Fees vary significantly, and they depend upon the size of the project and the quality of the firm retained.

Table 12-5   Participation of Financial Intermediaries in the Largest Acquisitions of 1983

Rank	Value of Deal (billions)	Companies	Financial Intermediaries	Fee (millions)
1	$2.3	Sante Fe Industries Southern Pacific	Salomon Brothers Morgan Stanley	$1.5 6.7
2	1.6	Xerox Crum & Forster	Goldman Sachs Salomon Brothers First Boston	2.5 2.5 0.6
3	1.5	Diamond Shamrock Natomas	Kidder Peabody Lazard Freres Salomon Brothers	4.0 3.0 3.0
4	1.1	Phillips Petroleum General American Oil Company of Texas	Goldman Sachs First Boston Kidder Peabody Blythe Eastman Paine Webber	5.0 5.7 1.2 0.8
5	1.1	CSX Texas Gas Resources	First Boston Goldman Sachs	3.3 3.3
6	1.0	Signal Wheelabrator-Frye	None Lazard Freres	– 2.5
7	1.0	Esmark Norton Simon	A.G. Becker Parlbas Oppenheimer Goldman Sachs Lazard Freres Salomon Brothers	1.5 1.5 2.5 2.5 2.5
8	0.9	Southland Citgo Petroleum	Dean Whitter Reynolds Goldman Sachs	1.5 N/A
9	0.9	Williams Northwest Energy	Smith Barney Harris Upham Goldman Sachs	4.0 5.0
10	0.9	Financial Corporation of America First Charter Financial	Bear Stearns First Boston	1.9 0.5

N/A = Not available

Source: "Deals of the Year," Fortune, Jan. 23, 1984, pp. 55–56

Attorneys. Attorneys, either internal or external, are involved in all acquisitions. Their primary functions are to perform a legal audit; evaluate legal issues, such as antitrust and taxation issues; assist in the negotiations; and draw up the detailed legal paperwork that accompanies most acquisitions. The legal audit is an extremely important step in the acquisition process, because it identifies potential liabilities (e.g., lawsuits pending, product liabilities) that could be inherited by the acquiror.

TABLE 12-6 Average Premium Paid Over Market

1978	1979	1980	1981	1982
46.2%	49.9%	49.9%	48.0%	47.4%

Source: W.T. Grimm & Co.

Accountants. Outside accounting firms are usually brought in to perform an accounting audit; to assist in evaluating such issues as valuation, taxation, and financing; and to provide financial advice during the negotiations. The accounting firm may be the acquiror's auditor if there is no conflict-of-interest issue (the firm may be the acquiree's auditor also). An accounting firm may be selected for its expertise within an industry or area.

Appraisers. Outside appraisers are usually retained to appraise specific assets, such as inventories, real estate, and physical plant and equipment. It should be noted, however, that appraising can be an extremely subjective process. For example, a piece of real estate could be appraised at $1 million, but there is no guarantee that the price could be obtained in the open market within a reasonable period of time. When valuing assets with fairly limited markets, such as industrial plants and equipment, the valuation becomes even more subjective.

ACQUISITION VALUATION AND PAYMENT ISSUES

Valuation

Almost every company is for sale if the price is high enough; therefore, one of the keys to the success of any acquisition is the price that is paid. A very good acquisition at $75 million may seem less attractive at $100 million.

There are no scientific rules that determine how a company should be valued. If the candidate is a public company, the market has already valued it; however, acquisitions usually require significant premiums over market value in order to obtain a controlling interest, as illustrated in Table 12-6.

One way to value a candidate is to analyze recent acquisitions of similar companies. The price/earnings (P/E) ratio of the tender offer, the premium over market price before the offer, and the market to book value ratio should all be analyzed for as wide a sample of comparable companies as possible.

Analyzing similar companies is not a straightforward task, however, since the definition of "similar" companies is often subjective, particularly for companies that participate in multiple businesses. For example, if one were trying to value Tiger International, would it be compared to trucking companies, air freight companies, or leasing firms? However, while this comparative analysis by itself is not a valid basis on which to value a company, it can provide some useful input for the valuation process.

Probably the most widely used method of valuing acquisitions is to discount their expected cash flows over a specified period of time. Although this process is relatively straightforward from a technical standpoint, projecting future earnings and cash requirements usually requires great familiarity with the company and its environment, and even then will involve subjective judgment.

Table 12-7 illustrates a simple model valuing an acquisition under two different growth rates. This example demonstrates how critical the assumptions are to the valuation (e.g., increasing the expected growth rate from 10 percent to 20 percent doubles the value of the acquisition, and therefore doubles the P/E ratio that could be justified). Since the development of the assumptions does involve subjectivity and risk, it is usually advisable to value the company under a variety of scenarios (e.g., optimistic, most likely, pessimistic) or to consider the impact of specific strategic jeopardies. Each of the major assumptions that drives this type of model is discussed below:

- *Time Period:* The cash flows should be projected for a time period that the forecaster feels comfortable in analyzing. Typically, this is either five or ten years.

- *Cash flow:* Cash flow is defined in this model as net income plus noncash items (e.g., depreciation), minus planned capital expenditures minus any changes in working capital. The example in Table 12-7 assumes that capital expenditures equal depreciation plus 10 percent of earnings but the actual projections of both earnings and capital expenditures should be based on analysis of the company's historical performance and announced plans (e.g., capital expenditure commitments).

- *Residual value:* The residual or terminal value of the acquisition often plays a major role in the valuation. This is the market value that the acquisition is assumed to have at the end of the forecast period. The example in Table 12-7 illustrates one method that is commonly used: setting the terminal value by using an anticipated P/E ratio. Another common method is to discount the value of the perpetual cash flows beyond the forecast period.[13]

- *Discount rate:* The discount rate allows for comparison of the acquisition to other available investment opportunities. The most widely used method is to use a discount rate equal to the corporation's weighted average cost of capital. However, as Alfred Rappaport points out, "the acquiring company's use of its own cost of capital to discount the target's projected cash flows is appropriate only when it can be safely assumed that the acquisition will not affect the riskiness of the acquirer. The specific riskiness of each prospective candidate should be taken into account in setting the discount rate, with higher rates used for more risky investments."[14]

---

[13] Robert W. Ackerman and Lionel L. Fray, "Financial Evaluation of a Potential Acquisition," *Financial Executive* (Oct. 1967).

[14] Alfred Rappaport, "Strategic Analysis for More Profitable Acquisitions," *Handbook of Mergers, Acquisitions, and Buyouts* (Englewood Cliffs, N.J.: Prentice-Hall, Inc., 1981).

Table 12-7 Conceptual Relationship Between Acquisition Earnings Growth Rate and Maximum Multiple Payable

PROPOSED ACQUISITION
Revenue: $200 million
Net Income: $10 million
Reinvestment = Depreciation + 10% of Earnings
Ending Value Multiple 8
Desired ROI: 14%

Year	10% Growth			20% Growth		
	Earnings	Cash Throwoff	Discounted Value	Earnings	Cash Throwoff	Discounted Value
1	$ 11.0	$ 9.9	$ 8.7	$ 12.0	$ 10.8	$ 9.5
2	12.1	10.9	8.4	14.4	13.0	10.0
3	13.3	12.0	8.1	17.3	15.6	10.5
4	14.6	13.2	7.8	20.7	18.7	11.1
5	16.1	14.5	7.5	24.9	22.4	11.6
6	17.7	15.9	7.2	29.9	26.9	12.3
7	19.5	17.5	7.0	35.8	32.2	12.9
8	21.4	19.3	6.8	43.0	38.7	13.6
9	23.6	21.2	6.5	51.6	46.4	14.3
10	25.9	23.3	6.3	61.9	55.7	15.0
Residual value	$185.0		$ 49.9	$442.1		$119.3
Total discounted value			$124.2			$240.1
Maximum multiple payable			12.4			24.0

Payment

The form of payment is also usually a critical factor in negotiations. Companies have the option of using cash, common stock, preferred stock, debt, or a combination of stock and cash. According to W.T. Grimm, in 1983 cash was used in 32 percent of the acquisitions, stock in 35 percent, stock and cash combinations in 33 percent of all transactions.[15] The advantages and disadvantages of payment with cash versus stock relate to the tax implications, the risk involved with stock, and the effect on earnings per share.

While cash probably offers a buyer more flexibility, if stock is used for at least 51 percent of the payment, the transaction usually can be structured so that any federal taxes can be deferred until the eventual sale of the stock. (Table 12-8 illustrates the various types of mergers that can take place and the resulting tax implications.) Alan L. Feld, author of *Tax Policy and Corporate Concentration*, states that "most mergers are not done primarily for tax reasons. But in the analysis of any deal you look at the numbers, and some of the numbers depend to a considerable degree on tax consequences."[16] Even if cash is used for payment, the deal can often be structured to reduce the tax liabilities; however, recent legislation reduces some of those opportunities. The Tax Act of 1982, in an effort to crack down on abuses, eliminated the incentive to structure deals as two-stage stock swaps, treating such transactions as if cash had been used. For example, as reported by *The New York Times*:

> In the Dome-Conoco case, Conoco owned 53 percent of the stock of Hudson's Bay Oil and Gas, which Dome Petroleum wanted to acquire. If Dome had purchased the Hudson's interest directly from Conoco, Conoco would have had to pay taxes on some $470 million in capital gains on those shares. But instead, to induce Conoco to part with its holdings, Dome bought shares of Conoco and then offered to swap them for Hudson's interest. By swapping the shares, rather than selling them for cash, Conoco saved an estimated $400 million in taxes.[17]

Another tax loophole in mergers that was closed by the Tax Act of 1982 involved the elimination of partial liquidations. Many authorities attribute merger tax reform to the widespread publicity of the partial liquidation involved in the U.S. Steel-Marathon Oil deal. Normally, the purchasing company tries to revalue the assets of the acquisition to generate higher depreciation and tax credits. This can be done by buying the assets of the company and technically liquidating the acquiree. However, as an offset to the tax benefits, the government requires tax payment on the recapture of past depreciation deductions and investment tax credits taken on the acquiree's assets prior to the buyout. To avoid these payments, U.S. Steel only partially liquidated Marathon, saving an estimated $500 million in taxes.

A potential disadvantage of stock deals is that the acquiree, by taking the acquiror's stock, has pinned the value of the acquisition to the future perform-

---

[15] W.T. Grimm & Co., *Mergerstat Review* (1982).

[16] "Tax Law's Effects on Mergers," *The New York Times*, Sept. 7, 1982, p. D-8.

[17] Ibid.

Table 12-8 Types of Mergers and Business Combinations

Characteristics	Statutory Merger (A)	Exchange of Stock for Stock (B)	Purchase of Assets for Stock (C)	Purchase of Stock for Cash or Nonvoting Securities	Purchase of Assets for Cash or Nonvoting Securities
Nontaxable to shareholders of acquiree if specific requirements met?	Yes, except for "boot"	Yes, except for "boot"	Yes	No	No
Transaction medium and steps	Generally 50 percent or more of purchase price must be in stock to meet continuity of interest rule	Voting stock only Voting preferred stock may be possible but not for pooling treatment	• Voting stock with possibility of up to 20 percent nonstock • Corporate shell of acquiree remains and may be liquidated	No restriction as to purchase medium	• No restriction as to purchase medium • Corporate shell of acquiree remains and may be subsequently liquidated to avoid double taxation
Type of accounting treatment	Purchase or pooling of interests	Purchase or pooling of interests	Purchase or pooling of interests	Purchase only	Purchase only

Source: James W. Bradley and Donald H. Korn, *Acquisition and Corporate Development* (D.C. Heath & Co., 1981).

ance of the acquiror's stock, especially if the acquiree's shares are encumbered by agreement in some fashion. For example, the Conoco stockholders who received Du Pont stock watched its value plummet from $54 a share in 1981 to the low 40s in early 1984.

The effect on earnings per share of using stock versus cash also must be considered. Depending upon the expected earnings per share issued (EPSI, i.e., the acquiree's earnings divided by the shares issued to buy it), the use of stock could potentially dilute earnings per share, with consequent repercussions in the investment community.

As shown in Table 12-8, straight cash deals require the use of purchase accounting. Table 12-9 compares the implications of purchase versus pooling accounting. As I. Robert Levine and Richard P. Miller view it, the following are some of the circumstances under which purchase and pooling accounting are preferred:

> Among the situations in which purchase accounting may be preferred are:

> • When the fair market value of the net assets exceeds the cost of acquiring the stock of the company. The resulting "negative goodwill" will have a positive impact on future earnings.

> • When the seller has had recent losses or poor earnings. A pooling would require restating all prior period earnings to include the seller's poor earnings performance, while a purchase would not.

> Among the situations in which pooling accounting may be preferred are:

> • When the purchase price significantly exceeds the fair value of net assets, and a material amount of goodwill would otherwise be recorded.

> • When the restated historic earning trends are improved by the pooling.[18]

GUIDELINES FOR SUCCESS AND REASONS FOR FAILURE

Despite the continuing popularity of acquisitions as a method to create shareholder value and the time and attention devoted to acquisitions in many companies, research indicates that, on average, almost 50 percent of all acquisitions fail. According to James B. Young, 45.3 percent of all acquisitions fail, and 6.4 percent more are likely candidates for failure.[19] He also points out that statistical sources indicate that there has been very little change in this failure rate for the past 40 years.

While there has been very little quantitative research performed on the reasons acquisitions fail, much of the qualitative research indicates that a gen-

---

[18] I. Robert Levine and Richard P. Miller, "Accounting for Business Combinations," *Handbook of Mergers, Acquisitions and Buyouts* (Englewood Cliffs, N.J.: Prentice-Hall, Inc., 1981).

[19] James B. Young, "A Conclusive Investigation Into the Causative Elements of Failure in Acquisitions and Mergers," *Handbook of Mergers, Acquisitions and Buyouts* (Englewood Cliffs, N.J.: Prentice-Hall, Inc., 1981).

Table 12-9   Purchase Vs. Pooling Accounting

Characteristics	Purchase Method	Pooling Method
Theory	Acquisition of assets or stock	Uniting of ownership interests. "Pooling of risks" concept is important.
Consideration	Buyer can use cash, notes, preferred or common stock, warrants or convertible securities. Contingent payment is allowed.	Must be an exchange of voting common stock for voting common stock. No shares to be issued can be contingent on future events.
Percentage sought	May purchase all or any part of assets or stock. May increase prior minority interest in stock.	Ninety percent or more of combining company's stock must be exchanged for issuing company's stock (10 percent or less can be cash or notes, *including* any stock acquired prior to the pooling).
Recorded amounts	Seller's assets and liabilities are adjusted to their fair value. Previously unrecorded assets and liabilities are also recorded.	Combining company's assets and liabilities retain same basis as before.
Goodwill	Amortized over not more than 40 years. Amortization is not tax deductible. If cost is *less* than net assets acquired, noncurrent assets are reduced; if they are reduced to zero, then "negative goodwill" is recorded and amortized over not more than 40 years.	No goodwill recorded.
Reported earnings	Earnings of seller included in operations from date of acquisition. Footnote disclosure of pro forma current and prior year earnings required. Subsequent periods' depreciation and other expenses are computed using adjusted asset and liability values.	All prior years' earnings must be restated to include pooled company and effect of additional shares issued. No adjustments to methods of computed earnings.

Source: I. Robert Levine and Richard P. Miller, "Accounting for Business Combinations," *Handbook of Mergers, Acquisitions and Buyouts* (Englewood Cliffs, N.J.: Prentice-Hall, Inc., 1981)

eral lack of acquisition planning and too little emphasis on the human aspect of absorbing a new organization play major roles in acquisition failures.

What can be done to ensure a successful acquisition? There is no one answer; each acquisition is unique, and success is never guaranteed. However, there are straightforward guidelines that, if applied to each acquisition, should significantly increase its chances of success:

1 Develop a comprehensive diversification plan as part of an overall development strategy. It is important that a firm has a clear definition of what business it is in and what business it wishes to be in. Should General Motors be in the automobile industry, the transportation industry, or the durable goods industry?

2 Buy a firm that meets sound strategic and economic criteria; do not buy simply what is available. Many firms become impatient or "lovestruck," and abandon their screening criteria.

3 Management must understand opportunity and have the resources to develop it and the commitment to exploit it. Companies should seek a good fit with their own operations; expecting perfection is not realistic. The buyer should take the time to understand its own strengths and weaknesses as well as those of the acquired company.

4 Evaluate the management of the acquired company for intelligence, style, energy, and motivation. Will they fit in as part of the corporate family? The value of sound management is difficult to overstate, but fit with corporate culture is equally important. Pharmaceutical companies for years have attempted to merge with cosmetic companies, but, very often, the managers of a "serious" business such as drugs are not comfortable with a business such as cosmetics.

5 Make the right advances, acquisition requires courtship. Gains for owners of both firms should be specified, and people should be absorbed into an organization with great care and sensitivity to needs for status and autonomy. Problems need to be anticipated and discussed openly with the management of the prospective acquisition. It is important that the top management of the acquiring company be involved in all aspects of acquisition planning and implementation.

6 Determine the price over which the deal ceases to be attractive. Keep in mind that, for the right price, almost any company can be bought. The key is to make the purchase at a price that allows for an attractive return.

7 Avoid a big mistake. Small mistakes can be solved or will dissipate over time. If a company bets on an acquisition and makes a mistake, there may be few options left.

Analyzing several recent acquisition failures sheds some light on the violations of the above guidelines by some of the largest, most successful companies in U.S. industry. Exxon's purchase of Reliance Electric, described by *Fortune* as "perhaps one of the worst mergers ever made,"[20] is an example of oilmen using a wildcatter's betting mentality to venture into manufacturing.

After Exxon paid $1.2 billion for Reliance Electric Company in 1979, it was shocked to learn that Federal Pacific, a company recently acquired by

---

[20] "Exxon's $600-Million Mistake," *Fortune*, Oct. 19, 1981.

Reliance, had been cheating on the safety testing of its equipment, and that Exxon conceivably could have a substantial liability for defective products. In addition, the product for which Exxon had purchased Reliance fizzled in the research lab and never came to fruition.

In 1978, Exxon Enterprises had drafted a plan to go into commercial production with an "alternating-current synthesizer" that was thought to have the potential to save a million barrels of oil a day in the United States by raising the efficiency of electric motors. Reliance was acquired to mass-produce and market the product, but, unfortunately, neither Exxon nor the consultants it employed on the acquisition questioned the fundamental assumption that the product was economically viable. When it proved not to be, the problems had already been compounded by the payment of a much higher purchase price than originally intended to avoid an unfriendly takeover and by the discovery of safety-testing cheating in Reliance's newly acquired Federal Pacific subsidiary. Reliance itself, it turns out, had made a poor acquisition that depressed the value of its stock and made it look for the unknown testing cover-ups. As *Fortune* viewed it:

> For a century-old oil company that has no desire to go out of business when its wells run dry, the logic of diversification is still compelling. At minimum, its experience with Reliance should have taught Exxon how not to go about negotiating a merger. The wildcatter mentality of playing your hunches may still be a good way to make money in oil but all the world isn't oil.[21]

In 1978, American Can had a reputation as being an active acquiror, having diversified into paper products, mail-order sales, and other unrelated fields. However, in 1978, after a supposedly sophisticated analysis, American Can acquired Sam Goody, Inc., a record store chain. Shortly thereafter, Goody's president and one of its vice presidents were charged with racketeering, interstate transportation of stolen property, and 12 counts of distribution of counterfeit recordings. In addition to the fines that were imposed, American Can's reputation within the financial community was tarnished. As Richard S. Palm, an analyst with Merrill Lynch Pierce Fenner & Smith, stated, "These indictments undermine industry confidence in American's ability to make sound judgments about acquisitions."[22]

DIVESTITURE AS A STRATEGY

Divestiture is the selling of a company, subsidiary, division, or a product line as a going business. Selling a business is just as important an investment decision as acquiring a business. The seller, in effect, believes that it can earn a greater return on the funds employed by that business by selling it (at market value)

---

[21] Ibid.

[22] "American Can: Diversification Brings Sobering Second Thoughts," *Business Week*, March 24, 1980.

and employing the funds elsewhere. Whether the proceeds of a divestiture are in the form of cash, equity, debt securities, or some combination, the implicit assumption, from the seller's point of view, is that those proceeds have better investment applications than in the divested property. The buyer, of course, is making a similar economic comparison, but in reverse. The fact that two opposite points of view can coexist, often to mutual benefit, simply reflects the different objecties, expectations, capabililties, or strategies of buyer and seller.

In most cases, the initiative is with the buyer. The business press typically covers a divestiture transaction from the buyer's side, i.e., as an acquisition. Much attention is paid to buying techniques, but little to selling. In part, this reflects the business community's preoccupation with size and growth. To divest a business may be seen as a sign of failure. Yet, a well-planned, well-executed divestiture can create significant value for the seller's stockholders. The seller's remaining business or businesses may benefit from increased management attention and the infusion of new liquid assets. Managers, employees, and customers of the divested unit may also benefit, as, for example, when the divested unit receives needed additional capital from its new owner.

A successful corporate divestiture requires specific, action-oriented skills. Corporate objectives and priorities must be determined first. The internal operations and external environment of the divestiture candidate must be analyzed in light of those objectives. Then, a divestiture sales plan can be developed, prospects contacted, negotiations conducted, and a transition smoothly managed. In the business environment of the 1980s, the skills to implement these activities are of increasing importance. The 1960s and late 1970s were boom times for mergers and acquisitions, and they represented—in many, if not most, instances—a seller's market. The 1980s, with high interest rates, stiff foreign competition, and corporate belt-tightening and restructuring, may be a buyer's market, with a heavier burden placed on the seller to plan for and consummate a satisfactory deal.

This discussion takes the perspective of the corporate, multibusiness seller, i.e., one with several different subsidiaries, divisions, or lines of business. It is also assumed that the selling organization will continue to be in business after the divestiture (perhaps in a significantly different form), although total liquidation will be briefly considered as an option. The issues faced by sellers of single businesses (e.g., following the retirement or death of the principal owner-operator) may be largely similar, but the decision to sell the entire enterprise may revolve less on economic considerations than on personal objectives and judgments of the competence of potential management successors. For purposes of nomenclature, the divestiture candidate is referred to in this section as "the division," although it may range from a free-standing, incorporated subsidiary to a single product line.

MAKING THE DIVESTITURE DECISION

In too many cases, the divestiture decision is a reactive one, arising from despair over a division's poor financial performance or from an unsolicited purchase offer that seems too good to refuse. Sellers who take a more proactive role, i.e., sellers who see the divestiture option as an opportunity, usually have better results than reactive sellers. In either case, however, a divestiture decision is usually harder to make than an acquisition decision, since divestiture requires a company to let go of something familiar. The division may still generate cash or may have some potential. It may once have been the core of the company, and it could still have strong emotional appeal and well-placed defenders. Divestiture will usually generate some difficult "people problems." Although the logical, analytical aspects of the divestiture decision is emphasized in this section, a sensitivity to the emotional aspects is also important.

Determining Objectives

If a company is considering a divestiture, it must know why it is doing so. Prospective buyers will be interested in the seller's reasons for divesting, and the seller's rationale should still leave them with convincing reasons to buy. An understanding of the objectives that the seller hopes to achieve through divestiture will also help the seller or its negotiators in structuring the proper deal. A classic reason for divestiture, for example, is to unload a disappointing acquisition. In such a case, it is critical to know why the division is falling short of expectations: poor financial results? Lack of fit with overall corporate strategy? Other reasons? And, the seller must decide how it will use the funds it gains from disposal of the division.

The reasons for and objectives of divestiture discussed below apply to most business situations, but they are not exhaustive. Objectives may overlap, since the sale of a division may serve several corporate purposes simultaneously.

Financial Reasons for Divestiture. Poor financial performance is probably the most commonly cited reason for divestiture, and a prospective buyer is likely to suspect this reason even when it is not the case. Intractable loss operations, which are unattractive to most potential buyers, are sometimes purchased by private investors, management groups, or employee stock ownership plans (ESOPs), particularly if the business is relatively small. Selling the division to such buyers may be seen as a better alternative, for economic or noneconomic reasons, than liquidating it. A small "dog" division in a large, high-overhead corporation, for example, may be turned around by entrepreneurs who can give it more attention.

In 1980, Colgate-Palmolive sold its Helena Rubinstein division, which had lost $50 million in 1979, to a private firm. Colgate received $1.5 million in cash and $18.5 million in notes payable over 15 years, but it agreed, in turn, to guarantee $43 million of the division's bank debt. Philip Morris was unable to turn its marginally profitable American Safety Razor subsidiary (makers of Personna and other blades) into a major industry contender. Philip Morris tried unsuccessfully for three years to sell the subsidiary, and it had almost liquidated it, when a management group agreed to purchase it in 1976 for $16 million. Squibb's sale of its Beech-Nut baby food division (1973) and Sperry's sale of its Remington electric razor division (1979) are other examples of well-known but unprofitable businesses sold by large parents to small investor groups. Some well-known ESOPs, where employees gained full or partial control of the business to strengthen it, include Rath Packing Company (Waterloo, Iowa) and Okonite Company (Ramsey, N.J.), as well as Chrysler and Pan Am.

A division may be profitable yet still be a candidate for divestiture for financial reasons. Some examples are as follows:

- *Not meeting corporate objectives:* In 1981, Beatrice Foods sold Dannon, the yogurt company, for $84 million, or 23 times Dannon's earnings. Although it was profitable, Dannon failed to pass rigorous, new corporate standards: 5 percent real sales growth per year or 18 percent return on equity (assuming one-third debt to total capital). Because of the recent entry of two well-financed competitors, Kellogg and General Mills, Dannon's positive cash flow was also threatened. The buyer, however, French dairy producer BSN-Gervais Danone, saw Dannon as a good vehicle for its own entry into the U.S. market.

- *Pressing capital needs:* A company may sell a profitable but nonessential division to cover losses in its core businesses. In 1982, LTV sold Lykes Brothers Steamship Company and its fleet of 46 ships to a new company for $150 million, posting a $30 million pretax profit. LTV had relatively little background in marine transportation, and it needed cash to strengthen its two large steel operations, Jones & Laughlin and Youngstown Sheet & Tube, which were suffering from a severe industry recession.

- *High debt burden:* Du Pont sold some of Conoco's oil and gas properties to Petro-Lewis for $716 million in order to reduce the large amount of high-cost debt it incurred in financing its 1981 acquisition of Conoco. (It should be noted that this transaction was more a sale of assets than of a going concern.) Occidental Petroleum acquired Cities Service for $4 billion in 1982 and, in similar fashion, tried to sell some of those assets to pay off loans. Chrysler sold its profitable combat tank manufacturing subsidiary to General Dynamics for $336 million in 1982, in order to satisfy creditors and other parties to its bailout agreement.

Divestiture as Part of a Larger Strategy. A divestiture may be part of a broader corporate strategy of asset redeployment. The seller's division may no longer fit with the rest of its business. It may be in a slow-growth market, or in an industry that is changing because of new technologies, mergers by large competitors, or other reasons. The division may be in an attractive, high-growth industry, but the seller may lack the capital required to maintain share, or it may prefer to channel its capital elsewhere. Or, the seller may want to remain in the industry but simply correct imbalances in size, product line, or geography.

Morton-Thiokol, the salt and household goods producer, sold its Norwich-Eaton division to Procter & Gamble for $371 million in early 1982. The division made Pepto-Bismol and other over-the-counter drugs, and had earned a healthy $22 million (pretax) in 1981 on sales of $216 million. Morton used $135 million of the proceeds to buy out a 20 percent minority shareholder, the

French company Rhone-Poulenc. Later in 1982, the balance of the proceeds helped finance Morton's $573 million acquisition of Thiokol, a chemicals firm.

In 1980, Esmark conducted a massive redeployment of assets to withdraw from both its profitable energy and unprofitable meat-packing businesses, in order to focus on its branded consumer products and increase stockholder values. Esmark first sold its Vickers Petroleum subsidiary to a French company for $347 million. It then transferred its ownership interest in Vickers Energy Corporation, which in turn owned TransOcean Oil, Inc., to Mobil Oil for 11.9 million shares of Esmark common stock (about 50 percent of shares outstanding) and cash with a total value of $741 million. Esmark then sold some of its Swift meatpacking units to a newly formed, public holding company for a 35 percent equity interest and a $35 million subordinated note. With its capitalization shrunk in half and with abundant cash, Esmark's shares rose from $26 to $60.

Richardson-Vicks sold its prescription drug business, Merrell, to Dow Chemical in 1981 in a complex, tax-free transaction worth $260 million. Richardson could not afford the high research and development costs needed to compete; it preferred to retrench in its strong over-the-counter drug business. Similarly, Computervision sold one of its two divisions, Cobilt, in 1981 in order to focus on its computer-aided design and manufacturing business. Both divisions were in high-growth electronics markets and required heavy research and development expenditures.

Burlington-Northern sold its single most profitable unit, Burlington Northern Air Freight, Inc. (BNAFI), to Pittston Company in 1982 for $177 million. BNAFI was the second largest competitor in a rapidly growing industry, but Burlington wanted to redeploy assets into its extensive natural resources businesses. From a timing standpoint, BNAFI's earnings were at a peak, and Burlington was concerned that the unit would require large amounts of capital to buy its own airplanes within a few years.

External Reasons for Divestiture. Some divestitures may be motivated less by operating strategy than by considerations external to the business. Some examples follow:

- *Improve market value of common stock.* This has become a major reason in recent years. A diversified firm may spin off a peripheral division in order to simplify itself for stock market analysts or to improve its image in the financial community. Cooper Industries, a manufacturer of drilling equipment and electrical products, sold its Airmotive jet engine repair division to an investor group in 1982, mainly to make itself easier to follow on Wall Street. Holiday Inns sold its Delta Steamship subsidiary for $96 million in 1982, in part because the stock market had typically accorded a higher price/earnings (P/E) ratio to firms in the lodging industry than to those in the maritime industry. A firm may also use its divestiture proceeds to acquire treasury stock and thereby increase earnings per share, much as in the Esmark case.

- *Avoid a takeover.* Divestiture of an attractive division may be used to thwart a potential takeover of the entire company. Brunswick sold its star Sherwood

Medical Group in 1982 to American Home Products, a large pharmaceutical house. Brunswick's low stock price made it vulnerable to a takeover attempt by Whittaker Industries, which planned to keep Sherwood and sell off Brunswick's other divisions. American Home bought 67 percent of Brunswick's outstanding shares for cash, then swapped the shares for ownership of Sherwood. Brunswick retired most of the stock, reducing its capital base and boosting share values. (It is interesting to note that, in the late 1960s, Brunswick sold 15 percent of Sherwood through a public offering. The spinoff was designed to improve the value of Brunswick's common shares by creating an implied market value for its remaining 85 percent interest in Sherwood.)

- *Domestic regulatory pressures.* Government regulations or court decisions, particularly antitrust actions, may require a firm to make a divestiture; other regulations may indirectly force a divestiture by increasing the cost of doing business. Schering-Plough, the drug company, acquired Dr. Scholl foot products in 1979, but was quickly forced by the Federal Trade Commission to sell Dr. Scholl's athlete's foot-powder product line because it competed with Schering's Tinactin remedy. On a larger scale, AT&T's 1982 modified consent agreement with the Department of Justice required it to divest its local telephone operating companies; this was the largest divestiture in history. As part of the agreement, however, AT&T will be free to compete in unregulated markets, leading many analysts to forecast a net increase in total stockholder values as a result of the break up.

- *Foreign pressures.* For companies with international operations, foreign government policy or political risk may encourage a divestiture or force a company to share ownership with local interests. Responding to nationalist pressures, Deere sold 26 percent of its Mexican subsidiary to the Banca Nacional de Mexico for $12 million in 1982. The same year, Honeywell reduced its interest in CII Honeywell Bull, a French computer company, for 47 percent to 20 percent by selling the difference to a French government-owned company for $150 million in cash. Honeywell received a premium price in this transaction as an inducement to remain in the business.

Other Reasons for Divestiture. Problems with management succession is a common reason for selling smaller or family-owned businesses, and this problem may also occur in a corporate division. The parent may believe that the division's junior managers are not qualified to replace senior managers who are about to retire. Divestiture may solve personality conflicts; for example, the division may be managed by a former owner who is unhappy in a large organization.

Divestiture may be simply an opportunistic response to an unexpected but attractive offer. Earnings may be at a peak and the timing may be right from the perspective of stockholder interests. Attractive offers, however, must be weighed against longer-term corporate objectives. Even if a company decides a division is not for sale, someone else's interest may provide new insight on a division's strategic opportunities.

Evaluating the Division

In addition to determining what corporate objectives might be served by a divestiture, the division's strengths, weaknesses, and future potential should be analyzed. Such analysis is needed so that management can make a sound decision regarding the unit; it also will provide data that can be presented to prospective buyers. The evaluation should cover (1) internal strengths and weaknesses, (2) environmental conditions that will affect future performance, (3) competitive position, and (4) the division's relation to the rest of a corporation.

Information for the analysis includes financial statements (at least five years, if possible), budgets and long-term business plans, market research data, competitive intelligence, and industry forecasts. Any unusual accounting practices or economic conditions that affect the division's reported performance should be identified. The capabilities of upper management and middle management should also be considered.

The evaluation process prior to divestiture is similar to that conducted during acquisition planning. Questions about strategic direction, business fit, and competitive position must be addressed. In principle, the corporate parent has an advantage over outsiders in obtaining information about the division, particularly in assessing the quality of earnings, confidential plans, and the caliber of division management. In fact, however, division plans may be overoptimistic. Smaller or more autonomous divisions may not be accustomed to providing detailed information to the corporate level, and attempts to gather accurate information may disclose the company's intentions prematurely. The use of outside assistance, such as consultants, investment bankers, or industry analysts, may be helpful in gathering information.

It may be necessary at this early stage to decide how involved the division's management should be in divestiture planning. It is generally best to let at least a few key managers know about the division's evaluation; they will find out soon enough, and their cooperation will be needed. General or specific assurances on the safety of their positions following divestiture may encourage the desired cooperation. During the divestiture process, it is also advisable to restrain the division from making long-term commitments that might hinder its sale. If the divestiture decision is relatively uncertain, such restraint must be imposed subtly and indirectly. Strict confidentiality is vital during the decision-making stage to avoid rumors and morale problems, which will only aggravate existing problems and reduce the division's market value.

An analysis of a divestiture candidate must also include its relation to the rest of the corporation. Selling an ailing acquisition, for example, may only undo the diversification or synergy that the acquisition was designed to accomplish in the first place. Are the division's earnings countercyclical to those of other divisions? Does it possess functional expertise, technology, distribution, or other assets that are of value to the rest of the company? Are its products needed for filling out certain product lines or for an internal, vertical source of raw materials or components? Can the indirect overhead associated with the division be eliminated upon divestiture, or will it merely be spread over the remaining businesses? What will be the impact of separation on the rest of the business, and how will it be perceived by employees, customers, suppliers, and the financial community?

Divestiture is a long-term decision that is generally irreversible. The evaluation of the division should therefore focus on its longer-term prospects. The macroeconomic, industry, and regulatory outlook will also have to be considered. The definition of "long term" will depend on the type of business, the level of risk, and the company's ability to make forecasts. However, five years should be considered a minimum. It may be useful to construct several environmental scenarios (e.g., optimistic, pessimistic, most likely) and attempt to assess probabilities for the division's future performance under each scenario. The evaluation of the division provides the basis for projecting its expected earnings, cash flow, and capital requirements, as well as making a qualitative determination of its role in the corporation's overall strategy.

Identifying and Evaluating Alternatives to Divestiture

Alternatives to divestiture depend on the company's objectives, e.g., poor earnings, slow growth, capital requirements, or a lack of fit with its other businesses. Each alternative will probably involve tradeoffs, the financial implications of which should be measured and compared. The tax implications of the alternatives may vary substantially, so attention should be given to after-tax effects. The specifics will depend on the structure of the final settlement. Tax effects are often critical, since tax basis and book basis frequently differ. In some cases, an ostensibly profitable transaction may turn sour when taxes are considered; in others, an unacceptable deal may become more attractive through proper tax structuring.

Unless a likely buyer has already been identified, the results of a decision to divest are highly uncertain, and an assessment of the probable outcomes may be helpful. The following alternatives are oriented toward the most common type of divestiture: a problem division.

Retain the Division. Retention should be regarded as a positive action rather than a matter of default. Several options are as follows:

- *Improve operations with a view toward keeping the division for the long term.* In several cases of problem divisions, an evaluation of disposal alternatives led instead to a turnaround plan. The cost and commitment required, however, must be well understood.

- *Improve operations in order to make the division more salable at a later date.* The time frame must be defined, and the incremental return on any additional investment must be carefully estimated.

- *Phase down operations.* This option could be undertaken for several reasons: (1) to squeeze cash out of the division, e.g., by raising prices, tightening credit terms, cutting inventory, selling nonessential assets; (2) to shrink the division's size and therefore make it easier for a smaller buyer to acquire it; and (3) to prune problem operations and retrench in strong areas. Implementation of a phase-down must be done carefully to avoid detrimental rumors.

- *Do not act.* No action is always an option, although it is often unrecognized as such. However, this alternative should be used only if more time is needed to make an informed decision. The problems that originally motivated the analysis of the division are unlikely to solve themselves.

Enter a Joint Venture. Through a joint venture, the division's problems can be shared with another company whose strengths, operating or financial, may help turn the division around. An example is Fiat-Allis, created in 1972. Allis-Chalmers' Construction Machinery Group had low market share, marginal profitability and difficulty in competing with Caterpillar, Komatsu, and others on a full-line, worldwide basis. Allis considered several alternatives, including more outside sourcing of finished product, becoming a short-line producer, and taking more component production in house to increase value added. Outright divestment was preferred to all of these; however, a buyer could not be found and liquidation was expected to bring less than book value. Fiat, which desperately wanted a foothold in the U.S. market, was willing to enter into a joint venture. Allis traded control of the division for cash up front and a deliberate, phased withdrawal from the venture.

Liquidate or Dissolve. This option may be preferred where sale of the division's individual assets would yield a better return than continuing to operate those assets or divesting the division as a going concern. Goodwill and patents can be liquidated as well as tangible assets. In instances where inflation in fixed-asset replacement costs has been very high, liquidation may realize more than book value. Any losses, on the other hand, will be partly offset by tax savings. If the division has a high profile in its community, attention should be paid to public relations; special efforts may be needed to minimize economic dislocation to the area.

Liquidation and dissolution of the entire corporation may create substantial value to public stockholders if the market has persistently undervalued the company. In early 1979, UV Industries was selling for about $20 per share, versus a book value of about $25. Stockholders approved management's liquidation plan, as follows: (1) UV's Federal Pacific Electric Company subsidiary was sold to Reliance Electric for $345 million in cash in March, and stockholders received a liquidating dividend of $18 per share in April; (2) UV's oil and gas properties were sold to Tenneco for $135 million; (3) UV's remaining assets, principally gold mines, coal mines, and other natural resource properties, were sold to Sharon Steel Corporation, which controlled 23 percent of UV, for $518 million in cash and subordinated sinking fund debentures. A final distribution of $7 in cash and $27 in debentures per share was made in September 1980. Shareholders thus realized a total of $52 per share (including the debentures at face value), versus a stock market value of $20 before the liquidation began. In addition, the liquidation plan complied with the nonrecognition of gain provisions of Section 337 of the Internal Revenue Code, which resulted in a tax savings to UV of about $42 million.

Shut Down. Under this option, the division's operations are ceased, but its assets are retained and "mothballed." A shutdown might be done while management waits for economic conditions to improve, looks for a buyer, or refurbishes facilities in order to transfer them to another division. Temporary shutdown will involve ongoing expenses such as maintenance, security, insurance, and property taxes.

Abandon. If the situation is desperate, a company may simply walk away from a business, taking whatever write-offs are necessary. U.S. business interests in Iran were abandoned during that country's revolution and the ensuing hostage crisis, although suits were later filed to recover compensation. RCA essentially abandoned its computer business in 1971, after years of losses and the prospect of a continuing cash drain. RCA reported a $490 million extraordinary loss (about $250 million after tax), although about $80 million was later recovered from the sale of its lease-customer base and other assets.

Spin Off to Investors or Take Public. A spinoff is a form of restructuring by which stockholders continue to own the same assets but in a different legal form. For example, the seller could create a subsidiary to own the divestiture candidate and then distribute shares of the subsidiary to the company's stockholders, severing or reducing the division's ties to the parent. The subsidiary must be large enough to be viable as a separate entity. Spinoff is sometimes done under court order, as in the landmark 1911 antitrust decision against Standard Oil of New Jersey, which forced the company to spin off its Indiana, Ohio, and California companies. Under its 1982 consent agreement, AT&T spun off its Bell operating companies in 1984; each share of AT&T common stock was exchanged for one share of the reorganized parent and prorated shares of the seven, newly organized regional operating companies. The Esmark and Brunswick/Sherwood spinoffs cited earlier, on the other hand, were purely voluntary.

One argument for voluntary spinoff is greater shareholder value. Consider a company with two unrelated divisions: Division A, in a high-growth industry, contributed $1.50 in earnings per share (EPS); Division B, in a static industry, contributed $.50. If the company's total EPS was $2.00 and its stock market price was $24, it would have a P/E of 12. As two separate companies, the stock market might accord Division A a P/E of 15, for example, and Division B a P/E of 9. Shareholders would then hold shares worth $22.50 and $4.50, respectively—an increase of $3 per share as a result of the spinoff.

Spin Off to Employees. Since the late 1970s, ESOPs have been increasingly used to keep financially troubled businesses afloat. ESOPs provide substantial tax advantages, and they are a means of giving employees a stake in the business and raising equity without going public. Under an ESOP, a trust is created that buys stock in the company or division on behalf of the employees. The stock purchases are typically financed by bank debt. The company then contributes up to 25 percent of its payroll expense per year to the trust, which uses these contributions to retire the trust's debt. The company gains a tax deduction for the total amount of its contributions, while also raising needed equity capital.

Choosing Among Alternatives

In choosing among divestiture alternatives, it is important to remember that disposing of a business is an investment decision. A useful economic concept for evaluating this decision is return on recoverable assets (RORA). Consider, for example, a division earning $5 million on assets with a net book value of $100 million—a 5 percent return on assets (ROA). The division's assets *recoverable* upon disposal, however, may be valued at $50 million, which could be invested in some other activity. The division's current RORA is then, in fact, *10* percent ($5 million ÷ $50 million), and this is the rate of return that should be used in comparing alternative investments of the recoverable funds.

Deciding to divest a division, particularly an older one, may be a difficult and even emotional process. For companies that are not accustomed to selling divisions, time may be required at top management levels to raise awareness, change values, and generate a consensus before presenting a divestiture plan to the board of directors for approval. James Brian Quinn describes this commonly observed process of strategic change as "logical incrementalism."[23] He cites General Mills' divestiture of its once dominant flour milling business, which was preceded by many staff reports, management meetings, the development of new data reporting systems, and the divestiture of smaller, less central businesses. How long a company's divestiture decision takes will depend on the decision-making procedures, the corporate culture, and the particular situation of the division. Once a decision has been made, however, it is important to begin the divestiture program as rapidly as possible. Otherwise, the division remains in a harmful state of limbo. A specific strategy for selling the division must be developed and implemented.

PLANNING DIVESTITURE STRATEGY

As with any complex transaction, there are no firm guidelines on the time required to complete a divestiture. The condition of the general economy, the stock market, and the industry will exert influences beyond the seller's control. Buyers who express interest but then back out will add to the time requirements.

Some practitioners suggest a target of six months from making the decision to closing, although this is generally a minimum. A rough schedule might be as follows: several months for gathering information and planning strategy; several months for contacting prospective buyers and making presentations;

---

[23] James Brian Quinn, "Strategic Change: 'Logical Incrementalism,'" *Sloan Management Review* (Fall 1978).

several weeks for conducting negotiations; and about two months for the detailed preparations prior to closing.

Key Functions in the Divestiture Program

One of the first questions to address is who should be involved in the divestiture program. Before staffing for divestiture, however, it is useful to consider the key tasks and functions that will be required. An overview of these is presented below.

Major Policy Decisions. This function will typically be the domain of the chief executive officer (CEO) and the board of directors. Final approval of the divestiture decision, program management, schedule, price, terms, and buyer will be required.

Overall Program Management. A senior manager must be selected to oversee the selection and contacting of prospective buyers; the "packaging" of the division for presentation to prospects; selection of and relations with outside consultants and intermediaries, if any; negotiations; and closing. The program manager should have direct access to the CEO. Since he or she is likely to have other responsibilities, the day-to-day management of specific aspects of the program may be delegated to key subordinates. It is important, however, that the program stays on schedule; any delays should be the fault of the buyer, not of the seller.

Data Gathering. This function will primarily involve assembling financial and operating information needed for presentations and negotiating. While the data collected during the divestiture decision-making stage provide a beginning, buyers are likely to require considerably greater detail concerning factors such as the quality of receivables and order backlog, the actual and book depreciation of major fixed-asset items, management agreements, labor contracts, and pension liabilities. The seller must exercise good judgment in determining the amount and format of information provided to prospects, in deciding whether this information is given voluntarily or on request, and in planning the timing of the release of information. Tax and other legal considerations that may affect the structure of the final agreement must also be identified, such as prior agreements with customers, lenders, creditors, lessors, licensors, and government agencies. The data gathering function may also assist in identifying prospective buyers.

Selection, Contact, and Presentation to Prospects. Active efforts are required to bring a suitable buyer to the negotiating table. As discussed below, prospects can be notified that the division is for sale in many ways, from a public announcement to a casual comment over lunch. Intermediaries may also be used. Skill is required to arouse serious interest in a prospect without distorting or omitting facts or weakening the seller's position. To avoid confusion, a single point of contact should be designated for communications with each prospective buyer.

Negotiations. Serious discussion of price and terms may be friendly or combative. It may involve a time-consuming chain of decisions, such as the signing of a letter of intent, a preliminary agreement, or supplementary agreements. A single, chief negotiator should be clearly designated, so that the buyer cannot take advantage of any conflicts within the seller's organization. The chief negotiator should have stature, credibility, experience, and thorough preparation. He or she should be given firm guidelines on the seller's primary objectives regarding price and terms, but there should be latitude to bargain over secondary issues. The negotiator should have the judgment to distinguish major and minor issues, but he or she will need direct access to the program manager or CEO when additional guidance is necessary.

Preparation for Closing. Considerable legal and accounting work will be required to document exactly what is and what is not included in the transaction, and to translate the two parties' understanding of their agreement into mutually satisfactory legal language. The legal documentation may be voluminous, but it is needed to avoid subsequent misunderstandings and possible litigation. The divestiture program is not completed until the final settlement has been signed, so the seller's management must be ready to see the program through to a successful closing. The seller should also be prepared to give some assistance to the buyer during a transition period after the closing. This transition period, in fact, is likely to begin before the final agreement, as the buyer gears up to take control of the division, and the seller should endeavor to make this transition as smooth as possible.

Staffing the Divestiture Team

The specific assignment of functional responsibilities in the divestiture program will depend on the relevant skills and experience of the seller's personnel, the pressure of their other responsibilities, and the size and complexity of the transaction. Some functions may be combined; for example, the program manager might also take responsibility as the key contact point and chief negotiator with serious prospects. Because of the range of functions required, however, it is likely that the divestiture program will be managed as a special project that cuts across existing organizational boundaries within the seller's corporation.

The initiative to consider divestment may have begun among corporate staff in the parent, for example, or at some management level between parent and division, such as group or region. Some of these people may also assist in carrying out the decision. Except in large conglomerates, it is unlikely that there is a designated staff function for handling divestitures, but personnel in an acquisitions, strategic planning, or financial planning department may have relevant experience or skills. It is generally best to take a team approach, with a senior manager and one or two other managers involved from start to finish.

This helps ensure unity of purpose, continuity, and timeliness. The corporation's chief financial officer and its top in-house attorney should also be involved. Tax and legal implications should be considered as early as possible.

Use of Intermediaries. It will probably be necessary to engage outside experts and intermediaries at different stages of the program, such as lawyers, accountants, management consultants, investment bankers, and business brokers. Ultimate responsibility for the success of the program, however, must remain in the seller's organization.

Outsiders may assist in negotiating and closing, as well as in identifying prospects and developing presentation materials. They should be selected on the basis of demonstrated experience and ability, but the program manager's judgment will be necessary. Most companies have established relationships, for example, with law and public accounting firms. These firms may have expertise in divestiture; if not, they can probably supply references of firms that do have such experience. It may also be useful to request references of previous clients. Any potential conflicts of interest should be identified. If outsiders are going to play a major role in the divestiture program, it is also important that they get along on a personal basis with key people in the seller's organization.

Compensation for outside consultants and others may be a per diem rate, a percentage of the divestiture proceeds, a contingency payment, or some other arrangement. Attorneys and management consultants often charge a man-day rate, while investment bankers typically charge a percentage fee. Fees can range widely, depending on the size of the deal, and they usually are negotiable. For large *Fortune 500* transactions, total fees to outsiders can run in the millions of dollars, although this may represent less than one percent of the proceeds. The value added by good consultants and other intermediaries is likely to be many times whatever fees they charge.

Involvement of Division Personnel. It is unavoidable that division personnel play some role in the divestiture program. During the presentation stage, the prospective buyer will visit the division's facilities, and it will probably want to meet its key managers in order to solicit their views of the division's prospects. The division's employees, moreover, are assets. A prospective buyer may be looking for certain management skills to augment those in its existing business. The buyer may even consider key division managers essential to the transaction. Even if the buyer is likely to make personnel changes or reductions after taking control, it will probably retain most of the division's employees, at least during a transition period. What division employees say and do during the divestiture program may have a major influence on a prospect's interest and subsequent negotiating position.

The division's managers are in an awkward position during a divestiture program, and their response to it may be hard to predict. If financial performance is a problem, they may feel unfairly blamed for failure and fear for their jobs. They may be bitter and feel that the fault lies with the parent. Or, they may see divestiture as an opportunity to strengthen the division and enhance their careers. In any case, division personnel can jeopardize the sale, or at least damage the seller's negotiating position. This remains so even as divestiture becomes more likely, since the division's managers may begin to transfer their loyalties from seller to buyer and curry favor with the buyer.

The seller's divestiture team must therefore take careful account of division personnel in its planning. A policy of openness and fairness is usually best. The seller should try to convince key division managers and other employees that their welfare is being considered, in the form of employment security, severance pay, and other benefits. The interests of division personnel, in fact, may provide useful guidance in planning the divestiture and identifying prospective buyers. Although confidentiality should generally be maintained during the decision-making process, once divestiture has been chosen, it must be dealt with openly. Disgruntled employees will hinder the sale; enthusiastic employees will help it.

Assessing the Division's Marketability

In order to set pricing parameters and identify and sell likely prospects, it is first necessary to conduct an inventory of the division's marketability. This enables the seller to tailor the sales plan and presentations for particular buyers. The process begins with a determination of exactly which items are for sale, which are excluded, and which are negotiable. Comparable asset values, P/E ratios, acquisition transactions, and other measures provide useful guidelines for valuation. The seller can then estimate the financial value of the division as an outsider might perceive it. This analysis should include an evaluation of internal strengths and weaknesses that an outsider might be less likely to know about, such as functional skills, technology, and other nonfinancial assets, that could have a significant impact on the division's attractiveness and value.

What Is for Sale? Unless the division is a fully freestanding entity, defining the business to be sold can be difficult. Facilities and equipment may be shared with other divisions. Certain functions such as legal, personnel, cash management, collection, and data processing may be performed by parent staff, and even general management personnel may be primarily affiliated with the corporation. Which employees go and which stay? While neither the buyer nor the seller can decide for employees, attractive compensation packages can be designed to help persuade them. If the division is not a complete business entity, it may be restructured as such, if that will make it more salable. On the other hand, it may not be desirable to sell the entire division as a single entity. The seller might want to break the division into pieces or reduce its assets to make purchase more feasible for smaller buyers. Profitable product lines might be segregated and sold on the basis of earnings power; assets associated with unprofitable lines could be sold for book value or whatever the market would bear. Other considerations include the following:

- *Fixed assets* that are essential to the business must generally be included. Unused or underutilized assets, however, such as real estate, buildings, or equipment, might be retained or sold separately.

- *Current assets* are more subject to negotiation. Receivables are likely to be discounted by the buyer, and if the seller has a strong collection function, it may be best to exclude them altogether. Marketable excess inventory might be sold separately, particularly if some of it has already been written off. Cash is a highly variable item, and it is usually divided up at closing based on previous negotiation.

- *Expense items,* such as fuel and office supplies, may have value not represented on the balance sheet. Insurance, a prepaid expense, must be carefully examined; disposition may depend on the type of policy or on whether the seller self-insures.

- *Liabilities* may often be excluded in order to facilitate a sale, or the seller may be willing to guarantee certain debts incurred by the division. Reserves and accruals must be examined for adequacy and relevance. Product or service warranties to customers must be identified and evaluated.

- *Patents and trademarks* may be included, or the seller could license them to the buyer. On the other hand, the division may hold certain licenses or distribution rights that are not transferable to a different owner.

- *Off-balance-sheet items,* such as order backlogs, long-term leases, and research and development, may have substantial value or liability, and should not be overlooked. The backlog, in particular, may be a better indicator of the division's future potential than recent operating statements.

Attractiveness to Buyers. Once the seller knows what it wants and what it is willing to divest, the division's attractiveness to prospective buyers can be assessed. The detailed analysis of financial and nonfinancial assets and liabilities discussed in the preceding section will provide a basis for this assessment, but industry, market, and competitive information must also be considered. Even if the division has been a poor performer, it is important to remember that the division's future, not its past, is being sold. Historical earnings are important, and they should be restated to account for any unusual or nonrecurring charges or corporate overhead allocations, but a wise buyer is likely to look at qualitative factors as well.

Attention must therefore be given to the division's functional skills in areas such as marketing, production, and research and development; current and projected funding needs, and whether those funds are needed for growth or defense; and the feasibility of division management's objectives. Even intangible factors such as the division's organizational culture may be of concern to prospective buyers.

Potential problems should also be identified, such as the following:

- *Antitrust considerations* may restrict the types of buyers that can be approached. Foreign governments may also impose restrictions, or may make it difficult to repatriate the divestiture proceeds.

- *Pension and benefit plans* may involve large obligations and may be unfunded or inadequately funded. Restructuring the plans, with IRS approval, may be necessary to attract a buyer. Employees will also be concerned about any changes. All plans and changes should be carefully reviewed by experts.

- *Labor unions* will certainly be interested in the divestiture program, although in most cases union approval is not necessary. Depending on the situation, union leaders may be advised of the seller's intent, although such disclosure is often left to the buyer. Most buyers will not want to walk into an unpleasant labor situation. If a union contract is about to expire, the seller should probably defer any disclosures about the divestiture program until a new contract has been negotiated, since the union may otherwise try to extract special concessions.

Determining Price and Structure

Decisions about price and structure cannot be addressed without a general determination as to the type of firm likely to buy the division. In many cases, some potential buyers will have been identified in earlier phases of the planning process; e.g., firms in the same industry or firms known to be making similar acquisitions. There are, moreover, no scientific rules to calculate one correct price and structure, because value is a highly subjective matter that will also be influenced by the changing market forces of supply and demand. Regardless of any other arguments, the price must permit the buyer a reasonable return on its investment. Too high a price could prevent the sale and could conceivably result in the buyer's bankruptcy and the seller's repossession of the business. Guidelines about desired payment and structure should therefore be flexible enough to permit negotiation and accommodate the needs and financial constraints of the buyer.

There are two main aspects to the structure of a divestiture transaction, each of which may have significant tax effects: (1) the form in which ownership of the division is conveyed to the buyer, and (2) the form in which the seller is compensated. The buyer typically receives control of the division in the form of stock, if the division is a subsidiary with its own ownership structure, or in the form of title to all or selected assets and liabilities associated with the division. The forms of compensation to the seller are virtually limitless. While most divestitures are for cash and notes, the seller may receive equity in the buyer's company, equity in the division, shares of the seller's stock previously obtained by the buyer, mortgages, merchandise credits, contingency payments, or a combination of payment methods. The timing of these transactions can vary from the closing date to a longer term schedule.

Expert tax counsel should be sought in order to determine an optimal structure, bearing in mind, where possible, the relative tax circumstances of buyer and seller. In general, for example, a seller would prefer to convey stock in the division in order to obtain capital gains treatment for any profit on the sale and to avoid recapture of accelerated depreciation as taxable income. A buyer would generally prefer to receive assets rather than stock in order to maximize the value of depreciable assets for cash flow purposes. Even if the division's legal structure permits a stock sale, the seller should be willing to consider the sale of specified assets as the more practical alternative for many buyers. The degree of flexibility required will depend on how the seller perceives its bargaining position.

Pricing Techniques. It may be useful first to establish minimum and asking prices on the basis of cash up front, if only for internal purposes, to serve as a reference for evaluating pricing alternatives. Book value, as stated for financial reporting purposes, is a useful starting point. The division's balance sheet may have to be adjusted to represent the corporation's true book investment in the division, since certain asset and liability items may not be carried on the division's books or may be commingled with those of other divisions. Book value should also be restated in light of the potential tax treatment of the transaction, since the division's tax basis is likely to differ from its financial reporting basis (e.g., accelerated versus straight-line depreciation of fixed assets).

While even an adjusted book value may bear little resemblance to the division's current liquidation value or future earnings potential, it nonetheless represents the seller's break-even point for financial reporting purposes. A prospective buyer, meanwhile, may look at book value as a benchmark for negotiating, believing that the seller has set book value as a minimum objective. Many buyers and sellers do in fact use book value as a standard, but too great an adherence to it can be unrealistic, since the business could be worth considerably more or less.

Various other techniques are available to assist the seller in determining a fair market price. Current liquidation value of the division's individual assets and estimates of its future earnings both provide useful guidelines. Comparison with similar companies may be helpful; the current market value of publicly listed companies can be readily obtained, and recent merger and acquisition activity should also be looked at.

Price/earnings ratios for comparable firms in comparable industries may be used as a reference. However, use of P/E ratios in negotiations may lead to disagreements, for example, over what constitutes a fair P/E ratio and which year's earnings should be used in the calculation. Discounted cash flow or net present value analysis is also a useful tool, but, again, disagreements may develop over estimated future earnings and the appropriate time horizon and discount rate. One author on the subject suggests that a buyer in its second year of ownership should be able to earn a return on its total investment equal to between one and one-half and three times the rate of high-grade corporate bonds or other low-risk investments.[24] While this formula may be somewhat simplistic, it highlights the fact that the buyer will be comparing the potential return on its investment in the divison with that of alternative investments. *Total* investment may be particularly important to a buyer, since it may expect to invest capital in the division beyond the price paid to the seller.

Negotiating Posture. During the presentation stage, before serious negotiations begin, the seller should be willing to quote a fixed or minimum asking price so that a consistent position is communicated to different buyers. Broad

[24] Gordon Bing, *Corporate Divestment* (Houston: Gulf Publishing Co., 1978), pp. 66–67.

objectives concerning divestiture structure may also be discussed, but the seller should avoid getting mired in details too early in the discussions. Successful negotiations typically proceed from the general to the specific, starting with agreement on the overall structure of the sale (e.g., stock or assets) and then moving to price. The terms of the sale permit the greatest flexibility and are usually dealt with last.

Regardless of the pricing techniques employed, the seller must be able to give convincing arguments to justify its price, and it must support these arguments with a logical analysis of the division's prospects. The asking price should be realistic, but, at the same time, sellers should not be afraid to be bold if the supporting analysis is well-founded.

Selling the Division

After determining the general attractiveness of the division and price objectives, an aggressive seller will actively seek prospective buyers, either directly or through intermediaries. An active approach is likely to speed the divestiture process and also give the seller more control over its outcome.

Finding Prospects. Compiling a list of prospects is analogous to the screening process in an acquisition search. Prospects should be screened on the basis of business fit, ability to pay, antitrust considerations, corporate objectives, and other factors. Suggestions can come from a variety of sources, including the seller's personal contacts, the board of directors, and the division's own managers, suppliers, and customers. The seller should not hesitate to use outside assistance when necessary. Consultants, bankers, lawyers, and accountants may suggest suitable public or private investors whose potential interest in the division might be totally unknown to the seller. Database services may be used in screening large numbers of prospects, for example, companies of a certain size range in certain SIC-code industries. Many corporations, moreover, have publicly announced acquisition programs. Publications such as *Who's Who of Corporate Acquisitions, Mergerstat Review,* and *Mergers and Acquisitions* may provide names of active acquirors and their acquisition criteria.[25]

Making Announcements. An alternative approach to prospecting is to announce publicly that the division is for sale and wait for interest to develop. This approach has been used successfully by many companies. If the division is relatively unattractive, a list of likely prospects may be difficult to compile. If the division is highly attractive, the seller may hope to conduct an auction among many bidders. Public announcement, however, often puts the seller in a reactive position and may give the division a bad name if much time elapses while buyers shop around. On the other hand, even a seller who actively seeks

---

[25] James J. Mahoney, *Who's Who of Corporate Acquisitions* (Tiburon, Cal.: Tweed Publishing Co., 1980); W.T. Grimm & Co., *Mergerstat Review* (Chicago, annually); Information for Industry, *Mergers and Acquisitions: The Journal of Corporate Venture* (Philadelphia, quarterly).

prospects on a confidential basis may eventually have to make a public announcement once rumors have begun to circulate.

Negotiating. Once a serious prospect has been identified through screening, initial contact, and sales presentations, the two negotiating teams can meet. The size of the teams is itself negotiable, but an expert lawyer (internal or external) should be included. Tax, accounting, and other analysts or consultants should also be available. Detailed analysis of counteroffers is generally best done away from the heat of the bargaining table, however. The chief negotiator should try to find general areas of agreement before discussing technicalities. Many minor details can be worked out in the period prior to closing, but the negotiators should reach agreement on all key points to prevent a deal from unraveling because of some later misunderstanding. It is common to allow the final price to fluctuate after negotiations to reflect the specific conditions at the time of closing.

Closing. Following the negotiations, the seller must provide updated, audited statements and documents for the division. A CPA should certify that the statements were prepared according to generally accepted accounting principles, but responsibility for their accuracy lies with the seller. Prior to settlement, the buyer is likely to try to uncover the division's worst problems, since afterward those problems belong to the buyer. The seller's divestiture team should cooperate with the buyer and avoid petty disputes to ensure that the divestiture program reaches a successful final settlement.

Guidelines for Success. In divestitures (as in acquisitions), the theme is simple: Careful analysis and planning—or executive homework—increases the chances of success. Moreover, experience suggests some guidelines that, if applied to each divestiture, should significantly increase its chances of success.

1. First and foremost, do the strategic homework—for *both* the parent and the division. Make sure that all attractive options have been fully considered. The benefits of the divestiture to the parent should clearly and substantially exceed both the direct and indirect costs of divestment.

2. Once the decision to divest is made, act quickly. The problems that originally motivated the decision will not solve themselves. Rumors can sap morale and harm the seller's negotiating position.

3. Approach the decision positively. In many cases, divestiture may be genuinely positive not only from the parent's perspective but also from that of the division. Where this is so, make every appropriate use of division management in carrying out the process.

4. Plan the divestment process carefully. Avoid a fire sale and try to reduce any personal trauma to the unavoidable minimum. The biggest risk in divestiture is the destruction of the division's economic value caused by the departure of key employees and other disruptions to the division's business. Therefore, it is

essential to have a clear strategy for approaching prospective buyers and for determining when and how to bring division management on board.

5. Responsibilities in the divestiture process should be clearly delineated and assigned. It is useful to have a dedicated, accountable team involved from start to finish.

6. Finally, anticipate the people problems. Where possible, take steps to mitigate them and compensate key people for the personal disruption they will experience. Even where substantial costs are involved, they may be a lot less than the indirect costs of perceived or real insensitivity.

13

Strategic Planning for Multinational Corporations

PATRICK F. DOLAN

Senior Consultant, Peat, Marwick, Mitchell & Co.

INTRODUCTION

During the 1970s and 1980s, the U.S. and world economies experienced the effects of the transition from a controlled, regulated, and fragmented world economy to a much freer, interdependent global economy in which world supply and demand factors determined prices. Now, there are freer world markets for energy, currency, trade, and labor. The economic transition of these two decades also has contributed to the growth of new global markets for products and services. In the United States, the deregulation of industries such as banking and transportation has permitted classic economic forces to dominate markets.

Overall, the change augurs well for U.S. multinational corporations (MNCs) in world competition. However, the transition has been both complex and turbulent, and the cost to the U.S. economy has been high. Some examples of these costs include the following:

- World oil prices increased from $13 per barrel in 1978 to $34 in 1980, after increasing from $3 per barrel to $11 during 1973–1974;
- Productivity growth in U.S. business was zero for the five years previous to December 1982;
- Interest rates rose to record levels;
- The trade-weighted value of the dollar declined from 120 in 1970 to a low of 85 in 1980, and rebounded in three years to 122;
- The 1983 business failure rates were the highest since 1932;
- International competition intensified; and
- Unemployment rates rose sharply.

Despite the gloomy outlook that the transition often produced in the United States, the international situation was much worse. Poland, Argentina, and Mexico were some of the victims of the economic upheaval. Growing protectionism and serious debt rescheduling problems in most of the less developed countries added to the economic instability.

This chapter discusses strategic issues, external events, and alternative strategies specific to a developed multinational corporation: a company that operates in many nations and that competes strategically on a global scale, in a world that is undergoing economic transition. Although this chapter focuses on MNCs based in the United States, the concepts, ideas, and approach discussed here apply to all MNCs, no matter where they are based.

Change Is Opportunity

This is a world of perpetual change. The courageous welcome this change, for without it, few people could greatly improve their economic situation. Change is opportunity; for MNCs, it is the opportunity to improve their relative standing in world markets.

In an ever-changing world, people as well as businesses face two strategic options: (1) do something, or (2) do nothing. Risk and opportunity are inherent in the "do something" approach. The "do nothing" approach harbors more risk, affords less opportunity, and, in the long term, results in failure. Change, and its constant companion, risk, have made both winners and losers in corporate America.

How can MNCs benefit from the recent changes in the world economy? They must first discern overall patterns and emerging trends in national and world markets, then position themselves to take advantage of them. Global strategy succeeds only when supported by thorough, informed forecasting and economic analyses.

Today, many MNCs forecast global and U.S. economic trends, as well as world trade patterns, and evaluate the effect of these trends and other external factors on their current business operations before setting strategies. This approach is analogous to sailing, where one attempts to find the currents and the winds before setting forth. The following sections of this chapter describe macro trends that affect most MNCs.

GLOBAL ECONOMIC TRENDS

In an interdependent world brought about by freer markets, freer world trade, and freer movement of resources, external events can shape the destiny of both a company and its industry. Many firms consider macroeconomic trends and forecasts before looking at each business within their industries. Naturally, a firm wants to pinpoint only those trends and events that may directly affect its own businesses. Later, the firm incorporates this information in its businesses and corporate planning. This approach has four steps:

- Identify major external trends and forecasted events in the economic, social, political, and technological environment;
- Target those trends and the events that directly affect the MNC;
- Analyze the potential impact of such trends or events on the MNC's operations; and
- Evaluate the impact in detail during the business and corporate planning process.

Few trends, if any, affect all companies and industries irrespective of location. One can isolate, however, three macro global economic trends that significantly affect today's MNCs: (1) standardized products and services, (2) evolving global industries, and (3) a restructured worldwide industrial base.

Standardized Products and Services

Customers and clients throughout the world want standardized products and services. Business has only recently recognized this fact, although global demand for uniform price-competitive products and services probably always has existed. For example, today's world wants Coca-Cola, and Pepsi; and Levi's jeans. Likewise, today, there are women throughout the world who are concerned with looking youthful, and they want Oil of Olay; surely the desire to look young has always existed. However, until the rise of the MNC such needs, latent or existent, could not be satisfied.

What is different today is that a global entity—the MNC—can provide standard products and services worldwide, and that consumers are aware of these standard items. This dual dimension of corporate existence and consumer knowledge is directly linked to freer markets, freer trade, freer movement of resources, and technological innovations in production, communication, transport, and travel. Now that business has recognized a global need for products and services that are more uniform, of high quality, and competitive in cost and value, the trend to standardize must inevitably lead to a world common market in many industries.

The demand of customers worldwide for standard products and services presents both opportunities and threats to the MNC. Opportunities are available to those firms that offer standard products and services globally and that are now global corporations or are becoming global corporations. Threats face those firms that continue to customize their products and services to accommodate perceived national differences among markets.

Evolving Global Industries

The trend to standardized products has directly contributed to the evolution of global industries. MNCs have had to make their products and services more uniform to compete successfully in the global marketplace. A global industry is one in which (1) customers throughout the world prefer and demand standard products and services, and (2) competitors have profited from exploiting the new global markets by adopting a global strategy. Most global industries are becoming increasingly dominated by companies with global strategies. These companies naturally benefit from economies of scale in production, distribution, marketing, and management. The trend toward globalization is comparable to the shift from regional to national competition in U.S. industry from 1890 to 1930.

Restructured Worldwide Industrial Base

The trend toward uniformity in products and services and the growth of global industries have contributed, in part, to the restructuring of the world's industrial base. For many years, the industrial countries of the West have been slowly moving from a manufacturing economy to a service economy. This transition was prompted by the two trends discussed above—standardization and globalization—as well as by technological innovation in production methods and greater competition from developing countries.

During the past four years, the restructuring of Western economics—from an industrial economy to an information-intensive economy—accelerated as a result of the 1980 and 1981-1982 recessions. Now, the Western economies are plagued with overcapacity and low demand in basic manufacturing; for example, such basic U.S. industries as steel, aluminum, automobiles, tires, farm equipment, and oil refining, have permanently reduced plant capacity. Companies in these industries, or companies serving those industries, must become the most efficient and lowest-priced producers to survive. Unlike the United States, other Western countries are also attempting to manage the transition by instituting explicit national industrial policies. However, as a group, developing countries have a comparative advantage over developed countries: They have opportunities to expand their manufacturing operations.

To keep from failing, many firms in the United States, Europe, and Japan have consolidated their manufacturing capabilities, and many others seek to reposition themselves in service industries. For those firms that remain in manufacturing, the dramatic shift from a supply-constrained environment to one that is constrained by demand will intensify competition. Relative cost position will strongly influence market share and ultimate survival.

WORLD TRADE PATTERNS

The successful MNC of the future must view the world (or at least its major regions) as one competitive market in which it must achieve and defend market share. Five world trade patterns affect the efforts of U.S.-based MNCs to compete in this global market: (1) U.S. integration in the world economy, (2) increased dependence on the U.S. dollar, (3) trade agreements, (4) comparative cost advantage, and (5) debts and nationalism in less developed countries (LDCs).

U.S. Integration in the World Economy

The United States has vigorously increased its involvement in the world's economy over the past decade. Before 1970, only a small portion of U.S. goods were exposed to world trade. In fact, from an economic standpoint, the U.S. economy represented the closest practical example of a closed economy.

That is no longer the case today. In 1980, 17 percent of the goods produced in the United States were exported (up from 9 percent in 1970), and more than 21 percent of its total sale of goods were imported (up from 9 percent in 1970). If one considers potential exposure to import penetration, over 70 percent of U.S. goods must now compete in an international marketplace.[1] These data show that the goods sector of the U.S. economy, which now represents one-third of the U.S. gross national product, operates in the global economy. U.S. basic manufacturing is being pounded by the waves of world competition. The result is that the goods sector is experiencing a severe restructuring throughout the world. In contrast, the service sector is relatively sheltered from world trade.

Based on historical trends, foreign manufacturers will make even stronger sales among U.S. consumers, unless U.S. industry competes globally. Two con-

---

[1] Ira C. Magaziner and Robert B. Reich, *Minding America's Business* (New York: Vintage Books, 1983), p. 32.

clusions can be drawn from this trend: Companies in industries exposed to world trade must compete successfully in a global market; and, companies in industries sheltered from world trade must compete successfully in a domestic market.

Increased Dependence on the U.S. Dollar

The U.S. dollar is the transaction currency of world trade, a reserve currency for central banks, and a safe haven in uncertain times. It remains a medium of exchange for 80 percent of noncommunist trade, and constitutes 75 percent of central bank reserves.[2] Therefore, the U.S. Federal Reserve System not only controls the domestic money supply; in effect, it controls the world's money supply. The stability of the world monetary system depends on the stability of the dollar.

During the past four years, the total world demand for dollars increased dramatically, driving up its value against other currencies. The trade-weighted value of the dollar is at its highest level since 1970, and the dollar's importance in world finance is at an all-time high.

But what will the relative value of the dollar be 5 or more years from now? U.S.-based MNCs must ask these questions: Can the dollar remain the medium of exchange for so much world trade and constitute such a large percentage of central bank reserves indefinitely? Will the European Currency Unit (the ECU) and the Japanese yen capture more of a share of the transaction and reserve use from the dollar? Will the dollar remain a safe haven for foreign investors in times of uncertainty? The answers will affect the most basic strategic options of MNCs.

Trade Agreements

Trade agreements increase the flow of goods and services among countries by reducing trade impediments or increasing trade incentives. The General Agreement on Tariffs and Trade (GATT) was signed in 1947 to promote world trade and commerce to restore prosperity to a war-torn world. Countries have worked within its framework for over 30 years.

The most important trade agreement since GATT has been the Tokyo Round-Table Multilateral Trade Agreement, signed in December 1979. It sets the rules for world trade for this and the next decade, in four key areas: (1) conducting international trade, (2) reducing tariffs, (3) setting rules for commerce in agricultural products, and (4) reforming the GATT framework. World trade should continue to become stronger under this agreement.

Application of Comparative Advantage

The theory of comparative cost advantage dictates that a country should produce only those goods for which it has a comparative cost advantage, so that it

---

[2] Robert B. Reich, "Beyond Free Trade," *Foreign Affairs* (Spring 1983), p. 793.

employs its economic resources efficiently. The value of this economic theory holds true only when applied to a theoretical, totally economic world. In the real world, governmental actions distort business patterns based on pure economics.

Recently, however, the development of abundant and cheap transportation, as well as the development of efficient financial and communication services through technology, has made comparative advantage less theoretical and more of a reality. It can be said today that "you can feed New York from Iowa and supply Iowa's entertainment needs from New York."[3] But for the Third World, without the free movement of the resources of capital, technology, know-how, and management, comparative advantage is still only an abstract concept.

Nevertheless, regional comparative advantage will soon exercise its true impact on world trade. An increasingly global technical and managerial personnel market and freer movement of capital are making it a reality. South Korea, for example, has become a new force in world production of low-priced, high-quality raw steel. Although its lower labor, energy, and transportation costs give it a comparative cost advantage over the developed nations, its success could not be achieved without state-of-the-art plants built by steel powers like Japan and West Germany and financed by major Western banks. Japanese, West German, and other Western resources were available to South Korea. The resulting South Korean resources are now available to Japan, the United States, and Western Europe. Flows of resources in both directions bolster additional world trade.

As the world becomes more economically interdependent, and as more global industries and companies develop, sovereign states, irrespective of political philosophy, will be exposed to the same global market forces. These forces will vary, depending on a country's stage of development, resources, and overall strengths, but each will be subject to equivalent economic rules. Since nations have been dragged into the same global economic ballpark through a changed set of rules, their response—and their proactive focus—must have an economic ingredient to succeed. Consequently, sovereign state responses and approaches to world trade and business will converge to a more uniform pattern, which, in turn, may affect political ideology as well.

Debts and Nationalism in LDCs

World trade is hampered by the debt service burden of LDCs. These countries have exhausted their hard currencies and their credit has suffered. Consequently, many subsidiaries of MNCs struggle under import restrictions. They are able to import fewer components and parts for their plants. That situation in turn limits exports. Compounding their difficulties is the fact that local credit restrictions inhibit local demand. In response, MNCs use counter trade in lieu of hard currency transactions to maintain business levels.

---

[3] James Cook, "You Mean We've Been Speaking Prose All These Years?" *Forbes* (April 11, 1983), pp. 143-146.

Most developed countries have policies directed toward creating independent high-technology industries with strong export-earning capabilities. These
industries have been greatly assisted by multi-billion-dollar government programs. In Europe, despite the European Economic Community (EEC) position
toward opening markets within the EEC, governments will continue to favor
locally established companies.

Economic nationalism, a natural response to difficult and uncertain times,
further suppresses global competition. The severe worldwide recession of 1981-
1982 exacerbated debt service problems and reinforced many governments' iso-
lationism, particularly in developing countries. Most LDCs are insisting on
more national value-added content, local management and ownership, and
transfer of technology before they will allow a foreign firm to sell to their markets. Many are also demanding export of their goods to trading nations, seeking substitutes for imports, and soliciting support for regional trade policies.

Why World Trade Will Continue to Expand

In spite of the LDC debt problem, which affects developed and developing
countries alike, and in spite of economic nationalism, at least nine factors suggest continued expansion of world trade over time:

- The enlightened self-interest of developed countries extends the limits to free
  trade further every year. MNCs in Western countries need a growing market for
  their products and services in LDCs, and LDCs need access to the U.S. market
  for their economies to grow through exports.

- The U.S. market is an ever-declining percentage of the world market. U.S.
  MNCs must seek other markets for products and services.

- Many countries are financially leveraged to the limit; these countries can grow
  only through equity capital from direct involvement by foreign MNCs. They will
  be forced to attract MNC investment aggressively, which, in turn, directly
  affects trade flow.

- The Tokyo Round-Table Multilateral Trade Agreement of 1979 has eased global
  trade restrictions.

- Governments are increasingly aware of the need to export their resources,
  goods, and services.

- Global competitors and sovereign states better understand and apply the theory
  of comparative advantage.

- Trading companies have increased their activity, and further development is
  likely.

- There is more uniformity of customer demands for both consumer and noncon-
  sumer goods and services, owing to increased communications through modern
  technology.

- MNCs desire a competitive advantage over national firms and other MNCs by
  adopting global strategies.

U.S. ECONOMIC TRENDS

The United States is no longer the world's dominant economic force. It produced 50 percent of the world's gross national product (GNP) just after World War II. Since then, the United States' percentage of world GNP has steadily declined. Now, it accounts for more than one-fifth of global production and nearly one-fourth of the total national product of all non-Communist nations.[4]

Four major trends specific to the U.S. economy affect U.S.-based MNCs: (1) shift from goods to services, (2) need for global service, (3) competitiveness of U.S. business, and (4) corporate consolidations.

Shift From Goods to Services

In 1982, the service sector of the economy generated 67 percent of the U.S. GNP and employed 7 out of 10 Americans. The goods sector, which includes raw material, manufacturing, and construction, now accounts for only one-third of the GNP.

Within the goods sector, U.S. MNCs now dominate manufacturing. According to Robert Reich, "Some 70 percent of the value added in American manufacturing currently derives from firms that have branches, subsidiaries, or joint ventures outside the United States; a similar percentage of manufacturing income in Japan, West Germany, Sweden, and Britain is earned by multinational enterprises."[5]

The gradual trend from goods to service became evident after World War II. At that time, about 50 percent of U.S. employment came from each sector. This trend continues.

In the future, U.S. manufacturing will produce much more in absolute terms than it does today, and, indeed, it may hold its relative share of GNP. However, just as agriculture now requires a small labor force,[6] so manufacturing soon will require a small work force.

Only by producing a higher quality or greater quantity of a product or service with less human labor can a society increase its standard of living. Most of the writing on strategy concentrates on the goods economy, and very little, if any, concentrates on the service economy. Strategic concepts and methods thus are not well developed for the most important sector of the U.S. economy. This chapter addresses the importance of both goods and services, their mutual interdependence, and their synergistic potential. The concepts, methods, and examples discussed here apply equally to both sectors.

The shift from goods to service has contributed to a polarization in income distribution. Now, there are greater numbers at the top and bottom, while middle-income families decrease as a percentage of the total.

Manufacturing, once the main stead of middle America, has given way to service, which provides low-paying jobs, well-paid jobs, and some jobs in

---

[4] Reich, op. cit., p. 793.

[5] Ibid., p. 802.

[6] In the United States today, 2.4 million farmers grow 170 percent more agricultural products than 7 million farmers did 50 years ago.

between. But, the service economy overall tends to produce a greater variation in family income. MNCs catering to consumers follow closely shifts in income distribution and demographic changes.

Need for Global Service

Many mature MNCs frequently require services for their worldwide operations. For example, it is important for service businesses, such as international banks, insurance companies, Big Eight accounting firms, advertising agencies, and oil service companies, to provide service to their MNCs' clients globally. If they do not, a competitor will provide a better global service and win the account. This is a relatively new trend, and the implications are far reaching.

According to a *Wall Street Journal* article on advertising agencies,[7] eight sizable acquisitions took place in the 18-month period ending July 1983. "Many of the acquisitions are based on the belief that the ad business soon will be divided into two parts: small shops serving mostly local accounts and a dozen or fewer huge, multinational agencies whose clients are huge, multinational advertisers." The *Journal* quotes Maurice Saatchi, a founder and director of Saatchi & Saatchi, Britain's largest advertising concern: "Those agencies that are farsighted enough to grasp this [trend] will do well, those that don't will suffer."

A *Wall Street Journal* bulletin on trends in industry and finance[8] reported that major law firms are opening more offices in new cities. "A major aim is to serve far-flung interests of corporate clients." The article cited Chicago's Baker & McKenzie, which pioneered opening branches in foreign cities. Baker & McKenzie represents Eli Lilly in Belgium, Brazil, and Britain, among other places.

Competitiveness of U.S. Business

Domestic operations of U.S. MNCs have a competitive disadvantage in export markets, in part because of the dramatic appreciation of the dollar from 1980-1983. Exports today represent only about 10 percent of the total output of goods and services. (About 20 percent of U.S. manufactured goods and half of U.S. crops are sold abroad; 40 percent of American exports normally are sold to LDCs.[9]

The underlying factors behind the reasons why U.S. exports are suffering include: (1) the strength of the U.S. dollar, (2) zero U.S. productivity growth during the five years before 1983, (3) competition from foreign companies subsidized by home governments, and (4) bilateral political deals between foreign

[7] Bill Abrams and Dennis Kneale, "Ad Agency Acquisitions Increasing as Firms Seek World-Wide Market," *Wall Street Journal* (July 11, 1983), p. 21.

[8] "A Special Background Report on Trends in Industry and Finance," *Wall Street Journal*, Business Bulletin (July 14, 1983), p. 1.

[9] Clyde J. Farnsworth, "Third World Debts Mean Fewer Jobs for Peoria," *New York Times* (Dec. 11, 1983).

governments. As a result of the first two factors alone, U.S. prices became 30 percent less competitive during 1980-82 than those of Germany and Japan.

Domestic operations competing against imports in the home market face the same disadvantages. More than 20 percent of goods consumed in the United States are imported. Some U.S. firms in the goods sector of the economy are counteracting this disadvantage by increasing their production in countries where costs are lower and then transporting these goods to both home and foreign markets.

Corporate Consolidations

U.S. firms often cannot defend their domestic market (which accounts for over one-fifth of global production) simply by operating as domestic businesses. Global competitors using the sources of global competitive advantage will erode their market share. Consequently, many of these firms, small and large, will consolidate, pool resources, or enter joint ventures to gain some of the advantages of their global competitors to defend their domestic market. MNCs are faced with two choices: they can go global and gain some of the advantages discussed below, or they can defend a market niche in a few national markets.

SOURCES OF GLOBAL COMPETITIVE ADVANTAGE

Global competitive advantage is the additional economic benefits gained by operating globally or in many national markets. These advantages are so great that few national firms will be able to compete successfully in major markets without government support or intervention. A national firm is one that operates almost exclusively within its own frontiers.

Many advantages exist for firms that compete globally, but five benefits clearly stand out: (1) global service, (2) total service synergy, (3) economies of scale, (4) capital resources, and (5) use of comparative advantage. These are discussed below.

Global Service

A global service advantage exists when a firm provides a uniform product or service to a global customer. Global capability to provide a product or service to other MNCs is itself a clear competitive advantage over domestic businesses.

MNCs that provide goods (e.g., oil service companies or capital goods) or services (e.g., Big Eight accounting firms, banks, advertising agencies, law and public relations firms, and insurance companies) to other MNCs have a clear competitive advantage over domestic companies in that market segment. For example, Peat Marwick International has a better chance of winning the audit engagement of a U.S. or British MNC than does a domestic accounting firm because Peat's worldwide office network is more efficient and more cost effective than a number of domestic accounting firms, from the point of view of a quality-conscious and time-conscious MNC client.

The Economist, in a review of the report "Who Audits the World?" compiled by Vinod Bavishi and Harold Wymen of the University of Connecticut, stated that "in the past decade, the big nine [accounting] firms have increased their dominance, particularly outside America."[10] The Economist reported the following market share percentages of the nine global accounting firms in three countries:

Country	Market Share 1971	1981
Britain	72	86
Canada	42	99
Australia	32	71

Clearly, the "global nine" stole the market from the small-and medium-size auditing firms (or, at least, acquired them) in those 10 years. Obviously, in the accounting business, the ability to provide a standard global service to MNCs has contributed to the market share growth of the very large accounting firms.

Total Service Synergy

Total service synergy potential exists when a firm provides new or improved services that complement existing services. Synergy is defined as combining activities in such a way that the combined benefits are greater than the sum of the benefits from the activities if they are kept separate. Synergy usually exists in the case of a global entity (sometimes, unknown to its management) simply because it operates in many national markets.

For example, an international air courier service recorded increased business in its Far East routes after adding more routes to Europe. Presumably, customers that used the new European routes also used the company's Far East routes. Here is a synergistic example on a micro level: A condominium in a New York City suburb has a private bus service to and from New York City daily. At one stage, the bus service had six trips to the city in the morning and four return trips home in the evening. When it added two more return trips home and left the morning schedule unchanged, the total number of evening passengers increased (just enough to cover the added expense) *and* the total number of morning passengers increased by 10 percent. This effect can be called "total service synergy."

In the first example, the firm's objective was to establish a greater presence in the air courier service business from the United States to Europe. The company ended up increasing business in its Far East routes as well. In the second example, the condominium's bus service wanted to improve the return bus service by adding two more trips home. As a result, it increased the morning passenger total as well. It seems that by improving one segment of a business or

---

[10] "Accountants: East, West, Who's Best?" The Economist (Sept. 3, 1983), p. 72.

adding a new one, goodwill is created for the other parts; this is reflected by the increased business that resulted without additional investment.

Economies of Scale

Firms that compete globally through shared business costs benefit from economies of scale. Greater volume and wider experience result in lower unit costs. These economies are particularly significant when high fixed costs are shared and when standard products are sold in large quantities throughout the world. According to Theodore Levitt, "Corporations geared to this new reality benefit from enormous economies of scale in production, distribution, marketing, and management. By translating these benefits into reduced world prices, they can decimate competitors that still live in the disabling grip of old assumptions about how the world works." [11]

Scale economies are normally associated with firms in the goods sector of the economy, but the advantages are equally achievable in the service sector. Large service firms benefit from scale economies in most business functions—marketing, finance, management, research and service development, and purchasing—that are centrally coordinated.

For example, large financial holding companies get better credit terms than their individual businesses; marketing and new service development are centrally coordinated in national and international accounting firms. The benefits and costs are shared by all offices in the company network, resulting in a lower cost to each office than if it had to conduct its own marketing and new-service development.

Capital Resources

The availability of capital resources to invest, the willingness to accept risk, and the longer-term payoff of a global strategy can offer a company a competitive advantage. For example, in the U.S. semiconductor industry, many industry experts believe that a chip maker can no longer survive on good technology and engineering alone. It must also acquire the resources of a very large company: superior financial discipline, marketing and people management. *Business Week* reports that Japanese chip producers enjoy a competitive edge: "Japanese producers will have a big advantage because they already are part of large, sophisticated corporations." [12]

In the semiconductor industry and in other price-sensitive product-based businesses, the strongest competitors forge a market-share strategy called "learning-curve pricing" to ensure continued market dominance. Learning-curve pricing severely restricts capital formation because prices are reduced to coincide with falling production costs, which should occur as volume grows and workers gain experience. This strategy is intended to create bigger demand

---

[11] Theodore Levitt, "The Globalization of Markets," *Harvard Business Review* (May/June 1983), p. 92.

[12] "Chip Wars: The Japanese Threat," *Business Week* (May 23, 1983), p. 81.

faster, reduce unit costs, push out weak firms—usually smaller companies—and discourage new competitors. The firm using learning-curve pricing thereby gains or at least holds, market share.

It is very difficult for a smaller firm to compete successfully against a global firm in a global industry using an aggressive market-share strategy like that used by Japanese firms:

> In any no-profits contest for market share, the odds are stacked heavily in favor of Japanese producers. More often than not, they are part of vertically integrated companies in the $15 billion to $20 billion class, so they can afford to subsidize their integrated circuits operations. This is a particularly telling advantage because of the chipmaking industry's daunting combination of enormous capital equipment needs, exceptionally high research and development spending (typically around 10 percent of sales), and brutal pricing policies.[13]

Use of Comparative Advantage

Product-based businesses depend on comparative advantage to succeed, more heavily than other types of firms. Global companies have the edge—they can set up operations in areas of the world where their product or the parts they need can be produced at a cost/value advantage over their competitors—in Southeast Asia, for example. As mentioned earlier, comparative advantage can be gained only if there is also free movement of resources—principally capital, technology, know-how, and management.

Another trend that affects this situation is the fact that as the world becomes more economically interdependent and more global industries and companies develop, sovereign states, irrespective of political philosophy, will be exposed to the same global market forces. These forces will vary according to each country's stage of development, resources, and overall strengths, but all nations will be subject to equivalent economic rules. They will be propelled into the same global economic arena. To succeed, their response must likewise have an economic ingredient. Consequently, responses and approaches to world trade and business will converge to a more uniform worldwide pattern, which in turn will benefit the global competitor.

Global economic trends, world trade patterns, U.S. economic trends, benefits for global competitors—these factors work behind the scenes, pushing companies into the global arena. On the scene, within the MNC itself, other factors are at work. The following section looks at the make-up of the MNC and its components, strategic business units.

MNC STRATEGIC BUSINESS UNITS

An MNC may have one or more business, but it most likely has more than one. Strategic management structures are shown in Figure 13-1. The most common

---

[13] Ibid., p. 83.

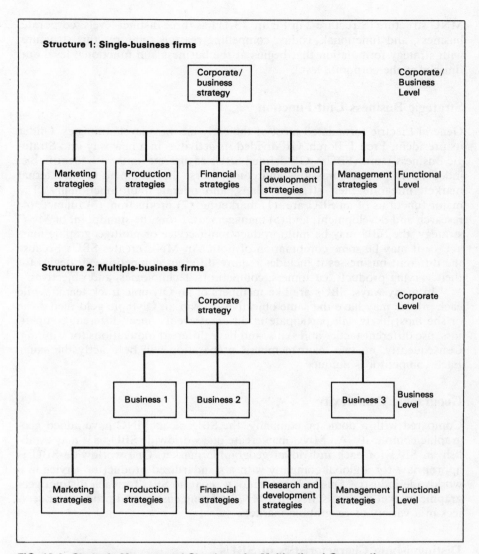

FIG. 13-1 Strategic Management Structures for Multinational Corporations

MNC structure (Structure 2 in Figure 13-1) has three distinct levels: corporate, business, and functional. Today, compelling reasons reinforce this structure, with strategy formulation that begins at the business and functional level and finishes at the corporate level.

Strategic Business Unit Function

General Electric formulated most of the early business-level strategies. Under its president, Fred J. Borch, GE divided its activities in a new way into Strategic Business Units (SBUs). GE defined SBUs as discrete units with identifiable, independent business missions and competitors; they compete in an external market, integrate their strategic plans, and operate multifunctionally. The major functions of an SBU are: (1) marketing, (2) production, (3) finance, (4) research and development, and (5) management. From the standpoint of MNC strategy, the SBU may be multiproduct/multiservice or multigeographic market, or it may be some combination of both. An MNC creates SBUs because the different businesses it includes require different competitive strategies for their varying products, customers, competitors, technologies, and objectives.

In many ways, SBUs are like members of an Olympic track team. While each athlete may have the same objective—to win an Olympic gold medal—he or she most likely will participate in different events, meet different competitors, use different tactics and skills, and have different motivations for winning. Consequently, no two team members' preparation will be exactly the same. Each competitor is unique.

Geographic Complexity

Compared with a domestic company, the SBU of an MNC have added geographic complexity. An MNC may create one worldwide SBU or it may establish an SBU for each individual geographic market. One worldwide SBU is appropriate for a global company with a standardized product or service in a worldwide industry. On the other hand, a separate SBU for each distinct geographic market is more suited to a MNC offering customized products or services in a variety of geographic markets.

Distinguishing Characteristics of SBUs

How does an MNC determine if two activities are part of the same business or if they are different businesses? First, it examines three characteristics: (1) products/services, (2) customers, and (3) technologies. If two of these three characteristics differ significantly, it is likely that these units are different SBUs. Second, it compares the direct competitors for each of these units. If they overlap significantly, the units may entail the same business, and they may not be separate SBUs. Third, it examines keys to success in each business. If they are the same, the units may not be separate SBUs; they may be part of the same business unit.

A profit center is probably not an SBU, and calling a profit center an SBU does not make it one. For example, the manager of a U.S. money center bank's corporate office in London is responsible for a profit center. The SBU might be the bank's corporate lending business worldwide (or in major regions of the world); the London profit center is thus just a subset of the SBU.

MNC BUSINESS STRATEGY

A business strategy is the means by which the management of an SBU plans to achieve its objectives. Selecting a business strategy for an MNC is a similar process to choosing a strategy for a domestic firm, yet it is usually more complex. This section highlights the attributes of MNC business strategy that distinguish it from the strategy of a domestic firm.

Characteristics of MNC Strategy

MNC business strategy differs in at least ten ways from domestic business strategy, as discussed in the following sections.

Strategic Focus. An MNC's strategic focus is global or multinational. The domestic firm's focus is predominantly, but not exclusively, national. The strategic focus of an MNC directly affects the remaining nine distinguishing features of MNC business strategy.

Business Strategy Elements. An MNC business strategy has at least six major elements or functions (as compared with the five elements in the domestic firm): (1) marketing, (2) production (or delivery in the case of a service business), (3) finance, (4) research and development, (5) management, and (6) focus. The focus strategy of an MNC clearly distinguishes it from that of a domestic firm. This sixth element of the MNC business strategy also lends complexity to the other five elements, as well as adds new subelements, such as foreign exchange exposure and tax strategy, to the finance function. The MNCs focus strategy alternatives—global or multinational—determine how the first five elements should be coordinated. For example, a global focus strategy, in which the world (or major regions of it) is viewed as one homogeneous market, requires a configuration of business elements that differ from that of a multinational focus strategy, in which each nation is viewed as a unique market. Therefore the MNC must address the focus issue before it selects other functional strategies.

Markets. An MNC's customers, present and potential, are found throughout the world. Its market may be global or multinational, depending on whether its customers accept a standardized product or service. A national firm, on the other hand, has one domestic market.

Products and Services. Today's customers seem to prefer high-quality, low-cost, mass-produced goods. As standard services become even more widely accepted, customers ultimately may view some of them as commodities not unlike oil, which they buy from the seller with the lowest prices. Many services are already much more uniform than they were only a few years ago, and they now are subject to increased pricing pressures. For example, the banking, insurance, audit, transportation, brokerage, and tax businesses offer standardized, comparable services. In such industries, price has become a devastating competitive weapon.

Competition. An MNC's competitors are other MNCs, global firms, state-owned or subsidized enterprises, and to a lesser extent, domestic firms in local markets. Competitors of domestic firms are other national firms, generally of the same size or larger. Because of the MNC's competitive advantage (achieved from its global or multinational focus strategy), few domestic firms are able to compete successfully against MNCs without government intervention or support. Consequently, national firms seek out submarkets and segments that the MNCs do not aggressively seek. The competitive arena is quickly becoming a two-tiered battlefield, with multinational and national firms each serving different market segments.

Government Policies and Regulations. MNCs, even at the level of the SBU, collaborate with many host governments. They must also comply with the regulatory requirements of each country in which they operate. Domestic firm SBUs operate within the constraints of the home government's policies and regulations.

Risk Vs. Return. MNC business units may have a higher risk/return profile than those of a domestic firm, particularly when dealing in countries with political instability, or high vulnerability to changes in patterns of world trade and/or finance. U.S. multinational banks pursued an aggressive strategy to increase market share of the world's credit markets, particularly during and after the dramatic increase in oil prices in 1979-1980. Most of the loans were made to developing countries; they were short-term, relatively expensive loans, repayable in dollars. Three dramatic shocks hit the credit markets simultaneously: (1) interest rates—the cost of credit—doubled; (2) the dollar exchange rate increased from 50 to 100 percent against foreign currencies; and (3) commodity prices dropped sharply. Many developing countries were unable to meet their covenants or service their debt. These countries, including Mexico, Poland, and Brazil, were forced to negotiate the rescheduling of their debt obligations with Western bankers. Obviously, the risks associated with this strategy proved much higher than anticipated.

Performance Criteria. When selecting a business strategy, both MNCs and domestic firms set targets and financial criteria to evaluate future performance. They also preset hurdle rates, such as return on investment (ROI) or cash flow,

and for incremental investment within the business unit. ROI is the most commonly used investment criterion. An MNC's measurements to assess the progress of a business strategy differ from those of a domestic firm in at least two ways: (1) MNCs are prepared to break even, or even to take a temporary loss, to hold or gain their share of a particular geographical market (they are also prepared to take a loss in one market to maximize their overall global strategy), and (2) some MNCs define early-warning signals to trigger alternative strategies.

Implementation Mechanism. Business strategy is implemented through systems, by people, and in an organizational structure; hence, the catch phrase "Systems, People, and Structure." The implementation mechanism of MNCs, comprised of people, systems, and structure, may span the globe. The implementation mechanism within a domestic firm is local and is much less complex. (This subject is discussed further below.)

Suppliers. Product-based businesses, whether they are MNCs or domestic firms, usually depend on input from outside the firm to conduct business. Such input may include raw material, semifinished parts, or, in the case of a trading company, a finished product. Service-based and product-based businesses rely on suppliers of credit, other business services, and equipment. Although suppliers are equally essential to the business units of MNCs and to those of domestic firms, three distinctions pertain to the MNC: (1) an MNC's SBU suppliers are frequently also MNCs, since "big business does business with big business"; (2) MNC SBUs obtain their supplies from many different sources worldwide (their business operations may be strategically placed to obtain the cheapest source of supply; domestic firms usually buy locally and from a fewer number of suppliers); and (3) MNC SBUs are often in stronger bargaining positions than their domestic competitors.

ALTERNATIVE BUSINESS STRATEGIES FOR MNCS

A business strategy is the means by which management of an SBU intends to achieve its objectives. Alternative business strategies are definable, mutually exclusive options available to an SBU or corporation. A firm may pursue only one alternative at a time.

As noted earlier, an MNC business strategy has six elements: focus, management, marketing, production (delivery, in the case of a service business), finance, and research and development. The focus element, which is the nucleus of an MNC business strategy, sets the philosophy, direction, scope, and approach of the other five strategic elements. Once the strategic focus is set, the other elements are designed to support the central strategic thrust of the business. Accordingly, alternative business strategies are described in terms of the focus strategy.

Focus Strategies for MNC Business Units

Today, MNCs are faced with two choices: Go global, and gain some of the advantages of a global competitor; or, defend a market niche in a few national markets. To those ends, MNC SBUs pursue one of five focus strategies. These strategies are discussed below.

Global Industry Focus. To gain a sustainable competitive advantage in a particular industry, SBUs pursuing a global industry focus view that industry as one worldwide homogeneous market. They use the sources of global competitive advantage, discussed above, to gain a cost/value advantage over national and multinational firms in the industry.

A global industry strategic focus may be appropriate under three conditions: (1) if customers or clients, as well as potential customers and clients worldwide, prefer or will accept substantially the same uniform product or service in most major markets; (2) if the business already has, or can achieve quickly, a dominant market position in the full range of the industry products or services; (3) if the firm has the resources, including capital, to launch and sustain the strategy on a global scale.

Global Segment Focus. To achieve a sustainable competitive advantage in a particular industry segment, SBUs pursue a global segment focus by viewing that segment as one worldwide homogeneous market. They use the same sources of global competitive advantage mentioned above. A global segment focus may be appropriate if previous conditions exist for the industry segment and the segment can be defended against attack from firms pursuing a global industry focus. This type of focus is within the resource capability of many businesses. However, it has its risks, since management must first find strategic market segments within an industry, not an easy task. Then it must identify the segment(s) in which it can achieve competitive advantage and concentrate on serving that one segment's needs. In the process it may forego some of the benefits of vertical integration, as well as limit the firm to an "all the eggs in one basket" strategy.

Multinational Industry Focus. To achieve a sustainable competitive advantage in a geographically fragmented industry, SBUs adopt this strategic focus by viewing each nation as a discrete and unique market. It may be appropriate under four conditions: (1) if customers or clients, as well as potential customers and clients, will not accept substantially the *same* uniform product or service in most major markets, but want *significant variations* in the nature of the product or the type of service; (2) if economic constraints other than governmental restraints limit global competition; (3) if the business already has, or can quickly achieve, a dominant position in major national markets within the full range of industry products/services; (4) if the firm has the resources, including capital, to launch and sustain the strategy on a multinational scale.

A multinational focus differs fundamentally from a global one, which views the world (or major regions of it) as one homogeneous market. Consequently, a global focus produces a uniform, highly competitive cost/value product or service for the "global" customer. The multinational focus, on the other hand, views the world as a number of unique national markets with different customer preferences in each market. Consequently, a business with a multinational focus modifies its products or services in each domestic market. Since these two strategies are so fundamentally different, selecting the less appropriate one could be disastrous for an MNC. For example, if an MNC competes in a global industry but pursues a multinational strategic focus (management believes that the industry is geographically fragmented), it will inevitably lose to the firm that adopts a global focus, all other things being equal. Likewise, the reverse applies. However, the real danger exists in viewing a global industry or segment as nonglobal, and therefore, multinational. In the past ten years, many geographically fragmented industries with distinctly national characteristics are developing into global industries, including steel, autos, shipbuilding, aircraft manufacturing, chemicals, consumer electronics, semiconductors, banking, insurance, transportation (goods and people), investment management, and telecommunications.

Today the trend is to global industries. Even if a business now pursues a multinational focus in a multinational industry, that industry is in constant change. Senior management must therefore continually review strategic focus.

Multinational Segment Focus. To achieve a sustainable competitive advantage in a segment or submarket of a fragmented industry, SBUs adopt this strategic focus by viewing each nation as a discrete and unique submarket. This strategy is appropriate for a business that does not hold a dominant position in the industry as a whole or that does not have the resources to do so.

A multinational segment focus may be appropriate if the conditions described for a multinational industry focus exist for the industry segment, and if the segment can be defended.

The potential dangers associated with a multinational industry focus apply equally to this strategic focus. Selecting an inappropriate focus may risk achieving the business objectives: survival, profitability, and growth.

National Focus. To achieve a sustainable competitive advantage in national markets protected from world competition (usually by governmental restraints, such as limiting imports of products being produced locally by the MNC or a consortium of local business and MNC), SBUs adopt this strategic focus. Businesses pursuing this strategy skillfully negotiate with local governments to obtain a protected niche from foreign competition. Such firms are cognizant of the need to blend their own objectives with the national policy of the local government.

A national focus strategy is often successful in developing countries where the local government wants to develop a local industry with the help of a small number of MNCs. This strategic focus can be very profitable, but it is distinctly limited geographically.

MNC CORPORATE STRATEGY

With corporate strategy, management orchestrates its SBUs (and their main functions or elements, such as marketing and research and development) to achieve a competitive edge. There are five major features of MNC corporate strategy that are not shared by domestic-company corporate strategy.

Foreign Exchange Management

With the introduction of floating exchange rates in 1971, foreign exchange management—the process of limiting the downside risk of a company's exposure in foreign currency—became probably the most important aspect of MNC corporate treasury management. Floating exchange rates that reflect and anticipate economic considerations have led to the development of forward markets and currency future contracts. These financial instruments, in turn, are used to moderate the risks of a multicountry operation. However, not all rates are allowed to float. The cruzeiro rate, for example, is fixed by the Brazilian government.

Foreign exchange exposure can be managed in three in three main categories: (1) fixed-rate currencies, (2) floating-rate currencies, and (3) currencies for which a forward market exists. This grouping is depicted in Figure 13-2. The third category gives the treasurer more options than the second, which in turn, offers more options than the first.

With a fixed exchange rate, the strategic alternative is to do nothing or do something. To do something will normally require balance sheet manipulation, such as deferring capital expenditure to be funded in dollars, or balance sheet restructuring, such as borrowing in local currency or obtaining a local partner to share the risk. Such partnerships structure deals that significantly limit the MNCs exposure without reducing its potential return or increasing the risks of the local partner. With a floating exchange rate but no forward market, the strategic alternative is again to do nothing or to do something. To do nothing, in this case, is more attractive because the treasurer knows that the currency is fairly priced in the market. Consequently, he or she can sleep without fear of an overnight devaluation. To do something also requires manipulating and restructuring the balance sheet, except that in this case the MNC will have easier access to local capital markets. In the Eurobond market, for example, an MNC can get financing for five years or more. Accordingly, to "do something" yields more options. With a floating exchange rate with a forward market, the treasurer has three strategic alternatives: (1) do nothing, i.e., do not hedge at any time for this currency, (2) do everything, i.e., hedge at all times in full for this currency, or (3) do something, i.e., hedge selectively in the currency. These alternatives are available for only one year ahead in a currency with an active forward market. The options available for category two also apply.

Of course, foreign exchange management is only one element of corporate treasury management. Because MNCs operate in more than one country, the MNC treasurer must manage remittance policies, financing in local capital markets, exchange control restrictions, specific legal and accounting conventions, and international taxation, in addition to foreign exchange exposure.

	Floating Rates	Fixed Rates
Forward Market	1	N.A.
No Forward Market	2	3

FIG. 13-2   Three Categories of Foreign Currency Used in Currency Exposure Management

Global Tax Planning

Tax codes influence every element of an MNC's financial strategy, including investment decisions, subsidiary capital structure, working capital management, and corporate profitability. Global tax planning attempts to minimize a firm's total worldwide tax bill without restricting its economic potential or ongoing business opportunities. Consequently, it is an integral part of corporate management.

Profits from domestic operations of MNCs are treated in the same way as profits from domestic firms. It is only when profits earned in one country accrue to a company that resides in another country that tax complications may arise. If the same profits are taxed in both countries, a double taxation situation occurs. To encourage foreign investment and trade, many countries make tax treaties with each other that allow the MNC to avoid double taxation.

When possible, global tax planning avoids double taxation. It reduces reported profits in high-tax countries and increases reported profits in low-tax countries, including tax havens; it also defers tax payments. MNCs use three methods concurrently to minimize global tax liability: (1) diversion, (2) extraction, and (3) deferral.[14]

Diversion occurs when profits are diverted from high-tax countries to low-tax countries, using trading techniques such as conduiting through other companies, setting up a domestic international sales corporation (DISC) that gives tax relief for export trade, or transfer pricing.

Extraction occurs when pretax profits in high-tax countries are reduced through charges such as interest, royalties, and corporate management fees. MNCs also extract profits indirectly in other ways.

---

[14] Derek F. Chanon and Michael Jalland, *Multinational Strategic Planning (New York: American Management Association, 1982), pp. 150-174.*

Deferral occurs when a tax liability is paid at a more distant time than normally required. Each approach has its own set of unique problems that must be managed and integrated with normal business activity.

Many corporations and their tax advisors use computer applications in tax planning because of the number of tax variables and the quantity of data to be evaluated. Although global tax planning is initially developed by tax planners—internally and externally—the corporate executive must be able to incorporate the tax implications before making a major business decision.

Political Risk Management

Political risk exists when potential government action or intervention may be detrimental to a firm's economic performance. Political risk management limits a firm's overall exposure to domestic and foreign government intervention by carefully selecting its business locations and integrating these business activities with the commercial objectives of both home and host governments. Political risk has three sources: host government, home government, and in some cases, supranational bodies. Their intervention can take three forms: (1) standard regulation, (2) discriminatory action, and (3) targeted intervention.

Standard regulations such as exchange controls apply to all firms and are usually known at the outset. This type of political intervention is the least severe.

Discriminatory action penalizes a group of companies. In the case of the host government, such intervention may focus on the foreign-owned corporation, such as requiring it to use some local product content or ownership. In the case of the home government, such intervention may focus on prohibiting MNCs from "trading with the enemy"—U.S. restrictions on high-technology trade with the U.S.S.R. for example.

Targeted intervention is the most severe form of government action, but it is limited to a small number of firms. In the case of the host government, targeted intervention may require the MNC to reinvest all profits locally, or, the host government may renege on agreements signed with a previous government. In the case of the home government, targeted intervention usually affects the MNC and its overseas operations. MNCs normally evaluate the likelihood and extent of host government intervention when planning or expanding foreign investment. Targeted intervention is their primary concern. At least four generic alternatives reduce the chances that an MNC will lose some or all of a foreign investment: (1) country selection, (2) pre-entry risk reduction, (3) post-entry risk reduction, and (4) emergency exit tactics. One or all can be used.

Country selection involves a set of criteria and an analytical framework to determine whether the firm should invest in a particular country. Pre-entry risk reduction minimizes detrimental political action by documenting the rights and responsibilities of the MNC and the host government in concession agreements, making local ownership an integral part of the strategy in politically sensitive LDCs, and/or insuring against the political risk of confiscation and war with the overseas private investment corporation. Post-entry risk reduction methods are tactics for managing the foreign-based business functions—marketing, production, finance, management, and research and development—to reduce host government intervention. Finally, emergency exit tactics are used to reduce the impact of seizure in the case of confiscation, by draining economic value from the beleaguered operation, and, in effect, leaving an empty shell.

The management of political risks, however, is still at the conceptual level; few concrete methods have been delineated to help manage exposure to this intervention.

Alternative Entry Strategies

Business can be expanded outside the domestic market in other ways than simply exporting goods and services. Exporting is an attractive way to test a new market or for a domestic firm to build a foreign market, but it is not a permanent competitive alternative for a developed MNC. Too many external factors affect the MNCs ability to compete when using an export strategy exclusively. For example, from 1980 to the end of 1983, the value of the dollar appreciated more than 40 percent against a composite of ten currencies (Figure 13-3). Today, U.S. producers are at a significant price disadvantage in the export market—through no obvious fault of their own. An exclusive export strategy is akin to the military strategy of positioning all military arsenals and resources on the mainland.

The most obvious reasons why MNCs expand their geographic presence are: (1) to reach new, profitable markets, (2) to obtain the advantages discussed in the section on sources of global competitive advantage, (3) to produce cheaper goods for both the home and the foreign market, and (4) to attack a competitor in its home markets, thereby indirectly defending their own U.S. market. Companies use four alternatives to extend their global reach: (1) direct investment, (2) merger and acquisitions, (3) joint venture, and (4) licensing.

With direct investment, companies set up a new operation in a foreign location. MNCs strictly control strategic moves into new countries at the corporate level to integrate the investment objectives into the company's global strategy. Management considers many factors when evaluating these opportunities, including market as well as infrastructure characteristics, political and labor conditions, and financial and tax considerations.

MNCs may also merge or acquire a foreign business to expand their global reach. The acquired business may or may not be related to the firm's current businesses. In recent years, MNCs have tended to acquire related businesses and divest unrelated businesses. A related business is one where a direct linkage exists between it and another business in the firm. For example, a company acquires an operation with a strong distribution network to gain an outlet for its existing products.

A joint venture is where two or more companies collaborate on a project. It is a high-risk strategy. For such an enterprise to succeed, each party must contribute a unique strength and yet share similar objectives, and the venture agreement must be strong and clearly documented. Today, joint ventures and consortiums are commonplace. This trend is likely to continue as companies realize that, in many instances, they stand to benefit much more from coopera-

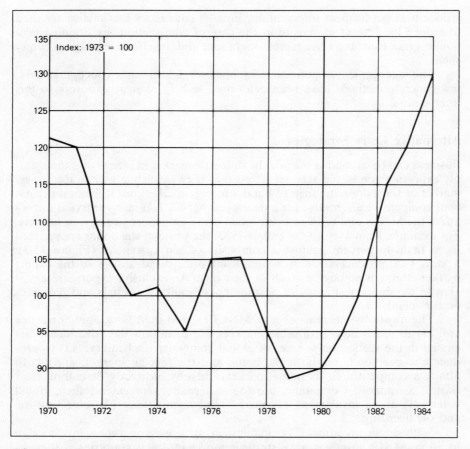

FIG. 13-3 Value of the Dollar Against a Composite of Ten Currencies, 1970–1984

tion than from all-out competition. And as potential synergy exists through collaboration, the purchaser of the joint venture product or services also stands to gain.

Licensing allows a firm to penetrate foreign markets with limited investment by giving a foreign partner the use of patents, trademarks, know-how, and support services in return for royalty payments. It is a particularly effective strategy for smaller markets and in countries the company cannot enter alone.

Foreign Government Regulations

MNCs compete for government favor and contracts to gain a competitive advantage in the domestic market or the region. Competition is fierce. MNCs with the greatest resources tend to win the favor of local government over smaller foreign firms, because the larger ones have more to offer the country. General Electric recently reported losing an important contract for the sale of CAT scanners to Austrian hospitals when a competitor, West Germany's Siemens, agreed to increase production of electrical goods (not CAT scanners) at a plant it owns and operates in Austria thereby offsetting the purchase with additional Austrian employment.[15] When MNCs coordinate their strategies to advance the economic development objectives of local governments, both parties benefit.

CONSTRAINTS ON GLOBAL COMPETITION

Constraints on global competition do exist, but for how long? In the past decade many geographically fragmented industries have developed into global industries. Yet today, four major constraints still limit global competition: (1) sheltered industries, (2) government restraints, (3) lack of resources, and (4) market fragmentation.

Four Major Constraints

Sheltered Industries. Unexposed to world trade, sheltered industries are predominantly in the service sector of the economy, such as health care, goods distribution, public transportation, housing construction, legal and tax services, etc. What they have in common is localized personal service. Certain businesses in the goods sector also fall into this category, including milk, which is difficult to keep fresh in transport, and steel beams and plastic moldings, which are expensive to transport compared to the value of the product.[16] The fact that a service or product requires a significant amount of local personal service is one of the most significant constraints on global competition.

Government Restraints. Governments limit global competition by placing barriers against trade to protect local firms or local employment.

Lack of Resources. Many firms lack resources as well as capital, personnel, and management skills to compete on a global scale.

Geographical Market Fragmentation. Geographically fragmented markets limit global competition. The additional costs of modifying a product or service in each national market may negate the advantages.

---

[15] John Zysman and Stephen S. Cohen, "Double or Nothing: Open Trade and Competitive Industry," *Foreign Affairs* (Summer 1983), p. 1,128.

[16] Magaziner and Reich, op. cit., p. 69.

KEYS TO SUCCESS IN MNC STRATEGIC MANAGEMENT

What internal factors contribute to a firm's potential success in setting and implementing strategy? In general, experience has shown that no simple set of rules or strategy imperatives will point to the right course automatically, and no planning system or technique guarantees the development of successful strategies. Nevertheless, some guidelines are listed below.

- Provide top-level commitment and leadership both to planning as a way of business and to strategic management as an approach.
- Take a long-term perspective.
- Delegate responsibility and accountability.
- Involve the right people from the very beginning, including strategy decision makers and key subordinates.
- Involve general managers responsible for implementation early in the formulation process so that ultimately it will be their strategy.
- Do careful preplanning, and educate the key people in strategic management concepts and international perspective.
- Get good information. This task is a bigger stumbling block than most people realize.
- Devote enough time to the process.
- Educate key business managers in strategic management concepts and issues.
- Designate key people as responsible for implementing specific aspects of the plan, and reward them accordingly.
- Install a strategic management information system.

CONCLUSION

Although many industries today are still fragmented by nation or region, the continued evolution of worldwide industries is inevitable. Global companies in both the goods and the service sector are emerging in this new arena. Global firms by definition require global strategies, which in turn demand that the strategist recognize and consider the firm's total worldwide profile. But first the MNC strategist must look at the SBU and ask the fundamental question discussed in this chapter, Does the SBU operate in a:

- Global industry (relatively uniform products-services worldwide)?
- Multinational industry (fragmented by nation or region)?
- Transition industry (changing from multinational to global)?

The answer will indicate the SBU's focus strategy, which in turn will determine the configuration of the SBU's functional strategies-marketing, production (or delivery in the case of a service business), finance, research and development, and management. An incorrect assessment of the industry's structure will place the SBU at a significant competitive disadvantage.

An accurate assessment of industry structure is one essential success factor for global firms. The MNC must also take advantage of two other factors that can determine its success or failure—strong, centralized leadership and direct access to current worldwide information. These two factors go hand in hand. A global firm's chief strategists must be able to formulate and evaluate global strategies based on accurate, timely strategic information. This information is now becoming more available and applicable through computers and other technological developments. In today's global environment, centralized information makes centralized decision-making a possibility.

BIBLIOGRAPHY

Channon, Derek F. and Michael Jalland, *Multinational Strategic Planning*, New York: AMACOM, 1978.

Fayerweather, John, *International Business Strategy and Administration*, Cambridge, Mass.: Ballinger Publishing Co. 1982.

Hout, Thomas, Michael E. Porter, and Eileen Rudden, "How Global Companies Win Out," Harvard Business Review, 98–108, Sept.-Oct. 1982.

Levitt, Theodore, "The Globalization of Markets," Harvard Business Review 92–102, May-June 1983.

Naisbitt, John, *Megatrends: New Directions Transforming Our Lives*, New York: Warner Books, 1982.

Porter, Michael E., *Competitive Strategy: Techniques for Analyzing Industries and Competitors,* New York: Free Press, 1980.

Yavits, Boris and William Newman, *Strategy in Action*, New York: Free Press, 1982.

Tools for Making Strategic Decisions

14

The Role of Science in Business Strategy

SIDNEY SCHOEFFLER

Founding Director, The Strategic Planning Institute

WHY EXAMINE THE ISSUE?

In most areas of human productive activity there is now, near the end of the twentieth century, absolutely no need to inquire what role science can and should play in that activity. The basic answer is obvious. Almost everyone understands that without science a modern doctor would be no better than a primitive medicine man, a modern engineer no more capable than a medieval artisan, and a modern farmer no more productive than a stone age hunter and gatherer. There *are* many issues on details and specifics (and always will be), and moral questions on use vs. abuse (and also always will be), but no disagreement on the basic notion that the laws of nature are capable of being discovered, important to know, and employable for the benefit of man. Moreover, the technology of making discoveries and applying them to human purposes is well developed, extensively tested, continually being further improved, and very extensively employed.

Curiously, this is not so in the area of business management, particularly strategic business management. The most popular concept here is still that business management is a craft. Strategic management is frequently seen as something that is learned by direct experience or from another craftsman, that consists of little more than the application of common sense plus native intelligence to a particular kind of problem, and that can be codified in relatively simple and unchanging procedures. In an increasing number of industries, one can see the remarkable spectacle of the product becoming better and better, the process of production becoming more and more efficient, but the business and its management remaining qualitatively stagnant. The situation is very similar to military strategy, where the quality of the weapons keeps improving, but the quality of the generals remains the same.

How can science improve the situation? This is not the place for a treatise on scientific method; in any case, that would amount to pontification about the well known. Instead, the question is approached from the negative side: What business blunders are occurring because science is not used in business strategy, and how might these blunders be minimized? A summary of the key concepts helps to clarify the major points.

WHAT IS "SCIENCE"?

"Science," as used here, does not mean test tubes or telescopes; it refers to a method of thought. This method has proven exceedingly powerful in all areas of human endeavor to which it has been applied; it produces insights and capabilities that are cumulative, expanding, and improving without end and without upper limit. Progress is not, of course, always free of misstep or error (or even fraud); but part of the essential nature of science is that these errors are discovered and corrected.

Some of the key ingredients of this method of thought are discussed in the following sections.

Observation and Evidence

One learns about the world by observing the world. (Likewise, one learns about business strategy by observing business strategy.) Observation must be careful rather than sloppy: The observer measures, records, compares, and checks. All opinions and theories are provisional until they are verified by adequate evidence, and all evidence consists of careful observation of the real world. If the real world is kind enough to show the observer what he or she wants to see, then it is observed; otherwise the observer tries to coax the world to reveal its secrets by arranging suitable experiments.

Analytical Rigor

Evidence is interpreted through the use of logic. One does not jump to conclusions, but works toward them. When an inspiration or a flash of insight does occur, it is necessary to go back and check to see if the insight is logically consistent with the evidence and if the evidence is adequate. If the idea is inconsistent with the body of available evidence, it is rejected as erroneous; if it is consistent with the evidence but the evidence is inadequate, judgment is reserved until the evidence is adequate. The standards of adequacy are tight rather than loose.

Significance

When a pattern or relationship is observed, it must be tested for significance before it is accepted as a "fact" or "law." Thus the risk that the observed relationship is accidental and ephemeral rather than systematic and dependable is minimized. If an observed pattern is not significant, little credence is placed in it. If it is not known whether the pattern is significant (perhaps because its significance has not been tested), the pattern is not considered significant and little credence is placed in it.

Probability

Patterns and relationships are not expected to be black or white; they can be shades of gray. Cigarette smoking does not always cause lung cancer, and not smoking does not always prevent it, but the probabilities are different (and the differences are significant). The important thing is to measure the probabilities. Unknown probabilities are poor guides to action.

Hypothesis and Test

Knowledge accumulates by a cyclical and repetitive process of hypothesis and test. The hypothesis phase is the driving force; the test phase keeps it honest. Imagination, creativity, energy, hopes, and dreams come into play during the hypothesis phase; conscience, caution, and "soundness" come into play during the test phase. It is important that both phases be kept active all the time. (In this context, "theory" is an advanced form of hypothesis.)

Representative Cross Section

Conclusions with respect to a particular case are almost always derived from similar other cases. The criteria for similar other cases are subject to hypothesis and test. A sufficient number of similar other cases must be examined in order to test for significance. Therefore, to find reliable action guides in any particular situation, the trick is to find an adequate number of other cases that are similar to the present case. Failing that, there are no reliable action guides.

Respect for Others

Evidence is assembled and conclusions are reached in a way that can be communicated to others and verified by them. This minimizes the risk of wishful thinking, error, or fraud. It also minimizes the wastage that comes from reinventions of the wheel. The habit of communicating both evidence and logic is a manifestation of respect for others. The conclusions or recommendations of those who are unwilling or unable to support their views are rejected.

Cost/Benefit

The principles of scientific observation may be deviated from for clear cost/benefit reasons. Sometimes it is simply too much trouble to do things right; for example, where the cost of error is small. When in doubt, however, all the principles should be applied in a conscientious and disciplined manner.

SCIENCE IN BUSINESS STRATEGY

The foregoing does not, of course, constitute a rigorous definition of science or a complete description of its methods. Emphasis has been placed on those precepts that, even though they are of great importance, are very frequently neglected in the formulation of business strategy and policy.

Strategic issues are, by definition, the critically important issues in a business—those that spell the major difference between success and failure. Therefore, they clearly deserve the best thinking and the most powerful methods and tools that can be brought to bear upon them.

Why, then, is the nonscientific approach to strategy-setting widely prevalent? Probably the most important fact is that the scientific base for business strategy is in a regrettably underdeveloped state and simply does not suffice as a guide to many of the decisions that must be made. It is not that the scientific approach is in principle unable to cope with business problems; it is that use of the approach has not been widely attempted. There is a vicious cycle at work here: The "supply" of the fruits of science is low, therefore the "demand" is low, therefore the "supply" is low, and so on.

The problem is how to break this vicious cycle, and to turn it into the kind of benign cycle that works so effectively in medicine, engineering, and agriculture. Fortunately, some very good beginnings have already been made.

Chief among these, in the specific area of business strategy, is the Profit Impact of Market Strategy (PIMS) Program. This program, organized at the Harvard Business School in 1972 and operated by the nonprofit Strategic Planning Institute since 1975, is a larger-scale continuation of previous work done at the General Electric Company. It is, in effect, a cooperative venture, involving about 200 major companies in North America and Europe, designed to provide a set of "observations," plus associated analytical procedures, for a more scientific approach to the planning efforts of the participating companies.

Each member company contributes information about its experiences in several different business areas to a combined data base. The PIMS staff analyzes this experience to discover the general laws that determine what business strategy in what kind of competitive environment produces what results. The findings are made available to member companies in a form useful to their business planning.

The program provides business managers and planners with tools and data to answer questions such as:

- What profit rate is "normal" for a given business, considering its particular market, competitive position, technology, cost structure, and so on?
- If the business continues on its current track, what will its future operating results be?
- What strategic changes in the business have promise of improving these results?
- Given a specific contemplated future strategy for the business, how will short-term and long-term profitability or cash flow change?

In each case, the answers are derived from an analysis of the experiences of other businesses operating under similar conditions.

More specifically, the purposes of the program are:

1 To assemble a data base reflecting the business strategy experiences of a group of participating companies;

2 To conduct a research program on that data base in order to discover the laws of the marketplace that govern (a) profit levels, (b) other outcomes of strategic actions, and (c) outcomes of changes in the business environment;

3 To conduct an applications program to make the findings of the research available to participating companies in a form and manner they can use effectively; and

4 To carry-out ancillary activities (publication, education, service to participants, study of planning methods, legislative recommendations) that will enhance the value of the entire program to its members and to the economy at large.

The unit of observation in PIMS is a business. Each business is a division, product line, or other profit center within its parent company which sells a distinct set of products and/or services to an identifiable group of customers in competition with a well-defined set of competitors and for which revenues, operating costs, investments, and strategic plans can be separated in a meaningful way.

Currently the data base consists of information on the strategic experiences of more than 2,000 businesses, covering a three- to ten-year period. The information on each business consists of about 100 items descriptive of the characteristics of the market environment, the state of competition, the strategy pursued by the business, and the operating results obtained. Each data item has been pretested for significance and relevance to profitability.

The PIMS staff has devised a set of standardized forms to be filled out by the participant company for the contribution of its experience records to the data bank. The forms are designed to break the required data items into simple elements that can be assembled readily from financial or marketing records, or that can be estimated by someone familiar with the specific business.

One of the most encouraging aspects of the PIMS Program, as a portent of things to come, is the growing volume of academic research being performed on the PIMS data base. To date, more than 20 studies by academicians (faculty research and doctoral dissertations) have been completed. These studies, plus the increasing amount of other scientific work now being done at such institutions as Harvard, Columbia, Purdue, Michigan, Stanford, and New York Universities, are providing a demonstration to both the business community and business schools that substantial progress is indeed possible in this area.

But it will take time for the fruits of the effort to cumulate to the point where most decisions in the areas of business strategy and business policy can become as "professional" as corresponding decisions in, for instance, medicine. In the meantime, what is the practitioner to do? Life must go on, whether science is fully ready to assist or not.

The first thing to do is, of course, take full advantage of the findings and the tools already available. They do not solve all problems, or even most, but they perform quite well as far as they go. Second, support the effort to keep improving the data, the research, and the tools. Third, develop a sense of discrimination between the "good stuff" and the makeshifts; in other words, become a more demanding consumer of business technology.

The field of health care, in addition to offering much instruction on how to become more scientific, also shows what can be done where the benefits of science have not yet reached. Where a disease can be cured, it is. Where enough is not yet known, (a) the patient is made as comfortable as possible; (b) his mind is occupied with good thoughts or distracting activities; (c) a miracle is hoped for; (d) if necessary, the process of dying is eased; and (e) work continues to do better the next time. A well-designed process of strategic planning does the same for the business executive.

CURRENT PERFORMANCE LEVELS IN THE BUSINESS COMMUNITY

The PIMS data base, in addition to providing observations for a scientific approach to business strategy, also affords a view of the damage done by the failure to use this approach.

The PIMS Program conducted a study to measure the shortfall from potential performance in a sample of 120 businesses. The approach took the following steps:

1 For each business in the sample, measurements were made of the results of a "no-change" strategy (i.e., the operating results that the business will probably achieve if it simply maintains its current strategic posture and floats with the

market). Operating results were measured in terms of the discounted present value of net cash flows plus capital gains (i.e., increase or decrease in the market value of the business) taken over a five-year period.

2 The potential operating results were then measured, using the same measure of performance. The potential was defined in terms of the results obtained by the good performers among "strategic look-alikes" (i.e., other businesses operating under strategically similar circumstances: having a similar position, in a similar market, facing similar competition, and employing a similar technology). The "good" performers were taken at approximately the eightieth percentile among the strategic look-alikes.

3 By direct comparison, a calculation was made for each business of its shortfall (if any) from potential.

The conclusions of this analysis certainly were not exact or indisputable, but they did produce a rough indication of the magnitude of the problem. The average business in the sample attained about *half* of its potential performance. This estimate of the current wastage of economic resources is in some respects too high (there is such a thing as simple bad luck, since the world operates on a probability basis, not a mechanical basis) and in other respects too low (the sample consisted of more outstanding companies than mediocre companies, and only of their surviving businesses). But there is little doubt that the possibility of improvement is huge and that a scientific approach can make most of the difference.

COMMON BLUNDERS IN BUSINESS STRATEGY

Some of the specific mistakes that lead to the waste of resources can be identified. This discussion does not concern unlucky moves, but those that can clearly be *expected,* on the available evidence, to fail.

Making Moves Inappropriate to the Position

Many businesses make moves and take actions that have a high failure rate for the starting position of the business. Examine the following examples of inappropriate strategies:

- XYZ, Inc., a business with a low relative market share, simultaneously carries out an expensive and innovation-oriented research and development program and an expensive and leadership-oriented marketing program.
- Continental Flange, a business with a product of mediocre quality, attempts to compensate for lack of quality by an energetic marketing effort.
- R.P.H., Inc., a business with a low relative market share, becomes vertically integrated.

Building Productivity in the Wrong Way

Many businesses, in an effort to improve the productivity of their work force, mechanize or automate excessively, increasing their fixed costs considerably. As a result they stand to lose the fruits of their improved productivity by becoming embroiled in frequent and severe price wars or marketing wars.

Underdeveloping Strong Positions

Many well-positioned businesses (good product quality, well-segmented market, high productivity) tend to rest on their oars and fail to take full advantage of the opportunities (e.g., for backward integration or for market-centered diversification) that their position provides.

Underdeveloping Weak Positions

Many businesses whose current positions have a few elements of weakness (e.g., slow market growth or low relative share) but other elements of strength, give up prematurely and underinvest in the business by a considerable amount.

Going Down With the Flagship

Many companies depend heavily on a major "flagship" business. When confronted with maturity in that business or with a major new competitive challenge (e.g., from Japan), they fail to either restructure the business to cope with the new realities or to redeploy their strengths to other businesses or markets.

"Zigzagging"

Lacking the fortitude and clear-sightedness to see a strategy through to a successful conclusion, many businesses change position or strategy frequently, dissipating resources through wasteful "zigzagging."

Joining the Other Lemmings

Joining the rush into apparently promising new markets or technologies without adequate competitive strengths to succeed in these new areas, a business may well be unable to survive the inevitable shake-out.

Inappropriate Turnaround Efforts

When a business gets into profit trouble or cash trouble, it may predicate its strategy on moves that produce only a short-run appearance of improvement at the cost of an erosion of the fundamentals of the business. A common example is saving money by reducing product quality.

COMMON BLUNDERS IN LOGIC AND METHOD

The blunders in business strategy are attributable, in a general way, to short-comings in logic and method. But under that broad heading, there are some specific errors that appear with particular frequency and cause an unusual amount of mischief.

Gullibility

Gullibility involves an uncritical acceptance of simplistic and/or unsupported principles of strategy and rules of business conduct. At least half of the most frequently cited principles of business strategy are not grounded in any visible evidence, or are inappropriate in major groups of businesses. It is easy to tell the sound principles from the unsound ones by examining the supporting evidence. If there is no evidence, or if the evidence is inadequate, the alleged principle is probably untrustworthy.

Failure to Test Consequences

Another common mistake is the adoption of a strategy for a particular business without a test of the consequences of that strategy. Many companies choose a strategy simply on the basis of where the business fits on a matrix, what their competitors are doing, what an "expert" recommends, or the prevailing consensus of the management team, without taking the trouble to test that strategy by a credible forecast of its consequences. It is not always easy to make this forecast, but it is always important to make the effort.

Poor Forecasting Logic

Inappropriate forecasting models are often used in strategy planning. The most frequent error is to employ time-series-based longitudinal models for strategic forecasting. This is almost always an error because any change in the basic structure of the business or its environment will invalidate a longitudinal model, and strategic changes normally do involve the basic structure. The answer is to use models with cross-sectional bases, whose range of applicability spans both the old structure and the new structure.

Wrong Peer Group as Basis for Evaluations

A business may use an inappropriate group of observations to evaluate its strategic options. Many business people compare their own situation to that of other companies in their industry. This is usually misleading, because other companies do not always share the same strategic problems. For example, the passenger car business of General Motors has little to learn from the experiences of Ford, Chrysler, or Toyota with passenger cars, but a lot to learn from the IBM mainframe business or the General Electric lamp business, which also hold top rank in a maturing industry under severe competitive attack.

Tunnel Vision

This error consists of exploring too narrow a range of strategic options, thereby missing opportunities for substantial (rather than merely incremental) improvements in the business.

Erroneous Discounting

In evaluating future incomes or outgos, businesses may use interest rates that are too high (thereby condemning the business to a harvest strategy) or too low (thereby ignoring an important element of opportunity cost). The villain is often inflation, which confuses many people as to which interest rate is really applicable. Most discount rates of less than 2 percent or more than 5 percent in *real* terms (i.e., relative to the rate of inflation) are suspect and probably wrong, unless the risk of the investment is very high. The use of a very short planning horizon (less than five years) is tantamount to a too high discount rate.

Cost/Benefit Errors

Overinvesting or underinvesting in the planning effort, relative to the benefits achievable, is another common blunder in planning. There is a frequent inverse correlation between the cost and the benefit of a planning process. This happens because an inadequacy of logic or method is often compensated for by elaborate bureaucratic busywork or expensive consultant studies. Good planning is not very expensive, compared to bad planning. But it is not cheap either, because it must be done with considerable care and attention to possible missteps and errors.

CONVENTIONAL WISDOM VS. SCIENCE

Science often challenges conventional wisdom, with the outcome being improved potential for effective health care, space exploration, data processing, corporate performance, and so forth. The following examples illustrate the role of science in challenging conventional wisdom in business strategy.

Investing in Technology

The "Unprofitability" of Modern Technology. Of all the findings on business strategy yielded by the study of the more than 2,000 businesses in the PIMS data base, the following is one of the most controversial: Businesses that are highly investment intensive, that is, those that use high levels of investment per dollar of sales revenue (airlines, bulk chemical-processing plants, or distributors of consumer goods requiring large inventories), are much less profitable than businesses with lower levels of investment per dollar of sales. Figure 14-1 illustrates this phenomenon in terms of return on investment (ROI).

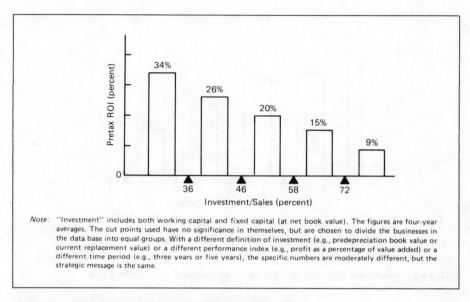

Note: "Investment" includes both working capital and fixed capital (at net book value). The figures are four-year averages. The cut points used have no significance in themselves, but are chosen to divide the businesses in the data base into equal groups. With a different definition of investment (e.g., predepreciation book value or current replacement value) or a different performance index (e.g., profit as a percentage of value added) or a different time period (e.g., three years or five years), the specific numbers are moderately different, but the strategic message is the same.

FIG. 14-1 Investment Intensity and Return on Investment

This finding is controversial not because the phenomenon is rare, uncertain, or weak—it is common, quite clear, and extremely powerful—but because it is so unexpected. The conventional wisdom is that there is a strong positive relationship between investment intensity and "modernity" or "progressiveness." Everyone knows that modern technology requires elaborate machinery, and thus heavy investments; that high labor productivity depends on extensive automation, and thus on heavy investments; and that consumer goods must be readily available to customers to sell successfully, and thus require large inventory investments. Since modern technology, high labor productivity, and readily available consumer products are judged to be "good" things, they are expected to *improve* profitability rather than to hurt it. What in fact happens is that (1) the commonly expected public benefits of investment-intensive technology (higher wages, lower prices, and improved product quality) do indeed occur most of the time; but, alas, (2) the expected private benefits do not occur. Instead, the profits of companies that use an investment-intensive technology are usually rather poor.

Why does investment intensity hurt profits? Before answering this question, it is important to confirm that we are in fact dealing with an issue that is real and substantive, not just an optical illusion. For example, it might be argued that the negative pattern in Figure 14-1 is due entirely to arithmetic: that investment-intensive businesses have large denominators in their ROI ratios, and that their returns are low for that reason alone. That possibility can be excluded by using another measure of profitability. For example, Figure 14-2 relates investment intensity to the ratio of residual income to sales. The

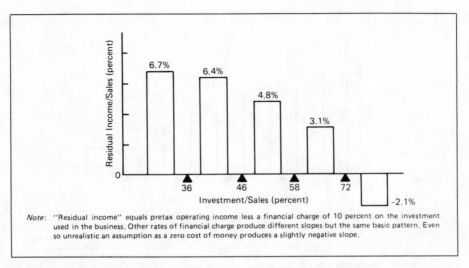

Note: "Residual income" equals pretax operating income less a financial charge of 10 percent on the investment used in the business. Other rates of financial charge produce different slopes but the same basic pattern. Even so unrealistic an assumption as a zero cost of money produces a slightly negative slope.

FIG. 14-2 Investment Intensity and the Ratio of Residual Income to Sales

similarity of the pattern to that of Figure 14-1 confirms that investment-intensive businesses are actually less profitable.

Another possible argument is that the negative effect on profit of investment intensity is actually due to something quite different. Specifically, it is well known that businesses with high shares of their served markets are considerably more profitable than those with low shares. One of the reasons for that relationship is that high-share businesses tend to be more efficient users of investment and are therefore less investment intensive, while low-share businesses are often inefficient users of investment and are therefore more investment-intensive. The negative effect on profit of high investment intensity might therefore be no more than the reverse side of the coin of the favorable effect on profit of high market share. To exclude that possibility it is necessary to establish that there is an effect on ROI from investment intensity *in addition to* that from market share. Figure 14-3 shows that there is indeed such an effect.

All the businesses in a given column have similar market shares, but investment intensity increases with each row. The fact that ROI decreases sharply moving down each column confirms that investment intensity has a negative effect on profit, regardless of market share.

Within each of the classes of investment intensity, one can examine not only ROI itself but also the degree to which the ROI of the group of businesses is lower or higher than would be expected from their levels of market share alone. Investment-intensive businesses are found to be even less profitable than would be expected from their market share, further confirming the phenomenon as a real and important one.

A third argument is that low ratios of sales to investment (i.e., high levels of investment intensity) are actually due to low levels of capacity utilization. A similar test of this hypothesis yields a similar result.

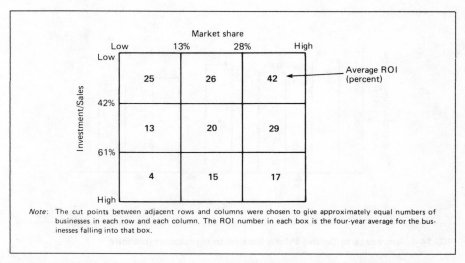

FIG. 14-3 Effect on Return on Investment of Investment Intensity and Market Share

The major reason for this negative effect seems to be that the game of competition is played in a very different way in investment-intensive industries than in others. When each of the firms competing in a particular industry has committed heavy investments on which a reasonable return needs to be earned, each becomes rather eager to keep its capacity loaded. In an investment-intensive facility, volume is commonly believed to be the key to profitability. (Perhaps surprisingly, this belief is as common in industries where the investment consists largely of working capital as it is in those where the investment is largely fixed capital.) So the competitive process in investment-intensive industries readily degenerates into a volume-grubbing contest, punctuated with frequent price wars, marketing wars, and other over-intensive competitive measures that take most of the joy out of being modern, automated, or otherwise investment intensive. In particularly good years, when every company's capacity is almost fully loaded, this effect may not appear at all, but when good years are averaged with bad, as in the figures presented here, the negative effect on profit is quite clear.

Figure 14-4 illustrates this point by relating increases in selling prices to investment intensity. The contrasts are most obvious at the extremes.

The profit-depressing price squeeze also shows up clearly in examining the value added per employee in industries that differ in their investment intensity. "Value added" is the degree to which a business upgrades the market value of the raw materials or components it buys, that is, the difference in market value between what the business buys and what it sells. Figure 14-5 shows that the value added per employee does not increase with added investment intensity over a surprisingly wide range.

Only on the extreme right of Figure 14-5 is there any significant favorable impact; in four fifths of all businesses, it appears that employees working with

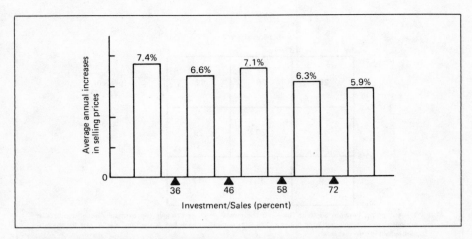

FIG. 14-4 Increases in Selling Prices Related to Investment Intensity

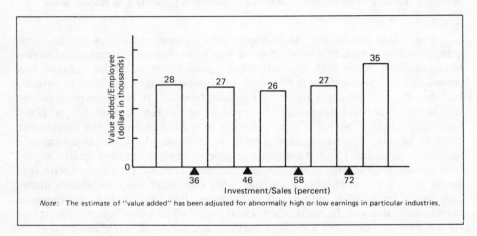

FIG. 14-5 Value Added Related to Investment Intensity

the support of large investments produce no more value than those working with only small investments. How can this be? It is possible that the first group of employees is simply less productive as individuals, that they are less capable people. More likely, however, is that the more intensive price competition occurring in investment-intensive industries reduces the market value of the product of companies in those industries, and hence the value added by their activities. Even on the far right of Figure 14-5, the increase in value added per employee is usually insufficient to justify the higher investment and cash required, as verified by examining the profit and cash results of most of these businesses.

A closely related reason for the unprofitability of investment-intensive businesses lies in their apparent inability to manage their personnel levels in a suitable fashion: The number of employees per dollar of sales is just about as high as in less investment-intensive industries. The increased numbers of people in administrative, commercial, and other functions on average counterbalance the savings of people in manufacturing functions.

Before leaving this subject, it is worth noting that Figures 14-1 through 14-5 have undoubtedly slanted reality in favor of investment-intensive businesses, and therefore have understated the magnitude of the problem. This bias occurs because the statistics are drawn from accounting records that are kept in the conventional way. It is becoming widely recognized that conventional accounting procedures overstate ROI, particularly of investment-intensive businesses, both by overstating the numerator and by understating the denominator. The reason is the same in both cases: Fixed assets are valued at their historical cost, rather than at their current inflated worth, understating both depreciation costs (and thus increasing apparent earnings) and investment levels.

What to Do About Investment-Intensive Requirements. If the technology of a business clearly requires a high level of investment intensity, either of plant and equipment or of working capital (or of both), what actions should the business take?

First, the business should not automatically assume that more is better insofar as investment intensity is concerned. A highly automated plant is not necessarily a better plant than a less automated one. Of course, the recent series of cash crunches in the economy has already cured many businesspeople of this knee-jerk reaction, but old habits of thought die hard, particularly in industries such as bulk chemicals where increased capital intensification has long been a way of life. Most businesspeople still unquestioningly assume that good technology is synonymous with automated production or long and full pipelines in distribution. And that assumption is valid just often enough in particular cases to save it from being ludicrous on its face. However, the proverbial "hard look" is clearly justified with regard to all investments that are larger than merely proportional to an increase in capacity.

Second, in evaluating a proposed investment that is clearly larger than merely proportional to an increase in capacity, the business should consider the strategic effect as carefully as it does the cost effect of the project. A negative strategic effect may more than offset a positive cost effect.

Suppose, for example, that a manufacturer is considering a capital-intensifying project (e.g., an increase in the degree of automation of plant) that on the basis of conventional cost calculations, will have an annual operating cost, everything included, of $1 million, an annual saving of $3 million in reduced labor costs or reduced spoilage, and therefore a net benefit of $2 million per year. Suppose further that all of these estimates are absolutely accurate, and that the net saving of $2 million per year does in fact materialize as promised. Even then, the project may not be, and very frequently is not, profitable. While the business *saves* the $2 million, it does not get to *keep* that $2 million.

Instead, it gives the $2 million away, mostly to its customers, secondarily to its employees, and thirdly in the form of higher marketing costs.

A business is forced into such a move by the changed competitive climate. First, its competitors' and its own increased desperation for volume (to keep those expensive plants with their high fixed costs loaded) leads to price and other concessions to customers, particularly after the new technology has become widespread; second, increased fear of plant shutdowns leads to higher wage settlements and a greater reluctance to discharge unneeded people; and third, the business becomes caught in more and more intense marketing wars. So, frequently the net effect of the new technology is that its benefits accrue to the customer and to the labor union, while the business is left with the costs and the investments.

Now, the message of this scenario is not, of course, that any capital-intensifying investment should automatically be rejected, but rather that its strategic effect should be estimated as carefully, before the event, as its cost effect. The net result in many cases will clearly be against the contemplated project, no matter how glamorous it may be. However, while the project may have a negative net prospect as far as percentage ROI is concerned, it may quite often have a favorable prospect as far as dollar results are concerned, because the lower percentage is applied to a larger investment base. In such cases, a rather difficult management decision is required—difficult because it involves a trade-off between an increase in sales and dollar profits on the one hand, and a decrease in the rate of profitability on the other.

Third, the business should adopt a market strategy that minimizes the profit-damaging effect of capital-intensive technology. The PIMS data base suggests several ways of accomplishing this, many of them leading to increased dollar earnings, if not increased ROI levels or higher percentages on sales. Three of these moves are examined here.

The first is suggested by Figure 14-3. The bottom row, where the highly investment-intensive businesses are located, reveals a sharp increase in profitability moving from left to right, from 4 percent average ROI to 17 percent. Even at approximately equal levels of investment intensity, the high-share businesses do much better than the low-share businesses. This observation may seem rather obvious and unhelpful, until it is recalled that market share is measured relative to the served market, that is, relative to that segment of the total potential market in which the business is making a serious competitive attempt. So one way in which a business can obtain high market share is to concentrate its efforts on a segment of the total potential market—for example, a smaller geographic area or a more specialized class of customers. Since market-segmentation efforts can often move a business toward the right on Figure 14-3, market segmentation or redefinition is clearly one strategic answer to the profit-depressing effects of capital intensity. The recent history of some segments of the specialty steel and pharmaceutical industries illustrates this principle.

A second approach is implied by Figure 14-6. Here businesses are divided according to their investment intensity and according to whether the breadth of their product line is narrower than what competitors are offering (to the same served market), about the same, or wider.

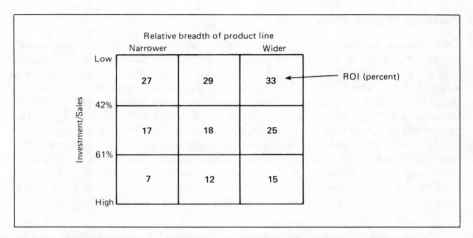

FIG. 14-6 Breadth of Product Line Related to Investment Intensity

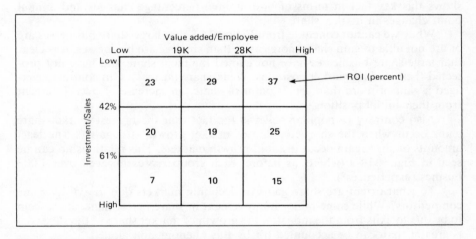

FIG. 14-7 Adequate Productivity Improvement for Increased Investment

Focusing on the investment-intensive businesses in the bottom row shows that a product line that is broader than competitors' is clearly preferable to one that is not. This observation can be combined with the previous one: An investment-intensive business can be quite profitable if it focuses on a relatively narrow and "conquerable" market segment, and covers that segment really well, with a broad and diverse product line tuned to the preferences of that segment.

A third approach to profit protection in investment-intensive businesses is to be sure to obtain adequate productivity improvement for the increased investment. Productivity rises more rarely than one would expect, but where it does rise, it certainly helps. Figure 14-7 gives the key facts.

Pursuing Market Share

Conventional wisdom has it that a business with a large share of its served market, especially if that served market is growing rapidly, not only finds it easy to gain additional market share, but also should pursue a share-gaining strategy. Many businesspeople believe that large-share firms possess advantages in resource availability, strategic position, and visibility—all of which facilitate a strategy of trying for an even greater market share. Rapid growth, meanwhile, helps to reduce the cost of the move, because the risk of triggering a major competitive donnybrook is lower in a growing market. It is also a common belief that weak-share businesses located in low-growth markets should, and usually do, harvest some of their share. The PIMS models in most cases confirm these judgments as to how businesses should act. But, the PIMS data base also indicates that this is not how businesses in fact do usually act.

Conventional Wisdom Vs. Observed Behavior. Businesses that already have high shares of their markets tend, on average, to gain less additional market share per year than do low- and medium-share businesses. Figure 14-8 shows this key fact in terms of both annual percentage changes and annual point changes in market share.

While we cannot conclude from Figure 14-8 that large-share businesses are or are not able to gain share more easily than small-share businesses, it is clear that large-share businesses have not gained the most share and have not protected their leading market positions. Weak-share businesses, in contrast, averaged a gain of more than a half point of share, an increase of over 7 percent from their initial position.[1]

Also contrary to popular belief is the fact that the highest market-share gains occur when the short-run rate of market growth is negative. The least amounts of share gain occur in rapid-growth markets. This relationship can be seen in Figure 14-9 (where, as before, each group represents well over 1,000 business experiences[2]).

To what extent are share gains in declining markets due to *exit* by some competitors? While some minor improvement in share performance does seem to be due to exits from the industry, the growth of market share of the survivors is greater than can be accounted for by this phenomenon alone.

Large-share businesses, on the average, lose share in rapid-growth environments, while weak-share firms gain share in such environments. Equally surprising, large-share businesses fare worse than weak-share businesses in negative market-growth situations. Figure 14-10 indicates the combined impact of initial share level and market growth rate on change in market share. It was the large-share businesses in rapid-growth markets that the conventional wisdom suggested would achieve the greatest share gains.

---

[1] The result is the same if initial *relative* market share is substituted for the initial simple market share.

[2] The PIMS data base has five or more years of data for close to 1,000 businesses. By taking every year-to-year move as a separate observation, over 4,000 year-to-year experiences are available for examination.

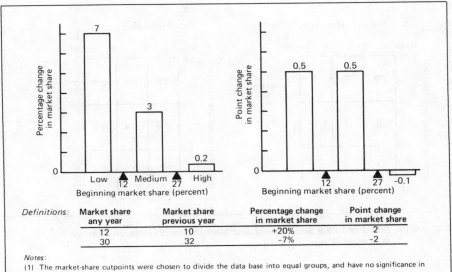

Definitions:	Market share any year	Market share previous year	Percentage change in market share	Point change in market share
	12	10	+20%	2
	30	32	−7%	−2

Notes:

(1) The market-share cutpoints were chosen to divide the data base into equal groups, and have no significance in themselves. Each group in the figure represents over 1,000 business experiences.

(2) The average market-share gain for the economy at large would seem to be *zero*, since whatever share one company gains another loses. The tables here do not average to zero because (a) more "good" than "poor" businesses are represented in the PIMS data base and (b) some businesses are implementing a segmentation strategy, in which almost everyone in the industry has a rising market share (though of a diminished served market).

FIG. 14-8 Market Share Gains

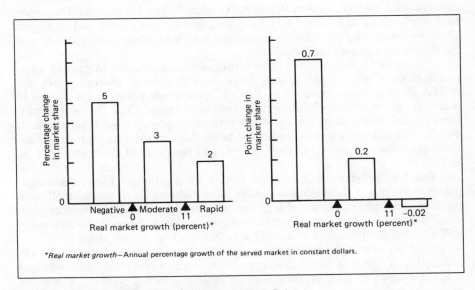

Real market growth—Annual percentage growth of the served market in constant dollars.

FIG. 14-9 Effect of Real Market Growth on Share Gain

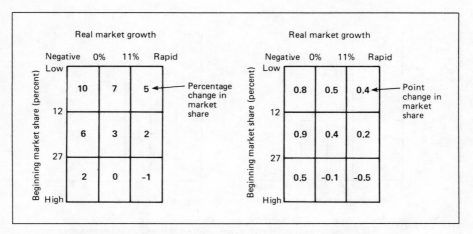

FIG. 14-10 Effect of Initial Share Level and Market Growth Rate on Change in Market Share

Why Do Businesses Act Counter to Their Beliefs? The focus here is on the large-share businesses, since they act in the most surprising manner. The observed results, counter to expectations, occur either because there really are natural market forces at work that lead such businesses to lose or give up share in rapid-growth markets, or because these businesses choose to follow that path. Among the reasons why large-share businesses may choose not to be aggressive could be the high costs of pursuing such a strategy.

Is it sensible, from a short-term performance perspective, for large-share firms to hold market position steady rather than to build it further? This question is examined in Figure 14-11 by comparing the cash flow, and in Figure 14-12 by comparing the ROI, of businesses that held market share steady and businesses that gained market share.

Figure 14-11 indicates the short-term cash costs incurred in gaining additional share. For example, among large-share businesses (bottom row), the market-share gainers earned a cash flow of 7 percentage points, compared to 10 points for the businesses holding their positions steady. Thus, the overall relative cash cost to the share gainers was 3 percentage points. Cash costs are moderately, but not significantly, lower for large-share businesses than for small-share businesses, both overall (-3 vs. -4) and per point of share gain (-1 vs. -2).

But, for short-term ROI cost, the story is quite different. Large-share businesses must pay a short-run cost in terms of reduced ROI, while small- and medium-share businesses are able to increase short-term ROI and market share simultaneously. (Over a longer time horizon, however, large-share businesses will reap the ROI benefits of having a higher level of market share.)

Looking now at market-share change segregated by rate of market growth rather than by level of initial market position, conventional wisdom holds that it is least costly to gain market share in rapidly growing markets. The belief probably derives from the ability of all competitors to build their sales simulta-

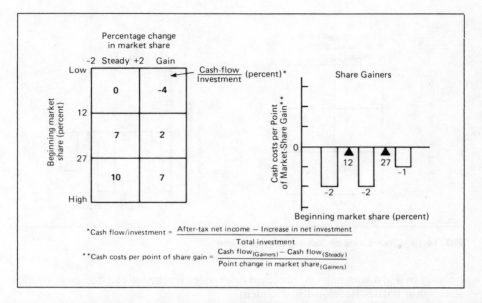

FIG. 14-11 Cash Flows of Steady Market Share Businesses Vs. Gained Market Share Businesses

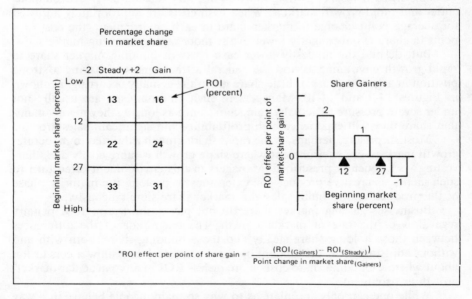

FIG. 14-12 Returns on Investment of Steady Market Share Businesses Vs. Gained Market Share Businesses

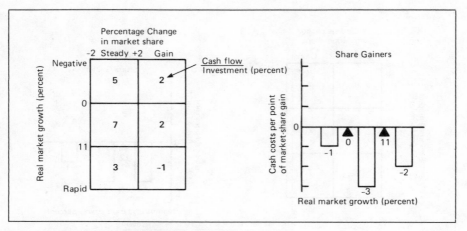

FIG. 14-13 Cash Costs of Gaining Market Share

neously in a growing market. Since no one's sales level needs to decrease, costly share-gain battles develop less frequently.

Cash and ROI performance, respectively, are illustrated in Figures 14-13 and 14-14.

Figure 14-13 indicates again that the process of building market share carries with it the cost of a lower short-term cash flow. Contrary to conventional wisdom, the cash costs of gaining share do not vary substantially between moderate- and rapid-growth markets. When cash costs are appropriately adjusted for average point change in market share in each environment, the cost of a point in share is only slightly lower in the more rapidly growing markets.

But, despite the modestly lower cash costs of building market share in rapid-growth environments and the general attractiveness of having a strong position in a growth market, little share growth is actually occurring, as shown in Figures 14-9 and 14-10. Managers in such environments are usually not under severe pressure to actually gain share, since as long as they merely maintain share they will experience high profitability and significant sales growth.

Most surprising, perhaps, is the rapid share growth exhibited in moderate-growth markets—an environment where share growth is more costly and "harvesting" is frequently prescribed. Managers in this environment often turn to such tactics as creative product-line extensions to prolong the maturity phase of the product, and to build sales and market share simultaneously.

Businesses gaining market share do not pay a short-term ROI penalty regardless of the rate of market growth. The magnitude of the differences between those holding share steady and those building share, both with and without adjustment for the amount of share gain, does not allow a conclusion about whether building share costs more or less ROI in any particular market-growth environment.

While one can only speculate as to why so many people behave in a way counter to what they probably believe, the evidence suggests the following explanations:

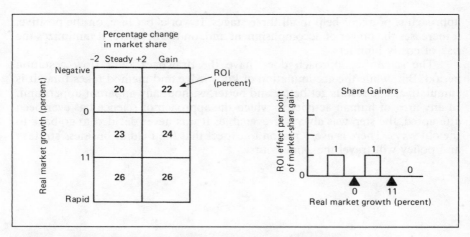

FIG. 14-14 Effect on Return on Investment of Gaining Market Share

1. Managers have a short time horizon. Most managers are concerned with current results—profits this year and perhaps the next. They are encouraged to have this outlook by the fact that their own salaries, bonuses, and promotions may be tied to *current* performance. Thus, managers would be unwilling to suffer either cash costs or ROI costs now for higher share and higher ROI in the more distant future.

2. "Management by exception" is a management style that focuses upon things and events that are not behaving "normally" *today*. This style, when applied to corporate strategy, may result in complacency about businesses that are very strong today, and encourage managers to focus instead upon bringing weak businesses up to average. From a portfolio perspective, such behavior may lead to investing in weak-share businesses that have lower ROI and cash-flow performance, rather than investing in strong-share, high-profit alternatives.

3. The large-share business may hesitate to use its share-gaining muscle out of fear of wreaking havoc in the market. Even a moderate expansionary move by a business with an already large market share could have quite substantial impacts on smaller competitors, and thus create quite a bit of market turmoil.

One conclusion: A strong *corporate* strategy is needed. Why? In the absence of such a strategy, it appears that natural business forces frequently push businesses in the wrong direction. Further, corporate strategy should be coupled with an appropriate reward system to induce managers to follow that strategy.

CONCLUSION

Good strategy planning consists of asking good questions, getting good answers, and effectively implementing the good answers. The scientific approach is of major help in all three stages. It works because, on the positive, it increases the power of accomplishment and, on the negative, it minimizes the risk of costly blunders.

The scientific approach does have the drawback of a slow gestation period. But, while the accumulation of knowledge and method takes time, it is cumulative. The results get better and better, without any apparent upper limit. In any area of human activity in which the approach of science has ever been attempted, the step was always irreversible: It was never decided to go back to the old ways. There is every reason to expect that the field of business strategy and policy will travel the same course.

15

Quantitative Tools for Strategic Decision Making

GUS W. GRAMMAS

Director of Technology and Company Programs, Graduate School of Business, Columbia University

THE NATURE OF STRATEGIC DECISIONS

Strategic decision making affects all managerial levels of the company. Specifically, it can be broken into two distinct components: decisions that affect the product/market scope of the company and decisions that affect the competitive posture of the individual businesses that are part of the company. Some of the major strategic decisions affecting product/market scope are:

1 Research and development expenditures—to ascertain new areas in which to expand;
2 New product introduction—to decide to enter new businesses through either acquisition or internal development (as an offshoot to decision 1);
3 Capital investment—to commit resources to a substantial addition to plant capacity, the success of which depends on future industry conditions and competitive activity;
4 Mergers and acquisitions—to increase market share;
5 Vertical integration—to extend the company's operational scope through forward or backward integration; and
6 Divestment—to withdraw from a specific industry.

Those decisions that primarily address competitive posture include:

1 Marketing—advertising programs, channels, promotion, and so forth;
2 Production/operations—such as automation (labor-capital relationships), size and location of plants (distribution costs vs. economies of scale);
3 Finance—working capital, credit terms; and
4 Human resources—personnel policies, union/labor relations (especially important in service industries).

After these decisions have been reached, a system must be designed to measure performance in light of specific goals. Moreover, financial, organizational, and timing arrangements must be decided in order to pursue the predetermined performance goals. Ultimately, these strategic decisions form the framework for middle management's day-to-day (tactical) and/or administrative decisions. In turn, the administrative decisions form the framework for line management's decisions. This chapter examines the analytical techniques and specific conceptual tools that are used for strategic decision making.

CHARACTERISTICS OF STRATEGIC DECISIONS

The presence of greater uncertainty, higher complexity, and longer-term payoffs are key elements that serve to distinguish routine action from strategic decisions. Successful management personnel usually possess a high tolerance for uncertainty and ambiguity, the ability to assess the likelihood and potential impact of future events on decision alternatives, and the commitment to make decisions in light of imperfect information.

The environment in which strategic decisions are made is more complex and uncertain than ever before. Technological change, governmental regulations, general economic uncertainty, and increased competition and customer sophistication all require corporations and governmental agencies to consider carefully the impact of their actions. For example, executives evaluating potential mergers or acquisitions must analyze social impact, political issues, antitrust suits, and other legal matters in addition to financial aspects.

Factors Affecting Complexity of Strategic Decisions

There are several factors contributing to the complexity and uncertainty of strategic decision problems. These interrelated factors are:

- Multiple objectives
- Difficulty of identifying good alternatives
- Intangibles
- Long time horizons
- Many interested factions
- Risk and uncertainty
- Interdisciplinary problems
- Several decision makers
- Value trade-offs
- Risk attitude
- Sequential nature of decisions

Multiple Objectives. It is typically desirable to achieve and/or make progress toward several objectives at once. In evaluating routes for proposed pipelines, a company wishes simultaneously to minimize the environmental impact and health and safety hazards, as well as to maximize economic benefits and positive social impact, while pleasing all groups of interested citizens. Since all these goals cannot be met with a single alternative, it is important to evaluate the degree to which each objective is achieved by the competing alternatives.

Difficulty of Identifying Good Alternatives. Because many factors affect the desirability of an alternative, the generation of good alternatives for careful analysis involves substantial creativity. In some problems, a good deal of thought is required to identify even a single alternative that seems possible, let alone reasonable, for achieving the problem objectives.

Intangibles. How should one assess goodwill of a client, morale of a work force, or distress of increasing bureaucracy and governmental regulations? Although it is difficult to measure such intangibles, they are often important factors in a decision.

Long Time Horizons. Many strategic decisions involve a commitment over an extended period of time, thus utilizing valuable (and often scarce) corporate resources that might be otherwise allocated. The consequences are not all felt immediately, but often cover (by intention or otherwise) a long time period. For example, the projected lifetime for most major facilities is 25 to 100 years, research and development projects routinely require 5 to 20 years, and the lead time for the installation of new nuclear power plant capacity is 10 to 15 years. Another aspect to consider is contingency plans should the project appear or become unsuccessful. The irreversibility of some decisions poses a major risk to the corporation. Future implications of alternatives now being considered must be accounted for in the decision-making process.

Many Interested Factions. Major strategic decisions often affect groups of people whose attitudes and values differ greatly. Because of these differences, concerns for equity and political pressure contribute to the complexity of a problem.

Risk and Uncertainty. With essentially all strategic problems, it is not possible to predict precisely the consequences of each alternative. Each involves risks and uncertainties: an advertising campaign may fail, a large reservoir may break, a government reorganization may result in an unwieldy bureaucracy, or a new product could turn out to be an Edsel. The major reasons for the existence and persistence of these uncertainties include:

1 Lack of sufficient data;
2 Expense and time associated with data retrieval and analysis;
3 Natural but unpredictable phenomena, such as earthquakes and droughts;
4 Shifts in population;
5 Changes in priorities over time; and
6 Uncertainty of actions of other influential parties (e.g., governments, competitors).

A general class of critical uncertainties concerns the risks to life and limb. Numerous personal and organizational decisions affect the likelihood that accidents or "exposure" result in fatalities or morbidity. Examples include decisions about foods and drugs, toxic or hazardous waste materials, product safety, and pollution control.

Interdisciplinary Problems. The president of a multinational firm cannot be professionally qualified in all aspects of international law, tax matters, accounting, marketing, production, and so forth. Qualified professionals should supply relevant inputs on these key factors in a major decision. In addition, the decision maker must decide whether or not the "right" inputs reach him. This analysis can be particularly problematic when professional input itself requires judgment.

Several Decision Makers. A single decision maker rarely has complete control over a major decision. Several decision makers, who may or may not think similarly, control crucial aspects in the overall decision-making process. To begin production and marketing operations in a new geographical area, corporate management may require approval from stockholders, several regulatory agencies, community zoning boards, and perhaps even the courts. The potential actions of others must be considered when a corporation evaluates its strategic policy.

Value Trade-Offs. Important decisions involve critical value trade-offs to indicate the relative desirability between environmental impact and economic costs today, immediate social costs vs. future social benefits, negative impact to a small group vs. smaller positive impact to a larger group, and sometimes the value of a human life versus the benefits generated by a hazardous technology.[1]

Risk Attitude. A firm operating with the status quo strategy may forecast small and declining profits in the next few years. Changing to an innovative strategy may have a chance of resulting in substantially higher profits, but also a risk of losses or even bankruptcy. Even if the likelihood of the various consequences is known, crucial judgments about an attitude toward risk are essential to evaluate the appropriateness of accepting risks that accompany each alternative.

Sequential Nature of Decisions. Rarely is one decision completely uncoupled from other decisions. Choices today affect both the alternatives available in the future and the desirability of those alternatives.

Common Characteristics of Strategic Decisions

Although the particular factors causing the complexity in specific strategic decisions may differ, all strategic decisions have the following characteristics:

- High stakes
- Complicated structure
- No overall experts
- Need to justify decision

High Stakes. The difference in perceived desirability between alternatives can be very large. It may involve millions of dollars or severe environmental damage, for instance.

Complicated Structure. Numerous features (discussed previously) make it extremely difficult to evaluate alternatives informally in a responsible manner.

---

[1] M. Parvin and G. W. Grammas, "Optimization Models for Environmental Pollution Control: A Synthesis," *Journal of Environmental Economic Management*, Aug. 1976, at 113–128.

No Overall Experts. Because of the breadth of concerns involved in most important decision problems and because of their uniqueness, there are no overall experts. Different individuals, however, have expertise in disciplines such as economics, engineering, and other professions which should be incorporated into the decision process. It may not be the case, however, that traditional expertise may be valid in the new situation. Some individuals mistakenly apply expertise that was appropriate for a previous problem but is not valid for the current one.

Need to Justify Decision. Because of their high visability, decisions may need to be justified to regulatory authorities, shareholders, bosses, and the public.

QUANTITATIVE APPROACHES TO STRATEGIC DECISIONS

Complexity cannot be avoided in making strategic decisions. It is part of the problem. There are, however, a variety of approaches used to deal with this complexity. On the one hand, complexity can be dealt with intuitively in an informal manner. On the other hand, formal mathematical models can be used to capture as much of the complexity as possible. Various approaches between these two are also possible.

In order to assess alternatives in the face of imperfect information, the individual must calculate the odds and weigh the risks of alternative courses of action. Recently, mathematical tools and techniques known collectively as risk analysis have been developed and proven useful in both government and industry. In any case, the process of obtaining and combining the available information is a difficult task that requires balancing all the pros and cons as well as recognizing the uncertainties for each alternative.

Specific quantitative tools exist to address the problematic characteristics that segment strategic decisions from routine ones. Mathematical models provide a systematic approach to strategic decision making and assist in the area of higher complexity by defining and quantifying key variables. Greater uncertainty is addressed by probability theory and risk analysis as a range of possible alternatives is devised. Decision analysis is used to make better decisions by structuring the decision and prescribing a strategy that indicates what action should be chosen initially and what further actions should be selected for each subsequent event that could occur.

MODEL BUILDING

Mathematical model building is not a precise art. In fact, it may be difficult to establish in real terms whether or not the decision that was made was optimal.

However, a set of tools exist that aid the decision-making process and alleviate some of the guess work.

In many firms today, the quantitative approach to model building is still a rather nebulous topic relegated to text books which adorn shelves. Consequently, an initial task for strategic planning executives may be the transformation of prevailing trends from qualitative approaches to a mix of qualitative and quantitative analysis. Thus, the integration of the skills possessed by quantitative analysts with the expertise of knowledgeable managers is proposed as the most productive method for effective decision making. One of the best ways to attain this integrated approach is through the use of a general quantitative model.

General Quantitative Model of the Decision

The formalization of decision making through the use of a quantitative model can be a useful and powerful tool in directing and controlling a company's limited resources to their optimal efficiency. Future situations and events can be identified, analyzed, and acted upon in a proactive rather than reactive way. To assess a strategic problem, whether economic, social, technological, or political in nature, a systematic approach should be taken in order to direct and control limited resources toward desired goals. The first step is identification and measurement of variables and their interrelationships that are controllable by managers of the firm. Some of the variables to consider in a typical firm are illustrated in Figure 15-1.

In the field of strategic management, little attention has been paid to the basic problems of methodology in research and explanation. Granted, many case studies and descriptive theories have been published. The complexity of the field coupled with its relatively new development seemingly result in an inapplicability of traditional deductive approaches. Some control and some knowledge is, however, better than none. Consequently, a need exists for an approach that takes into consideration degrees of uncertainty and a degree of control over certain situations rather than the absolute and general nature of the deductive approach.

Guth, for example, argues for a systematic approach to model building, recognizing its limitations:

> Without the use of a systematic approach to the problem of formulating organizational objectives and strategy for the future, managers are often not able adequately to anticipate critical problems and issues which will have significant longer-term effect on overall performance. In the press for operating effectiveness and efficiency in the short-run, it is all too easy, without the discipline of systematic analysis, for managers to escape awareness of basic changes in the environment relevant to their organizations which might require significant change in the commitment and structuring of the organization's resources. Even with a systematic approach ... there is some considerable margin for error in measuring the speed and direction of change and its impact on the organization. The potential for error, however, is considerably reduced, and the capacity to respond quickly and

effectively to new knowledge about the changing environment is enhanced by the employment of such an approach.[2]

The degree of control that an approach of this sort permits is a function of:

1 The choice of variables used and their significance in the determination of specific events and outcomes;

2 The degree of accuracy in the quantification of these variables and their interrelation; and

3 The extent of modification of the variables by the decision maker or makers.

Specific methodological implications result from these attributes. First, the variables and their interrelation must be specified in terms that are as precisely defined and measurable as possible, with the limitations on this process noted. Second, the observations that validate the explanation must be described, and approaches to achieving a more powerful explanation should be developed. Third, the level of modification of variables by the decision maker or makers must be included. In addition, the mathematical limitations of the model should be analyzed.

A standard assumption often included in models is that decisions made by individuals or companies are rational. This assertion is often incorrect when the reality of decisions is considered. There are both psychological as well as analytical aspects that affect strategic decision making. If a model is to be integrated successfully into the decision process, its role must be specified and clearly understood by both the analyst and the decision maker. For the communications process to be effective between the model builder and the manager, there must be a level of mutual understanding between them. The main goal of models, after all, should be the clarification of the insights and improvement upon the cognitive structure of the decision maker.

Computer Models

A full study and evaluation of strategic issues often requires sophisticated forecasting techniques and quantitative approaches to decision making under risk and uncertainty. However, the initial task of identifying the issues and problems by top-level decision makers must occur before staff planners can effectively utilize sophisticated forecasting and decision analysis techniques. The most recent developments in strategic planning have been in the area of expansion of formal models and their capability to assist in the analytical function. The primary aim of these systems is the generation of more timely, accurate, and cost effective planning information. As a result, decision makers are able to consider a greater range of alternatives in more detail and with more information than was previously possible using traditional planning methods. Potential benefits derived from these systems are great, but many of the current

---

[2] W. D. Guth, "Formulating Organizational Objectives and Strategy: A Systematic Approach," *Journal of Business Policy*, Autumn 1971, at 25.

1. Growth rate

2. Profitability performance (return on investment)

3. Strategy of the company

   a. Product/market scope

   b. Marketing policies, by product/market area:

      i. Product policy:
         ● Cost of competitive features
         ● Performance characteristics
         ● Quality level

      ii. Price policy—level of prices

      iii. Distribution policies—cost of distribution

      iv. Advertising and promotion policies—cost of advertising and promotion

   c. Product policies, by product/market area served:

      i. Plant and equipment policy—unit cost of manufacture

      ii. Labor policy—cost of labor

      iii. Inventory policy—cost of carrying inventory to smooth production output

   d. Financial policies:

      i. Debt to total asset ratio

      ii. Cost of debt funds

   e. Research and development policies, by product/market area—expenditure on research and development projects

4. The resources of the company allocated to each product/market area served

5. Demand potential in product/market areas served by the company

6. Resources allocated by competitors to the product/market areas served by the company

7. Aggressiveness of marketing policies of competitors

8. Organizational effectiveness and efficiency of the company (the degree to which decisions and actions affecting operations are taken in the organization in a manner consistent with the strategy, at minimum cost)

9. Level of aspiration of top-level managers with power to influence key strategic and organizational decisions for growth and profitability

10. Level of commitment of top-level managers to other than economic values

11. Willingness of top-level managers to accept risk

FIG. 15-1 Key Variables to Consider in a General Quantitative Model [3]

[3] For a thorough discussion on viable measurement, see W. D. Guth, "The Growth and Profitability of the Firm: A Managerial Explanation," *Journal of Business Policy*, Spring 1972, at 31–36.

applications lack proper systems support and optimization capabilities, that is, the facility to select rather than just evaluate alternatives.

Computer-Based Planning Systems

Most existing strategic planning models are computer-based financial simulations that evaluate proposed planning alternatives under specified environmental conditions and generate projected financial statements for each set of inputs. They contain managers' judgment on forecasts (financial, marketing, production, and so on) as well as the relationship between controllable variables and outcomes. Optimization models that analyze multidimensional problems and assess the marginal economic effects of strategic alternatives are of greater benefit to the individual decision maker.

Strategic management can be seen as a problem solving activity requiring formulation, analysis, choice, and implementation. The key to effective analytical support for the strategic decision-making process is not simply a computer-based corporate planning model. Instead, Hamilton and Moses propose the development of an integrated computer-based planning model with the following characteristics:

1 Optimization function for selection rather than evaluation of alternatives;
2 Simulation capabilities; and
3 Supporting information system to allow effective interaction between model and user by streamlining input preparation and output analysis.[4]

The process begins with corporate level definition of objectives which are then translated into a set of quantifiable goals and guidelines for the management of corporate resources. For example, corporate goals may include market share criteria, stockholder net wealth, and return on equity; guidelines may involve limits on financial ratios or expense constraints, legal limitations, and government restrictions. Other data, such as economic analysis, tax considerations, prime interest and foreign exchange rates, and inflation, are also communicated to corporate groups at the beginning of the annual planning cycle.

Within such a framework, a set of internal and external strategies are generated by each planning unit. Some of the internal strategies analyzed are:

1 Build/grow: which new and/or existing products/projects should receive emphasis;
2 Maintain:
   a. Which products/projects should be *aggressively* maintained (e.g., what type of program should be instituted to maintain market share);
   b. Which products/projects should be *selectively* maintained (e.g., choosing one or two items in a product line on which to concentrate efforts);

---

[4] For a discussion of mathematical programming, see W. F. Hamilton and M. A. Moses, "A Computer-Based Corporate Planning System," Management Science, Oct. 1974, at 148–159; and W. F. Hamilton and M. A. Moses, "An Optimization Model for Corporate Financial Planning," 22 *Operations Research* 677–692 (May-June 1973).

    c. Which products/projects should be *harvested* (e.g., letting a product run its useful life cycle, especially in a monopolistic setting); and

    3 Divest: which products/projects should be wound down, ceased, or sold.

Several factors are key to the success of the system as an integral part of the strategic decision-making process. First, the model should reflect a corporate-level focus with a financial orientation that analyzes the full range of variables including internal capital budgeting, acquisition and divestment, debt creation and repayment, stock issue and repurchase, and dividend payout. Usually a 5- to 10-year planning horizon comprised of one-year periods is considered appropriate. Second, the system should contain "what if" capabilities to allow the analysis of various scenarios. This capability, often referred to as simulation or sensitivity analysis, allows the decision maker to evaluate a number of different strategy alternatives and environmental conditions. Thus, the analytical requirements include the flexibility to evaluate investments in stages and variations on a wide variety of planning problems. Third, the system should contain the computational advantages offered by optimization methods so that an excessive number of cases need not be considered. Evaluation and selection regarding combinations of corporate strategies, financing programs, and planning assumptions can be greatly improved. Last, the creation of a supporting information system is essential to permit effective interaction between the user and the model. Remote terminals should be utilized to allow direct access to the system, resulting in the most effective use of the model as a planning tool. Input/output flexibility should be achieved through alternative computer programs that facilitate standard as well as special planning studies in batch and interactive modes. Software packages should be geared to the needs of the end user and provide useful management information. However, the development of an appropriate model is only an initial step toward its successful application to planning problems. Ongoing support through the creation of an information system to permit interaction between the model and the decision maker is essential.

RISK ANALYSIS

In every management decision there is some degree of uncertainty that represents the manager's lack of knowledge of future occurrences. Sometimes, the decision maker is quite sure of the outcomes of various possible choices, in which case the problem is one of evaluating some or all of the potential outcomes. However, the decision maker often is not at all sure of the results of various possible decisions and consequently must use a different approach if he or she is to make the best decision under a given set of circumstances. Whatever path is chosen, the possibility exists that an alternative choice of action would have been more advantageous over time.

    For many people, the concept of uncertainty is addressed explicitly only in some form of gambling. It is often difficult to think of uncertainty explicitly when assessing sales forecasts and future costs. Several techniques can be used in this environment of risk and uncertainty. They range in complexity from the traditional approaches, such as "single-point" projections, to computer simulations where risk and uncertainty are factored into the calculations. The following sections show how a decision maker can decompose a complex problem into smaller elements, assess the uncertainty and consequences associated with these elements, and ultimately relink the components to enable him or her to make the best possible choice under the circumstances.

Traditional Approaches

Historically, there have been a number of approaches used for handling uncertainty in a strategic context. Traditional approaches to the analysis of proposed capital expenditures, referred to as "single-point" analysis, assume a degree of certainty that is often nonexistent in the real world. In this approach, all investments, costs, income, and cash flows are assumed to be known and certain, as estimated. For example, assume that two mutually exclusive projects (A and B) are being considered and both are projected to have the same internal rate of return (IRR). Estimates regarding required investment, costs, projected income, and cash flow are based on the "best" single-point estimates. No uncertainty factor is attached to any of these values. For the purpose of this example, the following values are assumed:

Required investment	$2,000, A or B
Cash flow	$1,000/year for 3 years, A or B
Hurdle rate	10 percent, A or B

Assuming that $1,000 is the best estimate for each year's cash flow for either project, the net present value (NPV) for either project (at a cost of capital of 10 percent is:

$$\text{NPV}_A \text{ or NPV}_B = \left(\frac{1,000}{(1.1)} + \frac{1,000}{(1.1)^2} + \frac{1,000}{(1.1)^3} \right) - 2,000$$

$$= (909.09 + 826.45 + 751.31) - 2,000$$

$$= \underline{\$486.85}$$

Because both projects have the same NPV, they are equally acceptable using this estimate of outcome.

However, this approach to the analysis of projects is often unrealistic in the real world. Several methods have been identified to incorporate the notions of risk and uncertainty in strategic decisions. Some of the more common procedures are:

- Certainty equivalent
- Risk-adjusted discount rate
- Simple average
- Expected value
- Decision trees

Each of these methods is analyzed individually. However, as discussed later, each of these methods has severe limitations when dealing with the issues.

Certainty Equivalent

The "certainty equivalent" may be defined as the amount of return that a decision maker would require with certainty to make him or her indifferent about choosing one of two alternatives. Suppose someone offered to toss a coin and agreed to pay $2.00 if the outcome was heads and pay nothing if it was tails. How much would a person be willing to pay to play this game? Most people would mentally calculate a 50-50 chance at $2.00 and a 50-50 chance at 0 and arrive at $1.00 as the maximum amount they would pay. If one has to make a choice between several alternatives in which the outcomes are uncertain, the weighted average of each alternative can be calculated using the chances as weights. As can be easily ascertained, this type of decision is personal to the decision maker and depends on an individual's willingness to assume risk along with their security level. The certainty equivalent analysis ignores risk altogether. If the decision maker is indifferent toward risk, then this type of analysis is sufficient. In most cases, however, it is pertinent to assess risk vs. reward. Consequently, it is practically impossible to use a formal model for financial analysis based on the certainty equivalent.

Risk-Adjusted Discount Rates

The risk-adjusted discount rate method is based on a decision maker's attitude toward risk. Thus, projects must have higher projected returns as risk increases to be considered acceptable. This method incorporates risk by using different discount rates for projects that have different degrees of risk. For example, a project that is considered to have a low degree of risk might have a discount rate slightly higher than government bonds, which are considered risk free and are usually used as a benchmark for comparative purposes. A greater and greater premium is added to projects as they become more risky.

To illustrate this concept, consider two projects, X and Y. Each project has a required investment of $20,000. Project X involves virtually no risk and will generate a cash flow of $7,000 per year for five years, while project Y is substantially more risky and has a chance of generating $7,500 per year for five years. The company has decided to use a 10 percent discount rate for project X and 15 percent for Y. Thus, the NPVs for the two projects are:

$$NPV_X = \left(\frac{7,000}{(1.1)} + \frac{7,000}{(1.1)^2} + \frac{7,000}{(1.1)^3} + \frac{7,000}{(1.1)^4} + \frac{7,000}{(1.1)^5} \right) - 20,000$$

$$= 26,535,50 - 20,000$$

$$= \underline{\$6,535.50}$$

$$NPV_Y = \left(\frac{7,500}{(1.15)} + \frac{7,500}{(1.15)^2} + \frac{7,500}{(1.15)^3} + \frac{7,500}{(1.15)^4} + \frac{7,500}{(1.15)^5} \right) - 20,000$$

$$= 25,141.17 - 20,000$$

$$= \underline{\$5,141.17}$$

Thus, the differential in yearly return between X and Y was not large enough to compensate for the increased risk, as evaluated by the higher discount rate on project Y. Using this method of analysis, project X has a higher NPV and is a better choice.

Although rates are adjusted for risk, there is still no analytical assessment of risk and uncertainty. The problem results from the adjustment for risk itself and becomes a matter of how much should the decision maker discount various projects. It is difficult to quantify in this rather informal style where the real uncertainties exist. Thus the selection of discount rates becomes more emotional than analytical.

Simple Average

In the "single point" method, an attempt was made at projecting the best estimate of future cash flow projections. A slightly more sophisticated method is limiting the number of likely occurrences and averaging the possible results. For example, the cash flow projections for the first example could be influenced by competitor activity, notably:

Competitor Activity	Project A	Project B
Weak	1,400	1,800
Normal	1,000	1,000
Strong	600	200
	3,000 ÷ 3	3,000 ÷ 3
	= 1,000	= 1,000

Note that project B is far more volatile with respect to competitor activity than project A, but by the simple average method, their estimated NPV remains equal. This approach is an improvement over the single point system, as it introduces and incorporates risk. However, no explicit assessment of risk is incorporated in the variability. There is no probability assigned to different scenarios. In the example, the implicit assessment is that there is an equal probability that competitor activity will be weak, normal, or strong. In most cases, a more sophisticated methodology is required.

Expected Value and Decision Trees

In the previous example, simple averaging was used to summarize the variability in competitor activity. The concept of "expected value" (i.e., the sum of possible outcomes multiplied by their respective probabilities, sometimes called a weighted average) is introduced to incorporate probabilities for each level of competitor activity. Whereas the implicit assumption in simple averaging is that all outcomes have the same probability, the concept of expected value allows for differentiation. In this example, the same projected cash flows are used. However, a probability of 20 percent is placed on weak competitor activity, 45 percent on normal activity, and 35 percent on strong competitor activity. The chart can be expanded as follows:

Project	Competitor Activity	Probability	Projected Annual Cash Flow	Expected Value
A	Weak	0.20	1,400	280
	Normal	0.45	1,000	450
	Strong	0.35	600	210
			Total expected value	940
B	Weak	0.20	1,800	360
	Normal	0.45	1,000	450
	Strong	0.35	200	70
			Total expected value	800

Project *B* has a lower expected value than project *A* due to the higher probability that competitor activity will be strong and project *B*'s sensitivity to strong competition. In addition, the range of probable returns is greater in project *B* (200 to 1,800) than in project *A* (600 to 1,400). In general, the smaller the variability of projected returns, the lower the risk.

The concept of expected value is most useful when there is one decision to be made, such as the number of units to produce. Note that it is necessary that the payoffs in the expected value calculation represent real "utility" (i.e., the "value" of $2 is twice the "value" of $1). Later in this chapter, the assessment and measurement of utility are discussed in more detail. However, there is still no risk assessment incorporated in expected value analysis.

The problem is even more complicated when a sequence of decisions has to be made. To cope with this situation, decision tree analysis is used. A sequence of the decisions that are to be made and the events that may occur are outlined, with probability estimates for each event used to evaluate the expected consequences of each decision option. The only information on uncertainty required in the decision tree model is an estimate of the probability of certain events transpiring. The following steps are required to use this method of analysis:

1 List the alternatives for the decisions to be made.

2 Assign probability estimates to each likely event that may result from each alternative.

3 Assign probability estimates to each subsequent decision in the same manner.

4 Evaluate the consequences of each sequence of alternatives according to the appropriate criteria.

5 Evaluate the expected consequences of each of the first stage decisions by weighing each branch by probability estimates.

Figure 15-2 is an example of a situation where a company must decide whether to import a product from overseas, conduct market research to determine more clearly the demand for the product, or do nothing.

Suppose a company has an opportunity to import a product from overseas which has enjoyed good market success in other countries. The offer is to buy

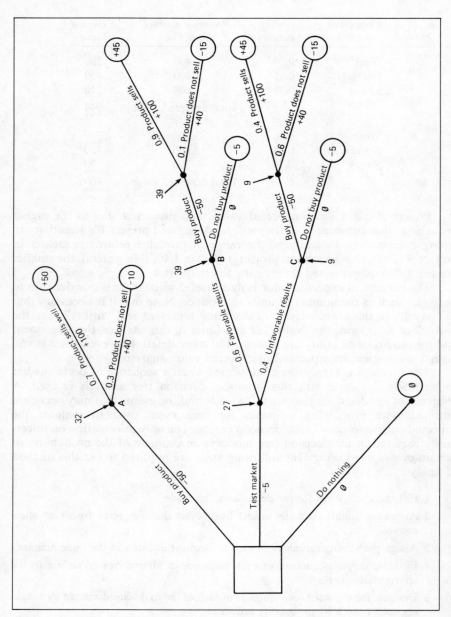

FIG. 15-2 Decision Tree Analysis

10,000 at a cost of $5 each. The company believes there is a good chance that the product will catch on, in which case they could sell all 10,000 at $10 each. Should the product not be well received, however, then it is projected that the firm will have to sell them on average for $4 each. The firm believes there is approximately a 70 percent chance the product will sell well.

Before the purchase decision is made, the company calls a marketing research company and inquires if they would be able to provide a better idea of the product's chance of success. The marketing research company indicated that for $5,000 they would test the market. If the results are favorable, the product will have a 90 percent chance of success. If the test results are unfavorable, however, there is still a 40 percent chance that the company's product would sell. The importing president believes there is a 60-40 chance that the test will be positive.

Figure 15-2 outlines the problem in diagram form. Each choice is represented by a branch with the various outcomes that might result fanning out from the ends in a sequential manner. Partial cash flows are added, as are the chance assessments associated with each branch. Net cash flows are placed at the end of each possible path.

The tree can eventually be "pruned" by replacing two branches with an expected value. For example, on the top two branches at point A, there is a 70 percent chance the firm will make $50,000 ($+50$) and a 30 percent chance it will lose $10,000 ($-10$). The expected value is $32,000 (0.7(50) $-0.3(10)-32$). This process is continued until the diagram is reduced to its original three branches. At points B and C, the company should choose the buy option because it has a greater expected value. The optimum choice is the one with the highest expected value: buy the product without the market research.

There are two alternative approaches to decision tree analysis. First, partial cash flows can be used in conjunction with the chance assessments for each branch to calculate the expected value. Forks can then be replaced with the certainty equivalents. The final result is the same as when using net cash flows. Second, each of the various possible strategies can be isolated and the expected value can be computed on each of these. As before, the strategy to maximize expected value is still to purchase the product without testing.

Decision trees map probability distributions, but do not assess risk. Each of the traditional analysis procedures contain important limitations in the presence of uncertainty. Specifically, they do not give information on the range and likelihood of possible outcomes and they do not quantify risk for assessment purposes. In the following section, a systematic approach to strategy evaluation is discussed.

Systematic Approach to Evaluating Strategy Risks

Due to the uncertainty that is inevitable in forecasts, particularly in the medium to long term, a strong need exists for a systematic approach to evaluating strategy risks. While some products and markets have shown stability in their historical development, most have not, making simple extrapolation of current developments into the future a rather risky approach to forecasting.

Intuitive processes possess a significant level of risk due to the influence of recent experience and implicit attitudes toward risk (aversion or preference).

Thus, a systematic approach should recognize uncertainty in the forecasts and the calculation of the payoffs of different strategic alternatives as well as identifying the role of attitudes toward risk in the final decision.

Some of the decisions that are relevant to this type of approach are:

- New product development
- Changes in competitive approaches with existing products
- New market entry
- Mergers and acquisitions
- Capital investment/divestment
- Production capability changes

The sequence of steps to follow consists of:

1 Determining key performance measure (e.g., return on investments, NPV).
2 Selecting an appropriate time frame.
3 Identifying key variables and their interrelationship.
4 Forecasting a range of possible values for each variable.
5 Determining the probability for each value.
6 Calculating the expected payoff.
7 Conducting sensitivity analysis.
8 Choosing the optimal alternative.

Forecasts and Probability Distributions

Until now, this discussion of decision making under uncertainty has treated chance as something the decision maker either knows or can calculate relatively easily. In real decision problems, however, the assessment of chance is often the most difficult part of the analysis. Usually a manager is faced with an uncertain future and very few tools to assist him in evaluating chance. In managerial decision making there are many times when an intuitive feeling about uncertainty is all that is required; there are other circumstances when very careful analysis and perhaps even some fairly elaborate computations are justified. The body of knowledge referred to as "probability theory" provides the means whereby a complex situation for which very little confidence in assessments of the chance involved can be made and a number derived in which a much higher degree of confidence is achieved. Probability can be defined as a number between 0 and 1 representing the decision maker's assessment of the chance of a future event.

Analysts can develop forecasts of future sales, profits, and so forth through the use of probabilistic modeling aspects of decision analysis. These projections can then be used to support decisions regarding investments, financial planning, and marketing. Because the relative costs of this type of computerized forecasting can be spread over a multitude of applications, their popularity is growing. The analysis assesses the chances that certain products will meet targets, the uncertainties inherent in the assessments, and the reason for the uncertainties.

Risk/Reward Relationship

As stated previously, different discount rates can be applied to the list of capital projects being considered to incorporate the varying degrees of risk associated with each. The higher the risk, the greater the premium applied should be.

A decision maker's propensity to accept risk will depend on the value of the potential gain or loss. For example, if there is a 50-50 chance to win $2.00 and a 50-50 chance to lose $2.00 by the toss of a coin, an individual may be willing to play. However, if the amount of money at stake is raised to $200.00, then many people would decline the chance. In general, however, the potential rewards must be commensurate with the risk taken, or the decision maker who is usually considered risk-averse will not take the chance.

Three statistics are important in the measurement of risk. The first of these is the "variance" of an uncertain quantity. Variance is a measure of the dispersion of possible values around the expected value, and is thus a measure of uncertainty. The larger the variance from the mean, the greater the uncertainty surrounding a quantity. Figure 15-3 shows probability functions for two uncertain quantities that have identical expected values but difference variances. "Standard deviation" is also used as a measure of dispersion of the outcome in the same unit as the mean. The standard deviation of an uncertain quantity is the square root of the variance. If the two investments or decisions have the same mean, then standard deviation is a good measurement to use in risk assessment. If two investments have different means, however, then the "coefficient of variation" (CV), which is the standard deviation divided by the mean, should be used. The CV can be used as an absolute measurement of risk as it expresses uncertainty as a percentage of risk. Thus, the higher the CV, the more risky the proposal.

Computer Simulation

The major pitfall behind "best estimate" methods is that it is impossible when comparing two opportunities to evaluate explicitly their relative risk if only "most likely" estimates have been made. Often, the decision maker is not the same person who made the original estimates. In the absence of any quantification of risk, it is difficult for the decision maker to know intuitively the thought process used to derive the estimates, that is, if optimistic, neutral, or pessimistic variables were used.

In the very broad sense, simulation involves the use of some kind of model to represent reality. The widespread availability of computers and software packages has facilitated the successful application of simulation techniques in many and varied fields of study. Simulation allows much more rapid and cost effective experimentation with a model that behaves like a real system. It involves the use of mathematical equations to either predict or determine the

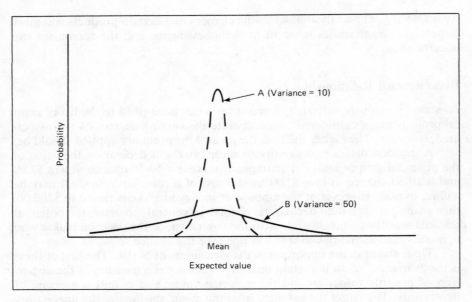

FIG. 15-3 Probability Functions

value of significant variables so that some predetermined objective is optimized. Once either the predictive or optimizing model is specified, replication
with given conditions always yields the same results. Invariability does not necessarily mean correct results with respect to the actual situation, as the results
depend on how representative the model is to reality.

In many systems, results for any given situation cannot be predicted with
precision. That is, there is a random element governed by the laws of chance,
implying that any model that ignores random fluctuations will be unrealistic.
Monte Carlo models differ from the more traditional simulation models in that
they do not yield invariable results. They generate empirical data to test suggested solutions rather than determine exact solutions. In essence, the Monte
Carlo method is a repeat-trials process of analysis, and it is proven as a valuable technique for analyzing problems involving uncertainties and complex
interactions among variables.

Usually, the computer package includes process generators that produce
statistical distributions of chosen variables. Next, the simulation takes random
samples from these distributions for the Monte Carlo trials to find the value of
a specific variable. At the time the program is run, the manager specifies the
number of trials required in order to produce meaningful results. Routines for
the calculation of basic financial criteria, such as rate of return and NPV are
included. The output is a distribution of possible outcomes containing information on means, standard deviations, and CVs. Thus, competitive simulation, as
shown later in this chapter with a case example, is really an application of risk
analysis programming. Uncertainty in the forecasted variables is translated

into a risk assessment vs. the expected reward. The output is a probability distribution of outcomes for any particular value of interest.

There are two pitfalls in this type of technique. First, simulation is a rather complicated approach, and executives may be reluctant to utilize a system that they do not fully understand. Second, considerable start-up investment is required for software development, debugging, and testing.

Sensitivity Analysis

Best estimates ignore several other possible estimates, ranging in value from the lowest to the highest values for each variable. Consequently, the following sensitivity analysis is proposed to treat uncertainty:

1 Project the range of values for each of the variables included in the analysis.

2 Assess the probability of occurrence for each value within the projected range for each variable. These estimates should be prepared by specialists either within or outside the firm.

3 Select at random a value and associated probability for each variable and compute a rate of return using these values for all variables. This process should be repeated with alternative selections.

4 Plot or list the various rates of return and their respective probabilities, and compute the variability for each combination. Generally speaking, rates with lower variability are preferred to those with higher variability.

DECISION ANALYSIS

The Nature of Decision Analysis

The basic assumption of decision analysis is that the attractiveness of alternatives depends on (1) the likelihood of the possible consequences of each alternative and (2) the preferences of the decision makers for those consequences. Even though all decisions require subjective judgments, the likelihood of various consequences and their desirability should be estimated separately using probabilities and utilities, respectively. These tools can then be used to calculate the expected utility of each alternative and the alternatives with higher expected utilities should be preferred. Decision analysis thus provides a sound basis and general approach for including judgments and values in an analysis of decision alternatives.[5]

Decision analysis focuses on five aspects fundamental to all decision problems, namely:

1 A perceived need to accomplish some objectives;

2 A selection from several alternatives;

---

[5] For an excellent overview of decision analysis, see Ralph L. Keeney, "Decision Analysis: An Overview," *Operations Research* 803–836 (Sept.-Oct. 1982).

3 The different consequences associated with alternatives;

4 The uncertainty about the consequences of each alternative; and

5 The possible consequences that are not all equally valued.

The decision problem is broken into parts, which are analyzed separately and then integrated by decision analysis to suggest which alternative should be chosen. This "divide and conquer" orientation is almost essential for addressing interdisciplinary problems. The methodology of decision analysis provides a framework to combine traditional techniques of operations research, management science, and systems analysis with professional judgments and values in a unified analysis to support decision making. Mathematical models, available data, information from samples and tests, and the knowledge of experts are used to quantify the likelihood of various consequences of alternatives in terms of probabilities. Utility theory is used to quantify the values of decision makers for these consequences.

The ultimate purpose of decision analysis is to help decision makers make better decisions. Even though the theory and procedures are straightforward, a price is paid for attempting to address the complexities of a decision problem explicitly. The implementation phase, that is, putting the methodology into practice, is more involved than other forms of analysis. A significantly greater portion of the overall effort in decision analysis is spent generating alternatives, specifying objectives, eliciting professional and value judgments, and interpreting implications of the analysis. Each of these steps requires interaction between the decision analyst and the decision makers or individuals knowledgeable about the problem substance.

For discussion purposes, the methodology of decision analysis can be segmented into four steps:

1 Structuring the decision problem;

2 Assessing possible impacts of each alternative;

3 Determining preferences (values) of decision makers; and

4 Evaluating and comparing alternatives.

There is, of course, a great deal of interdependence among the steps.

Structuring the Decision Problem

Structuring the decision problem includes the generation of alternatives and the specification of objectives. The creativity required for these tasks is promoted by the systematic thought processes of decision analysis.

Decision analysis captures the dynamic nature of decision processes by prescribing a decision strategy that indicates what action should be chosen initially and what further actions should be selected for each subsequent event that could occur. For instance, a decision strategy might suggest an initial test market for a new product and then, based on the results, either canceling the product, initiating further testing, or beginning a full scale marketing and sales effort. Thus, in describing the alternatives, one must simultaneously specify the decision points, the events that may occur between them, and the information that can be learned in the process. This dynamic structure can be conveniently represented as a decision tree.[6]

Two major problems are associated with generating alternatives. First, there may be a large number of potential alternatives, many of which are not particularly good. However, early in the investigation of the decision problem, it may be difficult to differentiate between the good alternatives and those that are eventually found to be inferior. In such circumstances, inferior options can be identified by screening models which use assumptions too crude for a final evaluation but sensitive enough to eliminate the "bad" alternatives. These models analyze a simplified decision problem by using (1) deterministic rather than probabilistic impact, (2) dominance or "almost dominance" rather than a complete objective function, and (3) constraints. This approach has the effect of eliminating alternatives so the decision tree is pruned to a manageable size. Consequently more time and effort can be expended to appraise carefully the remaining viable alternatives.

A second major problem associated with generating alternatives is that there sometimes seems to be a complete lack of reasonable alternatives. In this case, it is often worthwhile to utilize the objectives of the problem to stimulate creativity. If the objectives are clearly specified, one can describe possible consequences of the problem that are particularly desirable. Working backward, one asks what type of alternatives might achieve such consequences. The process of quantifying the objectives with an objective function (i.e., a utility function) promotes additional thinking about worthwhile alternatives.

The starting point for specifying objectives is the creation of an unstructured list of possible consequences of the alternatives. The consequences must be organized into a set of general concerns. For instance, with many problems involving the siting of large-scale facilities, the general concerns may be environmental impact, economics, socioeconomics, health and safety, and public attitudes. To determine specific objectives, the question may be, for example, what is the environmental impact of a particular alternative. The process of answering such questions is essentially a creative task. Previous studies on related topics and legal and regulatory guidelines should be of significant help in articulating objectives. For problems requiring external review, the potential reviewers (i.e., intervenors, shareholders, or concerned citizens) may contribute useful ideas for objectives.

Assessing Possible Impact of Each Alternative

If it were possible to forecast impacts with precision, the evaluation of alternatives would result in the choice of the best consequence. Unfortunately, the problem is complicated by uncertainties surrounding the eventual consequences. Probability theory can be successfully used in portraying all available information about uncertain quantities. Graphical displays convey information

---

[6] H. Raiffa, *Decision Analysis* (Reading, Mass.: Addison-Wesley, 1968).

concerning the *range* and *likelihood* of possible values of an uncertain quantity. Thus, for each possible alternative, the set of feasible consequences and the probability associated with each choice should be determined. This task can be undertaken by determining a probability distribution function p_j for the set of attributes for each alternative A_i.

There are several methods for quantifying probabilities. Three of the more common approaches are:

1 Use of a standard probability distribution function and assessment of parameters for that function (e.g., mean and standard deviation for a normal distribution);

2 Assessing points on the cumulative probability function (fractile method); and

3 Use of a professional familiar with the subject to specify probabilities at each distinct level.

The simplest way to visualize this structure is through the use of a payoff matrix, illustrated in Figure 15-4.

In addition to addressing the risk and uncertainty aspects of the decision problem, the time in which consequences may occur should be indicated. Through the utilization of skills from the various disciplines to develop and structure models as well as provide information and professional judgments, the interdisciplinary substance is automatically included.

Determining Preferences of Decision Makers

This process involves the creation of a model to assess the alternatives through a structural discussion between analysts and decision makers to quantify possible consequences of a problem. For decisions with single or multiple objectives, rarely is one alternative guaranteed to yield the best available consequence. In fact, there are usually circumstances that could result in undesirable outcomes with any given alternative. Attitudes toward risk and value trade-offs are complicated because there are no right or wrong answers. What is in fact required is a utility function that aggregates the various attitudes toward risk. Thus, the higher the expected utility of a consequence, the more it is preferred.

Determination of the utility function can be segmented into five steps:

1 *Introducing terminology and ideas*—to develop the lines of communication between analysts and decision makers. The goal of the assessment process is consistent representation of preferences for evaluating alternatives.

2 *Determining the general preference structure*—to structure preferences with a model indicating the general functional form of the utility function.

3 *Assessing single-attribute utility functions*—to determine the appropriate risk attitude and then to set the utility corresponding to two consequences, with the utilities of all other consequences relative to the two chosen for the scale.

4 *Evaluating scaling constants*—to assess the relative desirability of specific changes of different attribute levels.

5 *Checking consistency*—to check initial assessments and, if necessary, to alter responses to reflect better the decision makers' basic values.

	Outcomes					B$_j$		
	B$_1$	B$_2$	B$_3$	•	•	•	B$_n$	
Alternatives								
A$_1$	P$_{11}$	P$_{12}$	P$_{13}$	•	•	•	P$_{1n}$	
A$_2$	P$_{21}$	P$_{22}$	P$_{23}$	•	•	•	P$_{2n}$	
A$_3$	P$_{31}$	P$_{32}$	P$_{33}$	•	•	•	P$_{3n}$	
•	•	•	•	•	•	•	•	
A$_i$	•	•	•	•	P$_{ij}$	•	•	
•	•	•	•	•	•	•	•	
A$_m$								

Note: If A$_i$ is chosen and outcome B$_j$ results, then there is a payoff P$_{ij}$.

FIG. 15-4 Payoff Matrix

Cozzolino has suggested the use of risk preference theory to construct an objective measurement of utility-based risk analysis. This new methodology is proposed in order to assess the company's willingness to assume the business risk of a project and maintain a constant risk-tolerance policy.[7]

Evaluating and Comparing Alternatives

Once the decision is structured, the magnitude and probable likelihoods of consequences determined, and the preference structure delineated, all information must be synthesized to assess the alternatives. The expected value for each alternative A$_i$ is:

$$E\,(A_i) = \sum_{j=1}^{n} p_j\,P_{ij}$$

Using the expected values established for each alternative, the decision maker can rank his or her preferences, with the highest expected value representing the most desirable alternatives. It should be noted that the expected utility associated with an alternative is directly dependent on the objectives originally chosen to guide the decision and is a reflection of the degree of achievement of these objectives. As a further step, it is extremely important to conduct sensitivity analysis on the uncertainties associated with the various consequences and different value structures. This task is made easier because both impact and values are quantified with probability distributions and the utility function, respectively.

---

[7] John M. Cozzolino, "A New Method for Risk Analysis," *Sloan Management Review*, Spring 1979, at 53–66.

AREAS FOR STRATEGIC APPLICATIONS

Capital Investment/Divestment

The following case study is a good example of a simulation model used to evaluate a capital investment/divestment decision. The choice between capital investment opportunities is one of the most difficult challenges for a manager. The difficulty does not lie in projecting return on investment opportunities under a given set of assumptions, but rather in the assumptions and their corresponding impact. Each assumption involves a degree of uncertainty, and when these uncertainties are combined, they can multiply to disastrous proportions. Consequently, risk should be evaluated at each possible level of return.

Evaluation of a capital investment project starts with the principle of discounted cash flows as a reasonable means of measuring the rate of return that can be expected in the future for an investment made today. At best, the rate of return information with which the decision maker is provided is based on an average of different opinions with varying reliabilities and different ranges of probability.

Management takes the various levels of possible cash flows, return on investment, and other results of a proposal and estimates the probability of each outcome. For example, a project with an IRR of 8.0 percent, has a 15 percent chance of being a complete failure and a 5 percent chance of earning 25 percent. Thus, the IRR by itself is not sufficient in some instances. The additional information on the chances of substantial loss or gain assists the decision maker by giving a more complete descriptive statement of a project's opportunities.

In the Fleming Chemical case study contained in Appendix I, the company is concerned about one of its divisions, which is considered to be heading for financial trouble. Asphalt prices have been declining and it is expected that profits could be negative within the next couple of years. Suppose that an offer to purchase the division for $41.5 million has been received. Should the company accept?

The key input factors management has decided to use an industry demand, selling prices (average price per ton), market size over the next five years, market share, manufacturing costs per ton, investment required (plant, working capital, additional capacity), operating costs, fixed costs, and useful life of the facility.

Using the assessments in the case, the information is plugged into a computer system that generates pro forma income and cash flow statements under varying assumptions regarding market and cost data. For example, industry demand growth is expected to remain relatively constant (input line 82). Market share growth (line 87) is expected to be at a 4 percent compounded rate over the period. The $24 per ton price (line 92) is used for 1976 estimates. Costs (line 97) are projected to grow at a 1 percent per annum rate. Thus, these four variables comprise the uncertainty variables, with the "best estimate" for each factor utilized. The remaining input is known with a greater degree of certainty.

Based on this one set of inputs, expected annual income, cash flow, and asset values are generated. Using a 5 percent rate (the 1972 Treasury bill rate) and a mid-year point, the present value of the asphalt division (discounted net cash flow plus after tax residual value at the end of year 5) is:

$$PV = \left(\frac{11,715,000}{(1.05)^{0.5}} + \frac{9,364,790}{(1.05)^{1.5}} + \frac{6,841,090}{(1.05)^{2.5}} + \frac{5,110,390}{(1.05)^{3.5}} + \frac{3,496,600}{(1.05)^{4.5}} + \frac{8,567,200}{(1.05)^{5}} \right)$$

$$= \$40,020,000$$

Based on these calculations, the offer received by the company to purchase the division is in excess of $40,020,000, but there may be strategic decisions why the company should not sell. Therefore, consideration must be given to nonfinancial aspects, such as:

- Synergy between divisions;
- Competitive aspects of selling the division, that is, could the competitor gain more by capturing additional market share through the purchase; and
- Future plans of the division.

Note that the model has not made the decision a "go" or "no go" choice. However, it has given the company some financial statistics with which to compare the purchase offer.

This "best estimate" scenario, however, does not assign any probabilities to the riskiness of the values chosen for each of the uncertainty variables. In the next example, 50 runs are conducted wherein the 1976 price per ton is varied between $23 and $25 to test price sensitivity. The remaining three uncertainty variables are held constant. The simple arithmetic average of all present values in this computer run is expressed as a mean ($40,020,000), with the square root of the variance (used as a measure of the dispersion of data) expressed as the standard deviation (1,884,500). Uncertainty can be expressed as a percentage of risk through the use of the CV, which in this case is 4.7 percent.

The next set of important data is the risk profile (distribution of possible outcomes) that the computer generates. Here, five values are given with the corresponding probability of attaining that particular value or less. That is, there is virtually no probability that the present value will be any lower than $37,274,000. On the other end of the scale, there is a 100 percent chance that the value will not exceed $42,766,000. Using these five points as a guide, a graphical representation can be plotted with the cumulative probability represented on the vertical axis and present value on the horizontal axis.

As can be seen in Figure 15-5, there is approximately a 32 percent chance that the present values will exceed the purchase offer of $41 million. Note that the mean of the 50 trials was the same as the initial run, but that the risk element was introduced in this scenario.

The next simulation varies the prices between $22 and $25 per ton for 1976. Using the same methods of calculation, the mean present value is now $39,171,000 with a standard deviation of $2,841,100. The CV is 7.3 percent. Now, however, the probability of achieving a higher present value than the offer to purchase is reduced slightly to approximately 31 percent.

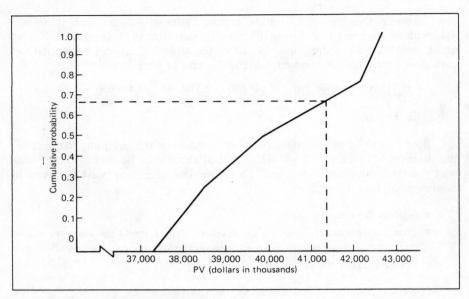

FIG. 15-5 Cumulative Probability Matrix

The final simulation accounts for variability in all four uncertainties: industry demand growth per year, market share growth per year, price per ton, and cost growth per year. The mean present value in this simulation is $39,098,000 with a standard deviation of $3,124,300. The CV is 7.99 percent. The probability of beating the offer is now assessed at approximately 26 percent.

Simulations can be continued by altering one or all of the uncertainty variables to ascertain which ones are more volatile. Through this approach of sensitivity analysis, management of the company can make a more educated decision on whether or not the purchase offer is indeed attractive. Although these models are not optimizing, they do assist the decision maker in his or her analysis by quantifying the inherent risks.

Mergers and Acquisitions

Consider now a large multidivisional firm that has decided to increase the concentration of corporate assets in one area (division X). This decision has been made based on the information provided by the business mix risk/return model. The notion of portfolio theory is to maximize return and minimize risk. The efficient frontier represents combinations of risk/return that maximize investment opportunities. Figure 15-6 indicates that assets in division Y should be redeployed to division X if the company as a whole is to move toward the efficient frontier. Any assets within the frontier could be utilized more effectively. Through this strategy, the firm can increase its expected return on equity without incurring any additional risk. This risk/return subsystem compares the

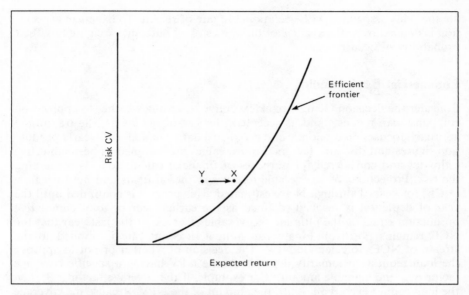

FIG. 15-6 Business Mix Risk/Return Model

standard deviation of the distribution of return on equity with the mean of the distribution. The points on the efficient frontier represent a unique allocation of corporate assets for each level of risk/return. Any point to the left of the frontier is considered an inefficient allocation of resources, as risk/return subsystems can show the user that particular asset allocation which would move the firm to a point on the frontier, which is preferable both from a management and a shareholder's point of view. The choice of which combination of risk and return is most compatible with other corporate goals is a discretionary call, based on the preferences of stockholders and potential investors.

New Product Introduction

A good application of risk analysis is the introduction of a new product line. The first task is to determine the key variables, such as advertising and promotion expense, total product market, market share, operating expenses, and capital investment.

The expected rate of return represents only a few points on a continuous curve of possible combinations of future happenings. Risk is influenced both by the odds on various events occurring and by the magnitude of the rewards or penalties that are involved when they do occur.

The company must then estimate the range of values for each of the factors and, within that range, the probability of occurrence of each value. Next, a random selection of a single value obtained from the distribution for each factor is combined for all factors and a rate of return is computed. This simulation process is repeated until a large enough sample is obtained to define and evaluate the odds associated with each possible rate of return. The average expectation is derived from the average of the values of all outcomes weighted by their probability of occurrence.

Commercial Bank Lending

Consider the decision facing a bank executive regarding whether to approve oil company loan requests and, if accepted, the size of the loan.[8] The traditional approach focuses on economic and geological data coupled with yearly production figures and discount factors. Future values are assigned as best subjective estimates and considered for purposes of financial calculations as containing the risk. Projections of recoverable reserves in the oil fields and net cash flow (NCF) for years 1 through N are estimated. This process is continued until the year of depletion is reached (defined as the earlier year of total cumulative production equaling the ultimate recoverable reserves, or the last year that the NCF remains positive). Finally, an annual discount rate is applied to the stream of NCFs to calculate NPV. The decision of whether or not to approve the loan request customarily depends on the NPV having a specific coverage factor over the loanable amount. For example, if the coverage factor is 3, then the loan cannot exceed one-third the amount of the NPV. Because the coverage factor is a subjective determinant and bears little correlation to the actual risks involved, a more scientific approach would be advantageous.

In a scientific approach, input data is divided into two categories: those factors that contain enough uncertainty to necessitate quantification and those factors that are subject either to little or no uncertainty and can be considered as constants. Some examples of uncertain variables are:

- Geological: area of reservoir, porosity, net productive feet, gas/oil ratio, production decline rate, and permeability; and
- Economic: oil production (year 1 to N), oil price (year 1 to N), gas price, fixed costs, variable costs, and discount factors.

Constants are items such as:

- Working interest
- Royalty interest (gas and oil)
- Carried interest

The uncertainty surrounding the first group of variables is quantified with the use of histograms, and a determination of the dependencies that existed is made. After numerous iterations (with the assistance of a computer), the histogram remains essentially unchanged.

Through the use of probability distribution, loan default can be assessed as well as other possible loan amounts. In addition, it is possible to assess loan

---

[8] For a thorough analysis, see Chi U. Ikoku, "Decision Analysis: How to Make Risk Evaluations," *World Oil*, September 1980, at 71–81, and Oct. 1980, at 157–162; Roger W. Berger, "Use Risk Analysis for Decision Making," *Computer Decisions*, March 1972, at 18–22.

requests from different oil companies. (For a thorough discussion of the use of decision analysis in petroleum exploration, see Newendorp, 1975.)

The preceding examples are only indications of the range of applications for risk analysis. Some other interesting examples include the use of decision analysis for settling legal disputes[9] and enabling managers to assess antitrust implications of product distribution strategies.[10]

BIBLIOGRAPHY

Berger, Roger W., "Use Risk Analysis for Decision Making," Computer Decisions, March 1972, at 18–22.

Bhandari, Narendra C., "Capital Expenditure Decisions Under Risk and Uncertainty," S.A.M. Advanced Management J., Autumn 1981, at 52–61.

Bodily, Samuel E., "When Should You Go To Court?" Harv. Bus. Rev., May-June 1981 at 103–113.

Brown, Rex V., "Do Managers Find Decision Theory Useful?" Harv. Bus. Rev., May-June 1970, at 78–89.

Cozzolino, John M., "A New Method for Risk Analysis," Sloan Management Rev., Spring 1979, at 53–66.

Garfield, Harry A. II, "Antitrust Risk Analysis for Marketers," Harv. Bus. Rev., July-Aug. 1983, at 131–138.

Guth, W. D., "Formulating Organizational Objectives and Strategy," J. Bus. Policy, Autumn 1971, at 24–31.

Guth, W. D., "The Growth and Profitability of the Firm: A Managerial Explanation," J. Bus. Policy, Spring 1972, at 31–36.

Hamilton, William F., and Michael A. Moses, "A Computer-Based Corporate Planning System," Management Science, Oct. 1974, at 148–159.

Hamilton, William F., and Michael A. Moses, "An Optimization Model for Corporate Financial Planning," 22 Operations Res. 677–692 (May-June 1973).

Hertz, David B., "Risk Analysis in Capital Investments," Harv. Bus. Rev., Sept.-Oct. 1979, at 169–181.

Hertz, David B., and Howard Thomas, "Decision and Risk Analysis in a New Product and Facilities Planning Problem," Sloan Management Rev., Winter 1983, at 17–31.

Hertz, David B., and Howard Thomas, Risk Analysis and Its Applications, Chichester, Eng.: John Wiley and Sons, Ltd., 1983.

Hertz, David B., and Howard Thomas, "Risk Analysis: Important New Tool for Business Planning," J. Bus. Strategy, Spring 1983, at 23–29.

---

[9] Samuel E. Bodily, "When Should You Go To Court?" *Harvard Business Review*, May-June 1981, at 103–113.

[10] Harry A. Garfield, II, "Antitrust Risk Analysis for Marketers," *Harvard Business Review*, July-Aug. 1983, at 131–138.

Ikoku, Chi U., "Decision Analysis: How to Make Risk Evaluations," World Oil, Sept. 1980, at 71–81, and Oct. 1980, at 157–162.

Keeney, Ralph L., "Decision Analysis: An Overview," 30 Operations Res. 803–836 (Sept.-Oct. 1982).

Newendorp, Paul D., *Decision Analysis for Petroleum Exploration* (Tulsa, Okla.: Petroleum Publishing Co., 1975).

Raiffa, H., Decision Analysis (Reading, Mass.: Addison-Wesley, 1968).

Ulvila, Jacob W., and Rex V. Brown, "Decision Analysis Comes of Age," Harv. Bus. Rev., Sept.-Oct. 1982, at 130–141.

APPENDIX

A CASE STUDY: FLEMING CHEMICAL COMPANY

The Fleming Chemical Company was concerned about the future of its asphalt division during early 1972. Industry prices had dropped sharply in the past two years and the following forecast had been made for the average price per ton for the next 5 years:

1972	$30.00
1973	28.00
1974	26.00
1975	25.00
1976	24.00

due to the substitution of alternative coating materials for asphalt.

Industry demand in 1971 had been 10,000,000 tons, and was expected to remain relatively constant during the period 1972-76. Fleming's market share of 20% during 1971 was expected to grow at the rate of 4% per year between 1971 and 1976 (to about 24.5% in 1976). Fleming's prices were equal to those of the industry. In 1971 the average price per ton had been $32.

Fleming's manufacturing costs per ton (excluding depreciation) were $22.00 during 1971, of which $17.00 was believed to be variable. Costs were expected to rise at the rate of 1% per year between 1971 and 1976. The divisions' working capital investment normally ran about 10% of sales.

The company's plant capacity was currently 3,000,000 tons per year. This had cost $50,000,000 three years earlier and was being depreciated over a ten-year period by the sum-of-the-years'-digits method. Additional capacity could be purchased in 100,000 ton increments at a cost of $1,500,000 each.

The company added a 10% (of sales) charge to each of its division's expenses for general and administrative expense, of which about half represented contribution above actual costs.

The company paid income taxes at a 48% rate.

CASH FLOW ANALYSIS

```
10 REM
11 REM   PROGRAM GENERATES PRO FORMA INCOME AND CASH FLOW
12 REM   STATEMENTS UNDER VARYING ASSUMPTIONS ABOUT MARKET
AND
13 REM   COSTS. THESE ASSUMPTIONS ARE ENTERED THROUGH DATA
14 REM   STATEMENTS STARTING LINE 77. AND HAVE SINGLE
15 REM   VALUED FORECASTS.
16 REM
17 REM   CASE ★FLEMING CHEMICAL COMPANY★
18 REM   NUMBER ★C41R★
19 REM
50 PRINT "FLEMING CHEMICAL DIVISION ANALYSIS"
75 DATA 0,4,0,0,0,13,3,5,10
77 DATA 1
80 REM INDUSTRY DEMAND GROWTH PER YEAR - C(1)
82 DATA 0
83 DATA 1
85 REM MARKET SHARE GROWTH PER YEAR - C(2)
87 DATA .04
88 DATA 1
90 REM 1976 PRICE PER TON - C(3)
92 DATA 24
93 DATA 1
95 REM COST GROWTH PER YEAR - C(4)
97 DATA .01
98 DATA 1
100 REM 1971 INDUSTRY DEMAND - A(1)
125 DATA 10000000
150 REM 1971 VARIABLE COST PER TON - A(2)
175 DATA 17
200 REM PLANT CAPACITY - A(3)
225 DATA 3000000
250 REM GSA PERCENTAGE - A(4)
275 DATA .10
300 REM WORKING CAPITAL PERCENTAGE - A(5)
325 DATA .10
350 REM DISCOUNT RATE - A(6)
375 DATA .05
380 REM TAX RATE - A(7)
390 DATA .48
400 REM 1971 MARKET SHARE - A(8)
425 DATA .20
450 REM 1971 PRICE PER TON - A(9)
475 DATA 32
500 REM 1971 FIXED COST PER YEAR Y - A(10)
525 DATA 10000000
```

526 REM CASH PCT OF GSA EXPENSE - A(11)
527 DATA .50
528 REM 1971 ENDING WORKING CAPITAL - A(12)
529 DATA 6400000
530 REM PERCENT RECOVERABLE BOOK VALUE - A(13)
531 DATA 1
535 REM ANTICIPATED PRICE PER TON - V(1)
540 DATA 5,30,28,26,25,24
550 REM DEPRECIATION - V(2)
575 DATA 5,6.36364E6,5.45455E6,4.54545E6,3.63535E6,2.72727E6
580 REM UNDEPRECIATED BALANCE - V(3)
585 DATA 5,1.90909E7,1.36364E7,9.09091E6,5.45455E6,2.72727E6

FLEMING CHEMICAL DIVISION ANALYSIS
BASED ON 1 TRIAL
EXPECTED ANNUAL INCOME, CASH FLOW, AND ASSET VALUES
ALL FIGURES EXCEPT PRICE ARE IN THOUSANDS
AVERAGE PRICE PER TON

30.	28.	26.	25.	24.

SALES IN UNITS

2080.	2163.2	2249.7	2339.7	2433.3

SALES REVENUE

62400	60570	58493	58493	58399

COSTS AND EXPENSES

58417	59226	60102	61280	62553

DIVISIONS NET PROFIT BEFORE TAXES

3982.8	1343.6	−1608.8	−2787.6	−4153.8

DIVISIONS NET PROFIT AFTER TAXES

2071.1	698.69	−836.62	−1449.5	−2159.9

CASH FLOW TO CORPORATION FROM OPERATIONS DURING YEAR

11555	9181.7	6633.5	5110.39	3487.2

CHANGE IN WORKING CAPITAL DURING YEAR

−159.99	−183.04	−207.66	−3.99000E-03	−9.3599

NET CASH FLOW TO CORPORATION DURING YEAR

11715	9364.79	6841.09	5110.39	3496.6

RESIDUAL VALUE AFTER TAXES AT YEAR END

−25331	19693	14940	11304	8567.2

PRESENT VALUE AT 5 PCT PER YEAR
                40020

---

77 DATA 50
92 DATA 23,0,24,.5,25

FLEMING CHEMICAL DIVISION ANALYSIS
BASED ON 50 TRIALS

EXPECTED ANNUAL INCOME, CASH FLOW, AND ASSET VALUES
ALL FIGURES EXCEPT PRICE ARE IN THOUSANDS

AVERAGE PRICE PER TON

30.	28.	26.	25.	24.

SALES IN UNITS

2080.	2163.2	2249.7	2339.7	2433.3

SALES REVENUE

62400	60569	58493	58493	58399

COSTS AND EXPENSES

58417	59226	60102	61280	62553

DIVISIONS NET PROFIT BEFORE TAXES

3982.8	1343.6	−1608.8	−2787.6	−4153.8

DIVISIONS NET PROFIT AFTER TAXES

2071.1	698.67	−836.62	−1449.5	−2159.9

CASH FLOW TO CORPORATION FROM OPERATIONS DURING YEAR

11555	9181.59	6633.39	5110.3	3487.2

CHANGE IN WORKING CAPITAL DURING YEAR

−159.99	−183.04	−207.66	−5.77000E-03	−9.3582

NET CASH FLOW TO CORPORATION DURING YEAR

11715	9364.7	6841.09	5110.3	3496.5

RESIDUAL VALUE AFTER TAXES AT YEAR END

25331	19693	14940	11304	8567.09

PRESENT VALUE AT 5 PCT PER YEAR
  MEAN   40020
  STD DEV   1884.5
  RISK PROFILE
  VALUE   PROB OF VALUE OR LESS
  37274   0
  38494   .25
  39715   .5
  42156   .75
  42766   1

---

77 DATA 50
92 DATA 22,0,24,.5,25

FLEMING CHEMICAL DIVISION ANALYSIS
BASED ON 50 TRIALS

EXPECTED ANNUAL INCOME, CASH FLOW, AND ASSET VALUES
ALL FIGURES EXCEPT PRICE ARE IN THOUSANDS

AVERAGE PRICE PER TON
29.944	27.889	25.833	24.777	23.722

SALES IN UNITS
2080.	2163.2	2249.7	2339.7	2433.3

SALES REVENUE
62284	60329	58117	57972	57723

COSTS AND EXPENSES
58405	59202	60064	61228	62485

DIVISIONS NET PROFIT BEFORE TAXES
3878.7	1127.1	−1946.5	−3256.	−4762.6

DIVISIONS NET PROFIT AFTER TAXES
2016.9	586.1	−1012.2	−1693.	−2476.5

CASH FLOW TO CORPORATION FROM OPERATIONS DURING YEAR
11495	9057.	6439.	4840.8	3136.8

CHANGE IN WORKING CAPITAL DURING YEAR
−171.56	−195.53	−221.13	−14.514	−24.969

NET CASH FLOW TO CORPORATION DURING YEAR
11666	9252.5	6660.2	4855.3	3161.7

RESIDUAL VALUE AFTER TAXES AT YEAR END
25319	19669	14903	11252	8499.5

PRESENT VALUE AT 5 PCT PER YEAR
```
  MEAN        39171
  STD DEV     2841.1
```
RISK PROFILE

VALUE	PROB OF VALUE OR LESS
34527	0
36968	.25
39410	.5
42156	.75
42766	1

```
82 DATA − .01,0,0,.5,.01
87 DATA .03,0,.04,.5,.05
92 DATA 22,0,24,.5,25
97 DATA .005,0,.010,.5,.015
```

FLEMING CHEMICAL DIVISION ANALYSIS
BASED ON 50 TRIALS

EXPECTED ANNUAL INCOME, CASH FLOW, AND ASSET VALUES
ALL FIGURES EXCEPT PRICE ARE IN THOUSANDS

AVERAGE PRICE PER TON
29.944	27.889	25.833	24.777	23.722

SALES IN UNITS

| 2081.6 | 2166.7 | 2255.4 | 2347.8 | 2444.3 |

SALES REVENUE

| 62332 | 60424 | 58261 | 58170 | 57978 |

COSTS AND EXPENSES

| 58459 | 59317 | 60249 | 61493 | 62839 |

DIVISIONS NET PROFIT BEFORE TAXES

| 3872.3 | 1107.5 | −1987.9 | −3322.3 | −4861.7 |

DIVISIONS NET PROFIT AFTER TAXES

| 2013.6 | 575.92 | −1033.6 | −1727.6 | −2528. |

CASH FLOW TO CORPORATION FROM OPERATIONS DURING YEAR

| 11494 | 9051.59 | 6424.7 | 4816.2 | 3098. |

CHANGE IN WORKING CAPITAL DURING YEAR

| −166.82 | −190.7 | −216.34 | −9.0747 | −19.264 |

NET CASH FLOW TO CORPORATION DURING YEAR

| 11661 | 9242.39 | 6641.09 | 4825.3 | 3117.3 |

RESIDUAL VALUE AFTER TAXES AT YEAR END

| 25324 | 19679 | 14917 | 11272 | 8525. |

PRESENT VALUE AT 5 PCT PER YEAR

| MEAN | 39098 |
| STD DEV | 3124.3 |

RISK PROFILE

VALUE	PROB OF VALUE OR LESS
33183	0
36795	.25
39681	.5
41685	.75
46809	1

16

Financial Tools for Strategy Evaluation

RONALD G. QUINTERO

*Senior Manager, Management Consulting Department,
Peat, Marwick, Mitchell & Company
Adjunct Professor, Corporate Finance, New School for Social Research*

USING FINANCIAL TOOLS

How do you support the selection of one alternative over another? How do you determine whether your company has the financial wherewithal to undertake a given project? How do you measure and evaluate performance? Financial tools provide objective means of analyzing these and other issues. Typical applications of financial tools include:

- Assessing the performance of a product, subsidiary, division, company, industry, or competitor
- Determining capital requirements
- Lease/purchase analysis
- Acquisition and divestiture analysis
- Product pricing
- Management evaluation
- Predicting business failure
- Deciding whether to make or buy a product
- Capital expenditure analysis
- Bond ratings

Financial tools transform financial statements from a myriad of data into useful information that can aid decision making. Any time a reader of financial statements uses them to draw certain conclusions, he or she is performing financial analysis. Financial tools aid the decision maker by providing an independent and objective means of supporting decision making. If properly used, financial tools can provide an unbiased assessment of past and future performance.

The Value Line Investment Survey, which for years has been recognized as an outstanding investment tool, is based entirely on financial and statistical algorithms, calculated on the computer. *Value Line* founder Arnold Bernhard claims that the times that he has deviated from the computer output, investment selections have frequently resulted in substandard performance. Consequently, his service tries to remain free of human bias by relying solely on the output provided by its investment tools, and to date it has been highly successful. Although this represents an extreme point of view, it reinforces the benefit of well-selected and properly-interpreted financial tools.

The financial tools on which this chapter focuses include financial ratio analysis, financial projections, capital investment evaluation methods, and valuation for acquisitions and venture capital. Some variation of these tools that can be useful in financial analysis will be discussed as well. All of these tools are closely related, as shown in Figure 16-1. Financial statements provide the raw data used to perform ratio analysis and to analyze the quality of presentation. Ratios, in turn, are valuable in financial projections, which in turn, are the basis for evaluating investment opportunities. Valuation analysis also relies on ratios.

Although financial analyses are invaluable elements in contemporary managerial decision making, they should not supplant good judgment. They should

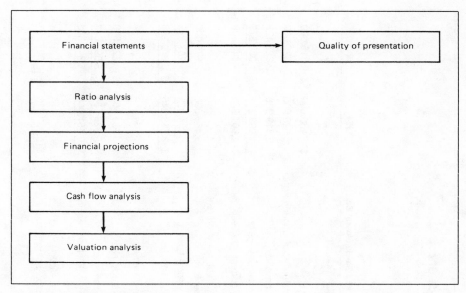

FIG 16-1   Integrating Financial Tools

enhance the decision making process, rather than replace it. An understanding of financial tools, including the assumptions on which they are based and their applications and limitations, can lead to better decisions and better results.

UNDERSTANDING FINANCIAL STATEMENTS

The concept of GIGO—garbage in, garbage out—is especially true in financial analysis. In order to use and interpret financial data properly, one must understand the data and how it was compiled. Essential issues that must be considered include data quality and integrity, reporting period, business unit, and accounting policies. The treatment of these issues and the assumptions and methodologies employed in compiling data can have a substantial impact on the resulting data.

The basic financial statements referred to in every auditor's opinion include the balance sheet, the income statement, the statement of changes in financial position, and the statement of stockholders' equity. The balance sheet is a "snapshot" of corporate financial position at a specific date, indicating assets, liabilities, and net worth. The income statement shows the revenues and expenses of the enterprise for a specified period. The statement of changes in financial position details the cash flow that is generated for a specified period. Annual changes in net worth are detailed in the statement of stockholders' equity. Examples of these statements are shown in Tables 16-1, 16-2, 16-3, and 16-4.

TABLE 16-1 Sample Balance Sheet

XYZ CORPORATION
BALANCE SHEET
December 31, 1984 and 1983

Assets	1984	1983
Cash	$ 605,324	$ 944,871
Accounts receivable, net of $75,000 allowance for doubtful accounts	3,727,018	3,129,256
Inventory (LIFO)	4,018,627	3,254,508
Prepaid expenses and other current assets	316,253	402,619
Total current assets	$ 8,667,222	$ 7,731,254
Property, plant and equipment, net of accumulated depreciation	4,109,614	3,241,828
Investment in ABC Co.	699,951	–
Goodwill, net of amortization	475,000	500,000
Other assets	1,057,526	1,223,719
Total assets	$15,009,313	$12,696,801

Liabilities and Stockholders' Equity	1984	1983
Liabilities		
Notes payable	$ 460,000	$ 315,000
Current maturities of long-term debt	525,000	325,000
Accounts payable	2,519,938	2,325,423
Accrued expenses	1,099,282	1,080,877
Total current liabilities	$ 4,604,220	$ 4,046,300
Long-term debt, net of current installments	3,450,000	2,575,000
Deferred income taxes	304,025	257,968
Total liabilities	$ 8,358,245	$ 6,879,268
Stockholders' equity		
Common stock, no par	$ 724,500	$ 724,500
Retained earnings	5,926,568	5,093,033
Total stockholders' equity	6,651,068	5,817,533
Total liabilities and stockholders' equity	$15,009,313	$12,696,801

TABLE 16-2   Sample Income Statement

XYZ CORPORATION
INCOME STATEMENT
For the Years Ended December 31, 1984 and 1983

	1984	1983
Net sales	$22,579,488	$18,923,504
Cost of goods sold	16,121,754	13,189,682
Gross profit	$ 6,457,734	$ 5,733,822
General and administrative expenses	2,647,321	2,405,804
Selling expenses	1,845,997	1,499,318
Operating profit	$ 1,964,416	$ 1,828,700
Interest expense, net	496,924	351,284
Gain on sale of fixed assets	111,897	–
Equity in earnings of ABC Co.	72,438	–
Income before taxes	$ 1,651,827	$ 1,477,416
Income taxes	502,792	593,921
Net income	$ 1,149,035	$ 883,495

The Balance Sheet

The balance sheet has been the financial statement to which the greatest amount of attention is paid. It is the first financial statement mentioned in the standard auditor's report, and is often the only financial statement submitted to trade creditors. It is the "primal" financial statement, evidencing the most important corporate objective: survival. A company can have an outstanding product, idea, market share, sales force, or many other desirable traits; however, if it has insufficient assets to meet liabilities, its existence may be jeopardized. Conversely, a mediocre company may wallow in mediocrity for years if it has a strong balance sheet.

The balance sheet is of great importance to creditors because it is an indication of what assets are available to satisfy debts. To the extent that the balance sheet reflects a company's prospects for survival, it also is of interest to shareholders, employees, customers, suppliers, competitors, and the community or communities in which the company is located. Management uses of balance sheet data include:

- Monitoring assets available for current and long-term needs
- Identifying collections of accounts receivable or measuring the turnover of inventory
- Determining capital requirements
- Analyzing debt capacity
- Evaluating efficiency of assets employed
- Identifying leverageable or salable assets
- Analyzing insurance needs

TABLE 16-3 Sample Statement of Changes in Financial Position

XYZ CORPORATION
STATEMENT OF CHANGES IN FINANCIAL POSITION
For the Years Ended December 31, 1984 and 1983

	1984	1983
Working capital provided		
Net income	$1,149,035	$ 883,495
Items not affecting working capital		
Depreciation	465,291	309,421
Amortization	25,000	25,000
Deferred taxes	46,057	39,274
Gain on sale of equipment	(111,897)	–
Equity in earnings of ABC Co.	(72,438)	–
Working capital provided from operations	$1,501,048	$1,257,190
Long-term borrowings	1,400,000	225,000
Proceeds from sale of equipment	167,000	–
Proceeds from stock options exercised	–	75,000
Total working capital provided	$3,068,548	$1,557,190
Working capital used		
Repayment of long-term debt	$ 325,000	$ 316,000
Additions to property, plant, and equipment	1,422,487	364,852
Purchase of minority interest in ABC Co.	627,513	–
Payment of cash dividends	315,500	283,950
	$2,690,500	$ 964,802
Increase in working capital	$ 378,048	$ 592,388
Analysis of changes in working capital		
Increase (decrease) in current assets		
Cash	$ (339,547)	$ 227,153
Accounts receivable	597,762	284,528
Inventory	764,119	308,196
Prepaid expenses and other current assets	(86,366)	62,731
	$ 935,968	$ 882,608
Increase (decrease) in current liabilities		
Notes payable	$ 145,000	$ (27,000)
Current maturities of long-term debt	200,000	15,000
Accounts payable	194,515	133,219
Accrued expenses	18,405	169,001
	$ 557,920	$ 290,220
Increase in working capital	$ 378,048	$ 592,388

TABLE 16-4 Sample Statement of Stockholders' Equity

XYZ CORPORATION
STATEMENT OF STOCKHOLDERS' EQUITY
For the Years Ended December 31, 1984 and 1983

	Common Stock (No Par)		Retained Earnings
	Shares	Amounts	
Balance, December 31, 1982	1,562,500	$649,500	$4,493,488
Stock options exercised	15,000	75,000	–
Cash dividends ($0.18)	–	–	(283,950)
Net income, 1983	–	–	883,495
Balance, December 31, 1983	1,577,500	$724,500	$5,093,033
Cash dividends ($0.20)	–	–	(315,500)
Net income, 1984	–	–	1,149,035
Balance, December 1984	1,577,500	$724,500	$5,926,568

Although generally accepted accounting principles (GAAP) prescribe permissible accounting methods, they allow sufficient flexibility such that a misleading impression of financial condition may be derived from the balance sheet if the accounting method that was used is not taken into consideration. Asset and liability balances can vary widely depending on the accounting method employed. Also, the character of certain assets and liabilities can vary substantially among enterprises. Dollar balances alone can belie the true financial condition of a business concern. Examples of issues relating to balance sheets that should be analyzed are shown in Table 16-5.

The Income Statement

Once we know how much a company is worth, the question becomes how much money it made. The earnings of a company directly affect its net worth, since net worth is the cumulative product of historical earnings.

Companies commonly compile an annual income statement, with quarterly or monthly updates. The income statement represents an estimate of financial performance over a specific interval of time. In his landmark volume on auditing theory,[1] Dicksee reduced all accounting to the "single voyage" model. According to this paradigm, a ship is acquired, goods are bought, and a crew is hired in order to transport the goods to another port, at which time everything will be liquidated and the profits will be divided among the partners. The voyage could last months or even years. Revenues are realized only at the end of the voyage, when the goods are sold; meanwhile, most of the expenses are incurred before the voyage ever gets under way. Assuming that

---

[1] Lawrence R. Dicksee, *Auditing: A Practical Manual for Auditors* (London: Gee & Co., 1892).

TABLE 16-5 Major Analytical Areas: Balance Sheet

Balance Sheet Item	Analytical Area	Implications
General	• Independent verification	• Relative degrees of assurance, in descending order are audited financial statement, review, and write-up.
	• Auditor's opinion	• Financial statement integrity depends on whether opinion is unqualified, qualified, restricted, or adverse.
	• Accrual vs. cash basis	• Cash basis, often used for federal income taxes, may distort actual financial condition.
	• Seasonal variations	• May suggest different levels of assets and liabilities are required.
	• Operating vs. nonoperating	• Assets not integral to the business should be analyzed separately.
	• Payment schedule	• Useful in determining means by which they will be satisfied.
	• Valuation method	• Historical cost, current value, replacement cost, general price level accounting, or liquidation level can result in significant variations.
Assets	• Restrictions	• May be pledged, collateralized, or subject of pending sale; hence not freely available for future use.
Cash	• Dedicated uses	• Debt agreements, bank restrictions, and impending liabilities may limit alternative uses.
Marketable securities	• Cost or market value	• Net proceeds are market value, less costs of disposal and taxes.
	• Liquidity	• Large blocks of debt or equity securities frequently cannot be sold at prevailing market prices.
Accounts receivable	• Aging	• Older balances may present higher risk of noncollection.
Bad debt allowance	• Percentage or specific identification	• May be inadequate.
Inventory	• Valuation method	• LIFO, FIFO, or average cost can result in significant variations.
	• Marketability	• Historical cost may exceed market value.
Fixed assets	• Fair market value	• Often varies substantially from historical cost.
	• Obsolescence	• Usable equipment may be technologically obsolete.
	• Depreciation	• Accelerated methods such as sum-of-the-years'-digits and double declining balance result in more rapid write-offs, hence, lower balances and earnings than straight-line methods, as can estimated useful life.
Unconsolidated investments	• Ownership	• Leased assets are capitalized, but not owned by the company.
	• Valuation method	• Equity accounting value may differ substantially from fair market value.
Intangible assets	• Amortization	• Method and estimated useful life affect value.
Liabilities and Stockholders' Equity		
Deferred taxes	• Rate of increase	• A growing company may never pay the net liability unless the "crossover point" is reached.
Long-term debt	• Interest rate	• Fair market value may differ from amortized cost, depending on relation between current and stated rate.
Convertible securities	• Conversion prospects	• May signal a potential modification to capital structure.
Treasury stock	• Costing method	• May be accounted for at cost or par value.

there must be a periodic accounting of voyage earnings, how do we estimate the portion of revenues and expenses attributable to each segment of the voyage?

This is the fundamental challenge of accounting: matching revenues and expenses. There is little dispute as to voyage earnings after the voyage has been completed and all accounts have been settled. Earnings are simply whatever is left over. The problem is that in most real-life situations, the voyage is still in progress.

There are two fundamental methods of accounting for earnings: cash basis and accrual basis. Cash-basis accounting is a simple tally of cash receipts and cash payments. It is commonly used in service businesses and by individuals and some corporations for filing income taxes. It is useful for depicting the financial reality of cash receipts and payments, which over the long run is the true measure of profitability. The problem with cash-basis accounting is that it fails to recognize that some revenues require several years to be realized, and some expenditures provide benefits that will last for several accounting periods. For this reason, GAAP requires in most instances that audited financial statements be presented on an accrual basis, which allocates revenues and expenses to the periods contributing to the income or benefiting from the expenses. Hence, a distinction is created between the realization and recognition of revenues and expenses.

Accrual accounting comes closer to approximating economic reality than accounting on a cash basis. Most financial data is prepared on an accrual basis. Major capital assets such as buildings or equipment clearly provide benefits that will last over several periods, and their expense should be charged accordingly. The problem lies in deciding what constitutes a reasonable basis for recognizing income and expenses. This problem is further complicated by the latitude that exists in income and expense recognition. The examples of income and expense recognition alternatives shown in Table 16-6 provide the potential for 165,888 different net earnings figures. Companies that are identical in every respect can report significantly differing results depending on how they recognize income and expenses. This does not mean that accounting data is simply a useless collection of numbers. Rather, it means that accounting data should be subjected to careful scrutiny before any conclusions are drawn. Accounting data is like a foreign language in that the substance of a message is the same irrespective of the language in which it is given. The economic reality of a company is largely unaffected by the accounting methods employed. The key challenge in using accounting data is correct interpretation.

The Statement of Changes in Financial Position

The income statement provides only a partial view of corporate performance over a given interval of time. It reflects revenues and expenses that have been recognized. However, as discussed above, there is often a disparity between the point at which revenues and expenses occur and the point at which they are recognized. This disparity is reconciled through the statement of changes in financial position, which bridges the gap between the recognition of income and the flow of funds. Also referred to as the statement of sources and application of funds, sources and uses statement, statement of changes, and funds flow

TABLE 16-6 Income/Expense Recognition Alternatives

Account	Method	Comments
Revenues	• Sales method • Installment sales method • Production method • Percentage-of-completion method	• Recognize at time of sale. • Recognize when payment is received. • Recognize when product is completed (applicable to extractive industries). • Proportional recognition over performance of a contract.
Sales returns and allowances	• Specific identification • Percentage of sales	• Appropriate for low volume and/or high-ticket items. • Assumes a discernible pattern.
Inventory cost	• First in, first out (FIFO) • Last in, first out (LIFO) • Average cost • Specific identification	• Assumes items sold in the order they are received. • Costing in reverse order to receipt. • Most accurate method.
Inventory write-downs	• Minimize write-downs • Realistic write-downs • Maximize write-downs	• Maximizes reported earnings. • Minimizes taxable income.
Overhead	• Absorption costing • Immediate recognition	• Allocates to each unit of production. • Assumes that overhead is an expense of the period.
Depreciation	• Straight line • Double declining balance • Sum-of-the-years'-digits • Units of production	• Assumes equal annual depreciation. • Assumes assets depreciate more rapidly in earlier years. • Assumes assets depreciate more rapidly in earlier years. • Depreciation is related to output.
Depreciation/amortization period	• Minimize write-off • Realistic write-off • Maximize write-off	• Maximizes reported earnings. • Minimizes taxable income.
Warranty/product service expense	• Percentage-of-sales method • Pay-as-you-go	• Matches future expense with period revenues are generated. • May contribute to earnings volatility.
Patents, maintenance, construction interest costs	• Immediate recognition • Capitalization	• Based on cash payments. • Assumes benefits in future years.
Officer/shareholder compensation and fringe benefits	• Minimize • "Fair" • Maximize	• Done only where necessary or to increase selling price of company. • Minimizes taxable income; common in closely held businesses.
Bad-debt expense	• Percentage of sales • Percentage of receivables • Specific identification	• Assumes a discernible pattern. • Assumes a discernible pattern. • Appropriate for low volume/high account balance activity.
Investment tax credit	• Flow-through method • Capitalization	• Immediate recognition. • Tax benefit coincides with asset usage.

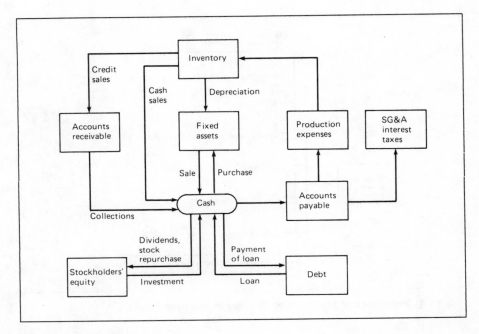

FIG. 16-2 Flow of Funds

statement, it provides the details of funds (working capital and long-term capital) received and used by the business (see Figure 16-2). Viewed by many analysts as the most revealing financial statement, the statement of changes provides the best indication of "cash" income. It can readily be converted into a
true cash-flow statement by using cash as the bottom line instead of using
change in working capital (see Table 16-13).

Another important attribute of the statement of changes is that it shows
how the company is spending its capital resources and where the money comes
from. The liquidity of the company is more closely related to the working capital generating capacity shown in the statement of changes than it is to the
amount of income shown in the income statement. Cash-flow projections and
discounted cash-flow analysis are usually made using the format of the statement of changes.

The importance of the statement of changes in relation to the other financial statements is best seen in Figure 16-3. To a greater extent than any other
financial statement, the statement of changes is fed by and flows into each of
the other basic financial statements. Using the prior year's balance sheet and
the income statement, it is usually possible to create a current balance sheet
and statement of stockholders' equity. The interrelationship of the financial
statements demonstrates the primacy of the statement of changes. And, it reinforces the importance of viewing the financial statements as an interdependent
unit rather than as individual perspectives of financial performance.

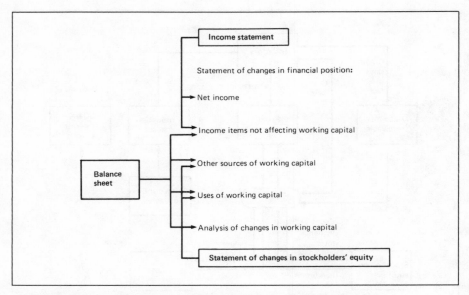

FIG. 16-3 Importance of Statement of Changes in Financial Position

The Statement of Stockholders' Equity

The statement of stockholders' equity depicts the net worth of the corporation. Stockholders' equity is the residual of assets, less liabilities, at the values presented in the financial statements. It should not be confused with the value of the company, since the two figures can be quite different. There are often substantial disparities between the traded market value of publicly held companies and their stockholders' equity, or book value. An example of this disparity is shown in Table 16-7.

The significance of stockholders' equity varies according to the group looking at the figures:

- To creditors, stockholders' equity represents a "safety cushion," since it shows the amount by which assets exceed liabilities.
- To shareholders, stockholders' equity represents the net investment in the company, and it reflects the original cost of their stock and retained earnings. The amount of stockholders' equity is often referred to as the capitalization of the company.
- To potential investors, stockholders' equity represents the net cost of entering into the business, at historical accounting costs. To the extent that the cost to potential investors of acquiring an interest in the company exceeds this amount or their pro rata share, stockholders' equity is often deemed to represent the downside risk of their investment.

The stockholder is more directly affected by transactions recorded in the statement of stockholders' equity than by those recorded in any other financial

TABLE 16-7   Examples of Disparities Between Book Value and Market Value, October 31, 1983

Company	Market Value/ Net Worth
American Telephone & Telegraph	1.31
Aetna Life & Casualty	0.84
Beatrice Foods	1.43
Boise Cascade	0.83
Bristol Myers	4.18
Chase Manhattan	0.54
Detroit Edison	0.83
Dun & Bradstreet	6.87
DuPont	1.43
B.F. Goodrich	0.60
W.R. Grace	1.03
Gulf Oil	0.81
Hewlett Packard	3.37
International Business Machines	3.81
R.H. Macy	3.04
McDonald's	2.49
Norfolk Southern	1.19
J.C. Penney	1.41
Procter & Gamble	2.11
St. Regis Paper	0.78
Teledyne	1.40
U.S. Steel	0.49
Xerox	0.94

Source: Merrill Lynch, Pierce, Fenner & Smith, Inc.

statement. Following are some examples of transactions recorded in the statement of stockholders' equity and their significance to stockholders:

- Changes in stockholders' equity normally result from earnings, losses, dividends, and changes in the number of shares outstanding.
- Earnings performance is perhaps the single most important factor affecting the value of stock.
- Prices are often referred to in terms of a multiple of earnings.
- Dividends and other distributions are the only cash flows that the stockholder receives from the company.
- Changes in the number of shares outstanding can signal changes in ownership control and dilution of ownership and/or earnings.

The statement of stockholders' equity reveals how the company is funding operations, exclusive of debt. It is important to note whether a company is "building up" its balance sheet (i.e., increasing net worth) as a result of profitable operations or through issuance of additional stock. The latter situation could indicate an inability of the company to fund operations internally, and the need to continue to issue additional stock in the future. Dividend payments may be evidence of superior earning capacity producing excess cash not required for reinvestment, or they may result from a policy necessitating periodic dividend distributions that essentially amount to non-tax-deductible expenses. Increasingly, analysts are saying that dividend payments are a confession by the corporation that it has nothing better to do with its financial resources. Average after-tax corporate returns on equity have generally ranged between 14 percent and 16 percent in recent years. It would therefore seem more economical to reinvest earnings in productive projects than to provide taxable dividend distributions on which investors normally earn less on a pretax basis. Many profitable companies that have been superior performers in the stock market pay few or no dividends. Consider the example in Table 16-8.

This example shows actual amounts experienced by corporations and investors. Obviously, the no-dividend policy provides the greatest benefit to shareholders.

Defining the Basis for Presentation

Financial statements can be prepared for any economic unit. This can include a single product, product line, department, division, subsidiary, geographical region, company, industry, or the entire national economy. The ease of preparing financial statements will depend on the availability and quality of underlying data. Often, the needed data is unavailable or requires so many assumptions as to be of dubious reliability. Competitor and industry profiles are frequently difficult to compile since most companies are privately owned and thus are not required to disclose financial information publicly. This is the case for small segments of some publicly held companies as well. Frequently, the financial data that is available fails to reveal the data needed. If you are preparing an analysis of how your company's labor costs compare to those of competing companies, for example, you may find that even if your competitors publicly disclose financial data, their labor costs are buried in the costs of sales and general and administrative expenses. Efforts to obtain such data should not be discouraged, since some information is better than none. And, there are often industry trade groups or data services that compile industry data. However, company and intra-company data generally is easier to secure than data from other companies.

In compiling data for a portion of a corporate entity, the question of allocating common costs arises. Overhead costs may be allocated among businesses on the basis of relative sales, assets, units of production, net investment, square footage of occupancy, or number of employees, to name a few of the commonly used methods. Each form of allocation is likely to produce different financial results. The results may vary so widely that they make a difference between whether a product seems profitable or not profitable. Business decisions and management bonuses are often based on information generated, in part, using allocated costs. The cost allocation system can therefore have significant strategic and behavioral implications. There is no simple solution for the com-

TABLE 16-8 Net Economic Benefit to Shareholders of Alternative Dividend Policies

	Dividend	No dividend
Pro rata income	$100	$100
Corporate income tax	50	50
Pro rata net income	50	50
Dividend	50	–
Individual income tax	25	–
Available for investment	$ 25 (a)	$ 50 (b)
Pretax return	8%	30%
Pretax income	$2.00	$15.00
Applicable tax	1.00	7.50
Economic benefit	$1.00	$ 7.50

(a) Available to individual
(b) Available to company

plicated issue of cost allocation. As a general rule, however, cost allocations should be designed to be both equitable and useful.

The use to which a financial statement will be put is an important factor in deciding on the amount of detail to be included in the statement. The format of financial data distributed externally is usually governed by GAAP and/or regulatory requirements. However, the format and the amount of detail in internal financial statements should be designed to facilitate decision making. The nature and content of financial information depends on the audience. The president of a diversified company may only require financial statements that provide an overview of the results of each business segment, while the executive in charge of the business segment may require much more detailed segmental financial data. Financial data should clarify rather than to obfuscate financial performance. It should be informative rather than exhaustive, and it should be user-oriented rather than accountant-oriented.

Another important issue in planning financial statements is distinguishing between variable costs (also referred to as incremental, marginal, or out-of-pocket costs), fixed costs, and total costs. Variable costs include only the costs of additional output, while fixed costs remain constant on a short-term basis, and are unaffected by output. Total costs reflect the combined total of fixed and variable costs, as shown in Figure 16-4. As long as the revenues derived from each incremental unit of production exceed the variable cost, it can be profitable to pursue production.

For example, suppose an opportunity exists to use excess capacity to produce for a variable cost of $1.75 per unit an item that we can sell for $2. If the

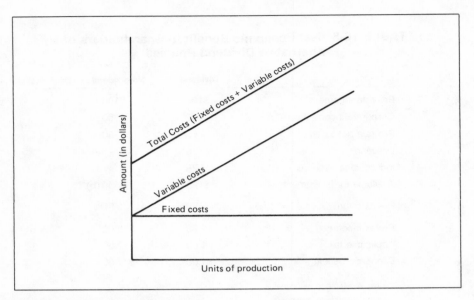

FIG. 16-4   Fixed and Variable Costs

cost allocation system would normally allocate $.30 of fixed costs to each unit
of production, the total cost per unit would be $2.05, seemingly making this an
unprofitable item to produce. However, since fixed costs are unaffected by
whether or not one elects to produce the item, it is evident that producing the
$2 item will result in an incremental profit of $.25 for each unit of production
that the company would not otherwise realize. In this case, variable costing and
total costing provide mixed signals that could lead to conflicting managerial
decisions. For opportunities that arise to employ unused capacity, incremental
analysis may lead to valuable business opportunities.

A final issue to consider in planning financial statements is the impact of
changing prices and costs. For example, the fact that a company's sales have
doubled in the last ten years is hardly praiseworthy if inflation has increased by
150 percent in the same period. If inflation is relatively modest, then historical
financial data provides a useful benchmark for comparing annual results. However, in highly inflationary periods, annual comparisons can be almost meaningless.

Three methods of accounting have been developed to reflect the impact
of changing prices: general price level accounting, current value accounting,
and replacement cost accounting. General price level accounting is required
as an additional disclosure of all large publicly held companies meeting certain financial criteria. Under this method, adjustments are made to certain
assets, liabilities, and income statement items so that they may be presented
on a common price level basis, as determined through the application of the
Consumer Price Index for All Urban Consumers. Current value accounting
and replacement cost accounting purport to do the same thing, except they

use current values and replacement costs, respectively, as their measurement benchmark. Differences between earnings reported according to these methods and historical earnings constitute the gains and losses attributable to price level changes.

These methods are useful in that they provide a means of presenting financial data in a manner that will diffuse the impact of inflation. Nevertheless, they have been slow to receive general acceptance, due to the difficulty of identifying appropriate benchmarks that fairly and accurately reflect changing prices on a uniform basis. Historical-dollar financial statements have the advantages of being relatively straightforward and more easily verifiable. They adhere more closely to basic accounting theory, and their cash-flow patterns are based on realized transactions. Furthermore, the majority of assets and liabilities in most companies reflect fairly current costs, and are accordingly valued close to current price levels. As long as most managers have been trained in and are accustomed to using historical-dollar financial statements, and as long as there are tolerable levels of inflation, there will be a reluctance to embrace accounting methods that reflect inflation.

FINANCIAL RATIO ANALYSIS

Financial statements report the aggregate results of operations and financial conditions of a company at a specific point in time. Absolute numbers can signal important trends or can provide material for public relations releases (for example, "We are proud to announce that during the past year, total sales for our company exceeded one hundred million dollars"). However, by themselves, the numbers have limited significance. Raw financial data is of little value unless there is a frame of reference in which to view it. Financial ratio analysis provides that frame of reference.

We intuitively perform financial ratio analysis any time we read a financial statement. Relationships among accounts that are noticed or trends that are observed are forms of nonquantitative financial ratio analysis. The more formal procedure of financial ratio analysis provides a basis for enhancing or supplanting intuitive judgment.

Financial ratio analysis can be used to compare the current year's financial data to that of prior years or future years, competitors on an individual or aggregate basis, or businesses within an entire industry. Within a company, it can be used to evaluate the performance of divisions, subsidiaries, departments, product lines, or individual products. Since it is based on ratios rather than on absolute numbers, financial ratio analysis mitigates the problem of comparing business units of different sizes. The basic categories of financial ratios include composition ratios, liquidity ratios, leverage ratios, activity ratios, profitability ratios, and trend analysis. They are each described in the following sections, with sample computations shown in Tables 16-9 and 16-10 (on pages 16-18 through 16-20) using financial data from XYZ Corporation in Tables 16-1 through 16-4.

TABLE 16-9   Financial Ratio Analysis of XYZ Corporation

Ratio	Components	Amounts as of or for Year Ended December 31, 1984 (in dollars)	Financial Ratio
Liquidity ratios			
Current	$\dfrac{\text{Current assets}}{\text{Current liabilities}}$	$\dfrac{8{,}667{,}222}{4{,}604{,}220}$	1.9
Quick	$\dfrac{\text{Current assets} - \text{Inventory}}{\text{Current liabilities}}$	$\dfrac{8{,}667{,}222 - 4{,}018{,}627}{4{,}604{,}220}$	1.0
Leverage ratios			
Debt	$\dfrac{\text{Total debt}}{\text{Total assets}}$	$\dfrac{8{,}358{,}245}{15{,}009{,}313}$	0.56
Debt/equity	$\dfrac{\text{Total debt}}{\text{Equity}}$	$\dfrac{8{,}358{,}245}{6{,}651{,}068}$	1.26
Long-term debt/equity	$\dfrac{\text{Long-term debt}}{\text{Equity}}$	$\dfrac{3{,}450{,}000}{6{,}651{,}068}$	0.52
Times interest earned	$\dfrac{\text{Earnings before interest and taxes}}{\text{Interest}}$	$\dfrac{1{,}651{,}827 + 496{,}924}{496{,}924}$	4.3
Activity ratios			
Accounts receivable turnover	$\dfrac{\text{Credit sales}}{\text{Average accounts receivable}}$	$\dfrac{22{,}579{,}488}{(3{,}727{,}018 + 3{,}129{,}256)/2}$	6.6
Average collection period	$\dfrac{\text{Average accounts receivable}}{\text{Credit sales}} \times 365$	$\dfrac{(3{,}727{,}018 + 3{,}129{,}256)/2}{22{,}579{,}488} \times 365$	55.4 days
Inventory turnover	$\dfrac{\text{Cost of goods sold}}{\text{Average inventory}}$	$\dfrac{16{,}121{,}754}{(4{,}018{,}627 + 3{,}254{,}508)/2}$	4.4

Days' sales in inventory	$\dfrac{\text{Inventory}}{\text{Cost of goods sold}} \times 365 = \dfrac{(4,018,627 + 3,254,508)/2}{16,121,754}$	82.3 days
Working capital turnover	$\dfrac{\text{Sales}}{\text{Average working capital}} = \dfrac{22,579,488}{(4,063,002 + 3,684,954)/2}$	5.8
Working capital per dollar's sales	$\dfrac{\text{Average working capital}}{\text{Sales}} = \dfrac{(4,063,002 + 3,684,954)/2}{22,579,488}$	0.17
Fixed asset turnover	$\dfrac{\text{Sales}}{\text{Average net fixed assets}} = \dfrac{22,579,488}{(4,019,614 + 3,241,828)/2}$	6.2
Fixed assets employed for each sales dollar	$\dfrac{\text{Average net fixed assets}}{\text{Sales}} = \dfrac{(4,019,614 + 3,241,828)/2}{22,579,488}$	$0.16
Total asset turnover	$\dfrac{\text{Sales}}{\text{Average total assets}} = \dfrac{22,579,488}{(15,009,313 + 12,696,801)/2}$	1.5
Total assets employed for each sales dollar	$\dfrac{\text{Average total assets}}{\text{Sales}} = \dfrac{(15,009,313 + 12,696,801)/2}{22,579,488}$	$0.61
Profitability ratios		
Profit margin	$\dfrac{\text{Net income}}{\text{Sales}} = \dfrac{1,149,035}{22,579,488}$	5.1%
Return on investment (ROI)	$\dfrac{\text{Net income}}{\text{Average stockholders' equity}} = \dfrac{1,149,035}{(6,651,068 + 5,817,533)/2}$	18.4%
Return on assets (ROA)	$\dfrac{\text{Net income}}{\text{Average net assets}} = \dfrac{1,149,035}{(15,009,313 + 12,696,801)/2}$	8.3%
Return on capital employed (ROCE)	$\dfrac{\text{Net income}}{\text{Average long-term debt and stockholders' equity}} = \dfrac{1,149,035}{(10,101,068 + 8,392,533)/2}$	12.4%

TABLE 16-10 Composition Ratios of XYZ Corporation

	1984	1983
Balance Sheet (percentage of total assets)		
Assets		
Cash	4.0%	7.4%
Accounts receivable (net)	24.8	24.6
Inventory	26.8	25.6
Other current assets	2.1	3.2
	57.7%	60.9%
Fixed assets, net	27.4	25.5
Investments	4.7	—
Goodwill	3.2	4.0
Other assets	7.0	9.6
	100.0%	100.0%
Liabilities and stockholders' equity		
Notes payable	3.1%	2.5%
Current maturities, long-term debt	3.5	2.6
Accounts payable	16.8	18.3
Accrued expenses	7.3	8.5
	30.7%	31.9%
Long-term debt	32.0	20.3
Other liabilities	2.0	2.0
	55.7%	54.2%
Stockholders' equity	44.3	45.8
	100.0%	100.0%
Income Statement (percentage of sales)		
Net sales	100.0%	100.0%
Cost of goods sold	(71.4)	(69.7)
Gross profit	28.6%	30.3%
General and administrative expenses	(11.7)	(12.7)
Selling expenses	(8.2)	(7.9)
Operating profit	8.7%	9.7%
Interest expense	(2.2)	(1.9)
Other income	0.8	—
Pretax income	7.3%	7.8%
Income taxes	(2.2)	(3.1)
Net income	5.1%	4.7%

Composition Ratios

The first step in performing any financial ratio analysis is to break down the balance sheet and income statement into their component parts. In breaking down the balance sheet, determine the percentage that each asset comprises of total assets, and the percentage of total liabilities and stockholders' equity represented by each item on the right side of the balance sheet. The income statement is broken down by calculating the percent of total sales that each expense and miscellaneous item constitutes.

Composition ratios are an excellent method for placing all firms on a similar scale. Irrespective of the sizes of the companies that are being compared, the sum of each category of accounts cannot exceed 100 percent.

Composition ratios highlight the relative magnitude of each asset account and indicate the proportional financing of total assets provided by each category of liabilities and of stockholders' equity. This type of analysis helps to isolate the reasons for shifts in profitability. There is no better tool for initiating the analysis of financial statements.

Composition ratios can also be used to develop common-size financial statements. Common-size financial statements make it easier to detect differences among units for which composition ratios have been calculated by placing them on the same scale. These statements can be developed by applying the composition ratios of another company to financial data of the company being analyzed, as shown in Table 16-11.

Liquidity Ratios

Survival is the most important objective of any company. Before the company can focus its attention on other plans and objectives, financial obligations must be met. Liquidity refers to the ability of a company to convert short-term assets to cash. Liquidity ratios measure the degree to which liquid assets are available to meet current obligations.

Current Ratio

$$\frac{\text{Current assets}}{\text{Current liabilities}}$$

The current ratio measures the relationship between current assets and current liabilities, which together are considered working capital. Current assets, which include cash, marketable securities, accounts receivable, and inventory, represent the most liquid assets of a firm. They are the assets from which cash most likely will be realized within a reasonably short period of time, and thus they are the most likely candidates to satisfy current liabilities. The higher the current ratio, the more liquid the company is said to be.

It would seem that a high current ratio is a desirable attribute. This is true only to a point. Although a high current ratio provides a measure of financial security, maintaining a needlessly high current ratio may reflect poor management of working capital. Most current assets earn little if any return, and they

TABLE 16-11 Using Composition Ratios to Develop a Common-Size Income Statement

(dollars in thousands)

Description	Composition Ratios (%) XYZ Corporation	AB Corporation	Common Size Income Statement AB Corporation
Net sales	$22,579	100.0	$22,579
Cost of goods sold	16,122	68.1	15,376
Gross profit	$ 6,457	31.9	$ 7,203
Selling, general and administrative expenses	4,493	22.6	5,103
Operating profit	$ 1,964	9.3	$ 2,100
Other expenses (net)	312	1.2	271
Pretax income	$ 1,652	8.1	$ 1,829
Income taxes	503	3.3	745
Net income	$ 1,149	4.8	$ 1,084

all have implicit, if not explicit, costs. It can be costly to tie too much into working capital.

A comparatively low current ratio should not automatically be construed as a negative attribute. There are many companies that thrive with barely enough current assets to satisfy current liabilities. They are able to do so if their current assets are highly liquid and can be converted into cash rapidly when current liabilities come due.

Quick Ratio or "Acid Test" Measurement

Current assets − Inventory
_____
Current liabilities

The quick ratio or acid test is similar to the current ratio except that it excludes inventory. (Some applications will also exclude certain nonliquid receivables.) It is called the quick ratio because it includes only those current assets that can quickly be converted to cash. The reason for excluding inventory is that it is generally considered less liquid than other current assets. While cash is the most liquid type of asset and receivables normally represent legal obligations to pay cash, inventories depend on successful sales efforts and cannot always be disposed of above cost. Many financially troubled companies have excellent current ratios only because large amounts of unsalable inventory are on hand.

Leverage Ratios

Leverage ratios measure the relative amount of leverage, or debt, employed and the ability of the firm to meet its financial obligations. The two issues are interrelated since the degree to which leverage is employed affects the fixed annual obligations.

Debt Ratio

$$\frac{\text{Total debt}}{\text{Total assets}}$$

This ratio is an overall measure of leverage employed. The left side of the balance sheet represents total assets, and the right side of the balance sheet shows how the left side is financed. The debt ratio calculates the proportion of the left side that is financed by debt.

It would seem to be desirable to have a low debt ratio. This is certainly true to the extent that it implies less risk. The more debt employed, the greater the fixed costs of interest and principal payments. However, this rationale overlooks the benefits that result from prudent use of equity. By "trading on the equity," it is possible to use leverage to help finance a company rather than to surrender control. This approach has been popular, and in several instances has been profitable, in the recent wave of leveraged buyouts, in which companies have been acquired almost exclusively through use of debt. Because debt is a tax-deductible expenditure, 14 percent debt costs 7 percent after taxes. This is often the least expensive form of financing.

Debt/Equity Ratio

$$\frac{\text{Total debt}}{\text{Total stockholders' equity}}$$

This ratio directly compares the two sources of business financing: debt and stockholders' equity, including preferred stock.

Long-Term Debt/Equity Ratio

$$\frac{\text{Long-term debt}}{\text{Total stockholders' equity}}$$

This approach measures the relationship among the two sources of capitalization for a business: long-term debt and equity. They comprise the "permanent" funding of a business. Short-term or seasonal needs funded by current liabilities are not deemed to be permanent funding.

The value of the business is often viewed as being the sum of the values of long-term debt and equity. To some extent these represent financing alternatives, because a business can normally be started or purchased using some combination of long-term debt and equity. Other common methods of assessing capitalization are to calculate long-term debt as a percentage of total capitalization or to calculate long-term equity as a percentage of total capitalization.

Times Interest Earned Ratio

$$\frac{\text{Earnings before interest and taxes (EBIT)}}{\text{Interest}}$$

Since periodic interest payments must be made when debt is assumed, interest expenses must be taken into account in the context of total pretax earnings. Income taxes normally are assessed only if net earnings exist after interest expenses. Interest expenses are therefore computed on a pretax basis, because the capability to pay interest is not affected by taxes. In the times interest earned ratio, a high multiple indicates that the company has demonstrated a considerable ability to pay interest, and there is substantial leeway in the amount that EBIT can decline before the company risks being unable to make required interest payments. It also is an important indication of a company's ability to secure bank financing.

Activity Ratios

Activity ratios, also known as turnover ratios or funds management ratios, measure the efficiency of working capital and fixed-asset use and management. Each activity ratio analyzes the relationship between an annual sales figure and an annual average of a balance sheet item or items. Annual averages are generally computed by calculating the average of beginning and year-end balances.

Accounts Receivable Turnover Ratio

$$\frac{\text{Credit sales}}{\text{Average accounts receivable}}$$

In what is gradually becoming a cashless society, the biggest source of cash for most businesses is accounts receivable. To some extent, sales and income, although recorded as accounts receivable on an accrual basis, are academic until receivables have been collected and cash has been received. Since accounts receivable are normally non-income-generating, and the financing of receivables may be expensive, it is important to collect receivables as promptly as possible. This is measured by the accounts receivable turnover ratio, which calculates the number of times that receivables "turn" annually.

It is generally more desirable to have a high receivable turnover figure than a low one. The exception to this statement is when a high turnover ratio is achieved because only the highest-quality credit risks were accepted, and several profitable opportunities of lesser quality were forgone. Also, analysis of an accounts receivable turnover ratio does not negate the need for analyzing accounts receivable in detail. It is possible that many of the accounts receivable currently outstanding were also uncollected as of the end of the previous fiscal year. An aging of accounts receivable, in which receivables are categorized according to length of time outstanding (e.g., less than 30 days; 30 to 60 days; 60 to 90; 90 to 180 days; and more than 180 days) is a good initial means of identifying problem accounts.

Average Collection Period Ratio

$$\frac{\text{Average accounts receivable}}{\text{Credit sales}} \times 365$$

This ratio converts the average collection period for accounts receivable into a figure expressed in terms of days. This figure is the multiplicative inverse of the accounts receivable turnover period times 365 days in a year. For example, if the accounts receivable turnover ratio were 6, then the average collection period would be approximately 60 days (360 ÷ 6).

Inventory Turnover Ratio

$$\frac{\text{Cost of goods sold}}{\text{Average inventory}}$$

Inventory, like accounts receivable, should be "moved" as quickly as possible. The costs of carrying inventory include financing, record keeping, storage, display, insurance, and losses due to damage, obsolescence, and theft.

Unlike the accounts receivable turnover ratio and other turnover ratios that use sales in the numerator, the inventory turnover ratio uses cost of goods sold in its numerator. This is because inventory is stated at cost; therefore, the volume figure that is used to express turnover—cost of sales—should also be stated at cost rather than at retail. The sales figure is often used in the numerator, which it is incorrect since it overstates turnover.

Normally, a high turnover figure is desirable. However, a few cautions are in order. Where companies that are being compared use different methods of valuing inventory (e.g., FIFO vs. LIFO), their turnover ratios may not be comparable. Seasonal fluctuations in inventory levels may make year-end balances nonrepresentative of balances that normally exist during the year. It may be more appropriate to use quarterly or monthly balances to calculate averages for purposes of estimating turnover ratios.

If a high turnover ratio is achieved because only high-volume items are in stock while profitable slower-moving items are not stocked, the high turnover figure may conceal the profitable opportunities that have been lost. Also, irrespective of turnover ratios, an analysis and aging of inventory should be done to ensure that the inventory is current and salable.

Days' Sales in Inventory Ratio

$$\frac{\text{Inventory}}{\text{Cost of goods sold}} \times 365$$

This ratio indicates the number of days' sales, based on annual sales volume, present in inventory at a specific time. It is not the same thing as the multiplicative inverse of the inventory turnover ratio multiplied by 365, since this measure is based on a year-end balance rather than on average annual balances. This ratio is a tool for management planning and for operations areas such as reordering inventory as well as being a measure of efficiency.

Since different lines of inventory are likely to move at different rates, this ratio should be calculated separately for each product line.

Working Capital Turnover Ratio

$$\frac{\text{Sales}}{\text{Average working capital}}$$

This measure is difficult to evaluate. A financially strong company with large cash balances may have a low working capital turnover ratio, whereas a financially distressed firm with a narrow margin of working capital may have an exceedingly high working capital turnover ratio. Notwithstanding the two extremes, it can generally be said that a high working capital turnover ratio is better than a low one.

Working Capital per Dollar's Sales Ratio

$$\frac{\text{Average working capital}}{\text{Sales}}$$

This ratio is the multiplicative inverse of the working capital turnover ratio, and is subject to the same limitations.

Fixed Asset Turnover Ratio

$$\frac{\text{Sales}}{\text{Average net fixed assets}}$$

The fixed asset turnover ratio is used primarily as an indicator of the productivity of net fixed assets employed. The various gradations can indicate whether a company or an entire industry is capital-intensive. Its inherent limitation as an evaluation tool is that companies vary in depreciation policies, purchase/lease preferences, and average plant age, which can have a substantial impact on the cost shown for the plant.

Fixed Assets Employed for Each Sales Dollar Ratio

$$\frac{\text{Average net fixed assets}}{\text{Sales}}$$

This ratio is the reverse of the fixed asset turnover ratio.

Total Asset Turnover Ratio

$$\frac{\text{Sales}}{\text{Average total assets}}$$

The total asset turnover ratio measures how asset-intensive a business is and the efficiency of total assets employed.

Total Assets Employed for Each Sales Dollar Ratio

$$\frac{\text{Average total assets}}{\text{Sales}}$$

This is the reverse of the total asset turnover ratio.

Profitability Ratios

Profits are the focus of most financial analysis. Each of the financial ratios discussed above is intended to enhance decision-making in order to improve profits. The financial ratios described below are those that relate most explicitly to profits.

Profit Margin Ratio

$$\frac{\text{Net income}}{\text{Sales}}$$

The profit margin is a common bench mark often used to characterize the profitability of a business. It refers to the percentage of each sales dollar that filters to the bottom line. A high profit margin is more desirable than a low one, and is one attribute of a lucrative business. It allows the luxury of occasional mistakes, which are likely to be less damaging than in a low-margin business where errors can result in red ink. The downside risk is usually less in a high-profit business than in a low-profit business.

The profit margin cannot be regarded as an entirely independent measure of performance. Before making any conclusions based on profit margins, it is important to analyze the contributing factors. In reviewing the financial statements and analyzing the composition ratios described earlier, it may become evident that superior profit margins are the result of a single event that is unlikely to recur in future years. Another factor to consider is turnover. A company earning an 8 percent profit margin on inventory that only "turns" once a year will earn less than a company earning 4 percent on inventory that "turns" three times annually. It is desirable to have a high profit margin, but it should be understood, analyzed, and placed in a proper context before any conclusions are drawn.

Return on Investment Ratio

$$\frac{\text{Net income}}{\text{Average stockholders' equity}}$$

Also known as return on equity, this is the most significant profitability yardstick employed. Return on investment (ROI) is a valuable management tool because it provides a basis for dissecting profits and isolating factors that can lead to profit improvement. It is also a valuable tool for investors because it identifies the rate of return on their net investment and provides a good base for comparing alternative investments.

The benefits of ROI analysis become evident when it is broken down into its component parts, as follows:

$$\underbrace{\frac{\text{Pretax income}}{\text{Sales}} \times \frac{\text{Sales}}{\text{Average total assets}}}_{\textit{Operating Factors}} \times \underbrace{\frac{\text{Average total assets}}{\text{Average stockholders' equity}} \times (1 - \text{Tax rate})}_{\textit{Nonoperating Factors}} = \text{ROI}$$

The operating factors—the pretax profit margin and the total assets turnover ratio—are those that relate to annual business operations, which management can most readily effect changes upon. ROI can be increased by improving the pretax profit margin (for example, by increasing prices or reducing expenses) or by improving the efficiency of asset usage. The asset usage issue, or turnover, referred to in the discussion of profit margins can be more clearly seen in the ROI analysis. It shows why a grocery store, for example, with assets turning over every few weeks, can be much more profitable than an art gallery requiring a similar investment, in which assets may turn over only once or twice annually.

The nonoperating factors are less easily controlled by management, but they can have a substantial impact upon ROI. The ratio of total assets to stockholders' equity reflects the net investment in the business, exclusive of financing, and is less subject to annual fluctuations. All other things being equal, a highly leveraged business will have a higher ROI than one that is well capitalized.

The final nonoperating factor to come into play is the tax rate. This aspect of the equation results in the net income after taxes. Since this amount is greatly affected by tax rates, management should arrange good tax planning in order to minimize the tax bite taken from pretax income.

ROI may vary substantially from company to company depending upon the capital structures of the companies involved. As shown in Table 16-12, two companies that are otherwise identical can have vastly differing ROIs as a result of their respective capital structures.

The ROI of a rapidly growing company will often show a steady decline even though sales and earnings are growing at a record pace. This frequently occurs simply because in the early stages the company was undercapitalized; adding earnings to a low equity base causes the ROI seemingly to skyrocket. The more normal but depressed ROI figures that result from a better capitalized position should not be viewed negatively unless they lag behind industry averages.

TABLE 16-12   Return on Investment Based on Alternative Capital Structures

	Company A	Company B
Capital structure		
Debt	–	$ 50,000,000
Equity (1)	$100,000,000	50,000,000
Operating results		
Sales	$120,000,000	$120,000,000
Operating profit	30,000,000	30,000,000
Interest	–	6,000,000
Pretax income	$ 30,000,000	$ 24,000,000
Income tax	15,000,000	12,000,000
Net income (2)	$ 15,000,000	$ 12,000,000
Return on investment ((2) ÷ (1))	15%	24%

Return on Assets Ratio

$$\frac{\text{Net income}}{\text{Average total assets (net)}}$$

An alternative to ROI is to ignore the capital structure of a business and simply to focus on the return on assets. The rationale for this approach is that the instrinsic profitability is unaffected by the method of financing. The financing method is simply a discretionary decision of management. The return on assets (ROA) ratio calculates a return on every asset employed in the business rather than only focusing on stockholders' equity. It is useful for identifying companies that have comparatively low returns on assets but appear attractive only because they are highly leveraged or undercapitalized, and as a result have a high ROI.

The problem with ROA is that the capital structure of a business should not be ignored, since it is an aspect of the business that cannot readily be modified. To focus strictly on ROA could lead to overlooking attractive investments in real estate, banking, or leveraged buyouts, which can have a low ROA but can be profitable in terms of ROI simply because of their susceptibility to leveraging. The best use of ROA is in conjunction with ROI and the other financial tools described in this chapter.

Return on Capital Employed Ratio

$$\frac{\text{Net income}}{\text{Average long-term debt and stockholders' equity}}$$

Return on capital employed (ROCE) is probably the best measure of the basic profitability of a business under the capital structure that is in place. It recognizes that the capital structure is often a discretionary decision of management; therefore, the return is calculated using all of the capital resources in place.

If the effect of financing alternatives is completely eliminated from our analysis, ROCE can be shown as:

$$\frac{\text{EBIT}}{\text{Average long-term debt and stockholders' equity}}$$

This format does not include interest expenses on long-term debt (it should include interest on short-term debt), or income taxes and the tax benefits resulting from the interest deduction. Considering, however, that these are bona fide expenses, the first format of ROCE is more commonly used.

ROCE gives a better perspective of the intrinsic profitability of the business. If we wish to view the business from a macroeconomic perspective, ROCE is the best measure. However, as investors we are most concerned with the return on our own investment; therefore, ROI prevails.

Trend Analysis

Trend analysis involves analyzing financial data over a multiple-year period in order to observe trends that seem to be in progress. The value of the financial ratios described above is only partially realized if we fail to see how they have evolved over time. Financial ratios are best used within a comparative framework, and there is no better bench mark for comparison than the company's performance in prior years.

Trend analysis should include data from at least two years, but preferably three to five years. The subject of the trend analysis should include some if not all of the financial ratios discussed above, as well as the growth rates of each significant balance sheet and income statement item.

Many observations may emerge as trends are analyzed. As with other forms of ratio analysis, trends should be compared to industry data and even to overall economic data in order to assess their significance. Growth rates should be analyzed, and the base upon which growth is measured should be considered. For example, if a high rate of earnings growth appears only because earnings in the base year were at a comparative low point, then this factor would have to be noted and other measures of performance in addition to earnings growth would have to be considered.

Using Financial Ratios

The objective of financial ratio analysis is not to calculate them but to use them. After the ratios have been calculated and analyzed, and appropriate comparisons have been made, a clear picture of corporate financial performance and corporate financial condition should begin to emerge.

Financial ratios are a good starting point for analyzing a company's financial condition, but they do not provide solutions. They can highlight potential problems, but they cannot solve them. They can identify potential strengths, but they cannot show how to develop these strengths. The purposes of financial ratios are to place financial data in a meaningful context and to highlight areas requiring further investigation. As with financial statements, the valuable skill is not in their compilation but in their interpretation and application to the decision-making process.

FINANCIAL PROJECTIONS

Financial projections should draw on the collective judgment and knowledge of executives from all significant activities within a business, including marketing, production, personnel, accounting, and finance. Incorporating information from these sources with data developed through the application of sophisticated analytical and quantitative techniques can lead to projections of which one can be certain of one thing: that they will probably be wrong. Given this probable outcome, why bother?

Financial projections are critical tools for business planning. To be without some sort of financial projection is like traveling through unfamiliar territory without a map. Financial projections provide a reference point around which business plans can be made.

Financial projections are frequently used for planning:

- Capital requirements
- Dividend policy
- Plant expansion
- Product development
- Wage increases
- Acquisitions and divestitures
- Debt amortization
- Income tax status

They are also commonly distributed to bankers and creditors.

Financial projections should include the four basic financial statements as well as a projection of net cash receipts. (The format for projecting cash receipts is shown in Table 16-13.) Omitting any one of these financial statements can lead to significant errors. For example, to project cash flow without projecting a balance sheet and an income statement can result in an erroneous projection of working capital requirements. In practice, however, many if not most projections fail to include at least one or more of the basic financial statements. Whether this failure is out of ignorance or out of expediency is not clear. However, the omission increases the potential for inaccurate projections. The advent of the microcomputer and the many financial spreadsheet software packages has taken much of the tedium out of developing financial projections. This should contribute to higher-quality and more timely and thorough projections.

TABLE 16-13   Sample Projection of Net Cash Receipts

XYZ CORPORATION

PROJECTION OF NET CASH RECEIPTS
For the Year Ended December 31, 1986

	1986
Sales	$26,000,000
Cost of goods sold	18,800,000
Gross profit	$ 7,200,000
General and administrative expenses	2,850,000
Selling expenses	2,125,000
Operating profit	$ 2,225,000
Interest expense	480,000
Income before taxes	$ 1,745,000
Income taxes	700,000
Net income	$ 1,045,000
Add:	
Depreciation and amortization	500,000
Deferred taxes	50,000
	$ 1,595,000
Repayment of long-term debt	(525,000)
Additions to property, plant, and equipment	(400,000)
Payment of cash dividends	(347,050)
Increase in working capital	$ 322,950
Working capital to be funded:	
Increase in accounts receivable	(300,000)
Increase in inventory	(275,000)
Increase in other current assets	(50,000)
Funding provided by current liabilities:	
Decrease in notes payable	(15,000)
Increase in current maturities of long-term debt	25,000
Increase in accounts payable and accrued expenses	325,000
Net cash receipts	$ 32,950

Financial projections should include, at the very least, quarterly projections for the next four quarters and an annual projection of the next fiscal year. They should be updated continuously as new data becomes available or as each quarter passes. Many companies have monthly projections as well as annual projections going as far as five years into the future. Granted, projections of more distant periods are less likely to conform closely with actual results; they are important because capital expenditures, production and sales planning often depend upon the profile of the business several years out.

Financial projections rival the religions of the world in the number of methods that have been devised and in the sincerity of their proponents. Each company must develop an approach towards developing and evaluating financial projections that is appropriate for the company's unique circumstances and for the purposes for which projections have been devised.

Projection methodologies run the gamut from being strictly judgmental to being entirely a function of statistical formulas. The degree of verification with outside sources of key assumptions such as interest growth rates and other macroeconomic data varies substantially among companies, as does the number of executives from various disciplines that are involved in the process. The thoroughness of the process undertaken to develop projections should depend upon the use(s) to which the projections will be put, the amount of accuracy required, and the business implications, or "downside," of inaccurate projections. Considerably less effort may be required if the implications of inaccurate projections are unlikely to be disastrous. At the same time, we should never lose sight of the fact that irrespective of the thoroughness of the process employed to develop projections, there will almost always be deviations between projected and actual performance.

The essential features of the financial projection process include:

- Determining the purpose of financial projections
- Identifying the target audience
- Selecting the required input and analytical tools
- Obtaining source data
- Developing a financial model and supporting algorithms
- Integrating input with financial model to produce preliminary projections
- Ascertaining the reasonableness of projected output
- Analyzing, evaluating, and revising projections until they are suitable for distribution
- Integrating projections with business plans and other uses to which they should be put
- Revising projections, projection techniques, and financial model as subsequent experience dictates is appropriate

Some of the analytical tools that are employed in the projection process include:

- *Trend analysis:* This tool involves developing economic and financial trends using quantifiable historical data, which is projected on a linear basis according to observation, moving averages, or statistical trend line analysis.

- *Regression and correlation:* Trends that are linear or curvilinear may be projected based on relationships between dependent and independent variables developed through regression or multiple regression analysis. In practical terms, all one needs to know about this tool is that it measures the desired relationship according to a stated degree of confidence, and that it can be done entirely on the computer or electronic calculator.

- *Time series analysis:* This type of analysis is based on the premise that some factors change more as a result of time than as a result of the interrelationship among variables. Projections are made on the basis of historical performance and the trends, cycles, seasonal patterns, and volatility to which historical performance was subject.

- *Research:* External data is obtained from published reference sources, on-line data bases, microeconomic and macroeconomic forecasting services, and surveys. Data obtained by these means becomes input to some of the other analytical tools. It is also a means by which their results can be evaluated.

- *Financial ratio analysis:* Projected financial data can often be evaluated, explained, or developed through the application of financial ratio analysis. This can also be a tool for plugging "holes" in the projections. For example, if sales are projected to be $40 million, and an appropriate sales/working capital ratio is deemed to be .35, then projected working capital could be $14 million; this could be further broken down according to composition ratio analysis of the balance sheet.

- *Mathematical algorithms:* Once projections of certain items have been established, other items will result as the product or sum of the projected inputs. For example, if projections have been made of personnel and compensation, labor expense will be the product of the two. Financial projections normally consist of a myriad of algorithms that generate the required financial statements. Several useful computer software packages have been developed for the microcomputer and the mainframe computer that can facilitate this process, and generate the required data promptly, while affording convenient manipulation and modification of data.

- *Simulation:* Analyzing alternative outcomes is critical to testing the validity of the model, its input and output, and its sensitivity to changes in certain variables. The final projections are often presented in a format that contains alternative scenarios that depict the worst case, best case, and expected results.

- *Judgment:* This is the most valuable tool of all those described.

It would be fruitless to attempt to provide a laundry list of areas requiring analysis in developing projections. Any general list would be incomplete, due to the unique attributes of every company. Examples of some of the areas that should be explored are presented in Figure 16-5.

EVALUATING CAPITAL INVESTMENT OPPORTUNITIES

There are four analytical tools used to evaluate and prioritize capital investment opportunities: the payback method, average rate of return, net present value, and internal rate of return. These tools are discussed in detail in any corporate finance textbook (see the bibliography at the end of the chapter for names of some books that discuss them in greater detail). The purpose of this section is to highlight the essential features of each method and to demonstrate how the methods can be applied in financial analysis.

Each capital investment evaluation method is deterministic in the sense that it provides a single discrete number based entirely on financial projections and related assumptions. Given that financial projections are subject to a fair

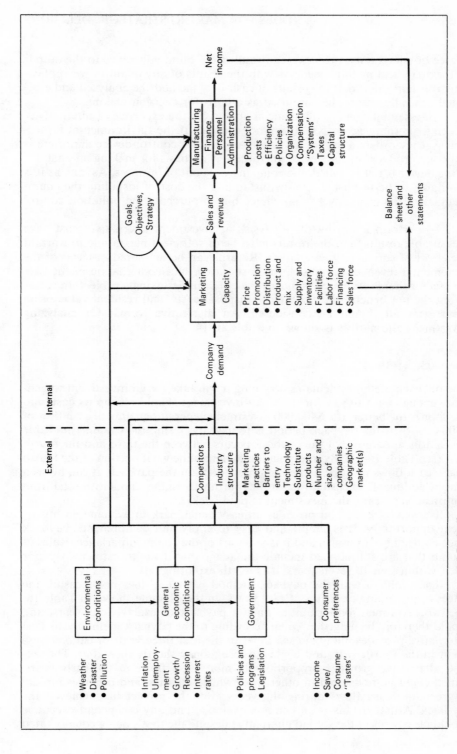

FIG. 16-5 Areas Affecting Financial Projections

degree of uncertainty, problems can result from blind adherence to the output of the analytical method used. As with the results of any quantitative application, it is important that the results of cash-flow methods be analyzed and evaluated critically before they are used as a basis for decision making.

An essential premise of financial analysis is the existence of alternatives. Lacking alternatives, analysis is a moot exercise. If the Environmental Protection Agency orders a factory to install a pollution control device and there is only one producer of the device, then there is no basis for making an analysis. If the device is not installed, the company goes out of business. As long as it is profitable to be in business, notwithstanding the cost of installing the equipment, then the company has no choice but to purchase the pollution control device.

To perform a worthwhile analysis, an investment alternative must have measurable results, and the results must be of sufficient magnitude to warrant the effort of conducting an analysis. Returns can be measured in terms of the incremental revenues generated, the costs saved, or a combination of the two. The factor that is evaluated is the *net* benefit of undertaking a project. In calculating the net benefit, the tax effects, disposal costs, and residual value of an investment all should be considered. An illustrative format for analyzing investment alternatives is shown in Table 16-14.

Payback Method

The payback method calculates how long it will take for an investment to generate enough cash to pay for itself. An investment should recoup its cost, and the sooner the better. If a $400,000 investment generates an annual cash flow of $100,000, then the payback period is four years. Using the example in Table 16-16, it is apparent that the payback occurs between the third and the fourth year (see Table 16-15). By interpolating to determine what portion of the fourth year's cash flows must be earned in order to attain the payback, it can be seen that by adding .42 of cash flows for the fourth year to the cumulative total from the preceding years, the investment is paid back.

The payback method provides an easy benchmark to evaluate an investment opportunity. It is simple and easy to apply and comprehend. Payback once enjoyed broad usage, and it is still part of the common parlance. Rules of thumb that are still applied include the adage that if the investment pays for itself within four to seven years, it is worth exploring.

The problem with the payback method is that it does not measure the effect of the timing or trends of cash flows. In the example shown in Table 16-16, two investment opportunities have a payback of exactly four years, and would therefore be judged as equal according to the payback method. The first alternative provides minimal cash flows in the first three years, a balloon payment in the fourth year, and begins to lose money shortly thereafter. The second alternative provides proportionally more cash flows in the early years, which could be reinvested in other worthwhile activities, and provides rapidly appreciating cash flows during the years after the project has achieved the payback. Although this is an extreme example, and any competent executive would clearly select the second alternative despite the first's being equally rated

TABLE 16-14 Format for Analyzing Investment Alternatives—Project Q

	1985	1986	1987	1988	1989
Investment cost					
Purchase price	$281,046				
Less: Investment tax credit	(18,746)				
Proceeds from sale of asset to be replaced	(15,000)				
Trade-in allowance on asset to be replaced	–				
Debt incurred to finance purchase (a)	–				
Add: Recapture of depreciation and ITC on asset to be replaced	3,085				
Installation costs	2,400				
	$252,785				
Investment benefits (b)					
Incremental revenues	$ 18,000	$21,000	$ 24,000	$ 27,000	$ 30,000
Net cost reductions	57,443	75,443	98,443	121,443	145,443
	$ 75,443	$96,443	$122,443	$148,443	$175,443
Less: Cost increases	–	–	–	–	–
Depreciation	(50,557)	(50,557)	(50,557)	(50,557)	(50,557)
Interest (a)	–	–	–	–	–
Pretax benefit	$ 24,886	$45,886	$ 71,886	$ 97,886	$124,886
Income tax	(12,443)	(22,943)	(35,943)	(48,943)	(62,443)
Incremental income	$ 12,443	$22,943	$ 35,943	$ 48,943	$ 62,443
Add: Depreciation	50,557	50,557	50,557	50,557	50,557
Net proceeds from disposal/terminal value	–	–	–	–	12,000
Less: Debt repayment (a)	–	–	–	–	–
Net increase in working capital	3,000	3,500	4,000	4,500	5,000
Net investment benefit	$ 60,000	$70,000	$ 82,500	$ 95,000	$120,000

(a) Many practitioners analyze investments independently from financing costs.

(b) For new business ventures, the format shown in Table 16-13 is preferable, provided that a terminal value is included.

TABLE 16-15 Calculation of Payback Period—Project Q

	Net Investment Awaiting Payback, Beginning (a)	Net Investment Benefit (a)	Net Investment Awaiting Payback, Year-End	Contribution to Payback Period (years)
1985	$252,785	$ 60,000	$192,785	1.00
1986	192,785	70,000	122,785	1.00
1987	122,785	82,500	40,285	1.00
1988	40,285	95,000	–	0.42
1989	–	120,000	–	–
			Payback period 3.42 years	

(a) From Table 16-14

TABLE 16-16 The Deficiency of the Payback Method

	Alternative 1		Alternative 2	
	Net Cash Flow	Cumulative Cash Flow	Net Cash Flow	Cumulative Cash Flow
Initial investment	$(100)	$(100)	$(100)	$(100)
Net cash flow:				
Year 1	5	(95)	20	(80)
Year 2	5	(90)	30	(50)
Year 3	5	(85)	25	(25)
Year 4	85	0	25	0
Year 5	0	0	40	40
Year 6	(10)	(10)	70	110
Year 7	$ (15)	(25)	95	205
Payback period	4 years		4 years	

by the payback method, it illustrates two basic flaws in the payback method: it fails to consider the timing of cash flows and their trends after the payback period. In less extreme examples it can be difficult to assess the impact of the timing of cash flows.

A second flaw that the payback method shares with all of the other cash-flow analyses tools is that it fails to distinguish between alternatives on the basis of the magnitude of the net benefit and to relate that net benefit to the original project cost. A $100 project that pays for itself in one year is deemed to be superior to a $1 million project that pays for itself in two years, even though the latter will clearly be of greater significance to the business.

The best use of the payback method is as an initial screening tool to ferret out investment opportunities that clearly cannot pay for themselves within any

Table 16-17 Calculation of Average Rate of Return—Project Q

	Incremental (a) Net Income	Net Investment Beginning of Year (a)	Depreciation	Net Investment Year End	Average Net Investment
1985	$ 12,443	$252,785	$(50,557)	202,228	$227,507
1986	22,943	202,228	(50,557)	151,671	176,949
1987	35,943	151,671	(50,557)	101,114	126,393
1988	48,943	101,114	(50,557)	50,557	75,835
1989	62,443	50,557	(50,557)	–	25,279
Total	$182,715				$631,963
	÷5				÷5
Average	$ 36,543				$126,393

$$\text{Average rate of return} = \frac{\text{Average incremental net income}}{\text{Average net investment}} = \frac{\$36,543}{\$126,393} = 28.9\%$$

(a) From Table 16-14

reasonable time period. That accomplished, other investment tools should be employed.

Average Rate of Return Method

The average rate of return, sometimes referred to as the accounting rate of return, is defined as follows:

$$\text{Average rate of return} = \frac{\text{Average net income}}{\text{Net investment}}$$

An example of this calculation is shown in Table 16-17. The average rate of return is often preferred by accountants because it is based on the net income presented on financial statements. It is consistent with the earnings figures reported to shareholders and quoted by the financial news media. Senior executives concerned with investor responses to reported earnings performance often prefer analyses that highlight reported earnings performance, since they satisfy investors by selecting investments that maximize reported earnings. Finally, the average rate of return shares with the payback method the advantage of simplicity—it is fairly easy to calculate and it provides a single percentage measure that can be compared against other investment opportunities.

The primary disadvantage of the average rate of return is that it fails to focus on factors affecting cash flow other than those reflected in net income. Other elements of cash flow, such as repaying the principal on loans or deferred taxes, are entirely ignored. The average rate of return also relies too much on the outmoded premise that investors rely on reported earnings to the exclusion of cash-flow information and other related data. Contemporary investment theory indicates that the stock market regards cash flow to be more significant than reported earnings in pricing securities.

Another fundamental weakness of the average rate of return, as with the payback method, is that it fails to attach any weight to the timing of income generated. Earnings generated several years in the future are treated no differently from earnings or losses presently generated. A project that requires several years to generate satisfactory performance levels may appear to be no worse than one that provides an adequate return within a more immediate time period.

Net Present Value Method

The net present value (NPV) represents the difference between the net cash flows of an investment and its cost, calculated on a present value basis to reflect the time value of money. The investment costs are deducted from the projected net cash flow, which are discounted at a rate that reflects the weighted average of capital to be employed. The result is the NPV. The higher the NPV of investment, the more desirable the investment becomes from a financial perspective.

NPV is regarded by many practitioners as the preferred method of investment analysis. Many businesspeople prefer to make decisions based on a single numerical value rather than a somewhat more nebulous rate of return or payback period. NPV is conceptually perfect in the sense that it provides a precise value for an investment opportunity. If the assumptions are correct, the NPV is the single "correct" net value of an investment. The problem is that assumptions regarding future events underlying the projected investment benefits are educated estimates at best, and assumptions regarding the cost of capital are not entirely straightforward. The uncertainty of projections is a weakness shared by each of the four methods of investment analysis; however, the issue of cost of capital is unique to NPV.

There is little controversy surrounding the cost of debt and the cost of preferred equity. The cost of debt is simply the rate of interest, adjusted for the tax deduction resulting from paying interest (calculated as pretax interest rate times (1-T), where T is incremental tax rate) and the cost of preferred stock is its dividend rate. Both calculations are shown in Table 16-18. The cost of common equity is somewhat less obvious, as demonstrated by the various interpretations shown in Table 16-19.

Proponents of each method swear that theirs is correct and have some justification for their beliefs. Fortunately, each method normally results in a cost of equity capital that is reasonably similar. The differences are further mitigated by the weighting process, whereby the incremental cost of each component of capital is weighted according to its proportional use in the capital structure employed in the investment (see Table 16-18).

Practitioners often have difficulty identifying the sources of capital used in calculating the weighted average cost of capital. This issue is more problematic when the amount of capital is small, and has no immediate effect on the capital structure of the company. An example is a project funded by the use of surplus

TABLE 16-18 Calculation of Weighted Average Cost of
Capital—Project Q

	Pretax Cost of Capital	Income Tax Benefit (1 − Tax)	After-Tax Cost of Capital	Weighting	Weighted Average Cost of Capital
Long-term debt	15%	(1 − 0.4)	9%	0.30	2.7
Preferred stock	14	—	14	0.20	2.8
Common stock	19	—	19	0.50	9.5
					15.0

cash. In such situations, the incremental market rates on the existing capital structure are used to calculate the weighted average cost of capital. Where the financial markets have been tapped to finance a transaction, the identification process is more direct. Any capital not attributable to long-term debt or preferred stock is normally regarded as equity capital.

The weighted average cost of capital resulting from these calculations becomes the discount rate used to determine the present value of the future cash flows. The resulting amount, less the original cost, is the NPV.

Table 16-20 shows the NPV of an investment at alternative discount rates. As expected, the higher the discount rate, the lower the NPV. The variation in the resultant calculations of NPV is an indication of the importance of carefully calculating the weighted average cost of capital and performing the calculation of alternative discount rates to provide a relevant range of value.

Internal Rate of Return Method

In order to calculate the NPV it is necessary to calculate the cost of capital to determine the discount rate to be applied to future cash flows. The NPV varies depending on the cost of capital employed. Several answers can result if alternative discount rates are used. The Internal rate of return (IRR) provides a single convenient quantitative measure of investment performance that eliminates the need to calculate the cost of capital. Many managers prefer using a single percentage rate of return resulting from IRR analysis that can be compared to other measures, such as cost of capital, investment "hurdle" rates (minimum rates of return required for an investment to be acceptable), and financial market rates. The IRR places investments of all sizes on common ground by providing a single percentage measure that can be used to compare them, instead of the absolute dollar amount provided by NPV.

The IRR is calculated through a reiterative process that determines the discount rate at which the NPV equals zero. Conceptually, this is arrived at on a trial-and-error basis. In the example shown in Table 16-13, the NPV is greater

TABLE 16-19 Alternative Methods for Calculating Cost of Common Equity Capital

Method	Basis for Calculation	Advantages	Disadvantages
Target rate of return ("hurdle rate")	Decision of senior management	• Management sets investment objectives • Simple	• Lack of precision • Unsubstantiatable
Risk adjusted rate of return	Risk-free rate of interest (e.g., 5-year U.S. Treasury notes) + risk premium (Beta × incremental return for equity investments) (a)	• Conceptually perfect	• May be unrealistic • Difficult to precisely determine the "correct" inputs
Return on equity (ROE)	Net income ÷ average equity, normally calculated over a 3- to 5-year period	• Over time, cost of equity capital will approximate ROE • Simple	• Variability among companies due to different accounting policies • Results in vicious circle of replicating prior performance
Analysts' proxy	Company's incremental borrowing rate on long-term debt + 4 percent	• Simple	• Lack of precision
Investor expectations	Expected annual appreciation in value of company's stock + expected dividend rate	• Correlates total returns on equity investments with expectations of sources of equity capital	• Nearly impossible to project

(a) Beta is a measure of variability in the value of the company's common stock in relation to stock market fluctuations. A beta of 1.00 signifies consonance with stock market fluctuations, whereas a beta below 1.00 signifies less volatility and above 1.00 signifies more. The equity risk premium is normally deemed to be at least 5 percent.

TABLE 16-20 Calculation of Net Present Value at Alternative Discount Rates—Projection Q

	Net Investment Benefits (a)	Present Value of Net Investment Benefits at		
		15%	18%	21%
1985	$ 60,000	$ 52,174	$ 50,847	$ 49,587
1986	70,000	52,930	50,273	47,811
1987	82,500	54,245	50,212	46,569
1988	95,000	54,317	49,000	44,318
1989	120,000	59,661	52,453	46,265
Total		$273,327	$252,785	$234,550
Net investment		(252,785)	(252,785)	(252,785)
Net present value		$ 20,542	–	$(18,235)

(a) From Table 16-14

than zero at a discount rate of 15 percent. If this calculation were to be performed manually, the next step would be to raise the discount rate in order to reduce the NPV. At 21 percent, the NPV is negative; therefore, the IRR must be between 15 percent and 21 percent. In this case, at 18 percent, the NPV is zero; therefore, the IRR is 18 percent.

In practice, the IRR is seldom a percentage that can be directly obtained from the present value tables found in most financial texts. Instead of being an integer such as 16 percent or 17 percent, it is more often a fractional amount, such as 16.14 percent or 17.23 percent. These amounts can be approximated using the present value tables through interpolation; however, they are more often precisely calculated using electronic calculators with financial functions or computers.

In most cases, the IRR leads to the same decision as NPV in ranking alternative investments. Occasionally, however, they do differ. Table 16-21 illustrates an example in which an investment with a higher NPV has a lower IRR. The reason for the difference is that the NPV discounts cash flows at the stated discount rate, whereas the IRR discounts them at the computed IRR. In situations where the IRR exceeds the company's cost of capital, the IRR discounts at an inappropriately high rate. Investments that produce relatively lower cash flows in early years may have an inferior IRR even though the NPV exceeds that of a competing investment. In these circumstances the NPV is regarded as a superior measure of investment performance.

An additional shortcoming of IRR is that it does not differentiate among investments on the basis of their relative size. A $10,000 investment with a 19 percent IRR would appear to be superior to a $10 million investment with an 18.5 percent IRR, even though the latter clearly has the potential to be of greater significance to the investors. As with any financial tool, blind reliance on results cannot supersede prudent application and interpretation.

TABLE 16-21 Example of Conflicting Results from Net Present Value and Internal Rate of Return Methods

	Initial Investment	Annual Cash Flows				NPV at 10%	IRR
		Year 1	Year 2	Year 3	Year 4		
Investment A	$25,000	$10,000	$10,000	$10,000	$10,000	$6,699	21.86%
Investment B	$25,000	—	5,000	10,000	30,000	7,136	18.20%

VALUING ACQUISITION CANDIDATES

Acquisitions of companies rank among the most significant capital expenditures made by businesses. The potential financial and business impact of acquisitions to the buyer can cause nearly any other type of capital expenditure to pale in comparison. For this reason, sound analysis of acquisition candidates is extremely important.

Well-publicized corporate bidding wars in which eager buyers increase purchase prices by tens if not hundreds of millions of dollars on short notice can make the valuation of acquisition candidates appear to be a superfluous issue that can be dealt with in a cavalier fashion. In fact, purchase price has the potential to be the determining factor of acquisition success, given that it is the benchmark against which subsequent results can be measured. An acquisition that is attractive at one price can be a money loser at a higher price. This is especially true in leveraged buyouts, in which purchases generate substantial principal and interest obligations that must be repaid.

Estimating the value of a company is not by any means a straightforward process. Well-trained experts can, at times, deviate substantially in their estimate of the value of an acquisition candidate. Unlike accounting, there are no generally accepted valuation standards that can be rigidly applied. Valuation is more an art than a science. Each situation must be uniquely analyzed, and often valued based, in part, on valuation methods peculiar to a specialized industry and/or the specific company.

Practitioners have developed several different valuation methods. Those that are most consistently applied are based on comparable companies, similar acquisitions, adjusted net worth, and discounted cash flow analysis.

Comparable Company Method

In contemporary portfolio theory, the stock market is presumed to be efficient in valuing publicly held securities. At any given point in time, the price of a company's stock reflects factors that affect the overall economy, the industry in which the company operates, the market for its products, and numerous factors specific to the company. They collectively determine the price at which a company's stock trades, a result of numerous independent transactions between value-maximizing investors.

TABLE 16-22   Calculation of Weighted Average Earnings of Z, Inc.

	Earnings	Weighting	Weighted Earnings
1983	$1,063,214	5	$ 5,316,070
1982	894,285	4	3,577,140
1981	952,193	3	2,856,579
1980	838,612	2	1,677,224
1979	725,484	1	725,484
Sum of weighted earnings			$14,152,497
Weighting			÷ 15
Weighted average earnings			$ 943,500

Stock market data on publicly held companies are particularly relevant in estimating the value of a closely held concern. Especially useful are data on comparable companies that possess similar investment characteristics to the closely held business. In determining what constitutes similar investment characteristics, it is important not to take the term "comparability" too literally. A comparable company that resembles the closely held business in every way can never exist, and is unnecessary for valuation purposes. Investors buy and sell stock in order to achieve a financial return; hence, the group of comparable companies identified includes a body of companies that collectively displays investment characteristics that offer investors the prospects of achieving a rate of return comparable to the rate achievable through an interest in the closely held concern. Investment traits used to assess comparability may include lines of business, customer type or industry, geographical concentration, marketing methods, competition, product complexity, sales and/or earnings trends, and overall financial condition. It is possible that none of the companies closely resembles the closely held company; collectively, however, they should display investment characteristics that would influence its value.

Value is translated from the comparable companies by applying their aggregate market capitalization multiples to the appropriate data of the privately held concern. The market capitalization multiples relate the stock prices of the comparable companies to certain per-share financial data, such as earnings, weighted average earnings (see Table 16-22), book value, and/or revenues. An application of these multiples to the related financial data of the privately held concern can result in several different values, as shown in Table 16-23. Each value constitutes a component of value that is not, by itself, fully indicative of value. The components of value are integrated into a single value by weighting them according to an informed judgment concerning the relative importance of each component in determining value, which may be supported by analysis such as that shown in Table 16-24. Other factors relevant to value may have to be considered that are not reflected in the stock prices of the comparable companies. Issues such as nonmarketability of stock, lack of man-

TABLE 16-23　Valuation of Z, Inc. Based on Comparable Public Companies

	Price/ Earnings	Price/Weighted Average Earnings	Price/Book Value	Price/ Revenues	Calculation of Value
Comparable public company					
P	9.1	10.2	1.24	0.33	
Q	14.0	12.9	1.36	0.49	
R	6.8	9.3	1.07	0.26	
W	15.0	16.8	2.28	0.81	
X	11.1	11.6	1.76	0.37	
Y	10.6	12.6	0.99	0.55	
Z	8.4	10.7	0.82	0.21	
Average of multiples	10.7	12.0	1.36	0.43	
	×	×	×	×	
Financial results of acquisition candidate	$ 1,063,214	$ 943,500	$6,343,518	$19,725,382	
Components of value	$11,376,390	$11,322,000	$8,627,184	$ 8,481,914	
Weighting (a)	× 30%	× 35%	× 20%	× 5%	
Weighted components of value	$ 3,412,917	$ 3,962,700	$1,725,437	$ 1,272,287	$10,373,341
Acquisition premium (b)					× 1.40
					$14,522,677

(a) Developed judgmentally or as shown in Table 16-24

(b) Based on general acquisition data of acquisitions with investment characteristics resembling Z, Inc.

TABLE 16-24 Method for Supporting the Weighting of Components of Value

	Price/ Earnings	Price/Weighted Average Earnings	Price/Book Value	Price/ Revenues	Total
Average of comparable companies (a)	10.7	12.0	1.36	0.43	—
Standard deviation	3.0	2.5	0.51	0.21	—
Coefficient of variation (b)	0.28	0.21	0.38	0.49	—
Reciprocal of coefficient of variation	3.57	4.76	2.63	2.04	13.00
Reciprocal as percentage of total	28%	37%	20%	15%	100%
Weighting system to be applied	30%	35%	20%	15%	100%

(a) From Table 16-23
(b) Standard deviation ÷ average

agement depth, appreciated assets, nonrecurring income or expense items, high cash balances, and others, may warrant adjustments to the value calculated through the application of capitalization multiples. Adjustments are normally made by applying premiums or discounts to the calculated value, and adjusting the earnings and book value of the acquisition candidate, where appropriate, so that the capitalized value is properly reflected.

The value developed by applying the aggregate market capitalization multiples of the comparable companies, with appropriate adjustments, is based on their stock prices, which are normally based on transactions for fractional interests in the underlying companies (e.g., 100 and 200 share-lots); consequently, the value reflects a minority interest. The value of the entire company can be estimated by applying an acquisition premium to the previously computed value. The acquisition premium may be based on premiums paid over the existing market prices of selected publicly held companies to acquire control. The extent to which the price is bid up above the level that existed before the announcement of an acquisition is referred to as the acquisition premium. For example, if a stock price of $10 prevailed before an announcement of an acquisition that was ultimately consummated at $13 per share, the acquisition premium would be 30 percent ($3 divided by $10).

The comparable company method has the advantage of providing an independent basis for arriving at value that is relatively less subjective than other valuation methods. It shares all the advantages of the stock market as a pricing mechanism in the sense that it reflects a plethora of factors that collectively influence value. Like the stock market, the comparable company method displays some volatility in value over time if applied to value a single company because of changes in stock price levels and trends within the market. Companies within the stock market experience fluctuation in their prices. The main caveat to keep in mind regarding the comparable company valuation method is that it is only as good as the capability of the practitioner applying the method, and the care taken to select appropriate comparable companies, and reflect them properly in a valuation formula.

Similar Acquisitions Method

Recent acquisitions of companies with investment characteristics resembling those of the acquisition candidate provide useful valuation benchmarks for many of the same reasons that comparable company are significant. Similar acquisitions may even be viewed as more relevant in as much as they represent informed purchases of entire companies, rather than the partial interests that constitute the basis of the comparable company methods.

Both the similar acquisitions method and the comparable company method rely on the premise that fair market value is established by transactions between willing buyers and sellers that are reasonably informed of the relevant information. The capitalization multiples from similar acquisitions are used to develop value in much the same way as is comparable company market data (see Table 16-25). Where appropriate, adjustments are made to the resulting data or the underlying data of the acquisition candidate that is capitalized in order to account for any unique attributes requiring special consideration.

The major problem of the similar acquisition method is the difficulty of obtaining sufficient data on acquisitions to provide a meaningful indication of value. There are more than 12,000 publicly held companies from which comparable company data can be drawn, but only a few hundred acquisitions occur each year that disclose sufficient useful data. Also, acquisition prices may sometimes reflect factors that are specific to the transaction and not applicable to others. Those factors may include the relative negotiating skills of the parties to the transaction; the financial capacity of the acquirer; perceived synergies that would cause the merged value of the acquired company to exceed its free-standing value; and other aspects of the acquisition agreement that may not be reflected in the purchase price, such as employment contracts. Because of these and other shortcomings, the similar acquisitions method is often used as one of several valuation methods to develop a purchase price, rather than as the sole method.

Adjusted Book Value Method

Conventional wisdom dictates that there should be some relationship between the price paid to acquire a company and the value of its assets, less liabilities, which constitutes the adjusted book value. Many unsophisticated transactions are based exclusively on this amount. Although the value of a business ultimately derives from the earnings that it can generate rather than its adjusted book value, the latter measure is important since any transaction occurring at

TABLE 16-25 Valuation of Z Inc. Based on Similar Recent Acquisitions

	Price/ Earnings	Price/Weighted Average Earnings	Price/Book Value	Price/ Revenues	Calculation of Value
Acquisition					
A	11.0	13.8	1.42	0.62	
B	15.6	14.7	2.01	0.93	
C	14.8	17.2	1.61	0.72	
D	8.9	9.1	0.97	0.39	
E	12.1	13.9	1.39	0.52	
F	17.4	19.1	2.28	1.04	
Average	13.4	14.3	1.52	0.67	
	×	×	×	×	
Financial results of acquisition candidate	$ 1,063,214	$ 943,500	$ 6,343,518	$19,725,382	
Components of value	$14,140,746	$13,775,100	$10,213,064	$13,807,767	
Weighting (a)	× 30%	× 30%	× 25%	× 15%	
	$ 4,242,224	$ 4,132,530	$ 2,553,226	$ 2,071,165	$12,999,145

(a) Developed judgmentally or as shown in Table 16-24

Table 16-26 Asset Valuation Methods

Valuation Method	Basis	Relative Dollar Value	Application
Book value	Net historical costs recorded on balance sheet according to generally accepted accounting principles	Variable	Accounting for a pooling of interests
Liquidation value	Net amount quickly realizable through a liquidation sale	Lowest	Liquidation; some asset-based loans
Current value	Net amount realizable through continued use in business or an orderly disposition	Middle	Purchase accounting; tax basis
Replacement value	Cost of replacing existing assets, without regard to enhanced functional performance of new fixed assets	Highest	"Make-or-buy" acquisition analysis

too substantial a premium over book value begs the strategic question of whether it would be more economical to build rather than to buy.

Adjusted book value is calculated by determining the fair market value of assets in place and reducing that amount by the market value of liabilities. Several interpretations are frequently provided for value that can confuse the issue, and are summarized in Table 16-26.

The result of adjusting the balance sheet to reflect the appropriate valuation is a calculation of adjusted book value. Table 16-27 provides an example of adjustments to the book value of Z, Inc. for purposes of acquisition analysis. The replacement value of assets is considered, as well as the cost of attempting to build a business of similar scope to the acquisition candidate. If the proposed purchase price were $14 million, the analysis in Table 16-27 indicates that there is an implicit premium of $554,439 associated with acquiring Z, Inc. instead of building it from the ground up. The advantage of starting a new business is greater control over determining many aspects of the organization that is ultimately established, while none of the bad aspects of the existing business are assumed. This must be weighed against the amount of time required to duplicate the business of the acquisition candidate, the risk that it may never be successfully duplicated, and the benefit of eliminating the acquisition candidate as a potential competitor.

TABLE 16-27   Using the Adjusted Book Value of Z, Inc. for Acquisition Analysis

	Amount per Balance Sheet	Adjustment	Adjusted Book Value	Explanation
ADJUSTED BALANCE SHEET				
Assets				
Cash and short-term investments	$ 862,557	$ 14,316	$ 876,873	Accrued interest on investments
Accounts receivable, net	4,279,118	(104,286)	4,174,832	Doubtful accounts receivable
Inventory	2,744,322	718,669	3,462,991	LIFO adjustment
Other current assets	293,517	–	293,517	
	$ 8,179,514	$ 628,699	$ 8,808,213	
Net fixed assets	2,823,424	1,923,562	4,746,986	Appraised value of assets exceeds depreciated book value
Patents	145,322	54,678	200,000	Analysis of current value
Goodwill	108,617	(108,617)	–	No tangible value
	$11,256,877	$2,498,322	$13,755,199	
Liabilities				
Current liabilities	$ 3,045,918	–	$ 3,045,918	
Long-term debt	1,867,441	$ (203,721)	1,663,720	Long-term debt at below-market rates
Net book value	6,343,518	2,702,043	9,045,561	
	$11,256,877	$2,498,322	$13,755,199	
USING ADJUSTED BOOK VALUE FOR ACQUISITION ANALYSIS				
Adjusted book value			$ 9,045,561	
Other costs to duplicate Z, Inc.:				
Start-up costs			1,000,000	Site location costs, employee recruitment expenses, professional fees, etc.
Replicative research and development			900,000	R&D costs to replicate product line similar to that of Z, Inc.
Differential of operating earnings of Z, Inc. during "catch-up" period			2,500,000	Estimated differential between operating earnings of Z, Inc. and start-up company during period of time required for start-up company to catch up to Z, Inc., not including start-up costs and losses reflected above
			$13,445,561	
Premium for buying ongoing entity			554,439	
Purchase price of Z, Inc.			$14,000,000	

TABLE 16-28   Valuation of Z, Inc. Based on Discounted Cash Flow Analysis

	Projected Amounts	Present Value of Projected Amounts (a)
Projected free cash flow:		
1985	$ 1,060,000	$ 929,825
1986	1,250,000	961,834
1987	1,463,000	987,483
1988	1,698,000	1,005,352
1989	1,952,000	1,013,808
1990	2,206,000	1,005,024
1991	2,493,000	996,296
Residual value ($2,493,000 ÷ 14)	17,807,143	7,116,399
	$29,929,143	$14,016,021

(a) Based on weighted average cost of capital of 14 percent

Discounted Cash Flow Analysis Method

The valuation methods described above are essentially price-based valuation methods. Value is based on the prices of similar businesses or assets. The implicit assumption is that the market provides the best indication of value. Discounted cash flow analysis (DCF) is a value-based concept, predicted on the economic concept that the financial value of a business results from the cash flows that it enables the owner to realize.

The heart of DCF is the cash-flow projections upon which value is based. A format such as that presented in Table 16-13 is used to project cash flows over some forseeable period—frequently five, seven, or ten years. The value of the acquisition candidate is deemed to be the present value of the cash flows that it can generate, discounted at the acquiror's cost of capital, adjusted for the risk of the acquisition candidate. The cash flows of the acquisition candidate have two components—the dividends or free cash flow that could be paid to the acquiror, and the residual value (also referred to as terminal value) that could be realized if the business were to be sold at the end of the projection period. The residual value is normally estimated by capitalizing the free cash flow at the cost of capital in the final year of the projection period (see Table 16-28), or by applying a conservative price/earnings ratio to the earnings in the final year, reduced to reflect the capital gains taxes that would result from the sale. The present value of these amounts is deemed to be the value of the acquisition candidate.

The process used in DCF is essentially the same as that employed in NPV calculations. Note the following similarities:

According to DCF:

Purchase price = Present value of cash flows + Residual value

By placing both components of DCF on the same side of the equation, it is evident that in applying DCF, the purchase price is always an amount where the NPV is zero. Applying another concept that has previously been discussed, with DCF, the purchase price is always an amount that will cause the internal rate of return to equal the cost of capital.

DCF shares the same major weakness as NPV: it is entirely dependent upon the reasonableness of the projections. A further weakness is the importance of residual value, which is often the most significant component of value. If it is difficult to estimate value at the time of purchase, it is even more difficult to estimate value several years hence. Some of this problem is partially mitigated since slight inaccuracies in the estimation of residual value are diminished by the discounting process. Also, sensitivity analyses are frequently performed under several alternative scenarios in order to arrive at purchase price parameters.

Despite these areas of concern, DCF remains an important valuation tool, often used in conjunction with the others to arrive at a consensus as to value or to establish price boundaries.

PRICING VENTURE CAPITAL

Pricing venture capital is one of the least well-defined areas of high finance. The process is a combination of horse trading, conartistry, and sophisticated analysis. The former skills are not readily imparted, nor germane to this chapter. The latter is important because it helps to clarify negotiating positions and establish a framework for arriving at an equitable arrangement. The use of analytical models can help remove part of the emotional element from what can be very difficult negotiations.

The central valuation issue is how large a portion of the company the venture capitalist will receive in exchange for the investment that is being made. Normally the companies receiving venture capital are not public, nor do they have a sufficient track record to be able to readily apply the valuation methods discussed in the previous section. Venture capital valuation methods are necessarily prospectively oriented, and tend to rely heavily on estimating future earnings and the timing and price at which the company will go public, since a public offering is normally the only means by which the venture capitalist can achieve the desired return on investment.

Traditional Pricing Method

The traditional pricing method focuses on the amount of the venture capitalist's investment, interim proceeds, and the value that it must have at the time of the initial public offering (target value) for the venture capitalist to achieve a target return on investment commensurate with the risk involved. The proportion of the total value of the company at the time of the initial public offering

TABLE 16-29 Traditional Pricing Method—Nu Corporation

	1985	1986	1987	1988
Venture capitalist's investment:				
Equity value of convertible				
debentures, January 1	$1,000,000	$1,420,000	$2,050,000	$2,995,000
Target total return at 50%	500,000	710,000	1,025,000	1,497,500
	$1,500,000	$2,130,000	$3,075,000	$4,492,500
Less: Annual interest on				
convertible debt	80,000	80,000	80,000	80,000
Target value, December 31	$1,420,000	$2,050,000	$2,995,000	$4,412,500
Venture capital recipient:				
Earnings (losses)	$ (350,000)	$ (50,000)	$ 350,000	$ 600,000
Assumed initial public				
offering price/earnings,				
December 31, 1988				× 15
				$9,000,000
Equity required by venture capitalist on				
January 1, 1985 to achieve target value		4,412,500 ÷ 9,000,000 =		49.0%

represented by the target value of the venture capitalist's investment is the amount of equity giveup required by the venture capitalist, according to the traditional pricing method.

The payoff on venture capital investments, if any, normally is realized when and if the venture capital recipient goes public or is sold. In the absence of an initial public offering (IPO) or a sale, it is unlikely that the venture capitalist will ever realize the 50 percent annual rate of return sought on successful investments. The apparently usurous rate of return on successful investments, giving rise to their nickname "vulture capitalists," is needed to compensate for the numerous failures that venture capitalists invariably invest in. Major venture capitalists generally prefer not to invest in companies that do not offer the prospects of an IPO within a three- to five-year timeframe. Although many venture capital investments are structured as debt (to give the venture capitalist a preferred interest in the assets of the corporation) with an "equity kicker," the venture capitalist is generally not content to receive a repayment of principal plus interest. The objective is to realize value through exercising the equity kicker.

The sample application of the traditional pricing method shown in Table 16-29 is based on a required annual rate of return of 50 percent, and what is deemed to be a conservative earnings figure and price/earnings multiple for the IPO four years in the future. By varying the earnings, IPO price/earnings ratio, target rate of return and/or timing of the IPO, different equity giveup percentages result. A matrix showing the equity giveup resulting from varying the aforementioned is useful for evaluating the giveup required. In practice, venture capitalists will make their decisions based on a conservative scenario, due to the risk and uncertainty of most venture capital investments. As a consequence, many successful venture capital investments yield considerably more than the required rate of return.

First Chicago Pricing Model Method

The traditional pricing method is simple and enjoys widespread use. By focusing solely on the returns required on successful investments, it addresses the major source of income for most venture capital firms. Unsuccessful investments yield nothing; mediocre investments yield comparatively little. A venture capitalist would not generally invest in a project that does not have the potential to achieve target rates of return achieved through an IPO or a sale of the company.

　　The flaw of the traditional pricing model is that it does not address the entire range of venture capital investments, the majority of which generally include companies that go under or fail to enable the venture capitalist to realize the benefit from his equity kicker. The broader portfolio issues of venture capital investments are reflected in the First Chicago Pricing Model (FCPM). This model quantifies the effect that alternative investment performance can have on required equity giveup.

　　The essential premise of FCPM is that, in the most basic sense, there are three potential outcomes of a venture capital investment: success, as demonstrated through an IPO or buyout; survival, which enables the venture capitalist to recover principal and interest on convertible debt, without exercising the "equity kicker"; and failure, which results in a complete loss to the venture capitalist. Between these extremes there are several hybrids that may be readily incorporated into the FCPM, but that are omitted in the following example.

　　In developing the input for the FCPM, the task is to quantify the financial impact of each alternative outcome and judgmentally assign a probability to each alternative outcome based on past experience or an assessment of similar investments. The data used for the example in Table 16-30 relate to the same hypothetical company analyzed through the traditional pricing method shown in Table 16-30. The successful scenario shows a more optimistic earnings figure and price/earnings ratio than was used in the traditional pricing model because there is no attempt to dilute these figures or show a conservative presentation to accommodate for failures. The resulting value of the equity kicker at the time of the IPO is higher. Also, a lower discount rate is used to reflect the present value of future outcomes because risk is directly reflected in the projections of alternative outcomes rather than by increasing the discount rate. The survival scenario reflects only the repayment of principal and interest, which is discounted accordingly, and the failure scenario reflects a complete loss providing no cash flows. This model is prepared on a pretax basis, although appropriate adjustments could be made to incorporate tax affects in the calculations.

　　The present value of the financial impact of each scenario is assigned a probability and weighted, so that the resultant value reflects each of the scenarios. The resulting equation is in the same form as a DCF equation: investment = present value of future investment proceeds. In this equation, the only

TABLE 16-30 First Chicago Pricing Model—Nu Corporation

	1985	1986	1987	1988	Present Value of Alternative Scenario	Weighting or Probability	Present Value of Probabilistic Alternative Scenario
Failure scenario							
Loss of investment and forfeiture of interest	0	0	0	0	0	30%	0
Survival scenario							
Interest	$80,000	$80,000	$80,000	$ 80,000			
Repayment of principal	—	—	—	1,000,000			
	$80,000	$80,000	$80,000	$1,080,000			
Present value at 40%	$57,143	$40,816	$29,155	$ 281,133	$408,247	40%	$163,299
Successful scenario							
Interest	$80,000	$80,000	$80,000	$ 80,000			
Present value at 40%	57,143	40,816	29,155	20,825	$147,939	30%	$ 44,382
Equity value of convertible debenture at December 31, 1988 initial public offering:							
Earnings of venture capital recipient				$ 900,000			
Price/earnings on initial public offering				× 25			
				$22,500,000			
Total valuation			V% ×	$22,500,000			
Equity value of convertible debenture				× 0.2603			
Present value factor at 40%			V% ×	$ 5,856,750	V% × $5,876,750	30%	V% × $1,763,025

$$
\begin{aligned}
\text{Total} \quad &\quad 207,681 \\
&+ \text{V\%} \times \$1,763,025 \\[4pt]
\text{Investment} &= \text{V\%} \times \$1,763,025 \\
\text{Investment} &= \text{Present value future} \\
&\quad \text{investment proceeds} \\
\$1,000,000 &= \$207,681 + \text{V\%} \times \\
&\quad \$1,763,063 \\
792,319 &= \text{V\%} \times \$1,763,025 \\
\frac{792,319}{\$1,763,025} &= \text{V\%} \\
\text{V\%} &= \underline{\underline{44.9\%}}
\end{aligned}
$$

unknown is the equity giveup (V). By solving the algebraic equation, the amount of equity giveup is computed.

The FCPM has the advantage of reflecting alternative scenarios more precisely than the traditional pricing model. As with other financial tools, the validity of the results of either of the venture capital pricing methods depends on the reasonableness of the underlying assumptions. At best, they provide an element of reason to a highly speculative area.

BIBLIOGRAPHY

Bernstein, Leopold A., *Financial Statement Analysis: Theory, Application and Interpretation,* Homewood, Illinois: Richard D. Irwin, Inc., 1978.

Foster, George, *Financial Statement Analysis,* Englewood Cliffs, N.J.: Prentice-Hall, Inc., 1978.

Gibson, Charles H., and Patricia A. Frishkoff, *Financial Statement Analysis: Using Financial Accounting Information,* Boston: Kent Publishing Co., 1983.

Gross, Charles W., and Robin T. Peterson, *Business Forecasting,* Boston: Houghton Mifflin Co., 1976.

Horngren, Charles T., *Cost Accounting: A Managerial Emphasis,* Englewood Cliffs, N.J.: Prentice-Hall, Inc., 1982.

Lee, Steven J., and Robert D. Coleman, eds., *Handbook of Mergers, Acquisitions and Buyouts,* Englewood Cliffs, N.J.: Prentice-Hall, Inc., 1981.

Loscalzo, William, *Cash Flow Forecasting,* New York: McGraw Hill, Inc., 1982.

Makridakis, Spyros, and Steven C. Wheelwright, eds., *The Handbook of Forecasting: A Manager's Guide,* New York: John Wiley & Sons, 1982.

Miller, Martin A., *Miller's Comprehensive GAAP Guide,* New York: Harcourt Brace Jovanovich, Inc., 1984.

Pratt, Stanley E., ed., *Guide to Venture Capital Sources,* Wellesley Hills, Mass.: Capital Publishing Corp., 1983.

Weston, J. Fred, and Eugene F. Brigham, *Managerial Finance,* Hinsdale, Illinois: The Dryden Press, 1981.

Van Horne, James C., *Financial Management and Policy,* Englewood Cliffs, N.J.: Prentice-Hall, Inc., 1983.

17

Productivity Analysis for Strategic Management

A. DUNCAN KIDD

Vice President, Corporate Development, Amstar Corporation

THE NATURE OF PRODUCTIVITY

The word "productivity" applied to manufacturing or production processes normally implies a ratio of output to labor input, such as units produced per man-hour. When applied to a business as a whole, however, the concept of productivity must be expanded. Labor is only one of the inputs involved; materials and energy, capital, and even the marketplace must be viewed as inputs as well. Thus the simple equation:

$$\text{Productivity} = \frac{\text{Output}}{\text{Input}}$$

becomes the more complex:

$$\text{Productivity} = \frac{\text{Output}}{\text{Manpower} + \text{Materials} + \text{Capital} + \text{Markets}}$$

Considering productivity in terms of all these inputs goes beyond manufacturing efficiency and human resources management into such seemingly unrelated business matters as pricing, inflation, capital planning, marketing, and strategic planning. Each of these affects the value of the output of a business or the amount or mix of inputs used to produce that output. Frequently there are trade-offs among inputs, and actions with regard to one input may improve productivity while actions with respect to another may reduce it. Improved productivity with respect to one input, such as labor, does not automatically mean improved productivity, profitability, or return on invested capital for the business as a whole.

For example, a small single-product manufacturing company makes a raw material change that improves the durability of its product, reduces materials costs, and eliminates a costly manufacturing step (Table 17-1). This business, like many manufacturing businesses, sets prices based on a markup of manufacturing costs to ensure its gross profit margin. In this case, this approach would lead to a price reduction (column B) greater than the cost reduction. Profitability would decline markedly even though labor productivity improved and materials costs were reduced. No rational company would price this way. Many, however, adjust prices annually, combining real cost savings and productivity improvements with inflationary cost increases to develop new standard costs. In the examples, pricing to maintain gross profit margin would produce the results shown in column C. Costs, prices, productivity, and profits would increase, but the profit increase would be only a fraction of expected cost savings. When all figures in column C are deflated by the 10 percent inflation factor, the profitability of the business in real terms declines markedly, as shown by the figures in column B.

The key to unlocking this barrier to greater productivity is value added. Value added is defined as revenue less the cost of purchased materials included in the cost of goods sold. It measures the net contribution of a business to the value of its products, as distinct from the value provided by its suppliers. In the example depicted in Table 17-1, the materials substitution maintained the utility and increased the quality of the product. It should have at least maintained its market value and, because of the material cost reduction, increased the business' value added. Instead, pricing by marking up costs negated all the cost reductions, and even some of the original value added. Although the example may seem farfetched, the basic problem is widespread and masked by the complexity of today's multiproduct, multibusiness companies.

This example involves only one of several ways of measuring productivity. Although these measurements and ratios may be unfamiliar, they are not new. They are variations of some of the most widely used business profitability ratios. But by being different they provide a different means of examining business processes and ascertaining productivity. Approaching productivity from a total business viewpoint provides new tools with implications not only in pricing, but also in capital investment decisions and in product, market, and capacity planning.

TABLE 17-1 Effects of Raw Material Change on a Single-Product Manufacturing Business
(dollars in thousands)

Situation: A purchased material substitution
- Improves durability but otherwise does not change appearance, quality, or utility of product;
- Reduces materials cost by $100,000/year; and
- Eliminates manufacturing operation involving five people to produce an additional $100,000/year savings.

	(A) Base	(B) Real Results	(C) 10 Percent Inflation
Units produced/sold	210,000	210,000	210,000
Sales revenue	$ 10,000	$ 9,690	$ 10,660
Materials costs	3,500	3,400	3,740
Value added	$ 6,500	$ 6,290	$ 6,920
Manufacturing operations	3,000	2,900	3,190
Gross profit	$ 3,500	$ 3,390	$ 3,730
Percentage	35.0%	35.0%	35.0%
Selling and administration	2,000	2,000	2,200
Operating profit	$ 1,500	$ 1,390	$ 1,530
Percentage	15.0%	14.3%	14.3%
Employees	150	145	145
Units output employee	1,400	1,450	1,450

PRODUCTIVITY OF A BUSINESS

The productivity of a business has been defined in the following equation:

$$\text{Productivity} = \frac{\text{Output}}{\text{Manpower} + \text{Materials} + \text{Capital} + \text{Markets}}$$

While it would be nice to have a single ratio that would reflect the overall productivity of a business, the various categories of input cannot really be combined. Mathematically, they have entirely different units of measurement. Operationally, they are managed differently and by different management processes. And the time horizon associated with each is different: changes in purchased materials and energy inputs (or in their unit costs) can be made or can occur in a relatively short time. Changes in manpower take a little longer, but usually can be accomplished within a fiscal year. Capital investment decisions, once implemented, seem permanent. Market changes can occur suddenly, but have effects stretching well beyond the tenure of present management.

In addition to the problem of noncomparability, strategic decisions frequently involve trade-offs among these inputs. The productivity of a business as a whole often is determined by the effectiveness of those trade-offs. Steps to reduce labor input generally require capital investment; to support capital investment, a business must derive profit from the marketplace. Materials substitution may reduce cost, but it may also adversely affect quality or market value.

To make wise trade-offs, productivity must be evaluated, input by input. There are four major means of evaluating productivity: (1) value added, (2) productivity ratios, (3) productivity standards, and (4) productivity patterns over time.

Value Added

Productivity is the ratio of output to the inputs required to produce it. But what constitutes output?

Those who have considered productivity at the corporate or strategic business unit level are increasingly turning to value added as the most appropriate measurement of output. Value added is the market price of products and services sold less the market cost of the purchased materials (or services) contained within them. It is the premium the market pays, over purchased costs, for the changes a business makes in materials or the utility value of the products it produces from them. It separates what a business does from what its suppliers and customers do, and recognizes differences in intangibles such as utility, quality, service, and reliability, as well as cost. Being an economic measurement, it is applicable to all kinds of businesses, and the value added of a corporation as a whole is equal to the sum of the value added for all its parts—divisions, business units, business segments, and individual products and product lines.

Value added is, at the same time, a measure of the economic value a business delivers to the economy in the form of goods and services and a measure of the resources it has at its disposal to produce those products and services and to support the future growth of the business. This duality frequently causes some confusion. In terms of financial statements, value added is revenue less the cost of purchased materials. Alternatively, it might be defined as the sum of all costs plus profit (which in itself is the cost of capital). The two are mathematically equal but conceptually miles apart. As used here,

Value added = Revenue − Purchased materials and services

denotes the amount of money the market is allowing the business to recover its costs and generate a profit. The internal operations of the business determine its profit, not its value added.

Frequently businesspeople say that they want to spend more on quality or service or integrate forward to increase their value added. The implication is that more costs automatically mean more value added. What they are really saying is that by spending more on or in support of their product, they are hoping the market will value it more highly and allow them more revenue. The distinction is subtle, but very important.

The importance of value added to the operation of a business is that it is the principal, if not the only, source of funds to finance all the activities that characterize a business:

- Manufacturing operations and funds for expansion
- Selling, administrative, and support functions
- Business development expenditures
- Return to investors or shareholders

Even capital expenditures are funded from value added, past (retained earnings) or future (debt). The only source of funds available to management that is not directly dependent on the past, present, or future value added is that provided by equity investors, and they must receive an adequate return.

One of management's tasks is to allocate funds among the various aspects of a business (Figure 17-1). When value added increases during periods of business growth, this allocation task is simple because "there is enough to go around," that is, funds allocated to one use can increase without reducing funds allocated to other uses. When value added is flat or declining, however, reduction of funds available to one area becomes the only way to increase the amount of funds available to any other.

In measuring productivity, value added lacks the certainty associated with unit volumes, standard costs, and headcounts as output. It involves uncertainty, change, and customer perceptions of value. It is a total amount rather than a rate. Value added may go down when volume goes down, in both cases on a real as well as nominal basis. One difficulty in using value added as a productivity measurement is that inflation can cause value added to increase in relation to noneconomic denominators, even though productivity has gone down. In productivity analysis, value added should be examined both on a current dollar basis and on a real basis, deflated to some constant dollar base.

In the balance of this discussion, value added is used when inputs are measured in current or nominal dollars, and real value added is used for noneconomic inputs such as man-hours.

Real value added may be superior to sales or profits as a measure of business growth. From its duality, it is a measure of the net contribution a business makes to the economy and the gross resources it has at its disposal, both of which most businesses would like to increase. Those who stress sales growth alone may be squeezed between increasingly competitive markets and increasing materials costs only to find that they are unable to generate the profits necessary to sustain sales growth. Others who focus solely on profits or earnings per share may find that they have sacrificed future market strength for short-term profits. A consideration of real value added alerts management to what is really happening.

Business Productivity Ratios

Personal, resource, capital, and market productivity ratios use value added as the output (Figure 17-2). In general, for personal and capital productivity

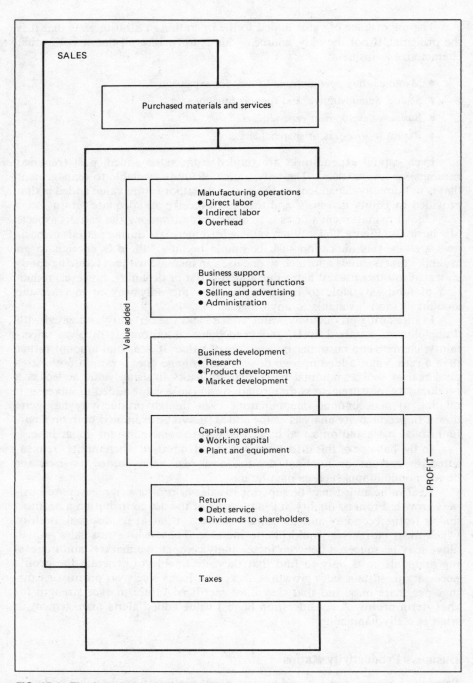

FIG. 17-1 The Importance of Value Added

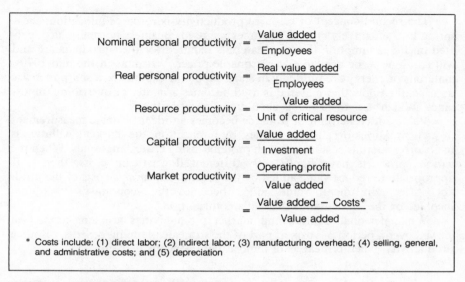

$$\text{Nominal personal productivity} = \frac{\text{Value added}}{\text{Employees}}$$

$$\text{Real personal productivity} = \frac{\text{Real value added}}{\text{Employees}}$$

$$\text{Resource productivity} = \frac{\text{Value added}}{\text{Unit of critical resource}}$$

$$\text{Capital productivity} = \frac{\text{Value added}}{\text{Investment}}$$

$$\text{Market productivity} = \frac{\text{Operating profit}}{\text{Value added}}$$

$$= \frac{\text{Value added} - \text{Costs*}}{\text{Value added}}$$

* Costs include: (1) direct labor; (2) indirect labor; (3) manufacturing overhead; (4) selling, general, and administrative costs; and (5) depreciation

FIG. 17-2 Productivity Measurement Ratios

ratios, the employees and investment categories should include all of those associated with the value added output of the business (including administrative and executive personnel), but should exclude those (e.g., diversified financial or real estate investment and portfolio managers) associated with income not related to the business and normally reported below the bottom line.

Profitability is not normally thought of as a productivity measurement, but it is profitability, or market productivity, that determines whether an enterprise is successful. Business strategy involves deploying people, material, and capital resources in relation to markets in order to realize an appropriate profit or return on investment over time.

There are many other productivity ratios that are appropriate to individual inputs and situations, but the set of ratios shown in Figure 17-2 is considered the most inclusive and, therefore, the most appropriate to examining the productivity of a total business. Substitute "sales" for "value added" in each of these ratios and they become very familiar business analysis terms.

Resource Productivity: A Special Case. Personal, capital, and market productivities are closely interrelated. Resource productivity is different and stands by itself. There are two distinct concepts of resource productivity, both measured by value added per unit of resource.

The first concept is yield, a cost or waste measurement that has long been a primary concern of line operating management. By definition, getting more useful product out of a given amount of raw material increases value added and, all other costs remaining the same, profits. The situation is more complex where multi-use process streams or possible byproducts are involved, and this leads to the second concept.

The second concept of resource productivity is resource allocation: measuring how effectively critical resources are used. Business normally has operated on the assumption that the materials required for their products are and will continue to be available at reasonable prices. When, as in the mid-1970s, materials or energy are suddenly in short supply or experience a sharp increase in price, then how that material is used becomes a matter of overriding importance. Which uses or products should receive priority?

Value added per unit of resource becomes an ideal strategic measurement in such situations because it includes, by implication, the market's willingness to absorb materials cost increases in products using critical materials. When the various products have significantly different downstream costs, then it is appropriate to reduce value added by the total *direct variable* costs of the product. After adjustment, value added becomes the economist's "marginal income" or the accountant's "variable contribution."

While personal, capital, and market productivities are long-term, best viewed over a period of years as part of the strategic planning process, resource productivity, when critical, is of almost daily concern.

Business Productivity Standards

Rate of change and long-term trends are more important in analyzing the productivity of a business than the absolute value of a particular ratio at a particular time. For those seeking an outside standard as a basis for comparison, there are several sources.

Published Financial Data. Publicly held corporations must prepare annual reports or 10K reports which contain many of the statistics required to construct strategic productivity ratios. These reports do not, however, break out value added, and sales must be used instead. When sales is used as the output measurement, capital productivity and market productivity become the familiar capital turnover and return on sales, respectively. While sales can be used to develop comparable productivity-type ratios for competitive businesses, the results are inferior to productivity ratios using value added. For businesses where material costs are a high percentage of sales or involve volatile commodities, comparisons based on sales dollars become virtually meaningless.

Government Statistics. For over 30 years the Department of Commerce's Census of Manufacturers has included statistics, broken down to the four-digit (and sometimes five-digit) SIC level on value added, employment, and value added per employee. Unfortunately, the census does not contain comparable useful data on profitability or investment, although data on inventories and capital expenditures by industry at least indicate trends.

Profit Impact of Marketing Strategy Data Base. The Strategic Planning Institute with its Profit Impact of Marketing Strategy (PIMS) data base has taken an approach to productivity quite similar to that described here and uses

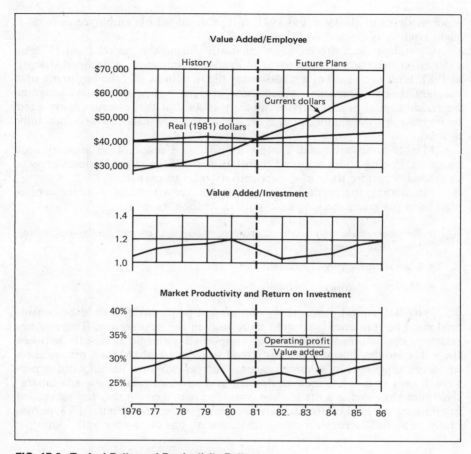

FIG. 17-3 Typical Pattern of Productivity Ratios

many of the same measurements. Using its data base of information representing 2,500 member business units, PIMS has developed benchmark productivity
standards for any business based on its structural characteristics, its capital
intensity, and the competitive characteristics of its markets.

Productivity Patterns Over Time

The most important standard for strategic analysis of the productivity of a
business is its own performance over time. Figure 17-3 shows several productivity ratios for a typical, reasonably well-managed manufacturing business. The
ratios shown are both historical and projected, based on the future plans of the
business.

Value added per employee is increasing steadily, with most of the increase
resulting from inflation as real value added per employee increases at a much

more modest rate. In 1980 and 1981, real value added per employee suffered a slight decline as a result of the recession.

Capital productivity increased modestly during the period from 1976 to 1980 as business steadily improved utilization of capacity. It declined sharply in 1981, both as a result of a recessionary dip in volume and the beginning of a substantial new capacity expansion program. The expansion program depressed capital productivity in the early 1980s, but that measure is expected to improve by the middle of the decade as the new capacity becomes fully utilized.

Market productivity fell sharply in 1980 as a result of inflationary cost increases. Pricing policy adjusted to inflation in 1981, and the business expects to gradually restore its market productivity ratio to past levels.

Eliminating the perturbations due to the recession and a major capital expansion program, the long-term pattern of these ratios is:

- *Personal productivity:* real—Increasing modestly; current dollar—Increasing faster than inflation
- *Capital productivity*—Essentially flat
- *Market productivity*—Essentially flat

Why flat capital productivity and market productivity should be considered good performance is covered more fully in the next section. These values relate to one another, and there are important strategic trade-offs between them. Day-to-day business pressures tend to reduce both. Market pressures on prices are supported by salesmen eager to increase volume; manufacturing personnel want to invest in new equipment and up-to-date facilities; administrative functions develop a life of their own. The management that has succeeded in attaining the kind of productivity pattern represented by Figure 17-3, particularly in an inflationary-recession environment, has done very well, indeed.

PRODUCTIVITY AND INVESTMENT

If there is one single measurement of the performance of a business that all would agree is significant, it is return on investment. But it is market productivity combined with capital productivity that determines return on investment:

$$\text{Return on investment} = \text{Capital productivity} \times \text{Market productivity}$$

$$\frac{\text{Operating profit}}{\text{Investment}} = \frac{\text{Value added}}{\text{Investment}} \times \frac{\text{Operating profit}}{\text{Value added}}$$

It is noteworthy that personal productivity is indirectly involved as it affects the costs deducted from value added to arrive at operating profit, as shown in the following ratio:

$$\text{Market productivity} = \frac{\text{Value added} \times \text{Operating costs}}{\text{Value added}}$$

Cost reduction does not automatically improve profitability and return on investment; it does so only when pricing allows the benefits of improved personal productivity to improve market productivity.

Return on investment is a complex measurement, affected by many things. The ratio alone does not reveal the problem or inform the management process. Consideration of return on investment in terms of its component parts, capital productivity and market productivity (i.e., asset utilization and profitability), can lead to an understanding of why this measurement is behaving as it is and of where efforts to control it should be concentrated.

Cost Reduction Investments

Businesses that have made extensive investments in cost-reducing equipment over the years are expressing concern about the returns on these investments. Many companies have instituted programs to "audit" capital investment decisions after the fact to determine if the projected benefits have been realized. Most have found that they have been and that the calculated incremental returns on incremental investment have been realized. The sum of these incremental improvements has not, however, shown up in the return on investment of the business as a whole.

The explanation may lie in pricing and inflation, as shown in Table 17-2. The analysis takes the same small manufacturing company presented in Table 17-1. and analyzes the effect of a capital investment in cost-saving equipment. Columns B and C show, in real or inflated terms, the net effect when the company applies cost markup pricing to maintain gross profit margin:

- The projected savings in people and costs are realized;
- The business' traditional 35 percent profit margin is maintained;
- Profits increase less than anticipated and on a real basis, decline; and
- Return on investment declines both before and after inflation.

Again, pricing simply to maintain profit margin decreases the real value added being sought from the marketplace, and inflation disguises the fact that this is happening.

But the cost reduction investment has done nothing to alter the market value of the real value added of the product. If pricing were left unchanged on a real basis and inflated to reflect the full 10 percent cost inflation, real value added would be maintained and the return investment objective of the new investment and the business as a whole would be maintained (columns D and E). The slight increase in return on investment in the inflated case, column D, is considered spurious. It results from the fact that inflation has been applied to working capital but not to fixed assets. Over the short term, this is mathematically correct but, given replacement costs, fixed assets will inflate over the long term also.

It is significant that even in columns D and E, capital productivity declines. Because value added has not been increased but investment has been, this is inevitable. To maintain return on investment, therefore, market produc-

TABLE 17-2   Effects of Capital Investment in Cost-Saving Equipment on a Single-Product Manufacturing Business
(dollars in thousands)

Situation: A $500,000 investment in cost-saving equipment will replace 10 workers with a net annual saving of $150,000:
- 30 percent return on new investment consistent with historic overall return of the business;
- No change in unit volumes; and
- 10 percent inflation of all costs.

	(A) Base	(B) Maintain Gross Profit Margin — Inflated	(C) Real	(D) Maintain Real Value Added — Inflated	(E) Real
Operations					
Net sales	$10,000	$10,750	$ 9,770	$11,000	$10,000
Materials	3,500	3,850	3,500	3,850	3,500
Value added	$ 6,500	$ 6,900	$ 6,270	$ 7,150	$ 6,500
Manufacturing operations	3,000	3,135	2,850	3,135	2,850
Gross profit	$ 3,500	$ 3,765	$ 3,420	$ 4,015	$ 3,650
Percentage	35.0%	35.0%	35.0%	36.5%	36.5%
Selling, general, and administrative costs	2,000	2,200	2,000	2,200	2,000
Operating profit	$ 1,500	$ 1,565	$ 1,420	$ 1,815	$ 1,650
Percentage	15.0%	14.5%	14.5%	16.5%	16.5%
Investment					
Working capital	$ 2,500	$ 2,750	$ 2,500	$ 2,750	$ 2,500
Fixed assets	2,500	3,000	3,000	3,000	3,000
Total	$ 5,000	$ 5,750	$ 5,500	$ 5,750	$ 5,500
Operating return on investment	30.0%	27.2%	25.8%	31.6%	30.0%
Employees	150	140	140	140	140
Productivity ratios					
Value added per employee	$43,300	$49,300	–	$51,100	–
Real value added per employee	$43,300	–	$44,800	–	$46,400
Value added investment	1.300	1.200	1.140	1.240	1.180
Operating profit/Value added	23.1%	22.6%	22.6%	25.4%	25.4%

tivity must increase. This implies that successive cost reduction investments require successive increases in market productivity to maintain return on investment. Even if the competitive environment would allow this, ultimately very high market productivity must invite new competition. Capital investment strategy must recognize these delicate balances among capital productivity, market productivity, and return on investment.

When the financial statements of competitors in the same industry are examined, their sales-to-asset ratios (and, by implication, their capital productivity ratios) are found to fluctuate over time around a constant value. An industry or market will support a given degree of capital intensity; the competitor with inadequate assets is at an operating cost disadvantage and may not generate enough gross profit margin to support a profitable business; the competitor with excess assets will not earn the return on investment necessary to continue a high level of investment.

The question of whether the market will allow a company to retain the savings generated by new capital investment is as important as whether or not the investment will produce savings. Incremental analysis of savings resulting from a cost reduction project answers only the latter. The answer to the former lies in understanding the industry and its markets, and considering all the various partial productivity ratios that enter into the overall productivity of a business.

When Productivity Investments Pay Off

From the foregoing, it can be seen that a business with higher capital productivity and lower market productivity than others in its industry may find that investment in cost reduction will improve its market productivity to a greater extent than the increased investment will depress its capital productivity. Alternatively, the cost reduction might allow it to become more competitive and increase volume and value added to the extent that, despite the investment, capital productivity declines very little. This is the case for a company that has been operating above practical capacity and combines productivity improvement with a capacity expansion investment.

Investment in cost reduction may also be appropriate when the return on the new investment is very high—high enough to allow substantial sharing of the savings with the marketplace and still provide a better than average return on the new investment. When such opportunities are substantial, they might be considered technological breakthroughs that will ultimately be pursued by all businesses in an industry. The advantage in these cases comes from being among the first because by the time the last few companies adopt the new technology or method, market forces will already have claimed the bulk of the savings.

For most businesses, most of the time, productivity investment decisions require an understanding of the marketplace and involve a higher degree of risk and uncertainty than is implied by analysis of the savings advantages alone. Investment is most apt to be an attractive approach to improving productivity when the business is insulated from price and real value added erosion by having proprietary products, products with high customized content, or a high market share. In such cases, there is a reasonable prospect that all or most of projected savings will appear at the bottom line as return on the additional investment.

At the other extreme are businesses where price is wholly determined by the market. For these businesses productivity investment generally pays off only when associated with capacity expansion or replacement. Volume expansion increases value added as well as investment, minimizing the sacrifice in capital productivity. Similarly, replacement investments using funds generated by depreciation do not affect net investment and are "free" as far as capital productivity is concerned. In both sound volume expansion and replacement investments, even if the market rather than the business is the beneficiary of the personal productivity improvement, capital productivity, market productivity, and return on investment should remain stable.

The example in Table 17-2 applies to a small product manufacturing company with moderate capital intensity where fixed asset investments are made incrementally. The situation is more acute for the large, capital-intensive process business where new plant investments are very large. It is normally several years before the capacity and value added potential of new plants are fully utilized; in the interim, there is an almost irresistible temptation to lower prices to increase volume. In many markets, the price reduction necessary to increase volume significantly may be so great as to produce a decrease rather than an increase in total value added and a decline in all three partial productivity ratios. PIMS has observed from its studies of the financial performance of a wide variety of businesses that the more capital intensive businesses tend to have lower average return on investment. PIMS attributes it to this effect.

Low profitability (i.e., low market productivity) in an industry is frequently an indicator of a low probability that returns on cost reduction investments will remain as long as increased bottom line profits. Competitive forces will gradually cause the return to leak away in the market.

The thrust here appears to run counter to the widely publicized view that U.S. industry must invest more capital in improving productivity. Extensive capital investment in producing present products and volumes at lower cost must inevitably depress real capital productivity.

Improving productivity on a national basis, however, means applying available manpower and resources to producing more value added, not just producing present value added more cheaply. If investments are made in new products, improvements that enhance the market value of present products, or cost reductions sufficient to recapture lost world markets or create new ones, then the increase in total value added will be much more than proportional to the capital invested and capital productivity will increase. It is the contracting business or economy, rather than the expanding one, that faces capital productivity problems.

PRODUCTIVITY IMPROVEMENT STRATEGY

The key to productivity improvement lies in one simple rule: Maintain or increase value added in relation to cost inputs. Without this, the benefits of anything else accomplished can be lost. Value added enters into the computation of all partial productivity ratios, and when value added output increases in relation to inputs, these ratios and return on investment increase. When real value added declines, painful cost and personnel reductions are necessary just to stay even.

Management of value added is more difficult than control of costs; it is also more important. Cost problems, although onerous, can be overcome by determined management action. Problems in the marketplace are deeper, take longer to resolve, and may be beyond management's control.

In approaching the problem of the overall productivity of a business, management should analyze its present productivity carefully, with respect to all inputs. What are the trends in the business' real value added, personal productivity, capital productivity, and market productivity? How do these trends compare with those of others in the industry and in closely related industries? Declining market productivity is as often a sign of poor pricing or changing market perceptions as it is of runaway costs. Capital productivity should also be examined: Is the business more or less capital intensive than others in the industry? Is investment increasing faster than value added in the business as a whole or in any significant segments of it?

With such information as a background, management can approach the problem of improving personal productivity. Improving personal productivity may be the only way to produce near-term results, but the real problem and its ultimate solution may lie elsewhere.

Improving Personal Productivity

Improving personal productivity is always worthwhile, providing it does not involve adverse trade-offs with output or other inputs. The low-cost producer in a market can enjoy the highest market productivity as well as the highest personal productivity. Determining the best way to improve personal productivity, however, requires knowledge and understanding of the business' partial productivities with regard to all inputs.

In general, the best approach to improving personal productivity is to seek to increase the output obtained from present inputs. Attempting to produce current output with less input is more difficult to achieve, presents fewer opportunities, and, in the end, improves only efficiency, not productivity. When the increased output is not needed in the market, then both output and inputs are reduced proportionately, with the freed inputs and resources made available to be applied to other productive pursuits. That is productivity.

Steps to improve personal productivity may be grouped into three categories: (1) motivating workers to work harder and produce more, (2) investing in higher output or labor-saving equipment, and (3) improving management methods and procedures.

Emphasis is frequently placed on the first two, but the third may offer the greatest opportunities because it avoids the capital trade-off problems. Even the best run business should frequently review scheduling, work flow, and organization, and administrative as well as production functions. The most

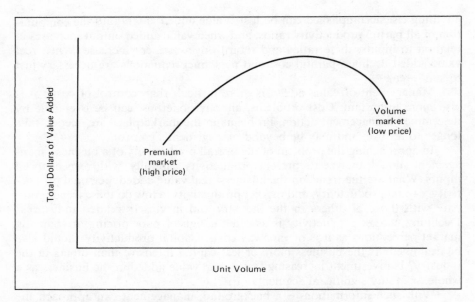

FIG. 17-4 The Value Added Potential Curve of a Product

highly motivated worker using the most sophisticated piece of equipment cannot be productive if poor management keeps him underutilized.

PRODUCTIVITY MEASUREMENTS AND BUSINESS STRATEGY

The various productivity ratios can be used not only to develop productivity improvement strategies but also to develop corporate strategies. They can help management in several important aspects of strategic planning:

- Analysis of value added and profit opportunities in the context of prevailing market conditions;
- Price vs. volume trade-offs in day-to-day operations; and
- Planning of capacity investments.

Optimizing Value Added

Value added is an amount, not a rate, and the amount of value added that a given business (product line) can deliver to and extract from its market is finite. Figure 17-4 portrays, in value added terms, the economist's classic price-demand curve. Each point on the curve represents the *amount* of value added generated by a particular combination of product volume and price.

The left-hand end of the curve represents the amount of value added generated with a high-priced premium product serving a specialized market niche. As price is reduced, the gain in volume more than offsets the sacrifice in unit margin, and total value added increases. Moving farther to the right, the proportionate sacrifice in margin becomes greater, and total value added passes through a maximum, subsequently declining at an accelerating rate. The shape of the curve differs from business to business, but it is difficult to conceive of a competitive product-market situation that does not exhibit an optimum somewhere between the extremes of price and volume.

In a growing market, the curve moves upward and to the right; during a recessionary period it moves downward and to the left. The curve represents the combined effects of all influences in a market: customers, their perceptions of value, competitors, and competitors' product and market strategies. When a new competitor or a substitute product enters the market, the curve tilts. When the new product or competitor enters at the lower price end, the right-hand side is affected more than the left, and the optimum moves downward and to the left.

As anyone who has ever tried to construct a price-demand curve for a product knows, the exact shape of this curve cannot be predicted and is changing all the time. Only one point is known, representing recent history, and there is uncertainty whether that point will be the same tomorrow. With a little informed judgment, however, it is possible to assess with reasonable certainty whether a business is operating on the left-hand side or right-hand side of optimum. Strategically, that is what is important.

New and growth businesses normally find themselves operating to the left of optimum, while aging and declining businesses probably find themselves on the right. Mature businesses in stable competitive environments probably are operating in the flat upper portion of the curve near the optimum. When mature markets are highly competitive, however, it is probable that most competitors are operating to the right of optimum. A company that can boast that its sales force has never lost an order on price is almost certainly operating far to the right.

In terms of the productivity ratios, if all increase with increased volume, the business is probably operating far to the left of optimum; if all are decreasing, it is operating far to the right. In the optimum range, all three ratios are relatively stable and capital productivity is probably declining slightly. Profitability is a less reliable indicator, affected as much by capacity as by position on the value added curve.

Balancing Price and Volume

Optimizing market position and value added maximizes profit opportunity. Whether that opportunity will be optimally realized depends on how well capacity is in balance with the market.

Figure 17-5 superimposes operating costs (excluding purchased materials) on the value added curve. The distance between the two curves represents operating profit. The cost curve is very similar to that found in the traditional breakeven chart, starting at the left with fixed costs. With materials excluded,

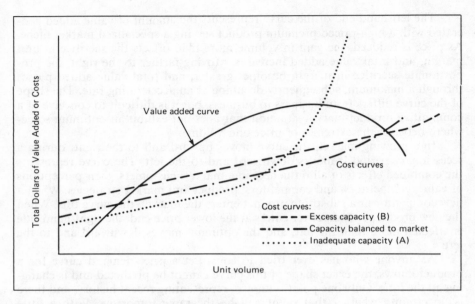

FIG. 17-5 Value Added and Capacity Costs

the variable portion has a much lower slope and, for many businesses where labor costs are not really variable, the line becomes almost flat. As volume reaches the practical capacity of a facility, interferences and delays force costs up at an increasing rate. A productive organization has an almost infinite capacity to absorb costs, but its ability to produce output is finite.

The solid cost line in Figure 17-5 represents a business where practical capacity is reached at approximately the same volume as optimum value added. Such a business can be said to be balanced with respect to its market. Maximum profit occurs at a volume slightly below that at which value added is maximized. Ideally, this business would seek to operate somewhere between the optimum profit and the optimum value added volumes. Over this range, profit is relatively stable and could, during mild recessionary dips, even increase slightly. The sacrifice in profit required to move a little to the right and improve market share is small. Finally, in terms of partial productivity ratios, this is the range over which market productivity is at its maximum. This last is another indication of where a business is on the value added curve and further support for stable market productivity.

The effect of capacity imbalance is illustrated by the two dashed cost lines, A and B, in Figure 17-5. When capacity is inadequate, as in curve A, fixed costs are lower but the business will run out of capacity before it can realize its market, value added, and profit potential. Although its profitability can be attractive, there are probably additional profit opportunities it cannot pursue. Also, its capacity-strained operations are probably creating customer service problems, which ultimately affect its market position and adversely alter its value added curve.

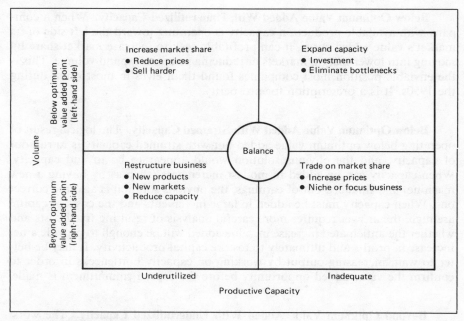

FIG. 17-6 Value Added/Capacity Matrix

Excessive capacity (cost line B) means higher fixed costs and therefore lower profit and market productivity at all points on the value added curve. It is worth noting that in this illustration of significant overcapacity, profits depend solely on where the business is operating on the value added curve, and not on capacity utilization. Many businesses have learned the hard way that pursuit of volume to maintain capacity utilization is not the right answer to a deteriorating market situation.

The Value Added/Capacity Matrix

The most appropriate strategy for a business depends on where the business is with regard to capacity utilization and where it is on the value added curve. This is portrayed in the popular decision matrix format as illustrated in Figure 17-6. In this matrix the target is the center, the area where capacity is in balance with the market. This is an elusive condition, and most businesses find themselves out of balance to one degree or another as market conditions change. Each of the four quadrants represents a position and suggests specific strategies. Starting in the upper left quadrant, and moving clockwise, there are four possible combinations:

1 Below optimum value added with underutilized capacity;
2 Below optimum value added with strained capacity;
3 Beyond optimum value added with underutilized capacity; and
4 Beyond optimum value added with strained capacity.

Below Optimum Value Added With Underutilized Capacity. When a company with available production capacity is operating toward the left side of its market's value added curve, it can profitably seek to increase market share by moving into lower margin markets or reducing prices to expand volume. This is the enviable position most companies found themselves in most often during the 1950s. It is a prescription for prosperity.

Below Optimum Value Added With Strained Capacity. The logical result of operating below optimum value added but with strained capacity is to run out of capacity, and the obvious solution would appear to be to add capacity. When capacity can be added in modest increments (such as by buying a new machine) and financed out of earnings, the obvious solution is also the correct one. When capacity must be added in large increments and the costs of capital are high, the answer requires more careful analysis of resulting fixed costs and whether the anticipated increase in value added will be enough to provide a net increase in profits and ultimately to restore capital productivity. It may be better to wait, increasing output by working on capacity bottlenecks in order to confirm the value added opportunity before the capital commitment is made.

Beyond Optimum Value Added With Underutilized Capacity. The worst position to be in is beyond optimum value added with underutilized capacity. All the alternatives are either difficult or unpleasant. The most attractive solution is to find new products or markets with which to utilize the excess capacity. The difficulty is that those products or markets must be truly new, part of a separate value added curve. If facilities are highly specialized, then the only solution may be disinvestment, closing down facilities to eliminate the fixed costs and redeploying the assets to other uses.

Beyond Optimum Value Added With Strained Capacity. If the over-used capacity results from prices that have caused the business to move into the right-hand side of the value added curve, then volume expansion has gotten out of control. This calls for a strategy involving niching or focusing, giving up business where reasonable margins cannot be obtained. Careful market analysis to define the least profitable customers or market segments can enable a business to climb back upward and to the left along the value added curve.

Economics of the Value Added Curve

Table 17-3 and Figure 17-7 relate the value added curve to the classic economic concepts of the price-demand curve and marginal income. The sets of volume and price shown at the top of Table 17-3 represent a hypothetical price-demand curve. The balance of Table 17-3 presents, in financial statement format, the economic consequences of this price-demand relationship. Figure 17-7 presents similar information graphically.

TABLE 17-3 Price-Volume and Value Added

Volume (units in thousands)	800	900	1,000	1,100	1,200
Price ($/unit)	$10.50	$10.30	$10.00	$9.50	$8.70
Employees	140	145	150	155	160
PRO FORMA OPERATING STATEMENT (dollars in thousands)					
Sales revenue	$ 8,400	$ 9,270	$10,000	$10,450	$10,440
Materials costs	2,800	3,150	3,500	3,850	4,200
Value added	$ 5,600	$ 6,120	$ 6,500	$ 6,600	$ 6,240
Variable operations costs	1,200	1,350	1,500	1,650	1,800
Marginal income	$ 4,400	$ 4,770	$ 5,000	$ 4,950	$ 4,440
Fixed manufacturing costs	1,500	1,500	1,500	1,500	1,500
Gross profit	$ 2,900	$ 3,270	$ 3,500	$ 3,450	$ 2,940
Selling, general, and administrative costs	2,000	2,000	2,000	2,000	2,000
Operating profit	$ 900	$ 1,270	$ 1,500	$ 1,450	$ 940
PRO FORMA INVESTMENT (dollars in thousands)					
Working capital	$ 2,000	$ 2,250	$ 2,500	$ 2,750	$ 3,000
Fixed assets	2,500	2,500	2,500	2,500	2,500
Investment	$ 4,500	$ 4,750	$ 5,000	$ 5,250	$ 5,500
PROFITABILITY RATIOS (percent)					
Variable contribution (Marginal income/Sales)	52.4	51.5	50.0	47.4	42.5
Gross profit margin	34.5	35.3	35.0	33.0	28.2
Return on sales	10.7	13.7	15.0	13.9	9.0
Operating return on investment	20.0	26.7	30.0	27.6	17.1
PRODUCTIVITY RATIOS					
Units/Employee	5,710	6,210	6,670	7,100	7,500
Value added/Employee	$40,000	$42,210	$43,330	$42,580	$39,000
Value added/Investment	1.24	1.29	1.30	1.26	1.13
Operating profit/Value added	16.1%	20.8%	23.1%	22.0%	15.1%

Cost assumptions:
- Materials costs, variable operations costs, and working capital are proportional to unit volume.
- All other costs and fixed asset investment are independent of volume.

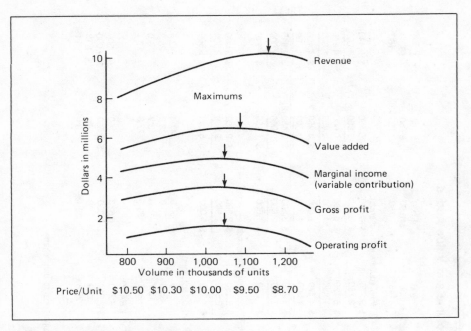

FIG. 17-7 Price-Volume and Value Added Curves

The business situation represented by the extreme left-hand column in Table 17-3 is one of high prices and margin, but a volume insufficient to provide an attractive profit after recovery of the full fixed costs of the business. As volume increases, marginal income (the accountant's variable contribution) and profits increase. Since price declines as volume increases while variable costs per unit and total fixed costs remain constant, the increase in revenue, value added, marginal income, and profits are not directly porportional to volume. All, even revenue, pass through maximum values and then decline with further increases in volume. The revenue maximum occurs at a very high volume, normally far beyond the range of consideration in most business analyses. Value added, however, reaches its maximum at a lower volume, and marginal income reaches its maximum even earlier. Assuming the remaining costs are fixed, gross profit and operating profit optimize at the point of maximum marginal income.

Economic theory says that a business should seek to operate at the point of maximum marginal income; this is the point at which marginal revenue equals marginal cost. At this point value added is still increasing; it reaches its maximum at a slightly higher volume. Significant considerations suggest that a business base its pricing, budgeting, and planning on a volume beyond the marginal income maximum up to, but not beyond, the value added maximum:

- Performance is relatively stable in the volume range between the marginal income and value added maximums.

- It is an aggressive posture, anticipating future growth. In a growth situation the value added curve expands to the right, and during the subsequent operating period the volume selected to provide maximum value added will probably provide maximum profits.
- It affords a cushion against mild economic downturns. By accepting a reduced volume and adjusting pricing to maintain or improve margins, planned profits can be preserved.
- It does not presume rapid response of variable operating costs to changes in volume. At the value added maximum, total value added dollars change little as volume fluctuates. Managers have found that budgeted operating costs are difficult to change. In a decline, so-called variable costs tend to behave as if they were fixed, just as in a growth situation so-called fixed costs behave as if they were variable.

Using the Value Added / Capacity Matrix

Some of the strategies suggested in the value added/capacity matrix (Figure 17-6) are tactical, to be pursued without capital investment, and others are strategic, requiring new fixed asset investment. The upper-left and lower-right quadrants involve tactical decisions regarding pricing, market segmentation, and direction of sales effort. Strategies are easily executed and may be pursued on a tentative basis testing the shape of the value added curve and optimizing profitability within the present market and capacity position. The upper-right and lower-left quadrants involve capital investment and all the associated risks. The upper-right quadrant may appear to be a very attractive position, but it entails the risk that if too much new capacity is added, the business may overshoot the balance point and find itself in the lower-left quadrant, with all its difficulties.

This matrix does not in any way simplify the hard and careful analysis that should accompany major capital commitments; it merely reemphasizes its importance.

By portraying opposing strategies as part of a single analytical structure, this matrix can help in communicating and understanding strategies within the management group of a business. Businesses pursuing a growth strategy often have great trouble adjusting when market conditions change. Often such changes mean that the value added curve has temporarily or permanently shifted, and the volume that placed a company near or to the left of optimum has suddenly left it far over to the right.

CONCLUSIONS

The productivity of a business is different from the productivity of its manufacturing operations as traditionally measured in terms of unit output per manhour. Labor is only one of the resource inputs business management must consider in assessing productivity. Capital and the marketplace are equally important inputs as the benefits of labor cost improvements can easily be lost through poor pricing and marketing or imprudent capital expenditures.

A different set of measurements is required to assess the productivity of a business as a whole. Value added is believed to be the best measure of output. It is an economic (dollar) measurement equating the combined effects of market conditions, competition, and market perceptions of value with the sum of all internal operating costs plus profit. Using value added as the output measurement, the major business productivity ratios are:

$$\text{Personal productivity} = \frac{\text{Value added}}{\text{Employees}}$$

$$\text{Capital productivity} = \frac{\text{Value added}}{\text{Investment}}$$

$$\text{Market productivity} = \frac{\text{Operating profit}}{\text{Value added}}$$

If there is a single measurement of overall business productivity, it is probably return on investment, which can be seen to be the product of two of the previous ratios.

$$\text{Return on investment} = \text{Capital productivity} \times \text{Market productivity}$$

Personal productivity enters into the equation in that, for constant value added output, improving personal productivity reduces internal operating costs and increases operating profit and market productivity. Return on investment is a very sensitive measurement affected by many things. For management, it is preferable to examine the business in terms of all three partial productivity ratios simultaneously rather than by return on investment alone. In this way the specific causes of change in return on investment becomes clear.

Absolute standards for the individual productivity ratios are of limited value. The important thing is the trend of each over time and the effect that specific future business strategies will have on each.

In managing and improving the productivity of a business, it is important to maintain or increase real value added. When real value added declines, all three partial productivity ratios decline, and restoring them to their previous values is very difficult. Despite all that has been said about the need to invest in improving productivity, investment in cost reduction not accompanied by an increase in value added is extremely risky. Such investments by definition reduce capital productivity, and there is a limit on how much offsetting improvement in market productivity a competitive marketplace will allow. The combination of the popular "maintain margin" (or markup on cost) pricing with cost-reduction investments is a prescription for declining return on investment. Inflation, which increases nominal value added, masks what is really happening. The safest approach to productivity improvement through cost reduction is in personal efficiency and management efforts to reduce idle time and wasted effort.

Consideration of the overall productivity of a business is most appropriate in the context of strategic planning. For almost any competitive business, the total amount of real value added that can be extracted from the marketplace is finite, passing through a maximum as price is reduced to increase volume. The ideal place for a business to be operating is up to, but not beyond, this maximum. The volume at which value added reaches its maximum is slightly greater than the economist's classic point at which marginal revenue equals marginal costs and profits are optimized. Such suboptimum (or post-optimum) operation is justifiable as it anticipates future growth of the market and affords management with the most attractive options in the event of an economic downturn.

The value added curve and its maximum point are abstract economic concepts and it is rarely possible to know the exact shape of the curve at a particular time. There are many indications, including the three partial productivity ratios, as to whether a business is operating below, beyond, or near the optimum; this position is the important thing, particularly in the context of capacity utilization and planning. Depending on whether the maximum of the value added curve occurs at a volume above or below practical capacity, diametrically opposite strategies are indicated. If volume is below the value added optimum, prices should probably be reduced and capacity should possibly be expanded. If volume is beyond the value added optimum, then reduction in capacity may be required and, paradoxically, prices should be increased to reduce volume. The position of a business operating beyond the value added maximum with underutilized capacity is extremely difficult and unpleasant. The best way to solve such problems is to avoid them.

PART VI

Formal Strategic Planning Systems

18

Designing and Implementing a Structured Strategic Management Process

SHARON LYSTER

Senior Manager, Peat, Marwick, Mitchell & Co.

INTRODUCTION

The aims of strategic planning may sometimes seem to exist solely in the minds of a company's top executives. An organization's ideals, goals, and needs frequently lack clear definition, and they may differ from executive to executive. Even when these concepts are well-defined and carefully conceived, they need a framework for their development into action plans. That framework is the process of strategic planning.

The process of strategic planning may be informal and unstructured; for example, it may be merely a mental exercise by the owner of a small, local enterprise. Or, it may be highly formalized and structured, as in the case of a project involving hundreds of managers of a multinational corporation. Whatever form strategic planning takes, it is the means to develop the answers to the question: How can the company achieve its strategic objectives?

Just as a good strategic plan is unique to the organization that creates it, the process of planning must also fit the organization's particular needs and reflect its size, structure, style, and product and geographic diversity. A process that is not tailored specifically to its organization is not likely to generate a strategic plan that will express the organization's ideals and enable it to reach its goals and fulfill its needs.

While every plan and the process through which it is implemented must be tailored to the individual situation, there are general guidelines for developing a formal planning process or modifying an existing one. The basic requirements for strategic planning are based on questions that each organization must ask about why it is planning, how it will structure the process, how it is going to conduct the process, what it can do to introduce change, and how it is going to ensure maximum support for and minimum resistance to the process. This chapter examines the *process* of strategic planning. Following are some of the elements that are essential to the process and the key questions that lead to a structured strategic plan for achieving the organization's objectives:

- *Establishing the strategic focus.* Why are we planning? What is the impetus behind the plan? Where are we on the planning phase "spectrum"?

- *Choosing the content.* How can we structure the plan to analyze the current situation and assess options? What type of plan do we need in order to facilitate strategic decisions and generate actions to implement the strategy? What must it include?

- *Creating commitment, linkages, and flexibility.* Where and how do we get the information we need? Which members of the organization are involved in and committed to planning? Who sets time lines, and how? Who reviews and approves plans and their outcomes? How is the plan communicated? Is it flexible and responsive to change? How are resources allocated? What are the tracking and measurement procedures? Have we linked the planning process, our long-term thinking, and the daily operations?

ESTABLISHING THE STRATEGIC FOCUS

Knowing the underlying reasons for the planning endeavor puts it on the right track from the start. What is the plan's impetus? Why is the company planning? Often, planners think that they know the answers to these questions, but closer examination and analysis may yield a more basic need for planning than was originally thought. Or, a shift in focus from an original need may surface.

Perhaps this is the first time the company has attempted to do structured planning. Or, maybe it needs to modify its present planning process in response to changes in its resources or environment. Depending on its needs and the compexity of its organization, a company may have one or many reasons for planning. Its goal may be better financial performance, sales growth, improved products, new-product development, geographic or market expansion, a new

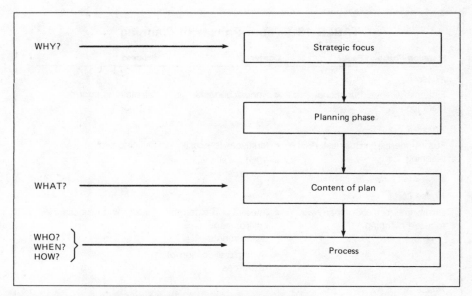

FIG. 18-1 Basic Questions Leading to the Planning Process

public image, better management, or a lower rate of turnover. The reason or reasons for strategic planning can be as diverse as the different kinds of companies that undertake structured planning. But no matter how many plans a company has designed and implemented, it must determine the focus of every new plan. A company must first know *why* if it wants to determine *what, who, how,* and *when* (see Figure 18-1).

An organization's strategic focus and its objectives indicate its place in the "evolution" of strategic planning, i.e., which phase of planning it is in and what type of planning it needs. (See the discussion of the four phases of planning below.) A plan for a small, single-product company will have a simpler focus and process than one for a multinational corporation of the size and complexity of General Electric, for example. Management's attitude toward strategic planning will also influence how far that company's planning process will have evolved. Generally, both management's planning philosphy and the planning process develop together as the company progresses in its evolution, although a company may remain in one phase indefinitely or even skip over certain phases.

Four Phases of Strategic Planning

The evolutionary spectrum as currently defined has four basic phases:

- Phase I: essential financial planning and control
- Phase II: future-oriented planning
- Phase III: environment-focused planning
- Phase IV: strategic management

TABLE 18-1 Four Phases of Planning

Planning Phase	Focus	Content	Process
Phase I			
Financial planning	Functional	• Annual budgets	Maintaining informal approach
Phase II			
Future-oriented planning	Business (SBU)	• Multiyear forecasts • "Static" allocation of resources	Defining process
Phase III			
Environment-focused planning	Companywide	• Internal and external environment assessments • Dynamic allocation of resources	Fine-tuning process
Phase IV			
Strategic management	Strategic	• Well-defined strategic framework • Widespread strategic thinking • Reinforcement of coherent management processes	Institutionalizing organization-wide process

Each phase is increasingly complex in terms of strategic focus, involvement of top management, complexity of analyses, and strategy formulation (see Table 18-1).

The phases are part of a learning process. With each phase, the focus changes and strategic decision making becomes more of an integral part of the management process. Determining where it is on this spectrum gives a company some indication of the degree of sophistication necessary for its planning process and what types of issues must be addressed if it wants to move into the next planning phase.

Phase I: Essential Financial Planning and Control. The focus of the initial planning phase is improved financial performance. This phase involves short-term quantitative analysis of financial goals and status. Smaller, functionally organized companies with limited product and geographic diversity generally do this type of planning. The actual strategic planning takes place within an informal system, and is directed by the chief executive officer (CEO) and the top management team.

Top management's ability to develop a strong business strategy based on their financial goals determines the success of Phase I planning. Management must translate the overall financial strategy into specific operational objectives. Phase I planning is successful only if the senior managers involved can make and implement the decisions that run the business.

Phase II: Future-Oriented Planning. As a company enters multiple markets or regions and adds businesses or divisions, the informal, implicit strategy formulation of Phase I, which is based on past performance, no longer meets the company's requirements. Planning for the future is now more important. In Phase II, the scope of planning broadens to include a longer time frame, and planning is focused on future needs and resources.

In this phase, managers attempt to forecast the longer-term results of business decisions. In addition, more managers become involved in making planning decisions during Phase II than the few top executives responsible for Phase I planning. At this stage, managers further down in the organization's hierarchy, with specific working knowledge of the different businesses, make strategic as well as operating decisions.

The planning concept of the business unit often emerges in this phase. The planning business unit may be the same as that used for daily management and reporting purposes, or it may be a newly defined unit for planning only: the strategic business unit (SBU). The SBU concept allows managers to plan for an organization structured along strategic lines rather than on product, geographic, or other operational lines.

As an organization becomes more complex, many management processes become more formalized and explicit. The process of planning is no exception. Planning tasks are delegated. Resource allocation improves. Calendars and timetables are prepared. More members of the organization become involved in the process as different levels of management prepare, review, and approve business plans.

A major planning pitfall often occurs in Phase II: The company fails to adjust its performance criteria and reward system to reflect its future-oriented focus. It continues to evaluate and reward its managers on the basis of their short-term or medium-term operating performance; i.e., on how they meet the budget. In this case, planning is merely an annual exercise. In effect, the plan sits on the manager's shelf until it is time to update the forecasts the following year.

Phase III: Environment-Focused Planning. In Phase III planning, the SBU concept is refined, and the focus of planning shifts from an analysis of internal company performance to an analysis of external marketplace and environmental factors. The company considers alternatives and makes contingency plans. In this phase, the role of the corporate officers expands to give direction to developing company-wide goals and objectives. Analysis of the external environment is as important as analysis of the company's internal environment in this phase of the planning process.

Organizationally, the planning effort focuses on the SBU. Gluck, Kaufman, and Walleck define the SBU as an "organizational entity large and homogenous enough to exercise effective control over most factors affecting its businesses."[1] Yet this entity is not always easy to define. In addition, focusing heavily on plans for the individual SBUs without developing a corresponding corporate umbrella plan can cause serious problems. The strategy for one SBU may benefit that SBU but may be highly detrimental to another SBU or to the corporation as a whole. Business opportunities that straddle SBUs are likely to be ignored unless higher management coordinates and consolidates strategies. Cash resources will not be allocated between producers and users unless higher management directs their allocation. Planning focused on SBUs demands a corporate-wide framework for allocating resources and developing the overall business.

However, the corporate plan is more than the sum of the individual business plans; it also includes those strategies that span business units or address specific corporate objectives. As a result of this need for an expanded corporate role, Phase III companies experience a shift in management style. The role of corporate management develops from that of reviewing, approving, and consolidating SBU plans to directing actively company-wide strategy development. A highly reiterative process begins to develop. Guidance comes from the top as plans are formulated from the bottom up. Multiple reviews, revisions, and approvals of plans are necessary to produce a coherent, consolidated plan.

Phase IV: Strategic Management. In Phase IV planning, the focus becomes that of linking a large, diverse organization through planning and managing it strategically. Strategically managed companies are generally large multinational, multi-divisional, multi-product organizations. Their management styles and systems and their organizational structures all operate within a strategic context as well as within a daily operational context. These complex organizations must plan for and respond to a multitude of challenges both from within the organization and from the external, competitive environment.

The design of the planning process itself is a critical factor in Phase IV planning. Effective planning in such a complex yet fluid atmosphere requires a well-defined and well-administered process that coordinates many activities on many organizational levels while remaining flexible and creative.

Corporate management continues to oversee and consolidate activities in this phase in order to ensure that the opportunities and challenges that face a specific business or that cross organizational lines are planned for and addressed. But planning now is done on multiple organizational levels. Depending on the requirements of the business, planning occurs on the product level, business level (which may or may not be the SBU), group level, and corporate level. In addition, "shared" plans may overlay the product, business, or group plans and may address shared resources (e.g., research and development) or shared needs (e.g., industry and customer base).

---

[1] Frederick W. Gluck, Stephen P. Kaufman, and A. Steven Walleck, "Strategic Management for Competitive Advantage," *Harvard Business Review* (July-August 1980).

The content of the plans and the timing of the planning process are individualized during Phase IV planning. The planning unit prepares formal plans that meet its individual planning requirements. For example, a well-run, stable business may review its general strategic performance quarterly and conduct an intensive strategic review every three years. On the other hand, a high-growth business in a competitive, volatile market may review detailed results monthly and repeat its rigorous, more detailed planning annually. This planning flexibility encourages managers to plan with a creative, long-term focus, and not become tangled in the annual exercise of detailed planning.

The strategically managed company removes the barriers between planning and operations. In this phase of planning, a strategic outlook and attitude permeate the entire organization. Influencing the future, not reacting to it, becomes the objective.

CHOOSING THE CONTENT OF THE PLAN

After the focus of a plan has been established, the content necessary for the plan becomes clear. Just as each phase of planning has a different focus, the content of the plan will vary in each phase to support that different focus.

A plan's contents may include financial analyses, budgets, financial projections, individual assessment of SBUs, analyses of technological resources, or industry analyses. Questions that a company must ask after it establishes the strategic focus for planning include: What information does the plan require to analyze the current situation? How do we assess options? What tools will help us to make strategic decisions? What methods will generate action plans to implement the strategy? The content of the plans will vary from phase to phase, depending on the strategic focus.

Phase-by-Phase Planning

Since the focus is financial in Phase I, the contents of Phase I plans often are the operating and capital budgets, which are based primarily on historical performance. The company in this stage of planning organizes and accumulates budgets by function (e.g., marketing, production), and it measures performance by comparing actual financial results against the budget.

Phase II's longer-term focus and the need to forecast the company's performance yields a different content for its planning. In this phase, the company expands the annual budget to include a longer term projection of business and financial results. It may use sophisticated forecasting tools such as regression analysis and computer simulation models to help predict the company's future. In order to allocate resources, a company will often include portfolio analysis in Phase II planning. But according to Gluck, Kaufman, and Walleck, the type of portfolio analysis that is practiced by Phase II companies "tends to be static and focused on current capabilities, rather than on the search for options. Moreover it is deterministic—i.e., the position of a business on the matrix is used to determine the appropriate strategy, according to generalized strategy.

Phase II companies typically regard portfolio positioning as the end product of strategic planning rather than as a starting point."[2]

In Phase III, the focus expands to include analysis and assessment of the external marketplace and of the firm's internal environment. The informal gathering and analysis of relevant market information collected by the CEO and key managers in Phases I and II becomes part of the plan's content. The planner analyzes information about buyers, suppliers, and direct and potential competitors in addition to changes in the economic and regulatory environment.

The focus of Phase IV planning is to unify and link an organization strategically. The content derived from that focus addresses the systems that are required to link strategic thinking with decisions made by the units of the company's diverse operations. Strategically managed companies link strategic planning decisions directly to operational decisions by designing structures and systems that integrate strategic thinking with operational decisions. The business strategy now defines the organizational structure. Strategic business units replace functional or geographic units as the primary organizational units. Management modifies its reporting, measurement, and compensation systems to support strategic as well as operational requirements. Management reporting systems accumulate and report the financial and operating information that is necessary to track strategic action plans. The company often links the operating budget directly to the first year of the strategic plan. Compensation systems include measurements and rewards for achieving strategic objectives.

CREATING COMMITMENT, LINKAGES, AND FLEXIBILITY

The strategic focus helps define a plan's content, the end product of which is a road map of goals and objectives. The content, in turn, leads to plans that must be implemented in order to achieve those goals and objectives. There are three requirements for success in this part of the planning process:

- Commitment to the plan at all levels of the organization: this is a function of the logic of the plan, how well it was communicated, and how much participation there was by all levels of the organization in creating it;
- Links between the long-term strategic thinking of the planning process and the daily management decisions made during the operating process; and
- Flexibility: the planning process must reflect the unique personality of the company; and, the process must allow for responses to changes within the organization and in the external environment.

Structuring the Process

Successful strategic planning for any company—from a small single-product company to a large multi-divisional, multinational corporation, and from a

---

[2] Ibid.

Phase I financially oriented firm to a Phase IV strategically managed one—must do the following:

- Specify objectives
- Generate strategies
- Evaluate strategies
- Monitor results

The way in which management chooses to assign, complete, and review these tasks defines the organization's planning process and system.

Commitment at All Levels of the Organization

To ensure that the four basic tasks of strategic planning are accomplished, a company must gain the commitment of all of its managers, at every level of the organization. The company's ability to gain this organization-wide commitment to its plans is closely linked to how it designs, introduces, and implements the process of planning.

Strategic thinking cannot be limited to the CEO. It must be an integral part of the daily management decisions of a line manager in the manufacturing plant as well as in the office of top management. Unless the supporting tactical plans are well executed, the objectives of the overall strategy will be impossible to achieve.

First, the planners must determine the following:

1 How many people and what levels of the organization will be involved in the planning process? When will they be involved?

2 Who will be responsible for setting the strategic goals and objectives?

3 Who will write the plans? Are the "planners" the same people who will be responsible for implementing the strategies?

4 Who will review and approve the plans? When and how often will they be reviewed?

5 Who will allocate the resources?

6 Who will gather and analyze the environmental and competitive information?

7 Who will gather and analyze the various market and financial information?

Answering these questions is a basic step in designing a structured planning system.

Assigning Responsibility

In order for top management to delegate the tasks of planning and involve managers in the planning process, it must define the tasks to be performed and decide at what levels of the organization they will be performed. The first question is: Who should become involved in the strategic planning process? Most organizations have three levels of management: (1) the corporate or executive level, (2) the business or division level, and (3) the functional level. (Smaller companies may have only the executive and functional levels.) The type and number of tasks that are to be performed and the number of people who make strategic decisions increase as the organization moves through Phases I to IV (Table 18-1). Managers on each level should perform planning tasks. Assignments of planning tasks should be made according to the type of task, the type of information to be gathered, and the impact of the task on the strategic direction. An important outcome of involving the operating managers in the strategic planning process and gaining their commitment to the strategic plan is that they gain a longer-term strategic perspective in addition to their short-term focus on operating decisions.

How responsibilities are delegated also depends on how top management directs initial planning. If the overall strategic direction is set by the office of the CEO, development is from the top down. If the business or functional managers develop the initial plans, the development is from the bottom up.

An example of assignment of responsibility can be seen in the goal-setting process, which has many variations. In a small, functionally organized company, the CEO alone may determine the company's goals, objectives, and action plans. In larger, more diversified companies, the setting of specific goals and objectives may be done throughout the organization, since the business is too complex for one person to perform this task. Frequently, the CEO and top corporate managers develop broad strategic guidelines, which the divisional and functional managers then develop into specific goals and objectives. Those specifics are then reviewed and approved by corporate managers.

How the broad strategic goals and objectives are set and how the tactical plans are developed both depend on the size and structure of the organization, the complexity of the business or businesses, the personality and style of the CEO, and the corporate culture. A financially oriented company (Phase I) requires commitment by its functional managers to a budget, as well as commitment by the CEO to the implicit general strategy. In a strategically managed corporation (Phase IV), each SBU manager must be committed to all facets of the strategic plan that apply to that particular SBU, e.g., developing an action plan to respond to a competitor's move, developing new products and markets, and generating operating budgets that meet profit goals.

Without this commitment, implementation of the strategic plan is extremely difficult, if not impossible. When the decision is made to structure the strategic process or when major changes are planned for an existing process (e.g., moving from Phase II to Phase III), the new planning process must be formally introduced and explained to the organization; key participants must understand the whys and hows of the process.

Planning is time-consuming. Generally, operating managers view it as an activity that is separate from daily decision making. If the planning process is not well defined, well organized, and well communicated, it will not be understood or viewed as an important activity; the plan will not be effectively prepared or implemented.

Peter Lorange, in *Implementation of Strategic Planning,*[3] discusses nine factors relating to the strategic process that must be communicated to those who will be involved in order to increase the probability that it will be effectively implemented:

1 The benefits of the plan must be clear to those who will put it into action. They must know what is in it for them and why they are doing it. They must also understand how it will lead to a better decision-making process. A planning system must improve the quality of business decisions in order to justify its existence.

2 The concept of planning must be understood by the managers affected by it. Is the logic of the process clear? Has it been communicated clearly? Is the manager able to understand what he or she is supposed to accomplish? Is the division of tasks sufficiently delineated among managers so that who does what is clear? Who initiates the planning? Who does the various steps? Who conducts the reviews? Who gives feedback to whom?

3 Is the sequence of various activities relatively clear? How well are the complex overall planning tasks broken down into smaller, manageable elements? Are there self-contained units or stages of the process that can be dealt with in a given period of time by a given group of managers? Have the appropriate units of analysis for planning been identified? That is, can the planning unit be analyzed in terms of market share, customer base, and competitive advantages? (If not, it may not be the appropriate unit for analysis.) Also, is the unit of sufficient size or does it have enough potential to justify the time and resources management will spend on it?

4 To what degree is the planning process a new experience? (If a new process is building on past experience of planning or budgeting, it is more likely to be accepted and succeed.) According to Lorange, "Evolution, not quantum leaps, seems to be an important lesson for implementation."[4]

5 The sponsor of the planning effort must be clearly identified. If the sponsor is not top management, the likelihood of success is greatly diminished.

6 The need for planning must be perceived as being important to the organization; top management must show that it values an improved planning process to achieve desired goals.

7 Planning must be able to produce some results relatively quickly. Too much time spent "planning" to plan may not pay off in improved results.

8 General line managers and their functional managers must endorse the plan. The planning activity must become part of the calendars and work habits of managers. Without the commitment to the process by middle management, planning will be a time-consuming, nonessential, and "academic" exercise.

9 Top management must be willing to commit the required resources. Staff support, computer resources, and time for research and meetings must be available. The resource requirements of planning must be seen as being as important as

---

[3] Peter Lorange, "The Task of Implementing Strategic Planning: An Overview and Introduction to the Book," in *Implementation of Strategic Planning,* ed. Peter Lorange (Englewood Cliffs, N.J.: Prentice-Hall, Inc., 1982), pp. 8–10.

[4] Ibid.

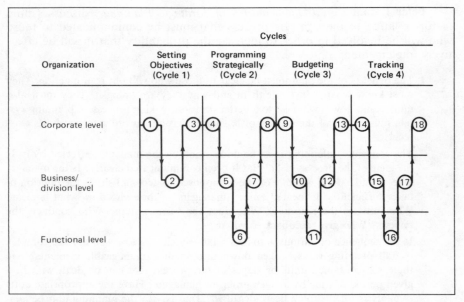

FIG. 18-2 Example of a Strategic Planning Model

those of the daily business activities. (Research has shown that the time and the funds needed for planning are frequently underestimated, which undermines the planning effort and diminishes its results.)

The Four Cycles of the Planning Process

The *who, what,* and *when* aspects of strategic planning can be viewed in terms of cycles of planning. (*When* is defined for the purposes of strategic planning as a sequence of events rather than as calendar dates.) Planning essentially involves four cycles (see Figure 18-2):

- *Cycle 1: setting objectives.* The tasks of this cycle include creating the corporate mission, defining the corporate objectives, formulating the business charters, setting corporate goals.

- *Cycle 2: programming strategically.* During this cycle, the tasks include preparing detailed strategic plans by business or functional area, developing and analyzing alternative strategies, choosing specific strategies, formulating action plans, and determining the strategy for resource allocation.

- *Cycle 3: budgeting.* In this cycle, the tactical plans to support the strategic plan— the operations plans, the operating budget, and the capital budget—are prepared.

- *Cycle 4: tracking.* In the tracking cycle, strategic performance is monitored and measured.

Figure 18-3 is a model of a structured planning process. It shows the merging of the various levels of the organization (in this case, the executive, business, and function levels of a three-tiered organization) with the cycles of the strategic planning process. The steps of each cycle (the circled numbers in Figures 18-2 and 18-3) and the elements that make up those steps are listed below. This model, developed by R.F. Vancil and P. Lorange[5] for a three-tiered organization, is only one process example. Any structured process will include these cycles, modified in detail as appropriate.

The major steps and the sample, elements of each cycle are outlined below. The numbers of the steps correspond to the numbered rules in the flow charts illustrated in Figure 18-3.

Cycle 1: Setting Objectives
Steps:

1 Formulate general guidelines; develop corporate mission.

2 Develop business charter, preliminary objectives, and strategy.

3 Review and consolidate business and corporate strategies; set preliminary corporate and business goals

Elements:

- Set financial goals and objectives.
- Identify new businesses and new product opportunities.
- Create resource management strategy.
- Set financing objectives.
- Assess competitive position.
- Assess company strengths and weaknesses.
- Examine key corporate risks and opportunities.
- Assess macroenvironment.

Cycle 2: Programming Strategically
Steps:

4 Request business tactical plans.

5 Develop business strategy, objectives, and tactics; request functional programs.

6 Develop program (functional) alternatives to meet business goals and objectives; analyze and select best programs.

7 Select the best mix of programs.

8 Set corporate and division goals.

Elements:

- Segment products and/or markets.
- Analyze keys to competitive success.

---

[5] R.F. Vancil and P. Lorange, "Strategic Planning in Diversified Companies," *Harvard Business Review* (January-February 1975)

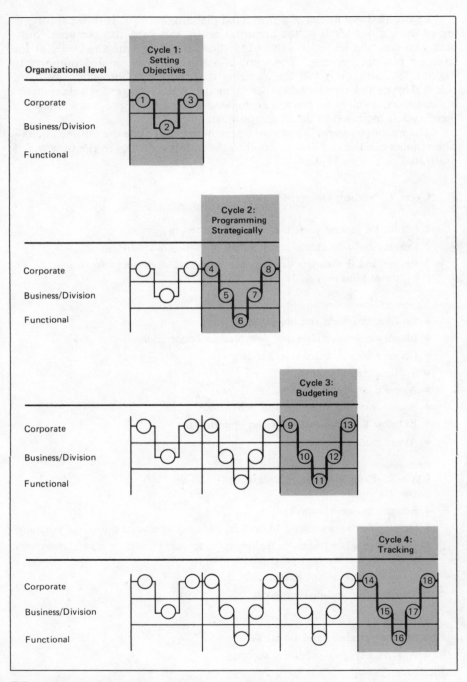

FIG. 18-3 Flow of the Cycles of the Planning Process

- Analyze major competitors and current positions.
- Define critical strategic issues.
- Set measurable goals and objectives.
- Develop resource strategies involving both production and technology.
- Develop financial resource strategy.
- Review business plans for analytical consistency.
- Review business plans for fit with corporate strategy.
- Review strategic resource expenditures.
- Determine methodology for resource allocation.
- Assess trade-off between short-term and long-term results.
- Determine integration of acquisitions and investitures
- Gather feedback on business objectives and strategies.

Cycle 3: Budgeting
Steps:

9 Make a tentative allocation of resources and request business budgets.
10 Request functional budgets.
11 Develop functional budgets and submit for approval.
12 Develop business budgets and submit for approval.
13 Approve business and corporate budgets and allocate resources.

Elements:

- Approve consolidated strategic plan and resource allocation.
- Develop business budgets.
- State business goals.
- Develop functional budgets.
- Review and consolidate functional and business budgets.
- Approve functional and business budgets.
- Develop corporate office budgets.
- Consolidate and review corporate and business budgets.
- Approve consolidated budgets and annual resource allocation.

Cycle 4: Tracking
Steps:

14 Identify strategic measurements to monitor performance.
15 Develop specific criteria to track business and functional performance.
16 Measure and reward actual functional results against measurements of functional performance.
17 Measure and reward actual business performance against measurements of business performance.
18 Review and reward actual corporate performance against measurements of performance.

Elements:

- Define financial and operational benchmarks to monitor strategic performance in the areas of capital spending levels, cash flow, profitability, productivity improvement, research and development efforts, and market share.
- Define action plan milestones.
- Develop calendar for strategic reviews of action plans and budgets.
- Develop management by objective (MBO) plans with components for strategic objectives.
- Develop compensation plans to reward achievement of strategic long-term objectives.
- Define link between budget and strategic plan.
- Monitor competitive, external environment.

Linkages Throughout the Process

The most notable aspect of the Vancil and Lorange model of the process of strategic planning is the reiterative flow of information and tasks, linking people, processes, and plans. All levels of management are involved in at least three of the four cycles. The primary role of the executive level in this model is to establish broad objectives and to set guidelines and directives for the company. These guidelines should be strategic, operational, and financial. The company's top executives then approve the plans and programs developed by the business units and consolidate the company-wide plan.

At the business level, the initial strategic guidelines established by the corporate executives are translated into broadly defined strategic action programs. The corporate level then reviews these programs to ensure that they are consistent with the overall resources and goals of the firm. After the corporate level approves the programs, the business level develops more detailed programs for specific action and sets guidelines for the functional level to follow in establishing specific programs to support the business programs. The business level, in turn, reviews and consolidates these functional programs and then sends them to the corporate level for final approval.

The strategic plans and action programs of the business level and the functional level form the basis for developing detailed operating budgets. The link between planning and operations is critical to the plan's successful implementation. Without this link, the plan and its program gather dust on the managers' shelves.

By the time the final strategic plans reach the corporate level and the operations budgets are prepared, inconsistent or conflicting goals and objectives should have been resolved. Each business or function should have a budget created by mutual agreement.

The model of the process of strategic planning described above illustrates top-down planning in a large, divisional corporation. The degree to which each level of management is involved in the planning cycles will vary depending on the company's strategic focus. A one-product, functionally organized company that prepares a formal budget (a Phase I company) will have a relatively simple planning/budget process involving the executives and the functional managers. Each company must tailor the process to fit its own situation.

However, no matter what the requirements of the company may be and in which phases of planning the company may be engaged, certain constants hold true. An effective strategy for any company must consider the strategic issues for each level of the organization. The strategy must address, formally or informally, the broad strategic direction of the company, specific strategic action plans, detailed operations plans or budgets, and implementation issues.

Companies generally revise and review their strategic plans many times as they assess alternative strategies and formulate action plans. In most companies, each cycle would also involve numerous smaller cycles. Reiteration helps ensure that the individual plans, at the functional level and at a higher level, are consistent with each other and that they support the overall strategic direction of the corporation.

Monitoring the Process

The planning process does not stop with the final review of the corporate strategic plan. As James Mills comments in his introduction to a Conference Board report:[6]

> Over the past decade, corporate planners from major companies have focused on the development and refinement of more effective planning processes. . . . The assumption behind all this effort was that better planning would lead to better plans.
>
> It was not a bad assumption as far as it went. But given the uncertainties of competition and of the external political and social forces with which companies must contend, it was only a matter of time before widespread disenchantment would arise over the practicality and realism of plans. That disenchantment has come with a vengence and with it, increased interest in the means with which the fulfillment of strategic plans can be measured.

The report[7] goes on to state:

> The development of formal strategic planning systems, a process still evolving in many firms, raises questions of operational and strategic control. In the initial years, of course, most company planning systems focus on developing planning as a discipline for managers to help run their business. The emphasis is on familiarizing managers with the idea of planning and with developing a planning system that they will accept. All of this stress on getting managers to plan has often deferred and even obscured the ultimate goal of a doable strategic plan with achievable objectives. But that stage has now come for many organizations; a time to see the results of strategies painstakingly wrought, and to be able to measure them credibly.

---

[6] James T. Mills, introduction to Rochelle O'Connor, *Tracking the Strategic Plan*, Conference Board Report 830 (1983), p. iv.

[7] O'Connor, op. cit., p. 1.

Until recently, more emphasis has been placed on preparing the plan than on its implementation. The tracking cycle addresses the critical tasks of monitoring and measuring implementation. It gives ongoing feedback as to how things are going; it should identify what is going right and what is going wrong.

As Mills states, the ultimate objective of a strategic planning process is to generate a plan with realistic, attainable objectives. The planners must first identify the key assumptions of the plan (e.g., predicted industry growth, increase in cost of materials, number of new product introductions by key competitors) and the primary expectations of the plan (e.g., sales unit growth, manufacturing efficiencies resulting from technology improvements, capital spending levels, cost of financing). These must then be measured against a quantitative or qualitative benchmark. The tracking of these key assumptions and expectations is assigned to managers responsible for monitoring actual performance against the plan. These managers must identify adjustments that must be made as a result of a changing marketplace, new government regulations, or unanticipated reactions by competitors.

Tracking and monitoring are not simple tasks. Two significant issues that emerged in the Conference Board study[8] of companies attempting to track their plans were "(1) valid measurement of performance that indicates long-term strategic results, and (2) the linkage between operational and strategic plans to ensure that they are compatible." Other major concerns expressed were the company's ability to react to and adjust for changes in basic forecasts and assumptions, the link between long-term performance goals and short-term compensation packages, and the commitment by top management to the tracking and review process.

The further a company's planning process is evolved toward management (Phase IV), the easier tracking becomes. This is because in later stages, the process becomes more fluid, linkages are made between planning and operations, and management commitment is stronger. Companies that are not in Phase IV should give increased attention to the tracking issue if they plan to develop a more effective system.

Maintaining Flexibility

Flexibility, which in the context of strategic planning is defined as the willingness to abandon or redraft plans when necessary, is perhaps the most important attribute of an effective planning process. Yet flexibility is the most difficult attribute to attain. A structured planning process must allow for change within the organization as well as within the external environment. Plans that are static from situation to situation and from year to year will fail.

Outside factors that affect a company do not determine its course: Its response to those factors makes it succeed or fail. Without the ability to change in response to uncontrollable conditions and events, and to anticipate change, a company's best-laid plans cannot accomplish the goals for which they were designed and implemented. Management must create a climate that encourages

---

[8] Ibid.

1. The primary purpose of any business plan must be to help its author to manage his operations more effectively.

2. The second purpose of a business plan is to establish mutually agreed upon commitment between the author of the plan and his boss.

3. A business plan must contain sufficient information to lend credibility to its promise.

4. A business plan must have strategic focus; that is, it must be part of an overall scheme to accomplish enduring objectives within the context of dynamic, interacting environmental forces.

5. A business plan must foster awareness of options and their likely consequences.

6. A business plan must boil up critical issues, choices and priorities on which management attention must be focused.

7. A business plan must be linked firmly to the system for allocating and committing capital funds.

8. A business plan must keep paperwork manageable.

9. Business plans must accommodate a plurality of managerial and planning styles.

10. Planning must be woven into the fabric of the organization to become a natural part of getting the job done.

Source: Walter B. Schaffir, *Strategic Planning: Some Questions for the Chief Executive*, P.A. Special Study No. 63 (New York: The President's Association, The Chief Executive Officers' Division of American Management Associations, 1976), pp. 15–16.

FIG. 18-4 Ten Do's of Planning

this realistic, practical willingness to shift direction in order to keep plans and planning on track.

The monitoring process should go a step further. The company should periodically reevaluate the aims, direction, and method of its plan. Some questions that a company should ask and some points that it should observe when reassessing its planning process are discussed in Walter Schaffir's "Ten Dos of Planning" (see Figure 18-4) and George Steiner's "Ten Don'ts of Planning" (Figure 18-5).

CONCLUSION

As businesses become more experienced in strategic planning, their plans become more complex, and the need for their integration throughout the entire organization becomes more important. The process of planning, therefore, takes on an even more important role. Focus, content, commitment, linkage, flexibility, and execution are the keys to a structured planning process. They hold the promise of turning once tentatively conceived, shadowy objectives into methodically planned, solid achievements—the results of successful plans.

1. Failure to develop throughout the company an understanding of what strategic planning really is, how it is to be done in the company, and the degree of commitment of top management to doing it well.

2. Failure to accept and balance interrelationships among intuition, judgment, managerial values, and the formality of the planning system.

3. Failure to encourage managers to do effective strategic planning by basing performance appraisal and rewards solely on short-range performance measures.

4. Failure to tailor and design the strategic planning system to the unique characteristics of the company and its management.

5. Failure of top management to spend sufficient time on the strategic process so that the process becomes discredited among other managers and staff.

6. Failure to modify the strategic planning system as conditions within the company change.

7. Failure to mesh properly the process of management and strategic planning from the highest levels of management and planning through critical planning and its complete implementation.

8. Failure to keep the planning system simple and to constantly weigh the cost-benefit balance.

9. Failure to secure within the company a climate for strategic planning that is necessary for its success.

10. Failure to balance and link the major elements of strategic planning and the implementation process.

Source: George A. Steiner, "Evaluating Your Strategic Planning System," in *Implementation of Strategic Planning*, ed. Peter Lorange (Englewood Cliffs, N.J.: Prentice-Hall, Inc., 1982), pp. 39–40. Reprinted by permission of Prentice-Hall, Inc., Englewood Cliffs, N.J.

FIG 18-5 Ten Don'ts of Planning

BIBLIOGRAPHY

Frederick W. Gluck, Stephen P. Kaufman, and A. Steven Walleck, "Strategic Management for Competitive Advantage," *Harvard Business Review*, July-August 1980.

Peter Lorange, editor, *Implementation of Strategic Planning*, Englewood Cliffs, New Jersey: Prentice-Hall, 1982.

Peter Lorange and Richard F. Vancil, editors, *Strategic Planning Systems*, Englewood Cliffs, New Jersey: Prentice-Hall, 1977.

Rochelle O'Connor, *Tracking the Strategic Plan*, Report No. 830, The Conference Board, 1983.

Alan J. Rowe, Richard O. Mason, Karl Dickel, *Strategic Management & Business Policy: A Methodological Approach*, Reading, Massachusetts: Addison-Wesley, 1982.

19

Multinational Strategic Planning Systems

DAVID C. SHANKS
Arthur D. Little, Inc.

TRENDS AND DRIVING FORCES IN MULTINATIONAL ENTERPRISE

Multinational operations can be considered as an element of corporate strategy that involves the geographic scope of the enterprise. Multinationalism can be portrayed on a matrix model of corporate development activity, as shown in Figure 19-1.

A multinational corporation (MNC) is a corporate entity with a cluster of affiliated firms located in a number of countries. The more countries in which an MNC operates, the broader its scope and its acceptance into the "big league" of worldwide business enterprise. The affiliated firms of an MNC share several characteristics:

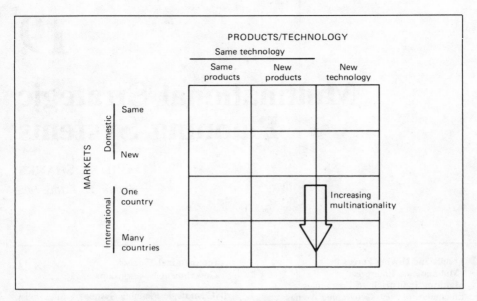

FIG. 19-1 Multinationality as a Function of Markets and Products

- They are linked by ties of common ownership;
- They draw on a common pool of resources, such as money and credit, information and systems, trade names and patents; and
- They respond to the same strategy.

Since the 1960s, there have been significant shifts in the world economic and business environment that have affected MNC planning strategies. Some of these factors arose from reactions to changes in the world economy; others are actually the result of heightened MNC activity. Taken together, these shifts have served as powerful driving forces that have shaped MNC strategy:

- Maturation of the economies of industrialized nations;
- Emergence of new geographic market/business arenas;
- Growth of a new order of risk factors in conducting MNC operations;
- A continuing increase in non-U.S. MNC ownership;
- The appearance of state-owned enterprises in the roster of large MNCs;
- Heightened scrutiny of MNC operations by U.S. (and other) governmental and regulatory agencies.

Maturing Industrialized Economies

Since the mid-1970s, the economic growth rate of the United States, Canada, the United Kingdom, France, and Germany has slowed; it is not expected to perform at mid-century rates of 5 to 7 percent real growth. Performance on the order of 2 to 3 percent real growth is projected, and with more cyclicality than in earlier years. Among the reasons for this decreased growth rate are the final closing of geographic frontiers, slowing population growth, and aging infrastructures that are no longer maintained at the rate of physical depreciation. This is not to say that these markets are not extremely attractive for an MNC—the developed world is by definition both a producer and a consumer of most of our planet's goods and services. For established concerns, however, high product sales growth rates must be found by other means—through replacement markets, planned obsolescence, fashion, new or substitute products—or in other areas of the world where population and consumer demand is rising more rapidly.

Emergence of New Geographic Arenas

New geographic and political arenas have emerged in recent years as market and business opportunities for MNCs. Under the Nixon Administration, the People's Republic of China was actively courted. Formal diplomatic relations were established and business activity expanded rapidly. For most MNCs, the Soviet Union is a largely untapped market. Soviet trade relations with the United States and other nations have been volatile and highly dependent on diplomatic and political conditions.

Other emerging nations, such as those with per capita incomes under $1,000 but with growth potential, also present future business opportunities. In fact, the U.S. Agency for International Development has designated several of these countries as opportunities for private sector investment by U.S. companies in joint ventures with locals. This is seen as a more effective way to promote economic growth than through direct government-to-government financial aid.

Increasing Risk Factors

Considering the history of commercial activity, trading risks have declined from the days when fire, shipwreck, piracy, and other business losses were commonplace events. Today's multinational strategist recognizes a new order of risks not present (or as prevalent) in earlier times: expropriation of assets, currency losses through exchange rate fluctuations and devaluations, unfavorable foreign court interpretations of contracts and agreements, social and/or political disturbances, import/export laws, tariffs, and suasions resulting in total or partial trade barriers.

Shift in Control

Over the past 20 years, there has been a gradual but definite shift in control of MNCs to corporations not based in the United States. Over half of the world's 500 largest corporations were controlled from outside of the United States in 1979, as opposed to 40 percent in 1963.

The list of countries controlling major MNCs is growing longer, and is also concentrating in certain areas. Japan, the United Kingdom, Germany,

France, and Canada have shown significant increases in the number of large MNCs. Also, emerging economies such as Korea, Brazil, the oil-rich nations in the Middle East, Venezuela, and Mexico have recently developed one or more large MNCs. These newer MNCs have different attitudes and incentives toward risk and return, fostered by different capital market structures (as in Japan), heavy government involvement (as with Mexico), or extensive international borrowings (as in Brazil).

State-Owned Enterprises

Multinational strategy must recognize the rise in nationally owned enterprises, which often are managed in ways and for objectives that do not match free-market economic theories. State airlines are an example of single-product MNCs that compete with privately owned carriers worldwide. Such organizations are often viewed as instruments of national policy or visibility, and may offer services that are subsidized by the government and represent offerings with which a self-contained business operation cannot compete. Other examples of state-owned MNC activity include British Petroleum, Alfa Romeo, and Renault.

Heightened Multinational Scrutiny

With the rise in U.S. multinational business activity during the 1960s came an increased awareness and scrutiny by governmental and regulatory bodies of the conduct of business in foreign countries. This intense examination was initiated, in part, by the realization that in some countries, foreign-owned MNCs represented effective control over a large sector of the country's economy. A case in point is U.S. oil interests in Middle East nations, especially in Iran and Saudi Arabia, prior to the formation of the Organization of Petroleum Exporting Countries.

Adding to increased interest is another problem: overseas business practices conducted by U.S. and other MNCs that violate home country legal and ethical standards. Most notable are various payment schemes to foreign officials in return for contract awards. These "corrupt practices," as defined by the U.S. Foreign Corrupt Practices Act of 1977, are all the more problematic to foreigners whose home country laws and customs often permit such practices.

These two factors, economic control and corrupt practices, have led to a series of rules and regulations—voluntary and imposed—regarding MNC business operations, including disclosure of information, corrupt practices regulation, and codes of conduct.

DOMESTIC VS. MNC STRATEGIC PLANNING: A COMPARATIVE VIEW

Today's MNC must make strategic choices at several levels. These choices have the potential to change significantly the nature of the corporation's future busi-

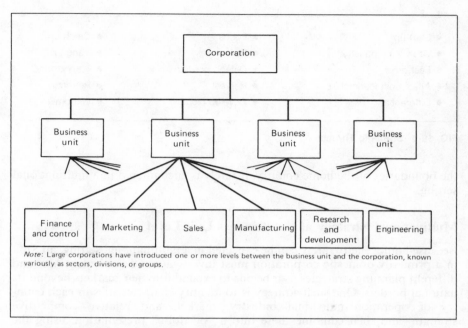

FIG. 19-2 Strategy Formulation Levels Within a Corporation

ness and performance. As shown in Figure 19-2, these choices exist at the corporate level, at the business unit or profit center level, and in the functions within each business unit, such as finance, manufacturing, marketing, sales, and research and development. This section concentrates on those planning concepts that are formulated, approved, and executed at the business unit and corporate levels. Functional strategies, although important to the MNC, are beyond the scope of this treatment.

Domestic Strategy at the Business Unit Level

Among the most commonly adopted generic strategies at the business unit level of a domestic corporation are differentiation, overall cost leadership, and focus. Implementation of these strategies often involves adopting one of several strategic thrusts, as summarized in Figure 19-3.

For a domestic corporation, the strategic business unit (SBU) arena is limited principally to the selection of product line, and associated technological breadth, depth, and diversity, and to the choice of markets and market segments within the home country's national boundaries.

In order for an accurate assessment to be made in most SBU strategic schemes, a microeconomic analysis of the industry is necessary. Success is greatest when there exists a more or less homogeneous set of factors, including a single market growth rate, competitor share concentration and structure, and level of demand saturation. Although such homogeneity may be found within

• Start up	• Focus	• Catch up
• Grow with industry	• Renew	• Hang in
• Fast grow	• Defend position	• Turn around
• Attain cost leadership	• Harvest	• Retrench
• Differentiate	• Develop niche	• Withdraw

FIG. 19-3   Strategic Thrusts

the boundaries of the home country, it rarely is encountered in a multinational setting.

Multinational Strategy at the Business Unit Level

Because homogeneity rarely can be expected in a multinational setting, an SBU in a primarily domestic corporation must investigate and implement new and different planning strategies as it begins to expand into new markets beyond its national borders. One such strategy is to identify characteristics in each country of operation—individual industry, market, and relative competitive strength—and then combine these into a "portfolio" presentation, using the same analytical matrix for all countries.

The strategic options selected by a domestic SBU as it develops a multinational strategy often follow a common pattern of development, which can be outlined in a step-by-step procedure:

- Export
- Licensing
- Foreign sales representation
- Joint venture
- Establishment of foreign manufacturing
- Creation of a foreign SBU
- Creation of multiple foreign SBUs
- Rationalization of foreign SBU operations by specialization of function (global strategy)

As illustrated in Figure 19-4, an SBU's strategic degree of freedom increases (1) as its state of development in each country in which it wishes to operate advances and (2) as the number and diversity of countries of potential operation increases. When an MNC has operations and markets for one SBU distributed throughout several countries, and when these operations present opportunities for selective geographic leverage or focus for overall economic advantage, the range of strategic options broadens substantially.

Recently, a clear distinction has been made between multidomestic and global industries. In the multidomestic case, business units follow separate

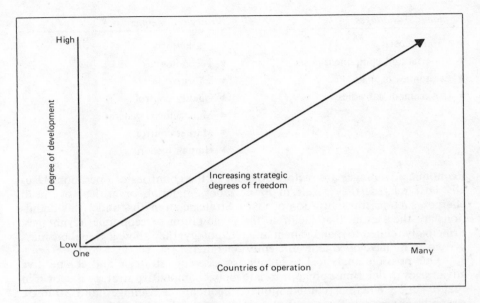

FIG. 19-4 Strategic Degrees of Freedom as a Function of Countries of Operation and Degree of Development

strategies in individual foreign markets relatively unconnected with one another. In sharp contrast, global competition involves marshaling a worldwide business system against similar MNCs, or domestically oriented companies in each country. Individual country opportunities may be sacrificed, for example, to support a thrust in another geographic area. Companies involved in global competition are more likely to have a highly centralized planning operation. Some examples of global industries and principal competitors in the global arena are listed in Table 19-1.

Some important clues as to whether an MNC is dealing with a multidomestic or global industry lie in the abilities of purely domestic firms to combat foreign entrants in the market. For example, personal service companies such as law firms, accountancies, and insurance companies in every country have strong natural barriers to foreign competitors in detailed and complex local regulation, legislation, customs, and practice. Conversely, heavy subsidies by a home country government for a particular industry or technology may create a formidable economic advantage that can be exploited worldwide. The long U.S. dominance in commercial aircraft began with government-sponsored military airframe and engine technology. Until recently, no purely domestic competitor could match the world market presence of Boeing and McDonnell Douglas in airframes, and General Electric and Pratt & Whitney in engines.

These clues, or criteria, can be divided into two areas: economic advantages and strategic strengths.

Economic Advantages

- Capital costs
- Material and component costs
- Economies of scale
- Government subsidies

Strategic Strengths

- Marketing
- Technology
- Information
- Quality control
- Management systems
- Market control
- Human resources

Economic advantages are factors inherent in the countries of operation. Usually cost related, they result in lower labor, material, or critical overhead charges, such as transportation or taxes. Strategic strengths, under this definition, are the factors that facilitate the exploitation of economic advantages. Principally related to management and technology, they allow a global business system to be developed and efficiently operated.

One possible analytical technique for assessing strategic and competitive advantages to determine an appropriate global competitive strategy is shown in Figure 19-5. Where a combination of economic advantages and strategic strengths appear low for global competition, as is the case with products such as Portland cement, beer, or glassware, a posture of defending individual

TABLE 19-1   Global Industries and Competitors

Industry	Competitor
Watches	Timex Seiko Citizen
Nuclear reactors	Combustion Engineering Westinghouse General Electric
Construction equipment	Caterpillar Komatsu
Power generation equipment (turbines, generators)	General Electric Westinghouse Siemens Mitsubishi
Motorcycles	Honda Suzuki Kawasaki
Automobiles	Ford General Motors Toyota Volkswagen

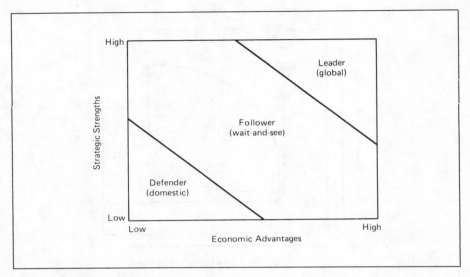

FIG. 19-5 Global Strategy Matrix

domestic markets by stand-alone business units may be appropriate (the "defender" posture). Where both strategic strengths and economic advantages can be exploited through a worldwide network of business operations, as in consumer electronics, commercial aircraft, or motorcycles, the successful strategy may be an aggressive pursuit of a global strategy backed by sufficient corporate resources and exploitation of existing competitive position. This is represented in the "global leader" segment of the matrix. The remaining intermediate zone (the "follower" position) is an area in transition, where traditional domestic defense is giving way to global competition at an identifiable rate of change. It appears to present the most interesting strategic challenge: to identify correctly how fast the transition is occurring so investment and operations can be set in place to take maximum advantage of the change. Preemption is important, but being too early may result in unacceptable market returns and cash-flow problems.

The color television industry, for example, moved through this transition in the 10 years from the late 1960s to late 1970s. During that period, Japanese manufacturers, notably Matsushita, Sony, Toshiba, Sanyo, and Hitachi, gained significant market-share advantages over U.S. and U.K. domestic producers, primarily due to their exploitation of the economic advantages of lower total costs and higher product quality, by means of exploiting strategic strengths in marketing and distribution.

This early identification of the transition from pure domestic to global competition is perhaps the most crucial element for both domestic and MNC-controlled SBUs. Obviously, the strategic strength and economic advantage factors illustrated in Figure 19-5 do not apply equally in all industries. These factors can be weighted and ranked according to relative importance, and the results plotted relative to time to assess the degree and speed of change toward

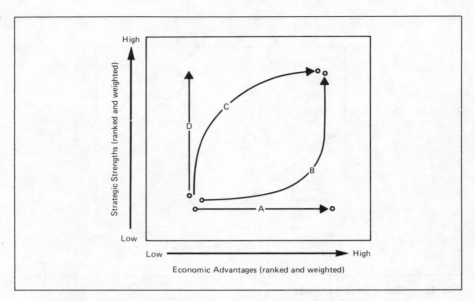

FIG. 19-6 Possible Development Scenarios Toward Global Competition

global competitor status. Figure 19-6 illustrates the tracks of four different companies in their progression toward global competition.

The linear development of industry *A* indicates that although it may potentially benefit from substantial international economic advantages, global competition may never materialize because no company in that industry is able to exploit sufficient strategic strengths. In industry *B*, economic advantages develop over time and ultimately are coupled with significant increasing strategic strengths that will precipitate global competition. In the publishing industry, for example, the electronic communication of densely packed information is enabling publishers to compose printed material centrally and print locally by remote command. Industry *C* has the advantage of significant strategic strengths. It is awaiting an economic advantage that will precipitate a globally competitive situation. Such a scenario existed when the U.S. government permitted engineering and construction firms to license nuclear reactor technology offshore, leading to intense international competition for power plant design and construction. Finally, in industry *D*, many companies may possess the necessary strategic strengths to compete globally, but economic advantages have not developed. Obviously, there are a number of different paths to global competition. By carefully monitoring movements of key economic and strategic factors, a corporation may identify the trends that animate the international competitive arena.

Domestic Strategy at the Corporate Level

Corporate strategy in a domestic business enterprise focuses on these major issues:

- Maintenance of the corporate entity
- Growth and renewal of the corporate entity
- Financing of the corporate entity
- Organization, measurement, and control of the corporate entity
- Management of external relationships

A domestic corporation contends with issues that are largely circumscribed within the boundaries of the home country. MNC corporate strategic planning must deal with these same issues; however, the complexity of the planning task increases with the introduction of new languages, cultures, currencies, and economic and political systems.

Multinational Strategy at the Corporate Level

An MNC must add several issues to the list of strategic priorities of a domestic corporation:

- International risk
- Logistics
- International finance
- Government relationships

International Risk. In recent years, international risk has been of significant importance in MNC corporate planning. The threat of economic and employee losses in operations increases when a corporation begins to move beyond its familiar frontiers. Expropriations in Cuba after the 1960 revolution and in Iran in 1979, executive kidnappings in Argentina, assassinations in Mexico, and contract repudiations in Nigeria are testimony to the multiform and multicausal business problems that are compounded by the world's diverse economic, social, racial, and political forces.

A number of methods for assessing international risk have been developed during the past 20 years. Most rely on scanning a variety of social, political, and economic factors in a given country and rating and ranking these to arrive at an index of the likelihood of some business interruption. A sampling of these techniques is presented in Table 19-2.

Current international risk-assessment techniques consider political development, societal achievement, technical advancement, and resource abundance of the host country in assessing three types of risk:

- *Business risk*—fluctuations in operating income
- *Financial risk*—fluctuations in debt repayments
- *Catastrophic risk*—termination of operating income

Beyond assessing risk, an MNC requires a mechanism for dealing with the social and political forces that exist in its host country. Conflict management

TABLE 19-2　Examples of Risk Assessment Techniques

Technique Originator	Technique	Characteristics
Frederick T. Haner (University of Delaware)	Business Environmental Risk Index	Expert weighting and ranking of 15 key economic and political variables
Frost & Sullivan	World Political Risk Forecasts	Multifactor analysis with probability of various disaster events
Probe International	Custom Forecasts	In-depth narrative discussions of present/future conditions
Charles W. Hofer and Terry Haller	Globescan	Comprehensive analysis incorporating several decision and support models
Concorde Group	CG Model	Scenario-based future planning
Arthur D. Little, Inc.	International Business Environment Assessment	Business profiles that identify risk factors and offer alternative strategy development

strategy is an important component of the overall MNC strategy for relationships with host countries.

Logistics. As operations expand throughout the world, logistics becomes an element of strategy with important dimensions. Attention to logistics must include data and information flow as well as physical product movement. Key issues in MNC information systems planning include:

- Transborder data-flow restrictions;
- Unionization of data processing departments outside the United States;
- Additional recordkeeping for compliance with the Foreign Corrupt Practices Act (and its equivalent in other governments);
- Increasing interdependence among operating units; and
- Rapid technological developments in information processing.

Facilities planning and location often determine the logistics of product movements. Capital-intensive manufacturing and distribution facilities often become a keystone in MNC strategic plans.

International Finance. All corporations must adopt financial strategies, including internal and external financing, debt and equity balancing, and other means of ensuring the growth and integrity of the enterprise. Multinationals, however, face significantly greater challenges in their financing operations than domestic corporations. Factors specific to multinational enterprises include:

- Currency exchange
- Currency translations
- Local inflation rates
- Local tax laws
- Regulations on repatriation of earnings

Beyond handling these factors, MNCs must deal strategically with pressure for local ownership and differing investment expectations. For example, Mexico has adopted a policy that requires local majority ownership of foreign multinational operations. In some instances, the local partner must be the government, as is the case with certain industries in France.

With local ownership often comes different expectations of appropriate business returns. Local owners, especially governments, may take a long-term view of profitability levels and the rates and timing of returns. For them, stable employment and the lack of more attractive alternative investment opportunities are the most important considerations. The foreign multinational may have better alternatives for investment, and typically desires a faster, higher return. Local borrowing has been one way to reduce foreign MNC direct investment and still enable the MNC to maintain control of the local venture.

Government Relationships. Some leading analysts of multinational enterprise maintain that relations with other countries is (or should be) the central strategic issue for an MNC. They believe that, depending on the circumstances, it is of strategic importance for a corporation to resist, comply with, or lead socioeconomic trends in a host country.

Most MNCs must pay special attention to their external relationships with host countries. It is not only in the Third World or less-developed countries that these relationships must be watched carefully. In France, the recent thrust toward nationalization by a Socialist majority has created, among other programs, a list of "essential industrial poles," which includes Pechiney Ugine Kuhlmann and Saint-Gobain Pont-a-Mousson. With the nationalization of these firms may come foreign ownership of some important U.S.-based companies.

MNC STRATEGIC PLANNING SYSTEMS

Given the range of planning factors and the variety of enterprises that must be considered, there are few hard and fast rules about MNC strategic planning systems. The factors needed to develop a sound plan vary, however, according to the level (SBU vs. corporate) and complexity (domestic vs. multinational) of the problem, making it possible to highlight those factors of key importance to a firm. The nature and scope of these factors in turn determine the type of planning system best suited to the strategic information and control requirements of that particular enterprise.

Strategic Planning Systems at the Multidomestic SBU Level

As illustrated in Table 19-3, a firm conducting a multidomestic SBU operation is faced with a geographic market portfolio planning problem. The individual markets have few, if any, points of commonality that call for centrally directed product or market strategies. Essential elements of a planning system for this type of MNC operation include:

- Wide latitude for individual countries to develop local (home country) plans and programs for dealing with unique products, markets, and sets of competitors;
- Tight central control over flow of funds and resource allocations, based on operating and financial performance indicators from local operating units;
- Central analysis, but with local input, of the overall SBU portfolio performance, including local political and economic risk, relative currency valuations, exchange rates, and operating and ownership policies and regulations.

Kawasaki motorcycles, which entered the United States two decades ago, is a useful example of a multidomestic business. Kawasaki's planning system allowed a great deal of flexibility, enabling it to permit U.S. operations to develop creative product and market strategies without threatening the company's central control over basic financial factors, including the overall level of reinvestment in the U.S. business.

Kawasaki motorcycles have become a world-class competitive product through the efforts of Kawasaki Heavy Industries, the Japanese conglomerate. In the early 1960s, the Kawasaki motorcycle was produced in Japan principally for the Japanese market. Domestic sales were leveling off and management sought further opportunities for growth. At Kawasaki, motorcycles are produced by the Engine and Motorcycle Group, which is responsible for small internal combustion engines, motorcycles, and jet engines. Although part of a much larger entity, the strategy of the motorcycle business unit approximates that of a single-business company. The major strategic milestones in the evolution of Kawasaki motorcyles as a multinational operation include:

- Establishment of a U.S.-based marketing and sales office in 1965;
- Introduction of export motorcycle sales to the United States, supported by heavy advertising and sales promotion expenditures in the late 1960s and early 1970s;
- Development of an extensive independent domestic distribution and dealer network;
- Establishment of a continuing stream of product innovations and models directed toward satisfying the recreational motorcycle buyer in the United States;

TABLE 19-3 A Comparison of SBU-Level Strategic Planning Factors

Factor	Single Domestic	Multidomestic	Global
Industry			
Demand	Stems from a single set of factors	Different demands/factors by country/area	Unified by a common product or selling theme
Driving forces	Homogeneous set	Heterogeneous set	Multivariate, but may be used to balance/optimize a global system of competition
Trends	A single set	Vary; may offset/balance	
Market			
Growth	Homogeneous growth rate for overall industry	Several different growth rates; can vary widely	Several different growth rates; can vary widely
Key segments	A single set	Different sets may exist	Different sets may exist
Customer groups	A single set	Different sets by country	Different sets by country
Trends	A single set	May vary by country	May vary by country
Competitor			
Nature/ownership	Single set	May vary among countries	Trend toward concentration
Concentration/shares	Single set	May vary widely among countries	Trend toward concentration in a few globally active competitors
Bases of competition	Similar for all competitors across the industry or niche	—	—
Strategic thrust	—	—	Complementary roles assigned by country or region
Technology			
Products	Similar sets exist within the industry offerings	Different sets may exist; vary widely country-by-country	Common themes exist across international boundaries
Substitutes	If existant, present for all competitors	May exist only in some countries/areas	May exist only in some countries/areas
Raw materials	Tend to be equally accessible to all competitors	Individual countries/areas may have advantages	Individual countries/areas may have advantages
Financial			
Cost structure	A single range exists within the industry	Varies by country	Varies by country; used to fine-tune a global system
Investment intensity	—	—	Varies by function emphasized
Profitability	—	—	

- Ensurance of a prompt parts supply system through its distributors and a company warehouse system;
- Establishment of the first Japanese motorcycle assembly facility in the United States, in Lincoln, Nebraska, in 1974.

In recent years, Kawasaki's domestic U.S. production was about one third of its worldwide total. The Lincoln facility has received considerable attention as a model of Japanese-style manufacturing within the United States. In a recent study of Kawasaki's 1,500 dealers, the majority found the overall quality of the machines built in the United States to be equivalent to or better than those produced in the company's main domestic motorcycle plant in Akashi, Japan.

This deep penetration of the U.S. market required a considerable initial investment. The motorcycle division ran its U.S. operations at a loss for 14 years, from 1964 to 1978. Today, Kawasaki continues to assemble motorcycles in the United States from parts manufactured in Japan. Kawasaki's overall U.S. entry strategy has proved remarkably successful in terms of gaining and holding a strong competitive position. The key elements of this strategy included (1) freedom for U.S. operations to develop distinctive products, distribution channels, advertising, and marketing, and (2) control over the flow of funds to ensure that the necessary investment was made to develop the market.

Global Competition

An MNC engaged in global competition, as shown in Table 19-3, tends to tailor its planning system along the following lines:

- Central (typically home country) control over the scope and contribution of individual countries' operations at the production, distribution, and marketing levels. This control is based upon varying regional advantages in skills, raw materials, and other resources; energy costs; transportation; or rates of market growth.
- Central monitoring and control of resource allocation, performance goals, and risk indicators.
- Central development, dissemination, and control of key factors in technological and product-related success, including product design, product quality, parts interchangeability, field service, and warranty provisions.

Operating a planning system for a globally competitive product implies (1) a higher order of detailed communications with line and staff personnel in all countries of operation and (2) a method to motivate and reward individual country operations effectively and equitably for what may be perceived to be a suboptimization of that country's potential.

Timex Corporation, the Middlebury, Connecticut watch manufacturer, is a classic example of the development of multinational business operations with a single product line. Over a 20-year period, from 1950 to 1970, Timex grew to dominate the worldwide wristwatch industry by radically changing the basis of competition. In doing so, Timex put into play a comprehensive mix of centrally controlled marketing, manufacturing, and distribution strategies.

The basic Timex product is an inexpensive pin-lever watch engineered for mass production and assembly. Most wristwatches in the early 1950s were of Swiss manufacture, built in a relatively labor-intensive process from individually fitted components. Unable to sell its watches through jewelry stores, the traditional distribution channel, Timex introduced its product through a wide variety of retail outlets, including drug stores, hardware stores, and large mass merchants. The product was backed by a generous one-year warranty, coupled with a lifetime low-cost service policy. Heavy advertising stressed high value in service, durability, and reliability. Timex built a worldwide network of over 15 manufacturing and assembly plants to support its sales. These facilities were designed for the lowest cost piece-part fabrication, and incorporated the latest in automated small-parts assembly and testing equipment. Manufacturing, designed to produce interchangeable parts, took place under rigid quality control. The lightweight watch movements, cases, and straps were shipped by air freight for subassembly and final assembly at locations that took maximum advantage of import duty and tariff regulations.

Timex's integrated business strategy was formulated and directed from the top of the company by its founder, Joachim Lehmkuhl. It is interested to note that the Timex strategic thrust remained essentially unchanged for more than two decades. Key strategic elements included:

- Low-cost manufacturing
- Broad, efficient mass distribution
- High product reliability
- Creative customer service

In recent years, Timex has been threatened by the advent of the digital electronic watch. Late to enter this technology, which calls for radically different movement manufacturing techniques, Timex saw its worldwide market share erode. Its current recovery strategy appears to have two main elements:

- Rejuvenate and consolidate its position by introducing competitive electronic watches; and
- Significantly diversify the product line, utilizing its existing, well-established retail distribution system.

Today, success in product diversification may be the crucial strategic element for Timex. Within a two-year period, Timex has introduced the Nimslo 3-D camera, the Timex/Sinclair home computer (as of this writing, the price leader in its segment at under $100), and a line of home-use electronic health care devices including digital scales, thermometers, and blood pressure and pulse rate monitors. All of these products build on Timex's precision, high-volume production and mass-distribution capabilities.

The Timex central planning system should be effective for manufacturing and physical distribution of these products, many of which are already established as globally competitive. However, the system now must deal with a much wider range of products in markets where Timex is not the initial, or even one of the principal, competitors. These challenges may test the adaptability of Timex's planning system as much as new technology has tested the focused manufacturing system.

Multinational Strategic Planning at the Corporate Level

As with the planning systems of domestic corporations, multinational strategic planning at the corporate level tends to address the business and environmental challenges and opportunities present in its planning horizon. However, these factors are usually more complex and varied than for a domestic enterprise. As outlined in Table 19-4, the multinational firm must usually pay close attention to these key factors:

- A corporate culture more varied and diffused throughout several countries (especially if the MNC has grown through acquisition);
- A broader range of shareholders and shareholder interests (especially if the MNC operates in countries where significant minority or majority interests are part of a national policy);
- A need to understand and deal with a broad range of world economic, social, and political forces;
- A need to communicate, control, organize, and reward employees worldwide, with sensitivity to local custom and practice, while supporting corporate goals and objectives.

Given these requirements, research and experience with MNC corporate planning systems show the following general trends:

- Multinational corporate plans are developed at the parent company's headquarters.
- Business unit plans are developed:
  a. Locally, if they are for domestic or multidomestic SBUs;
  b. Centrally, with local input, if they are for globally competitive SBUs.
- Environmental factors are recognized as crucial to planning.
- Financial considerations dominate corporate plans.
- Contingency planning is receiving increased emphasis.

An interesting example of a corporation with a centralized, corporate-level plan development is Akzo, N.V., a chemicals and fibers MNC based in the Netherlands. It was formed in 1969 through a merger of Aku, a synthetic fiber manufacturer, and KZO, a chemicals manufacturer. In 1971, the Akzo Board of Management, dissatisfied with prior planning methods, called for a revised approach. The new system consisted of these major elements:

- Division of the corporation into units appropriate for strategic planning (about 100 within Akzo).

TABLE 19-4 A Comparision of Corporate-Level Strategic Planning Factors

Factor	Domestic	Multinational
Internal environment		
Culture, values, heritage	Homogeneous	Homogeneous (parent nation); coupled with heterogeneous satellite country operations
Compensation and reward system	Simple; single-country customs, laws, regulations	Complex; multicountry customs, tax laws, regulations
Corporate strengths and weaknesses	Single set	Multiple set; satellite operations may either complement or offset parent company
Financial control system	Focused on single country operations control	Multivariate; requires understanding of each host country's regulations
Stakeholder interests/influences	Relatively homogeneous	Potentially heterogeneous; especially with widely distributed ownership situations
External environment		
Economic driving forces	Single set	Multiple sets
Social and political factors	Uniform set	Diverse and dissimilar; potentially clustered by stage of national economic development
Overall risk of operations	Usually well understood; managed by balancing investment in domestic business portfolio	Less predictable; managed by balancing investment in individual businesses and in overall multinational portfolio mix
Business portfolio		
Mix and diversity	Often more diverse than with multinationals; more industry sectors	Diversity often achieved through geographic scope rather than through product proliferation
Relatedness	Trend away from conglomeration; toward common themes	Varies; high degree of relatedness in globally competitive multinationals
Number and complexity of units	Varies	Varies
Ownership and control	Units tend to be wholly owned/controlled by parent corporation	High degree of parent corporation influence/control; tempered by local national regulation of foreign ownership

- Initial classification of each planning unit according to its strategic position and role for growth and funds.
- Development of a strategic plan for each unit, with emphasis on:
  a. Environmental analysis;
  b. Portfolio positioning;
  c. Strategic options;
  d. Proposed strategy and required resources.
- Development of divisional and corporate objectives and strategies, including resource allocation guidelines.
- Allocation of resources to the planning units.
- Development of planning unit action programs, targets for financial performance (especially cash flow), and targets for capital expenditures.

Akzo strategic plans for a five-year period are developed and revised each spring. Return-on-investment targets are established for each unit, based on that unit's strategic position, corporate expectations, and unit strategies. Unit plan reviews are conducted in three meetings between the Akzo Presidium and divisional boards of management. Although planning units are responsible for development of detailed strategies and programs, Akzo has placed ultimate responsibility for portfolio strategy and resource allocation with the central authority. Recently, Akzo has begun to link research and development planning with its corporate and planning unit strategies—an important step for a technology-based corporation.

As evinced by Akzo, centralized portfolio planning is an important tool at the corporate level of an MNC. Although individual SBU plans may be prepared by local or regional management (depending on the global nature of competition), a centralized approach is usually taken to monitor risk and exposure, adjust the overall mix of business activity, and achieve a coherent strategy for growth and renewal.

SOME IMPLICATIONS FOR FUTURE MNC PLANNING SYSTEMS

From the perspective of the United States, and probably of Japan and Europe as well, three developments—world environmental trends, advances in strategic planning methods and techniques, and MNC performance and the outcome of existing strategic directions—imply the following shifts in MNC planning systems:

- More use of strategic management techniques to enhance planning and analysis;
- An emphasis on technology as a major issue in strategy development;
- Recognition of specialization of function in country operations in global strategy formulation;
- A search for more relatedness in business unit portfolios;

- An increase in risk-sharing through joint ventures, research and development partnerships, and other multicompany business operations.

Implications for Strategic Management

In contrast to strategic planning and analysis, strategic management encompasses the implementation of a corporation's plans and programs. Domestic corporations are integrating "linkage" mechanisms—techniques to ensure plan accomplishment—into the corporate strategic planning process. These include tying the budgeting and control process to plans, adjusting the reward and compensation system to fit business unit mandates, and finding ways to ensure that business unit accomplishments are in line with the strategy selected. Highlights of this process include:

- Overall planning assumptions, goals, and objectives, and a statement of strategic guidelines are developed by corporate planning, and presented and discussed at a meeting of worldwide line and staff managers.
- Individual country business plans are developed and submitted to corporate management following overall planning guidelines.
- A corporate analysis of country plans is made and country business managers are notified of necessary adjustments.
- At an annual meeting, corporate and country business managers present and discuss plans:
  a. A corporate operating plan covering the first year of each five-year plan, containing the necessary budget and program detail for financial and operational control.
  b. The five-year corporate strategic plan, establishing overall business directions.

This process places high importance on the implementation aspects of the firm's strategy. As a result of focused discussions during planning meetings, strategic plans are prepared with specific program elements, key milestones, responsibility assignments, and associated expense and revenue targets, which are reported, monitored, and controlled.

Effects of Increasing Influence of Technology

With the proliferation of manufacturing locations, MNCs have created a diffusion of state-of-the-art process and product technology throughout the free world. Japanese and U.S. electronics companies have trained locals in Hong Kong, Singapore, Sri Lanka, and other developing Asian countries. These countries are now producing their own "me too" products, which often do not carry the overhead and research and development costs of the originators. The impact of technology diffusion will probably be to truncate lead times, and possibly shorten product life-cycles.

The natural reaction of technological leaders will be to protect lead time, which represents the recovery window for capital investment. Centralized research and development facilities in the home country and the careful division of manufacturing responsibility to avoid "complete systems" knowledge may be one way to achieve this objective. Another is to consider maintaining strict confidentiality on processes, formulas, and techniques, instead of placing them in the public domain through the patent system. Coca-Cola's secret soft drink formulation is a case in point. More recently, IBM has maintained a high degree of secrecy regarding its entry into the microcomputer industry with personal computers.

Specialization of Functions

The trend to maximize the efficiency of globally competitive businesses fosters the rational consideration of MNC functions. The search for low-cost labor in Latin America and Asia has been the most visible evidence of this trend. Other countries may offer different advantages, such as low-cost energy, inexpensive or readily available raw materials, low taxes (or high subsidies), favorable trade regulations, or available technical, scientific, and other critical skills. In a process similar to that used by domestic corporations that "rationalize" facilities by adding more efficient units and closing inefficient ones, MNCs will gradually focus each country's resources on areas of strength and away from areas of relative disadvantage.

A scan of recent national industrial develpment advertising sections in business periodicals demonstrates the emphasis that some countries have been placing on their relative advantages to the international business community:

- *Ireland*—productive assembly labor force, tax advantages, European Economic Community access

- *Germany*—skilled labor, technology

- *Brazil*—abundant natural resources, developing markets, attractive potential for foreign ownership

- *Japan*—skilled, productive workforce; access via trading to world markets

- *Argentina*—natural resources

Search for Relatedness

Recent studies have shown that the earnings performance of pure conglomerates has not met that of single-business or closely related business companies. Current corporate portfolio analysis seeks relatedness among business units, as opposed to the pure financial "portfolio balance" models of the 1970s. Relatedness, or fit, can be achieved in many dimensions, including markets, customers, products, technology, management skill, and geography. Although many MNCs appear to have a single—or related—industry focus, future acquisition and divestiture programs may produce even more of a fit as MNCs, like domestic corporations, strive to perfect what they do best.

Increase in Risk Sharing

Entry into markets of significant size and growth requires heavy investments. Many high-growth areas of the world are also relatively unstable socially and politically. Furthermore, many countries require a local ownership share. For these reasons, joint ventures between two or more MNCs, a foreign MNC and a local partner, or between an MNC and a local government, will become increasingly common.

BIBLIOGRAPHY

The following references were used to prepare this chapter. The author is especially endebted to William H. Davidson for the concepts of economic advantages and strategic strengths, which, taken together, form a useful framework for analyzing global competitiveness.

Basche, James, *International Dimensions of Planning*, Research Bulletin No. 102, New York: The Conference Board, 1981.

Birnbaum, Jeffrey H., "Falling Profit Prompts Timex to Shed Its Utilitarian Image," *Wall Street Journal* (Sept. 17, 1981), p. 29.

Brady, Rosemary, and Desiree French, "Go Ahead and Dream," *Forbes* (Oct. 25, 1983), pp. 111–112.

Buss, Martin D. J., "Managing International Information Systems," *Harvard Business Review* (Sept.-Oct. 1982), pp. 153–162.

Capon, Noel, John V. Farley, and James Hulbert, "International Diffusion of Corporate and Strategic Planning Practices," *Columbia Journal of World Business* (Fall 1980), pp. 5–13.

Davidson, William H., *Global Strategic Management*, New York: John Wiley & Sons, 1982.

Davidson, William H., and Phillipe Haspeslagh, "Shaping a Global Product Organization," *Harvard Business Review*, (July-Aug. 1982), pp. 125–132.

"Doing Business in Unstable Countries," *Dun's Review* (March 1980), pp. 48–55.

The Economist Intelligence Unit, Ltd., "State Ownership for More French Multinationals," *Multinational Business*, No. 3 (1981), pp. 49–52.

Ellis, Harry B., "U.S. Production, Japanese Style," *The Christian Science Monitor* (March 6, 1981), p. 1.

Gladwin, Thomas N., and Ingo Walter, "How Multinationals Can Manage Social and Political Forces," *The Journal of Business Strategy* (Summer 1980), pp. 54–68.

Gotcher, J. William, "Strategic Planning for Multinationals—The Views of Governments and Scientists," *Long-Range Planning* (Feb. 1981), pp. 23–31.

Hofer, Charles W., and Terry P. Haller, "Globescan: A Way to Better International Risk Assessment," *The Journal of Business Strategy* (Summer 1982), pp. 41–55.

Hout, Thomas, Michael E. Porter, and Eileen Rudden, "How Global Companies Win Out," *Harvard Business Review* (Sept.-Oct. 1982), pp. 98–108.

Johnson, Howard, "Assessing Risks in International Lending," *Burroughs Clearing House*, Detroit: Burroughs Corporation, 1980.

LaPolombara, Joseph, and Stephen Blank, *Multinational Corporations in Comparative Perspective*, New York: The Conference Board, 1977.

McDowell, Edwin, "Japanese Investment and the Growth of Kawasaki," the *New York Times* (June 3, 1979), pp. D1, D-4.

Porter, Michael E., *Competitive Strategy*, New York: The Free Press, 1980.

Sampson, Anthony, *The Seven Sisters*, New York: Viking Press, 1975.

Sethi, Narendra K., "Strategic Planning System for Multinational Companies," *Long-Range Planning* (Jan. 1982), pp. 80–89.

Skinner, Wickham, *Manufacturing in the Corporate Strategy*, New York: John Wiley & Sons, 1978.

Stobaugh, Robert B., "Where in the World Should We Put That Plant?" *Harvard Business Review* (Jan.-Feb. 1979), pp. 106–114.

Uttal, B., "A Computer Gadfly's Triumph," *Fortune* (March 8, 1982), pp. 74–84.

Uyterhoeven, Hugo, Robert M. Ackerman, and John W. Rosenblum, "Timex Corporation," in *Strategy and Organization*, New York: Richard D. Irwin, Inc., 1973.

Vernon, Raymond, *Storm Over the Multinationals*, Cambridge: Harvard University Press, 1977.

Vernon, Raymond, and Louis T. Wells, Jr., *Manager in the International Economy*, Englewood Cliffs, N.J.: Prentice-Hall, Inc., 1976.

Wheelwright, Steven C., "Japan—Where Operations Really Are Strategic," *Harvard Business Review* (July-Aug. 1981), pp. 43–51.

Wind, Yoram, and Vijay Mahajan, "Designing Project and Business Portfolios," *Harvard Business Review* (Jan.-Feb. 1981), pp. 70–82.

20

Strategic Resource Allocation and Control

CHARLES H. ROUSH, JR.

Vice President, Management Analysis Center, Inc.

INTRODUCTION

Over the past 10 years, many companies have jumped on the strategic planning bandwagon and created substantial, even elaborate, strategic planning capabilities. The need for an organized process for considering business from a strategic perspective has resulted in emphasing strategic planning functions. The growing diversity of businesses that characterizes most large companies accentuated the need for a methodology that enables top management to make strategic decisions in a complex, multi-divisional environment.

While the capability to formulate strategy was being enhanced, relatively little attention was given to the management processes required to implement strategy effectively. All too often it was presumed that strategy, once formulated, could be implemented within the framework of existing management processes and operating procedures. The problems that resulted from this inherent assumption ultimately led managers to recognize that an effective implementation capability is necessary if the results of strategies—no matter how brilliantly formulated—are to produce desired results.

Strategic management as a concept encompasses both strategy formulation *and* implementation. Because it provides a complete framework for dealing with the total management challenge, it is a very rich concept.

Two management processes must be designed correctly and work effectively to ensure successful strategy implementation. The first is the resource allocation process. If a process to support top management decisions on where scarce resources are committed is not in place and aligned with the strategic planning process, it is unlikely that the benefits from sophisticated strategic planning, no matter how well done, will be achieved in any systematic way. The second is a control process that enables top management to evaluate performance against strategic objectives. Strategic objectives typically have a rather long time horizon and involve issues that transcend routine, day-to-day operations. Traditional control systems that are oriented toward short-term performance cannot provide top management with the insight required to assess performance against strategic objectives. A different type of management process—a strategic control system—is needed.

STRATEGIC RESOURCE ALLOCATION

Resources should be committed to operating units in support of the strategies approved for those units. To do otherwise is to relegate strategic planning to an interesting theoretical exercise. Yet all too frequently these processes are not sufficiently linked together.

The problems involved stem, in large measure, from the notion in some companies that a strategic plan is simply a narrative description of newly discovered opportunities and threats, and a statement of where the business should or could be heading. The plan serves as a focal point for discussions with top management and the development of a directional strategic commitment. After this dialogue, the plan is shelved. Later, traditional processes are used to propose various types of projects, particularly capital projects, and these proposed projects are not likely to be fully compatible with agreed-upon strategy. Instead, they may tend to emphasize a variety of nonstrategic objectives. An example is boosting short-term operating performance, as determined by traditional measurement criteria such as return on investment, at the expense of strategic goals.

Effective operating budgets cannot be developed by business units without complete knowledge of the new capital they are scheduled to receive during the budget year. But in many companies the budget development process is not properly linked with either decisions on capital expenditures or business unit strategies.

A well-developed budgeting process can be found in almost every large company. The only important differences concern the rigor with which budgets are administered as instruments for management control. Elaborate budget-development processes that have been institutionalized over many years, however, may not incorporate provisions to reflect the effects of projected resource allocations, particularly new capital projects. For example, departmental budgets for various support functions are often determined on the basis of departmental strategies, rather than on the basis of requirements that are keyed to the flow of new resources to operating units. Likewise, budgets may not reflect overall strategic direction unless that direction can be defined and made explicit to all organizations that develop specific budgets.

Forging these necessary linkages to create a completely integrated planning and resource allocation process is absolutely essential to the effective use of available resources and the achievement of strategic objectives.

Description of an Integrated Planning and Resource Allocation Process

An integrated planning and resource allocation process, as illustrated in Figure 20-1, consists of five distinct cycles:

1 The financial input cycle
2 The planning cycle
3 The programming cycle
4 The budgeting cycle
5 The budget execution cycle

The Financial Input Cycle. The first step in making effective resource allocation decisions is developing the corporate financial strategy. A viable financial strategy is required for many reasons, but it is an essential prerequisite to developing capital availability estimates. Important ingredients in financial strategy include expected profits, debt/equity ratios, and dividend payout ratios. These factors play a major role in determining the amount of financial resources that can be committed to strategy implementation. They have a direct impact on the rate at which a growth strategy can be implemented without securing additional funds from the sale of equity.[1]

A clear understanding of financial strategy defines the boundaries within which resource allocations eventually will be made. As a simple example, if the strategy is to make a major investment to gain market share, sufficient funds must be available. These funds depend on operating cash flow and on debt and

---

[1] Increasing importance is being attached to the development of financial strategy. Two relevant publications are: William E. Fruhan Jr., *Financial Strategy* (Homewood, Ill.: Richard D. Irwin, 1979); and James K. Malernee, Jr. and Gary Jaffee, "An Integrative Approach to Strategic and Financial Planning," *Managerial Planning* (Jan.-Feb. 1982).

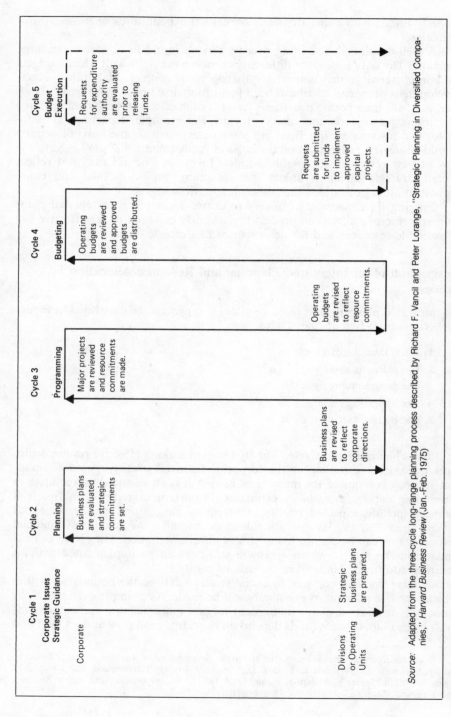

Source: Adapted from the three-cycle long-range planning process described by Richard F. Vancil and Peter Lorange, "Strategic Planning in Diversified Companies," *Harvard Business Review* (Jan.-Feb. 1975)

FIG. 20-1 Diagram of an Integrated Five-Cycle Planning and Resource Allocation Process

dividend policies. If sufficient cash cannot be generated, the strategy must be modified or the policies on either debt or dividends, or both, will have to be changed.

The Planning Cycle. The purpose of the strategic planning process is to provide an orderly evaluation of existing business activities in comparison with new opportunities that could be pursued. New opportunities include entering new businesses or modifying existing businesses in response to changing environmental conditions.

In some companies this systematic strategy assessment process is carried out at the corporate level. The result is a set of instructions (cycle 1) transmitted down to the business units for use in developing their strategic plans. Other companies use a "bottom up" approach. In either case, as strategies are formulated by business units and submitted to top management for decisions, they are accompanied by financial plans that project the general level of required resources. These estimates, though at an aggregate level, should be as realistic as possible and justified appropriately. In that form, they enable top management to decide upon those business strategies that not only are best from the overall perspective of the firm, but also are affordable. During the review of these strategic business plans, top management makes its first general determination of where, and in roughly what amounts, resources will be directed.

A strategic plan usually covers several years. Decisions by top management affect resource flows for extended periods. In many companies the period is set arbitrarily at five years, while in a few the period is 10 or even 20 years. An oil company, for instance, might use a 20-year planning horizon because a long period is necessary for it to integrate oil field development and production with transportation capabilities and refining sitings—all investments with very long lives.

Financial planning provides a means for evaluating alternative strategies and their resource implications over these long periods, and of comparing those requirements with estimates of the resources that will be available in future years. Decisions that result from this process provide guidance to lower level business units so that their proposed plans can be modified, where necessary, and fine-tuned to reflect top management's decisions.

The Programming Cycle. After business unit plans are modified, they are resubmitted to top management along with more detailed information on required financial resources. Major capital projects are justified in greater detail, and proposed operating budgets for the first year of the planning period are made to reflect both capital projects and approved strategies. Traditional capital budgeting processes are emphasized at this point to support decisions by top management on specific projects or programs, as proposed by the business units. Top management's decisions take into account the anticipated returns from particular investments, the projected availability of funds, corporate needs for funds, requirements for funds by the business units on a time-phased basis, and many other factors. The result is an integrated plan for expenditures that is consistent with corporate strategy, business unit strategies, investment opportunities, and the projected level of financial resources that will be available to fund the plan.

The Budgeting Cycle. As a result of top management's decisions on how resources are to be applied, budgets can be specified for the first year of the planning period (also called the budget year). The budget includes operating targets, such as revenue, operating expenses, and profits, as well as capital expenditure estimates for each business unit. Business unit budgets are based on the capital resources received by the units and the underlying strategies that formed the basis for the resource allocation decisions.

The Budget Execution Cycle. Many companies require a business unit to submit formal analyses to top management when requesting funds for approved capital projects. These requests are submitted throughout the budget year when the business unit is ready to move forward with an approved project. The analysis and justification for the project give top management a further opportunity to examine in detail the economics and overall desirability of the project before releasing funds. These justifications are often prepared and submitted in a very standardized format and are frequently limited to relatively large capital projects.

The Capital Budgeting Process

Making decisions on capital expenditures is one of top management's most important responsibilities. It is not surprising, therefore, that an elaborate process to assist management in making decisions on proposed uses of capital and other types of resources has been developed. This process is called the capital budgeting process. It places heavy emphasis on the techniques and methods for analyzing alternative investment opportunities, although in some companies considerable attention is also focused on process issues: how and when to submit investment proposals and how top management decides on which opportunities to pursue.

Although the capital budgeting process focuses on the use of capital, there are other types of resources that top management also must decide on, often in conjunction with decisions on capital.

Variations in the Process. The nature and sophistication of the capital budgeting process vary widely from one company to another. Companies that are capital intensive with numerous, long-lived capital projects need a capital budgeting process that is quite different from companies that are not capital intensive. Overall strategic directions also dictate different capital budgeting processes. For example, companies with a high-growth strategy need a process that is different from those with an aggressive acquisition strategy.

Different management styles and operating philosophies also affect the character of the capital budgeting process. For example, companies that are highly decentralized tend to delegate greater responsibility for capital budgeting decisions than companies with centralized decision making. In some firms the process is highly analytical, while in others greater importance is attached to more qualitative criteria, such as the historic performance of operating managers. In the latter situation, managers with strong performance records can expect to receive more resources than managers with less successful performance records.

The type of capital budgeting process used also may be affected by the amount of capital regularly available for investment, which reflects both a particular financial strategy and the economics of the businesses the company is in. Where capital flows are relatively high, management may encourage the submission of numerous proposals so that it has a rich base of opportunities to evaluate. When capital flows are relatively constricted, top management may want to limit the submission of proposals to only those that are highly promising. Thus, the capital budgeting process can and should be tailored to meet the objectives of top management across a very wide spectrum.

Given the number and variety of factors that affect the choice of a budgeting process within a company, only a normative capital budgeting process can be discussed with any confidence. There is no such thing as an "average" company. To describe the process completely, all aspects of a fully developed process are covered in this chapter. It should be noted, however, that this process must be adapted to the specific needs of each individual company.

Description of the Process. The capital budgeting process focuses on the systematic identification and analysis of capital investment opportunities. In this way the process supports top management's efforts in making decisions on capital resources. For business performance to be favorable, investment decisions must be consistent with strategic objectives and reflect returns that are consistent with both the nature of the business and the risks that are taken.

During the strategic planning phase of the integrated planning and resource allocation process, alternative business strategies are examined in the light of corporate strategy, and directional strategic commitments are made. Rough approximations of capital requirements, including those for capital projects, are made for each business unit to provide top management with sufficient information on capital requirements to make the necessary strategic decisions. Capital budgeting thus links the resource allocation process to strategic planning.

The nature of the capital budgeting process during the strategic planning phase varies considerably from company to company. In a widely diversified company with 40 to 50 divisions, top management needs information in summary or aggregate form. Companies with numerous long-term capital projects (e.g., refineries, chemical plants, paper mills) have significant capital carryover requirements from one year to the next. In this environment, management must spend a large portion of its time reviewing the progress of existing capital projects. Also, although large new starts may be few in number, they may be so significant that capital projects are analyzed and reviewed separately on an ongoing basis throughout the year. In most companies, however, strategic decision making focuses largely on the new capital resources required to implement the business strategies proposed by the operating divisions.

During the programming phase, top management must make more detailed decisions on the specific uses of capital sought by its operating units. The focus at this time is on a thorough evaluation of specific proposals for the capital resources that are incorporated in each unit's strategic plans. The proposals are evaluated independently to assess the reasonableness of the expected returns, and collectively to ensure the overall capital budget is consistent with the company's financial strategy and sufficient to fund and complete projects on schedule.

Once decisions are reached on planned capital commitments, the operating units proceed with developing their operating budgets for the budget year. These budgets should reflect not only operating revenues and expenses, but also capital commitments based on their approved capital projects. The incorporation of capital funds into the budget provides top management with a detailed estimate of funding commitments by project, as well as an approximate schedule of when the funds will be required. This information is necessary to support near-term financing plans that might be needed to generate committed funds.

Capital Budgeting Horizons. A capital budgeting horizon defines the period through which it is reasonable to forecast and schedule capital requirements so that near-term decisions can be made in recognition of longer term needs. The horizon used in evaluating the expected returns from a particular project varies depending on the nature of the project and the analytical techniques used to evaluate it.

Most large companies have both a five-year and a one-year capital budgeting horizon. The five-year capital budgeting horizon often coincides with the five-year strategic planning horizon. The one-year capital budget details the capital requirements and the timing of expenditures in the budget year. A variety of actions may be necessary to provide necessary capital resources in the short run. Thus, there is a greater need for accuracy in both the dollar amounts and timing of the expenditures during the budget year. In some companies (e.g., high-growth technology firms) the one-year horizon is the primary capital budgeting planning period, because with growth rates of 30 percent or higher, the deployment of capital resources for the next (or budget) year severely taxes the abilities of both operating unit managers and top management.

Basic Decision Criteria. Top management's review of proposals for capital is based on two types of decisions. The first involves economic considerations, including an assessment of the projected returns from a particular project. The second relates to how well the proposed project fits the company's strategy. This assessment concerns the manner in which the proposed project supports both the strategy of the business unit proposing the project and overall strategic objectives. Examples of the latter include corporate objectives to increase productivity, enhance customer service capabilities, or maintain desired growth rates.

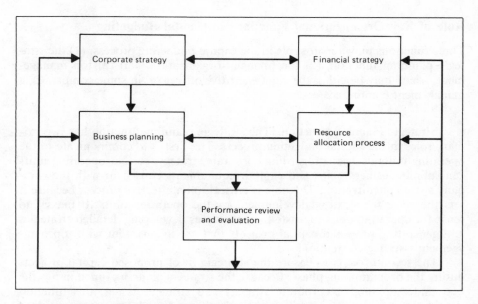

FIG. 20-2   Role of Financial Strategy in Integrated Planning and Resource Allocation Process

The two decision criteria are applied in both the strategic planning and the programming phases. In the strategic planning phase, overall or summary data on proposed projects are examined in conjunction with various strategic criteria to evaluate proposed business strategies, and strategic issues are of relatively greater importance. In the programming phase, the economic issues tend to be of greater importance. In many companies a comprehensive and detailed examination of each capital project is often not carried out during the programming phase. Instead, an in-depth analysis that addresses specific economic considerations is carried out when the operating unit requests funds to implement the project during the budget year. In this way top management can focus its limited time for detailed review and analysis on those major projects that are in a clear go-ahead stage and require a decision to authorize the expenditure of capital resources.

The economic criteria used to evaluate capital projects—from an overall perspective during the programming phase and in more detail during the budget execution phase—should reflect financial strategy. This suggests that financial strategy decisions not only provide guidance in the form of goals or constraints during the strategic planning phase, but also provide a framework for the development of economic decision criteria that are used during the evaluation of capital projects. This relationship is diagrammed in Figure 20-2, which shows the effect of financial strategy on the overall process. The decision criteria are developed through the use of various analytical techniques that are employed to evaluate capital projects.

Role of Key Organizational Functions in Capital Budgeting

Three functions play a major role in the capital budgeting process: (1) the strategic planning function, (2) the financial organization, and (3) top management, which may be either the chief executive officer or, in some companies, a management committee.

Strategic Planning Function. The strategic planning function has two primary roles in the capital budgeting process. The first is to communicate to the operating units decisions regarding corporate strategy, so that operating units can submit business plans and capital requirements consistent with the company's strategic direction. This role is critical to an effective process because it sets the stage for strategy development by the operating units. It makes no sense for operating units to waste their resources developing detailed strategies and generating proposed capital projects that are inconsistent with top management's strategic intentions.

The second role is to ensure the strategic fit of proposed capital projects during the programming phase. Because the strategic planning function has the best understanding of corporate strategy and strategic issues, this function should play a major role in determining whether capital projects are consistent with strategic objectives. In some companies, the strategic planning function is required to sign off on proposed capital projects. In other companies, someone from the strategic planning function is included on a review committee that evaluates proposed capital projects.

Financial Organization. The financial organization is normally the function that administers the capital budgeting process. Often, it is charged with most of the work required in both the preparation and justification of proposed capital projects, as well as for the corporate-level analysis of proposed projects.

At the corporate level, the financial organization is responsible for analyzing the capital budget to ensure it is consistent with overall financial goals and financial strategy. Another responsibility is the development of procedures and standards to make the process effective. This responsibility often extends to the specification of mandatory information that must accompany proposed capital projects and standard analytical techniques that must be incorporated into project analyses.

The analytical responsibility is a major one during the programming phase, but is also important during the strategic planning phase when the financial organization provides support to strategic planning in the form of an analysis or critique of strategic plans. During the budget execution phase, the financial organization usually has responsibility for preparing detailed analyses of capital projects for top management prior to the release of funds to the operating units. During the preparation of these analyses, input may be received from the strategic planning organization, depending on the nature of a particular capital project. Alternatively, the financial organization provides staff support to a committee or broader management group that has overall responsibility for the analysis, and, in many companies, it makes recommendations directly to top management on the desirability of each proposed project.

At the operating unit or division level, the financial organization typically is responsible for administering the capital budgeting process and preparing analyses and justifications that support the desirability of proposed projects. In making these analyses, most companies provide a wide degree of latitude to the operating unit. The operating unit is encouraged to use whatever analytical approaches are deemed appropriate, and is expected to address all relevant issues and business considerations during its analysis. This freedom is designed to encourage an analysis that is broader than the mandatory requirements called for in policies or standards established at the corporate level.

Top Management. The five phases of an integrated planning and resource allocation process provide top management with a sequential, step-by-step decision process, moving from broad strategy issues to substantive issues involving the allocation of resources, to the determination and execution of specific budgets. This process links decisions on long-term strategic objectives to decisions on specific capital projects. For the process to function smoothly, top management must play a major role in both the design of the process and in its execution.

Because of the long-term importance of decisions on capital expenditures and, in many companies, because of the large size of the capital budget, capital budget approval is sometimes vested in the board of directors. In other companies the responsibility is vested in the chief executive officer, and in some cases in a top management committee that includes the chief executive officer. Rarely, however, are major decisions on the capital budget delegated to a group below the level of the chief executive officer.

Top management uses its capital budget decision authority to guide the corporation to its long-term objectives. By linking the capital budget to clearly understood strategic objectives, top management exerts a strong influence over the future course of the business. In addition, the signals sent by top management's decisions on the use of capital represent a major method of communicating with key operating managers. For these reasons, the capital budgeting process can consume a significant portion of top management's time.

Criteria Used by Top Management to Make Decisions

Capital budgeting is normally seen as a highly quantitative process, even though the extent to which quantitative data are prepared and used to support top management's decisions varies from one company to another, depending primarily on the basic need at the top management level for quantitative data. In companies with a very analytical orientation, proposals for capital projects include much more sophisticated quantitative analyses than in companies where top management is less insistent on this type of analysis.

But in most companies, top management's decisions on capital projects are influenced also by subjective criteria. Such judgment calls are made on various assumptions presented in the justification of the proposed project. These judgments by top management are based on years of practical experience, and involve subjective considerations above and beyond the explicit quantitative information.

Analytical Techniques.[2] Over the past 20 years, a variety of analytical techniques has been developed for evaluating proposed capital projects. Different companies use some or all of these techniques to support decision making on resource allocation. These decisions take place during the programming phase of an integrated planning and resource allocation process and, later on, in the budget execution phase when specific projects are examined in greater detail, prior to releasing funds.

The use of any particular set of techniques and the importance accorded to each vary from one company to another for many reasons. For example, top management may prefer a particular technique because it is easy to understand and use.

Description of Commonly Used Analytical Techniques. Most companies use and place relatively greater emphasis on analytical techniques that reflect the time value of money. Three methods are in widespread use:

1 *Discounted rate of return.* Also called the discounted cash flow method, discounted rate of return is probably the most widely used of all the analytical techniques. It determines the discount rate at which the present value of cash receipts equals the present value of cash expenditures.

2 *Net present value.* The net present value method uses a discount rate determined from the company's cost of capital to establish the present dollar value of a project. The discount rate may be adjusted to reflect other criteria set by management, such as an adjustment to compensate for perceived risk or an arbitrary cut off rate that serves as a screen for capital projects proposed by a particular division. This method uses the discount rate to determine the present value of both cash receipts and cash outlays. The difference provides a net present dollar value for a given project. Although it is frequently used, net present value is often considered less important than discounted rate of return.

3 *Profitability index.* Also called the present value index, the profitability index creates a ratio by dividing the present value of cash receipts by the present value of cash outlays. A discount rate, similar to net present value, is used to determine the present value of the cash inflow and outflow. Seldom used, this method is generally considered less significant than the other two.

---

[2] Various researchers, including the author, have surveyed corporations during the past 10 years on their use of analytical techniques or capital budgeting methods. Generally these surveys result in findings that are not markedly dissimilar. Two surveys that are both interesting and thorough are: J. M. Fremgen, "Capital Budgeting Practices: A Survey," *Management Accounting* (May 1973), and J. William Petty, David F. Scott, Jr., and Monroe M. Bird, "The Capital Expenditure Decision-Making Process of Large Corporations," *The Engineering Economist* (Spring 1975).

Two other analytical techniques are in general use, but neither reflects the time value of money. Therefore, they are not as effective in discriminating between alternative capital projects. They are:

4 *Return on investment.* Also called accounting rate of return, return on investment is simply the ratio of the average annual net income from a project divided by the initial investment in the project. Although less sophisticated than the three methods described previously, it indicates how the financial results of a project will appear on a company's financial statements. As a result, it is widely used and generally viewed as being of considerable importance, but it is probably not as important as the discounted rate of return method.

5 *Payback period.* This is a commonly used method. Although it is technically deficient, payback period is widely understood and still used frequently. It determines the period of time required for the cumulative cash inflow from a project to equal the initial investment. Thus, it specifies how long it takes to recover the initial investment in a capital project.

Occasionally other more specialized techniques, most of which reflect modifications in some way of the five major methods just described, are used. For example, the payback period can be computed using a discount factor. The particular combination of techniques used by a company reflects existing management preferences. In some instances, techniques may be varied to reflect the nature of a specific capital project. For example, proposed investments in new products might be analyzed using a set of techniques different from those for a proposed project for equipment replacement. The relative importance attached to certain techniques may also be varied in a similar manner.

Adjusting for Risk and Uncertainty. A major problem arises for top management in attempting to use the information generated by the various analytical methods, because the methods do not, in and of themselves, discriminate on the basis of risk. Risk is dealt with in a number of ways, from the use of very simple methods to the use of very sophisticated techniques.

When dealing with the concept of risk, management generally thinks in terms of the likelihood that projected returns or values will not be achieved. There are several ways of dealing with the risk associated with specific quantitative values. First, in some companies the payback period is seen as a simple surrogate for risk and is used specifically for this purpose. Second, some companies arbitrarily adjust their discount rates to reflect the increased risk inherent in particular types of projects. Third, even though adjustments are not incorporated in the analytical techniques, top management makes intuitive adjustments based on judgment and experience, and consequently demands a higher projected return from a project perceived as being relatively more risky.

A more fundamental problem management must confront is the variability of the projections and the reasonableness of the assumptions on which they are based. Many different factors—volume, market share projections, unit production cost estimates—can result in a capital project not achieving projected returns. Many companies use a sensitivity analysis that shows the variation in returns resulting from variations in different types of projections. This type of analysis permits top management to make a more reasoned assessment of the riskiness of a particular capital project. A more elaborate approach is the use of simulation models based on probabilistic techniques. Because of their cost and complexity, however, simulation models are rarely used; when they are used, they are applied to only large and very significant projects.

In the final analysis, risk must be evaluated by top management on the basis of experience and judgment. Quantitative methods assist and simplify this process, but they can never substitute for top management's judgment. Some companies that have tried to quantify the process have discovered that elaborate and sophisticated analytical processes were not worth the additional effort. Instead, relatively simple sensitivity analyses are more widely used because they give top management reasonable insight into risk without resorting to highly complex and cumbersome analytical techniques.

The Capital Budget Execution Process

During the budget year, operating units are required to submit requests for capital funds when they are ready to proceed with approved capital projects. In many companies these submissions are called "appropriation requests." As might be expected, the rigor and formality of this process tend to increase as companies increase in size and in the number of major capital projects undertaken. An appropriation request is supported by a detailed analysis of the project, which provides a basis for top management to decide whether or not the commitment of capital resources is still justified.

Having reached a decision on resource allocations during the programming cycle, why should top management require a further detailed justification of capital projects? First, the financial circumstances of the company may have changed during the course of the budget year. A temporary shortfall in funds availability—due, perhaps, to a swing in the economy—may require that some projects be deferred or modified. Second, appropriation requests are generally required only for large capital projects that have a major impact on the company. It is appropriate for top management to examine these projects in detail from an economic perspective before releasing the funds to implement them. And third, although capital requirements for all operating divisions are reviewed during the budgeting process, top management cannot examine each project separately—particularly from an economic perspective—with the rigor and thoroughness that are applied to an appropriation request.

Because the appropriation request review process is an ongoing one, and the number of requests over the course of a year can be substantial, information submitted to top management is usually highly standardized. Commonly, a standard form is required, along with backup analytical information. The standardized aspects of the appropriation request are not viewed as limiting factors, because supporting analysis to whatever depth is deemed appropriate by the submitting unit is also encouraged. Because the appropriation request is standardized, top management can review the request efficiently without spending excessive time locating particular types of information or discovering that some necessary information has been omitted. If more detail is needed, the backup analyses can be reviewed.

The information required in an appropriation request typically includes a description of the project, its costs and duration, and a discussion of its purpose and significance to the business unit. This discussion could include a competitive analysis and information on business strategy or other relevant facts that were considered when the business unit strategy was developed. Also included are specified quantitative analyses, which include some or all of the analytical data discussed previously—a discounted cash flow analysis, a present value analysis, a payback analysis, and a return on investment analysis—as well as other information, such as a year-by-year cash flow schedule for the life of the project. Usually some specialized information is required on important subjects such as productivity and energy conservation.

The specific use of these criteria and their relative importance, as well as the possible requirement for a sensitivity analysis, varies from one company to another depending on management style and orientation toward quantitative decision criteria. In addition, the standard submission may be supplemented by special market studies or other analyses as deemed appropriate by the submitting operating division.

Most companies classify appropriation requests by purpose, because different types of projects have different analytical and information requirements and necessitate the establishment of different decision criteria. For example, different hurdle rates are assigned for different classes of projects, based on the inherent business risk associated with each type of project. Classification schemes also segregate capital from operating expenditures for subsequent tracking and analysis. This after-the-fact reporting provides top management with summary information on the uses to which capital resources are put, which can provide additional insight on the extent to which capital resources are being directed toward overall corporate objectives. In addition, classifications specify different levels of approval authority. Approval authority for large projects in a specific category (e.g., maintenance projects) can be delegated to the operating divisions, while approval authority for small projects in other categories, such as business expansion, is retained by top management.

The wide range of classifications employed depends on the nature of the business, top management's objectives, and the need for after-the-fact analysis. Four major classifications are widely used:

- *Business expansion* involves additional investments to expand capacity for present products or to spread existing business activities to new geographic locations.

- *New products or ventures* reflects an investment in a new product or a new market that might include a new customer segment. This category is usually viewed as having the highest risk of any class of investment.

- *Cost reduction* covers all investments made to increase operating efficiency, thus leading to increased productivity and lower costs.

- *Maintenance* includes all investments required to maintain operating effectiveness or productive capacity, such as replacement of wornout plant and equipment and renovation of facilities.

Most companies that use an appropriation request process have specified capital project approval levels. The approval level may vary by the project dollar amount and organizational level, depending on the classification of the project. Another factor that influences the setting of approval levels is the size of the company. In a very large firm, an approval level for the head of an operating division may be set at $1 million for a specific type of project, while in a smaller company an approval level of $50,000 may be set for a similar type of project. The dollar threshold for approval levels is also influenced by the degree to which the company is committed to a decentralized operating concept. Companies emphasizing decentralization as an element of their operating philosophy have relatively higher dollar thresholds for division-level managers.

Generally, very large projects—certainly those exceeding $10 million to $20 million—require a decision by the board of directors. Where the board is very active and highly involved in the decision process, this amount may be much smaller, even in companies that are quite large. In other situations, approval authority rests with the chief executive officer or a committee, usually the regular management committee, that has been delegated the responsibility for corporate-level decisions on capital projects. In some companies there is also an investment committee that reviews all capital projects and makes recommendations to the management committee.

Those capital projects reviewed by top management during the appropriation request process are, by definition, relatively large ones that must be sent upward in the organization for final decisions. Small projects, such as maintenance projects of a routine nature, are usually grouped together and reviewed as a unit. The requirement for capital to support these projects is often budgeted as a lump-sum amount to the division, and the size of this budget, in aggregate, is reviewed by top management and adjusted as necessary depending on the availability of capital funds. Division managers have the responsibility for spending these funds, and they are usually guided by various policies or directives established to control how the funds are spent.

The criteria for top management's decisions on appropriation requests are similar to those used during the programming phase, except greater emphasis is placed on economic assessment and critical implementation issues are examined in greater detail. Basically, top management challenges key assumptions about projected market size, market share, and unit production costs. Top management seeks assurance that major risks have been identified and that there is a basis for believing the expenditure of capital will lead to satisfactory returns. In making final decisions, top management relies heavily on the division-level and corporate-level analyses prepared for each appropriation request and on its experience and judgment in assessing the merits of specific projects.

Because of the heavy economic orientation of appropriation requests, the financial organization plays a major role in the process of evaluation. In some companies, it is the only organization involved in this process in a meaningful way. At the corporate level, the financial organization performs three important functions:

1 It reviews each appropriation request to ensure it is complete and has met established procedural guidelines.

2 It analyzes the appropriation request to establish the credibility of the financial data in the project plan, and comments on the reasonableness of basic business assumptions inherent in the financial data. Critical success factors that must be achieved for the project to be successful are usually delineated as a part of this analysis.

3 It makes recommendations to top management on the merits of each project. These recommendations may take into account a broader set of corporate-level issues on overall strategy and resource allocation.

The nature of the financial organization's input to top management is determined by its basic role in the corporate-level decision process. Where the financial organization is very strong, the scope of its input is very broad. Where the financial organization does not play a major role in decision making, the scope of its input tends to be limited to an economic assessment of the proposed project.

Many successful firms have a defined process for tracking and evaluating performance on capital projects, ranging from simple collection and reporting of expenditure data by project to a process requiring resubmission of the appropriation request for projects exceeding a set threshold—perhaps 10 percent of the approved budget—and a post-completion audit to determine whether or not the project achieved projected objectives.

Allocating Noncapital Resources

The resources required to implement proposed strategies extend beyond necessary capital funds. Various noncapital expenses, such as research and development costs, advertising and marketing costs, and training costs, are directly related to the achievement of strategic objectives. Other types of resources, such as the availability of experienced management talent, special expertise in scarce and technically oriented skill areas, and access to limited supplies of raw materials, may also be important. Although strategic expenses and strategic resources can be very significant during the resource allocation process, most companies have not developed the capability to routinely identify and evaluate these resources, particularly strategic expenses, in their resource allocation processes.

The Importance of Strategic Expenses. During the development of business strategies, it is relatively easy to identify the new capital expenditures that will be required to implement the strategies. New fixed assets can be defined, their costs can be estimated, and they can be evaluated as relatively discrete entities. New working capital requirements may be harder to specify precisely, but reasonable estimates can be made based on the nature of the proposed strategy and on existing systems and procedures for managing inventory, billing customers, and paying for supplies.

Estimates of the various incremental expenses associated with implementing a strategy can, on the other hand, be quite difficult because incremental expenses are incorporated into the operating budgets of many different units that control the resources, and a provision usually has not been made to account separately for those expenses that would be strategic in nature. Because expenses of a strategic nature could occur in any functional unit, the process of identifying and estimating these expenses is complicated and requires the rigor of an appropriate accounting system. If incremental expenses are not classified and accounted for in the first place, of course, it is unlikely that an effective process can be established to monitor them, and management will not have the information it needs to evaluate and control strategy implementation.

Although this general problem has been identified,[3] relatively few companies have addressed the issue directly by developing a systematic process to define and record strategic expenses so that they can be evaluated when resource allocation decisions are made.

Benefits of Using Strategic Expenses. The ability to identify strategic expenses usually requires accounting systems and a budget process that records and reports this information. Once this capability is in place, strategic expenses can be systematically identified and related to proposed business strategies. Projections of strategic expenses can be incorporated into the financial plans that are part of business unit strategic plans, which permits top management to take these expenses into account during the programming cycle. In this way the full impact of strategic resource requirements can be considered when making strategic commitments.

Furthermore, during the budgeting cycle, operating budgets can be distributed with the strategic component clearly designated, which provides a better basis for management decisions during the budget execution phase. Expenses incurred to meet current operations can be separated by top management from expenses incurred to support long-run strategic commitments. This capability, in turn, provides a means for tailoring control systems and reward criteria to reflect strategic objectives, and it improves the ability of managers at all levels to emphasize strategic commitments in their decision processes.

Finally, because strategic expenses are often incurred by units outside any particular division (e.g., research and development or advertising) it is difficult to obtain an integrated projection of the total requirements for any given strategic expense category. If several business units are proposing strategies that require significant advertising expenses, for instance, the combined effect could have a major impact on both the advertising function and the overall corporation. A system that routinely provides for the identification of strategic expenses enables top management to assess both the specific impact of these

---

[3] See Richard F. Vancil, "Better Management of Corporate Development," *Harvard Business Review* (Sept.-Oct. 1972).

expenses on particular divisional strategies and the combined effect of these expenses on various functional organizations. Top management can use this critical information when making decisions on strategic commitments.

STRATEGIC CONTROL

If a company has developed an effective strategic planning capability and is striving to make strategic management a reality, then the need for a process that will provide top management with information on performance against strategic objectives seems obvious. Yet, all too often the need for a process that will provide top management with information on strategic issues is neglected. The result is that top management is not able to exert its influence on strategic matters—and in this sense to control them—in the same way it does on routine operating matters.

This serious limitation can frustrate even the best commitment to strategic planning and strategic management. But without a means to obtain information that permits the evaluation of performance in a strategic sense, top management can make informed decisions only on short-run matters. It must trust to luck that performance against strategic objectives is proceeding as expected.

Definition of the Problem

Most corporations expend considerable resources and incur substantial operating costs to record, produce, consolidate, and analyze a huge assortment of information necessary for managing the business. Some of this information is required to meet a variety of government or regulatory requirements. The remainder is developed largely to meet the specific needs of managers at all levels, from top management down to the shop foreman. Although practically all this information contributes to better operating decisions, it does not give top management useful feedback on performance against strategic objectives.

In most companies, strategic objectives are established and action programs to implement them are developed around criteria that are not normally reported in routine management information systems. Because strategic issues are almost by definition nonroutine, systems designed to report on routinely developed operating information cannot address strategic issues.

What top management needs to control the implementation of strategy is a system that can provide, on a regular basis, information on strategic performance against predetermined success factors. The critical success factors can be internal (the ability of the company to execute the strategy successfully) or external (technology, markets, competitors, government agencies). Together they represent the critical events that can influence whether or not strategic objectives are met.[4]

---

[4] This requirement is addressed thoroughly in John F. Rockart, "Chief Executives Define Their Own Data Needs," *Harvard Business Review* (March-April 1979).

A system that generates and reports information to top management on strategic performance is called a strategic control system. This type of system identifies and monitors the critical success factors, measures performance against these factors, collects the necessary information, and reports this information to top management. These parts of a strategic control system are discussed in more detail in the following sections.

Benefits of a Strategic Control System

A system that permits top management to track and evaluate strategic performance against objectives is valuable because it forces the strategic planning process to be more rigorous. Strategic objectives that are to be measured and tracked must be defined, during the formulation of strategy, in action-oriented terms. This means that strategic objectives cannot be expressed in vague generalities, but must be defined concretely and specifically. The result is more credible and realistic strategic plans.

A strategic control system also provides a means for top management to discuss strategic issues and performance with lower level managers whenever necessary, rather than once a year during annual strategic planning sessions.

In addition, a strategic control system can influence managerial behavior throughout the organization. When a new strategy requires a major change in behavior, the signals sent through the process of collecting information and tracking and evaluating performance against strategic goals can reinforce the type of behavior change management is seeking. In fact, there is probably no more powerful stimulus to changing managerial behavior, particularly if the compensation system is altered to reward managers on the basis of results achieved.

Types of Information for Strategic Control Systems

To develop and use a strategic control system, information needed to measure and evaluate performance against critical success factors must be gathered in a systematic way. Because this information is not normally generated by existing information systems, a new process for collecting and aggregating information is necessary.

This process must be oriented toward output rather than input information, since strategic performance tracking requires information on the results expected from the expenditure of budgeted funds. It also must be capable of gathering various types of internal information from different departments to create new performance measures. This requires skilled technicians, extensive inter-unit coordination and cooperation, and the commitment of sufficient resources. Corporations that have been successful in developing an effective strategic control system usually create a special unit at a high level in the organization dedicated solely to this task.

Finally, the process must be capable of collecting external information on technological trends and changes in government regulations, for example, to provide a basis for monitoring the achievement of objectives developed in light of perceived external opportunities.

Companies without experience in collecting and using external information have a tendency to view it as an impossible task with a low payoff. Companies that have aggressive programs to obtain this type of information, however, value it highly. Effective strategic management requires that a company develop this capability to support its strategy formulation activities and to track its progress against externally oriented strategic objectives. It is this latter requirement, in particular, that cannot be developed sufficiently without appropriate external information.

The central organizations created to develop internal information can also be used to seek out and provide external information. Special expertise is required to be successful. Often it is more efficient to locate this expertise in a single organization. In a company where such a unit exists, it plays an important role in the planning, programming, and budgeting process discussed earlier. For example, it provides a means for developing independent external and internal information that can be used to evaluate assumptions incorporated into capital projects proposed by operating divisions.

Outline of a Strategic Control System

A strategic control system, as illustrated in Figure 20-3, consists of six major steps:

1 *Formulate strategy and specify strategic objectives.* This is accomplished during the strategic planning phase of an integrated planning and resource allocation process. It presumes that top management has made a strategic commitment and that approved operating unit strategies are consistent with this commitment.

2 *Identify critical implementation factors and compare them with strategy.* An assessment must be made of the company's ability to execute the strategy as it is being developed. Of interest would be an assessment of the organization's structure, human resources, culture, and management processes or operating systems. If major barriers to the likely achievement of the strategy exist, they must be dealt with explicitly. If the barriers cannot be eliminated or reduced, then the strategy must be revised. This step requires an iterative process during the formulation of strategy to provide assurance that agreed-upon strategies are realistic and attainable.

3 *Specify performance criteria for the successful achievement of strategic objectives.* Top management must identify the critical factors, both internal and external, for strategic success. These critical success factors must be defined in sufficient detail so they can be measured and performance against them can be tracked, and they must represent both strategic objectives and implementation requirements. If the critical success factors raise questions about the achievement of strategic objectives or implementation capabilities, then a reassessment of the strategy itself may be necessary.

4 *Develop measurement techniques.* Criteria for measuring progress against achieving the critical success factors must be developed. These criteria can encompass a wide range of measurement indicators to depict the extent of the progress being achieved.

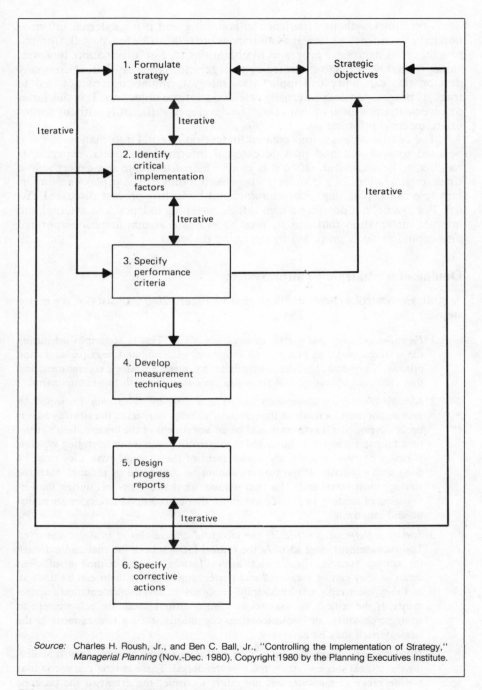

Source: Charles H. Roush, Jr., and Ben C. Ball, Jr., "Controlling the Implementation of Strategy," *Managerial Planning* (Nov.-Dec. 1980). Copyright 1980 by the Planning Executives Institute.

FIG. 20-3   Diagram of a Strategic Control System

5 *Design progress reports.* Data sources must be developed and an information system capable of collecting the necessary data and converting them into a form appropriate for use by top management must be created. The reporting process should be consistent with top management's methods and procedures.

6 *Specify corrective actions.* When critical success factors are not being met, corrective action is required. Either the actions taken by the organization or the strategy itself must be modified. This provides top management with control over strategy implementation.

Responsibility for Developing and Operating a Strategic Control System

A strategic control system is of limited benefit if top management has not made a conscious commitment to strategic management as a concept and taken the steps necessary to implement it. Once top management makes a firm commitment, a strategic control system seems to be an essential requirement to support the management processes. It is then seen as a very useful, even essential, management system, not only in its own right, but also because it is a major factor in shaping the behavior of managers at all levels.

The requirements of a strategic control system and the resources needed to develop it are such that no single entity in a company can be expected to design and implement a system without significant and continuing support from the chief executive officer and the management team.

There is also a need for a similar system at the operating division level, particularly where the operating division is defined and managed as a separate strategic business unit. Diverse operating divisions require different types of control systems that can take into account the needs of their various strategies. For example, divisions that have a high-growth strategy require control systems different from those that have a cash-generation strategy. The critical success factors and performance indicators are quite different. A strategic control system at the division level provides for these differences and enables division managers to better control the implementation of strategies that are unique to their particular divisions.

CONCLUSIONS

This chapter focuses on two important aspects of strategic management. The first is a resource allocation process that is tightly linked to the development of strategic plans and overall corporate objectives. The second is a control system that enables top management to evaluate performance from a strategic perspective. While each is important individually, together they provide a powerful decision support capability that can make strategic management a reality.

If either of these two processes is missing, however, serious deficiencies exist in the corporation's ability to translate its strategies into results through meaningful decisions and purposeful actions. Strategic planning then is relegated to an annual theoretical event, rather than an essential function that is oriented to clearly defined objectives. Further, there is an enormous risk that major mistakes can occur, almost routinely, because decision processes lack rigor and do not provide top management with the insight and reassurance it needs.

In the resource allocation process, the risk of directing scarce resources to projects that are not consistent with overall strategy is a major concern. Such an occurrence obviates the significance of strategic planning in the first place, while unwise resource allocations reflect on the level of competence and judgment of top management.

As for strategic control, to proceed with major strategic programs without a means for tracking progress that is anticipated against strategic objectives, or in developing essential capabilities to implement the strategies, is to invite disorder. The losses incurred by many corporations as a result of strategies that did not work—sometimes running into the hundreds of millions of dollars—are evidence that a control system to monitor the implementation of strategy is not a luxury, but a necessity.

Most companies have already developed processes that incorporate some of the capabilities required for a fully integrated planning and resource allocation process. For example, they may have a strategic planning function, and the capital budgeting process may be fully developed. Also, it is highly likely that they have a budgeting process, although it may or may not be used effectively to improve decision making and control. Only an exceptional company, however, has a well-developed system to incorporate strategic expenses into its decision process.

The systematic integration of these processes is also important. Strategic resource allocation means that decisions on capital projects, operating budgets, and the actual expenditure of funds are carried out in a way that reflects the underlying strategies that top management has agreed to or decided on. When there is a direct link between the processes, top management can be assured that approved strategies are indeed being furthered by the resources that have been committed.

While most companies have developed some of the processes needed for effective strategic resource allocation, very few companies have developed processes that are oriented to the control of strategy implementation. Those that have developed this capability have been working at it for many years. Although there are several reasons why this is the case, the fundamental problem is an overemphasis on short-run operating performance, which is fostered by the business community in general and by numerous groups, such as regulatory agencies, financial institutions, investment managers, and even individual investors.

Because of the pressure for short-term performance to meet short-term reporting requirements, top management has responded with control systems that focus on the measurement of short-term results: They understand the importance of this information and they know how to use it. But most top managers have not yet perceived the need to measure performance against long-term strategic objectives, in part because these are not seen as important or are not understood by outside groups.

Indeed, this information is normally treated as "confidential" by top management and withheld from the public eye. Without an external stimulus to develop this information, and combined with the continuing emphasis on short-run performance, it is not surprising that strategic control as a concept is emerging at a rather slow pace. There is a growing recognition, however, that a new approach may be needed, similar, perhaps, to that used by Japanese competitors. The Japanese clearly have a long-term strategic perspective for assessing business performance.

How can a company develop an integrated planning and resource allocation process and a strategic control system to evaluate performance in a strategic sense? While it should not be difficult, it is. It is not technically a problem, because most reasonably large companies have the internal resources to develop and administer these processes. Instead, the difficulty can be traced to two underlying problems. The first problem is that the management processes that must be integrated are the responsibility of several different organizational functions and some of the resources needed to carry out the processes are located in still other organizational functions. Integrated management processes require that these organizations work together in a very cooperative and extremely coordinated manner, which is difficult to achieve, particularly when there is not a major unifying force from top management to guide their actions. This leads to the second problem, which is the lack of perceived need by top management for these integrated processes. Without a clearly understood requirement that emanates from top management, it is unlikely that major integrated systems can be designed and implemented effectively. This places the responsibility for the development of these processes in the executive suite, where it belongs.

As the trend toward strategic management becomes stronger, it is likely that top management will feel the need for those processes that are essential to an effective strategic management capability. Included in their requirements will be an integrated planning and resource allocation process and a strategic control process, because of the critical role these processes play in the implementation of strategy. Strategic management includes strategy implementation requirements. Without these processes the implementation of strategy will be a questionable and uncertain activity that will limit the many benefits to be derived from strategic management.

21

Developing Strategic Information Systems

JOHN A. TURNER AND HENRY C. LUCAS, JR.

Graduate School of Business Administration, New York University

INFORMATION SYSTEMS AS STRATEGIC TOOLS

Strategic information systems are systems that serve the information needs of upper management. They can be computer based or manual, and formal or informal. It is generally accepted that executive management performs functions different from those of middle or lower levels of management, for example, in crafting long-range strategies and in providing corporate-wide leadership, in making decisions and in resolving problems, and in serving as the primary communications link with the external environment. The information needs of executive management are different from those of other management levels. Consequently, strategic information systems (SISs) have characteristics different from those of management control or operational-level systems. These differences are evident in the data used by the system and in the functions performed.

SISs tend to use data on activities external to the firm. The data is highly aggregated with a current or future time frame. Other information systems generally use data about internal activities that is detailed and that pertains to past events. SISs are flexible systems that are designed to change easily. They often contain models that can be manipulated interactively by an analyst, and they provide analytic procedures that can be called upon as needed until the analyst and the client are satisfied with the result. Other information systems tend to be more rigid in their operation, with predetermined procedures and outputs. These systems are concerned primarily with the transformation of data from one form to another in ways that have already been decided upon by the system designer. Finally, SISs differ from other systems in their scale. SISs often operate on relatively small data bases, and they have one or, at most, a few users. In contrast, the firm's operational systems are often massive, with extremely large files (e.g., 5 million policy holders) and thousands of users.

While there has been some reference to decision-making systems in the literature, most strategic information systems provide assistance in some aspect of the decision process rather than actually recommending or making a decision. Most systems are limited to delivering information on a wide range of subjects necessary for planning, to assisting in the exploration and evaluation of alternative courses of action, and to provide structure for the planning process. This situation is due largely to a lack of knowledge about what executives actually do and how they do it. In all likelihood, because of the ever-changing nature of top management work and its fragmentation, verbal nature, and political essence, most of these activities are probably not amenable to heavy computer support.

Information systems and computer or communications technology can contribute to strategic activities in four ways. First, this technology has the potential of refining the planning process by the use of improved data sources and analytic methods in forecasting and evaluation. Second, a firm's internal information systems are the source of targets used to measure current operational performance. Knowledge about current performance is needed to establish a base from which strategic moves can be made. The ability to implement a new strategic information system successfully rests on an objective assessment of the strengths and weaknesses of the firm's data processing capabilities.

Third, information systems may be used to reduce the cost of current products or to improve the delivery of services, thereby obtaining a competitive advantage. Finally, information system technology may present opportunities for opening new markets through the development of novel products or services.

The importance of SISs to a firm largely depends on the nature of the firm's business and on its industry structure and its size. Firms engaged in dynamic industries with high rates of technological change frequently need more information about their environment than firms in more stagnant industries. Dynamic industries are characterized by emerging scientific knowledge, unstable markets, and a variety of customer needs that make the dominant competitive issue the ability to innovate.[1] Information about these factors contributes to innovation by expanding the number of options considered by decision makers and by improving decision quality. In a similar way, companies that must respond to the moves made by a price or product leader need information about what that leader is doing, as well as general economic forecasts, in order to devise a counter-strategy.

In more static industries, with mature technology, stable markets, and stable competitive dynamics, knowledge about the environment is less important. A competitor's moves can be more easily anticipated; thus, factors influencing the timing of major moves are more likely to be internal to the firm rather than external. However, even firms in static industries must be aware of general economic conditions in order to adjust plant capacity and production schedules to demand and to technological change that might lead to competitive or market unstability.

Large organizations need strategic information systems more than small ones because their planning process involves gathering data from a wide variety of external and internal sources and communicating this information to a relatively large number of players. Strategic information systems provide one strategy for accomplishing this coordination.

It should not be presumed that the use of some form of computer or communication technology in some strategic activity will, in and of itself, ensure an improvement in that activity. As with all organizational change, the use of technology must be well-conceived and properly implemented and managed. Under these conditions, technology has the potential that is discussed in this chapter.

DATA FOR STRATEGIC PLANNING

The quality of strategic decision making is often determined by the data upon which these analyses are based. There are two broad categories of data used in strategic information systems: internal data about one's own firm and products; and external data describing the industry, competitors, and the general economy.

---

[1] For a more detailed discussion of environmental uncertainty see P.R. Lawrence and J.W. Lorsch, *Organization and Environment* (Homewood, Ill.: Richard D. Irwin, Inc., 1969).

Internal Data

One important source of data is the company's own operational information systems. (See Figure 21-1 on pages 21-6 and 21-7.) These include: (1) production, consisting of scheduling, work in process, job costing, and labor distribution; (2) logistics, involving inventory control and forecasting, purchasing, receiving, and distribution; (3) sales and order filling; (4) general accounting, including accounts receivable, accounts payable, cash receipts, check writing and reconciliation, and invoicing; (5) payroll; and (6) personnel. These systems provide inputs to management control systems consisting of: (1) budgeting, (2) general ledger, (3) fixed assets and depreciation, (4) financial statements, (5) project control, (6) sales analysis, and (7) profit analysis.

Gaps in these systems may result in a lack of information about the current status of a particular activity. This, in turn, may cause a decision to be made to adopt a particular strategy based on a presumption that later proves incorrect. If this presumption is central to the selection of the strategy, it may result in an incorrect selection, with unfortunate consequences. Furthermore, the significance of much internal information for strategic purposes may not be apparent without additional data from sources external to the firm.

External Data

Because of the broad nature of questions that are considered at executive levels of an organization and the long time horizons involved, most data pertains to factors external to the organization, such as data on sales of competitors' products, product demand, the costs and availability of raw materials, and the economy. Historical and forecast data is needed as well as current data. The purpose of analyzing this data is to recognize strategic opportunities that may exist in a market, as well as to detect threats to the firm's established lines of business. Market data of this type is often collected and distributed by private firms (for a fee), by an industry association, or, sometimes, by the government (e.g., the Bureau of Labor Statistics). It is not unusual for a firm to commission a market research study involving surveys of respondents or laboratory experiments to determine demand for or acceptance of a product. The firms that provide this data and related services are called data bank publishers.

Characteristics of External Data. While executives are familiar with buying data in printed form (e.g., consolidated airline schedules and catalogues), a whole new industry has emerged to serve the data needs of business and government. The products provided by this industry are varied; they involve the following factors:

- *Product content:* Products can be as small as a single piece of data, such as the credit rating for an individual, or as large as the complete profitability analysis of a new product.

- *Product format:* Products may be printed, such as a directory or guide, or they may be provided on demand at a computer terminal at the customer's site, using a public or private network.

- *Standardization:* Products can be standard in sense that the programming required to search the data bank has already been accomplished, or, they can be customized, requiring a new program to be written or a new analysis performed.

Printed directories are attractive when (1) the data do not change frequently, (2) access to the data is needed at only a few locations, and (3) only a few data elements need be considered. Computer terminal access is called for (1) when the data is volatile and a computer is used to update the data bank frequently (distribution is required only when a data element is used), (2) when the data is needed at many locations, since it can be distributed over a computer network, and (3) when there is a great deal of data.

Categories of External Data. There are several hundred organizations—private companies, government agencies, or not-for-profit groups—that function as data bank publishers, providing data, analyses, or related services. The market is divided into the following broad categories:[2]

- Business and Finance
    a. Econometric statistics and modeling
    b. Stock, bond, and commodity prices
    c. Corporate statistics and news
- Marketing
    a. Consumer credit
    b. Business credit
    c. Marketing and demographic statistics
       —Surveys
       —Forecasts
- Bibliographic
    a. General news abstracts
    b. Scientific and technical abstracts
    c. Legal
    d. Library

Business and finance subject areas involve the planning tools for economic analysis and strategic planning, security and commodity price and volume data, and general corporate news for buy/sell decisions and for portfolio evaluation. Marketing areas consist of individual and business credit ratings, customer location, and estimated demand for different types of products. Surveys provide information on current patterns and forecasts that indicate future trends. Bibliographic uses include abstracted articles from newspapers and magazines; summaries of technical writings; statutes, decisions, administrative rulings, trademarks, and patents; and filing and cataloging of library material.

---

[2] For a more detailed description see Darrow and Belilove, "The Growth of Data Bank Sharing," *Harvard Business Review* (Nov.-Dec. 1978).

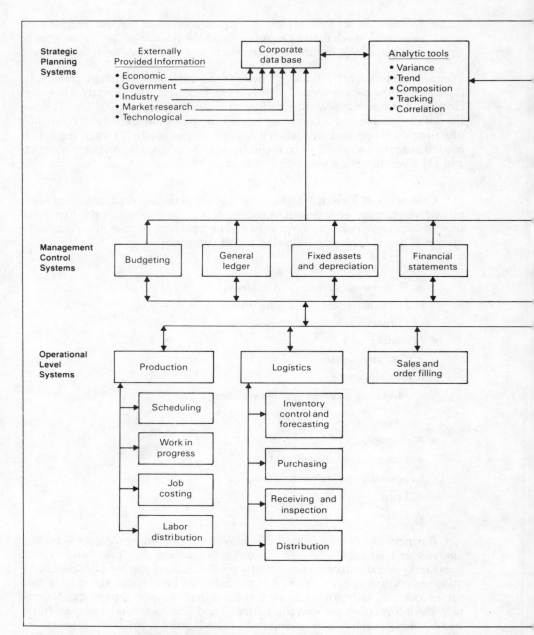

FIG. 21-1 The Information System Structure of a Typical Manufacturing Company

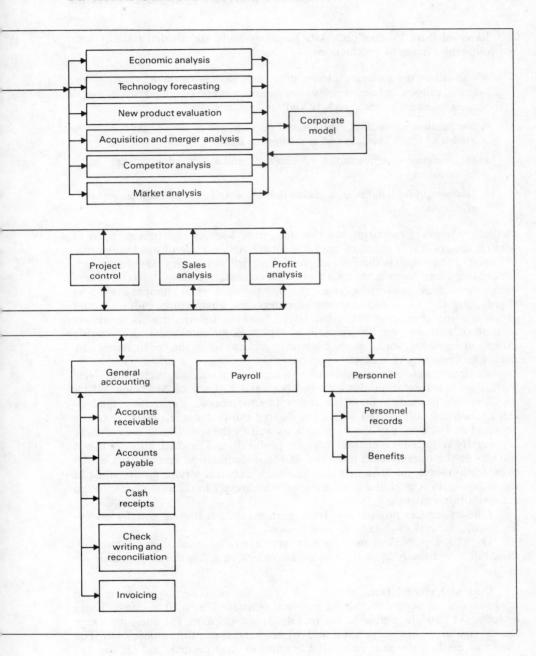

External Data Production. Data bank products are divided roughly into the following phases of production:

- *Collection:* the gathering of raw data from records of public corporations, banks, utilities, industry associations, government agencies, newspapers, magazines, technical journals, reports, and the judicial system;

- *Organization:* data bank creation and development of the computer software needed to access the data and to manipulate it;

- *Dissemination:* distribution of the data bank and associated analytic programs to customers; and

- *Liaison:* professional help to clients in using data banks and associated information tools.

Collection involves capturing the raw data from sources and translating it to printed, microfilm, or machine-readable form.[3] An example of machine-readable unedited raw data is the Federal Reserve Board's monetary statistics, which are provided on magnetic tape. Organization consists of coding the data, verifying its correctness, correcting errors, revising the data when changes are made, aggregating the data into meaningful categories, abstracting, indexing, and cross-indexing. For example, Abstracted Business Information is a weekly mailing of abstracts on 100 specialized topics. Some publishers also provide exception reporting, for example, informing a client when the credit rating of a particular company changes.

Computer networks permit on-line access to data banks, such as the New York Times Information Bank or the National Library of Medicine MEDLINE system of medical literature abstracts. Customers use searching, analytical, and editing software to obtain the desired information. Knowledge of the contents and structure of the data bank as well as the specifics of the software are usually required, or charges become prohibitive. The distinction between services at the organization level and at the dissemination level is that at the organization level, the customer deals through a central service group, while at the dissemination level, the tools are available directly to the customer through a distribution network.

Liaison services provide experts to perform special studies, usually involving small amounts of data from many sources.

Data bank publishers may provide services in one or all phases of production, but they usually limit their activities to one or a few data categories.

Cost of External Data Services. Various financial arrangements can be made to obtain access to the information contained in a data bank. These include: (1) outright purchase, (2) rental, (3) subscription, (4) one-time usage fee, (5) cost on a per-datum basis, and (6) surcharges on a time-sharing bill. The choice of method depends on (1) the amount of data needed, and (2) the fre-

---

[3] Machine-readable form is data on a medium that can be directly read by a computer peripheral device, e.g., magnetic tape that can be read by a tape drive, and encoded in the proper format so that it can be interpreted by a computer program.

quency with which the request will be made. Purchase and rental are suggested when the amount of data is large and the usage frequency is high; one-time and per-datum charges are good approaches when small amounts of data are needed infrequently, or when a company is engaged in an initial exploration.

Rough estimates of what a customer might expect to pay for typical products are:

- Single datum or small set of related data: $0.01–0.50;
- Report requiring no new computer programming: $5.00–250;
- Report requiring new computer programming: $100–2,500 and up; and
- Complete data bank with one year's updates: $200–10,000.

The "make or buy" decision applies to using data bank services. A firm has a choice between gathering the data itself and constructing its own data bank or purchasing the data from a publisher. Creating a data bank is suggested when (1) the data is proprietary and valuable; (2) the organization expects to make such extensive use of the data bank that the cost of using an outside publisher would be prohibitive; (3) the internal staff has the necessary expertise to organize the data bank and develop the computer software; (4) the data base is small enough to be tractable; and (5) the contents of the data base may be marketable to others. Buying is recommended when (1) the data bank is available from a publisher; (2) the data bank will be large and the data will be difficult to collect; (3) the data requires frequent expert updating; (4) the data is needed only on a periodic basis; and (5) there is no undue risk in relying on outside services.

Issues

Internal Organization. A firm just starting out purchasing services from a data bank should designate a person, or a unit, to have primary responsibility for liaison with publishers. This is a specialty area that requires knowledge of the data and analytic procedures that are available and their costs, capabilities, and limitations. Publishers have no incentive (except their honesty) to point out deficiencies in their data or analytic procedures. Over time, a group within the firm should learn about the various publishers in sufficient detail to advise other members of the firm.

Initially, data bank usage should be controlled centrally. The major problem to be faced is coordination of products among potential users and encouraging them rather than restricting or controlling usage. Frequently, internal users do not know how much information is available; a centralized service unit can help disseminate information about the data bank market. If necessary, transfer charges can be used to allocate the services of this unit and the data bank charges to those other units using its services.

The central unit should keep track of publishers from which the firm is currently buying services, since there frequently are discounts for multiple use by a firm. It is also desirable periodically to inventory the strategic information needs of the key units within the company. This permits identifying potential data bank suppliers before their services are needed internally.

As the use of data bank products grows, consideration should be given to decentralizing control to divisions, or other subunits, in order not to constrain usage.

Quality of Data. The contribution of strategic information systems to corporate planning depends greatly on the quality of data used as input to analysis and model building: Data should be timely, accurate, and complete. The historical nature of certain analyses and the long time horizon of strategic planning require that data be gathered on an ongoing basis.

Because of the likelihood of obtaining data bank products from more than one supplier, it is important to consider the relation of the products to each other. Particularly difficult is the different time periods covered by specific products, especially fiscal years and lags of certain statistics. There is also a need to ensure compatibility in terms of format and meaning.

Internal Information Sources. Because of the cost savings associated with operational-level systems as a result of improved efficiency, most information system investments have been at the operational level. As a result, most machine-readable information available in a firm pertains to operational-level activities. In contrast, at the corporate level, the need is to consolidate information reported by various parts of the organization into a consistent picture of the firm. This consistency is not achieved without considerable effort.

Several factors can assist in this consolidation:

- Corporate-wide data definitions ensure that a term has the same meaning throughout the company. For instance, "goods in inventory" may mean the goods are in the warehouse in one division, while in another division it may mean that goods have finished final inspection, but have yet to be shipped to the warehouse. If a corporate analyst is trying to determine the value of goods available to be sold, it is important for "goods in inventory" to have the same meaning in each division.

- A corporate chart of accounts should be established that is followed by each division and that has enough subcodes to permit splitting transactions among programs. Units tend to expend by program, while the corporate level is interested in reporting by category. The internal accounting systems should support mapping between these different views.

- Standard reporting categories permit aggregating of data reported by divisions. Both reporting categories and time periods should be common for all units.

Absence of a major internal system can create data gaps that, in turn, may reduce the completeness of analysis. The degree of compatibility among a firm's internal systems, in terms of data meanings and timing, becomes a major issue in developing and operating a strategic information system. In general, the less compatibility among a firm's internal systems, the more difficult it will be to develop its strategic information system.

SYSTEMS FOR ANALYSIS AND PRESENTATION OF STRATEGIC INFORMATION

Strategic information systems are composed of two parts. One provides access to a data base containing needed data, both internal and external. The other part of the system provides the capability to perform analyses and build models. Categories of analyses include:

- Variance analysis, to detect and explain deviation from a standard;
- Trend analysis, to track changes over time in sales, markets, and material prices;
- Composition analysis, to detect changes in composition of costs, competition, and markets;
- Competitor analysis, to discover and track behavior of competitors; and
- Correlation analysis, to discover meaningful relations between sales, costs, advertising, profits, and other important factors.

Building models requires the ability to perform computations and to display data in a variety of ways. It is generally agreed that model building frequently reveals insights about the dynamics of business function that are almost impossible to obtain in any other manner. As David C. Hickson, a vice president of Bankers Trust, observed:

"Our model building was a most revealing task. Star shells of insight burst around us and we have been busy doing things as a result of what we saw revealed. I wish to emphasize that these insights came out of the building of models rather than the operation of them."[4]

Thus, it can be said that strategic information systems contribute to the planning process both by making available a great deal of necessary information and through insights gained in building and running models.

While many analytic techniques are used in strategic planning, there are two approaches that represent the kinds of computer support available today. In both cases, the essential element is the ability to answer "what if" questions in order to understand the implications of different courses of action. The first, spreadsheet analysis, provides the analyst with facilities for creating a spreadsheet in which a line on the sheet can be related to another line by means of a simple formula. Thus, one can write: "PROFIT = GROSS SALES − COST OF GOODS SOLD". New columns can be created by changing the value of a variable, for example, increasing gross sales by 10 percent, and the changes will be reflected in the other entries in the spreadsheet.

The second approach makes use of a more extensive system to build financial models of a company. In this system, features are available for data entry and editing, data retrieval, and various analytic procedures. The system is more difficult to learn and use than the previous system, but it is more powerful.

---

[4] Daniel C. Hickson, "A Banker's Appreciation of System Considerations," Annual Meeting, American Society of Engineering Education, UCLA (June 1968).

Spreadsheet Analysis

A spreadsheet program permits the screen to be viewed as a window on a large spreadsheet consisting of columns and rows. By defining the relationship among various rows and columns as algebraic expressions, entries are created in the spreadsheet.

As an example, a spreadsheet could be built with the first column (A) containing period names: first quarter, second quarter, and so on. The second column (B) might contain actual sales data, while the third column (C) might have actual data on returns of goods. Then, the fourth column (D) could be defined as returns as a percentage of sales by entering the expression C1/B1*100 while the cursor is positioned at Column D, Row 1. This expression means that the entry at Column D, Row 1 is the result of dividing the contents of Column C (sales), Row 1, by the contents of Column B (returns), Row 1, and multiplying by 100 to obtain the percent figure.

The program provides a simple language for defining the relationship among various rows and columns in a table. When a number is changed, all of the related information on the spreadsheet is automatically recalculated. Thus, it is possible to see easily the effects of various changes and to answer "what if" questions.

Financial Modeling

General-purpose modeling programs consist of a modeling language that permits (1) identifying the elements of the model by name, (2) describing computations in a simple algebraic format, (3) describing portions of the model as systems of simultaneous equations, (4) calling of external functions, and (5) interactive debugging. These systems contain routines for many commonly used functions, including (1) depreciation, (2) rate of return, (3) loan payment and amortization, (4) compounding, (5) investment yield, (6) percentage distribution, (7) regression analysis and forecasting, and (8) sum, average, maximum, and minimum.

Flexibility in the selection and formatting of output documents is provided by report writing and graphic features. Customized report features include (1) ordering of information in reports independent of the ordering within the model, (2) formatting of text within reports, (3) interchange of rows and columns, and (4) full editing, including variable column widths, precision, brackets, prefixes, suffixes, and zero suppression. Graphic display features include (1) line or bar graphs, (2) standard or user-defined plotting symbols (plotting of any item against time or against other items), (3) automatic scaling, (4) controllable plot size, and (5) interchange of axes.

To aid in data management, these programs often have the following features: (1) data input, with error checking and prompting, (2) inquiries, to permit the examination of values without processing reports, (3) temporary changes, and (4) consolidation of multiple sets of data.

Interactive analysis features allow the analyst to test assumptions and evaluate alternatives. They include:

- Sensitivity analysis, to show the effects of incremental or percentage change to any model elements;
- "What if" analysis, to show new computed values as a result of different sets of assumptions;
- Impact analysis, a ranked listing of all model elements that will, if changed, have an impact on any element selected for study; and
- Target value analysis, which computes the values needed for any specified input items to achieve a target value for a model element.

Risk analysis may also be performed by specifying the ranges of possible values, that is, the probability distributions for key variables. The system then randomly selects values for these variables and executes the model logic, to provide a composite profile of computed results. To analyze time series data, these systems often provide (1) regression, (2) exponential smoothing, and (3) moving average computations. An example of a financial modeling system is EMPIRE,[5] which is available for many types of computer systems.

Integrated Planning Systems

Integrated planning systems have been described at length in planning literature.[6] Forecasting data obtained from data bank publishers are contained in a data base system running on the company's main computers. A set of analytic tools, including mathematical programming routines and econometric and risk analysis models, are used iteratively, over a corporate network, by members of the planning staff to evaluate the implications of following alternate courses of action over a multiyear planning horizon.

In large corporations, some mechanization of the planning and control function is necessary just to process the large quantity of data. The design of effective plans over multiyear horizons implies the ability to maintain historic plans as well as historic realities. Key to the notion of integrated planning systems are standardized reporting formats that specify the content and form of information flowing from lower to higher levels in a company. Each higher level consolidates and evaluates the performance and plans of lower-level units. Plans are revised in light of conflicts and interdependencies in strategies proposed by the units as well as rapid changes in the environment. The implied model is that of a feedback control system with an overall response time measured in years.

The requirements for integrated planning systems are:

- A flow of information to create strategies;
- Analytic tools for evaluating alternate strategies;
- Information describing changes in the external environment; and
- Measurement of actual performance.

---

[5] EMPIRE is a financial modeling package developed by ADR Inc., Princeton, N.J.

[6] For a more complete description, see Hamilton and Moses, "A Computer-Based Corporate Planning System," *Management Science* (Oct. 1974).

The process is one of translating strategies to plans, plans to projects, and projects to actual performance. Then, the process is reappraised and repeated. The key to this effort is the ability to view the corporation as a whole, no matter how diversified the individual components (it is this that differentiates corporate-level planning from top-level divisional or business planning). This implies being able to consolidate information from the components to determine corporate profitability both at the present and at forecasted future points in time. Then, alternate strategies are generated and evaluated in the context of top management's goals, which may be as diffuse as maintaining a certain level of corporate profitability independent of cyclic or economic fluctuations. This requires the ability to perform "what if" analyses and impact analyses. The selected strategy is then reflected in division plans and projects, thus disaggregating the previously consolidated information. All of this must be done iteratively and consistently.

The evaluation of alternate strategies requires considering the following factors:

- *Management viewpoint and values:* the predominant perspective and style of the leaders of the company; the corporate culture;

- *The company's strengths and weaknesses:* what the company does best, and where it has the greatest problems;

- *Business and industry criteria:* those factors that determine success in a particular business, as well as factors that are important due to industry structure;

- *Competitive actions:* the courses of action being followed by the firm's competitors; and

- *Environmental conditions:* the opportunities, risks, and pressures associated with changes in the environment.

Management's viewpoint may not be consistent or homogeneous, but it is the context in which key corporate decisions are made. Objective recognition of a company's strengths is necessary to prevent establishing unattainable goals. Competitors' actions are tracked in order to recognize their probable strategies, facilitating the design of counter-strategies. Awareness of changes in environmental factors permits positioning the company to take advantage of these changes.

The key problem at the corporate level is not one of obtaining enough information: It is distinguishing *relevant* information from the overwhelming amount of data available. Top management cannot afford to wait until all relevant information is known; it frequently must act on partial information and analysis.

Issues

Use of Formal Systems. One popular image has the chief executive officer (CEO) operating his or her own terminal and making key corporate decisions based on the programs he or she runs. This notion has several flaws:

- Most important decisions require analysis of data from many different, incompatible sources. It requires considerable skill to run the analyses and to interpret their results. It is not just the running of a program that is involved. There is an analytic process that takes many years to master. Most top-level executives have neither the patience nor skill for this type of work.

- Descriptions of the work that executives do indicates that it is fragmented by interruptions and paced by external events rather than being thoughtfully analytic. Thus, the mode in which executives function and the mode necessary to be a good analyst are incompatible.

- Executive decision making involves negotiating and bargaining with other power centers within the company, a process requiring face-to-face meetings and two-way communication. Evaluation of competing strategies is more the result of the interaction of key players than it is the reasoned weighing of alternatives; thus, it is not amenable to being made completely by computer processing. The decision outcome is influenced by the decision-making process.

The arguments above do not mean that systems with good display features cannot be used to *present* information. In many cases, backup data or operating data can be presented much more conveniently by a computer system than by stacks of printed data. However, there will still be a staff performing the analyses and packaging the material for presentation.

Decision-Making Systems. The issue of decision-making versus decision-aiding systems frequently comes up in discussions with top executives. Since most decisions at top management levels are nonrepetitive (i.e., the decisions tend to be unique), where the factors involved in the decision and their relative importance change from decision to decision, they do not lend themselves to programming. In order to do so would require the system to have general knowledge about the decision. Because it is difficult to ensure that the system contains all of the necessary knowledge for the decision (the system cannot know what it does not know), general decision-making systems, for business, are a long way in the future.

There are also political reasons for not relying on decision-making systems. If a decision is made by a system, then the outcome may be predicted by someone who has access to the system. No top-level executive feels comfortable with the notion that others may be able to predict his or her moves.

As problems become more narrowly defined and more routine, and are performed by more people in the organization, it becomes worthwhile to do the necessary analysis and to build the knowledge base needed to program the decision.

For the present, top management decision making will rely on skilled analysts supported by a variety of analytic tools and data, many of them based on computer programs. These clusters of data, analytic tools, and procedures are frequently referred to as decision support systems, especially when a subset of these tools has been configured to apply to a particular decision-making situation.

Benefits of Modeling. As mentioned above, the main benefit of computer modeling and simulation often is not the solution of a specific problem, but, rather, the insight gained from a more precise description of the decision-making situation and an identification of critical parameters.

DETERMINING SIS REQUIREMENTS

A number of experienced executives have observed they seldom have the information they need to manage their companies. As a rule, the higher a manager is in a company, the greater the flow of information with which he or she must contend and the less clear are his or her real information needs. Various techniques for defining information needs are described later in this chapter.

Three factors determine how a firm should go about determining its strategic information system requirements. First, the business that the firm is in and the structure of the industry imply certain information categories that are critical to success. For example, companies in dynamic fields with frequent technological innovation need information about new technological developments and trends. For these firms, strategic information systems are important devices in tracking technology, in forecasting environment change, in monitoring competitors' actions, and in coordinating the firm's activities. SISs should reduce the time necessary to recognize a threat or opportunity and decrease the response time required to respond. While companies in more static industries may be less willing to invest in strategic information systems because they are not as vulnerable to environmental change, they still must monitor competitive actions, introduce new products, and control the company's activities.

Second, firms with little experience in developing information systems may have difficulty in integrating internal strategic systems. Because of the range of skills required to build SISs, a firm should be well advanced in applying computer technology before developing strategic systems. It is generally accepted that firms go through states of data processing growth.[7] Stage 1, initiation, usually involves cost-reducing accounting and other operational applications. In this stage, a firm is coping with understanding the technology and gaining experience in how to apply it.

In Stage 2, expansion, data processing seems to take off, with applications often seeming to have been selected at random. There is a steady rise in expenditures for hardware, software, and personnel. This stage frequently ends in crisis, when top management becomes aware of explosive data processing growth without corresponding bottom-line benefits.

In Stage 3, formalization, top management attempts to rationalize and coordinate the firm's data processing activities. This stage is characterized by the withdrawal from innovative applications development, the initiation of formalized management reporting systems for computer operations, and the

---

[7] See Gibson and Nolan, "Managing the Four Stages of EDP Growth," *Harvard Business Review* (Jan.–Feb. 1974).

establishment of elaborate quality control methods. Frequently, applications with real potential for increasing revenues and profits and for facilitating management decision making have not been developed by this time.

Stage 4, maturity, involves developing applications that touch directly on critical business operations. The relationship between top management and the highest-level data processing officer is sound enough, at this stage, to permit him or her to be accepted as a member of the key decision-making group. It is at this stage that strategic information systems most easily can be developed. Attempting to build strategic systems before attaining mature data processing growth may impose unnecessary problems.

The stage model of data processing growth is useful for identifying general problems and issues related to a firm's experience with data processing. However, it implies a step-by-step progression through stages. This need not be the case. Firms can successfully bypass one or more stages of growth, or a small firm can develop a strategic information system, as long as the necessary prerequisites are met and key issues are resolved.

The third factor a firm should consider in selecting an information system requirements strategy is the condition of its operational systems. If its operational systems are well-developed and high-performing, and if they cover the core technology (i.e., the key production technology) of the company, then most of the requirements for a strategic information system will deal with obtaining external data, integrating this with internal data sources, and performing the necessary analytic procedures. However, if operational systems are underdeveloped, or if they do not provide the necessary internal information for strategic planning, then these systems must be developed. One way to assess the status of internal systems is to perform a systems audit (discussed below).

Management control systems require the establishment of standards against which various activities can be measured. The question many executives face is deciding at what level or value a standard should be set. Strategic information systems can be of assistance in establishing these performance standards by showing the relation between desired performance and the standards for measurement. For example, a CEO may desire a certain level of profitability from a division. However, profit figures may not be available on a division basis. The CEO may decide, therefore, to control the division on monthly sales and cost data through the use of a model that relates the division's sales and costs to estimated division profit.

Although there are many methods for determining system requirements, two—systems planning and success factors—represent examples of different approaches to requirements analysis that lend themselves to strategic information systems planning.

Systems Planning

Systems planning is a structured analysis approach to establishing an information systems plan in order to satisfy short-term and long-term information needs.

Underlying this approach is the notion that an information systems plan for a company should be integrated with its business plan, and that it should be developed from the point of view of top management and with the active participation of top management. Systems planning is composed of two phases:

- An identification phase attempts to understand the business. This involves identifying the information systems that are needed to support the business and grouping them into clusters of related systems. This process permits management to set implementation priorities and become more aware of relationships among systems.
- A definition phase validates information gathered in the first phase and defines the systems that are most needed (i.e., those with the highest priorities). This phase includes defining major actions, resources, and schedules required to build these systems.

Frequently, gaps in operational-level systems develop because of a lack of past user demand for mechanization in certain areas or because of an inability to justify a particular activity based on its cost. Also, operational-level systems often have a scope that parallels organizational boundaries (however, sometimes even operational-level systems cross functional boundaries, such as in the case of inventory control). The vertical orientation of these systems may restrict data sharing, which is needed for strategic information systems. Systems planning is a top-down analysis approach that starts with business objectives and problems, relates these to processes and organization, and then identifies the application systems, data files, and data classes needed to perform the business processes.

Systems planning usually involves a group of executives from different levels of the company, and from different functional areas, as well as staff support from an outside consultant. A top executive sponsors the study, and a manager with a broad perspective who commands the respect of management is appointed team leader. The team then agrees on its objectives and begins gathering data. This includes information on (1) organization structure, (2) financial and product reviews, (3) market analysis, (4) current plans, (5) environmental analysis, (6) profile of information systems, and (7) results of previous related studies.

The major business processes (i.e., the essential decisions and activities required to manage the resources and operations of the business) are identified and represented in a table. The team then interviews key executives to gain knowledge of management's views, values, priorities, and information needs. The team asks questions about (1) objectives and responsibilities, (2) methods of measurement, (3) major problems, (4) satisfaction with current information, and (5) information requirements. The team then reviews the current data processing support, and it identifies gaps between the information systems that are currently in place and those that are needed. All of this material is assembled in tables and matrices, analyzed, and then presented to top management in the form of a recommended action plan, with backup material. An example of the systems planning approach is Business Systems Planning (BSP) developed by the IBM Corporation.[8]

It takes many months to perform a systems planning study because of the large amount of data that must be gathered and because of the methods used to present the data. Critics of this approach point out that it is expensive and time-consuming, and that it deals primarily with current needs rather than with future needs. And, by trying to produce a complete systems plan, much more information is gathered than is really needed. Analyzing the data produced by the study is somewhat of an art. Furthermore, critics observe that the documentation produced by a systems planning study is seldom read by top-level management within the firm (because they already know most of it), and that it does not address the information needs of top management.

On the other hand, supporters of systems planning report that the process produces a corporate-wide information systems plan that permits identifying gaps in coverage and facilitates establishing development priorities.

Success Factors

In contrast to systems planning, the success factor approach to determining information requirements focuses directly on the information needs of top management. Short interviews are held with top-level executives to identify their goals and the success factors that underlie these goals. Success factors are three to six key elements, related to both the industry and the job, that must be handled exceedingly well in order for a company to be successful. For example, in the automobile industry, styling, an efficient dealer organization, and tight control of manufacturing costs are critical to profitability. Success factors are then refined, and an initial cut at identifying measures is made. Knowledge of these success factors, methods of measuring them, and the systems that need to be present in order to deliver this information help to identify a firm's strategic information systems.

Follow-up interviews are used to sharpen the factors and to define measures and reports in depth. There are four sources of success factors:

- Industry structure, which determines those particular factors that must be effectively dealt with if the firm is to be successful;
- Competitive strategy and industry position, which identify those factors related to a firm's history and current strategy that are important for success (e.g., an industry leader's approach to marketing products is a success factor to other firms in the industry);
- Environmental factors, such as the gross national product and inflation rate, that influence the behavior of consumers in certain industries; and
- Temporal factors, involving internal organizational considerations, which may influence the success of a company over a particular period of time.

---

[8] For additional information, see "Business Systems Planning Guide," IBM Corporation, GE20-0527-1 (Aug. 1975).

A number of benefits are attributed to this approach to information systems planning. First, the process helps a manager determine those factors on which attention should focus. Then, identification of success factors defines the type and amount of information that must be gathered, limiting the collection of costly, unnecessary information. Third, this approach moves an organization away from the trap of building systems around data that is available or easy to collect. Rather, it focuses on data that is needed, but that otherwise might not be collected. An example of the success factor approach is critical success factors developed by Rockart.[9]

Critics of the success-factor approach observe that much more detailed information is needed to design a firm's information systems than is gathered by a handful of interviews with top managers. Then, success factors are directed at the management control function rather than specifically at the process of strategic planning. One also must wonder if a manager's reflections about factors that are critical for success are stable information needs or if they are transient demands of the moment.

STRATEGIES FOR BUILDING INFORMATION SYSTEMS

Once a firm's strategic information systems have been identified and their requirements have been determined, the resources necessary to build these systems have to be allocated. The approach selected for building a particular SIS requires an assessment of (1) the quality of the firm's existing information systems, (2) the skill level of the firm's information systems staff, and (3) the firm's capacity to commit to building additional systems. Information systems involve two very different activities: operating a computer facility and developing information systems.

Information Systems Activities

Operations. Operating a computer facility involves running a computer system on a day-to-day basis. It is similar to running a production line in that the work is routine and the skill level required is not particularly high until a failure is encountered, although a fair amount of training is needed.

Development. Developing information systems consists of performing studies of system requirements, designing systems, programming and testing them, providing operating procedures and user training, and then supporting them once the systems become operational (e.g., making changes to enhance systems and keep them current). The development staff is highly skilled, somewhat similar to research and development engineers. They frequently have strong ties to their profession, and weaker ties to their company. Because of the

---

[9] John F. Rockart, "Chief Executives Define Their Own Data Needs," *Harvard Business Review* (Mar.-Apr., 1969).

great demand for people with knowledge about designing and building information systems, there is a large amount of staff turnover.

There are good reasons for making a distinction between operations and development. First, the people that staff each function tend to have different values and culture. Operations tends to have blue-collar workers, while development tends to have white-collar workers. Second, the two functions involve different management jobs. Managing operations is like running a production line or a power plant, where the product being produced is clearly defined and performance standards exist, while managing development is more akin to running a group of professionals. The product is different in each situation, and performance standards are very nebulous. Then, a firm may have a well-run operations unit and a relatively poor performance in systems development (or vice versa). This would affect a firm's strategy for developing SISs.

Performance Measurement and Control

Unless top-level executives are able to control the quality of information services provided in the firm, they are unlikely to take the risk of relying on these services in making a major strategic thrust. Two factors—performance measures and incentives—are particularly critical to successful management of the firm's information systems activities.[10]

Performance Measures. Operational performance measures usually include both the percentage of availability of a computer facility and the number of interruptions of a system over a time period. The specific measures used are far less important than the fact that top management is sufficiently concerned about the performance of the computer facility to have measures reported on a regular basis.

It is considerably more difficult to measure development performance than it is to monitor a computer facility. Frequently, schedule and cost are the only performance measures used (i.e., how close a job was to the original implementation schedule and the ratio of actual to estimated development cost). While these are objective, and they do represent important factors, it is not easy to adjust for the difficulty of projects, and they tend to obscure other issues. For example, an application system may be delivered on schedule and within cost, but users may not be satisfied with it and they may not use it. Should the system be considered successful?[11]

The following factors are suggested for monitoring development of information systems:

- Percentage of actual to budgeted cost of system development;

---

[10] A more complete discussion of the issues and techniques involved in managing the data processing function is beyond the scope of this chapter. For additional information, see Lucas and Turner, "A Corporate Strategy for the Control of Information Processing," 23 *Sloan Management Review* 3 (Spring 1982).

[11] For a detailed discussion of the implementation of information systems, see Lucas, *Implementation: The Key to Successful Information Systems* (N.Y.: Columbia University Press, 1981).

- Percentage of actual to scheduled delivery, measured according to when the system is accepted by the user;
- Evaluation of whether the anticipated benefits of a system are achieved (this requires identifying the rationale for a system—usually found in the requirements study—and seeing whether it is actually met);
- Determining whether a system is actually used;
- Measuring perceived user satisfaction with a system; and
- Determining the number of problems reported after a system is delivered to the users and the average time to repair these problems.

Incentives. The other important determinant of staff behavior is incentives. Discounting extrinsic rewards such as salary or job title, the act of simply including key members of the information systems staff in symbolic activities, such as strategy sessions, can improve their performance. Of course, consistently meeting performance objectives, such as developing systems on schedule, within cost, and with anticipated bottom-line consequences, should be rewarded by salary increases and promotion. What is important is that the measures and criteria applied and the incentives be coordinated and consistent.

Strategies for Developing SISs

There are two broad strategies for developing strategic information systems. The first is to develop a system internally. This approach involves determining the requirements for, designing, and programming various forecasting, econometric, and analytic systems needed for planning and evaluation as well as for the consolidated internal information system. Considering the diversity of these systems and the multiple sources of data, this course should not be attempted unless the company has a proven track record in building systems as well as an experienced staff.

The second approach is to buy (or lease) packages and data banks from publishers. This course is followed by most companies. The challenge is then to integrate the packages so that data can be transferred between them and to reduce the amount of manual handling required to run the system. Leasing has the advantage of permitting use of the systems and data without full commitment. Until cost factors become prohibitive, this course is attractive.

The importance of an information systems plan is that it permits identification of gaps in internal systems and it helps establish a sequence for obtaining various packages and data banks on a priority basis. The plan also can become the framework in which compatibility issues are resolved.

Issues

Role of the Information Systems Department. Frequently, internal information systems departments are not familiar with the tools or process of policy analysis. This area is a specialty, involving economics, management science, and information systems. A company beginning to do policy analysis may have to bring in help from the outside, which has the potential of creating a conflict with the information systems department.

Unrealistic Expectations. The assumption is frequently made that a heavy investment in strategic information systems will necessarily result in improved strategic decision making. Many factors other than a SIS influence decision-making quality, including the skill of the staff performing the analysis, the scope of the analysis as defined by executive management, the staffing process, judgments about probable outcomes, and the role of politics. SISs may contribute to improved decision-making performance when they fill a clearly defined need, such as a particular analytic procedure (e.g., being able to answer what-if questions or considerably improving the data upon which decisions are based), but they should not be viewed as a cure-all for some other factors involved in strategic decision making.

USING INFORMATION SYSTEMS TO IMPROVE CURRENT OPERATIONS

Thus far, the focus of this chapter has been on using strategic information systems to support strategic planning and decision making. This section considers the use of information system applications to improve the competitiveness of products and services, which is the ultimate purpose of strategic planning.

Information systems can contribute to profitability by providing opportunities to improve operational efficiencies. The need for systems of this type is usually perceived by an operational unit, based on changes in procedure. For example, it may be observed that capturing data about clients at only one point in the company will decrease redundant manual record-keeping. The primary objective of such systems is to reduce cost, frequently by substituting machine procedures for human data processing. Since, in general, the cost of data processing machines is decreasing, while the cost of labor is increasing, this substitution can result in a lower total cost.

New systems, however, involve changes to peoples' jobs, changes to the structure of an organization, and changes to the distribution of power within a firm. As such, they involve risk, and they are frequently resisted. If system implementations are to be successful, they require active executive participation, careful preparation, and strong leadership.

Another way that computer and communications technology can contribute to current products is by extending or enhancing the features of a product to give it a competitive advantage. For example, many of the computer-generated displays and engine controls on recent automobiles (e.g., timing and mixture) fall into this category.

Methods for identifying high pay off applications and the barriers to implementing systems are described in more detail below.

Routine Applications

The first use of computers in business was for routine financial applications, such as payroll and accounting. The rationale for these applications was error reduction and variable (i.e., transaction-related) cost control. Workers performing routine clerical functions, such as posting debits and credits to a journal, were replaced by a computer program that did the posting. The number of errors introduced by the application program was far less then the number of mistakes made by humans. A secondary benefit of these applications was that they frequently either reduced per-unit processing costs or made them independent of transaction volume.

Systems of this type, called transaction processing systems, have similar structures. They accept a transaction (input), check it to be sure that the data it contains is valid (editing), post the transaction to a file of some sort (file maintenance), and produce reports from the file (report writing).

Business systems had to have two characteristics in order to be programmed:

- All conditions that might be encountered in the system had to be known in advance; and
- Rules for handling each condition had to be completely specified.

If the application was an accounting system, then all transaction types had to be defined in advance. And, the procedures for posting each type of transaction had to be completely defined. If an undefined transaction was encountered, it would be treated as an error.

These characteristics are typical of activities at the operational level of organizations. These systems are termed "programmed" systems and they are, for the most part, of a routine clerical nature.

The motivations for building programmed computer application systems provides clues for potential opportunities. They are intended to:

- Reduce errors in data;
- Reduce costs of production and services;
- Process data within set schedules and with acceptable dependability;
- Carry out large calculations that would otherwise not be possible;
- Provide compatability between different parts of a system;
- Facilitate planning and orderly growth; and
- Respond to a mandate to use a computer.

The last item requires some explanation. Sometimes, it is necessary to report or record certain information, for example, when that information is to be requested by the government. Under these conditions, a computerized system may be directed, rather than cost-justified. For example, starting in the middle 1970s, many firms installed computer-based personnel information systems, so that they could meet affirmative-action reporting requirements of the government.

More specifically, direct benefits of programmed systems include: (1) reduced inventory, (2) reduced back-office processing time, (3) better customer service, (4) more efficient use of funds, (5) availability of new funds, (6) improved data accuracy and speed, and (7) improved access to files. Indirect benefits include: (1) improved company image, (2) better tracking of work processes, (3) improved decision making, (4) better information flow in the firm, (5) improved planning, (6) increased organizational flexibility, and (7) organizational learning.

The extent to which these advantages will be realized depends on many factors, including readiness by management and operational staff to consider new ways of doing things, the presence of a trained and experienced staff, and the availability of good data.

Decision-Aiding Systems

Another type of system is the decision support system. These systems support semistructured and unstructured decision making and problem solving by providing access to data and modeling tools. They also may assist in structuring a problem solution and enhancing coordination among decision makers. Since use of these systems is presumed to be discretionary, the decision-making process and user-control aspects of decision support systems tend to be customized for individual users in order to take into account a user's preferred style of interacting with a system.

Decision support systems can improve current products and services by helping people perform their jobs better. For example, a major oil company observed that one of their most important decisions was bidding on leases. They applied statistical and game theory analysis techniques to assess the risk of losing a bid. The performance of bidders improved dramatically when they began to use the system to help them establish their bids.

Evaluating Alternate Implementation Projects

A firm has only limited resources, both financial and human. There are many competing uses for these resources. Consequently, a key management decision is how resources are to be parceled out among opportunities, especially new computer applications. Thus, a top executive may be faced with the problem of deciding which of a number of potential cost-reduction or service improvement opportunities should be pursued.

When evaluating alternate opportunities, one should:

- Identify all benefits and impacts of a candidate project;
- Estimate the magnitude of each benefit or impact on a scale that allows comparison across benefit/impact type; and
- Compare the total package of benefits offered across alternate projects in order to find those projects that represent the best use of the company's resources.

Although these steps are conceptually simple, they are difficult to apply in practice. For example, often, only a small number of benefits are identified for each project considered instead of the full range. Sometimes, no estimate is made of the magnitude of the benefit, usually because this is difficult to quantify. Comparisons across projects tend to be qualitative; when quantitative comparisons are made, they often neglect uncertainty.[12]

One method that is frequently used to compare project candidates is a weighting and scoring approach. The characteristics of projects are divided into a number of major classes, or factors, such as operational cost savings, project development cost, improved customer service, probability of success, and importance of the project to the company. A weight is then attached to each factor in relation to the relative importance of the factor. Each candidate project is then scored according to the degree it possesses the desired characteristics. The scaled weights and scores for each factor are then multiplied together and summed to get the weighted score for the project. Projects are then ranked high to low on the basis of their weighted score; they are selected for implementation in this order until the amount allocated to application system implementation is exceeded.

This method has the advantage of being simple to apply. It ensures that the candidates are evaluated on the same factors, and it makes subjective factors identifiable. However, it also has a number of disadvantages. First, the evaluation technique assumes that the factors are independent and that trade-offs can be made between them. For certain factors, this may not be true; for others, such as cost of operation and cost of implementation, the trade-off may be more complex than portrayed by the weighting scheme. Second, it is extremely difficult to identify all of the factors needed for evaluation. Third, it is often difficult to place values on many system benefits, especially intangible ones. Finally, there is a tendency to focus on system features, just because they are part of a system, even when these features may not be particularly useful for an application.

A complementary approach is to calculate the return on investment (ROI) of the projects, using a discounted cash-flow analysis. This permits identifying potentially high-return projects, but it tends to favor cost-saving projects because their benefits are easier to quantify. A strict ROI analysis may eliminate a large class of innovative systems that may have a high—but a priori uncalculable—benefit to the firm.

One important part of evaluation is to assess the risk associated with each project. Possible risks include the following: (1) projects may fail to deliver anticipated benefits; (2) the cost of implementation may exceed planned levels; (3) the time for implementation may be much greater than planned; and (4) the performance of the system may be below estimate. Three factors contribute to risk:

- *Project size:* The larger the project is, the more communication is needed among project members and the more likely is a serious misunderstanding. In general, the larger the project, the greater the risk.

---

[12] See McFarlan, "A Portfolio Approach to Information Systems," *Harvard Business Review* (Sept.–Oct. 1981).

- *Experience with the technology:* Because of the likelihood of unexpected technical problems, project risk increases as the project team's familiarity with the hardware and software decreases.

- *Project structure:* As procedures, functions, and outputs become less well-defined, project risk increases.

One method of measuring risk in each of these categories is to use a questionnaire, answered by the project manager and key users, several times over the life of the project. Top managers should ask themselves whether the benefits of a project are great enough to offset the risks.

Barriers to Implementation

In addition to the resources needed to accomplish a strategic information systems project, there are often other factors that management should consider. Building an information system usually involves changes to peoples' jobs. These changes can involve the tasks performed, the procedures followed, the interdependence among workers, and the clients served. Workers frequently are reluctant to change the way they do things. This reluctance stems from a fear of the unknown, habit, and an unwillingness, as people grow older, to learn new things. One way to cope with this reluctance is to make workers aware of the shortcomings in the way things are done. This "unfreezing" makes users more willing to change. After this, the changes involved in a new application system can more easily be made.

Often, new systems involve redistribution of power within an organization. Individuals (or groups) that lose power as a result of a system are likely to resist it, while those who gain in power are likely to promote the system. The uncertainty surrounding the implementation of a new system creates opportunities for political game-playing.

Another barrier to building information systems is lack of knowledge about how to apply computer technology to business problems. Frequently, people with the necessary skills are not readily available. And, building a system can be expensive (although the cost is decreasing), and many managers are reluctant to spend this money for uncertain returns. Experience to date has been problematic, increasing the fears of management.

Issues

Implications of Investing in Information Systems. What effects do information systems have on productivity, on the structure of organizations, and on the quality of working life of the people within them? At operational levels, the evidence is strong that computer-based application systems increase productivity. This is because the cost of computers has been dropping, while the cost of labor has been rising. However, the high cost of capital partially offsets this. Packaged application systems have reduced the cost of systems development, and there are now a reasonable number of trained people to apply the technology.

Along with this productivity improvement, there seems to be a decline in working life quality, especially in routine clerical jobs where workers have no choice but to use a system. The reason that job quality is poorer is because computers permit designing a mechanized job, where the system paces and controls a worker. Frequently, decisions about job design are made on the basis of this model rather than on one that takes advantage of a new job to give workers more control over their work tasks. Mechanical jobs come about because system designers are not experienced in job design and because management is not particularly interested in using technology to improve the quality of working life. [13]

There is no evidence of a consistent structural change in organizations related to using computer systems. The current low cost of equipment encourages decentralization of equipment, data, and staff using private or public networks. Computer-based mail and other message systems provide new techniques for communication and coordination. It is generally accepted that the internal structure of an information services function should match the structure of the larger organization. That is, the system should be decentralized if the organization is decentralized, and it should be centralized if the organization is centralized.

BUILDING NEW SERVICES AND PRODUCTS FROM INFORMATION SYSTEMS

A number of companies have extended their product line offerings or modified their products based on expertise in information systems that was developed internally to serve planning and decision-making needs. One exciting strategic opportunity is to use computer and communications technology to create new products and services. This is where the most freedom of action lies, where the most creativity is needed, and where the greatest returns exist.

There is an advantage in being first to market a new product or service; if a demand has been identified and the product has been well-executed, then a huge success may result. Other firms attempting to imitate this success may find legal barriers, start-up costs, and lead times so great that by the time they get their product to the market, it is already committed to the original product. However, there is also a risk in being first. The technology may have problems that delay product introduction or reduce product capability over that planned. Then, the market may not exist. Judgment on timing is critical to success.

Computer and communications technology expands the range of strategic alternatives available to a firm. In this sense, it is a subcategory of all technology that can be transformed into new products or services. At this level, the dominant relationship is between technology and strategy rather than between

---

[13] See Turner, "Computers and Clerical Jobs: The Missed Opportunity for Work Redesign," presented at the ACM SIGCPR Conference, Georgetown University, Washington, D.C. (June 1981), available as Research Report 24, Graduate School of Business Administration, New York University, and Bjorn-Andersen and Hedberg, "Designing Information Systems in an Organizational Perspective," *TIMS Studies in the Management Sciences* (1977).

information systems and planning, as was the case with the direct contribution of strategic information systems to strategic planning. Technology forecasting thus becomes a central part of corporate planning, and the opportunities presented by computer and communications technology becomes advanced product planning.

For example, a company recently announced plans for a chain of retail stores that contain no merchandise; they provide only mail order catalogues and a computerized index to the catalogues. Customers come to the store or telephone it; the customer or a salesperson uses a terminal to search an index in order to locate the goods requested by the customer. A computer system then aids in generating merchandise orders. The customer gets the advantage of one-stop shopping, and the company obtains a discount for quantity orders and for providing machine-readable order data. In this situation, computer and communications technology permits treating merchandise from many different suppliers as if it came from one source, thereby creating a new service to market.

These opportunities are not just limited to the service sector. A number of years ago, McDonald Aircraft Corporation invested heavily in computer equipment and application systems to support the manufacturing of their line of military aircraft (as did many of the other major defense contractors). McDonald Automation, the outgrowth of this effort, is now one of the country's largest suppliers of computing services (as are Grumman Data Services and Boeing Data Services). The banks and insurance companies have also spun off data processing subsidiaries.

Methods for recognizing opportunities to create new products or services that incorporate computer technology are described below, along with the barriers to and implications of investing heavily in these systems.

Recognizing Opportunities

While recognizing opportunities requires both entrepreneurial skill and knowledge of computer and communications technology, several patterns have emerged that are useful.

Using Computer and Communications Technology to Differentiate Products From Those of Competitors. Home ovens have long used mechanical timing devices to control cooking time length, to compute the relationship of the weight of the item being cooked with oven temperature and cooking time (this is a feature of deluxe models), to show the time, and to do countdown timing. These units have an average failure period of about three years. It would not be difficult, from either a design or manufacturing standpoint, to build a solid-state microprocessor-based control unit that also controlled oven temperature. Such a unit would be easier to use, more reliable, and cheaper to produce. Yet, no U.S. manufacturer has introduced an oven with these features, probably because of the industry's commitment to existing products, (which is based on factors such as an established production line and a trained service staff). Yet, this represents an opportunity to improve and differentiate a product.

In contrast, consider the electronic control features in microwave ovens. Almost all manufacturers have products with microprocessor-controlled power, time, timer, and delayed-cooking start/stop. This is probably because microwave ovens are relatively new (thus meeting less resistance to change) and because the market is competitive. Electronic control features result in product differentiation.

Using Computer Technology to Create a Unique Product. For many years, games were static; that is, the human's interaction with the game was one way. Chance, in the form of a drawn card or thrown die, provided the system response. Incorporating microprocessors into games permitted creating a whole new family of dynamic games that provide more competitive and realistic responses.

Cable television has become a major industry. Cable provides more channels, programming that is not available on commercial television, and clear reception. However, most of the cable networks do not permit the viewer to send messages (except in several trial systems, and, even then, the messages are extremely limited in content, and they can be sent only to the transmitting station). The exciting possibility of cable television is not in the expanded number of television channels, the programming, or the improved reception, but in the potential changes in marketing and financial institutions when consumers are linked together by local networks that permit two-way, computer-based communication.

Firms that make a heavy commitment to information systems at the operational, management control, or strategic level have greater technological capability (through the skill of professionals and managers) to provide computer and communications technology-based products to new markets than those firms that have passing familiarity with the technology. A considerable investment is required before a firm becomes sufficiently experienced with a technology (e.g., with suppliers, applications, and implications) to base a new product or service on it.

Some Examples

Examples of ways in which computer and communications technology has allowed firms to gain a strategic advantage are presented below. The examples are diverse, and they are drawn from many different industries. The common thread running through these descriptions is that computer and communications technology was used to create a new product or service. The organizations involved had enough confidence in their ability to apply and manage this technology to rely upon it for major changes in company direction.

Real Estate Applications. Some 250 of the more than 1,800 realty boards in the country have installed computers. It is estimated that there are more than 37,000 terminals linking real estate offices to regional systems, which provide brokers with services ranging from listings of properties for sale to financial analysis.

Commercial firms have led the way in applications, but now the greatest growth is in analyzing customer finances in the residential market. ROI, amortization schedules, and evaluation of alternative forms of financing are provided as customer services. Programs also help match customer needs with available properties by enabling the realtor to find houses in a location that fit a customer's budget.

Library Innovations. Libraries are undergoing a dramatic change in their mode of operations. In the next decade, they are likely to be smaller, but they will be able to provide users with more services and access to more information.

The Southeastern Library Network links 260 libraries from Virginia to Louisiana. Some 2,400 libraries across the country are tied into another network that provides access to a data bank in Ohio with 7 million titles. Bell Telephone Laboratories has 22 libraries linked together in a private network sharing specialized research resources.

Many people believe these events are the first step in providing home service. In the future, it may be less expensive to have people access library data from home computer terminals than to provide services at the library itself.

A Hospital System. American Hospital Supply Corporation (AHS) is the number-one firm in the hospital supply business, with over $2 billion a year in sales. It is the only company offering automated order entry and inventory control systems to hospitals. Approximately 40 percent of the 7,000 hospitals in the country deal with AHS, using computer terminals for direct communication.

Incoming orders are forwarded over the network to the company's distribution center located nearest to the hospital. The hospital immediately receives an order confirmation with prices and delivery dates. AHS claims that they have been able to cut the price of products by 20 percent through efficient handling and reduced shipping costs. Hospitals can reduce inventory because AHS can ship 95 percent of the orders on the day they are received.

The firm believes that the system is responsible for increasing profitability. The average hospital orders 5.8 items per order from AHS, compared with an industry average of 1.7 items per order.

Market Research. Information Resources, Inc. developed a unique service to perform marketing studies. The firm invested $2 million to buy point-of-sale scanning equipment and provide it, free of charge, to markets in two selected towns, one in Indiana, the other in Massachusetts.

The firms enlisted 2,000 households in each town and provided them with identification cards that trigger the point-of-sale terminal to send a record of the customer's purchases to the company's computer in Chicago. The system is used to measure consumer reaction to special coupons, free samples, advertising, various kinds of displays, and pricing.

An early experiment involved determining the effectiveness of free samples in place of or accompanying television commercials. The household panelists were divided into four groups of 1,000 each, and were given various combinations of advertising and free samples. Sales doubled in all groups having free samples, but the group exposed to advertising in addition to samples proved to be more loyal over time.

This new marketing analysis technique, with its increased accuracy, gives Information Resources an advantage over its competitors.

Discussion. The firms described above all used computer and communications technology to embark on new products or services. In the real estate market, early adopters are able to offer better service, at reduced cost, than their competitors can offer. Libraries, through the opportunities provided by networking and computer technology, are examining ways in which they can provide increased service at lower cost, by distributing information to individuals at home or at their office instead of at a central location.

American Hospital Supply has been able to improve customer service and lower product cost, thus tying customers more closely to them. Information Resources built a new market research business using this technology.

These firms view computer and communications technology as a means of creating new roles and new markets for themselves instead of just using it to improve operational or internal performance. In this case, technology provides opportunities for new products and services.

Forecasting Technological Trends

In order to integrate computer technology into strategic planning, it is necessary to forecast technology trends. Forecasting techniques can be grouped under three headings: (1) extrapolation of trends, (2) classification analysis, and (3) intuitive projections. Trend extrapolation depends on finding some suitable quality—frequently, a measure of performance—that describes the technology and projecting the value of this quality forward in time. The common experience is that the shape of this curve rises steeply initially and then levels off. A major improvement in the technology or a new device is then found that moves the performance up to a new curve. It is often possible to draw the envelope of the family of performance curves that shows the progress, over time, of the technology as a whole. Of course, it is not possible to predict whether a new device will be invented to extend the envelope.

Classification analysis involves studying a set of devices or processes having the same function. These items are then grouped into classes according to features they possess or parameters that can be identified. From this grouping, it is sometimes possible to recognize a missing member of the group, or, one may be able to anticipate performance from a precursor event or device.

Intuitive projections are derived by inviting experts or informed persons to speculate about technological possibilities, often by arranging some interaction among them. One might generate a list of potential or desirable technological breakthroughs, and follow through to the consequences. Another approach is to enact scenarios where participants take on various roles and improvise responses to situations. One approach that is quite popular is the Delphi method, where participants are given a list of events of high significance and asked to indicate the date at which the events might happen. On a second iteration, participants are given the average prediction date (compiled from responses to the previous round) along with the interquartile range (containing 50 percent of the estimates), and they are asked if they wish to revise their predictions. After a few iterations, a consensus is often reached on the part of the participants about what is likely to happen.

While all of these techniques are useful for technological forecasting, drastic changes in the political, military, cultural, or economic environment may invalidate the underlying assumptions of an analysis, rendering it useless.

Methods of Incorporating Technology Into Strategic Activities

The executive is faced with the question of how to go about incorporating computers in new products and services. It is first necessary to recognize likely trends in computer technology. Then, two approaches can be used: technology push and needs pull.

With technology push, the capabilities of the technology suggest new products and services. For example, the existence of inexpensive microcomputers in a significant number of homes created a market for video games. Successful games are more lucrative to their distributors than movies, and they provide a much higher ROI. The key to this approach is to be able to forecast technological trends (especially in the consumer market) and to be able to interpret the implication of these trends.

In needs pull, a service or product need is identified that can be filled using computer technology. For example, a West Coast entrepreneur decided there would be a market for a service that scanned the newspaper for information on subjects selected by clients. He observed that late-evening air time could be purchased inexpensively. This time could be used to broadcast a reading of the newspaper, preceded by a coded header that contained information on the content of the article. He then had a microprocessor device designed that accepted a list of subject codes as input from the client. The device contains an FM radio pretuned to the station. The broadcast subject headers are scanned by the device to see whether the code matches one of the codes on the client's active list. If so, the device turns on a recorder. In the morning, the client hears only articles of interest, read aloud over the recorder.

Another approach is to analyze a firm's strategic objectives in order to identify opportunities for the use of computer and communications technology and to plan for its use. While this generally results in recognition of gaps in internal information systems and in identification of application systems for development, a by-product can be the recognition of a new service or marketable product. A firm's strategy set consists of the following:

- *Company mission:* what the company does, and what it does *not* do;
- *Company objectives:* descriptions of desired future company positions;
- *Strategies:* general directions in which the company expects to move in order to achieve objectives; and

- *Organizational attributes:* organizational strengths or important factors that should be taken into consideration in using information systems.

The company's strategy set can now be transformed into an information systems strategy set, made up of the following:

- *Application system objectives:* the purpose of each project in operational terms;
- *Constraints:* internal and external considerations that must be followed; and
- *Design principles:* operational guidelines for system design.

An interest group structure made up of (1) customers, (2) creditors, (3) employees, (4) management, (5) creditors, (6) stockholders, and (7) the public all exert pressure on the company. Each company mission can be identified with the principal interest group advocating the mission as well as with objectives and strategies associated with that mission.[14] This process permits identifying the source of each component of the company's information systems plan, and it links that plan to the company's mission. Computer and communications technology can also enhance the company's mission by providing a strategy for mission accomplishment.

While many companies do not formally or systematically attempt to recognize opportunities for applying computer and communications technology, analyzing a firm's strategic goals does provide a practical method.

Barriers to the Use of Computer and Communications Technology

One of the major barriers to using computer and communications technology in new products and services is that these new activities often compete with existing power centers for limited resources. For example, a major metropolitan police department installed a computer-based command and control system to dispatch patrol units to reported incidents. A new unit, the communications division, was created to develop and staff the new system. After the system became operational, the department became concerned that precinct commanders were not using the system to manage their patrols. It turned out that the commanders felt that the new division was now responsible for the patrols, since they had taken over the assignment function, even though the department management had not relieved them of their responsibility. They felt the communications division had encroached on their turf, and they responded by relinquishing the responsibility for their patrols.

Another barrier to the use of new technologies is a lack of familiarity on the part of top management with technology and the opportunities it presents. Experience with information systems at all levels of the company can help develop a cadre of experienced specialists and managers.

Finally, some companies are unwilling to accept the risk involved with a new and rapidly changing technology. Decisions that are perfectly reasonable

---

[14] See King, "Strategic Planning for Management Information Systems," 2 *Management Information Systems Quarterly* 1 (March 1978).

today may be undercut by technological change. The only defense against this possibility is to allocate resources to technology forecasting.

Issues

Risk. With any new technology, there are a number of uncertainties. One is that the technology will not be available when promised. Another risk is that the technology will not meet its performance or cost objectives. Technological change tends to move unevenly; there is always a chance that once one is committed to a path, new developments will occur that cause the existing technology to become outmoded. For example, third-party computer leasing firms that committed heavily to the IBM 370 line found the value of this equipment greatly reduced after the announcement of the firm's 4300 line of computers that afforded enhanced price performance.

Applying Technology. It is often difficult to obtain the skilled staff needed to apply a new technology properly. Workers who are knowledgeable about a new technology tend to be in high demand and few in number. Therefore, it is important to acquire the necessary human resources before embarking on a technology-dependent strategy.

22

Formal Corporate Strategic Planning Analysis Systems: A Computer-Based Approach

MICHAEL A. MOSES

Professor, Graduate School of Business Administration, New York University

THE STRATEGIC PLANNING PROCESS

The concept of strategy is applicable to a business as well as to a portfolio of businesses within a multibusiness corporate structure. The strategy-making process is viewed in this chapter as a problem-solving activity requiring formulation, analysis, choice, and implementation. Strategic planning processes are effective when they facilitate formulation of viable strategy alternatives, support systematic analysis of these alternatives, clarify goal structures as the basis for choice, facilitate design of internal structures and processes to implement the choices, and increase decision efficiency.

Strategic planning at the business unit or planning unit level requires, at a minimum:

- Situational analysis: the analysis of opportunity and threats, resources, competitive strengths and weaknesses, and current and projected performance;
- Generation of generic business-level strategy alternatives;
- Formulation of specific strategic alternatives for particular environments;
- Analysis of strategic alternatives;
- Choice among strategic alternatives; and
- Internal design considerations for implementation.

In the multibusiness firm, strategic planning processes, in addition to facilitating and supporting effective problem-solving at the business level, must integrate different business-level strategies into a portfolio of strategies that effectively balances opportunity and risk for the corporation as a whole. This integration effort may result in adding new businesses to the portfolio, or in deleting existing businesses from the portfolio.

This chapter concentrates on a formal planning system designed for use at the corporate level rather than at the strategic business unit (SBU) level. The corporate level produces strategic problems that are very complex and that require the largest amount of data for analysis and resolution.

For a firm organized into many strategic planning units (SPUs), the formulation activity is the creative activity of strategy development. Analysis, in this case, deals with the study of the complex interaction between SPU strategies and their external environments. Strategic choice involves finding portfolios or subsets of SPU strategies that meet organizational goals and/or making changes in organizational goals to meet SPU capabilities. The success of any problem-solving task—independent of the depth of sophistication of the formulation, analysis, and choice phases—usually hinges on the efforts involved in implementing the chosen solution alternative. Organization design, executive compensation, performance measurement, and financial reporting and control are the major organizational processes that have been incorporated into the solution implementation activity in this chapter.

Strategy Formulation

The strategy process starts with the corporate decision maker. In this process (Box A, Figure 22-1), the corporate decision maker has direct responsibility for formulating organizational goals and constraints and for issuing a set of initializing assumptions that guide the development of strategic planning unit strategies. An SPU is defined as the lowest-level unit within an organization where there is a manager directly responsible for the development of a strategic plan for that unit. For this analysis, it will be assumed that the organization is made up of many SPUs, and that they are independent in a product/market sense. The initializing information usually contains—in addition to the broad organizational goal/constraint environment—data on areas such as the corporate view of a "most likely" macroeconomic environment; tax, prime interest, and exchange rates; and particular legal, social, and regulatory environments. This information is transmitted to the SPU via the communication channels that are described and defined by the structure of the organization. The structure of the organization (Box B, Figure 22-1) is one of the most important determinants of successful strategy implementation; it is discussed in more detail below.

Upon receiving the plan initializing documentation, the SPU's responsibility is to formulate its strategic plan (Box D, Figure 22-1). The end result of this formulation is, usually, a verbal description and a multiyear financial statement describing the product/market strategic alternatives available to the SPU and the impact of these alternatives on corporate-level goals, constraints, and resources. In many organizations, an analysis of the key issues confronting the SPU is also included. The resulting strategy for the unit takes into account the unit's products, markets, any need for diversification or contraction, management and other resources required to support a product/market commitment, and plans to meet these requirements. Once these plans are formulated, they proceed back through the organizational structure (Box B, Figure 22-1) where, after intermediate-level reviews, they are submitted to the corporate decision maker (Box A, Figure 22-1) and the corporate planning staff (Box I, Figure 22-1) for corporate-wide analysis and choice.

Corporate Analysis

Since most organizations are made up of more than one SPU, and each SPU often will have several product/market diversification, expansion, and/or contraction strategies, the task of the corporate decision maker at this point is to determine which subset of strategies should or could be undertaken by the organization (Box H, Figure 22-1); (possibly, the whole set should be undertaken). The corporate-level manager's ability to understand the complex interdependencies among the available SPU strategies and to respond precisely to continuing changes in external and internal environments is greatly enhanced by the use of an analytic computer-based strategy evaluation system. Such a system should have the ability, at a minimum, to do the following: (1) generate macroeconomic and microeconomic scenerios and investigate their effects on proposed strategic alternatives; (2) use the corporate-level "what if" business analysis models of the strategic planning units; (3) allow a sophisticated management user to formulate and report on alternative solutions to his or her particular strategic planning problem, in a language that is readily understandable to the user; (4) collect, edit, and make changes to his or her strategic planning data base simply and efficiently; (5) permit the management user to be able to analyze the interdependencies and risks inherent in available strategic alternatives, utilizing modern analytical techniques. Figure 22-2 illustrates a system with these capabilities.

Decision Making

The corporate strategic decision-making process (Box A, Figure 22-1) is obviously one that can proceed independent of any supporting system or structure.

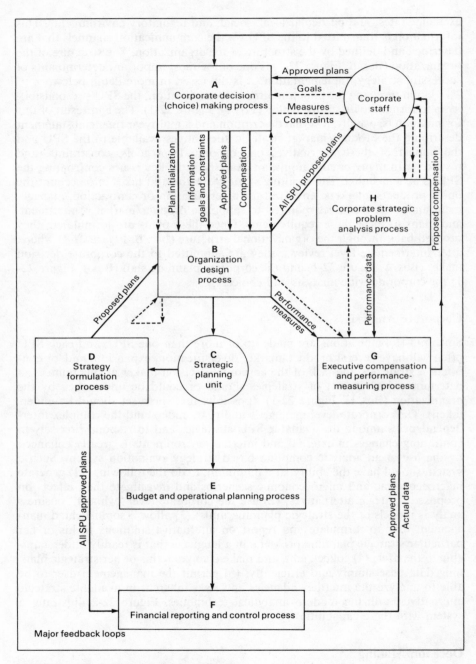

FIG. 22-1 Corporate Strategy Process Model

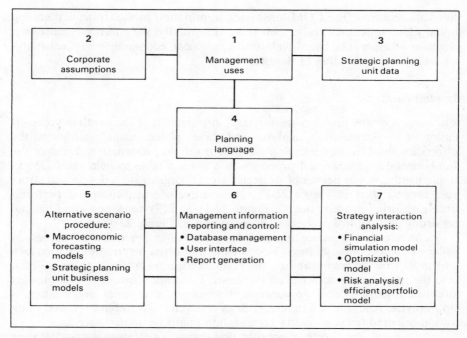

FIG. 22-2 Corporate-Level Strategy Analysis System

And, in many organizations, strategic decisions are made without formal attention being given to strategy formulation or analysis. Since strategic decision making requires some degree of intuition, it cannot be proven empirically that the lack of a formal system or structure will lead automatically to the making of incorrect or ill-advised decisions. But, these facts also do not negate the need for a system or structure. The decision-making process itself and the methods of linking and/or enticing the decision maker to use a particular system or structure should be studied. If a formal system exists, then the interaction of decision maker with the system is in the form of a feedback-generating catalyst. The review of an SPU-formulated plan by the corporate decision maker (CDM) often generates a set of desired plan alternatives or responses to "what if" questions that bring the CDM closer to understanding the economics of a particular SPU. A review of the interactions between competing SPUs triggers questions on issues such as the sensitivity of the accepted set of proposed SPU strategies to changes in the firm's environment, the dependence of the plan on the success of other strategies, the benefits of changing constraint-limitation values, and the costs of undertaking nonoptimal but intuitively appealing strategies. When used in this manner, the system serves as a decision-aiding tool—not a decision-making tool—by supplying information to the CDM that would not have been available otherwise. However, the choice of incorporating or ignoring this information is always up to the decision maker. Not infrequently, in the search for a robust corporate strategy, several formulation/analysis iterations are required. The CDM feeds back information to the strategic planning units, which must then revise their plans. Eventually, the end result must be a decision, whether it be based on intuitive judgment, economic/analytical analysis, or an artful blending of the two.

Implementation

The success of any problem-solving task, independent of the depth or sophistication of the formulation, analysis, and choice phases, usually hinges on the efforts involved in implementing the chosen solution alternative. Three of the fundamental organizational processes that are available to help the CDM in implementing his or her set of strategies are: (1) organization design and structure process (Box B, Figure 22-1), (2) executive compensation and performance-measuring process (Box G, Figure 22-1), and (3) budgeting and financial reporting and control processes (Boxes E and F, Figure 22-1).

The selection of an organization design can often determine the success or failure of a corporate strategy, since this design often determines factors such as the location of responsibility, the communications channels to be utilized, and the need for concurrence on decisions. For some firms, a formal production-line organization is appropriate. For others, a regional organization is appropriate. And, for still others, such as research, high technology, and innovation-oriented firms, a matrix organization might be appropriate.

In general, the choice of organization design for strategy implementation depends on the types of environmental uncertainty the organization faces. Future events may be classified as to types of uncertainty, as follows:

1 *Events that are relatively certain or inevitable:* These are the events that can be forecasted with a relatively high degree of certainty.

2 *Specified uncertainties:* These are uncertain events whose identity and probability of occurrence can be specified. Planning for these can be approached by:
   a. Risk planning, i.e., devising one plan of operations that is designed to maximize expected profit (subject to other constraints), given the specified probability distributions of these uncertain events; or
   b. Contingency planning, i.e., the creation of alternative plans so that, at the occurrence of a random event, the plan contingent upon it would be chosen for action.

3 *Unspecified uncertainties:* These are events whose identity is unknown.

An organization's design should allow it to function, both ex ante (through planning) and ex post, in a cost-effective manner, under the types of uncertainties described above. As environmental uncertainty increases and as more information is acquired, emphasis in organization design shifts from preplanning to organizational adaptation during task execution.

Thus, a repertory of organization design strategies is needed that is contingent on environmental uncertainty and on associated information-processing requirements. In general, the greater the environmental uncertainty, the greater the amount of information that must be processed in order to achieve given performance levels. The use of organization design strategies that reduce the need for information processing (creation of slack resources and creation of self-contained tasks) or increase organizational capacity to process information (investment in vertical information systems and creation of lateral relations) helps to manage the increase in data. The last approach—use of lateral relations—involves selective formalization of relationships that cut across the line organization. As uncertainty increases, these lateral relations include the following: (1) encouraging direct contact among participants sharing a problem, (2) instituting liaison roles, (3) setting up temporary task forces, (4) establishing permanent project teams, (5) creating integrating roles for experts, (6) formalizing managerial linking roles through budgeting power, and (7) establishing a matrix organization involving dual authority relationships to management and linear authority.

When uncertainty increases to the point that the above organization design strategies are still not effective in meeting given performance levels, performance goals may be reduced. Or, new operational goal dimensions may be chosen by invoking a referral process between goals and underlying values. Organization design should provide for activation of this referral process and for evolving design of the organization itself.

Another key variable for successful implementation of a corporate strategy is how SPU and division-level management is measured and compensated. In any multi-SPU organization, the reason for accepting strategies from different SPUs will almost always vary. Some are accepted for cash flow, while others are accepted for earnings growth, and others for earning stability. Thus, to increase the likelihood of successful strategy implementation, the measurement and compensation of these SPU managers should be based on different indicators, ideally, on those parameters that caused their strategies to be accepted. As a result of the corporate strategy analysis process and the use of a portfolio concept towards risk management, a concise business mission can be defined for each SPU, as well as a clear set of performance measures of that SPU. When creating compensation systems for the managers and their SPUs, the mix of current, deferred, and incentive compensation must reflect the mission and measures that were established previously. Thus, the compensation package of the manager of an SPU with high earnings-per-share growth should weigh future financial results and project completion more heavily than the manager whose SPU is slated for divestment. The manager in the latter case will have a compensation package based on short-term income and/or cash-flow generation and the successful completion of the divestiture. Along with short-term and long-term financial measures, the managers of some components, such as those selected for their stability, will be measured on a long-term moving average of selected characteristics that have been chosen to define stability. Still other managers, such as those responsible for new-venture SPUs, may have no financial measure at all. Their measures may focus on the successful design, development, and production of a new product on a predefined time/quality continuum. The failure to use differentiated compensation systems among SPU managers that differ as to financial criteria, percentage weighting of short-term and long-term results, and the use of nonfinancial measures can easily negate the work done in the strategy formulation and analysis phase. This is especially true when approved SPU strategies require managerial action that may be contradictory to those actions required if the manager desires to maximize current compensation under an unenlightened compensation system. Unfortunately, most of the work done in the area of executive compensation has dealt with what should make up an adequate package rather than with what the package should be related.

The ideas of budgeting, financial reporting, and control are not new, but they must be emphasized, since controlling to a strategic plan is fundamental to successful strategy implementation. The natural response of an SPU manager is to create a strategy that will be accepted by the CDM. This almost always yields a forecast that tends to be optimistic. If future SPU performance is not controlled to the strategic plan, the credibility of the entire strategic planning process can be subverted and eventually destroyed, since there is little credibility in the financial information contained in the plan. The other extreme is also possible, where pessimistic estimates are constantly submitted so that the SPU can easily perform at a level higher than planned. Controlling this strategy is more difficult, but it must be done.

The minimum requirements of such a control system are that it be structured to facilitate variance reporting and that it have available an adequate history of the organization's environment. Most organizations use variance analysis to assess the degree to which monthly and/or quarterly "actual" data of SPUs is meeting the budget targets previously agreed upon. When there are significant differences between actual results and planned results, the differences have to be explained in some manner, such as lower sales or higher costs. This concept must be pursued at the strategic level also, so that significant differences between the conceptual strategy of one year and that of the next or between the actual financial results of the subsequent years of the strategy and the original plan can be explained. This means that the control system must have a memory for the original strategy and its financial projections. And, it must contain key environmental parameters that might help to explain these variations.

Some Conclusions

This introduction presents a model for the corporate strategy process. The model is generic and descriptive but, at the same time, it may be viewed as satisfactorily perscriptive (i.e., normative) in the sense that it defines and solves the strategy problem that emerges in the planning process. Needless to say, there are alternative process descriptions; this one was chosen because it allows for the interaction of the corporate decision maker with an analysis system, and it can be used to demonstrate the need for the interaction of the analysis system with the formulation and implementation tasks.

In this chapter, the computer-based system briefly discussed above is developed in more detail. This chapter also discusses how these systems can be implemented and used.

CORPORATE STRATEGY ANALYSIS SYSTEMS

Most existing corporate planning models are computer-based financial simulations that are used to evaluate proposed planning alternatives. They normally compute the financial implications of alternative marketing, production, and financial policies under different environmental conditions, and they generate projected financial statements for each set of inputs. In all but the simplest cases, there are a great many planning alternatives to be considered.

Of course, the development of an appropriate corporate planning model is only one step toward its successful application to planning problems. Another step is the creation of a supporting information system to allow effective interaction between model and user. Although corporate models can reduce the effort required to evaluate and select plans, many require such extensive input preparation and output analysis that useful results may be difficult to obtain. This can seriously limit the operational effectiveness of the model and preclude consideration of a full range of planning alternatives. Where input/output functions can be relegated to a flexible computer-based information management system, however, model implementation can be greatly enhanced.

The nature of the interface with corporate planners is also important. Corporate planning is inherently an interactive, investigative process in which intermediate results may indicate the direction for successive analyses. Experience with both batch modes and interactive modes for periodic and ad hoc planning studies strongly suggests that on-line access to the model and its supporting system is necessary to permit their most effective use as creative planning tools.

The system presented here has been designed to operate as an integral part of the strategic planning process. Emphasis is placed on providing useful decision-aiding information within the practical limitations of available computational capabilities and established planning practice. Experience to date has demonstrated that an integrated system is both operationally feasible and appropriate for strategic planning.

System Requirements

Organizational Context. For purposes of strategic planning, the functional organization of the corporation is determined by the delegation of responsibility for planning, usually paralleling communication routes and authority patterns that have already been established for other corporate purposes, such as accounting or performance control. The system discussed here was designed for a large firm in which the corporate-level planning responsibilities are concerned primarily with SPU portfolio selection and finance. The lower levels are fairly independent; operating responsibility is within the limits of a corporate plan. Through this division of planning responsibilities, the specialized knowledge of managers close to the actual operations is employed most effectively, while corporate-level attention is concentrated on those decisions requiring an overview of resources and opportunities.

In applying the current version of the planning system in other corporate contexts, it is necessary only that planning units be independent. Financial and decentralized holding companies, conglomerates, and single-product/multioffice firms are representative of the many organizational types for which appropriate planning units can be defined. Firms with highly integrated product lines and/or a high degree of vertical integration require simple modifications in each subsystem to reflect the effects of internal transfers of products, resources, and services.

Planning Process. As discussed above, the corporate planning process begins with a corporate-level definition of objectives, which is then translated into a set of quantifiable goals and guidelines for the management of corporate resources. For example, corporate goals might relate to market share, net wealth of the stockholder, return on equity; guidelines or restrictions might involve acceptable financial ratios, legal limitations, or availability of scarce resources. These and other data on factors such as economic conditions and tax and prime interest rates are communicated to corporate groups and SPUs at the beginning of the annual planning cycle.

Within such a framework, a set of alternative internal and external strategies are generated by strategic planning units and relevant corporate groups. Internal alternatives defined by each planning unit can be structured for planning purposes as follows:

- Momentum strategies, which reflect continuation of present activities in existing lines of business;
- Development strategies, which reflect the incremental effects of all proposed changes in the nature or level of momentum strategies;
- Financing strategies, which reflect alternative opportunities for financing existing and proposed activities at the corporate and subsidiary levels; and
- Divestment strategies, which reflect the discontinuation of an existing momentum strategy through its sale to an external agent.

External opportunities can be defined by the subsidiary or by the divisional planning units, but they are more often defined by corporate-level planning units, such as corporate development and finance. For example, acquisition strategies reflect alternative ways of incorporating new companies and undertaking new ventures in new industries.

Once a set of internal and external alternatives has been generated, a composite plan must be formulated that achieves the corporate goal within corporate guidelines and restrictions. Often, some modification of goals or restrictions is called for, which means that changes are fed back into the system and new analyses are conducted. Facilitating this planning process was a major reason for the development of the system described below.

System Characteristics

General System Specifications. The key to effective analytical support of the strategic planning process is not a corporate model but an integrated system. The corporate-level focus, the need to develop balanced portfolios of SPU strategies, financial orientation, and the distant planning horizon that characterize corporate strategic planning in most organizations are reflected in the system. In addition to capabilities offered by simulation modeling and econometric analysis, some form of optimization or optimum-seeking capability generally is desirable. This should assist in selecting strategies and funds sources, rather than simply evaluate selected alternatives. Another desirable system feature is direct access to the system via a remote terminal to permit creative planning applications. Provision should also be made for alternate input and output options to facilitate use for different studies, in both batch and interactive modes. Finally, the system should be flexible enough to analyze a wide variety of planning problems. These range from subsidiary strategy and funds source selection to acquisition/divestment evaluation, portfolio selection, and business-mix evaluation.

The System Overview. In general terms, the system presented here is a specialized, computer-based management information system with extensive analytical capabilities. Its power derives from the integration of diverse but complementary planning models with user-oriented information storage and handling features.

The central analytical component is a large mixed-integer mathematical programming model that maximizes corporate performance over a multiperiod planning horizon by selecting appropriate operating, acquisition, and financing strategies. A corporate simulation model computes the detailed implications of selected alternatives under specified environmental conditions and generates projected corporate financial statements for each set of inputs. Econometric models supply projections for the national economy, specific industries, and selected subsidiary companies. SPU business models allow the user to determine the sensitivity of SPU performance to changes in factors such as its market share, price/cost structure, and inflation. Risk analysis models provide insights for evaluating business mix and the implications of various strategic alternatives. The flow of information, maintenance of the planning data base, and interfaces with data sources and users are controlled through the information management subsystem. Use of the system—and of each of the subsystems, when they are used independently—may be in either on-line or batch mode. Conversational interaction with the system provides direct management access to the data base and analytical models as an integral part of the planning process.

At the start of the planning period, corporate management assumptions on pertinent planning data are communicated to group and subsidiary management so that the preparation of the planning information by the strategic planning units will be based on uniform global assumptions. Each SPU submits, at a minimum, the following financial data:

- *Strategic planning unit data:* A profit and loss statement, balance sheet, and a statement showing sources and applications of funds are submitted, assuming the acceptance of all proposed momentum, development, acquisition, and financing strategies necessary to fund all projects.

- *Strategy data:* Each momentum, development, and acquisition strategy proposed by an SPU is documented by abbreviated profit/loss and source-of-funds/application-of-funds information.

- *Financing data:* Information is also submitted, if appropriate, for each existing or proposed financing instrument, indicating principal amount, repayment schedule, compensating balance, cost, type, and restrictions on the use of funds.

When the SPU data and other management assumptions on goals, restrictions, business mix, and the like are assembled at corporate headquarters, the use of the planning system can be initiated. Communication between the user and the system is via an interactive/interrogative language especially designed and structured for this system. Thus, all questions and procedures are task-related or problem-related. Once the SPU financial data has been edited, analyzed, and placed in the appropriate data files, all requests for information or transfer of information between subsystems are handled through the information management subsystem.

Use of the systems begins with a tranfer of SPU financial data to the econometric and SPU business models subsystems, where alternative data bases are prepared for various assumptions on areas such as projected macroeconomic conditions, market share, and inflation rates. Simultaneously, other data bases are developed by the risk analysis subsystem to determine confidence levels for the performance of all selected SPUs. All of these systems require on-line interaction to ensure appropriate data base formulations. Once alternative data bases have been established, the information is transferred to the optimization subsystem, where a goal/constraint-achieving plan is formulated for each alternative data base. The financial effects of these plans (as reflected in statements such as the statement of profit and loss and the income statements) are determined by the simulation subsystem. All reports produced by the system are communicated to the users at their terminals throughout this process. Nonfeasible solutions require changes in management assumptions or submission of additional strategies that are requested by the user through the management hierarchy. The iterative process is continued until a plan that is acceptable to management is reached. This will usually require restatement of some constraints or objectives, a blend of acceptable alternatives for the different environments, new financing strategies, and requests for additional strategies caused by restructuring of the business mix. The approved plan is communicated back through the organizational hierarchy, where implementation plans are developed, with short-term items being incorporated into quarterly operation reviews.

THE SUBSYSTEMS AND THEIR USES

Information Management Subsystem

The multitask component illustrated in Figure 22-3 controls the use, the internal information flow, and the final reporting of the modeling system. The user interacts with the system via a planning language. This language is designed specifically to be understandable to the management-oriented user. The computer

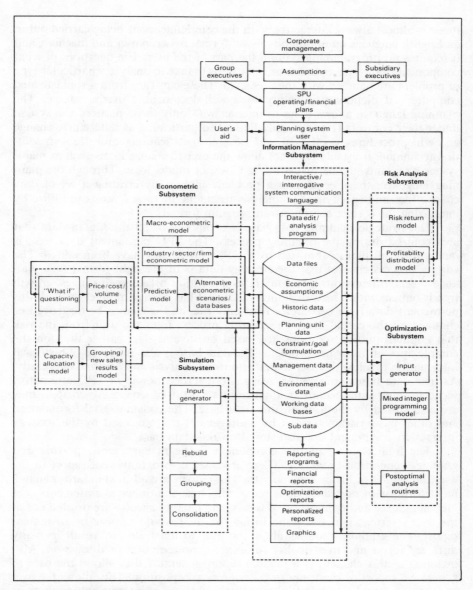

FIG. 22-3 Integration of Subsystems

mode is almost always interactive, with the communications being carried out in an English language question-and-answer format between user and machine, and it requires no programming skill on the part of the user. The questions of what component of the system to use or what steps to take to analyze a particular type of problem are handled with the user's aid. These can vary from a sophisticated computerized dictionary/directory to a well-documented user's manual. The planning language allows users to interact with only those parts of the system under their control. This is usually limited to parts such as data entry, change and edit procedures, coefficient and variable specifications, and problem solution technique. It usually does not allow the user to change items such as major system programs, the permanent data bases, or model logic. Through the planning language, the user sets up a problem analysis by creating a set of data change files and specifying the analysis technique he or she wants to utilize by initializing the correct computer-run program formats.

The strategic planning data base is composed of all the sets of data that are required during the planning process. The SPU permanent data base is made up of all plans submitted by the SPU after they have been edited. The editing process ensures that the strategy data is in the right format (e.g., balance sheets, interest rates, and tax rates are within preassigned ranges, growth trends remain within historical limits). Once it has been completely edited, this permanent data base becomes a read-only file, and it cannot be destroyed or changed by the casual user. This editing process frees the user from the risk that counterintuitive solutions are based on invalid data rather than on the complexities of his or her problem. The data base is also made up of historical information to allow the user to perform trend analysis and comparisons easily. As new data bases are created, using the macroeconomic or SPU alternative scenarios, and intermediate or final results worthy of saving are created, they are also stored by the user on this data base. The constant/goal formulation and other basic parameters set by management that are used by the strategy interaction component are also stored on this data base.

The final element of this component is the management-reporting and graphics generation programs. These are a set of programs that report to the user the results of his or her analyses. The reports are all in standard management form, with no translations required. Thus, the financial statements—net income, source and application of funds, and balance sheets—are printed out at the user's terminal in the same format as they would appear in an annual report. The graphics routines allow the user to illustrate any result in many different forms and in a quality suitable for presentation or discussion. Also included in this element is a flexible report generator that allows the user to generate a report of his or her own design or composition. This allows the user to create financial ratios and other statistics that are of interest only to them or that they feel better portrays the results of a particular analysis without having to have this data printed out for all users.

Consolidation Simulation Subsystem

The consolidation simulation subsystem performs a deterministic financial simulation for a redesignated set of momentum, development, divestment, acquisition, and financing strategies. This component contains a rebuild module, a grouping module, a corporate elimination/consolidation module, and a performance measure module. Like most corporate financial simulation models, it is based largely on accepted financial accounting variables and relationships. The user submits selected particular SPUs and strategies for consolidation. If the user desires to pick and choose among possible strategies within an SPU, the rebuild module is used to construct a new SPU by summing the available financial data for the selected strategies and meeting any cash imbalances from the corporate funds pool. This also permits entry of additional SPU financing and allows for subgroupings of strategies into business lines. The rebuild module generates a balance sheet and a profit and loss statement for each restructured SPU. At the next stage of the simulation process, the user specifies desired SPU groupings (e.g., along functional lines or by business type). The group consolidation module then combines the SPUs into groups, and it can generate a balance sheet and a profit and loss statement for each of the proposed groups. This module also permits conversion to a common currency, and divestment of SPUs as desired. Completion of the corporate consolidation is accomplished using the elimination/consolidation module. This eliminates all existing and new intercompany flows; finances funds deficits from a corporate pool; incorporates all proposed divestments; permits entry of additional parent company financing and accounting entries; and produces annual consolidated corporate financial statements. The corporate performance module can be used to determine the value of corporate performance measures deemed appropriate by management.

Corporate Optimization Subsystem

The corporate strategic planning optimization subsystem maximizes corporate performance over a multiperiod planning horizon by selecting an optimal set of strategic funds sources and uses subject to a complex set of financial, legal, and operating limitations imposed at both the corporate and SPU levels. The mixed-integer mathematical programming model is the basic element of this subsystem, with operating support provided by a matrix generator, a matrix modification processor, and postoptimal analysis routines.

The most operationally effective planning objective found to date is maximization of a linear approximation of undiscounted earnings per share over the planning horizon. Other performance measures, including discounted measures of return and risk-adjusted measures, can also be evaluated by the model. The primary planning variables represent all available momentum, development, acquisition, divestment, and financing strategies.

Strategy selection frequently implies decisions of the go/no-go type (e.g., divestments), except where explicit provision is made for partial strategies (e.g., financing, stock acquisition). The definition presented above implies that a development strategy can be selected only if its associated momentum is also selected. Momentum strategies are available for divestment; thus, all momentum strategies must either be totally accepted or totally rejected. The rejection of a momentum strategy implies that it should be sold to an outside party at the proposed price submitted as input by the system user.

The financing of selected strategies may be arranged through a variety of funding sources at both the corporate and SPU levels. Stock issues, both common and preferred, treasury repurchases of securities, and short-term and long-term financing instruments are considered. Long-term debt may be arranged at the corporate level for internal allocation to strategies, or, it may be contracted at the SPU level for a particular strategy. Voluntary early retirement of corporate debt is treated as a variable in the model.

Corporate earnings are subject to various financial and operating restrictions. Some are imposed by management policy, and others by external forces. Among those represented explicitly in the optimization model are restrictions on the pattern of earnings-per-share growth, return on assets and equity, corporate funds flow, common financial ratios (e.g., debt equity and interest coverage ratios), short-term debt, and stock transactions.

A matrix generator draws the appropriate management data files and strategic planning data files from the data base and organizes them in a form consistent with the functional relationships described by the model and the requirements of the solution algorithm. Due to their complex nature, matrix coefficients in the corporate planning models often are functions of a number of basic input parameters. Frequently, they allow no meaningful financial or management interpretation. Therefore, to facilitate analysis, a matrix modification processor has been developed to compute automatically the effects of new point estimates or ranges from the strategic planning data files and/or the management data files.

One of the major reasons for developing a corporate strategic planning optimization model was to permit testing of the robustness of proposed solutions and to determine optimal reallocations of corporate resources in response to changes in the planning environment. The combined capabilities of a post-optimal analysis routine, the matrix modification processor, and available mathematical programming systems make this possible.

Econometric Subsystem

Effective strategic planning requires some projections for the economies and industries in which the corporation operates or plans to operate. The econometric subsystem is designed to provide such insights through use of both macro (i.e., national level) models and sector (i.e., industry level) models. These forecasting models make it possible to test the reasonableness of projections submitted by SPUs and to generate information on projected economic conditions, which can be used in the formulation of SPU plans. The econometric forecasting capabilities currently used were not created for this system, but they are among the many forecasting models that are commercially available. (These include Data Resources, Wharton Econometric Model, and Chase Econometrics.)

Another part of the econometric subsystem, the acquisition data preparation model, uses computerized financial information available from several Wall Street firms in conjunction with the econometric forecasting models to generate financial planning data for companies that are being considered for possible acquisition. Of course, the optimization model is the perfect vehicle for testing the desirability of proposed acquisitions. It can easily evaluate hundreds of proposed acquisitions at a time. Only with the capabilities of the econometric subsystem, however, can the needed data be obtained on many companies in a short period. When the optimization subsystem chooses one of the proposed acquisitions, a more detailed study must be undertaken.

SPU Business Model Subsystem

The SPU business models give the corporate user the ability to determine the effects on SPU performance of changes in SPU operating characteristics such as market share, price, and major component cost in a what-if question format. This activity begins with the strategies submitted by an SPU and a set of cost/ volume relationships that further describe the SPU. The model is basically a simulation model, with added analytical capabilities available for the management user who desires to use them.

The model was designed to be a time-shared computer model that could answer a set of what-if questions posed by a management-oriented user. The questions under the manager's control deal with major changes in the following:

- Volume of orders; market share; revenue
- Component cost structure (e.g., labor and raw materials)
- Manufacturing delays in items with long production cycles
- Customer delays in desired delivery dates of finished products
- Inflation/escalation parameters
- Finished product performance warranties
- Methods for allocating fixed costs
- Methods for generating cost and capacity data as a function of volume of sales
- Grouping for reporting purposes

In its current form, the model requires the user to predetermine any new parameter value, since it does not include forecasting, cost accounting, or optimal joint cost allocating models. It was assumed that this could be done by other models, which could then be easily linked to the current one. When a set of changes have been made, the model computes their effect on the financial performance.

The model is capable of estimating performance for up to 20 years in the future. The model is based on average costs within quantity of production steps, and thus it was not designed to be a budgeting tool. Its results are approximate, but they have enough consistency and validity to be very useful for strategic planning purposes.

The model is based on a breakdown of output products into projects. Each project will then have its profile containing project-related average prices, costs, and balances and specific order volumes. The expenses for all SPU services and facilities that are not directly project-related are also input data. Whether and how these joint costs are allocated to projects is up to the user. The generic effects of speed-ups and delays for all project and nonproject data, warranty provisions, and capacity additions as a function of volume are also input data. The original set of this data is provided by the SPU.

The logical flow of information through the model is very simple. The user (1) specifies an order volume for all projects; (2) alters price, cost, and volume data for any or all projects; (3) creates a project margin report file for all projects; (4) groups projects into organizational subdivisions for reporting purposes; (5) calculates or changes directly non-project-related data, such as capacity and fixed costs as a function of volume; (6) if desired, chooses an allocation procedure for relating fixed costs to organizational subcomponents previously established; (7) chooses reports desired; and (8) generates reports and new SPU strategy form.

The model is used in an interactive mode, with all required changes being initiated by the user. The user is free to enter the model at any point and make as many changes as necessary to generate the desired SPU alternative operating scenerio. The capabilities that are most often used are those for changing order volumes, costs, and allocation procedures.

Risk Analysis Subsystem

The risk exposure of any corporate strategic plan is one of the most important factors to be considered by a strategy analysis system. Unfortunately, this is the area in which little has been done using analytical techniques. Trying to develop the risk exposure of a particular SPU strategy is difficult; trying to do the same for all combinations of these strategies becomes close to impossible. Some firms get around this problem by trying to analyze risk on an industry level. Thus, the question is, how can assets be allocated among various industries that have historically demonstrated particular risk characteristics. Two of these characteristics are the mean and standard deviation of return on equity. Given these data, a firm can develop an efficient portfolio that maximizes expected return for a level of variance in that return, by allocating its assets to the indicated industries in the indicated proportions. Once this has been completed, the risk of each SPU strategy is ignored since it is assumed that, on the average, all the chosen strategies will conform to the risks inherent in the efficient portfolio.

Most planning data come to corporate planning staffs as point estimates or, at best, with high and low estimates as well. The second component of the risk analysis subsystem generates alternative data bases to provide insights into the possible effects of the inherent variability in these estimates. A profitability profile model, used in conjunction with the forecasting models, determines probability distributions of performance for strategic planning units based on historical data and subjective management evaluations of possible future conditions. These distributions can then be used to estimate confidence limits for different profit levels. Once a new profit level has been derived, the simulation subsystem is used to create revised financial data based on this new profit estimate. A worst-case level, called the minimum income level, is derived for every strategy, and this is incorporated in the optimization analysis via a constraint that requires the minimum income of all selected strategies to exceed some minimum level set by corporate management.

SYSTEM IMPLEMENTATION AND APPLICATION

Implementation

To increase the probability of successful implementation, the most important function of a corporate strategy analysis system must be to increase the decision efficiency of executives. Decision efficiency increases the effective use of executive time and decision-making capability by focusing attention on key variables, providing rapid feedback and economic implications on the effects of policy alternatives on corporate goals and alternative allocations of scarce resources, and allowing implementation instructions to be transmitted in unambiguous terms. This is accomplished by a system that facilitates the ordering of priorities, standardizes and simplifies information form and flow, maintains an appropriate time horizon and decision sequence, comprehends the simultaneity of strategic decisions, formalizes performance measures and corporate goals, reports all outputs in a language familiar to the executive, and warns of incompatibility of policy decisions with goals. The system discussed in this chapter was created with these thoughts in mind. Two of the most important characteristics of decision efficiency provided by the system are: (1) maximizing the number of alternative opportunities considered simultaneously and evaluating the effect of each combination on the goal performance measure; and (2) minimizing loss of information and time in communication by reducing intermediaries and language barriers. The first is accomplished by the functions and interrelationships of the previously described subsystems: the optimizer and the simulator responsive subsystems; the risk-analysis and econometric business model supportive subsystems; and the omni-controlling information management subsystem. The second attribute is provided by the program formats. Run introductions consist of questions to be answered by the user that are interactive and conversational and that preclude inadvertent omissions. The reports are in familiar language, and are uncluttered by irrelevant computations, so that a user conversant with management goals and preferences directly controls the input and output of each phase, dynamically formulates policy alternatives, and can determine results of different planning scenarios all at the terminal. A coherent series of planning runs can be made by a user who understands what the output means for the corporation.

In order to achieve rapid acceptance of the system, it must be designed to run on current data that is almost entirely collected and reported by the organization. Some exceptions to this rule are possible. But, to design a system—no matter how elegant—that uses data that is not currently being collected or reported dooms it to eventual failure.

The user of the strategic planning system is typically a member of the corporate-level planning group who interacts with corporate executives for confirmation of data and performance/constraint level estimates. It is assumed that the system is well-established. Hence, all relevant participants are experienced with the full procedure and with their responsibilities and channels of authority, communication with respect to the system are well understood, and the information management system contains a full complement of timely data bases.

Before the SPUs prepare their strategies, they should receive corporate guidelines concerning interest rates for the corporate pool, tax rates, general and industry-specific economic trends, etc. Initially, SPU strategies should be related to the "most likely" environment assumption. The financial information comprising the SPU strategies should be presented on uniform forms, so that they can easily be edited for completeness and consistency and transferred to the data base. This also allows orderly comparison among SPUs.

The elemental strategies are accumulated at the subsidiary and at intermediary corporate levels before they reach the corporate staff. These intermediate stages give the responsible executives an opportunity to check strategies for consistency with goals and forecasts and to avoid conflicts within their groups. Acquisition strategies and alternative development and financing strategies may be added. It is not desirable at this level to reject strategies or to discourage SPUs from submitting many strategies or risky strategies. Since the broader corporate perspective may be different, and the planning system requires many alternatives to develop a plan, there is value in the elimination process itself and in the tension between constraints and performance measure. After the group executive has approved the group plan, a set of operating strategies, divestments, acquisitions, and financing alternatives is communicated to the corporate planning group for analysis.

Since all the groups have submitted plans for a most likely economic/business unit scenario, it is at this time that these plans—in conjunction with the econometric business unit and risk analysis subsystem—are used to generate multiple data bases. In conversations with corporate management, the planning group has delineated a set of alternative economic/business unit scenerios and risk distributions for which they would like to analyze the effect on the submitted plans. Wage/price guidelines, capital cycle, loss of market share, increases in raw material prices, and inflationary/disinflationary economic scenarios are but a few of the alternative data bases that are prepared. As this process is going on, the simulation subsystem is used to prepare the first corporate consolidated financial reports based on the most likely data base. This is simply the corporate consolidation and elimination of any intercompany flows of all the group plans. Usually, the summation of all the group plans as submitted vastly exceeds corporate resources and does not meet corporate goals and constraints. At this point, the optimization subsystem is brought into play. It is the dynamic interaction between the corporate planner, corporate management, and the simulation and optimization subsystems that allows a goal/constraint achieving corporate plan to be developed. It is due to the dynamic nature of this process that the planning system was designed to be highly interactive and common-language-dependent. Thus, the reports, verbal or graphic, are in forms that are readily understandable by all corporate management. As alternative data bases become available, the simulation/optimization process is reiterated so that a goal/constraint achieving plan can be developed for each alternative economic/business unit scenerio. Once all the economic scenarios have been analyzed, it is corporate management's responsibility to choose the final acceptable plan. This will usually require restatement of some constraints or objectives, a blend of acceptable alternatives for the different environments, new financing strategies, and, most often, the request for additional strategies from certain groups. The approved plan is communicated back through the organizational hierarchy (top to bottom), where implementation plans are developed. Short-term items are incorporated into the quarterly operating reviews.

System Applications

For discussion purposes, two general types of planning studies can be distinguished, and their implications for systems operation and applications are discussed here. Planning studies are conducted at regular intervals, and, they typically relate to planning decisions encompassing the full scope of corporate activity. Ad hoc planning studies are conducted in response to particular problems or opportunities that arise during the regular planning period, and they require at least limited analysis prior to the next overall corporate review. While the distinction between these two types of planning studies is often blurred in practice, it is helpful in considering the range of system operating options and applications available to the user.

Periodic Studies. As indicated earlier, the heart of the analytical system as it is used during the annual planning cycle is the optimization subsystem. Its inputs are drawn from several sources, via the input or matrix generator program. Analysis of projected profitability distributions (generated by the profitability profile model) for key industries and companies not only provides reasonable parameter values for certain optimization model relationships, but it also provides inputs to the business-mix risk/return model. This, in turn, generates appropriate limits on investment/divestment programs for the optimization model. Typical results from the optimization and postoptimal analyses indicate those investment and financing strategies that offer the best corporate performance over the defined planning horizon.

An important capability of the optimization model is simultaneous consideration of financing, operating, and investment decisions. Too often, financing strategies are selected after operating and investment decisions have been made. Financing alternatives are of major importance, and they can affect corporate goals as much as major acquisitions or new operating strategies. The question of equity or debt financing, the importance of financial measures (e.g., liquidity, interest coverage) can be comprehended only when they are considered simultaneously with the major operating alternatives of the firm. Extensive parametric analyses of these policy restrictions have allowed management to evaluate the implications of the traditional financial rules of thumb. In one study, for example, the high marginal cost associated with the interest coverage restriction and subsequent parametric analysis revealed that the planned divestment of a subsidiary with no significant debt would prevent acceptance of a highly profitable, but debt-financed, expansion of an existing subsidiary. The result was an explicit determination of the trade-off between the policy limit (interest coverage) and earnings per share (EPS). This information led to a management decision to lower the required interest coverage, and to subsequent completion of the planned divestment and acceptance of the expansion strategy. Thus, the financing of any alternative cannot be determined in isolation; it must be evaluated with all other corporate alternatives.

The optimization subsystem is also uniquely equipped to evaluate corporate acquisition and divestment alternatives. Acquisitions are not considered as unique and independent alternatives, but, rather, as the contribution of the acquisition to earnings per share. Its implications for corporate constraints are evaluated as part of the total corporate pool of opportunities.

The optimization model assists in deciding not only what to acquire but also how it should be financed and when during the planning period the acquisition be undertaken. In the annual planning cycle and in special studies, acquisition candidates are generally proposed to the model with a range of pooling options (e.g., common stock financing) and purchase options (e.g., equity, debt, or cash financing). For example, a major subsidiary proposed several small pooling acquisitions that were accepted by the model, but only as cash purchases, in view of the low projected price of common stock and the unexpected availability of cash generated by divestments. In another case, the model recommended delay of two planned subsidiary acquisitions in favor of immediate purchase of a corporate acquisition opportunity. In another study of common stock financing, three major acquisitions, each in excess of $100 million, were considered both individually and in combinations. Taken one at a time, Acquisition A (the smallest) showed a positive contribution EPS over the planning horizon; Acquisition B resulted in slight dilution (reduction in EPS); and Acquisition C (the biggest) caused significant dilution. Traditional acquisition evaluations would have recommended accepting A and rejecting the other two. When all three were submitted for evaluation, the optimization analysis suggested acceptance of both A and B and indicated that rejection of B would have reduced the optimal EPS value by an amount nearly 20 times the expected dilution effect. Further examination revealed that the funds balancing constraint became limiting in periods 3 and 4, when Acquisition B was expected to contribute substantial cash flows. Since the debt/equity constraint was also limiting in these periods, rejection of Acquisition B would have forced the use of expensive equity financing to meet corporate cash requirements or curtailing of promising internal investments.

In view of the approximations inherent in most corporate optimization models, such as the linear approximation to earnings per share used in the model, the results can be considered only as approximate. Since solutions using the above approximation deviated by only 3 percent from the computed maximum values, they represent desirable, if not optimal, selections from among the vast number of alternatives considered. By way of contrast, the simulation model requires few assumptions and allows detailed examination of selected strategies. Its role in the planning system is, therefore, to validate the optimization results and to provide more detailed insights into their implications than is possible using only the optimization model. For example, the simulation model will compute corporate earnings per share very precisely for any selected set of strategies; the optimization model can only estimate this figure because of the nonlinear effects of expansion and contraction in the stock pool.

The operating pattern described here for periodic planning studies takes on many different forms in practice. This flexibility is a basic design feature of the planning system. In some cases, additional iterations between models are performed where variances or new insights are found. On other occasions, only parts of the system may be used.

Ad Hoc Studies. Several examples illustrate the scope of the system operation and application in support of ad hoc planning studies:

- *Exogenous events.* The impact of unanticipated variations in interest rates, taxes, and foreign exchange rates on existing plans can be quickly evaluated using the simulation model. Where reallocations of certain corporate resources are possible in the short run, optimization studies may also be conducted with strict constraints on decisions already committed to in the past planning cycle.

- *Acquisitions/divestments.* Opportunities to purchase or sell corporate holdings under favorable terms may require prompt analysis at any time during the planning period. Simulation of the new corporate system and analysis of implied changes in business mix are obvious possibilities, with the additional option of an optimization analysis to identify potential gains from responsive adjustments in other financing and investment strategies. Furthermore, where new companies or industries are involved, econometric studies and profitability profile studies may be required.

- *Corporate structure.* Differences in borrowing power, funds-flow regulations, and tax rates for different strategic planning units make the analysis of organizational structure a complex task for multinational corporations. The consolidation process employed by the corporate simulation model permits efficient exploration of structural alternatives in response to changes in both internal and external factors.

Many other ad hoc studies, including direct interrogation of the system data base via the information system, are easily conducted using various combinations of system capabilities.

Use of the System for Acquisition Analysis: Some Implementation Experiences

This example uses a large multifirm/multidivision corporation with an established corporate strategy analysis system (as described above) at some point after the annual plan has been formulated. An exogenous executive decision is made to increase the concentration of corporate assets in one of the groups (Group A). This decision is based on information provided by the business-mix risk/return model. It has shown that the firm's asset concentration in Group C, a mixed set of companies involved in the capital goods industry, must be reduced and redeployed to Group A if the firm as a whole is to move towards the efficient frontier (i.e., to increase its expected return on equity at the current level of risk).

For a more general evaluation of corporate policy that is not related to a specific acquisition but, rather, to the corporate-wide allocation of assets, the risk/return subsystem compares the standard deviation (i.e., the risk-dispersion indicator) of the distribution of return on equity with the mean of the distribution. Historic data for each of the major industries represented in the corporation (capital goods, ocean shipping, agriculture, and trucking) are the source for the set of points. The point on the efficient frontier represents a unique allocation of corporate assets among groups for each level of risk/return. If the corporation as a whole is inside the frontier, the risk/return subsystems can show the user that asset allocation that would move the corporation to a point on the frontier that can easily be shown to be preferred from the point of view of management and stockholders.

Choice of which efficient point is most compatible with other corporate goals, policies, and financial considerations must be left to executive judgment and to the executive's perception of the preferences of stockholders and future investors. The decision requires evaluation of the trade-off between risk and return goals and EPS or other performance goals. The graphic analysis package clarifies this procedure. The group executive of Group A is requested to submit a proposal for an acquisition to the corporate planning group, described by the data on the acquisition strategy form. Various transformations of this data and management data will be needed for the matrix used by the system. From the strategy data, two alternative acquisition strategies are formed for each of several years in the plan cycle, one financed by purchase and one by pooling. The corporate characteristics will be different in each planning year due to shifts in internal structure and environmental conditions, so an acquisition might be valuable in one year and a burden in another. The econometric/business unit subsystem can be employed to convert each of these strategies into four additional strategies, to correspond to the high and low economic growth scenario alternatives and to a high and low market share business unit scenario alternative. The result is a total addition to the data base of many strategies representing several combinations of years, methods of acquisition, and economic environments.

The other important matrix change is in the management data base. This is a change in the position of that constraint, or boundary, within which the system must seek an optimal solution. Introduction of both types of changes to the data base is done by an interactive question-and-answer process. The full process of generating the new inputs and entering them to the files requires only a few minutes of computer time.

For a quick look at the characteristics of Group A when the proposed acquisition is included, the user can request the simulator subsystem to provide financial statements. The simulator will add each data item of the user-chosen acquisition strategy to corresponding totals for the other strategies in the accepted plan. The user can test each of the full versions of the acquisition strategy, or any part, in a similar manner.

The acceptance or rejection of an acquisition proposal should be based on successful competition with other strategies for the financial resources, which are not unlimited, of the corporation. This analysis requires the optimizer subsystem. A particular strategy may not meet some profit or other criterion on its own, but it may be acceptable to the corporation when it is undertaken in conjunction with other strategies. After all, a corporate-wide perspective for executives' decisions is one of the primary purposes of a corporate planning group.

For example, the Group A acquisition proposal may generate income sufficient to contribute five cents per share over the five-year planning period. This may not seem adequate. Suppose it is a debt-free company with a high cash yield expected in a future planning year, and that cash can be used in a high-yield activity elsewhere in the corporation, whose proceeds can then be reinvested in other alternatives. Thus, rejecting the acquisition proposal means missing the opportunity of undertaking a set of investments that will yield 37 cents per share; this does not mean merely forgoing the five cents per share produced by the acquisition if considered in isolation. This type of analytical consideration of secondary and tertiary effects of strategies in alternative combinations can be vital to the long-term health of a large corporation, and it can be obtained efficiently only through the use of the optimization subsystem.

After the appropriate changes in the strategy and constraint files have been made, the optimizer itself can be run. The output at the terminal will be a consistent set of recommendations based on strategies, constraints, and environmental data submitted as input. Each run output will be available at the user's terminal in a form similar to Table 22-1. The strategies will be identified by code number and name. The selected strategies are meaningful only as a complete set. A portion of one run œay not be compatible with portions of other runs if there have been major changes in one of the inputs. After a series of manipulative runs, the user should be able to present corporate executives with the net impact of several well-defined alternatives for the acquisition. To be acceptable, the acquisition must have justified itself in competition with existing and alternative strategies. The characteristics of this acquisition may suggest changes in the previously optimal plan (before the group asset allocation constraint was eased). For example, this acquisition may be financed most efficiently under certain circumstances by the divestment of another company. Manipulation over several optimizer runs can indicate the cost of not making a particular divestment or of not accepting an acquisition as recommended by the optimizer. Management judgment may choose to ignore certain optimizer results, since human perception may be far more acute than gross data machine input allows. But, this judgment will be informed: The operational cost of these counter-decisions can be described.

In addition to listing the optimal set of strategies, the printout indicates which corporate-level group-level management constraints were binding. This is particularly useful feedback to the executive goal-formation process. Thus, the operational impact of a particular limit on the level of return on equity, for example, can be communicated to goal setters. By parameterizing (varying) the constraint level slightly on only this parameter in successive optimizer runs, the optimal solution (strategy set) for one constraint level can be compared with the optimal solution for another level. The difference is an indication of the cost of maintaining the constraint at the original level. This is not to say that a binding constraint ought to be changed, but only that there is some cost (in terms of the corporate goal) that should be considered when a constraint level is chosen by traditional rules and customs or other forms of entrepreneurial wisdom. For an example, the optimizer may report that for every million dollars the Group A asset constraint is increased, total EPS over the planning horizon could be raised two cents for the same strategy and constraint input.

TABLE 22-1 Sample Optimization Results—Terminal Output Company XYZ

Consolidated EPS	Increase Over Previous Year
1982: 5.25	—
1983: 6.91	31.4%
1984: 7.42	7.3%
1985: 8.37	12.0%
1986: 8.76	4.6%
1987: 9.93	13.0%

DIVESTMENTS

Name	Percent Divested	Reduction to Total EPS If Not Divested	Net Cash Received
Company 26: ABC Tool Co.			
Strat 3—Steel market	100%	0.2532	$10,321
Strat 5—Auto market	100	0.0331	2,423
Company 35: EFG Valve Co.			
Strat 1—Momentum	100	0.6231	37,311

ACQUISITIONS

Name	Percent Acquired	Reduction to Total EPS If Not Acquired	Acquisition Price in Kilo $
Company 351: North Sea Oil— 1983 pooling 2M common shares	100%	0.3714	115,132

BINDING CONTRACT RESTRICTIONS

Name	Change in EPS Per Unit Change in Constraint Level
Funds balance—85	0.000312
Funds balance—86	0.001432
Debt equity—84	0.000231
Group C assets—85	0.005231

NEW CORPORATE FINANCING

Issue	Type	Year	Kilo $ Amount	Number of Shares
93	Long-term debt	1984	50,000	—
97	Short-term debt	1986	75,000	—
84	XYZ—Common stock	1985	—	2,000,000

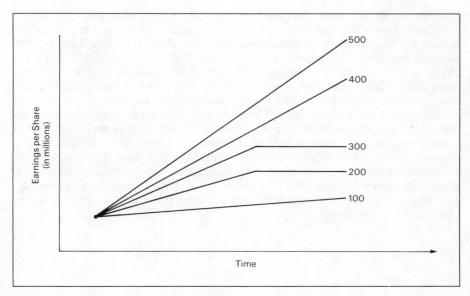

FIG. 22-4 Group C Contraction

To facilitate comparison of different parameterization runs, a printout is available (see Figure 22-4). For example, Group C assets can vary from $500 million to $200 million in three feasible steps, and the system will describe the effect on EPS of each change. Figure 22-4 indicates that the firm can reduce its concentration in industry (recommended by the risk/return model) only to $200 million. Below that, the EPS growth goals are no longer met. This would indicate that in order to reach the frontier, the firm must generate more productive opportunities in its other groups, or else assets cannot be reduced in Industry C below the $200 million level.

The new optimal set of strategies should now be returned to the simulation subsystem for generation of financial reports, including the acquisition with the selected time and financing procedure. The results are then communicated to group executives through the normal communications channels available in the organization.

CONCLUSIONS AND EXTENSIONS

As firms grow larger, become more complex, and increase the number of products that they sell or industries that they serve, the need for rational allocation of scarce resources at the corporate level increases. The system discussed in this chapter is a first step in this process. Although it is financial in nature, the usefulness of the corporate strategy analysis system discussed here is not limited purely to diversified nonfinancial institutions. In its present form, it is applicable to (1) any firm whose products, offices, or services are independent and whose major scarce resource is money and managerial talent, or (2) an integrated firm whose product transfers are made at known market prices. The system has been implemented in a large multisubsidiary firm, and it has proven to be an invaluable management tool. Not only has it been useful in doing the things it was designed to do (such as picking acquisitions and divestments, facilitating what-if questions, and allowing for rapid and understandable information processing), but it has helped management become accustomed to thinking on more than one level. Thus, systems thinking is more apparent than before the planning system was implemented. Most choices are made with a total corporate view, and multilevel information is constantly desired. It has also stimulated the search for new opportunities, since the apparatus for their evaluation is now readily available. Thus, decision efficiency has been heightened. The author believes that because of the system's successful implementation and its modest cost, in a few years no large firms will be without major portions of this system.

PART VII

Organizing for Strategic Management

23

Organizational Structure and Management Process

PETER LORANGE

Professor of Management and Chairman, Department of Management
The Wharton School, University of Pennsylvania

INTRODUCTION

There has been strong interest over the past few years in the role an organization's structure and management processes play in effective strategic management. Important progress has been made regarding these issues within the research community,[1] and practitioners have added important insights based on their experience. In this chapter, a firm's structure and its related management processes are presented as highly interrelated phenomena, and an integrated point of view is offered for considering management structures and processes as complementary vehicles for implementing strategies effectively. Treatment of only selected aspects of a firm's structure or management processes is likely to have significantly less effect on implementation; it is the con-

---

[1] Bala S. Chakravarthy and Peter Lorange "Managing Strategic Adaptation: Options in Administrative Systems Design," *Interfaces*, Vol. 14, No. 1 (1984).

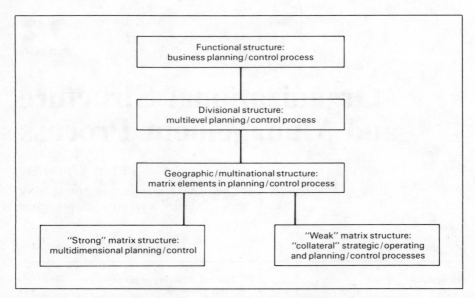

**FIG. 23-1   Archetypes of Structural Forms With Accompanying Management
Process Supports**

sistent consideration of both structure and process that will prove to be effective.

A key to assessing the appropriateness of a particular structure and its accompanying management processes is an understanding of the strategic pressures that a firm faces from its environment, both for pursuing new opportunities and for coordinating internal activities to compete efficiently in already existing businesses. Thus, this chapter begins with a brief discussion of how environmental pressures affect the structure and processes a firm adopts. It then moves on to discuss major, broad patterns in the evolution of organizational structures and their accompanying processes, with particular emphasis on seeing them as vehicles for an organization to achieve a better alignment between its environment and its internal capabilities.

The discussion in this chapter of alternative structures and processes focuses on five different archetypes: the functional form, accompanied by a business planning and control process; the divisionalized structure, with its multilevel planning process and decentralized control support; the geographic/ multinational organization, with its associated process backups; and two full-blown multidimensional structure/process alternatives, one that emphasizes the structural approach, and another that emphasizes process considerations (the so-called strategic/operating structure approach). These are illustrated in Figure 23-1.

To a large extent, each structural process builds on the former, and significant parts of one archetype can also be found in the next. That there are common elements among the archetypes underscores that, in real life, a continuity of hybrid options will evolve rather than the dichotomized archetypes presented. Typically, management will anticipate emerging environmental pressures, and it will respond by modifying the firm's management structure and processes. Structural modifications usually affect only certain parts of the organization at one time, not the entire corporation. Different aspects of the management processes also tend to be strengthened on an ongoing basis. More "clean sweep" realignments of structure and process at one discrete point in time are typically much more difficult; hence the emergence of hybrid structural/process patterns.

Since a company normally consists of a multitude of businesses, each facing different strategic realities and challenges, the effect of different structures and processes on particular business elements *within* the firm also needs to be addressed. For this reason, structures and processes must be designed to fit different strategic business settings within the firm, just as the firm's overall structure and processes must be tailored to its general environment.[2]

Throughout this chapter, an attempt has been made to emphasize up-to-date information that will be useful to the practitioner. This current information, however, builds on the long and rich traditions of research on the interrelationships between strategy and structure.

STRATEGY AS A DETERMINANT OF STRUCTURE AND PROCESS

This section focuses on the interrelationship between the strategic challenges, the resulting pressures an organization faces, and the organization's need to develop a formal structure and an associated management process to respond to these pressures.

A basic, overriding task of strategic management is to increase the value of the organization through the following steps:

- Attempt to identify a set of attractive business opportunities, judged in terms of the market.
- Attempt to develop organizational strengths that meet the requirements for success in the attractive business segments.
- Set aside resources today in order to be able to build the strengths required to carry out future strategies. This strategy-implementing activity takes place in tandem with the organization's ongoing efforts to keep the present pattern of business activities going.

Thus, there is a complex challenge for management that requires an understanding of a diversity of issues. For example: What makes some environments more attractive than others? What are the critical requirements for succeeding in each setting? How can a firm assess the appropriateness of the match

---

[2] Peter Lorange, *Corporate Planning: An Executive Viewpoint* (Englewood Cliffs, N.J.: Prentice-Hall Publishing Company, 1980).

between its position in the environment and its internal capabilities? As a firm strengthens this match by building new strategic capabilities, what resources is it applying?

A precondition for addressing questions relating to structure and process is an analysis of the environmental setting or settings at hand. Then, the firm can establish a view of the critical strategic pressures that it may be facing. In a competitive business setting, one way to succeed is by having a product that is sufficiently unique to allow a firm to charge a higher price than its competitors, and to enjoy thereby a higher margin of profit. Alternatively, the profit margin can be created by bringing the product to the market place at a lower cost than the competition. An organization's choice of business strategies, therefore, when it comes to decisions about products and costs, depends on two major considerations of the environment: (1) What opportunities does a particular business environment provide for the *adaptation* of a firm's product to the environment so as to emphasize the product's distinguishing features (e.g., novel design, unique quality, better service, a reliable source of availability), and to what extent can this environment create a basis for more or less continually modifying a product to keep ahead of a competitor's products? (2) What opportunities does a particular business environment provide for the *integration* of organizational activities so as to achieve comparative cost advantages, for example, through attempting to standardize in order to achieve so-called experience-curve effects in manufacturing, distribution, or marketing.

An organization must face up to a combination of pressures to adapt to its environment and to integrate its activities; the importance of each of these tasks will be dictated by the environmental setting at hand, will tend to differ from business to business and from company to company, and will probably change over time.

Of course, the complexity of the firm's environmental strategic exposure depends on several underlying factors, three of which are particularly important. First, the diversity of the firm is critical; e.g., how many businesses it is in, and how these businesses are related, and whether the firm can be managed so as to benefit from a common core of know-how. Second, the stability of each of the firm's particular businesses is likely to differ, for example, in terms of sales growth rates, evolution of the business, and the effect of environmental factors such as consumer shifts, technological change, or initiatives from government and other stakeholder interests. Third, the fierceness of the competitive climate that each business faces varies depending on the type of competition, the structure of the particular industry, and the competitive strengths enjoyed by the competing firm in a particular business.

The complexity of the firm's strategic response is, of course, derived to a large extent from environmental factors. The environment determines what it takes to compete successfully. Environmental pressures might lead to a variety of responses, depending on what level of the organizational hierarchy is affected: the business element level, the business family level, or the corporate/portfolio level.

At the business element strategy level, a firm's response to environmental pressures may be manifested in its decisions on whether to remain within the present product/market configuration or to extend into the new product or market applications. Conceivably, a business element strategy may also be simplified further by concentrating on an even narrower set of products or markets. At the business family level, the environment might lead a firm to emphasize coordination among business elements in the external competitive arenas, as well as to attempt to achieve competitive advantages from clearer internal coordination of research and development (R&D), manufacturing, sales, and so forth. At the corporate, or portfolio, strategy level, environmental pressures might affect the degree to which management chooses to pursue corporate-wide transfer of strategic resources (e.g., funds, key management talent, or technological know-how). Or, alternatively, management may rely on having the business families consider redeploying strategic resources among subsets of business elements within themselves. The latter method implies that a smaller fraction of resources might be reallocated with a corporate-wide focus in mind. The corporate portfolio strategy might be said to be more complex if the environmental circumstances call for a corporate-wide strategic resource allocation.

It should be noted in passing, however, that how effective an organization wants its strategy to be greatly affects its willingness to face up to environmental complexity. With a highly ambitious vision and performance challenges for itself, the organization can tolerate less evasion of environmental reality. Pressures to modify the organizational structure and processes thus might be expected to be felt earlier and stronger in such instances.

By choosing an appropriate organizational structure and management processes, an organization can develop a relevant strength posture for meeting environmental challenges. However, an organizational structure (i.e., the delineation of the patterns of formal tasks and authorities assigned to the members of an organization) cannot, of course, be changed too frequently. The costs associated with reorganizing should not be ignored. To reorganize represents a fairly drastic way of bringing the organization's capabilities in line with its environmental requirements; such discrete adjustments from one organizational setup to another can uproot working relationships and otherwise affect motivation. Reorganization may be disruptive, and it may be some time before the organization is back to working at full speed. These considerations should be kept in mind when considering the properties of the five major organizational forms that are discussed later in this chapter. A firm cannot easily switch back and forth between the archetypes.

The development of management processes can be seen as complementing choices about a firm's structure, in that they further delineate specific patterns of executive interaction and behavior, *within* the basic organizational framework chosen. Tailor-made management processes represent an overlay on the formal structure; that is, they are a more incremental, flexible mode of adjusting a firm's ability to integrate its activities and otherwise adapt to its environment. As long as the organization's structure is designed to meet the strategic pressures it faces in the first place, the management processes can help extend the firm's ability to adapt to those pressures. Management processes can thus be seen as complementary, more dynamic fine-tuning on top of structure. It should be stressed that even though an organization may have matched its adaptive and integrative capabilities to the strategic challenges at hand, such a fit does not tend to be a stable one. Environments tend to change more or less

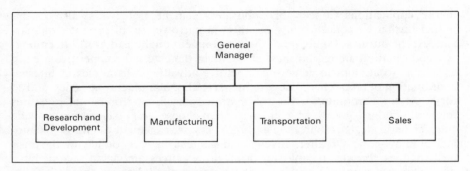

FIG. 23-2 Functional Organizational Structure

continuously, revealing new opportunities as well as emerging threats, and putting pressure on management to develop and modify continually the firm's ability to respond to such environmental challenges.

An important implication is that an organization must continually channel resources into building future positions of strategic strength, at the expense of its immediate performance. An accurate assessment of the environment is thus essential for determining the trade-off between building for the future and attempting to achieve immediate short-term results. An appropriate structure and process for a given setting is critical for making such decisions. It is a major challenge to management, functioning through a particular structure and its associated management processes, to allow for a realistic commitment of resources to strategic change, by channeling appropriate resources into building new strengths, that is, by "protecting" them from all being used to meet today's short-term performance pressures.

THE FUNCTIONALLY ORGANIZED FIRM

Figure 23-2 provides an example of a functional organizational structure. This type of structure is used when the various tasks engaged in by the business have been specialized as much as possible. Each major function is assigned to a particular department in order to take advantage of employee experience and the benefits of scale that result from the specialized activities that might be carried out within each of these departments. Duplication of effort is kept to a minimum.

This form of organization has major benefits as well as limitations, all of which are well known. It is used primarily by corporations with uncomplicated strategic settings, primarily ones that focus on one business or on a few highly interrelated ones. The general manager in such a firm must be closely associated with the business, because he or she must provide the generalist's "glue" to pull the specialist functions together into a cohesive business. The major strength of this form, above all, is that it offers strong integrative capabilities; it provides a basis for carrying out each function in a cost-efficient manner, for

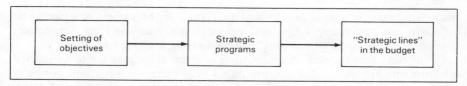

FIG. 23-3 Direction-Setting Steps in a Business Planning Process

building a specialized organization that can benefit from the accumulation of focused efforts, and for investing in specialized equipment. Its major limitation is that it provides a relatively poor vehicle for adapting quickly to new opportunities and threats from the environment. Because each functional unit in the organization has a specialized and narrow purpose, a relatively inflexible pattern is created. Thus, for this setup to be an appropriate structural choice for a firm, there must be some degree of stability in the business's environment. Rapidly changing external circumstances would easily defeat the very purpose of this form, which is to provide a stable, efficient organization by pursuing the benefits of integration.

The functional structure is suited to a firm that finds itself in a relatively narrow span of business. Such a business may frequently be well established and relatively mature, in which case its environment is likely to be relatively secure. The strategic success of such a firm typically hinges on its ability to achieve lower costs than its competition. The functional organization lends itself to such a requirement, because it represents a structural vehicle that is well suited to pursuing integrative, efficiency-oriented strategies. The functional structure may also be well suited to the smaller, rapidly growing firm in which the lack of size justifies choosing this relatively "inexpensive" structure and in which the pressure to maintain profit margins sufficient for the firm to survive calls for integrative discipline.

The strategic management process in this type of organization needs to strengthen further the integrative focus of the business. This can be achieved by continuing to improve the coordination of internal activities as well as by developing related products or markets. A formal planning process might be established to facilitate this. The process would help management reassess the strategic direction of the business, delineate strategic programs for implementing the business strategy, and reserve room in the budget for the tasks required to carry out the strategic programs. Figure 23-3 outlines key steps in such a business planning process.

The process of setting objectives consists of reassessing the basic strategic direction of the business by considering changes in the environment and by articulating the internal requirements for pursuing new business opportunities vigorously. Several useful analytical models have been suggested for carrying out this step, most of which are extensions of the original Boston Consulting Group's business growth/market share grid concept.[3] The delineation of

---

[3] See, e.g., Charles Hofer and Dan Schendel, *Strategy Formulation: Analytical Concepts* (St. Paul, Minn.: West Publishing Company, 1978).

underlying assumptions or factors that are critical to the success of a particular objective is a particularly important aspect of this planning step. Subsequent changes in these assumptions may lead to a revision of the objective.[4]

The next step focuses on articulating *how* the objectives are to be carried out through appropriate strategic programs. Many strategic programs normally call for a cross-functional team effort. For example, the development of a new product might require close cooperation between R&D, manufacturing, and marketing. Similarly, a strategic program for improving the efficiency of the production process might require the combined involvement of R&D and manufacturing. Thus, although each functional department is engaged in specialized cost-efficient operating activities, each will need to carry out additional roles if the firm is to implement the overall strategic program successfully.

The link between the strategic programming step and the budgeting step of the planning process thus becomes critical. Each functional department's role in carrying out the overall strategic program should be clear, and each department should receive sufficient resources earmarked for realistically carrying out its share of these tasks.

Figure 23-4 provides a formalized picture of how strategic programs link up with the budgeting process. For each strategic program, the tasks that must be performed by each functional department and the required resources are described. The overall resource requirements for each strategic program are provided in the right-hand column of the figure. The total set of derived strategic implementation roles that each functional department is requested to carry out, and the associated resources that each function would need for this, can be seen in the bottom line of Figure 23-4. The budget for each functional department should have specific lines that articulate these resource needs.

The setting of strategic direction within a business can be aided by making use of a business planning process in a functionally organized company. Such a process should delineate business objectives and identify strategic programs that enable the firm to remain competitive. Process improvement, renewal of products or markets, or a move into new businesses less directly related to the core business might be the result. Also, each functional department's part in the team effort to carry out a strategic program, as well as the resources needed to carry out the required activities, must be spelled out carefully. And, finally, functional departments should be given the resources necessary to carry out their derived strategic roles (as illustrated in the bottom line of Figure 23-4).

There must be a trade-off if a firm is to meet both strategic and operating pressures; sufficient resources must be provided for strategic purposes, and each functional department should get adequate resources in order to be able to carry out its strategic roles. These resources should not be made available to meet operating crises and day-to-day demands.

To recapitulate, a corporation engaged in a limited number of highly interrelated businesses adapts to its environment by choosing an appropriate organizational structure. Normally, the functional form is selected so that the corporation can develop a focus for pursuing an efficient way of competing.

---

[4] For a discussion of critical assumptions, see Richard Mason and Ian Mitroff, *Challenging Strategic Planning Assumptions* (New York: John Wiley & Sons, 1981).

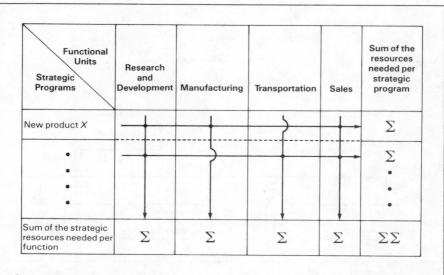

Source: Richard F. Vancil, "Better Management of Corporate Development," *Harvard Business Review* (Sept.-Oct. 1972), p. 59

FIG. 23-4   Delineation of Strategic Program Tasks to be Carried Out by Functional Department, and the Implied Resource Requirements

Management processes are also needed so that objectives can be modified and the necessary strategic programs can be delineated and executed. By choosing a proper combination of structure and process, an organization should be better able to cope strategically and prepare for its future.

THE DIVISIONALLY ORGANIZED FIRM

Many organizations find themselves at one time or another in situations where they face a highly heterogeneous environment. This often stems from attempts by the firm to diversify as it grows; it may also result from changes in the environment that present the firm with emerging opportunities to engage in several businesses rather than in one. The consequence of increased environmental complexity is an increased need for adaptation.

In a divisionalized structure, a firm attempts to adapt to its environment by developing relatively self-contained organizational entities around each of its businesses. Thus, although the chief executive of the functional organization is the only general manager in the firm, responsible for coordinating the various functional activities into an overall, consistent business strategy, in a divisionally organized firm there are several general managers, and of two different types. The chief executive is faced with managing the portfolio of businesses, and the division managers are charged with managing their own businesses.

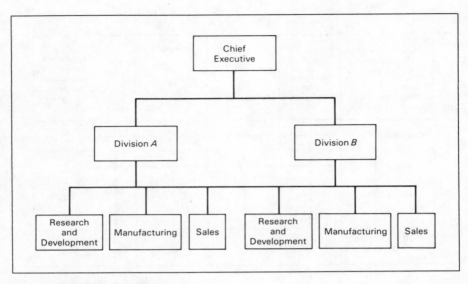

FIG. 23-5 Divisionalized Structure

The chief executive faces the task of achieving a balance among the firm's various businesses. He or she must focus on the generation and use of strategic resources—most notably, funds and human resources—and decide which of the firm's businesses should generate net funds and to which businesses these funds should go. He or she will also have to balance the firm's know-how base, as embodied in its management, which requires careful judgment in the development, evaluation, and assignment of key executives. And, he or she must also attempt to achieve an overall portfolio balance in the risk exposures—economic as well as political—that the different businesses face in their environments.

The second type of general manager is in charge of a self-contained business entity; these managers are frequently called division heads. They face tasks similar to those faced by the CEO of a functional organization; that is, they coordinate the division's functional activities into a particular business strategy. Thus, within each of the divisions, the focus continues to be one of specialization, as is the case with the functional organization.

A divisionalized structure (Figure 23-5) provides a firm with the ability to adapt to its environment at two different levels: At the business level, it allows the firm to address specific opportunities and requirements for each business, and at the corporate portfolio level, it helps the firm achieve a more explicit way of balancing its overall resource commitments and risk taking. A divisionalized structure may also be able to counteract the potentially negative effects of large, bureaucratic, and unfocused functional organizational entities that might otherwise develop when the firm grows.

The major potential drawbacks of this form, however, might include lost opportunities, or a weakening of the firm's cost position owing to duplication of effort caused by having several parallel organizational entities pursuing similar functional tasks. Within each division, too, there might be the familiar problems involved in adapting to environmental changes, as with a functional structure. To change drastically the balance between existing divisions may also be difficult; each division might have developed a vested interest in pursuing its business, and there might be resistance to redrawing the borders between the business charters of the divisions. Changing significantly the portfolio of businesses would make adaptation at the corporate level all the more difficult.

The management processes that reinforce the structure of a divisionally organized corporation must also support different business strategies as well as an overall corporate-wide portfolio strategy.

There is a need to articulate a business strategy for each of the businesses by delineating a business objective, strategic programs, and ways to implement the budget. The processes also need to help managers address the trade-off between using resources for the future repositioning and self-renewal of the business, and using them to meet operating pressures and achieve shorter-term, bottom-line results. Each business or division, then, requires management processes similar to those found in a functionally organized business.

There is an additional need, however, for a corporate-wide assessment of strategic resources to determine how much the corporation as a whole can afford to allocate for future growth, and where these strategic resources should be allocated among all of the firm's existing and potential businesses. The planning process should thus be extended to provide a corporate-wide, portfolio view in order to come up with a balanced set of business objectives. This should lead to a prudent overall balance among factors such as the generation of funds and their use, human resources and know-how, and exposure to economic or political risk. Objectives for all the businesses in the firm should be reconciled in terms of how they fit into the overall corporate-wide, portfolio point of view, and all strategic programs should compete for strategic resources.

To accomplish this sort of interaction, a divisionally organized firm must establish a top-down/bottom-up dialogue between the corporate level and each of the businesses within the corporation. The top-down signals should be based on a broad perception of the environment and should emphasize the firm's overall "architecture," the "fit" of each business within this overall portfolio, and the broad feasibility constraints on the corporate-wide allocation of strategic resources. The aim is to enhance the development of the overall portfolio. The bottom-up signals should describe the nature of the various business environments and identify opportunities for employing a particular business's strengths. Further, they should articulate realistic strategic programs, and include requests for the necessary strategic resources. These top-down and bottom-up interchanges are interrelated, contingent on each other, and mutually reinforcing. They require a process that is based on close cooperation and interaction.

Figure 23-6 illustrates an interactive top-down/bottom-up planning process that attempts both to develop business plans for each business and to reconcile these in a corporate-wide portfolio. The steps of this multilevel process are directly analogous to the business planning process delineated in Figure 23-3. And, the four cells at the bottom-right of Figure 23-6, encircled by a double

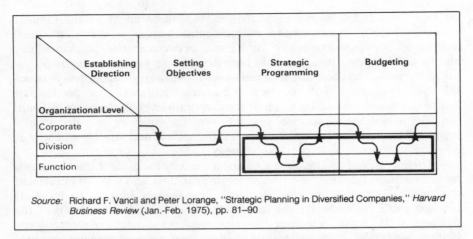

Source: Richard F. Vancil and Peter Lorange, "Strategic Planning in Diversified Companies," *Harvard Business Review* (Jan.-Feb. 1975), pp. 81–90

FIG. 23-6   An Interactive Process to Develop Both a Corporate-Wide Plan and a Business Plan

line, represent the linking of strategic tasks to the various operating functions, as delineated in Figure 23-4.

A divisionalized organization, then, is in a strong position to adapt to its environment. Beyond the advantages stemming from its organizational structure, which pushes authority closer to each business area, it benefits from an accompanying elaboration of the strategic processes that attempts to have an impact on the allocation of strategic resources at several levels. This helps each business adapt to its situation, and it helps the corporation as a whole to balance its efforts to enter promising areas and to disengage from others. The strategic process facilitates the vigorous pursuit of business strategies among the firm's many businesses, and it also helps the corporation to pursue selected opportunities on a larger scale by channeling strategic resources into a few emerging business opportunities in a more proactive manner than otherwise might have been possible.

THE GEOGRAPHIC STRUCTURE

As a consequence of their success over time, many corporations end up with manufacturing facilities and markets scattered over large geographic areas. In discussing their structure and processes in this section, multinational corporations are used as an example, although the following considerations could apply to any geographically diverse corporation.

One type of multinational firm is a worldwide, product-organized corporation.[5] It might manufacture cars, farm equipment, chemicals, or pharmaceuti-

---

[5] Peter Lorange, "A Framework for Strategic Planning in Multinational Corporations," *Journal of Long Range Planning* (June 1976).

ORGANIZATION STRUCTURE AND PROCESS

cals; characteristically, its manufacturing lines or products require heavy R&D or massive investment in manufacturing in order to turn out products at a reasonable cost. Such product types tend to be marketed worldwide, and they tend to be of uniform design and quality. This type of firm can be contrasted with a multinational that produces consumer-oriented products, such as foods, spirits, toiletries, or clothing. Here, a primary challenge is to adapt the products to the particular circumstances of each country. Standardizing the products on a worldwide basis would defy local preferences and requirements. This type of firm might be called a geographically organized corporation.

The worldwide, product-organized corporation has strong needs for cost-efficient development, manufacturing, and distribution of its products. Hence, it would typically adopt a divisional structure as its organizational form, based on its products. This type of firm, of course, must also adapt to local circumstances, perhaps by further fine-tuning its marketing and by modifying its products, even though such concerns might not tend to be equally important. Local country organizations typically are in place to take care of sales and distribution for each worldwide division.

Such a company might thus find itself with parallel sales/distribution organizations operating in a given country. At times, it might find it useful to consolidate some of these activities, so as to strengthen its position. This consolidation may take the relatively weak forms of shared office and support functions or of efforts to coordinate actions among governmental agencies and other external stakeholder groups, or it may appear as stronger forms of coordination such as joint marketing, distribution, and sales. The emergence of a second organizational dimension can be seen here: the seeds of a matrix structure. Although the worldwide, product-organized dimension is clearly the dominant one, a complementary geographic-area dimension might be "grown."

As with a normal divisional structure, a key task for the worldwide, business-divisionalized firm is to balance the portfolio of global businesses. Such a global portfolio strategy must take into account funds-flow characteristics as well as economic and political risk considerations stemming from its combinations of worldwide business activities. Assessing economic and political risk may be particularly difficult, in that each worldwide business strategy will be exposed to different risks in different countries. Consequently, although the basic characteristics of the management process will be similar to those of an ordinary divisionalized corporation—that is, multilevel, with both business and portfolio dimensions—additional planning and control processes might also be established for each country in order to coordinate the various business strategies as they come to apply to particular countries.

The other type of multinational corporation, organized by geographic area, should have separate organizations in each country so it can adapt to local circumstances. Each country organization may, in fact, have its own divisions, and business strategies are built up around local markets. The firm's corporate portfolio is determined largely by achieving a balance among its country divisions. Such an organization must focus on each local market and attempt to reach a balance among country exposures. For this, a country-based divisionalized structure is appropriate.

Here, there might also be opportunities for country organizations to coordinate aspects of their business operations, such as, for example, new business developments, approaches to manufacturing, or the sharing of process innovations. Thus, there might also be a need for worldwide coordination across particular products or processes.

The strengthening of the management processes should reflect this multidimensional challenge. To complement the hierarchical divisionalized process approach developed around the country division structure, a dual planning and control process might also be developed to strengthen the firm's ability to coordinate its production of global goods and to adapt its processes.

THE MATRIX STRUCTURE

From the discussions of both the worldwide divisionalized structure and the geographic-area structure for multinational corporations, a so-called matrix organization can be suggested, one in which both a product *and* an area dimension can be more fully integrated into the organization's structure and processes, allowing considerations of adaptation *and* integration surrounding *both* dimensions to be dealt with more fully.

As discussed above, one potential drawback with a divisionalized structure is the cost associated with the duplication of efforts among several organizational subunits within the firm, leading possibly to a loss of competitive edge. At least to some extent, the improvements in a firm's ability to adapt to changing circumstances provided by a division structure come as a trade-off against a lowering of the ability to achieve cost-efficient integration. The so-called matrix structure, illustrated in Figure 23-7, attempts in part to ameliorate this by emphasizing how to achieve both adaptive and integrative capabilities in a cost-beneficial manner by borrowing features from both the divisional and functional structures.

In a company with a matrix structure, each business is run by a business manager responsible for the general management task of setting and implementing the business's direction. The business manager's role in this respect is similar to that of a typical division manager; the business manager will not have full autonomy over a set of functional departments. Instead of reporting directly and exclusively to the business manager, several businesses will be served by a shared set of functional resources. Thus, by consolidating the functional activities of divisions, the firm might gain in integrative capabilities and keep down the costs resulting from duplication of efforts. By maintaining the general management focus on each business as well, however, the firm might still preserve the ability to adapt effectively.

The general management role of the chief executive officer in a matrix structure is concerned with the overall balance of the corporation, which is affected by the firm's resource-flow patterns and risk implications stemming from its particular mix of businesses. The chief executive officer is in charge of adapting the firm to new environmental circumstances by modifying the overall portfolio. In addition, he or she takes on two added roles: making sure that the

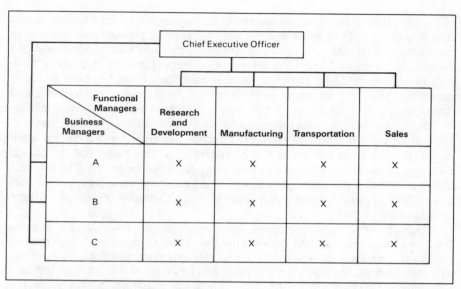

FIG. 23-7 Matrix Organization Structure

company's functional activities are coordinated so that the cost advantages of integrating the firm's activities can be achieved; and monitoring the significant differences of opinion that can arise between functional managers and business managers regarding whether to emphasize integration or adaptation. Potential conflicts between the two dimensions should, of course, be addressed early on.

This particular structural form, with its greater balance between the pressures of adaptation and integration at both the business level and the portfolio level, nonetheless does come with specific costs attached. Above all, these stem from the inevitable additional costs of communication, interaction, and fatigue from friction and ambiguity associated with the approach. The intricate pattern of structural interrelationships in the matrix structure also might create a de facto inertia against major shifts in strategic direction, and thus make it difficult to achieve adaptation in practice.

For a business manager in an organization with this structure, there will be heavy emphasis on negotiating with functional managers to persuade them to carry out the various tasks necessary to run each business. This might be achieved through extensive formal and informal meetings or one-to-one encounters. At times, it may be necessary to institute additional planning or control processes in order to achieve better coordination. Committees composed of business and functional representatives might be involved in this effort. Such processes help to delineate tasks in more detail, that is, who is to interact with whom, about what, and when. It should be stressed again that structural features alone do not automatically ensure appropriate strategic focus; an organization's structure needs to be complemented by appropriate management processes if it is to integrate its activities and adapt to changing circumstances successfully.

The nature of the planning process in an organization with a formal matrix structure (Figure 23-7) must address the challenge of providing the firm with the ability to deal with a hierarchy of strategies, much like the process used in a divisionally organized firm to develop both a corporate-wide plan and a business plan (Figure 23-6). However, in this case, instead of business divisions interacting with the corporate level, there will be a balance of business and functional elements providing the bottom-up inputs. All of the business managers should be deeply involved in the setting of objectives, so that they can attempt to set a meaningful strategic direction for their businesses. Environmental conditions in particular will be addressed at this stage, and the critical assumptions underlying the business strategy must be reassessed. The business managers should, however, consult with the functional managers so that they can realistically assess the organization's ability to actually implement particular strategies.

During the strategic programming stage, the business manager and the functional managers should decide how the different functional departments will coordinate their activities to carry out strategic programs for each business. The managers should interact extensively and come up with several preliminary solutions. The challenge facing each functional manager in this respect is attempting to accommodate the strategic programming tasks from each business in such a way that the function's task still can be carried out with a reasonable degree of efficiency.

During the budgeting stage, this two-dimensional dialogue will continue; however, the functional departments will be even more centrally involved now, because they outline the detailed activity patterns for next year. The relative shift in involvement from the business to the functional dimension as the planning process moves along, in terms of having the initiative in delineating the bottom-up planning inputs as a basis for the interaction with the corporate portfolio level, is illustrated in Figure 23-8.

Although the matrix structure is conceptually very intriguing, there are several potential problems associated with making a planning process work within this complex kind of organizational structure. First, the costs of interaction may be considerable, both because of the time involved and because of the potential for disruptive conflicts. Managers may be forced to take extreme views, associating themselves with the one dimension they represent, when good strategies should be based on an eclectic synthesis. The process of reaching broad commitment to a strategy throughout the organization might easily get bogged down. Thus, by institutionalizing the functional and divisional dimensions, as is the case in a matrix structure, managers might, through their vested interests, limit the firm's ability to adopt to complex strategic changes.

THE "WEAK" MATRIX CONCEPT

An approach closely related to the matrix structure, but still a distinct design in its own right, is the "weak" matrix concept. This is based on the so-called dual

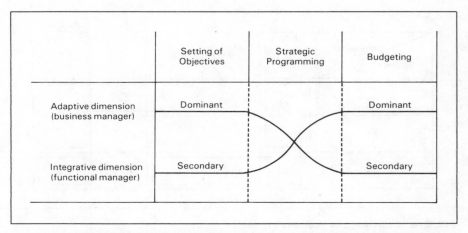

FIG. 23-8   Shifts Between the Business Manager's and Functional Manager's Relative Involvement in Providing Bottom-Up Inputs of the Planning Process

strategic/operating structure. Like the matrix structure, this approach is appropriate for corporations that face both strong adaptive and integrative pressures. The matrix form might be an appropriate *structural* response for an organization to meet such strategic needs, but there are also strategic *process* options available that might strongly complement the matrix structure. Therefore, the weak matrix concept places less emphasis on the matrix *structures,* and more emphasis on developing matrix interrelationships through *processes,* by emphasizing how the same managers within the organization might wear two hats; that is, they develop strategies as members of business teams, which then provide the direction for them in their operating dimension roles.[6]

The emergence of strategic business units (SBUs) signifies the rapidly gaining prominence of this approach. SBUs, or business elements, as they are referred to here, are the basic units of analysis a firm uses to create adaptive strategies to meet challenges from the environment. These units of analysis around which adaptive strategies are delineated are identified *without* taking the organization's formal organizational structure as the point of departure. They should be expected to change, since environmental conditions frequently change, although changes in such units of analysis may not necessarily have an impact on the formal organizational structure.

It is useful to think about business elements as specific products or services that go to particular markets. The first task in testing this initial definition of a business element is to see whether the product or service can be meaningfully described, including the identification of who the customers are. If so, a preliminary grid pattern of product/market cells should be obtainable, as shown in Figure 23-9. Other issues can then be raised in order to further fine-tune the business element definition. For example, one can seek to establish the

---

[6] Peter Lorange, "Implementing Strategic Planning at Two Philippine Companies," *The Wharton Annual*, Vol. 8 (1984).

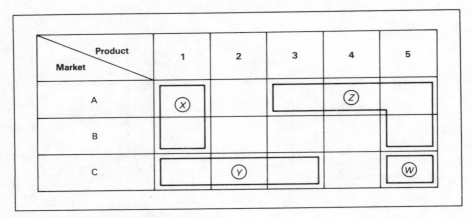

FIG. 23-9 Delineation of Business Elements

rate of growth as well as the overall market potential for each particular product/market setting. And, one can specify who the firm's competitors are and what the firm's own competitive advantages are in comparison. A related issue is to explore whether there might be alternative ways for customers to satisfy their demand, that is, whether there are available substitutes. If these questions can be answered in a reasonably ambiguous way, a firm can determine whether each product/market cell is internally homogeneous, that is, whether it represents a distinctive strategic setting with its own business attractiveness and unambiguous competitive strength position. If these questions cannot be answered clearly, the initial, or "trial," product/market delineation may have been drawn too broadly, thereby creating a mix of rather unfocused business elements.

It may be impractical, however, for a firm to pursue entirely homogeneous business elements, because it may end up with too many planning units. It may be necessary, therefore, to carefully recombine units that, in fact, represent more or less similar competitive settings. As long as business attractiveness and competitive strength can be assessed in a relatively unambiguous way, the basic uniqueness of each strategic setting can be maintained, while cutting down on the degree of fragmentation. Figure 23-9 shows four such combinations of basic cells, or business elements.

It is important to recognize, of course, that imagination, intuition, and common sense have to play key roles when delineating business elements. A reasonable trade-off is necessary: On the one hand, the business elements should not be so small and so numerous that they are entirely impractical to work with; on the other hand, overly large, excessively heterogeneous entities should not be created either. Business elements sometimes turn out to be very asymmetric in their patterns, as can be seen in Figure 23-9. The major criterion should remain valid, however; namely, that a minimum of internal homogeneity must be maintained for each business element.

The term "strategic business unit" has become very popular for referring to business elements. Unfortunately, there is confusion over the meaning of this term, because some companies use it to represent a cluster of several closely related business elements that need to be considered together strategically for synergy reasons. This was, indeed, the original meaning of SBU at General Electric Company, where the term seems to have been coined. The term refers to two different types of entities for strategic analysis; one emphasizes the pursuance of an adaptive, competitive business strategy for a particular product/market segment, and another emphasizes how to achieve a coordinated strategy for a set of closely related product/market strategies, based on pursuing synergies. In this chapter, the terms "business element" and "business family," respectively, are used to differentiate between the two types of entities. Thus, the ambiguous term SBU, which does not make this distinction, can be avoided.

A business family thus consists of a set of closely interrelated business elements, identified in terms of the following two classes of synergies:

- *Market-derived synergies:* Two or more business elements serving the same or closely overlapping customers, or competing against the same or closely overlapping competitors, may find that their product lines or service offerings complement each other, particularly if conscientious efforts are made to achieve this through coordination of the business element strategies.

- *Internal synergies:* Two business elements may be integrated vertically, which might make it difficult to assess the competitive advantage of one in isolation from the other. Also, there may be technologically determined interrelationships, the use of a common sales force, or joint production. Business element strategies may be modified to make such integrative efforts more feasible.

Although business element strategies may be changed considerably in response to environmental circumstances, the business family level can be expected to be more stable, because there will be an "averaging" effect among the family's various business elements. There might be a considerable degree of strategic self-renewal within a business family, however, in that resources might get shifted from more mature business elements to new, high-potential business elements within the business family. Since the formal operating structure of the organization coincides (to a considerable extent, if not completely) with that of the business family, it might be relatively stable—which is important for organizational commitment—while still allowing the firm to adapt realistically at the business element level in response to environmental and competitive realities. Thus, executives can feel relatively confident that they will be transferred to new, high-growth business elements within the family after they have managed a more mature business element to the end of its life cycle. Without such a sense of security, management teams may be hesitant to manage mature businesses out of fear of self-liquidation.

This concept of delineating business elements and business families can be applied to a corporation organized along divisional lines, such as the one portrayed in Figure 23-5. For example, assume that the management of such a company has analyzed its product/market involvements and identified a dozen or so business elements. Furthermore, these business elements fall into a few clusters, or business families, owing to their interrelatedness. The four business elements indicated by X, Y, Z, and W in Figure 23-9 form one such business family (which coincides with Division A in Figure 23-5). Top management may wish to appoint a business element planning team for each of the four business elements. The chairperson of each team should be a senior manager, for example, a key functional manager. The members should be the best talents available, forming a representative cross-section of the firm's functions, but they may also come from central or division staffs.

A team of managers should also be established to cope with the business family level. The chairperson of this team should be the division manager, and the members should include the chairperson of each business element team. A few key staff executives, and possibly a few managers from other parts of the corporation, might be added to the team to make sure its views are sufficiently broad and eclectic.

Each business element team should prepare objectives and strategic programs for its respective business element. The team's output at each stage becomes the bottom-up ingredient of an interactive and iterative process, first with the business family team and then with the corporate level (similar to the one portrayed in Figure 23-6).

The bottom-up/top-down dialogue in the planning process regarding portfolio balance and overall resource allocation is thus carried out between the business families and the corporate portfolio level. This two-level portfolio approach may be seen as suboptimal, in that each family is allowed to delineate its "mini-portfolio" to take care of its self-renewal, and managers at the corporation level are left with developing a "portfolio of family residuals." However, the positive behavioral effects and political acceptance accompanying this approach might more than counterbalance the potential problems with resource allocation.

The strategic direction established for each business element and each business family by each team then becomes the basis for guiding the operating departments in carrying out their part in the implementation of the firm's strategies. Through a process analogous to the one portrayed in Figure 23-4, each operating department is given its assignments as part of the team for implementing the derived strategic program, as well as the necessary strategic resources, articulated through their strategic budget lines, to carry out their strategic tasks.

There are several important implications that should be pointed out about these emerging strategic and operating structures, which are illustrated in Figure 23-10. First, the strategic "structure" is not a structure in the sense that the term has been used previously in this chapter. Rather, it is an analytical dimension that the organization chooses to make use of when delineating its strategic direction. Thus, the same people wear two hats. One role is that of an employee performing a specific job assignment in the formal organizational structure; the other is that as a member of a business element team or business family team analyzing and determining strategic direction.

Second, this approach enhances the organization's integrative and adaptive capabilities. The operating organizational structure can be delineated in such a way that it lends itself to at least some degree of specialization, and it may remain relatively stable over time, so long as pressures to adapt do not

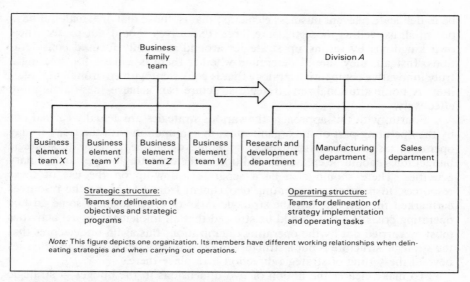

FIG. 23-10 Strategic and Operating Structures

have to be responded to by reorganizing the firm's structure. Thus, there should be organizational stability and efficiency; that is, the firm should be able to pursue experience-curve effects and take advantages of economies of scale.

The firm's adaptive capabilities, on the other hand, are provided for through the strategic structure, which can, and should, change frequently, in response to changes in the environment. Thus, adaptive strategies can be developed more freely on the basis of a realistic consideration of the environment, without being overly hampered by institutional considerations and vested interests. The strategic structure is, thus, intentionally unstable, while the operating structure is intentionally stable.

Third, this combination of strategic and operating structures also enhances the organization's ability to adapt by intentionally focusing on promising new opportunities early, and in a systematic manner. Business element teams delineate strategies that allow them to answer the following type of questions affirmatively: Does a business element seem to possess sufficient future potential? And, does the delineation of the business element seem right as the basis for identifying creative, imaginative competitive strategies; that is, can a good manager associate himself or herself with it? When answering these two questions, it is important to recognize that it is the potential rather than the actual size, that is important. All business elements, large or small, require management attention; unfortunately, management often ends up paying relatively too little attention to the small, emerging, and truly promising businesses, while too much emphasis goes to the larger, well-established ones.

Classic structural approaches might thus lead to a deemphasis on new business development and a perpetuation of the firm's present business involvements. One of the main purposes of a strategic structure, therefore, must be to delineate relevant business elements; that is, those that are small but have potential, as well as those that are large. Executives should not protect their own kingdoms by setting up strategies around internally focused considerations. Instead, they should determine whether there is a basis for creating a truly innovative competitive strategy that is consistent with environmental realities. A noninstitutionalized strategic structure can achieve these aims more effectively.

Fourth, with this approach, the various strategies are actually carried out by the operating part of the organization, in conjunction with their day-to-day operating tasks. Thus, within each operating department, separate strategic budget lines should be created in addition to the operating budget for ordinary activities. There should also be a separate follow-up on the use of these resources, to prevent an operating department from borrowing the resources earmarked for carrying out the strategic tasks in order to meet some ad hoc operating crisis. And, it should be stressed that all implementational activities must be carried out by the operating organization; this again underscores that the strategic structure is not a structure in the ordinary sense, since no activities beyond the setting of strategic direction take place there.

To make clearer the notion of two dimensions in the budget—a strategic one as well as an operating one—it is useful to describe in some detail how each type might be defined. Failure to define clearly what constitutes strategic resources as opposed to operating resources may actually hamper the realistic implementation of strategy. The organization should appreciate that strategic resources are not "gifts" on top of the ordinary budget. When the dual strategic/operating budget concept is implemented, each unit in the organization develops a lean operating budget with no fat or frills, and then adds back the resources necessary to execute the strategic tasks. Without a clear definition of what is "strategic" and what is "operational," activities may be classified incorrectly. Units may be less than stringent in classifying activities, and they may feel tempted to move some operating activities into the strategic pool in order to relieve bottom-line pressure.

Strategic resources should be aimed at changing the direction of a particular business; that is, they should be used to carry out a change in business strategy. It follows that strategic resources are discretionary when seen in the context of current operations. In contrast, operating resources should be consistent with the expected operating activity level for a unit in the organization; they must take into account incremental changes from last year that affect this year's activity level target. Operational resources are used to achieve the best possible year-ahead results.

In practice, it is necessary to realize that strategic resources will normally be scarce, and that careful choices should be made to select priorities among a small set of strategic program activities. This focus on a few truly significant strategic activities may also make it easier for the organization to come address the difference between a strategic budget and an operating budget, and to manage the two types of activities together on a day-to-day basis within the various units in the organization.

Strategic resources can be classified into several types. The most important are the human resources needed to carry out strategic activities. People's skills can be difficult to assess, but it is essential that the best-suited people are assigned to the key tasks. This central aspect of resource allocation, unfortunately, is often not well handled in management processes. One way to help keep track of the allocation of human resources is to institute some broad accounting for the time-spending patterns of the most talented managers. Too often, it tends to be exactly these people who are drawn away from strategy implementation by various ad hoc "fire fighting" tasks.

Another class of strategic resources is discretionary finances allocated to enhance a given strategy. These may include investments in assets, such as plants or equipment; expenditures associated with R&D, such as product testing and introduction, market research, and process modification; and specific investments in working capital requirements stemming from inventory changes, changes in credit volume, or term changes. Such shifts in expenditures should be considered strategic resources when they are part of a specific effort to change strategic direction.

Even though all strategic resources can be classified into one of the above categories, it does not follow that all of these types of expenditures or investments are always strategic. For instance, expenditures for R&D may be incurred as a normal part of keeping an ongoing business moving. Similarly, investments may have to be made to modernize or to respond to ordinary increases in demand; such spending reflects business as usual, and not a change in strategy. This argument highlights the important point that when there is no clear and explicit distinction between strategic and operating resources, the bulk of a firm's investments may be nonstrategic; that is, they are plowed back into existing strategies in order to perpetuate them further. As a result, the existing businesses may become too capital-intensive because of over-investment, and they may gobble up such a large part of the firm's funds that too little is left for strategic self-renewal.

If an organization hopes to run smoothly and to get its members to accept the dual strategic/operating structure concept—in which everyone must wear two hats—the company will have to face the challenges of added job ambiguity. This calls for executives who appreciate that they have responsibility that is broader than their formal authority; they must have a broad attitude, and they must be skilled in resolving conflicts and adept at interpersonal relationships. It will be easier to get people to accept this setup if the strategic and operating structures are somewhat similar, so that the two structures can become associated as a common organizational identity. For example, the strategic and operating structures might come together at the division level/business family level, as shown in the Figure 23-10. In fact, the strategic structure and the operating structure almost always come together at the business family level, and these business families normally coincide with the division level of the operating organization.

A final management process for monitoring progress in strategy implementation is strategic control. This process is particularly important in strengthening an organization's ability to adapt. It helps a firm modify and improve strategies in between planning periods, as critical underlying assumptions change. For a corporation that must be able to adapt quickly and extensively to new circumstances (e.g., a firm active in new, rapidly changing busi-

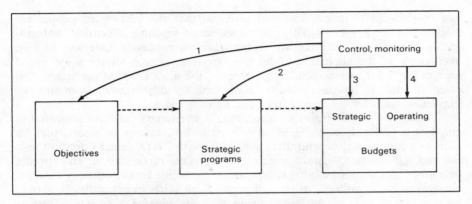

FIG. 23-11 The Control Process: Operating and Strategic

nesses), the elaboration of a strategic control process to complement the management structure and the strategic processes discussed so far becomes a necessity.

Figure 23-11 suggests an overall, simplified picture of the strategic control process and how it interlinks with the setting of strategic direction (see Figure 23-3). It also indicates that the control process monitors both operating performance and strategic progress.

The strategic control processes shown in Figure 23-11 assess how well the critical assumptions underlying an objective are actually holding up (1). Changes in the assumptions may force the firm to revise that stated objective. The strategic control process should also include explicit follow-up on the progress of strategic programs (2), including an evaluation of the critical assumptions underlying the strategic programs. Also, the control process should exercise budgetary control over both the strategic budget (3) and the operating budget (4). The four dimensions of strategic control are indicated by the four solid arrows in Figure 23-11.

A key issue in strategic control, as it now has been more broadly defined, is that it must enable a firm to reconcile the trade-off between near-term and long-term performance in a more explicit manner. Thus, the control process should be able to monitor progress both in terms of an organization's ability to adapt (its effectiveness) and to integrate its activities (its efficiency). All the elements of performance measurement are interrelated, although they must be seen in context to give a meaningful picture of how an organization is progressing.

An organization's strategic focus, then, is greatly affected by its structure and accompanying management processes, whether it has a functional structure, a divisional structure, a geographic structure, or a weak or strong matrix structure. In many cases, a firm's structure is more important in simpler, more stable strategic settings, while the emphasis on processes increases when the firm faces more complex strategic settings. It would be futile to argue, however, whether a firm's structure or processes are most important, because they complement and reinforce each other. The challenge for an organization is, thus, to find a proper balance between structure and process and to achieve an overall consistency reflecting the strategic setting at hand.

INTERNAL TAILORING OF STRATEGIC PROCESSES AND STRUCTURE

Thus far, the discussion of organizational structures and management processes has been primarily from a corporate-wide perspective; however, within a firm, the various business elements face different competitive environments. Thus, they face different adaptive and integrative challenges. A new, rapidly growing business segment, for example, must be able to adapt to changing circumstances effectively, while its integrative capabilities are relatively less important. The contrary is true for a mature business element located in a more stable business niche where it enjoys a strong leadership position. For such a business element, (often called a "cash cow"), it is much more important that strong integrative capabilities be developed; adaptive capabilities in overabundance might be distractive, and, thus, dysfunctional. For the so-called star business element, located somewhere in between, a relatively balanced set of adaptive and integrative capabilities may be necessary.

A firm's strategic processes and aspects of its structure, then, must be modified to fit different internal organizational setups; that is, they must be tailored to fit diverse settings. In describing how this might be accomplished, examples of two business elements are used: a new business that needs to be able to adapt quickly and efficiently, and a more mature business that needs to effectively integrate its activities. The former might, for example, be a business element in a new, rapidly evolving segment of the electronics business; the latter could be a stable, mature entity in the food business.

To tailor a business element to its environment, the following aspects of the firm's strategic processes and structure must be addressed:

- The nature of the top-down/bottom-up interactive planning dialogue and review between the corporate headquarters and each business element (or business family);
- The choice of variables or focus to be emphasized in the planning process;
- Managers' time-spending patterns;
- The degree to which resources constrain decision making;
- The flexibility of each business element's charter;
- The control process; and
- The management incentive

The Top-Down/Bottom-Up Dialogue

For a new business element, the critical strategic issues involve articulating an objective, modifying strategic direction, and adjusting frequently strategic programs for implementing strategy. Strategy must be seen as fluid, for a variety of reasons; for example, the needs of the customer are still changing rapidly; the competition tends to try out new variations for capturing business; and changes in technology force frequent reexamination of the business concept. The planning and review dialogue conducted between corporate headquarters and the business element (or business family) should never lose sight of the fact that the business setting is fluid and that the rules of the game are not yet finalized. It is, thus, essential that the business element bring to the discussion a detailed knowledge of the business and a true feel for the situation. The substantive expertise of the business element team is essential, and its members must be skilled in entrepreneurship if the business is to succeed and is to be in a position to take advantage of the emerging opportunities that frequently appear. What the corporate level can contribute to the discussion is a pool of experience, seasoned judgment, the ability to add encouragement, and a sense of perspective. It is essential that the dialogue allows both sides to reason together—openly, informally, and frequently—in the attempt to reduce the distance between the corporate level and the business teams.

In the more mature business element, there are different requirements for the two management levels in their top-down/bottom-up dialogue. The business level must be geared to succeed within a much more clearly defined competitive arena; it contains, for example, firmly established customer preference patterns and less pressure to leapfrog from one technology to another. This calls for a tighter, more integrative emphasis on developing efficient strategies and maintaining costs at a competitive level. The challenge here is to take advantage of the greater maturity of the business by streamlining the internal activity patterns to achieve economies of scale, process efficiencies, and experience-curve effects. The dilemma, however, is to know how far to go along these lines without weakening the business's adaptive abilities excessively. There is always some need for adaptation in a business, and this must be recognized, even at the expense of a somewhat less focused integrative effort. The business level should bring a sensitivity for these issues to the discussion table.

From the corporate side, there are two important considerations. First, corporate headquarters must satisfy itself that the business is carrying out a sufficiently integrative strategy. It is normal for there to be a certain degree of resistance to moves to achieve integration; after all, measures such as trimming and standardization of product lines, plant rationalizations, and the combination of several sales and distribution forces into a more efficient one can be painful. Thus, the dialogue with the business element may involve directives from the top that set specific performance demands or apply more explicit pressure. Second, the corporate level must provide specialized staff advice on how to achieve the benefits of integration. There is often a body of knowledge and a pool of experience to draw on, in such cases, and the dialogue will tend to be dominated by this contribution of top-down substantive inputs to the strategies in question.

The management, then, needs to tailor its review style to the particular business element in question. In practice, however, upper managers are often content to review businesses in a more or less uniform manner, resorting to personal styles—developed over a lifetime career—that fail to distinguish among different settings.

Choice of Variables

For a new business that needs to be able to adapt to changing circumstances, the essential variables to be focused on differ from those of a mature business, with its need to achieve integration. This is the case both for the setting of objectives and for the strategic programming phase.

The key challenge in the setting of objectives for a new business is to establish a "strategic window," that is, to identify an attractive business niche and indicate how the organization can compete in this niche.[7] To assess such a business niche, the business should focus on factors that might affect its growth potential, by performing a growth scenario analysis. To assess its own strength, the business needs to evaluate the comparative strength of its new products. And, a business should also assess the extent to which it can build distance between itself and its competitors.

For a mature business with an integrative need, the key variables are different. In assessing the business niche's future, such a business is much more concerned with analyzing its ability to get early warnings about cycles in demand and to assess factors that might cause the business to decline, such as the introduction of substitutions and demographic changes. Thus, the emphasis on discovering factors that might derail the business demand rather than on upward potential. Similarly, the firm's assessment of its competitive strength will differ; here, it will emphasize variables having to do with cost advantages related to process, plant technology, and other efficiency issues. The firm's strength is determined through its ability to maintain the strategic window, by developing further entry barriers based on economies of scale, process superiority, and modern plants.

At the strategic programming stage, a new business usually centers its strategy around the introduction of new products or entry into new markets. Thus, it must focus on variables that assess customer acceptance as well as the potential responses of competitors. The mature business's strategic program, on the other hand, is more concerned with how to improve efficiency, and with how to keep or improve market share through price promotion and other means.

The differences in top-down/bottom-up management review style and in the key variables focused on by a new business and an established business can be described as shown in Figure 23-12. It helps make clear that the nature of the review process and the formats of the business plans should be tailored to a considerable extent, or, if they are not tailored, they should be slanted in such a way as to highlight the differences among the essential variables to be discussed in each setting.

Time-Spending Patterns

Executives spend different amounts of time on the different stages of a planning process: the setting of objectives, strategic programming, and budgeting. In a new, adaptive business, ample management time and energy must be spent

---

[7] Derek Abell, *Defining the Business* (Englewood Cliffs, N.J.: Prentice-Hall Publishing Company, 1979).

Tailoring Feature of Management Process \ Type of Business Element	New Start-Up Business, with Predominantly Adaptive Needs	Established, Mature Business, with Predominantly Integrative Needs
Nature of top-down/ bottom-up dialogue	Open; bottom-up driven ("reason together")	Directive; top-down
Setting of objectives stage: choice of key variables	Growth; upward potential	Stability; viability
	Product quality advantages	Process/cost advantages
Strategic programming stage: choice of key variables	Customer acceptance of product/market, entry moves, and competitor responses	Customer acceptance of price, promotional competition to defend position, and competitive responses

FIG. 23-12 Process Tailoring of Basic Review Style and Choice of Key Variables for Business Elements With Adaptive and Integrative Needs

on the "front end" of the process; managers must pursue the novel formulation of an objective and the creative activity of articulating accompanying strategic programs. In more mature, well-established business elements, on the other hand, the issue is not to spend time on reexamining the assumptions behind the business objectives, since they will have become relatively well understood and can be expected to change relatively little from before. Rather, time should be spent on articulating efficiency-oriented strategic programs and on developing the typically complex patterns necessary to integrate them into the budget. In this case, executives tend to spend more time on the "back end" of the process.

Resource Constraints on Planning and Decision Making

A new business element needs to allow for considerable flexibility in its patterns for spending resources, since there are often dramatic changes in the assumptions that underlie its strategies. Thus, it should not narrow down its options for pursuing its objectives too drastically or too quickly. Instead, it should develop contingency plans to build in a reasonable degree of flexibility.

A mature business element vs. on the other hand, become much more clear over time. As a result, the business can commit itself to them strongly and not worry as much about decision making flexibility in the planning process.

The Flexibility of Each Business Element's Charter

A new, emerging business element should have a charter broad enough to allow it to develop gradually what might be the most useful definition of its boundaries. A charter that is too tightly and narrowly drawn might unnecessarily hamper creativity in forming a new business concept. For a mature business, on the other hand, the charter should be much more explicit to enable the business to focus on its relatively well-understood field, and to guard against distraction into exotic but probably less relevant, tangential opportunities.

The Control Process

The full-blown strategic control process is discussed toward the end of the section on the weak matrix concept, and is illustrated in Figure 23-11. The process can be tailored to particular business elements, however. A new business element must focus on controlling the assumptions underlying its objectives and the accompanying strategic programs. Clerical budgetary control, on the other hand, is probably not as important, except for monitoring the actual strategic budget lines.

For a mature business, the control needs are different. Here, tight budgetary control is essential if the business is to monitor efficiency levels effectively. This depends to a large extent on the successful coordination of different operating functions, a task for which the operating budget is indispensable. Control of the critical assumptions behind objectives and strategic programs, on the other hand, is normally less of a pressing issue. Strategic control is deemphasized even more by the fact that the strategic resource function of the overall budget tends to be much smaller for a business of this type than for a new, start-up business.

Management Incentives

In a new business, management incentives should focus more on the ability to implement the business strategic programs and to modify objectives and strategic programs in a proactive manner. In a mature business, the incentives should focus on rewarding classic responsibility-center performance.

From the discussions above on how to adjust strategic processes to enhance the adaptive or integrative focus of a business, it should be clear that tailoring a business's processes to its setting represents an important approach to fine-tuning a given company's ability to meet is differentiated needs. The discussion in this section has emphasized the need to see the choosing of management processes as a micro issue that complements the macro dominated views of structural design and process choice, presented earlier in the chapter.

CONCLUSIONS

The needs of an organization for support in coping with a multitude of strategic pressures stemming from its environment are fundamentally what dictate its choice of structure and process. A firm needs to be able to adapt to changing circumstances and to integrate its activities in order to compete effectively. It must pursue organizational self-renewal by shifting resources from mature businesses to emerging ones. Its top management should be cognizant of pressures it faces, and it should recognize that, in part, all challenges can be met by the adoption of an appropriate structure and processes. Top management, in particular, must attempt to assess the balance between the company's various sources of needs. Short-term demands for performance, for example, might create a tendency within some corporations to put too great an emphasis on the integrative dimension, particularly when determining the firm's structure.

Structure and process choices are highly interrelated. In fact, it is difficult to distinguish among the effects of different structures without considering them together with their accompanying processes at the same time. Management teams must guard against the tendency to see structures and processes as independent design alternatives. This would probably lead to less than optimal choices.

But, even though structure and process are highly interrelated, there are still important differences among these complementary tools. Structural choices tend to be associated with more discrete or finite attempts by an organization to adjust to its environment; a change in structure signifies a major shift in an organization's potential ability to deal with its strategic challenges. Process choices, on the other hand, tend to bring about more incremental changes in the firm's ability to cope strategically. Management processes might thus be seen as a further fine-tuning or amplification of the basic structure.

Although in this chapter structure/process choices have been described as five separate options, in practice there might be a continuity of choices. Hybrids of the basic structural models might evolve; for example, a firm might end up with a matrix structure within one part of the organization, while the rest of the company remains divisionally organized. The firm's management processes also will contribute toward a continuous shift in its capabilities, since they are continually fine-tuned. Management needs to approach the task of developing a firm's abilities to adapt and integrate on a continuous basis, rather than addressing them only at certain intervals and then imposing dramatic shifts in structure and process. Major reorganizations should be undertaken only during exceptional circumstances, because the real costs to an organization of such interventions might indeed be greater than anticipated. Uprooting of management teams, disruption of communication channels, relocation of existing experience bases, managerial uncertainties, and diminishing of executive morale—all frequently associated with major changes in an organization's structure—may diminish the firm's ability to cope with its strategic challenges until the new organization is working. Such periods can be precarious. It is, therefore, a welcome alternative to see structure and process as one vehicle through which a steadier evolution can be achieved.

As an organization evolves in order to cope with more complex strategic challenges, and as it adopts a multidimensional structure and processes, there is a tendency to emphasize process considerations over structural ones. Management process considerations tend to be of continuous concern in complex organizations. To meet the diversity of needs faced by specific businesses within such a diversified firm, the management processes can be tailored to the particular settings of different businesses. Management processes thus offer a multiplicity of internal tailoring opportunities, all of which reinforce the basic structure chosen by the firm.

Decisions about structure and process should be seen as one of top management's normal ongoing tasks. By managing the organizational context within which strategic decisions are made, management can have a critical impact on the firm's strategic direction. If insufficient attention is paid to managing structure and process, on the other hand, it is unlikely that top management will be able to achieve if its intended strategic results.

BIBLIOGRAPHY

Abell, Derek F., *Defining the Business*, Englewood Cliffs, N.J.: Prentice-Hall, Inc., 1980.

Aldrich, Howard, *Organizations and Environments*, Englewood Cliffs, N.J.: Prentice-Hall, Inc., 1979.

Browne, Paul, *The Role of Top Management in Shaping Organizational Design*, Boston: D.B.A. Thesis, Harvard Business School, 1981.

Chandler, Alfred D., Jr., *Strategy and Structure*, Cambridge, Mass.: MIT Press, 1962.

Davis, Stanley M. and Paul Lawrence, *Matrix*, Reading, Mass.: Addison-Wesley Publishing Company, 1977.

Galbraith, Jay R., *Designing Complex Organizations*, Reading, Mass.: Addison-Wesley Publishing Company, 1963.

Galbraith, Jay R., "Organization Design: An Information Processing View," *Interfaces*, Vol. 4, No. 3, 1974.

Galbraith, Jay R., *Organizational Design*, Reading, Mass.: Addison-Wesley Publishing Company, 1977.

Galbraith, Jay R. and Daniel Nathanson, *Strategy Implementation: The Role of Structure and Process*, St. Paul, Minn.: West Publishing Co., 1978.

Kimberly, John R. and Robert H. Miles (eds.), *The Organizational Life Cycle*, San Francisco: Jossey-Bass Publishers, 1980.

Lawrence, Paul and Jay Lorsch, *Organization and Environment*, Homewood, Ill.: Richard D. Irwin, 1969.

Lorange, Peter, *Implementation of Strategic Planning*, Englewood Cliffs, N.J.: Prentice-Hall, Inc., 1982.

Mintzberg, Henry, *The Structuring of Organizations*, Englewood Cliffs, N.J.: Prentice-Hall, Inc., 1982.

Vancil, Richard F., *Decentralization: Managing Ambiguity by Design*, Homewood, Ill.: Dow Jones-Irwin, 1980.

24

Measuring and Rewarding Strategic Performance

MARK R. HURWICH, *Principal*

RICHARD A. FURNISS, JR., *Vice President*

Towers, Perrin, Forster & Crosby

INTRODUCTION

Samuel Butler once said, "All progress is based upon a universal innate desire on the part of every organism to live beyond its income." Although this statement may be somewhat extreme, nearly all managers agree that linking pay to performance helps to harness executive motivation. This chapter deals with the subject of executive compensation from the strategic planning perspective: How can (and why should) executive compensation be made to reinforce the planning discipline and motivate strategic performance?

Other chapters in this book show how the art of strategic planning has progressed in recent years. As plans have become more powerful and sophisticated, managers have become aware of a need to *implement* them better. A key element in implementation is the enterprise's reward system, that is, its executive compensation mechanisms. When this system reinforces the strategic plan, chances of success are increased considerably.

This chapter examines the elements of executive compensation and their linkage to corporate performance. It shows how rewards and incentives differ, discusses the relationships between incentive programs and business goals, and points out some imperfections in current compensation design. Finally, it presents an approach to motivating strategic performance through compensation, and discusses the design issues compensation planners must address.

Why Link Compensation to Strategy?

Before delving into how strategy and compensation can be linked, consider why this subject has generated such interest. Most incentive compensation plans are designed to reward executives for achieving planned results. Too often, however, the "results" that generated rewards were not relevant to either management or shareholders, and incentive plans became simply a conduit for pay. Many organizations now wish to focus executive attention more specifically on taking the steps necessary to achieve strategic objectives, and to attain the real goal of an enterprise: increasing its value to the owners.

However, saying that compensation plans motivate strategic performance does not make them do that. An incentive plan that is truly linked to business objectives must cause deliberate actions, not just good intentions.

Some managers now believe that the way executives are compensated is a key impediment to implementing strategy. It may even be an impediment to getting executives to take strategic plans seriously. These managers perceive a need not only to get compensation plans to promote strategic activities, but also to prevent them from inadvertently penalizing executives for taking actions required for long-term results.

Developments in the technology of strategic planning—as well as advances in related fields—have increased the ability to align compensation and strategy. Many of the qualitative techniques in strategic planning, such as portfolio analysis, were useful in generating strategies, but they did not lend themselves to compensation design. However, the recently developed quantitative approaches to strategic planning and the determinants of shareholder value create new opportunities in compensation design.

Probably the most important reason for attempting to link compensation to strategy is a perceived discrepancy between executive and shareholder interests. On the one hand, shareholders and directors press for an explanation and justification of executive compensation (particularly when stock market performance is disappointing). On the other hand, companies legitimately need to motivate and reward executive performance and to maintain a competitive compensation stance if they are to retain key executives. Those who determine

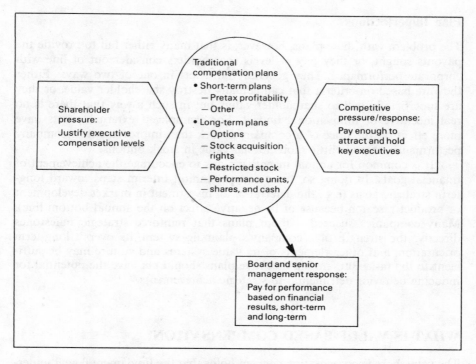

FIG. 24-1 Pressure on Traditional Compensation Programs

top executive remuneration have the difficult task of balancing these interests (see Figure 24-1).

Background

Attempts to structure executive compensation plans to satisfy both shareholder and executive interests began several decades ago. During the 1950s and early 1960s, when the marginal tax rate on ordinary income was 91 percent, the qualified stock option—the return of which was taxed entirely at capital gains rates, and only upon sale of the stock—was overwhelmingly attractive.

The Tax Reform Act of 1969 brought about the introduction of performance plans. In such plans, the major determinants of award payout value were financial measures of corporate performance instead of—or in addition to—changes in market price. Growth in earnings per share, return on equity, and the like formed the basis for calculating award payouts. These plans were regarded as improvements over qualified stock options because of their relative cost-effectiveness and tax-effectiveness, and also because they achieved a linkage between executive rewards and the attainment of financial goals.

Plan Imperfections

The problem with these plans, however, is that many either fail to provide the payouts sought, or they pay at levels shareholders consider out of line with corporate performance. They generally fall short in one of two ways: Either they are based on criteria that can actually destroy shareholder value, or they are superficially tied to shareholder value, but in such a way that there is no real incentive or motivational impact. For example, if external events have more effect on the price of a company's stock than improvement in company performance, there is little motivational value in stock options.

It is common for annual incentive plans to encourage the achievement of financial goals. In doing so, some actually inhibit interim steps toward long-term strategic goals (e.g., the deferral of an investment in market development or product research because of its negative effect on the annual bottom line). Many companies succeed without plans that reinforce strategic milestones directly; the strength of a company's planning system, its overall long-term orientation, and other elements of its value systems and culture may be sufficient to the task. But, annual incentive plans should *not* have the potential for inducing behavior detrimental to strategic achievements.

WHAT IS VALUE-BASED COMPENSATION?

The value-based compensation concept holds that the fundamental goal underlying an executive's work, whatever specific function he or she carries out, is to maximize return on company resources over time and, hence, increase the organization's value to its owners, the shareholders. By linking executive incentives to the true determinants of corporate worth over the long term, and by identifying and rewarding managers for taking those key actions required in the near term to position a company for future success, an incentive program can both meet executives' needs and further shareholders' interests. A popular term for plans that do this is "strategy-based compensation," because these plans reinforce strategies, rather than inhibit them. However, this term puts the emphasis in the wrong place; after all, strategies are themselves a means to fulfill corporate mission and increase shareholder value. The term "value-based compensation" is preferred in this chapter, because it keeps the ultimate objective of increasing shareholder value more prominently in mind.

Incentives Vs. Rewards

To highlight the characteristics of value-based compensation, a distinction must be made between incentives and rewards. The primary difference between an incentive and a reward is that of activity versus passivity:

- A *reward* passively reflects results after they have occurred; if the company has performed well (e.g., earnings grow, stock price increases) over a certain time span, managers receive a payment. There is little or no direct connection, however, between the actions that caused the performance and the payout.

- An *incentive*, on the other hand, can cause managers to take specific actions that will lead to good company performance. This difference between rewards and incentives is fundamental to the design of value-based pay systems.

Both incentives and rewards incorporate pay/performance relationships, and they share the financial benefits of good results with those who helped achieve them. But, incentives also address the issue of how the compensation program can mesh with other corporate activities, integrate with its systems, reinforce its strengths, and help compensate for its weaknesses to produce better performance. A reward has no enabling force; an incentive has the power to make good performance a more likely possibility. An effective incentive plan not only rewards executives for taking appropriate actions, but, in conjunction with other management systems, it also helps identify what executives must do to improve corporate performance and increase shareholder value.

There is a considerable body of well-tested management theory that explains what makes a company competitive and successful. Most business planning systems use some formulation of the theory to devise company strategy. Value-based incentives are designed to integrate with planning systems, in order to encourage actively the executive actions required to develop good business plans and make them work.

Incentive Programs and Business Goals

Traditionally, the focus of executive compensation has been on equity and competitiveness. Equity, of course, means treating everyone fairly, but, too often, it is construed to mean treating everyone alike. Competitiveness, in the traditional sense, means determining the compensation practices of competitors and—often—copying or transposing them.

In contrast, value-based compensation focuses on determining the kind of performance that will increase shareholder value, identifying the executive actions needed to bring it about, and then designing the compensation program to reinforce both the desired means and the desired ends through pay. Rather than merely design competitive compensation programs, the objective is to design compensation programs in a manner that makes the company itself more competitive.

At the outset, it is emphasized that value-based compensation is a concept; its application differs from company to company. Moreover, the concept often touches on areas traditionally outside compensation design, such as goal-setting systems (even the best plan does not work when it is linked with a poor goal-setting system), communication, and implementation (which often makes the difference between a fully effective plan and one with negative impact or no impact).

The most difficult task in developing a value-based compensation system is determining just what performance goals are desired and what actions are needed to achieve these goals. (Of course, no two companies will have exactly the same strategies or goals, nor can they use the same incentive formulas.)

Annual incentives should be designed to encourage the implementation of strategies. Long-term incentives should foster those enduring corporate values that guide the choice and development of strategies. Increasing shareholder value over the long term is probably the most universal and important value to reinforce.

DEFINING AND MEASURING STRATEGIC PERFORMANCE

Before a system that uses pay to reinforce strategy can be designed, the concept of strategy must be understood. Most executives view strategy as a plan that states how the company's many resources will be used during the next several years to accomplish the enduring mission. A strategy defines in some detail (e.g., tactics, operating plans) what will be done this year and, in more general terms, what will be done over the next two, three, and more years.

Some companies believe in elaborate, highly detailed strategic planning systems, and their cultures attribute great importance to these systems. Others have a far less formal system; often, it is no more than a general notion in the CEO's mind of where the company should go and how he or she intends to get it there. But, as companies become successful and larger, they usually become more complex. Their once simple strategies become, of necessity, more elaborate, encompassing several businesses and orchestrating the activities of hundreds or thousands of employees.

Whether strategies are formally or informally stated, however, managers act out of their assumptions. They decide what is expected of them, what resources will be available, how to allocate resources, and how they must interact with other managers to reach a common goal. Therefore, the more explicitly the strategy is stated, the better the guidance in making critical decisions. Linking pay to strategy can ensure that the messages managers get are the right ones!

This section discusses elements of strategy and strategic planning systems—common to all companies, whatever they are trying to do—that are critical to designing a value-based compensation system.

Figure 24-2 illustrates the basic elements of a planning and control system. At the top is the mission or purpose for which the enterprise exists. Next, the strategies express how the resources will be used to accomplish the mission. Finally, the operating plans and budgets translate the strategy into action.

Mission

Before designing a strategy, management (and shareholders) must decide on the company's mission and state it in clear, unambiguous terms. There should be no doubt in the minds of management and staff about the purpose of the organization and what its fundamental tenets are. "Making money" is not a sufficient statement of purpose. It does not indicate factors such as how the enterprise intends to reach this goal, what types of businesses will be pursued,

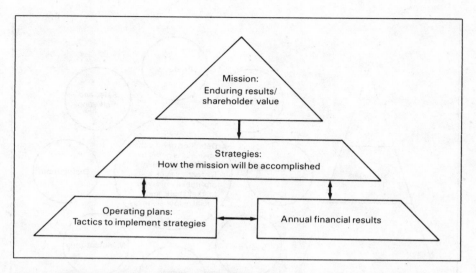

FIG. 24-2 Strategy: The Critical Element of the Planning and Control System

what kind of working environment will be maintained, who the customers will be, and what products and services will be provided.

These and other questions must be resolved and accepted by both management and shareholders before proceeding to develop strategy. Without this agreement, the enterprise lacks focus, strategies for various units may be inconsistent, and, worst of all, there is no single set of criteria or standards against which alternatives can be tested.

No matter what else an organization intends to do, the mission for most profit-making enterprises includes increasing shareholder value over time. What value means, and how it is measured, depends on the nature of the shareholder. Holders of publicly traded common stocks often regard the sum of dividends and share price increase over a relatively long time period as a measure of how well a particular company is doing. When comparing two different companies, high-risk businesses may be required to return more than low-risk ones to justify the investors' chances of loss.

Privately owned companies may set somewhat different missions or priorities and, accordingly, they include other measures of success, such as service to the community. Often, they include elements of personal satisfaction for the owners. Nevertheless, an increase in shareholder value usually remains a primary goal, and it can be measured by the cash that owners take out plus growth in company value, or by proceeds from the sale of the company.

A third kind of shareholder value is the worth of a subsidiary to its parent. This is more difficult to measure than the other two types, because there is usually no common stock price to establish a monetary value, and the parent exercises authority over such matters as dividends, reinvestment, and choice of business. In most cases, however, it is possible to identify a set of financial

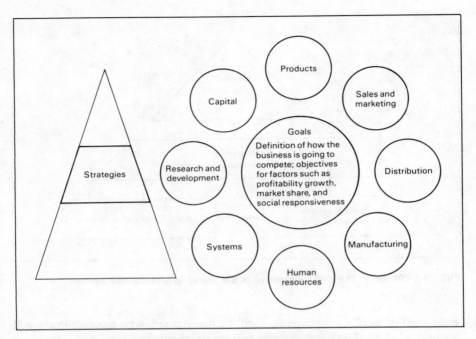

FIG. 24-3 Strategy Combines Ends (Goals) and Means (Resources)

parameters that, measured over time, reflect value and can therefore be used as performance indicators.

Strategies

Strategies determine how management intends to use the shareholders' resources to accomplish the mission. Resources include the major assets of any enterprise: cash, staff, technology, and fixed and current assets, as well as less tangible strengths such as market position, culture, unique management skills, and product advantages. Each functional area may also be viewed as a resource. Figure 24-3 illustrates key functional areas to be considered when developing strategies.

Strategies assign priorities, specify and allocate resources, and establish time frames and schedules. Corporate or business unit strategy is the basis for functional strategy, that is, what the managers of each resource must do to ensure that the enterprise as a whole is moving toward its goal. Individual unit tasks, priorities, and time frames depend on what a company is trying to accomplish. For example, if market conditions and the competitive environment offer an opportunity to achieve a profitable and growing position on a price basis, various functional units may have to do the following:

- *Research and development:* Develop a product that can be produced at low cost to satisfy the needs of the greatest number of customers.

- *Marketing:* Withdraw from markets demanding costly, customized product models; concentrate on promoting a standardized, off-the-shelf product.

- *Manufacturing:* Develop production techniques and establish facilities to manufacture the product in long runs at lowest possible cost.

On the other hand, if a company were following a high price/performance market niche strategy, the tasks of the functional units might be quite different. The sales force would seek customers whose needs are unmet by the present offerings; research and development (R&D) would design products with unique (perhaps expensive) features, and the manufacturing unit would strive to meet the stringent product performance requirements set out by their demanding customers, with less concern for cost.

Measuring performance against a strategic plan requires that each functional area have a reasonably detailed set of objectives. These must be expressed in quantitative—or, at least, observable—terms to the extent possible, and they must include accomplishments critical to strategic success. For example, using the previous example of a company seeking a *price* position, measures of success could be the following:

- *Research and development:* Demonstrating success in designing a low-cost product through its acceptance by a key potential customer's engineering department.

- *Marketing:* Obtaining a specified share of the target market.

- *Manufacturing:* Bringing a new, highly automated plant on line within budget.

Clearly, many strategic goals require more than one year to attain. Interim steps must be accomplished, and various units must do their part. Marketing cannot sell a product until R&D designs it and the manufacturing area produces it. Management has to orchestrate and monitor each unit's progress, adjusting plans and tactics as succeeding milestones are reached.

Operating Plans

Operating plans translate strategies into action; in a sense, they bring strategies to life. Operating plans form a statement of what must be accomplished in the first year of a long-term strategy. They must be clear and explicit, spelling out the key tasks each manager must perform.

Operating plans should include what is to be done, when, and how. For example, if the task of marketing is to increase its share of a target market by the end of the year, there would be a set of tasks to accomplish this: redesign the package by May 1, add six new salespeople by June 1, launch a new advertising campaign by July 15, and increase inventories in warehouse locations by July 31.

Similarly, if manufacturing is to support the marketing effort, its tasks might be to increase raw material inventories by February, ensure that the new production line is on line by March 1, increase production 20 percent by June 1, and meet unit cost targets throughout the year.

Measuring management performance against operating plans requires the establishment of clear, unambiguous, observable standards, both financial and nonfinancial. The measures for each manager should be few in number, and they should relate both to the day-to-day operation of the enterprise (e.g., reduce inventory levels to 10 percent of sales volume) and to the implementation of the long-term strategy (e.g., complete the first phase of laboratory testing on a new product). Also included should be the assumptions under which each manager is operating (e.g., what resources are available and what other units will accomplish).

Budgets

In the same way that operating plans are the tactical expression of a company's strategy, budgets are the financial expression of the annual operating plans and strategy. Budgets are important in monitoring the performance of operating units and the company as a whole. Comparing performance against budget is a way of monitoring the enterprise's financial health. Budgets allow the financial officer to know what funds will be available or needed at the beginning of the year and during the period.

The major problem with budgets as tools for implementing strategy is that they do not reflect many of the critical tasks needed to carry out a plan. And, because they *seem* to be an expression of how well business is going, they can mislead management. Budgets, by their nature, can only deal with internal measures expressed in financial or accounting terms. They do not show, for example, what market conditions led to an increase or a decline in volume. For instance, if management achieved a budgeted 10 percent increase in sales, but the market grew 20 percent, market share actually declined, but the budget failed to show it. Budgets provide little insight into R&D, personnel, organizational effectiveness, competitive environment, market trends, customer needs, and many of the critical areas of strategy implementation. Therefore, although budgets are an important indicator of performance, they are not the only important indicator. Progress in carrying out action plans should also be considered in evaluating business performance.

SHORTCOMINGS OF CURRENT INCENTIVE DESIGNS

The elements of a typical planning and management system—what executives want to accomplish over time and how they intend to do it, over both the short-term and long-term—are discussed above. Actions and results that can be measured and observed, and to which incentives can be linked, will flow out of such a system. Why have these links not been made successfully?

To an extent, they have been. For years, human resource professionals and executive compensation consultants have been working to structure programs so they have a positive impact on corporate results, with the ultimate aim of increasing shareholder value. Value-based compensation is evolutionary; in part, it makes explicit the implicit design criteria, so that plans can be better tested against them. New concepts from general management and finance also can be incorporated to magnify the impact of incentives on corporate performance and to direct it more accurately toward increasing shareholder value.

To understand the opportunities for structuring incentives more effectively, some of the shortcomings of current approaches should be discussed. Financially oriented annual incentives, objective-based programs, long-term incentives, and some general plan structuring principles are examined below.

Flaws in Financially Oriented Annual Incentives

The immediacy of the annual bonus probably makes it the most powerful device for focusing management efforts; it communicates what management ought to do, this year, to meet company goals. Unfortunately, many plans today are driven almost entirely by financial targets (e.g., increase in division profits), rather than by a combination of financial and tactical objectives (e.g., bringing a plant on-stream, increasing market share, and developing a new product). This creates a fundamental problem, because long-term business strategy cannot be captured by financial measures alone; it does not translate. As important as profit growth is, using it (or other financial measures) as the sole measure of annual executive performance and concomitant bonus awards has several negative results:

- Managers may be penalized for taking steps that reduce annual financial performance but that are essential for implementing and achieving long-term strategies.

- The annual plan loses its ability to motivate individuals (e.g., the head of R&D) whose impact on profits is, at best, indirect; payoff is not linked to individual performance.

- Nonfinancial goals of the operating plan become totally subservient to financial goals.

Many incentive plans are expressed in financial terms alone, as are long-range forecasts. However, current management practice accepts the need for something more than a forecast, which is just an extrapolation of present circumstances into a possible financial future. Strategic planning—in contrast to forecasting—introduces the element of directing fundamental business change; e.g., change in organizational profile and change in market position. An incentive plan with goals expressed exclusively in financial terms—however complete, challenging, and relevant they may be—cannot fully reflect strategic goals, just as annual budgets and long-range forecasting cannot substitute for strategic planning as a managerial tool.

Explicitly rewarding managers for attaining short-term financial goals while only ostensibly valuing important operating goals can have insidious effects. As many executives have observed, "The problem with incentives is that they work!" The performance you reward is the performance you get, and what you do not pay for becomes more difficult to accomplish. Although managers are motivated by considerations in addition to their paychecks (at least, they say so), it does seem foolish to structure plans that, in effect, actively discourage important management functions. Yet, some do.

Clearly, it is the lack of balance of financially based plans that creates problems. Financial measures are certainly important ways to judge business success. Unless a company achieves the short-term financial results it needs to remain viable, it will not survive to realize long-term success. Moreover, it is conceivable that financial-measures-only incentives could be appropriate for some firms or some units; there may be no other measures. But, financial measures can obscure, overwhelm, or eliminate the nonfinancial measures, thereby losing the power of the incentive for managers whose performance cannot be captured in financial results alone.

Flaws in Objective-Based Annual Incentives

If exclusively financially based incentives are not the answer, can objective-based programs work? In order to answer this, one must understand how objective-based annual plans operate. Many programs that seem to have nonfinancial objectives really do not. One company, for example, had a program where financial measures determined a target bonus that was modified through objective-based criteria. But, in reality, everyone knew that the financial results were all that mattered. To an outsider, the plan looked as though it had both financial and objective-based criteria (indeed, in another company, this program might have worked well). But, in this company, the "secondary" application of nonfinancial criteria was perceived by many to have little impact—and their perceptions were right. Bonus amounts averaged within a few percentage points of what the financial results alone would have determined.

Many companies do not incorporate the right objective elements into incentives. They include objectives that were developed for salary review, career growth, and similar personnel-oriented functions. In these applications, such objectives work well, but they cannot be routinely applied to developing annual incentives, which require a strategic focus. Strategic objectives should include only those few specific steps that must be taken this year to accomplish long-term strategies. The plans of many companies say, "Begin objective-setting by reviewing your job description." This will result in routine objectives, not in the few critical change-oriented and strategic objectives. Obviously, the incentive objective-setting process should be integrated with the strategic planning objective-setting process. It is necessary, across the organization, and up and down the line, for executives to establish compatible goals whose attainment results in implementing the strategies chosen. Effective incentives should be integrated with management systems.

In some organizations, the objectives used in incentive systems are unrelated to human effort or individual considerations. The objectives may be appropriate for the overall strategy, but, without "ownership," they are often ignored by those who must carry them out. Usually, what is needed is to build in a good, explicitly stated objective-development process. (This process, by the way, *is* usually present in well-designed management-by-objective programs, but the focus needs to be more strategically oriented.) Thoughtful and dedi-

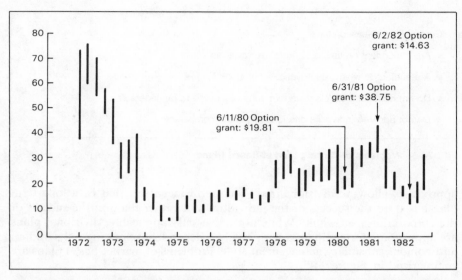

FIG. 24-4 Current Market-Based Mechanisms Do Not Always Reflect Long-Term Share Value

cated implementation of this process is also a requirement for success. Often, executives need training to ensure that they fully understand and can carry out the objective-setting process.

Flaws in Stock Market-Based Long-Term Incentives

For many years, companies considered the stock option the most appropriate long-term vehicle for rewarding executives. Options have value only when market price increases, and market price is a direct measure of shareholder value; therefore, the argument went, the match is appropriate. But, is it?

Figure 24-4 shows a company's recent stock performance and timing of three option grants. During the period, the company's stock price fluctuated considerably from quarter to quarter, but its underlying long-term value seems to have changed very little. Yet, an executive whose options were granted near the stock's 1981 peak would find them worthless now, while another executive who received options a year later would have a sizable gain if the options were exercised now. As with most option plans, the timing of grant and exercise, more than long-term performance, determines the magnitude of the payout. The problem lies in the "signal to noise" ratio: There is so much "noise"—reaction to outside events, for example—in the price of a share of stock at any given time that the market's "signal" of its underlying value can be completely washed out. Other market-based incentives (e.g., restricted stock) suffer similar problems.

Another difficulty is that for privately held companies, market-based approaches are not available. Nor do any of the traditional market-based

---

Current market-based plans:

- Are dependent on timing of grant, exercise, and sale
- Are subject to whims and cyclicality of stock market
- Do not communicate clear performance objectives to management
- Do not apply to individual divisions or private companies

FIG. 24-5 Problems of Current Market-Based Plans

approaches allow a "divisionalized" long-term incentive; that is, a long-term plan based on the success of the individual unit rather than on the success of the corporation as a whole. While not universally applicable, divisional plans are appropriate for companies with highly independent operating units and an autonomous subsidiary management style. Problems of market-based plans are summarized in Figure 24-5.

Flaws in Internal-Measure Performance Units

The earnings-per-share (EPS) based performance unit was an attempt to relate shareholder value to performance measures within the executive's control. In the belief that "real" value is created by earnings growth, this incentive was designed to provide payouts to executives based only on internal company performance: actual EPS vs. target EPS over a specified period.

EPS-based performance units (or any of their variants) reduced the problems of market-based plans, and they can be used in decentralized and privately held companies. However, many of these strictly internal measures have turned out to be poor determinants of shareholder value. For example, of the 172 of Standard & Poor's 400 industrial companies that achieved compounded EPS growth rates of 15 percent or more during 1974 to 1979, including dividends:

- Shareholders had negative returns in 16 percent of the companies; and
- Shareholders' returns were inadequate to compensate for inflation in an additional 35 percent.

Thus, despite their high EPS growth, less than half of the sample generated adequate shareholder returns. Further evidence is given in Figure 24-6, which shows the relationships between earnings growth and the Dow-Jones Industrial Average. Although the two figures maintained a close relationship through 1971, they soon diverged radically, as inflation destroyed the value of the dollar and high interest rates provided attractive return opportunities to investors in debt securities. One effect of single-measure plans, such as those based on EPS growth or return on equity (ROE), is that they can encourage executives to unconsciously (or consciously) reduce company value over time. There are

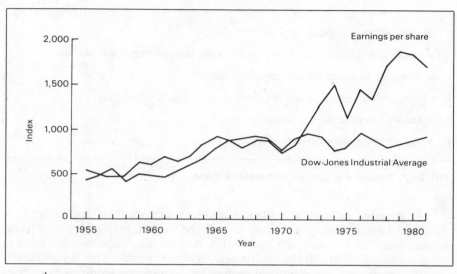

FIG. 24-6   Current EPS-Based Plans Do Not Reflect Long-Term Share Value

companies driven by EPS growth whose managers make every decision in the context of earnings increase. Invariably, return on investment erodes. On the other hand, if ROE is the sole target, investment is inhibited and the company's future can be jeopardized.

Using *two* measures in a long-term plan is a step in the right direction. The relative importance of the measures is often determined arbitrarily, however. This may cause undue focus on one measure at the expense of the other, and may lead to decisions that do not maximize shareholder value.

Many performance plans have problems even beyond their predominant use of inappropriate measures. One such problem arises in setting targets. Who knows what a reasonable return will be for the next three to five years? A rate of 14 to 15 percent was not bad in the past few years (and it would have been outstanding before 1970), but it will be inadequate if interest rates and inflation return to 1980 to 1981 levels. Many companies that thought they had these questions answered at the beginning of their performance cycles are facing them again as lower-than-forecasted years make plans inoperable.

In addition, the goals selected for inclusion in longer-term incentive plans often are not fully integrated with a company's financial planning process. Rather, they are designed to provide "competitive" levels of executive compensation at the end of some predetermined period. An EPS growth rate representing acceptable or average performance is usually selected, primarily for its inconspicuousness compared with the goals chosen by peer organizations. This approach may be reasonable, but it can hardly be defended as supportive of a strategic plan that is not acknowledged, communicated, or in any other way built into the performance measures that trigger compensation at the end of the performance cycle.

Current performance plans:

- Usually are based on EPS or EPS growth (often poor performance measures)

- Rarely are related to the true company mission

- Frequently are based on arbitrary formulas (often counterproductive)

- Make it difficult to set appropriate targets

- Are not integrated with planning systems

FIG. 24-7 Problems of Current Performance Plans

It is naive to believe a plan that offers an executive, for example, a $200,000 bonus three years from now if the corporation grows at a compounded annual EPS rate of 12 percent, will at all encourage that executive to take any actions that will change the organizational profile. This is particularly true if changing the organizational profile (for example, by acquiring businesses in an industry with greater growth potential 10 years from now) could jeopardize either the annual bonus in the year the acquisition is made, or the longer-term award payable. These problems of performance plans are summarized in Figure 24-7.

Flaws in Plan Design Characteristics

Throughout industry, participation in long-term incentive plans has extended too far down the organization ladder. To be competitive, companies have included many managers who have no direct effect on long-term organizational results. This clouds the purpose of the long-term incentive, and tends to skew emphasis to the short-term reward.

The CEO of a multibillion-dollar organization has a much greater ability to influence corporate results than an executive, for example, three levels lower. Yet, both could have the same long-term plan. Either the lower-level manager is being measured in dimensions unrelated to his or her function, or the CEO is being judged by criteria more appropriate to a lower-level manager. Neither situation is desirable (although the latter is probably worse).

Finally, many companies have performance cycles that are too short. Three years—the most common length—is, in many cases, not long enough to average out business-cycle fluctuations that are outside executive control. Moreover, a three-year cycle does not provide much balance against an annual incentive. If the target annual payout is the same as the target long-term payout (an arrangement that is not unusual), then at the conclusion of a three-year cycle, outstanding awards from previous cycles are no bigger than the annual payout on an accrual basis. If each year accrues one-third of the total award, the accrual value for the three years just equals the annual incentive. Actually, since salaries and incentives have been inflating over the period, the accrued value of the long-term plan is less than the value in the annual plan. It is no wonder that many managers are short-term-oriented: They're paid to be!

There is no question that compensation mechanisms can be structured to communicate an organization's strategic plan in a powerful and persuasive manner. Longer-term incentive awards can be better oriented toward rewarding managers for attaining the specific goals incorporated in an organization's strategic plan and increasing shareholder value. Such plans link executive remuneration with true corporate performance more effectively, and they will constitute coming trends in longer-term incentives.

DESIGNING VALUE-BASED INCENTIVE PROGRAMS

Nobody deliberately sets out to design an ineffective incentive plan, of course. When that happens, it is usually due to the use of inappropriate measures for capturing desired future performance. In many cases, it is difficult to see that the measures are wrong, because increased shareholder value coincidentally parallels the measures selected (the plan can be a good reward, but still not an active incentive).

The discussion above shows how the mission, strategy, operating plans, and budgets are linked together and are dependent on each other. This section shows how incentives can be designed to support these elements of the planning system. The authors' concept, illustrated in Figures 24-8 and 24-9, is essentially this:

- The long-term incentive plan should be tied to the corporate mission: increasing shareholder value. This might be done through financial measures influenced by management that reflect changes in shareholder value, or market-based devices constructed to avoid volatility and timing problems. Participants should be those few managers who have primary responsibility and authority for decisions and actions relating to long-term success. In effect, participants in the long-term plan should be those executives who set the course of the enterprise, develop a strategy, and ensure that it is implemented.
- The annual plan should parallel operating plans and budgets. Annual incentives should:
  a. Be linked to those financial results needed that year to ensure the organization's continued viability; and
  b. Reinforce the interim nonfinancial actions necessary for accomplishing this year's portion of the strategic plan. This structure ensures that specific steps and directions are identified, and preserves the balance between short-term (profit) objectives and long-term (strategic) objectives.

These principles ensure that plans developed pay for the right results. To ensure that they are motivational—that they are incentives, not just rewards—the plans should be designed so that participants can see valid pay/performance relationships and can influence results.

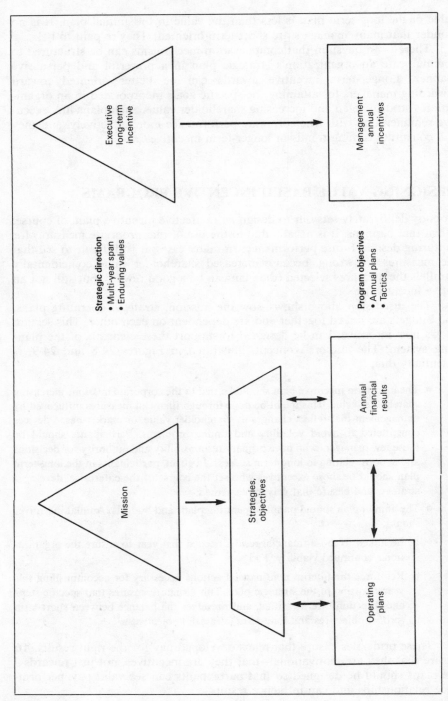

FIG. 24-8 Planning Systems and Incentive Systems Are Linked

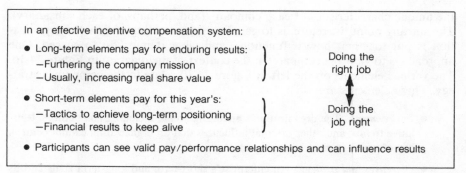

In an effective incentive compensation system:

- Long-term elements pay for enduring results:
  - —Furthering the company mission
  - —Usually, increasing real share value

      } Doing the right job

- Short-term elements pay for this year's:
  - —Tactics to achieve long-term positioning
  - —Financial results to keep alive

      } Doing the job right

- Participants can see valid pay/performance relationships and can influence results

FIG. 24-9   Effective Incentive Compensation System

This concept recognizes that the job of senior management is to develop an effective strategy that leads to increased shareholder value over time ("doing the right job"). The long-term incentive plan directs their attention toward shareholder value, as reflected in appropriate long-term financial measures.

Below the senior level, the primary job is to implement the strategy senior management has developed ("doing the job right"). Attention is properly focused on the near term, but the tasks these managers must accomplish are vital to long-term success. When they accomplish these tasks, the annual plan pays off.

Why not partially base compensation directly on long-term strategies? Because strategies change, and, as noted above, they are themselves only a means to the end of increasing shareholder value. Suppose a company pays its executives for accomplishing a five-year plan. It is likely that three years into the strategy, a different plan will be called for, making the compensation program obsolete. More important, what incentive has been created to develop the best strategy, and refine it to produce the best results over time? By reinforcing the company's mission through long-term incentives at the top of the organization, and including nonfinancial elements directed at implementing strategies lower down, compensation can facilitate the process of choosing and implementing correct strategies.

This section outlines the steps involved in designing an effective incentive plan that is linked to the strategy, that fits with the characteristics of the organization, and that management and shareholders can accept.

There are four principal requirements for designing effective incentive plans. The first is to develop a deep understanding of the characteristics and objectives of the organization, and to integrate incentive plans explicitly with them. The second is to develop annual incentives that support an organization's operating plan. The third is to design long-term incentives that relate closely to increasing shareholder value. The last requirement is to be pragmatic in applying the theoretical principles, and to pay as much attention to plan implementation as to design; plan performance criteria must integrate with the decision-making process.

Effective value-based pay plans aren't packaged. While the basic concepts can be applied to most enterprises, the plan itself must be custom-tailored to the unique characteristics of each company (and, perhaps, of each subsidiary). The starting point, therefore, is to gain an understanding of how the organization is put together, how it functions, and what it must do to suceed. One approach is to view the company in the context of the diagram in Figure 24-10. The various elements on the left in Figure 24-10 relate to the company's strategy. These elements are:

- *Environment:* The organization's operating arena, including competitors, legislative trends, and other external influences that an organization cannot control, but of which it must be cognizant.

- *Objectives and strategy:* An enterprise's short-term and long-term goals and its plans to achieve them. The goals or objectives define the organization's reasons for being—including increasing shareholder value over time—and determine what key tasks the organization must do well to survive and operate effectively.

- *Key success factors:* Those relatively few tasks that the enterprise must perform well in order to carry out its strategy. They can differ greatly among companies in the same industry, as each develops a unique strategy.

The elements on the right in Figure 24-10 show how the enterprise is arranged to carry out those tasks called for in the strategy. These elements are:

- *Structure:* The manner in which the tasks of an organization are broken down and regrouped. Structure also encompasses the responsibilities and authorities assigned to individuals. The structure must fit the organization's goals and strategy, and it must be reinforced by other elements of the organization's design.

- *Resources:* The human, financial, technological, physical, and other resources needed to support the strategy and design of an entity.

- *Culture:* The organization's history, beliefs, and shared values. Culture represents a powerful, and usually persistent, organizational element. Any change, as well as the manner in which change is introduced, must be evaluated in light of an organization's culture, and its role as a force facilitating or inhibiting change.

- *Systems:* The variety of planning, data processing, financial control, human resource, and reward systems that jointly play a critical role in communicating, energizing, focusing, and controlling the disparate activities within an organization.

- *Distinctive competencies:* Those relatively few things that the enterprise does particularly well and that, if properly focused, can enable it to achieve competitive advantages and carry out the requirements for success.

- *Executive leadership:* The bonding ingredient that glues all the elements together and ensures that tasks are carried out as they should be to accomplish the organization's mission.

An organization's competitive success can be modeled as a function of the "goodness of fit" among these characteristics:

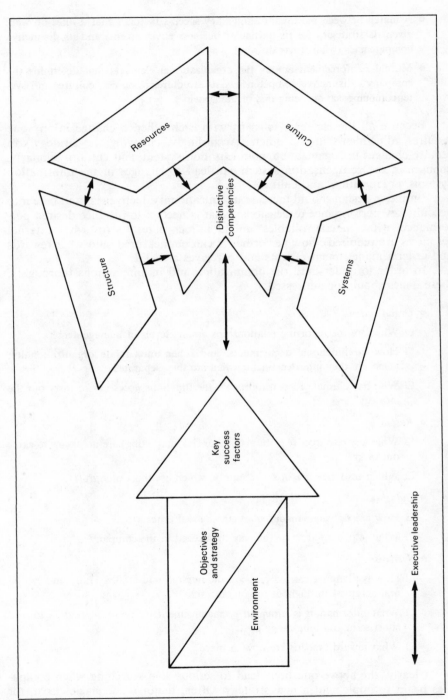

FIG. 24-10 The Organizational Effectiveness Model: A Fit Between Strategic Elements and Organizational Elements

- A match between the organization's key success factors (what it *must* do well, given its strategies for its particular business environment) and its distinctive competencies (what it *can* do well).

- Mutual reinforcement among the organizational elements that determine the company's distinctive competencies: its structure, resources, culture, and systems (compensation being one of the systems).

Because all the elements must fit with each other, a change in any one requires adjustments in the others. Accordingly, changing the strategy can require changes in organization, compensation system, and culture. Similarly, changes in the compensation system can lead to changes in the information systems, organization, and culture.

Incentive design should increase organizational effectiveness and take into account key performance dimensions: what is needed to produce desired performance, what "uncontrollables" might influence results (or what external resources are required), how performance can be measured, and what rewards and criteria management expects and perceives as valid.

In order to understand the organization and its interactions thoroughly, these issues should be addressed:

- *Organization*

  □ What are the reporting relationships among levels of management?

  □ How do functions, departments, and other units relate organizationally; when are they interdependent; when are they separate?

  □ Who has ultimate responsibility for the functions necessary to carry out the strategy?

- *Resources*

  □ What key resources (e.g., human, financial, marketing) are necessary to carry out tasks?

  □ Which resources are in short supply; which are most plentiful?

- *Culture*

  □ How are decisions made; what are the real criteria?

  □ What is perceived to be the way to succeed in the company?

- *Systems*

  □ How is planning carried out; are the mission and strategy fully understood and accepted throughout the organization?

  □ What information is provided to management to monitor progress toward short-term and long-range goals?

  □ What reward systems are now in place?

Clearly, the above questions lead to serious soul-searching when companies begin to implement a new strategy. Often, major inadequacies exist, for instance, in the alignment of responsibilities among various managers who must carry out certain tasks but who do not have access to the resources they need. Addressing these issues directly may be beyond the scope of normal compensation design. But, by being aware of problems in the areas where they exist, plans can be developed that, at least, do not compound problems in related areas, that do not fail because of these problems (when other designs would have worked), and that may even lead the organization in solving related difficulties.

Annual Incentives

Paradoxically, value-based incentive plans may give more weight to annual individual performance measures than to long-term performance measures. The measures themselves, however, will be very different from those in conventional long-term incentive plans and in most annual plans. For example, significant weight will be placed on attaining strategic milestones as well as on achieving annual financial goals. Incentives will not only reward managers for achieving results, but will encourage actions leading to them (especially when the results will not be evidenced for a number of years). The only way to accomplish this is by incorporating annual performance measures.

To establish performance measures, management needs a good strategic objective-setting process that is integrated with planning and control systems. Each manager's objectives are the few critical goals his or her unit must achieve if the company is to succeed. In that context, a useful objective should not concern "business as usual"; instead, it should do one of the following:

- Focus on a significant improvement opportunity;
- Deal with an important problem; and/or
- Establish or improve a management process or program.

These criteria are often useful in establishing good objective statements:

1 The objective is instrumental to reaching corporate goals, and its relationship to those goals is evident. All managers' objectives together constitute an operating plan, which in turn is the first year of the strategy.

2 The objective is not routine; it extends beyond the day-to-day requirements of the job, and its accomplishment demands something more than the standard operating procedure.

3 The objective is feasible; within reasonable limitations and capabilities, it can be done.

4 Major aspects of accomplishing the objective are identified; how it will be done is at least implied to the extent that other resources are required.

5 Major resources and conditions essential to meeting the objective are identified; what it depends on is at least implied.

6 The time period over which the objective will be measured and/or the target completion date is given.

7 The objective contains one or more quantity measures of attainment.

8 The objective contains one or more quality measures of attainment.

9 The objective is specifically and accurately stated, with no references that might mean different things over the course of a year. It is the most precise definition possible of what must be accomplished.

10 The objective is a "contract" to which plan participants are willing to commit. Since participants have specified their intentions, and have identified critical resources and factors likely to affect accomplishing the objective, they willingly accept their role.

Once managers' objectives have been set according to the criteria outlined above, the annual incentive plan can be built around them. This requires weighting the objectives to reflect their relative importance, calibrating the plan so that actual performance above and below targets results in a commensurate payoff, determining awards at competitive levels for desired performance, and funding the plan.

An objective-based plan might be applied as follows:

(1) Objectives	(2) Weighting	(3) Degree of Performance	(4) Weighted Performance
A	50%	90%	45%
B	20	110	22
C	20	50	10
D	10	80	8
	100%		85%

For example, the manager has four objectives, the first of which, A, accounts for half the overall weight. During the year, he attains 90 percent of the target for A. Multiplying the weights (column 2) by the performance (column 4) results in the figure used to calculate his annual payout, in this case 85 percent of target. If the executive's target award is $20,000, the payout is 85 percent of $20,000, or $17,000.

Value-Based Long-Term Incentives

Many internally based financial measures used in developing long-term incentives do not relate well to shareholder value. Market-price measures also have disadvantages. Furthermore, market price is not always available (for example, in a private company or a subsidiary). There are some alternatives: different ways to use market price; creating market price "surrogates" (measures determined from variables within management control but parallel to market price); and combination and hybrid approaches.

Value-Based Market-Price Measures

Much of the difficulty with market-based long-term incentives derives from the volatility of options. As shown in Figure 24-4, the "noise" of price fluctuation outweighed the "signal" of increasing company value. As a result, decisions about grant and exercise timing are potentially more powerful than company performance in determining plan payouts.

One solution is to filter out the noise. This might be done by:

- Using stock price averages in performance plans;
- Making grants more frequently (so the impact of statistical fluctuations is dampened); or
- Eliminating or reducing the "game-playing" aspects of market devices (e.g., rather than permitting options to be exercised at market price at any time, use shorter exercise windows or even fixed performance periods).

Assuming that some or almost all of the noise in the market-price measure has been eliminated, is there a basis for a value-based incentive system yet? The answer is: It depends.

By developing a market-based measure with less noise in it, a better, more accurate reward has been created. Whether that reward is also an incentive depends upon whether the organizational elements in the company (its structure, culture, and systems) create an instrumental linkage between executive actions and the market-based reward. For example, in a new, small, single-business company where entrepreneurial top managers hold most of the stock, have developed a strategy, and are pursuing it, the link between pay and performance is strong: Executive actions are perceived to impact shareholder value. In a larger, more bureaucratic organization, the linkage is weaker.

It may still be necessary to create an explicit linkage between executive actions and market price in order to develop pay plans that are truly incentives. One means of doing this is to create market-price surrogates based on measures within executive influence.

Market-Price Surrogates

The concept of a market-price surrogate is simple. The objective is to create a measure that closely parallels a company's underlying stock price (eliminating short-term fluctuations), but that is determined by operational variables. If this can be done in a reasonably straightforward and comprehensible manner, then a way has been found to link pay to performance that provides the best of both worlds: It represents shareholder interests (because it tracks basic trends in market price), yet it directly reflects management actions (because it is made up of the factors management influences or manages).

Can such a surrogate be constructed? Are there variables that explain shareholder value? Theoretical and empirical research conducted by the academic, financial, and business planning communities suggests that, in fact, there are. Creating shareholder value is primarily a function of sustained good performance in two dimensions:

- *A positive spread* in return on capital; that is, a true return on shareholders' investment above the average return available for businesses of equivalent risk.

Intrinsic value = Book value/Share × Leverage factor

Leverage factor depends on:

- Spread in return on equity
  (return on equity − cost of equity)

- Book value growth

FIG. 24-11 Intrinsic Value Is Determined by Measures Within Executive Influence

- *Growth, when a company is achieving positive spread* (growth in a negative-spread situation can actually reduce shareholder value, in that more capital is committed to an investment with a below average return).

By incorporating measures of spread and growth—or other measures related to them—in long-term incentives, and by modeling the results, plans can be developed that track a company's market price, or that even create a market price for privately held firms and divisions.

The sections below briefly discuss two such surrogates—intrinsic value and economic return—and how they are determined and applied.

Intrinsic Value

Intrinsic value (IV) is a surrogate for long-term market value. It is directly developed from the fundamental financial performance measures within management's control. It combines spread (return on equity, less its cost) and growth in equity to create a "leverage factor": the multiple of a company's book value per share at which its stock sells (see Figure 24-11). It is based on evidence that the financial markets assign a premium over book value to the stock of companies that earn a positive spread. This premium can be enhanced by growth in the underlying equity. The relationships are examined below, step by step.

Figure 24-12 shows the empirical relationships between spread and the leverage factor. At 0 percent spread (return on equity equals the cost of equity), the ratio is 1.0 (market price equals book value). As the spread increases, so does the market premium. With a negative spread, market price falls below book value.

Figure 24-13 illustrates the effect of growth rate. With a positive spread and a positive growth rate, the market value further increases. With a negative spread and a positive growth rate, the market value decreases. These graphic relationships are translated to a matrix in Figure 24-14. (The values shown are illustrative only.)

From an investor's point of view, the relationships are obvious: A company adds to real value only when the return on funds invested is greater than that available from alternative investments the investor might have chosen. And, the faster the company makes (or loses) "real" money, the greater the effect on the spread. (This does not mean, however, that a company's spread

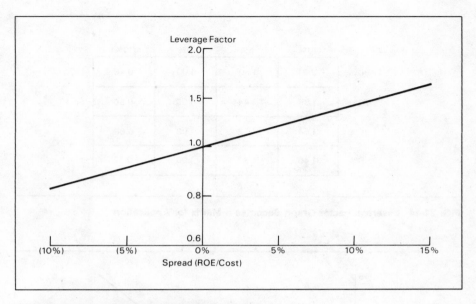

FIG. 24-12 Leverage Factor Depends on Spread

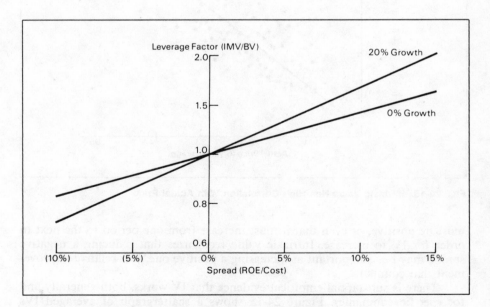

FIG. 24-13 Leverage Factor Depends on Spread and Growth

	Spread			
Growth	10%	5%	0%	(10%)
30%	2.21	1.60	1.00	0.40
20%	1.88	1.44	1.00	0.56
10%	1.64	1.32	1.00	0.68
0%	1.46	1.23	1.00	0.77

FIG. 24-14 Leverage Factor Graph Becomes a Matrix for Application

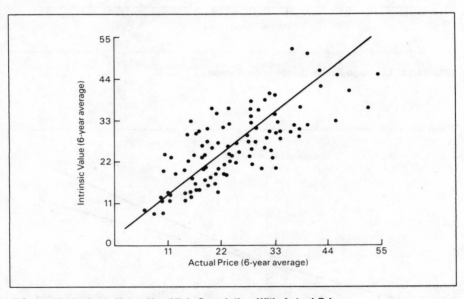

FIG. 24-15 Intrinsic Value Has High Correlation With Actual Price

must be positive, or even that it must increase from one period to the next in order for IV to increase. Intrinsic value recognizes that reducing a negative spread may be as important as increasing a positive one. It is relative improvement that counts.)

There is substantial empirical evidence that IV works, both generally and for specific companies. Figure 24-15 shows a scattergraph of averaged IVs against average market price for a sample of over 100 firms, demonstrating a close statistical relationship between IV and actual market price. Figure 24-16 adds an IV line for Figure 24-6, between IV and actual market trends.

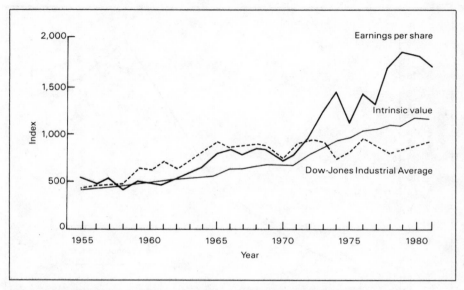

FIG. 24-16 Intrinsic Value More Evenly Tracks Underlying Market Value

Economic Return

Intrinsic value creates a surrogate for market price by using spread and growth to generate a leverage factor applied to book value. Another recipe uses growth in cash generated, less a charge for equity, also calculated at the risk-adjusted rate shareholders should expect.

Simply stated, economic return per share in any year is the excess of cash generated over the cost of equity where:

- Cash generated is defined as after-tax net income plus depreciation, amortization, and other noncash charges;
- Cost of equity is defined as beginning book value times expected return; and
- Expected return is defined as the 90-day Treasury Bill rate for the year (the "risk free" rate), plus a risk adjustment for equity securities.

The economic return concept holds that a company's stock price will move in relation to the average (or total) annual economic returns for a period of prior years. Clearly, increasing economic return requires management to increase earnings, increase real return on equity, or both. Therefore, the same financial objectives apply to economic return as to intrinsic value. Similarly, economic return can be demonstrated to parallel share prices as shown (in this case for a particular semiconductor company) in Figure 24-17.

Using Market-Price Surrogates for Incentive Plans

The two measures described above can be applied to a long-term incentive plan by creating a surrogate for stock price and rewarding participants for an

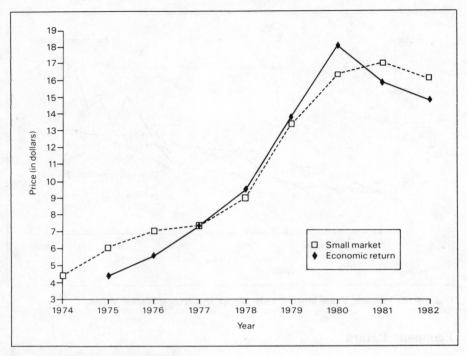

FIG. 24-17 Price Vs. Economic Return

increase in value, as illustrated in Figure 24-18. Using one of the models, a hypothetical per-share value is calculated at the beginning of a performance period (based on historical performance) and again at the end (based on performance during the measurement period). The payout is determined similarly to that of a stock option; number of shares times increase in value. In actual practice, many refinements are necessary to tailor the plan to individual companies. Variables include:

- Years in the averaging period
- Treatment of dividends
- Cash flow vs. profits
- Method of calculating measures such as cash flow and equity
- Treatment of extraordinary items
- Use of conventional options in tandem with value-based cash incentives
- Additional performance measures
- Appropriateness of an open-ended (no cap) plan

Once these issues have been addressed, and an appropriate payout level has been determined (i.e., how much the executive should receive for a specified level of increase in shareholder value), the plan can be designed, as outlined below.

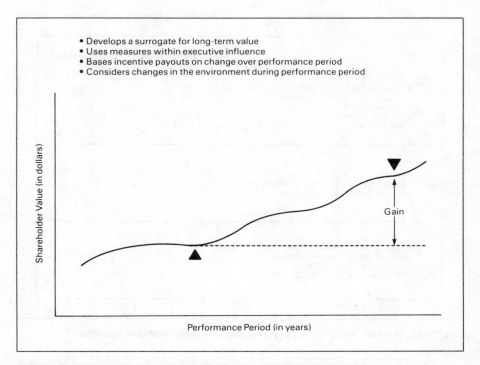

- Develops a surrogate for long-term value
- Uses measures within executive influence
- Bases incentive payouts on change over performance period
- Considers changes in the environment during performance period

FIG. 24-18 New Approach to Rewarding Increase in Shareholder Value

Intrinsic Value Approaches

The intrinsic value approach uses a formula to derive the leverage factor, which is multiplied by book value to obtain the intrinsic value. Figure 24-19 illustrates how a payout is calculated for a particular company in four steps. The steps are as follows:

1 In the period before the start of the new cycle, the company showed a spread of 2.50 percent and growth of 10.00 percent, resulting in a leverage factor of 1.16. With a beginning book value (BV) of $10.00 a share at the start of the cycle, beginning IV is $11.60, or an intrinsic price of 16 percent over book value.

2 Units are granted on the basis of the initial IV. (For example, to match a competitive option grant worth $100,000 at a beginning IV of $11.60, 8,620 units would be granted.)

3 At the end of the cycle, the company's performance for the period is calculated. Assume, for example, the spread is now 5.00 percent and growth is down to 7.50 percent, resulting in a value leverage factor of 1.30. If ending book value is $15.00 a share, ending IV is $19.50.

4 The value of each unit is the difference between beginning IV and ending IV: $7.90 ($19.50 − 11.60). With 8,620 units, award payout would be about $68,100.

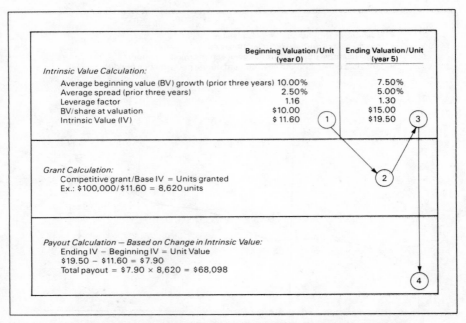

FIG. 24-19 Intrinsic Value Units Parallel Options in Grant and Unit Valuation

Unlike most traditional performance plans, the IV approach does not require plan designers to set arbitrary performance targets based on best guess of future economic scenarios. Rather, IV includes a built-in measure of the economy against which it measures management performance.

Economic Return Approaches

Table 24-1 shows economic return as calculated for one year. Assume earnings per share of $3.70, and $1.80 in depreciation and amortization added back to get cash available (generated by the business). The beginning equity is $25.40 per share, multiplied by a charge of 15 percent (the risk-free rate plus a risk premium), resulting in a cost of equity of $3.80. Cash available ($5.50) is reduced by $3.80, to give $1.70, the economic return on a one-year basis. These one-year figures are then added for several years to give a measure that parallels stock price (Figure 24-20). (Unlike intrinsic value, economic return is only a relative measure; it provides an index to change in stock price, whereas intrinsic value produces a result numerically close to stock price.)

Hybrid and Combination Approaches

Although intrinsic value and economic return surrogates can be used in incentives to track shareholder value more accurately than many internally based

Table 24-1   Calculation of Economic Return Per Share Data

Financial Data

Net income	$ 3.70
Depreciation and amortization	1.80
Cash flow	$ 5.50

Equity Charge

Book value	$25.40
Equity cost	15%
Charge for equity	$ 3.80

Economic Return

Cash flow	$ 5.50
Equity charge	3.80
Economic return	$ 1.70

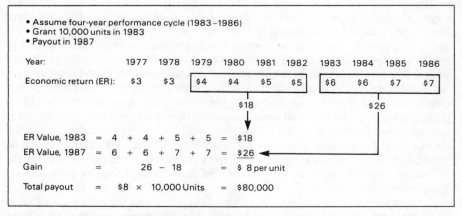

- Assume four-year performance cycle (1983–1986)
- Grant 10,000 units in 1983
- Payout in 1987

Year:	1977	1978	1979	1980	1981	1982	1983	1984	1985	1986
Economic return (ER):	$3	$3	$4	$4	$5	$5	$6	$6	$7	$7

$18 $26

ER Value, 1983 = 4 + 4 + 5 + 5 = $18
ER Value, 1987 = 6 + 6 + 7 + 7 = $26
Gain   =   26 − 18   = $ 8 per unit

Total payout   = $8 × 10,000 Units = $80,000

FIG. 24-20   Change in Shareholder Value Equals Change in Economic Return Unit Value

approaches, are they always the best choice for incentives? A plan will not be a true incentive unless management understands and accepts it and it is appropriate to the strategy and organizational variables noted previously. In some situations, the complexities of a surrogate-based plan make it hard to accept.

Of course, part of the difficulty in accepting such a plan may lie in learning new performance measures. To the extent that ingrained and previously accepted measures are simply wrong, changing them may be a difficult but necessary process. However, it is not realistic to expect that change to take place solely through incentive design. A workable plan that takes steps in the right direction is probably a better choice than one that is theoretically perfect but grudgingly accepted.

Fortunately, the lessons learned in developing value-based surrogates can be applied in designing a hybrid plan: an incentive structured around a relatively conventional plan, but with measures selected and payout calibrated using the value-based concepts. Advanced technology is confined to the design and calibration of the plan, but the plan itself is traditional in appearance. How this can be done is described below.

The first step in developing a hybrid plan is to agree on the performance measures (probably some variations of growth and real return) that link company performance to shareholder value. These measures are then embodied in a performance plan, and they are tested under a number of pay/performance scenarios. They should be discussed and analyzed, not only to compare modeled plan payouts against expectations, but also to develop an understanding of the variables under management influence that are most critical to performance. This discussion can assist management in understanding (and, therefore, accepting) different performance concepts, and it can suggest dimensions for a compromise between a pure approach and one that is close, but better understood. When management understands the new concepts reasonably well, training should be conducted for other participants, and the new measures should be included in information systems.

For example, suppose management accepts the importance of spread in return on equity and equity growth as determinants of shareholder value, but wishes to express its plan in familiar terms and to eliminate calculating an artificial measure at the beginning and end of each period in order to determine payout value. Suppose also that management accepts that returns should be judged relative to an external rate. Assuming that the firm's risk adjustment is constant over the performance period, "spread" (ROE less cost of equity, when cost of equity is a risk-free rate plus a company-adjusted risk premium) can be translated into a simpler measure. The first performance measure selected is the difference between the company's ROE and the average Treasury Bill rate over the performance period.

Suppose also that earnings per share is ingrained in the culture, and management does not feel that it can change this situation overnight. Moreover, EPS is currently the language in which operational decisions are made. Therefore, equity growth is translated (through simple financial modeling, with an assumed dividend rate) into its impact on EPS. Average EPS growth then becomes the second measure used in the hybrid plan.

Two measures that correlate with shareholder value have now been selected. From the pay/performance scenario analysis, each scenario can be expressed in terms of the two performance measures chosen as well as in terms of the payout that would result. Through simulation or correlation analysis, a table can then be constructed directly relating the selected company performance variables into incentive payouts. An example is illustrated in Table 24-2.

The incentive calculations have now been greatly simplified. Suppose that ROE over a four-year performance period has been 15 percent. Further,

Table 24-2 Indirect Approach: Use Surrogate to Calibrate Payout Matrix

AVERAGE (1989–1993) INTRINSIC VALUE LESS BASE
(1983) INTRINSIC VALUE

Spread Above T-Bill	Earnings Per Share Growth From 1983		
	10%	20%	30%
0%	$ 0	$ 5	$ 25
5	10	30	75
10	20	60	125
15	30	90	175
20	40	120	225

suppose that the average Treasury Bill rate during that period is 10 percent, so the company has achieved a return of 5 percent above the Treasury Bill rate. If, during that period, the company's average EPS growth was 10 percent per share, the table shows that each incentive unit awarded will be worth $10.00. Since the payout for that cell was determined from a value-based model, it is also known that shareholder return would roughly parallel that increase.

In developing these hybrid plans, it is important to realize that simplicity can have its costs. Each step away from a surrogate that truly tracks shareholder value may make a model easier to understand, but it may also reduce its accuracy. Further, surrogates capture a dimension of change that hybrids do not: transition. The stock market (and IV) recognizes that increasing the level at which a company operates increases its value during the interval the change takes place. (Suppose that a company is operated in such a way that it generates a 5 percent return to shareholders. One day, management realizes how to make it generate 15 percent, and implements that decision immediately. Over the year that follows, will the return to shareholders be 15 percent, or something greater? It will be greater: During the period when modes of operation are being changed, the value leverage factor will increase until it reaches its higher steady state. In addition to the 15 percent return the shareholders realize from the new mode of business operation, they will benefit from the transition in the leverage factor.) The matrix, because it is based on conditions at only one point, cannot as easily reflect transitional changes (unless it is done over each year).

Design Considerations

The authors believe that the issues discussed above have an impact on the creation of value-based incentive systems. Nonetheless, other steps can be considered to increase effectiveness.

- *Eligibility.* For incentive purposes, most companies should move toward the goal of weighting long-term incentives much more heavily at the top of an organization than many do now, and shift the bulk of the incentive at lower management levels to annual plans. This would align pay better with responsibilities, and it would use the power of the annual plan to cause desired actions.

- *Performance Cycles.* Along with narrowing eligibility for long-term plans, it is suggested that longer cycles be used. A primary reason is that the more accurate measures of long-term performance discussed above allow a plan to run longer without need for frequent changes caused by factors such as poor forecasts and incorrect measures. Further, if full business cycles can be included, management performance (vs. external factors) is better reflected. Finally, creating shareholder value is not simply doing well for three or four years; it is the achievement of sustained performance. Longer cycles reflect this.

SUMMARY AND CONCLUSIONS

Apart from its uses a compensation tool, the notion of value-based performance measurement seems likely to gain acceptance because of its applicability in other areas, especially in strategic planning. Executive compensation plan designers should become familiar with these tools, both because of their own intrinsic merit, and because corporate boards and management will expect experts to know about such devices.

This chapter has discussed how traditional and annual management incentive plans attempt to link pay and performance, but they may actually inhibit managers from implementing their long-term strategy. Many annual incentive plans are driven by short-term annual financial performance (e.g., profit vs. budget) and they not only fail to provide an incentive for nonfinancial performance (progress in the development of a new product), but actually inhibit it. Traditional long-term plans pay off if the timing is right (such as in stock option plans) or they focus on measures that, by themselves, have little to do with long-term value and can result in its destruction (as in the case of EPS growth).

The chapter discusses the difference between incentive plans, which can cause managers to take action they might not have otherwise taken, and reward systems, which are based solely on results. The point here, of course, is that incentives can focus everyone's efforts on the tasks (i.e., the strategy) that will achieve an increase in shareholder value. Incentives do not merely reward good results: They can make good results more likely.

This chapter outlines an approach to using the power of incentives to support the strategy, and outlines basic concepts in both short-term and long-term compensation plans:

- Annual incentives should be geared to the few key elements of the long-range strategy that must be done this year (nonfinancial steps) as well as to financial results.

- Long-term incentive plans should reflect management's success in accomplishing the mission: generally, increasing shareholder value. Success should be measured not only in share price on a given day, but in management's ability to improve the underlying or intrinsic value of the enterprise. The best internal performance measures seem to be return, relative to alternate opportunities, and growth, each weighted appropriately.
- Incentives should be designed so that participants see the relationships between their actions and plan results.

Finally, the chapter outlines approaches to annual and/or long-term plan design that combine economic and strategic planning theory with the practical considerations of pay plans that participants understand.

The value-based concept offers the promise of incentive plans that produce payouts that parallel shareholder gains and incorporate performance measures that can be influenced by executive action. Of course, neither the IV model nor the economic return model nor their variations should be applied blindly. A standard plan is unlikely to meet any one company's needs because it will not be sufficiently integrated with its culture, information systems, and processes. The value-based concept must be tailored to specific needs.

Designing value-based compensation plans is a process that varies from company to company. To be successful, the process must meld pragmatic attention to what the organization can accept with an understanding of factors that create shareholder value.

25

Developing Managers for Strategic Management

H. MICHAEL HAYES

Graduate School of Business Administration, University of Colorado at Denver
Formerly with Management Development Institute, General Electric Company

INTRODUCTION

Since World War II, interest in the practice of management and in the work of the manager has increased tremendously. Studies of management systems and managerial work have blossomed into full-fledged academic disciplines. Books on management routinely make the best-seller lists. Many schools of business, at both graduate and undergraduate levels, are changing their names to "schools of management." Regardless of the name, enrollment in schools of business and management has increased dramatically. More and more companies are establishing internal management development programs, and the growth in nondegree seminars, workshops, courses, and other educational programs offered by trainers, consultants, and universities has been explosive.

Rightly or wrongly, management (used here to mean management systems and practices, as well as individuals in managerial positions) gets much of the credit or blame for national economic performance. In the 1960s, Servan-Schreiber warned Europe of the "American Challenge" based on his view of excellence in U.S. management. In the 1970s, it was Japanese management that surprised the world with its competence. In the early years of the 1980s, U.S. management is increasingly being questioned with respect to both its basic values (particularly its emphasis on short-range results) and its ability to achieve strategic organizational objectives.

Although the ability of management to influence national destiny is open to question, there is no question about the importance of managers to an organization. As Drucker has said, "Managers are the basic resource of the business enterprise."[1] They are, he elaborated, "the most expensive resource in most businesses—and the one that depreciates the fastest and needs the most constant replenishment." For all organizations, therefore, a significant question has been and must be: "How do we ensure the quantity and quality of managers necessary to achieve the goals of the enterprise?" Increasingly, the answer to this question starts with some kind of management development system. Today concepts of strategic management provide both a new dimension to management development and new ways of thinking about the nature of management development activities.

MANAGEMENT DEVELOPMENT AND STRATEGIC MANAGEMENT

The increase in numbers of directors of management development, the adoption of succession planning systems, and the increased use of education programs, both internal and external, all attest that an increasing number of firms have concluded that management development activities should be treated explicitly and proactively. However, the precise nature of these activities and their effectiveness varies tremendously. In many instances, management development activities seem to take place independently of the objectives of the firm; occasionally, they seem to be in conflict with those objectives. There are a

---

[1] Peter F. Drucker, *People and Performance: The Best of Peter Drucker on Management* (New York: Harper & Row, 1977), p. 3.

number of reasons for such independence or conflict. In some instances, business objectives and strategies lack clarity or are not adequately communicated to those involved in management development. Where management development is a staff activity, it may be outside the organizational mainstream or the necessity for its existence may receive only lip service from top management. Basic values of those charged with the responsibility of management development activities can be at odds with the values of the line management and so raise questions about the appropriateness of development activities.

Even where management development activities are part of the organizational mainstream and closely integrated with business strategy, opportunities for conflict still exist. One authority, for instance, has observed that the truly successful executive education program is one that does not induce any new behavior in the participants and so allows them to return to their work with a minimum of disturbance to the organization.[2] Although this may have been stated partly with tongue in cheek, it underscores a fundamental dilemma of management development; that is, how to ensure that changes in behavior induced through development activities are consistent with organizational objectives, systems, and practices.

Resolution of this dilemma starts with a clear articulation of the nature and objectives of management development, on an organization-specific basis, and a high level commitment to integrate management development activities into the mainstream of organizational work. The purpose of this chapter is to assist in such articulation and integration. Given the focus of this chapter on developing managers for strategic management, it is necessary first to establish the relationship of management development to concepts of strategic management.

In his comprehensive treatment of the subject, House[3] defined management development as "any attempt to improve current or future managerial performance by imparting information, conditioning attitudes or increasing skills." He continued, "Hence, management development includes such efforts as on-the-job coaching, counseling, classroom training, job rotation, selected readings, planned experience and assignments to understudy positions." According to House, possible outputs of these efforts include desired changes in knowledge, desired changes in attitude, desired changes in skills, desired changes in job performance plus unintended conflict, anxiety, and frustration. Implicit in House's definition is the need to specify desired knowledge, skills, attitudes, and dimensions of job performance and to conduct management development activities that optimize desired changes while minimizing unintended conflict, anxiety, and frustration. However these may have been specified in the past, strategic management will require new knowledge, skills, attitudes, and job performance above and beyond what has traditionally been associated with managerial work. The nature of these increased requirements is suggested throughout this book. Their flavor is nicely captured in a 1977 address by Reginald H. Jones, then chairman and chief executive officer of the General Electric Company, and in a 1980 article by Gluck, Kaufman, and Wallech.[4]

---

[2] H. R. Smith, "Executive Development Program," *Business Horizons* (April 1974), pp. 39–46.

[3] Robert J. House, *Management Development: Design, Evaluation and Implementation* (Ann Arbor, Mich.: University of Michigan, 1967).

[4] Frederick W. Gluck, Stephen P. Kaufman, and A. Steven Wallech, "Strategic Management for Competitive Advantage," *Harvard Business Review* (July-August 1980), pp. 154–161.

In his talk, "Strategic Management for the 1980s," Jones described changes in General Electric's management system and then identified the following benefits that the refined management system should provide in the years ahead:

1 It should strengthen the ability to leverage opportunities into sustained earnings growth, while containing the downside risks.

2 It should provide even greater assurance that new ventures get the attention, resources, and continuity they need to succeed.

3 It should increase the ability to cope with complexity, uncertainty, and accelerating change.

4 It should produce a more effective approach to the integration of international activities.

5 It should improve company-wide management of basic resources—human, financial, and technological.

6 It should ensure the availability and motivation of trained, seasoned top-level executives.

In their article, Gluck, Kaufman, and Wallech defined strategic management as "a system of corporate values, planning capabilities, or organizational responsibilities, that couple strategic thinking with operational decision making at *all* levels and across functional lines of authority in a corporation" (emphasis added). In tracing the evolution to strategic management, the authors develop a four-phase model in which strategic management is the last phase, joining strategic planning and management in a single process. They go on to state that firms that manage strategically are characterized by the thoroughness with which management links strategic planning to operational decision making, a process largely accomplished by:

1 A planning framework that cuts across organizational boundaries and facilitates strategic decision making about customer groups and resources;

2 A planning process that stimulates entrepreneurial thinking;

3 A corporate values system that reinforces managers' commitments to the company's strategy.

These views of strategic management suggest expanding our perspective of managerial work. Strategic planning skills will become a requirement for all managers, either because strategic planning will occur at more levels and more managers will be included in the planning process, or as a way to ensure the strategic understanding necessary to better link strategic planning and operational decision making. While emphasis will still be on managerial skills necessary to achieve the objectives of the enterprise, increasingly managers will need to have the skills necessary to develop new objectives and methods for their accomplishment. In other words, an uncertain, complex, and changing environment will put a premium on entrepreneurship and innovation.

The complexity of strategic management will emphasize the importance of developing skills appropriate for unique business situations. That is, managers not only will need basic managerial, strategic, and entrepreneurial skills but also will have to understand how to apply them in a given organizational culture, structure, or stage of business life cycle.

Finally, the concept of strategic management does not imply that something is learned in addition to traditional management. Rather, and as this chapter attempts to convey, concepts of strategic management should permeate all management development activities.

CONCEPTS OF MANAGEMENT DEVELOPMENT

Strategic management is good management practice applied in the context of the individual firm's objectives and strategies. The imperative of strategic management is to connect the work that is done in the organization to its strategy. This means that management development objectives, systems, and practices should be rooted not only in a generic understanding of the nature of managerial work and how individuals develop but in an understanding of how the nature of managerial work is influenced by the individual's position level in the organization, by the characteristics of the organization, and by the nature of the business situation.

This perspective leads to six basic premises regarding management development activities:

1 Development is an ongoing learning process involving the individual's knowledge, attitudes, and skills. It occurs through the interaction of the individual with his or her total environment. Hence, the majority of development occurs on the job. It is enhanced by coaching, mentoring, courses, and other activities.

2 Ultimate responsibility for developing managers for strategic management rests with the individual. The role of management development, as an organizational activity, is to facilitate and encourage individual pursuit of development.

3 Developing managers for strategic management, particularly with respect to knowledge and skills, is a hierarchical and sequential process. Required knowledge and skills vary according to organizational level. Development activities must be keyed to the individual's past development and current needs, and must have a finite horizon with respect to development for the future.

4 Developing managers for strategic management must take into consideration the current strategy, vision, or grand design of the firm and its internal and external environments, preparing the managers to participate in new strategy development.

5 The ability of an organization to pursue a particular strategy is inextricably linked with its corporate culture. Therefore, the development of managers for strategic management must have as one of its fundamental purposes either reinforcement or change of corporate culture. Further, attitudes toward management development are a significant part of the corporate culture.

6 In developing strategic management skills, a wide range of knowledge and skills can be imparted in a variety of ways. Therefore, each organization must decide what knowledge and skills are important in its environment and what methods should be used in their achievement.

How Managers Develop

The traditional academic view associates management development with formal education: undergraduate, graduate, or, increasingly, nondegree short courses offered by a department of management education within the university. In industry, however, there is general agreement that most development occurs on the job. Much of this development is informal and ad hoc. Its nature and extent are driven by the particular job situation: the demands of work at the moment and the work group with whom the manager interacts. In this environment, some individuals will learn more than others, or learn more rapidly, because of intelligence, previous background, or personal initiative. On-the-job development can be enhanced by sequenced work assignments, on-the-job coaching, special assignments, and classroom education.

A Career-Spanning View of Manager Development

Most managers start their careers as individual contributors in a technical specialty or functional area. Work experience as an individual contributor is, at least in the United States, generally confined to one such specialty or area. Promotion through a series of managerial positions is generally within one function, and most promotions to general management are made from the ranks of those who reached senior functional positions.

There are exceptions to this pattern, of course. In some firms, cross functional assignments for both individual contributors and managers are the norm. In others, the nature of even a first-time manager assignment is multifunctional and managers are exposed to all functions in a relatively low risk, low complexity environment.

The pattern of significant time in a single function is more prevalent in manufacturing organizations with large research and development, engineering, or manufacturing functions. It is less likely in service organizations. However, most managers have a strong technical or functional background and have demonstrated significant competence as individual contributors prior to promotion to managerial positions. Management development, therefore, first must concern itself with building on this technical competence within the function and then, for those who rise to the top of the function, must facilitate the transition to general or multifunction management.

In broad terms, then, management development should concern itself with the personal growth and development of an individual over a career that spans a series of assignments. Ideally these assignments should:

- Appropriately recognize the variation in individual learning rates, with respect to both the nature and the length of assignments;
- Ensure that each assignment builds on a previous assignment;
- Take into account not only growth on the current assignment but preparation for transition and enhancement of growth on future assignments;
- Have a sense of trajectory but recognize that trajectories may change;
- Have a reasonable time horizon.

Notions of how managers develop and the concept of a career-spanning sequence of assignments suggest both the complexity of the process and some of the problems associated with its management. Inevitably this raises questions as to the extent to which individuals can pursue their own development and the role the organization should play in management development.

Responsibility for Management Development

There is a wide range of practice and opportunity with respect to assigning responsibility for management development. At one extreme are examples of what might best be described as omnipotent paternalism. In such cases extensive management development activity may exist but decisions regarding promotion or education are made by upper management with essentially no input from the individual involved. At the other extreme are organizations where, either because of managerial philosophy or resource constraints, overt management development activities are essentially nonexistent. In these cases promotion or placement decisions are made solely on the basis of the short-term needs of the firm, and formal training or education is entirely the responsibility of the individual.

Between these two extremes there is opportunity for significant variation in approach. In the ideal model for management development, individuals

- Have comprehensive understanding of themselves and their strengths, weaknesses, and goals;
- Have complete understanding of the various career paths available to them and the knowledge and skill required to pursue a particular path;
- Have available a wide array of means by which to pursue personal development; and
- Take the initiative to identify and pursue specific development activities.

The role of the organization in this ideal model consists essentially of supporting individual effort and initiative.

Achieving this ideal model, however, is unlikely. Individuals in their early career stages are not likely to have the personal insights the model requires of them, nor are they likely to have sufficient understanding of the knowledge and skills required to pursue a chosen career path. The nature of organizational life is such that management systems and practices and the availability of specific development opportunities can significantly influence the climate for development. Further, there is general agreement that the immediate manager plays a key role in subordinate development. How this role is viewed by the management population and how it is carried out can materially influence the extent to which individuals can take control of their own development.

A more practical model of responsibility is one that recognizes the shared responsibility of the individual, the immediate manager, and the company in the development process. Such a model is shown in Figure 25-1, which represents the extent to which each group is able to take the lead in development. Management development systems and practices must fully exploit the development potential inherent in individual, immediate manager, and company ini-

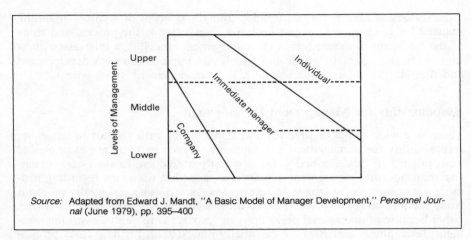

Source: Adapted from Edward J. Mandt, "A Basic Model of Manager Development," *Personnel Journal* (June 1979), pp. 395–400

FIG. 25-1 Locus of Development Opportunity

tiatives. Before these systems and practices can be discussed, the nature of managerial work as a basis for developing managers for strategic management must be considered.

DEVELOPING OBJECTIVES FOR STRATEGIC MANAGEMENT DEVELOPMENT

As those who are experienced in management development well know, moving from broad concepts involving the need to improve knowledge, skills, attitudes, and job performance to more operational objectives is both challenging and frustrating. Management, and managerial work, is not a science. As Drucker[5] has pointed out, the terms themselves are slippery and mean different things to different people. Nevertheless, without some reasonably well-developed, organization-specific model of the nature of managerial work, management development activities will lack direction and purpose. Although it is beyond the scope of this chapter to review all the thinking on management, it may be helpful to review certain concepts as a preface to presenting an approach to developing such a model.

The Nature of Managerial Work

In broad terms, there are three major schools of thought regarding what managers do. The classical view of management that influenced much of early management development was a simple one. Managers, it was deductively asserted, plan, organize, coordinate, command, and control to maximize the profits of

---

[5] Peter F. Drucker, op. cit., p. 47

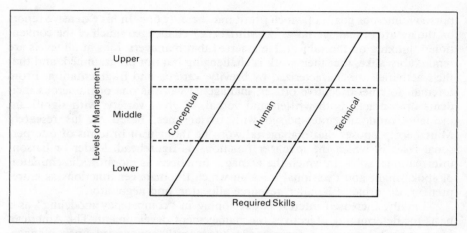

FIG. 25-2 Skill Mix as a Function of Organizational Level

the firm. The basic theme was introduced by Fayol in 1916.[6] There have been variations, of course. MacKenzie[7] described the work of managers in terms of planning, organizing, staffing, directing, and controlling. Ralph Cordiner, President of General Electric in the 1950s, said managerial work at General Electric involved planning, organizing, implementing, and measuring. While precise development activities that focus on these dimensions of managerial work occasionally seemed elusive, the dimensions at least provided a sense of direction.

In the early 1950s, Katz[8] proposed that managerial work could be considered in terms of conceptual, human, and technical skills. While these skills are required for all managerial work, they are required in differing amounts as a function of the manager's level of responsibility. This variation is illustrated in Figure 25-2. In an update of his original work, Katz divided human skills into two categories: leadership ability within the manager's own unit and skill in intergroup relations. He stated that technical expertise at top management levels is far more important than he originally thought, to the extent that this requirement for technical expertise may be the constraint that limits the ability of a professional manager to move easily from one industry to another.

Increasingly, the classical and deductive views of managerial work have been modified by research that focuses on what managers actually do. In their landmark work on deductive organizations, March and Simon[9] developed the theme that managers do not single-mindedly pursue profit but, rather, that they

---

[6] As described in Henry Mintzberg, *The Nature of Managerial Work* (Englewood Cliffs, N.J.: Prentice-Hall, Inc., 1980, 2d edition).

[7] R. A. MacKenzie "The Management Process in 3-D," *Harvard Business Review* (March-April 1965), pp. 131–147.

[8] Robert L. Katz, "Skills of an Effective Administrator," *Harvard Business Review* (September-October 1974), pp. 90–102.

[9] James G. March and Herbert A. Simon, *Organizations* (New York: John Wiley & Sons, Inc., 1958).

pursue numerous goals, of which profit may be only one. In his extensive report on the nature of managerial work, Mintzberg[10] challenged much of the conventional thinking on the subject. He asserted that managers' jobs at all levels are remarkably alike, that their work is challenging but not programmed, and that their activities are characterized by brevity, variety, and fragmentation. From foreman to chief executive officer, managerial work is one of numerous incidents or contacts, both written and verbal, of great variety, with significant incidents randomly interspersed with trivial ones. Based on his research, Mintzberg proposes that managerial work be thought of in terms of interpersonal roles in which the manager functions as figurehead, leader or liaison; informational roles, in which the manager functions as monitor, disseminator, or spokesman; and decisional roles, in which the manager functions as entrepreneur, disturbance handler, resource allocator, and negotiator.

Finally, increased interest is developing in "competency modeling" as a basis for determining objectives for management development. The American Management Association, for instance, has recently announced a new management education program developed from a research-based competency model.[11] Analysis of over 2,000 job studies that focused on managers who were outstanding performers identified 18 generic management competencies which cluster into four groups identified as goal and action management, directing subordinates, human resource management, and leadership. In addition, certain generic business knowledge (e.g., accounting, marketing) was determined as a threshhold competency for effective managers. The program specifies desired levels of competency, assesses individual competency, and then provides education tailored to individual need.

Whether objectives for management development are driven by the classical school, the behavioral school, competency models, or a synthesis of all three, the development of managers for strategic management needs to take additional factors into consideration.

Ability to Think Strategically

It is perhaps surprising that the three streams of thought about managerial work seldom make explicit reference to strategy. This may simply reflect the fact that strategy is relatively new as a major factor in business management thinking. Alternatively, it may be that strategy has been seen as something of concern only to strategic planners or to high-level managers, unnecessary to broad management development. Clearly, this is not consistent with the concept of strategic management.

In an excellent treatment of the topic, Uyterhoeven, Ackerman, and Rosenblum[12] described the "general manager as strategist" and made the case

---

[10] Henry Mintzberg, op. cit.

[11] Harry F. Evarts, "The Competence Program at the American Management Associations," unpublished paper dated January 4, 1982.

[12] Hugo E. R. Uyterhoeven, Robert W. Ackerman, and John W. Rosenblum, *Strategy and Organization: Text and Cases in General Management* (Homewood, Ill.: Richard D. Irwin, Inc., 1977)

that general management is everybody's business. As they pointed out, the number of general manager jobs (meaning the manager of a multifunctional business unit at a level below the chief executive) is growing, as more and more firms move toward divisional forms of organization. Within the framework of overall corporate strategy, these general managers are charged with executing business unit strategy.

These strategies, however, are seldom formulated in isolation from the rest of the organization. Functional managers frequently provide input to the strategic planning process and, increasingly, may be assigned major responsibility for strategy development. More importantly, these functional managers continually make operating decisions that have strategic implications. In a complex and uncertain environment, strategy must inevitably be broad in terms of methods specified for its achievement. Functional managers, and in fact all managers, have increasing discretion as to the activities they engage in to pursue organizational objectives. As they exercise that discretion, their actions may either further define or modify strategy formulated at higher levels. It is imperative, therefore, that they understand and accept responsibility for how their actions either support or modify the organization's strategy.

Such strategic thinking—that is, the thought processes that the manager brings to bear on matching organizational capability and aspirations with opportunities that exist in the external environment—has several major elements:

- Understanding the relevant external environment;
- Understanding the capability and objectives of the organization;
- Understanding the linkages between loosely connected events;
- Recognition of multiple influences on outcomes;
- Ability to analyze "messy" or undefined problems;
- Ability to sense new opportunities and establish appropriate objectives based on environmental analysis;
- Ability to envision a broad array of strategies or solutions to achieve organizational objectives.

The Unique Business Situation

The great business legend of the past half century is that of the "professional manager" who can step into any business or division and run it well.

Now this legend is reduced to myth. And the advice from Harvard's John P. Kotter to the millions of American executives who want to move up is this: Stay put and learn your trade. Successful managers are made very slowly—not born or bought.[13]

Beyond the need to develop an understanding of strategic concepts and formulation, perhaps nothing more strongly defines the development needs of

---

[13] From the jacket of John P. Kotter, *The General Managers* (New York: The Free Press, 1982).

strategic managers than the elements of the particular business situation in which the manager must operate: the position of a business in its life cycle, how the business adapts to its environment, the business' form of organization, and its corporate culture.

Business Life Cycle. The personal characteristics, knowledge, and skills required to manage a business in its introductory or growth stages vary considerably from those required to manage a business in either its maturity or its decline. At General Electric, for example, investment priority categories of invest/grow, select earn or grow, and harvest/divest (roughly corresponding to the business life cycle stages of introduction/growth, maturity, and decline) require different managerial skills. [14]

- *Invest/grow.* Manpower emphasis is on entrepreneurs oriented to expansion— whether organic, by acquisition, or by joint venture.

- *Select earn or grow.* Manpower emphasis is on sophisticated businesspersons capable of intensely critical and complex analysis, strong strategic planning, clearly articulated plans, innovative cost and productivity improvement programs, and real time control of results. Top managers *must* be able and willing to make tough trade-off decisions.

- *Harvest/divest.* Manpower emphasis is on solid, experienced "hard nosed operators" with proven track records in generating cash and in utilizing tight controls.

These requirements suggest criteria for both selection of managers and their developmental needs. Few organizations remain static, however, and most have patterns of adaptation to their environment that must be considered in developing managers for strategic management.

Types of Organizational Adaptation. How organizations adapt to a changing environment as they make product-market decisions, select technologies for development, and put in place administrative processes varies significantly. Miles and Snow[15] have identified four patterns of organizational behavior which suggest significantly different adaptive approaches, each requiring very different managerial skills:

- *Defenders* are organizations that have narrow product-market domains. Top managers in this type of organization are highly expert in their organization's limited area of operation but tend not to search outside their domains for new opportunities. As a result of this narrow focus, these organizations seldom make major adjustments in their technology, structure, or methods of operation. Instead, they devote primary attention to improving the efficiency of their

---

[14] From a General Electric policy manual.

[15] Raymond E. Miles and Charles C. Snow, *Organizational Strategy, Structure and Process* (New York: McGraw Hill, Inc., 1978).

existing operations. In these organizations, critical skills focus on current technology and problem-solving (rather than problem-finding) behavior.

- *Prospectors* are ogranizations that almost continually search for market opportunities. They regularly experiment with potential responses to emerging environmental trends. Thus, these organizations often are the creators of change and uncertainty to which their competitors must respond. However, because of their strong concern for product and market innovation, these organizations usually are not completely efficient. In these organizations, critical skills are the ability to monitor a wide range of environmental conditions, trends, and events, and to develop creative responses to selected opportunities.

- *Analyzers* are organizations that operate in two types of product-market domains: one relatively stable, the other changing. In their stable areas, these organizations operate routinely and efficiently through use of formalized structures and processes. In their more turbulent areas, top managers watch their competitors closely for new ideas, and then rapidly adopt those that appear to be the most promising. Critical skills focus on both managing the internal environment and understanding the external environment.

- *Reactors* are organizations in which top managers frequently perceive change and uncertainty occurring in their organizational environments but are unable to respond to these changes effectively. Because this type of organization lacks a consistent strategy-structure relationship, it seldom makes adjustments of any sort until forced to do so by environmental pressures. Critical skills are not consistently defined and the organization tends to be unstable.

These patterns of adaptation not only suggest varying managerial skills but also emphasize the difficulty of developing these skills when organizational strategy is not clear. For firms that successfully pursue appropriate patterns of adaptation, however, it is likely that the organizational structure will change. This too will influence the development of strategic management.

Organizational Structure. Most industrial organizations initially produce one product, or a limited product line, for one market. If market growth provides sufficient opportunity for sales growth, the firm may continue in a single product, single market mode. Other companies may elect to add new products and seek out new markets, thus evolving into multiproduct, multimarket forms of organization and, ultimately into a global multidivisional structure. Possible paths of organizational growth and forms of organizational structure are shown in Figure 25-3.

The nature of organizational growth and the type of structures used to accommodate this growth affect the nature of managerial knowledge and skills. For firms that grow in size in single markets with limited product lines, or are already at this stage, emphasis is on technology and in-depth market knowledge. Interpersonal skills focus on the use of power to ensure control of resources. Conceptual skills are primarily concerned with management systems designed to improve the efficiency of the organization or to refine relationships with the external environment. On the other hand, for firms that grow through

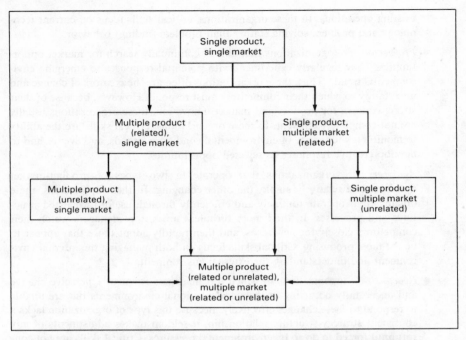

FIG. 25-3 Evolution of Product Market Approach: A Determinant of Organizational Structure

product line proliferation in multiple markets, or that are already at this stage, in-depth knowledge of technology and markets is no longer feasible. Instead of relying on their own knowledge of technology and markets, managers must become skilled at extracting what they need to know from specialists. Traditional forms of authority are unlikely to exist and interpersonal skills must focus on persuasion rather than power. Conceptual skills are more concerned with multiple linkages in which relationships between cause and effect are not clear.

Culture. Increasingly, corporate culture is being recognized as a major influence on management development. Culture can be described as the set of habitual and traditional ways of thinking, feeling, and reacting that are characteristic of the ways a particular society meets its problems at a particular point in time. Within a corporation these habitual and traditional ways can enhance communication, reduce intra-organizational conflicts, establish well-understood problem-solving behavior, and facilitate achievement of organizational objectives, provided they are consistent with the attitudes and values of the individuals in the organization. Conversely, if new objectives and new strategies are not consistent with corporate culture, the probability of their achievement is low because of misunderstandings resulting from poor communication and increased intra-organizational conflict.

Schwartz and Davis[16] have recently developed a useful framework for examining the match between corporate culture and business strategy. Their framework requires, first, defining corporate culture in terms of tasks of innovating, decision making, communicating, organizing, monitoring, and appraising and rewarding, and then defining it in terms of company-wide relationships, boss-subordinate relationships, peer relationships, and interdepartment relationships. Once culture and other organizational dimensions have been defined in similar terms, their compatibility can be assessed systematically.

In the event of incompatibility, a judgment can be made on how (or if) compatibility can be increased by management development activities. For management development, therefore, it is important to decide whether the purpose of management development activities is to reinforce the existing culture or to effect its change because of new objectives and strategies. In particular, it is important for management development activities not to increase cultural conflict in the organization. In simple terms, if the predominant culture is theory X, and this is the desire of top management, then training or developing managerial skills to operate in a theory Y mode can only have negative results. Similarly, it is not likely that managers can be educated to single-mindedly pursue maximum profits this year if it is a certainty that this year's results are the floor for determining next year's budget.

The Changing Nature of Business in the Future

Much of the current understanding of managerial work is based on what has occurred in the past. In an increasingly uncertain future, it is reasonable to expect that the nature of managerial work will change. In the 1980s, it will be increasingly important for managers to:

- Be technically competent in basic business functions
- Have intellectual breadth and be comfortable in the world of ideas
- Have good strategic planning capability
- Be socially responsible
- Be politically sophisticated
- Be world-minded
- Have high ethical standards

The American Assembly of Collegiate Schools of Business in conjunction with the European Foundation for Management Development sponsored an international conference in Paris to discuss "Managers for the XXI Century: Their Education and Development."[17] Some of the conclusions of this conference were:

---

[16] Howard Schwartz and Stanley M. Davis, "Matching Corporate Culture and Business Strategy," *Organizational Dynamics* (Summer 1981), pp. 30–48.

[17] Clarence C. Walton (ed.), *Managers for the XXI Century* (Washington, D.C.: American Assembly of Collegiate Schools of Business, 1981).

- The concept of lifelong learning will spread, with growing recognition that management schools cannot teach everything the future manager needs to know. This suggests an ongoing process of learning on the job, coupled with appropriate returns to the classroom.
- Increased attention will be needed on noncognitive skills (e.g., communication, negotiation, and other interpersonal skills), but this increased attention must not come at the expense of technical or cognitive skills.
- With respect to the manager's external functions:
  a. The number of claimants (or stakeholders) will increase and greater diversity will be required for organization structures, especially for enterprises operating both nationally and internationally (suggesting that shared authority will become a more prevalent organizational characteristic).
  b. Sharply rising public demand for social as well as economic accountability will in many cases require managers to play a leadership role in modes not defined by recent industrial history or understood in traditional theory.
- With respect to the manager's internal functions:
  a. Internal responsibility to mobilize, develop, and deploy resources will continue. Style, however, will have to change.
  b. Authority derived from property rights and meritocracy will yield to industrial democracy as a legitimate basis for authority.
  c. Managerial style will change from a predominantly hierarchical, authoritarian pattern to a more consultative one.
  d. The kind of person attracted to management, especially to management in a large corporation, may change because the fundamental nature of the managerial role is changing.
  e. Because of greater organizational complexity, more innovation will be required of managers.

DESIGNING A STRATEGIC MANAGEMENT DEVELOPMENT PROGRAM

In designing a program for developing managers for strategic management, management must shape the system to the specific organization in which it will operate. Shaping the system requires answers to several critical questions;

- In this organization, what are the major generic aspects of managerial work important at all managerial levels? This should include such things as work planning, interviewing, performance appraisal, objective setting discussions, salary planning, career counseling, and, for strategic managers, strategic planning or thinking.
- In this organization, what knowledge and skills are particularly important to manage within a given function? That is, in addition to the basic techniques of the function, does the functional context influence the mix and intensity of generic knowledge and skills?

- In this organization, what knowledge and skills are required at each level, regardless of function? For the first-time manager, this usually focuses on basic or generic skills. For the second-level manager, this may broaden to include multifunctional understanding. For the third-level manager, this broadens to include concepts of strategy and strategy formulation.
- In this organization, how are these broadly defined requirements for knowledge and skills modified by the business situation, company culture, and changing corporate objectives?

The systems available for developing managers for strategic management fall in three broad categories:

1 Those that influence the nature of the work itself and so establish the broad environment which directs and within which development occurs;

2 Those that deal with selection, promotion, and placement; and

3 Those that deal with education and training.

Influencing of Work

As stated previously, most manager development occurs on the job. Obviously jobs vary in their potential for development, both because of their inherent nature and because of the ways they are structured or influenced. Maximum potential exists when work is challenging and clearly relevant to the business strategy.

The number of employees who give "lack of challenging work" as their reason for moving to other jobs emphasizes that challenging work cannot be taken for granted. Similarly, instances where employees are engaged in activities that appear inconsistent with the business strategy are sufficiently numerous to emphasize that the relevance of work to the business strategy also cannot be taken for granted.[18] In developing managers for strategic management, ways of increasing the likelihood of challenging work that fits with the business strategy must be considered. Job descriptions, work planning systems, strategic planning systems, measurement and reward systems, and special assignments are useful tools to accomplish this objective.

Job Descriptions. Because "challenging work" is an ambiguous term, managers and subordinates can have legitimate disagreements about whether work is challenging or not. In addition, not all work can be challenging, and managers and subordinates can have legitimate disagreements on the potential for challenging work in a given job. Although resolving these disagreements involves judgment calls, good job descriptions improve the quality of such calls and increase the likelihood that all jobs will be structured to maximize their potential for challenging work.

---

[18] See John M. Hobbs and Donald F. Heany, "Coupling Strategy to Operating Plans," *Harvard Business Review* (May-June 1977), pp. 119–126.

A job description system that holds managers responsible for job descriptions of their subordinates and that subjects job descriptions to evaluation and periodic review by others imposes discipline on what otherwise is likely to be a fuzzy and unclear area. This is not a popular activity with most managers. Some fail to see its importance. Some find it difficult. It is, nevertheless, an important first step in increasing positive results from on-the-job experience.

Work Planning Systems. Challenging work is both complex and dynamic. It involves multiple objectives that are difficult to quantify and subject to change. It requires independent initiative and judgment with respect to method, timing, and application of resources. Therefore, some sort of system is required at every level in the organization for establishing, adjusting, and meeting these multiple objectives.

Variously called work planning, management by objectives (MBO), and performance management, systems that establish performance objectives and how they will be accomplished are widely used. They often have mixed results. In some instances the systems are oversold and expectations are too high. In others, the systems are improperly designed or installed or are not adequately understood by those who implement them. On the other hand, where expectations are reasonable and where the systems are designed for the particular organization or business and carefully installed with thorough communication, results are generally excellent. Key characteristics of successful planning systems are mutual understanding between boss and subordinate, and mutual agreement on objectives and the broad basis for their accomplishment. Where these characteristics exist, potential for on-the-job development increases.

Strategic Planning Systems. Establishing a strategic planning system has a powerful impact on the organization. Its very existence indicates that strategic planning is important and strongly suggests the need to think strategically. With appropriate linkages, a strategic planning system provides the opportunity to increase significantly the likelihood that work throughout the organization is relevant to the business strategy.

These linkages deal with the connections among the strategic plan, the operating plan, and the individual work activities. These connections cannot be taken for granted. There are innumerable instances of excellent strategies that have not lived up to their potential because the work in the organization did not support the strategy. At a minimum, these connections require:

- Broad communication of the business strategy throughout the organization; and
- Specific connection of the strategic plan to the work planning system.

There is much evidence to suggest reluctance to do the former and failure to do the latter. The reluctance stems from the view that strategies are proprietary and they should be carefully disseminated on a tightly controlled "need to know" basis. Secret strategies, though, are seldom secret from competitors, who can determine them with good analysis. They are, however, likely to lead to nonstrategic behavior within the firm. Failure to connect the strategic plan to the work planning system is, in the final analysis, a defect of the strategic planning system itself and reflects management's failure to consider the behavioral requirements of the strategy. It is not enough just to communicate the strategy throughout the organization. Good strategic planning anticipates ways in which corporate culture, past practices, and imperfect communication can result in behavior that does not support the strategy, and zeros in on specifically identified behavioral changes.

Measurement and Reward Systems. Perhaps more than any other factor, performance measurement and reward systems established by organizational leaders send a message throughout the organization about the activities top management thinks are important. If the performance measures focus on short-run results (e.g., this month's profits, sales, or billings) and if the rewards are totally driven by these measures, then the organization clearly focuses its attention on short-term operational activities, frequently at the expense of long-term strategic objectives. If, on the other hand, organizational leaders expect strategic thinking and expect on-the-job experience to develop managers for strategic management, the performance measures and reward systems will recognize strategic results as well as short-term operational results.

For example, in the 1950s, General Electric established eight key results areas for measuring managerial performance. They included both current profitability measures, such as ROS and ROI, and longer-term measures, such as market share position and trends, productivity, product leadership, and personnel development. In the 1970s, with the establishment of a strategic planning system and an investment priority classification system, the relative emphasis on key results measures varied according to the nature of the business. For managers in invest/grow businesses, for instance, strategic results such as growth in volume and growth in market share received greater emphasis, while for managers in harvest/divest businesses, more emphasis was put on cash flow.

The appropriate measures of strategic results are highly dependent on the individual firm's strategy and so will be unique to that particular firm. Without such a set of measures to ensure that organizational members perceive commitment on the part of organizational leaders to an appropriate balance of long range and short-range goals, it is unlikely that the nature of the work experience will be conducive to developing managers for strategic management.

Special Assignments. Increasingly, a multifunctional perspective is necessary for strategic management. Matrix organizations or those that frequent form project teams generally demonstrate such a perspective. For most organizations, however, the nature of work and managers' career paths are not likely to develop a multifunctional perspective. Special assignments, either as members of task forces or special study teams, or as individuals on short-term loan to another function, can materially enhance strategic management.

Identification/Selection, Promotion, and Placement

In broad terms, the objective of selection, promotion, and placement is to match the talents and expectations of individuals to the needs of the organization. With respect to management development, the object is to ensure that the right individuals are provided with the right kinds of work assignments to enhance their personal growth, consistent with the present and future needs of the organization. The selection, promotion, and placement systems that assign individuals to accomplishing the work of the organization also accomplish this manager development objective. Generally these systems encompass positions at three levels in an organization.

At relatively low organizational levels, job moves tend to be in function and within a given business. Development objectives tend to focus on technical competence and assessment of managerial potential. Job opportunities and individuals come together through personal knowledge or job posting, with selection made by the hiring manager assisted by recommendations from the former manager.

At middle levels in the organization, job moves tend to be in function, sometimes across business components but in related businesses. Development objectives are to enhance technical competence and managerial skill and broaden functional perspectives. Job opportunities and individuals come together through personal knowledge, enhanced by "networking," company-wide manpower registers, and personnel specialists. Selection still tends to be made by the hiring manager, but reviewed by the next level of management and assisted by recommendations of the former manager and personnel specialists.

At high levels in the organization, job moves are cross-function as well as cross-business component in order to develop multifunctional competence and further enhance managerial skills in varied settings. Job moves also may involve promotion to multifunctional management. Individuals are identified for job opportunities by formal succession planning systems. Candidate slates are developed, the hiring manager makes the selection, but there is extensive input from personnel specialists and previous managers, and extensive review by upper levels of management.

There are clear variations on this basic system. In very large, single-product businesses, such as the automotive industry, all moves are essentially "in business component." In contrast, in diversified organizations there is more emphasis on cross-business component moves, particularly at higher levels in the organization. In some businesses, such as Exxon, a formal corporate system starts tracking individuals and managing their career moves at relatively low levels. At General Electric, on the other hand, career moves, while driven by a corporate-wide annual manpower review, tend to be managed within individual businesses for all but high-level managers. In some firms such as AT&T, assessment centers are widely used to determine the suitability of individuals for managerial work. In others, managerial judgment is the primary basis for selection and promotion.

All these systems have certain elements in common. They recognize the developmental value of every assignment and consider the developmental needs of the individual in selection, promotion, and placement. They focus on manager development in terms of future needs of the organization as determined by its mission and its long-range strategy. They approach manager development with a sense of trajectory; that is, they look beyond the next assignment to subsequent assignments over, perhaps, a ten-year period.

Education and Training

Management education and training has been one of the major growth businesses of the post-World War II period. Today, courses on every aspect of management are offered by universities, professional associations, consultants, and others. This array of courses, the variety of educational approaches, and the claims for their effectiveness attest to the increased importance organizations are placing on the role of education in management development and to its complexity.

For firms considering the role of education in developing strategic managers, there are four basic questions:

1 What can be legitimately expected from education for strategic managers?
2 How does education for strategic managers differ from traditional management education?
3 What should the nature and extent of the education curriculum for strategic managers be?
4 How should the educational effort be managed?

Expectations for Education. There is clearly a wide range of opinion on what can legitimately be expected from education with respect to management development. Educators argue that formal education plays, or should play, a major role. Many organizations, including very large firms such as DuPont, rely heavily on work experience for development. Others such as General Electric, AT&T, and IBM believe education plays a major role in manager development, and have extensive in-house education programs.

This wide range of approaches derives from the nature of management education. Even when analytical techniques are the object of instruction, they tend to be frameworks for understanding and approaching "messy" problems rather than formulas for generating pat solutions. Participants internalize the subject matter in terms of their own frames of reference, diverse backgrounds, and diverse current and expected future assignments. What individuals get out of a management education course, therefore, is highly individualistic and, in many instances, not amenable to testing or other traditional methods of evaluation. Where testing is appropriate, it still must be recognized that mastery of a given skill does not guarantee that the skill will be used on the job.

For most firms this means that the benefits of management education must, to a large degree, be taken on faith. That is, they can seldom be quantified in absolute, economic terms. Rather, the justification for management education efforts rests heavily on the subjective collective judgments of participants, educators, managers who send participants, and those who fund the educational effort.

Given the nature of management education, attempts to develop specific objectives whose achievement can be precisely measured and that satisfy all the various constituencies of management education are likely to prove frustrating. Broad objectives can be established, however, and they might include the following:

- Teaching basic skills and techniques and providing the opportunity for practicing them in a low-risk environment;
- Providing frameworks for analyzing "messy" problems;
- Providing frameworks for organizing random on-the-job experience, thus increasing the development potential of the experience;
- Enhancing self-understanding and interpersonal relations;
- Broadening individual managers' perspectives by considering issues outside their normal purview;
- Providing knowledge in specific areas (e.g., cost analysis, long-range planning, international management); and
- Strengthening or altering corporate culture.

Not all these objectives would necessarily be included in every organization's list. All the behavioral changes associated with these objectives are complex and subtle; they are likely to occur for a variety of reasons, with classroom education only one. All need to be elaborated to take on appropriate organizational context. Without such a set of expectations, reasonably well understood and generally agreed to, it is unlikely that education will have the desired impact on developing managers for strategic managements.

Unique Requirements for Developing Strategic Managers. Basic management skills have been widely taught for many years, courses in strategic planning are offered with increasing frequency, and a wide variety of other courses are available to enhance strategic management ability. For education to fulfill its role in developing strategic managers, however, the curriculum offered must be company or organization specific.

The curriculum must be a reasonably well-defined sequence of educational courses and experiences for various career paths. It should be targeted at specific organization levels and functions, should be well integrated, should build on previous courses, and particularly, should be career spanning. Specific courses in the curriculum should derive their necessity from the company's specific organizational strategy. Those charged with responsibility for educating strategic managers must, therefore, be a part of the main stream of corporate life.

A Strategic Management Curriculum. It may be helpful to consider the current array of General Electric management courses, not as a prescription for other firms but as an illustration of how one curriculum reflects corporate needs, the concepts of career spanning, sequencing, and position-level targeting. As indicated in Table 25-1, the current General Electric management education curriculum starts with individuals in premanagerial assignments and continues with a sequence of courses to meet the needs of individuals in jobs up to and including department general managers. In addition to the courses shown, special executive workshops for department-level managers and above are scheduled on an ad hoc basis in response to special corporate needs.

The courses listed in Table 25-1 represent only a small portion of General Electric's overall education program. However, they represent that part of the curriculum that deals with developing and training strategic managers. They require frequent updating as corporate needs change, as new understanding of the nature of managerial work is acquired, and as new teaching methods become available. Attention to the strategic dimension is ensured by establishing a dotted line relationship from all courses to a "strategic dimension coordinator" charged with monitoring both the nature and extent of the strategic dimension in all general management courses.

Managing the Educational Program. For most firms considering education for strategic management a significant issue is the extent to which is should be an in-house activity. Options include a totally internal approach, a totally external approach, or a mix of both.

In a totally internal approach, internal staff have full responsibility for the complete management education curriculum and for design, development, and administration of all courses, including responsibility for course content, faculty or instructor selection, and location. Course attendance is limited to employees and is encouraged as a matter of company policy; in some instances it may be mandated.

In a totally external approach, all course attendance is at publicly available courses, such as those offered by the American Management Association, business schools, and various consultants. Responsibility of internal staff is limited to evaluating and recommending various external courses and, possibly, to administering participant selection and enrollment processes.

In a mixed approach, some courses are designed, developed, and administered by internal staff, principally to ensure company relevance. External courses are used either because of economic considerations or to take advantage of the opportunity to broaden perspectives through interaction with managers of other firms. In some instances external contractors are used to design, develop, and administer courses that focus on company-specific needs, either because of economic considerations or because of unique skill requirements.

In deciding which approach is preferable, management should consider the following factors:

- *Relevance.* Although the total internal approach provides the most opportunity for company-specific relevance, the internal/external mix provides the opportunity to target relevance where it is critical while maintaining the opportunity to broaden perspectives inherent in external courses.

Table 25-1 General Electric's Management Curriculum

GENERAL MANAGEMENT COURSES

Course	Length (in weeks)	Focus	Criteria for Participant Selection
Management Skills Development	2	Accelerate upward mobility by teaching or sharpening managerial skills, interpersonal skills, and self-understanding.	Individual contributors identified by present managers as having a high degree of managerial potential.
Management Practices	1	Teach basic managerial concepts, techniques, and skills for effective utilization of human resources to meet the needs of business components.	Primarily for the newly appointed, first-time manager.
Manager Development	4	Increase understanding of business as a multifunctional activity, improve skills to implement business strategies, enhance understanding of company's systems and objectives, enlarge knowledge and understanding of company's worldwide business environment.	Generally for individuals in the first or second managerial assignment, identified in the annual manpower review as having potential to move up at least one additional organizational layer.
Business Management	4	Increase knowledge and skills necessary to operate as member of a multifunctional business team with particular emphasis on business strategy: concepts, formulation, and implementation.	Senior functional manager.
Executive Development	4	To improve the effectiveness of the newly appointed multifunctional manager to set strategic direction, build an effective organization, and provide personal leadership.	Identified by corporate staff as having high potential for appointment to department level in the relatively near future.

SPECIALIZED MANAGEMENT COURSES

Course	Length (in weeks)	Focus	Basic for Participant Selection
Strategic Planning (workshop)	1	To introduce participants to concepts of strategy and the strategic planning process at the company.	Experienced individual contributors or managers who will be extensively involved in strategic plan development.
International Management	2	To develop a global business perspective and enhance knowledge and skills to plan and operate in a global environment.	Experienced managers, particularly in businesses that face global competitors and/or market opportunities.
Advanced Marketing Management	3	To develop a more effective professional approach to marketing through a series of studies emphasizing marketing strategy and its elements.	Experienced managers, primarily in the marketing function.
Impact	3	Advanced study of manufacturing techniques and processes and the relation of manufacturing strategy to business strategy	Senior manufacturing managers.

- *Sequencing.* The total internal approach allows the most precise sequencing. However, at least some university-sponsored executive programs offer sequencing. At Pennsylvania State University, for instance, the Emerging Executives Program is followed by the Executive Management Program. At Harvard University, the Professional Manager Development Course is targeted at a lower level executive than its Advanced Management Program. For many firms this sequencing may fit organizational needs.

- *Quality control.* Generally, quality control is achieved through selection of faculty and course materials. The internal approach allows an active approach to quality control whereas the external approach is essentially passive. Assuming a competent internal staff, management can expect the internal approach to have the most potential for achieving high quality. The mixed approach, however, provides an external yardstick against which to constantly calibrate the quality of internal programs.

- *Culture sharing.* In most management education courses a frequent comment is that at least half the learning comes from interaction with other participants. Internal programs attended solely by employees offer the opportunity to reinforce or disseminate corporate culture. The value of culture enhancement, however, must be weighed against the opportunity for broadened perspective afforded by external programs.

- *Brand identification.* "Buying" management education is not easy and so there is significant information value in a well-established "brand name." The internal approach provides the opportunity, over time, to establish "brand names" that come to be known and respected throughout the organization.

- *Administration.* Clearly, the total internal approach requires the most significant numbers of internal administrative staff who have the knowledge and skills to develop and run such courses. At least some of this staff cost, however, is a cost that would be included in the tuition for participants in external courses. The use of external programs, properly managed, can still require a significant administrative effort, depending on the degree to which external attendance is orchestrated.

Other Issues in Strategic Management Education

Development of an appropriate management education curriculum involves several other considerations. Four that merit particular attention are (1) the international dimension, (2) course development as an element of strategy formulation, (3) education vs. experience, and (4) "learning how to learn."

The International Dimension. Few firms can operate successfully without taking into account competitors, markets, and technology on a global basis and without taking account of global economic, political, and social systems that influence the environment in which the firm operates. For companies like General Electric with a long history of international business involvement, the international dimension has long been a part of the management education curriculum. Its increasing importance in recent years led to the establishment of a separate course in international management. Whether the international dimension is included in general management courses, in a separate international course, or in both, an important objective of strategic management education should be to increase the ability of managers to *think* and *act* effectively in a global environment. More particularly, education for developing strategic managers should include educational experiences that

- Develop a company-relevant global *perspective*; .
- Improve knowledge and skills to *plan* effectively in a global environment; and
- Improve knowledge and skills to *operate* effectively in a global environment.

Course Development as an Element of Strategy or Policy Formulation. Management education is frequently prescribed to acquaint managers with new strategic directions or with new policies. The process of developing appropriate education with respect to new strategies or new policies can serve as a valuable check on the logic of the strategy and the appropriateness or clarity of a new policy. This is often the case where significant changes in behavior are contemplated and where the educational experience is not supported by or accompanied by structural changes. In many instances, therefore, it is most appropriate to consider development of education concomitantly with strategy formulation or policy development.

Education Vs. Experience. Although on-the-job training is invaluable in developing management talent, especially when development programs match individual and organizational needs, there are limits to what can be gained on the job. In some instances assignments are becoming longer, reflecting concern that a pattern of many relatively short assignments may lead to superficial learning and may fail to provide a solid base for performance appraisal. Fewer assignments will reduce the variety of potential learning experiences. Simultaneously, the dramatic increase in scope and complexity of managerial work emphasizes the need for more learning. Education will increasingly be relied on to compensate for a reduced set of managerial experiences and as a way to facilitate currency in a field of exploding knowledge.

Learning How to Learn. The concept of "learning how to learn" posits that learning skills, and motivation to learn, cannot be taken for granted. This can have significant implications for educator and manager alike.

For the educator, the concept of learning how to learn suggests that, above and beyond learning objectives relating to course content, enhancement of learning skills should be an important objective in management education. For the manager, learning how to learn emphasizes the importance of learning as a process to be managed. In essence this suggests that every manager should have a personal learning strategy which focuses on career objectives and takes into account developmental needs and personal learning style.

SPECIAL ROLES FOR STRATEGIC MANAGERS

There is much evidence to support the intuitive notion that the immediate supervisor has an enormous effect on the personal development and growth of managers. All corporate systems that influence the nature of work and that measure and reward performance do so through the immediate manager, who assigns the work, establishes the basis for performance evaluation, conducts the performance appraisal, and makes salary recommendations. More than any other individual, the immediate manager acts as a career counselor, providing advice on development needs and methods. Generally, the immediate manager has the most to say about when, or if, a subordinate is ready for promotion.

Some managers are extremely effective as counselors and developers; they are interested in people, assume responsibility to help their development, and devote substantial time and effort to development activities. Unfortunately, this is not the norm. Considerable evidence indicates that most managers are uncomfortable with performance appraisals, thus reducing the likelihood that performance appraisals will identify real developmental needs. Few managers are truly effective in career counseling sessions, which require a substantial degree of maturity as well as interest and skill. Even fewer have the strategic perspective necessary to identify and develop the skills necessary for strategic management.

The Manager as Career Counselor

Recognizing both the importance of the manager's role in development and the scarcity of managers who can effectively carry out that role, many organizations have turned to "mentors." Bell Labs, for instance, has a host-adviser mentoring program specifically tailored for its new employees, which number about 1,500 each year. Jewel Cos. Inc., a Chicago-based retailer, has conducted since the early 1960s a corporate sponsorship training program for managers considered for rapid advancement. Job candidates are often selected to become someone's protege even before being hired.[19] Where such systems have worked effectively, the mentors were seasoned managers, many of whom had volunteered to participate in the program.

This approach has its drawbacks, however. In many instances, mentoring takes on the characteristic of grooming "crown princes" and so induces conflict between the mentored and the unmentored. The personal chemistry between mentor and protege is critical, and if volunteerism does not produce good matches it is likely that at least some mentoring assignments will be strained or ineffective. Finally, there is significant opportunity for conflict between the mentor and the protege's immediate manager.

Despite the interest in mentoring systems, and despite the difficulties many managers have with their role as human resource developers, most firms will continue to rely heavily on immediate managers to guide the development of subordinates. The experience to date with mentoring systems suggests that they are difficult to develop and maintain. Although employees may, from time to time, establish an ad hoc mentoring relationship with a high-level manager, the natural inclination is to turn to one's immediate manager for career advice and counseling. The inherent potential in a system in which *all* managers are involved in developing their subordinates is great. Capitalizing on this potential requires managers who are skilled in developing managers for strategic management and who will ensure that subordinates carry out appropriate development activities. For most firms, this involves:

- A management population committed to strategic management;
- Clear definitions of the manager's responsibility for personnel development;
- Management training in performance appraisal and career counseling;
- Systems that ensure performance appraisal sessions and career counseling discussions take place with appropriate documentation and review; and
- Systematic audits that measure the effectiveness of performance appraisal and career counseling discussions.

---

[19] See Margaret Price, "Corporate Godfathers," *Industry Week* (June 29, 1981), pp. 71–74.

This list suggests a role for the manager that requires significant involvement in subordinate learning. A special aspect of this role is that which the manager can play as formal teacher.

The Manager as Teacher

When identification of development needs indicates that formal classroom education or training is necessary, the U.S. corporate norm is to assign the task to the personnel department, either to teach the subject or to arrange for its teaching, generally by professional educators. There are exceptions, of course. At Intel Corporation, senior managers are routinely required to teach a variety of basic management practices to first-level managers. At Rolm Corporation, managers are strongly encouraged to teach appropriate topics to their subordinates. The frequency of "train the trainer" sessions in many organizations suggests the use of some employees to teach, although generally on an ad hoc or volunteer basis. An extreme example is found in Japan, where Toshiba requires *all* managers to take a course to prepare them for their roles as classroom teachers.

In the training of strategic managers, the notion of "manager as teacher" appears to have unexploited potential. Because one of the best ways to learn a subject is to teach it, requiring managers to teach strategic management or strategic planning, for instance, could be an extremely effective way of ensuring widespread understanding of strategic management concepts. Involving senior managers in teaching basic management practices to lower-level managers also establishes a valuable channel of communication that can reduce the isolation of senior managers. Finally, the increased interaction among hierarchical levels in the organization helps to articulate and reinforce the existing corporate culture.

CONCLUSION

As with business strategy, the approach each firm takes in developing managers for strategic management will be unique. Some view it as a process best allowed to operate incrementally, driven primarily by modest changes in the firm's strategy or environment. Others see it as a process to be managed proactively, driven by a vision or grand design that juxtaposes the firm's strategy and its view of the managerial behavior appropriate for that strategy. Some focus on one major method of development; others use a multimethod approach that links all development activities into a comprehensive system. In some instances, responsibility for orchestrating the development of strategic managers is centralized with tight controls and much corporate initiative. In others, it is dispersed widely throughout the organization with loose linkages connecting the process across components and across organizational levels.

Whatever the pattern of process and responsibility, the critical ingredients of developing strategic managers, inextricably intertwined, are conscious choice, high-level commitment, and widespread understanding and acceptance of its importance.

Conscious choice involves an explicit decision to initiate strategic manager development based on well thought out assumptions about the nature of managerial work and how manager development takes place. At General Electric, for instance, the present emphasis on strategic management development can be traced back to its famous "Blue Books," written in the 1950s, which described a comprehensive view of the nature of the work of a professional manager, and to the establishment of its Management Development Institute, which provides the corporation with a source of management education.

While some sense of high-level commitment is clearly implicit in any decision to initiate development of strategic managers, more than just approval is required. For most organizations a move to strategic management development will be a significant cultural change and is likely to occur only if high-level commitment is publicly displayed and ongoing. Without this commitment, frequently repeated, a new concept such as the development of strategic managers can easily get lost as other strategies and structures evolve.

Finally, the nature of strategic management development requires widespread understanding and acceptance of its importance throughout the organization. In the organization dedicated to educating managers for strategic management, this means communicating how the firm defines strategic management and how it sees development occurring.

26

Role of the Chief Executive Officer in Strategic Management

KARL D. BAYS

*Chairman and Chief Executive Officer,
American Hospital Supply Corporation*

THE ROLE OF THE CHIEF EXECUTIVE OFFICER IN STRATEGIC MANAGEMENT

When I became chief executive officer (CEO) of American Hospital Supply Corporation, I took over a good company. In 49 years, American had grown from a small local distributor to a large, diversified corporation, from a tiny Chicago office to a farflung network of distribution centers and manufacturing plants. In the process, it transformed its industry. Since American worked to upgrade hospital purchasing techniques, other distributors were forced to upgrade theirs. Foster G. McGaw, American's founder, had also set new standards for quality in the nation's hospitals. "Growth through service" was McGaw's philosophy. I was a believer in those words, then and now.

I had had time to absorb his values. I had come to the company as a 25-year-old fresh from graduate school. By the time I became CEO, I had been with American 13 years. Positions during that time included sales representative, office manager, region manager, and management posts in four divisions as well as the corporation itself. I had seen the international side of the business; I had experience with its manufacturing. I felt I knew the company. I knew American's traditions and values. And I also shared them.

NEEDED: A MANAGEMENT SYSTEM

But I had my own ideas about what the company needed. Health-care dollars from both the government and private insurers were flooding us in those days. We were moving very fast. Sales were doubling every five years. Earnings had jumped as much as 24 percent in a single year. Overnight, it seemed, we had grown from a $66-million company (sales the year I joined American) to one of about $500 million. And some old rules of management no longer applied.

We had the weaknesses of any high-growth company. Among other things, neither the lines of authority nor the lines of communication were always clear. (I myself can recall some memorable squabbles with fellow salesmen who had somehow been assigned the same account as I had.) But we were in an excellent position to benefit from the explosion of growth in the health-care field. Foster McGaw had seen to that. We had the customers. We had the selling skills. We even had the sales. But the corporation cried out for fresh strategy. We needed a system.

I had envisioned for several years what that system should be. I learned it at Indiana University from John F. Mee, a professor of management who emphasized fundamental principles—the basics—that major corporations have followed since the late 1800s. Such principles are classic, and they have been more valuable to me than some of the contemporary strategic notions such as experience curve and portfolio analysis.

Plan, organize, motivate, control. That's the core of the system Mee taught me, in four words. As I was moving up in the corporation, I spoke those words so often that they became an acronym: POMC. We scribbled it on the backs of napkins. We extolled its virtues at meetings. It became a private password, almost a source of humor.

Yet it works. POMC. All we have to do today is say it: People know exactly what we mean. What's more, they understand the organizational muscle behind it. They know what the business is about. They know where the business is heading. They know their specific areas of responsibility.

Some executives tend to forget such basics as they climb the corporate ladder. The higher they go, the more easily they forget. But I firmly believe the basics are essential. They bring order to a complex world, simply because they do *not* change. Markets change. So do regulations and technology. So does competition. But the system stays. POMC. Without such a framework, the successful positioning of any company—and that is the crux of strategic management—is impossible.

GETTING STARTED ON STRATEGIC MANAGEMENT

At the time I was named CEO, American was a loosely organized collection of approximately 40 businesses. It was somewhat untidy. In one division, we even sold student uniforms. We were also decentralized, which meant division presidents ran their units the way they saw fit. They received just one set of instructions each year, outlined in a one-page letter from the chairman. Those instructions basically said sell—sell in a way that allows the corporation's earnings to grow 20 percent a year.

Some divisions starved themselves to make that goal. Others were rolling in cash and did not care. Beyond this, planning did not exist. Certainly, we all had to provide detailed financial statements and budgets. But our horizon was very short. Vision did not seem necessary: Our products were selling vigorously and so was our stock. Price-earnings multiples were 60 to 70 times earnings. Capital was readily available. Controls, financial and otherwise, were loose. Bonuses were based on a boss's mood instead of clear standards.

The bubble burst just as I was made president.

Our earnings grew just 3 percent in that year, 1970. The first six months earnings actually declined. The numbers we were reporting added up to a negative—but highly powerful—statement of the need for a management system. I took them as proof of the opinion I had had for years. It was also a painful prod to get the management system into place and working.

Planning

Today we have come to describe that overall system as strategic management: management that positions the company in line with opportunities. But it meant doing many things differently. It meant taking a longer view. It meant doing a systematic study of changes in the environment, including the economy, the industry, and our competitors. It meant examining our markets and products, as well as alternative ways of doing business. All that had seemingly endless implications for our systems of planning, organizing, motivating, and controlling.

In our first steps, we put planning first. We needed someone in charge of planning. We needed to involve all managers throughout the organization. And we needed information.

So I appointed a vice president of planning, reporting directly to me. I also named a long-range planning committee, including both staff and line managers. We wrote an instruction manual, entitled "Business Planning," which represented our view of the management basics as well as the most current planning tools. In the manual we requested data on competitors. We asked for data on the health-care environment. Most important, we asked for a strategy: a formal plan for taking each business unit from here to there.

We were very methodical. We gave examples and definitions of what we wanted, making clear the change from the old way. We sent the manual off to all our divisions.

It is accurate to say our first attempts at strategic planning were awful. Our divisions had never done it. All of us at the top, too, had a lot to learn. We struggled with definitions of markets and competitive assessments. We developed numbers we later learned were wrong. We dickered about investments in research and development, products and pricing. Today we accept such negotiations as routine. But the first time through they were awkward.

Many grappled with the concept of strategic planning itself. They were used to thinking only of profits, and preparing what amounted to a budget. Preparing strategies, with attendant focus on the environment and markets, was unfamiliar. Some line officers thought planning meant simply envisioning their hopes and dreams. As a result, we got "wish lists" with no basis in reality, rather than true strategic plans grounded in market research. The fact that some divisions were suspicious about the entire exercise (a few feared corporate headquarters was usurping power, while others disliked the extra work) didn't help.

So there were several stumbles during our first steps toward strategic management. Previously, American had run things simply by the numbers. Now we wanted to run things according to a true business plan. It involved a whole new way of thinking—a new way for people to do their jobs. Today that is called changing the corporate culture. At the time, it seemed a somewhat grim exercise in survival.

Changing Values

Fortunately, that bad year had shocked everybody. Many of our managers were ready for fresh ideas. Those who were not left. Our newly appointed planning vice president and his staff also provided a lot of education, via seminars, speeches, and individual consultation. We were not shy about rejecting bad plans, and we were clear about what needed improvement. We worked hard to simplify the instruction manual, as well as the system itself. Ultimately, we instituted a whole new set of criteria, and compensation, for jobs well done. Each of these steps helped shape behavior and instill new values.

The planning initiative also helped motivate people. That, I thought, was one of my chief jobs in those early years. I cheered. I waved the flag. I kept the lines of communication open. I dropped into people's offices. I gave formal speeches. I ran meetings. I let people know we had a system, a new way of assessing the environment and collecting ideas about the way the place ought to be run, while solidifying a clear corporate strategy.

We kept the message pretty simple: POMC, with emphasis on the P to start. The top management team, including myself, all stumped, politicked, explained, and talked up the new way of planning and managing. Beyond that, I let all my managers and my staff know I trusted them and had confidence in them. After that, I left them alone—unless they failed to perform.

Meanwhile, the planning committee and I kept assessing the plans. We stayed with two basic issues: what American was and what we wanted it to be. We asked every question we could.

Who are we? Where are we going? How shall we get there? Such questions obviously form the heart of any strategic plan. As a result, they also involve some very hard-headed assessments. We looked at American's strengths and weaknesses. We examined the ways its products and services might match the needs of the marketplace. We learned the characteristics of each of American's markets. We learned what our competitors had to offer and what we could offer, too. We spent many days, nights, and weekends asking, answering, analyzing.

Out of this exercise, two results emerged. One, we got our planning system. That's the formal process of preparing the strategic and operating plans that double as Bible and road map for our 33,000 employees today. Two, we got a new organizational chart.

Organizing and Motivating

American was a decentralized, loosely organized collection of some 40 different units. They were divided into a handful of business groups, roughly the same size in sales and earnings. We had an administrative staff, of course, but it was sketchy.

We kept our decentralized organization. But we now grouped our major operating units according to the primary markets they served, in line with the market analysis we had just completed. We came up with nine groups—medical services, hospitals, science specialties, medical specialties, dental, pharmaceuticals, dietary, capital goods, and international—that are the ancestors of a smaller number of groups today. We put six new group vice presidents in charge of them, reporting to a new senior vice president in charge of operations.

This put the customer at the top of our organizational chart, so to speak. That reminded everyone of our corporate mission. It also put the daily operations of the business under one man, freeing me as CEO to handle long-range issues. It further allowed us to expand the administrative staff in such areas as planning and finance, without losing sight of the corporation's traditional service philosophy.

Our planning department had already been strengthened. We had improved financial controls by adding three assistant corporate controllers, as well as a national credit and collection manager. Now we clustered other corporate service functions—personnel, legal, regulatory and consumer affairs, distribution services, and manufacturing services—under one senior vice president. This put corporate headquarters in a better position to serve the new "groups."

The process was wrenching, as reorganizations usually are. No matter how it is handled, some people are viewed as losers—often, some very good people. It is disruptive, and earnings may reflect the upheaval for several quarters. For a CEO, it is time-consuming, distracting, and pervasive. As a result, many other important issues take second place.

Yet I felt, as I have from time to time since then, that reorganization was critical for the long-term health of the corporation. The timing then was right, which is essential for selling the corporation on the change. That bad year had shocked all of us. But with the growing pressure of inflation on our costs, we had to become more efficient.

We did what we could to ease the process. We explained the logic of the reorganization in speeches and memos. We made clear who was now reporting to whom. We waved the flag of what was good for the corporation.

Motivation was a critical factor in accomplishing the change. Many employees were enthusiastic about what was being done. They believed we were setting American on the right road and they backed us 100 percent. Besides, they were hungry for new organizational and management tools. They had read the literature. They knew what others were doing. They hadn't seen those tools here and they wanted them.

As I have noted earlier, I continue to spend a fair amount of time—as did all of top management—selling the idea, motivating people in the process. I ran meetings at the divisions: meetings for managers, meetings for salesmen. I said we would become what I called a "Tiffany" company, raising the quality of the corporation across the board. We set a goal of reaching $1 billion in sales by 1975, doubling our size from 1970. All this created an atmosphere of enthusiasm and excitement, and made believers of us all.

Controls and Culture

At this juncture, then, we had begun planning. We were also organizing and motivating. We then began to design and install control systems, which were sorely needed. I recall, for example, that we had several hundred bank accounts all over the country. American had $20 million floating in the system at any given time, overcompensating banks beyond belief. Moreover, inflation had begun to affect the economy and our costs. We realized we could not afford to grow the way we had been growing. The days when managers were given all the cash and resources they wanted to achieve earnings targets had to come to an end, and they did.

We installed a broad range of financial controls. We began to think in terms of managing the balance sheet, not just the earnings statement. A new financial language was applied within American: Managers began using terms such as NEACC (net earnings after cost of capital) and RONWA (return on net working assets). These constitute comfortable jargon for us now. Back then, they were new and somewhat foreign.

We also continued to computerize all of American's operations. That would prove a critical move. It laid the foundation for a key strategy for American in the 1970s, a strategy of automated product distribution. Today, for example, American's network of computer terminals (installed inside the hospital) allows some 3,000 hospitals to order supplies directly from our distribution centers. Such supply and inventory-control techniques distinguished us from other suppliers. They also provided a significant competitive edge, especially as efficiency and cost-control became issues in the health-care industry.

Telescoping the steps we took makes it sound as if we revolutionized American Hospital Supply Corporation's world. But we did not change everything. We didn't have to. Foster G. McGaw, then honorary chairman, continued to personify the value system around the corporation. Year after year, he had hammered away at a few basic tenets that characterize the culture of the company. His philosophy of growth through service, for example, drove the corporation during its first 50 years. It continues to drive the corporation today.

Growth through service. McGaw put it another way: "If you serve the real needs of the customer, then sales and profits will follow." Such tenets could not, and should not, be changed. To maintain them, we remind employees of McGaw's legacy every chance we get. They can all tell the story of how McGaw rode freight trains across the Midwest, assuring that he visited his customers regularly, not just once or twice a year as was standard practice at the time. That is part of corporate folklore by now. It is vitally important to keep that alive.

Foster McGaw taught me one other principle that I still follow: Never settle for seconds in your employees. Hire the best people, he often said. Hire those with the will and confidence to win. Pay whatever you need to get them. Support them. Teach them. When you want something to happen ask them to do it. Then let them do the job. More often than not, they will succeed.

That is the way I tried to manage, from the beginning. I saw the CEO's role in those days as that of leader: the single person responsible for the overall direction and control of the business. I still do. But the way in which the CEO leads takes many different forms. The form it took for me back then was simply providing a visible presence for the corporation, by way of those speeches, meetings, and office visits. I was the one with the system. I needed people to understand that system and believe it, because without it, we could not get American anywhere.

DEVELOPING OBJECTIVES, GOALS, AND STRATEGIES

American's planning and management system has improved sharply since it was established in the early 1970s. But the basics remain the same.

Plans are still written by operating people, not by corporate planners. Planners provide just the methodology. We produce two sets of plans each year: one for strategy, one for operations. The strategic plan extends five years for most of our business units (our high-technology units run a little longer, eight years, due to the nature of research and government approval). The operating plan extends three. Those plans are revised each year. As a result, changes in corporate direction are subtle, emerging gradually over time.

The planning process serves two functions. First, it prompts communication and negotiation about the direction of the corporation and its units. Second, the process sensitizes people to environmental change. Both functions are critical to positioning a business.

Strategic and Operating Plans

American kicks off its planning year by gathering all its division presidents and other upper-level managers at corporate headquarters for a two-day meeting in February. I give a state-of-the-corporation speech and my assessment of the health-care environment. We then issue broad "marching orders": a statement of the corporation's objectives, strategies, and five-year goals for sales and profit margins.

Our business objective is very simple: to increase the value of shareholders' investment by improving the corporation's competitive position. Financial goals stem from continual review of the corporation's performance. Our strategies—the way in which American will reach its objective and its goals—are based on maintaining distribution leadership in health-care and related products, with emphasis on the marketing of products manufactured by American.

Division presidents then return home to produce strategic and operating plans for their individual units. They work the first half of the year on strategy, in accord with instruction manuals issued by our corporate planning department. Industries and markets are scrutinized. Strengths and weaknesses of the unit, and of its competitors, are examined. Goals and strategies are reviewed. Those plans are then passed up to the company's major groups, or sectors. Managers there review and condense the information. They also do some significant scrutinizing and strategizing of their own.

Various managers at the corporate level then receive five strategic plans submitted by our sectors—hospital and medical specialties—and by international, and corporate marketing (a unit responsible for serving our largest corporate customers). We begin *our* review. I review the plans myself. I read them, ask questions at formal presentations, make suggestions. So do senior officers, as well as corporate planners. I make a summary presentation of the corporate strategic plan to our board of directors, whose members provide a constant review of the strategic direction of the company. And ultimately, we write the full corporate strategic plan.

Operating plans are similarly developed. They outline specific tactics for achieving strategies, and financial goals for the first three years of the strategic plan. Managers pay special attention to the first year. We accept them, assuring the financial goals of each business add up to the goals of the corporation. Often they do. If they don't, we spend December revising plans.

Staff functions also create annual and longer term plans. Can we actually plan legal services, public affairs, personnel administrations, and other functions? We must and we do.

Commitment and Compensation

By the end of the year, we have distributed innumerable three-ring binders throughout the corporation. We have taken considerable care to ensure they do not simply sit on the shelves. Because the operating managers themselves write the plans, they tend to use them. More important, they know they will not get corporate support for a project if it is not in their plans. Requests for capital, for example, would be denied. The plans also are a rich resource for business presentations throughout the year. They hold the answers to a number of everyday business questions: market share, growth, cost of research and development projects. They also provide the basis for still other plans, such as plans for managing human resources.

In short, these three-ring binders are used religiously because they are woven into the way American does business. But there is one other way we ensure they will be used: compensation.

Key managers receive an annual bonus if they achieve the profit goals set in their operating plans. It's called "making plan," and the critical importance of that is made clear in many ways. Motivating forces range from the "carrot" of our Annual Awards Night to the "stick" of monthly reporting sheets, published in a widely circulated newsletter for managers, which show who is on target and who is not. Managers also get a bonus for *overachieving* plan. They get still another bonus for achieving their MBOs (management by objective), which spell out tactics for any given manager that help his or her business unit reach its goals.

Key employees develop their own MBOs, in accord with negotiations and approval by their supervisor. Each has about half a dozen. A research director, for example, might have an MBO such as "I will complete the prototype of a new product by May of this year." A sales manager may agree to hire and train five new sales representatives to cover a new region by June. MBOs always include deadlines, as well as a way of measuring the achievement. The bonus is based on how fully the manager meets his objectives.

The top manager, the CEO, is not exempt from this. I set MBOs myself, and publish them. The board of directors rates my performance.

The system of compensation tied to plans has been modified several times since the early 1970s. We have installed new incentives that are more closely tied to long-term thinking at the corporate level. We have instituted a management planning and development department, a sort of in-house university. We have also substantially improved our analysis of the marketplace. American has now, for instance, an environmental assessment panel consisting of 11 people within the corporation who represent "environmental segments." Our director of investor relations represents the investment community; our director of government relations conveys governmental issues. The panel identifies environmental issues that affect the company's strategic direction. Those issues, which in 1983 ranged from the growing number of elderly to new federal regulations, become the springboard for the next planning year.

Yet this is all just fine-tuning. Overall, our basic system of planning and management has remained the same. It has allowed me and the top managers I work with to position American well. That is the key task of strategic management. The system is only a tool. It prepares the organization for opportunities. After that, it is all judgment and execution.

ORGANIZING FOR STRATEGY IMPLEMENTATION: KEY STRATEGIC MOVES

Some key strategic moves we have made serve as examples of how the judgment and execution part works. They arose from trends we highlighted in the environmental assessments of our strategic plans. All were executed under tactics subsequently spelled out in our operating plans. The examples illustrate several points.

First, it is not just the formal system of planning that counts. It is being "out among 'em": out among the customers, the employees, government officials, and others. Such people informally provide valuable information that helps shape strategy. Sometimes they even provide flashes of insight that point the way. As a result, it is critical that managers spend time with these key groups. We all plan for it, making room in our schedules. The practice is fundamental to our entire system of strategic management.

It is also fundamental to the CEO's role. It is the way the CEO gathers information. In part, it is the way ideas are sold—both inside and outside the corporation. But—and this is my second point—the role a CEO plays in strategic management does vary widely. There is never just one way to get the job done. Sometimes a CEO is the one with the "vision" of where an organization should go; just as often, a CEO backs the vision of others. On very rare occasions I give orders. More often, I offer encouragement and support.

A CEO must have a number of tools in his or her management kit, plus the wisdom to know which one to use, and when.

Corporate Marketing

The decision to establish a corporate marketing program, which we did in 1977, illustrates one example of organizing for strategy implementation. Today this program provides a vehicle to attract and serve our largest customers. Special services offered through the program range from consulting that helps customers control costs to a microcomputer/software package that helps calculate those costs. American also provides discounts to corporate customers, in return for purchases of a certain volume of supplies each year.

The program has been very satisfactory. It has saved money for customers and also brought sales to us. Here is how it developed.

By the late 1970s, we had been observing consolidation in our marketplace for some time. Hospitals were under pressure to contain costs. Many were simply buying each other up, forming "multihospital systems," while others were banding together in purchasing groups. Everyone hoped to cut expenses by sharing services and effecting such economies of scale as centralized purchasing.

Now, we could have panicked over our "shrinking marketplace." Instead, we decided to try to meet the changing needs of the customer. We felt such a program would be critical, and could form a key marketing strategy for the 1980s. But we did not act immediately. Instead, we debated.

Our thoughts crystallized in the second half of 1977, as the American Hospital Association came out in clear support of hospitals' voluntary effort to contain skyrocketing costs. That support was their response to the threat of government control over hospital costs. It was also the trigger we needed. It showed that hospitals would be receptive to a cost-cutting program, provided we could assemble the right package. It also gave us ammunition to sell such a program within the corporation—a tactic no CEO can afford to forget when it comes to change.

We took two steps. One of our most successful managers was given the charter to develop a "corporate approach" to group purchases. Others in top management began the task of politicking and persuading to sell the concept within American and get the program off the ground.

Persuasion was sorely needed, as some restructuring of our sales force was required. Divisions at the time were accustomed to operating as independent companies. Each sent out its own sales representative to sign separate agreements with separate hospitals. But suddenly, we were proposing to sign one contract at corporate headquarters with one group of hospitals to buy products from all American's divisions. Division units would sell separately for many of their customers, but not for the largest hospitals and groups.

That was a tough sell. Divisions did not want to surrender their best customers. They also did not want to relinquish power to a single corporate sales force. They felt their autonomy challenged. They charged the program was a needless expense. They argued it would not work.

But the program made sense. It was more efficient. It saved hospitals money. It brought sales to American. It was the right response to changes in the health care environment.

So I put it on my personal agenda of priorities. I held breakfast meetings with key executives. I personally signed the early agreements. I took the flak that goes along with such a new program, including an antitrust lawsuit from several competitors (decided, on appeal, in our favor). Most important, I worked to create a ground swell of support by publicly backing the program while giving free rein to the smart, aggressive people I had in charge. It became their program as much as mine, a technique critical to success.

We took other steps within the company to sell the program, too. Our public affairs department profiled the new program for in-house publications and gave it play in the annual report. We gradually made resources available for more corporate marketing positions: New opportunities and career paths opened up, attracting some of our best managers. Word spread that the corporate marketing department was the place to be. And I did my share to spread that word.

These political processes are crucial for achieving change within the corporation. That is easy for a CEO to forget amid the countless demands of the job. Yet support never comes by blind obedience to orders by top management. It is much more subtle. It requires talk, timing, and the type of tactics described here.

Success, of course, is the best selling tool a CEO can have. During the next two years we signed a number of corporate agreements. Today American has such agreements covering about 10 percent of all U.S. hospital beds. Sales within the program are growing at about double the corporate growth rate. Our competitors are now adopting the same approach.

Home Health Care

More recently, and in similar fashion, we have entered the home health-care market. Our environmental assessment had for years highlighted the trend toward care provided outside traditional hospital settings. Such "alternate sites" included the home, as well as assorted freestanding medical centers. Studies showed the market was huge and growing fast. Analysis also showed that hospitals themselves were expanding into these alternate sites. Those studies confirmed my own observations. As a result, we believed hospitals would be a key player in the emerging markets.

Once again, we heard some cries of alarm about our "shrinking marketplace." Once again, it was—at least to us—more a question of figuring out how to meet the needs of our changing customer. We debated. We got input from all sides, from aggressive managers eager to enter the new market to customers and financial analysts. Everyone was anxious to know what we had in mind.

This time, we moved into one segment of the market with an acquisition. We bought Abbey Medical, a national network of outlets that sell, rent, and service medical equipment for home use. Abbey was, for American, a good entry to the market. Its "key buying influences" were people within the hospital, including discharge-planners and respiratory therapists. That formed a good fit with our existing businesses. We emphasized in many ways—meetings, speeches, conversation—that the corporation should be in the market.

Since then, Abbey has continued to grow with additional acquisitions. We have developed other products for home use, such as intravenous nutritional products, and spawned a new business unit within the corporation to guide growth in that area. We have entered other alternate site markets, such as the market for physicians' products.

Our business in these markets is now growing at a rate of about 20 percent in sales. Recently, we have begun marketing a program to further improve results. Under the program, American and the hospital together provide services and products for the patient at home, and together share in the revenues. The program backs our belief that hospitals will play a major role in the new market. It is also a feature that distinguishes us from competitors—a key to any successful corporate strategy.

Entering Medical Specialties

Strategic moves such as corporate marketing and alternate sites result from efforts at various levels within the company, from the top to the bottom. But one corporate move—one of American's best—originated wholly with a manager who is now one of our executive vice presidents. He heads our medical specialties business, which sells products to medical specialists such as ophthalmologists and cardiovascular surgeons. He came to corporate headquarters in the late 1960s. At the time, his business unit sold one chief product, heart valves. He wanted to expand that franchise.

We listened to his arguments, based on the observation that the "age of the medical specialist" was upon us and that American should provide a broad range of products to meet that market's needs. He wanted the freedom to have an off year—"profit plan relief," as it is called—in order to make the necessary investments. The expenditures he wanted would have reduced his projected earnings increase to about 5 percent at a time when we were asking managers to aim for 20 percent.

Yet his arguments made sense. He received the go-ahead. And we have since watched him turn his operation into one of the most profitable businesses in the company. Sales have grown at an average compound rate of 25 percent for the past ten years, and net earnings at almost 32 percent. The business develops and sells hundreds of products, from surgical lasers to diagnostic catheters.

It has been one of our best strategic moves for two reasons. First, the business will continue to grow quickly. Second, it has led the entire corporation to place greater emphasis on research and development. The latter is critical to coping with today's environment as hospitals ask for new, cost-efficient products.

Making Adjustments

American's strategic management process does not always work perfectly. At times, we are detoured by unforeseen events.

For example, the Food and Drug Administration once questioned sterilization procedures at one of our manufacturing plants for intravenous solutions. We were forced to shut down the plant in February 1975 and recall some products. The recall prompted a $2.9 million after-tax charge against first quarter earnings. That was a devastating blow to corporate plans for the year, since the division contributed about 10 percent of the corporation's net earnings at the time.

But the planning system stood the company in good stead. We called division presidents together and said we had to alter our course for the year. Could they implement "contingency portions" of their 1975 profit plans to make up for lost income? In short, could they overachieve plan?

I believed they could: Since we grant bonuses to our managers for overachieving their plans, they always have what one could call a "bottom drawer" strategy for pulling out all the stops. I told them that I believed we would still make our corporate profit plan for the year. That was the message sent to the investment community, and although some were skeptical, neither they nor I were disappointed. In 1975 our net earnings rose 18 percent from the prior year, just as we had planned.

Unforeseen events are not the only development to detour a plan. We have also made our share of mistakes. For instance, American invested heavily in the dental business in the mid-1970s because we thought dental insurance, which was becoming part of many union contracts and corporate benefit programs, would create a good growth market. It did not. The economy turned soft and the expected increase in dental work did not appear. Moreover, we learned that we could sell only through dealers. At American, we believe that customers prefer to deal with us directly. So in 1982 we sold our dental operations.

We clean house like this regularly, a task critical to any strategic management system. We do not mind taking a risk, but once we know it is not working out, we try not to waste time getting out. In the three years ending in 1982, for example, although we bought 14 businesses, we also sold 12 more.

Aggressiveness is a trait that is widely praised in strategic business development. Another vital trait, one that needs to begin with the CEO, is patience.

That fact is something our Japanese counterparts have proven. It also was demonstrated in American's building of a business in Japan itself.

We began doing business in Japan 12 years ago. For two and a half years, we didn't write a single order. After that point, our business in Japan achieved excellent growth and we expect it to continue. Several factors have been key. They include the leadership of an outstanding Japanese manager. But perhaps the most important factor was patience in committing to the market—in learning it well and developing it strategically.

How does the CEO know when to keep the company in a market and when to get out? There is no formula. Only a general rule that CEOs ought to be patient when they see a strategic and financial payoff down the road. And that kind of vision comes only through judgment and experience.

THE ROLE OF THE CEO IN STRATEGIC MANAGEMENT

Experience simply takes time. But judgment is more elusive. It comes from being out among those customers, hospital administrators, employees, and public officials who directly influence American's customers. It is not enough to read the environmental assessments in strategic plans. A CEO needs to feel that environment. He needs to see it for himself.

For example, I give about 30 public speeches a year, mostly to customer groups. I mingle with the audience before and after, asking questions, hearing what is on people's minds. I also serve on a number of boards and industry committees. I even work the cafeteria at my own company during the breakfast and lunch hours. Such activities are not just for fun. They help me see my business through the eyes of others; customers, suppliers, employees, regulators, competitors. Their perceptions guide their behavior, and their behavior affects American's business. If I do not understand how they think, I cannot do my job.

That is how I hone my judgment—whether to buy or sell, get into a new market or stay out. It is the part of strategic management that is toughest to explain. But it is the heart of the CEO's role.

To do it well, a CEO must absorb information through every available channel, from the formal system to the informal process just described. That means listening, talking, asking questions, observing. It also means a constant flow of facts, figures, and opinions. Out of it easily come 50 issues that clamor for attention. The vital task is to sift that flow for data to make daily business decisions and determine long-range priorities.

Only a handful of issues, four at the most, should have a CEO's full commitment at any given time. Call it a personal agenda. These are usually issues out of the corporate mainstream, yet critical to the long-term health of the corporation. My own agenda, for example, has ranged from getting more women into management to reshuffling the corporate organization.

Once the list is developed, one has to work through it. That inevitably involves the political processes I have described. The CEO must create a ground swell of support, a consensus, a belief among key players that this is how the corporation should go. Reaching this consensus means more talk: a little push, a little pull. A CEO also needs to develop a group of people who will go to the mat on that issue. They will execute the project, and they should get enough headroom to make it theirs.

As all this is going on, the CEO should be sending signals to other players in the corporate world, both inside and outside the company itself. These signals should make it clear the project is a priority. And they can take many, many forms. Signals can be direct and quite personal: For example, a CEO can make a point in a casual phone call or office chat. Other times, signals are more symbolic. A CEO may himself or herself sign a particular corporate agreement, instead of delegating it to another. That says, loudly and clearly, that the agreement is important. The CEO can also leverage the organization itself to strengthen messages: The creation of a new corporate unit or position, for instance, helps legitimize a new program.

If a CEO has the corporation's trust and respect, its people will respond accordingly. They also will be reinforced by the reaction of outsiders who observe the change.

Such political processes are the tougher side of strategic management. But they are the stuff that go beyond the system to make it work. They are also the most important part of the job. Strategic management is not just issuing orders to carry out some vision from the top. It comes down to managing people. It comes down to developing a responsive system. It comes down to knowing the industry very, very well.

An additional role unique to the CEO is assuring the involvement of the board of directors in the strategic management process. The CEO has two obligations here. One is to assure that planning and strategic management do occur and that the board shares in determining the strategic direction of the company. The second is to see that investment opportunities brought before the board are tied to the stated strategic direction. At American, the key strategic issues are shared with the board at the very outset of the year's planning process. Each time an opportunity is brought to a board meeting, board members are clearly shown how the decision ties to the strategy. We also use the board to great advantage in discussion of strategic issues and subsequent investments; its members represent a real resource to help guide the strategic direction of an organization over the long term.

ISSUES

To be sure, American still grapples with a number of strategic management issues. Spirited and sometimes intense rivalry among business units, for example, is a classic problem of decentralized organizations. We are no exception. The company promotes from within, and many of our managers are former salesmen trained to get ahead by expanding territory. Moreover, we publish rankings of every kind: profits, productivity, who is making plan, who is not; who is on top and who is on bottom. As a result, the various divisions compete for everything from sales to research and development projects.

Turf wars are destructive if they last too long. But they usually do not. I can recall interfering only once, when several divisions were squabbling for the right to market an exciting new product. Usually, such rivalry is settled at levels far below the CEO by the parties themselves.

Rivalry, in short, is something we have decided to accept. A truly decentralized organization does not have a choice. A CEO cannot give managers autonomy and the chance to stick their heads above the crowd while retaining the right to call off occasional skirmishes. Besides, at times we can turn turf wars to our advantage. It is a fine way to see whose techniques work best.

Another issue crops up from time to time. I am asked occasionally if our planning process has grown a little slick. Skeptics suggest that some managers "think strategically" by repeating last year's corporate line about environmental trends and the "proper" corporate response. Meanwhile, they focus on the first year of the operating plan. Skeptics also note that by the time formal plans reach me, they are well polished. They argue that such finely honed presentations hide issues from me, rather than reveal them.

I agree, to a point. We do risk having the system become a bit rote and ingrained. But we take steps to counteract that. For example, during the formal presentation of business plans we began to include more time for open discussion. That gives top managers a chance to dig in for strategic issues. If we uncover critical topics, we immediately appoint a task force of the necessary talent, and name one of the corporation's senior managers to chair the group.

From time to time we also make an effort to reinvigorate strategic thinking. We challenge managers repeatedly throughout the planning process. I make such efforts when I am in the field. I ask them, and I ask myself, are the real issues bubbling up in our strategic plans? Are we putting enough money into key programs? Are we actually using the playbook as it was written? Occasionally, we will call on outside consultants to challenge our methodology as well. We also require that all managers spend time with customers and industry groups.

Beyond such steps, I do not worry about the issue of strategic "slickness." We have many incentives tied to performance. If people are not strategizing correctly, it will show up in their results and their income. Moreover, the health-care marketplace keeps changing. That keeps us all alert.

Short-Term Vs. Long-Term Thinking

A related issue: American, like many other companies whose stock is traded publicly, promises the investment community a strong financial performance, quarter after quarter. That involves what many call short-term thinking. Therefore I am often asked how we can encourage long-term thinking in our strategic management, especially when the cost of subsequent long-term projects bites into short-term performance.

That is a perennial issue that may not have an all-purpose answer. Yet our marketplace is changing quickly, and our fate increasingly rests on factors further down the road. As a result, it is critical that a corporation be capable of both approaches.

So we have established some practices that help us examine the trade-offs. For example, managers who wish to make special investments that will bring returns in years to come but will cut near-term profits may ask for profit plan relief. That eases a business unit's immediate financial goals and it frees up cash needed for investment. Typically, managers make their requests during strategic plan negotiations. They know that their case must be strong, but they also know that the option is available if the payoff is clear.

We have also established some financial incentives keyed to the longer term. In addition to traditional stock option plans, in recent years we have set up a new compensation program for some 40 key managers of the company. Under the terms of the program, these managers receive stock provided the corporation achieves stated three-year financial goals (such as improvement in profit margins). The program ties corporate strategic plans to long-term, bottom-line results. It also ensures that managers work for the good of the corporation and not just their own business unit.

The strategic planning process lays the groundwork for such programs. It creates an atmosphere for long-term thinking. American builds on that to encourage special long-term efforts in areas such as research and development.

Here, we have done a number of things within the corporation. We have created an organizational unit, the technology and ventures division, that clearly highlights that area's importance. As part of the corporate practice, we have ruled that no division manager can make a profit plan by cutting its research and development budget. All corporate officers also make it a point in any speech to emphasize the fact that American's research and development investments are growing, despite the slowing increases in health care expenditures.

Such moves signal that research and development has become very important to the corporation. Quarterly earnings are still important, too, and we are not in danger of having managers forget that fact. Too much depends on short-term performance, from stock price to bonuses. But with the proper incentives, managers are getting better at looking further down the road. I try to set an example for that.

LOOKING AHEAD: THE CHANGING ROLE OF THE CEO

I am certainly not alone in wrestling with these issues. All CEOs must think hard in the years ahead about how they do their jobs and, thus, how well their companies work. That is not a new challenge. While CEOs have always led their companies, how they lead has taken different forms. The emphasis has changed from decade to decade.

The clarion call in the 1950s, for example, was to make operations more efficient. Corporate plans were based on that goal; so was corporate management. So CEOs dutifully shrank their accounts receivable, reduced their inventories, and tended a host of other minutiae in response to that call.

In the 1960s, our collective attention turned to competitive postures and attendant strategies. CEOs all worried about who had what share of the pie, and how to get more. In the 1970s, the power of special interest groups led to new government regulations and social pressures. CEOs and their firms struggled to be good corporate citizens, taking on issues such as minority hiring and environmental impact.

Today CEOs still must worry about all the issues of the past decades. We make sure our operations are efficient. We fret over competitive postures. We respond to special interest groups and new legislation. But we hear more these days about global competition, innovation, and productivity. It seems we must add more tools to our manager's kit.

Productivity is the biggest issue by far. Not blue collar productivity, but white collar productivity: the work of managers, officers, and staff. The CEO can have a direct impact here, and it is surely just as critical a strategic issue as entering a new market. As a result, I have gotten behind it in the same way. I first "sent the signal" that productivity was a priority of mine with a rare night meeting of top management in my office. We had to watch the number of white collar workers in the corporation, I said. We had to ruthlessly set our own priorities to improve our individual productivity. We had to do more with less. The issue was kept before the corporation in speeches, emphasizing some of the same themes. We began to publish rankings of managers' head counts in relation to performance. I even had productivity improvement as one of my own MBOs for several years running: again, trying to set the example.

Productivity is just one issue. I also believe the attention of CEOs should increasingly turn to the need for innovation. Customers everywhere want and need new products, in health care and virtually every other industry. An even tougher issue, and just as important, involves the U.S. CEO's counterparts abroad. Some of us have felt the squeeze from those competitors. But many of us also see the tremendous opportunities offered by their home territory. Both trends indicate that the CEO of tomorrow must think globally, broadening an information-gathering network as well as utilizing formal studies of markets, competitors, and organizational strengths. We highlight the need for this in our own strategic plans, signaling that it is a priority with the corporation. The operating plans provide the framework for us to develop our tactics.

Productivity, innovation, and global competition are all growing concerns now. They will continue to be in the years ahead. They result from a changing environment that will, in turn, change some of the requirements of the CEO's job.

But some things will not change. At American Hospital Supply Corporation, the philosophy of growth through service should always govern strategy as well as daily action. The job of the chief executive officer will always rest on his or her responsibility for the overall direction and control of the business. If CEOs have sound management systems in place—if they work their networks of contacts within the business and outside of it—issues such as global competition will rise to the top. Strategies and tactics will emerge. A few of them will be on the CEO's personal agenda. The corporation ultimately will do what needs to be done.

This philosophy does not guarantee great strategic management. But it raises the chance of success.

BIBLIOGRAPHY

Abell, Derek F., *Defining the Business: The Starting Point of Strategic Planning,* Englewood Cliffs, N.J.: Prentice-Hall, Inc., 1980.

Ackoff, Russell L., *Creating the Corporate Future: Plan or Be Planned For,* New York: John Wiley & Sons, Inc., 1981.

Burger, Chester, *Chief Executive: Realities of Corporate Leadership,* Boston: CBI Publishing Co., Inc., 1978.

Deal, Terrence E., and Allan A. Kennedy, *Corporate Cultures,* Reading, Mass.: Addison-Wesley Publishing Co., 1982.

Donaldson, Gordon, and Jay W. Lorsch, *Decision Making at the Top: The Shaping of Strategic Direction,* New York: Basic Books Inc., 1983.

Drucker, Peter F., *Changing World of the Executive,* New York: Times Books, 1982.

Drucker, Peter F., *Managing in Turbulent Times,* New York: Harper and Row, 1980.

Freeman, R. Edward, *Strategic Management: A Stakeholder Approach,* Marshfield, Mass.: Pitman Publishing Inc., 1983.

Henderson, Bruce D., *Henderson on Corporate Strategy,* Cambridge, Mass.: Abt Books, 1979.

Kotter, John P., *The General Managers,* New York: Free Press, 1982.

Mintzberg, H., *Nature of Managerial Work,* Englewood Cliffs, N.J.: Prentice-Hall, Inc., 1980.

Ohmae, Keniche, *The Mind of the Strategist,* New York: McGraw-Hill Book Co., 1982.

Pascale, Richard T., and Anthony G. Althos, *Art of Japanese Management,* New York: Simon & Schuster Inc., 1981.

Peters, Thomas J., and Robert H. Waterman, Jr., *In Search of Excellence: Lessons from America's Best-Run Companies,* New York: Harper & Row, 1982.

Porter, Michael E., *Competitive Strategy: Techniques for Analyzing Industries and Competitors,* New York: Macmillan Publishing Co., 1980.

Quinn, James B., *Strategies for Change, Logical Incrementalism,* Homewood, Ill.: Richard D. Irwin, Inc., 1980.

Rothschild, William E., *Putting It All Together: A Guide to Strategic Thinking,* New York: American Management Association, Inc., 1976.

Sloan, Alfred P., Jr., *My Years with General Motors,* New York: Doubleday & Co. Inc., 1972.

Steiner, George A., *Strategic Planning: What Every Manager Must Know,* New York: Free Press, 1979.

27

The Role of the Board in Strategic Management

MILTON C. LAUENSTEIN

Lauenstein & Associates, Inc.

INTRODUCTION

Over the past few decades, the role of boards of directors in many corporations has evolved to include expanded responsibilities, often encompassing advice, consent, and monitoring of a firm's strategic direction. The level of involvement ranges from boards that simply question managers concerning corporate strategy to the elaborate system at Texas Instruments, where the entire board attends an annual four-day strategic planning conference and a corporate objectives committee of the board meets an additional 10 days during each year.

A major reason for this growing participation in corporate strategy has been the increasing accountability of boards of directors. Harvard Law Professor Detlev F. Vagts has written that the traditional legal view of the directors' functions "has been a rather vague and relaxed one", but he notes "a growing body of indications that the present relaxed condition of the law towards boards of directors will not continue."[1] The collapse of Penn Central brought new requirements for monitoring a firm's financial policies, the corporate bribery scandals of the 1970s resulted in new board responsibilities under the Foreign Corrupt Practices Act, and both public and shareholder actions have begun to attack the business judgment rule, which has traditionally insulated board members from legal liability. Even though the pace of change in this area may have slowed somewhat of late, a board's passive involvement in major plans and decisions of a firm has become increasingly risky, both in terms of potential legal liability for negligence and in terms of fulfilling the board's mandate to protect shareholder interests. A recent publication summarizing the legal responsibilities and liabilities of directors listed the following as "Things for Which a Director Might Be Sued":[2]

- Conflict of interest
- Mismanagement of corporate affairs
- Misrepresentation in Securities and Exchange Commission (SEC) registration statements
- Antitrust violations
- Insiders' trading of stock
- Corporate failure to comply with antipollution laws
- Illegal campaign contributions
- Misleading proxy material
- Failure to include in proxy statement material requested by stockholders

The list covers a wide range of possibilities, a number of which could be avoided through adequate board attention to strategic issues. Two additional strategically significant areas of board concern, executive compensation and corporate acquisitions, have received considerable public and media attention, and they seem to be likely areas for increases in board accountability.

A more positive incentive for active board involvement in corporate strategy is that a strong and effective board can offer a wide range of experience and special talents, which in itself provides a major potential source of competitive strength.

A corporate strategy may be thought of as a basis for expecting favorable results. Its success depends on recognizing and balancing the interests of all the parties involved in corporate operations: shareholders, employees, customers, suppliers, and the community at large. The role of the board of directors is to recognize these various interests and to ensure that the company is being run in a way that takes them all into account.

---

[1] "Directors: Myth and Reality," 31 *The Business Lawyer* 1231–1232 (March 1976).

[2] *Corporate Director's Guide* 5 (Wash., D.C.: Financial, Government and Public Affairs, 1978).

However, many boards have failed to perform the critical functions necessary to help a company succeed. The National Association of Corporate Directors has categorized boards into four groups:[3]

- *Minimum boards,* which meet only to fulfill minimum statutory requirements;
- *Cosmetic boards,* which serve as a rubber stamp to management prerogatives;
- *Oversight boards,* which function primarily to review programs, policies, proposals, reports, and the performance of corporate managers; and
- *Decision-making boards,* which are involved in setting corporate policy, determining management objectives, and authorizing their implementation.

Those boards in the oversight and decision-making categories are clearly in the best position to contribute to the strategic success of a corporation.

While boards are becoming increasingly active in contributing to the formulation and implementation of strategic plans, many business leaders would prefer to see this trend accelerate. A recent survey of new corporate directors found that over half of them believe that assuring the strategic plan for the future is a primary responsibility of board members. By contrast, only 21 percent felt that long-range planning was an area over which they had a strong influence in key management decisions, and only 43 percent reported even receiving the company's long-range plan when they joined the board.[4] Despite considerable academic and business press attention to the concept, relatively few companies have established strategy committees or corporate objectives committees of the board. The vast majority have concentrated on the board's traditional powers and responsibilities.

AUTHORITY OF THE BOARD, BY LAW AND BY CUSTOM

By law and by custom, there are a number of specific areas in which the board of directors uses its authority to direct the affairs of a company. However, whether the exercise of that authority is real or is only nominal depends on the individual circumstances and the relationship between a particular board of directors and chief executive officer. Traditional duties of strategic importance are discussed below.

Hiring and Firing the Chief Executive Officer

The board of directors' selection of the chief executive officer (CEO) is probably its strongest means of influencing corporate strategy. Although boards also elect the other corporate officers, they seldom exercise authority over subordinate managers with respect to strategy matters. The key issue is the CEO.

---

[3] "Evolution in the Boardroom" I Corporate Director's Special Report Series, National Association of Corporate Directors (Aug. 1978).

[4] *The New Director: Changing Views of the Board's Role* 20–21 (N.Y.: Arthur Young & Co. 1981).

It is the CEO's personality, ambitions, biases, and tolerance for risk that have a pervasive effect on corporate strategy. Once a strong-minded CEO is in office, some boards find that they have limited ability to influence the strategy pursued by the corporation. The selection of the CEO by the board should not only be a means of determining the kind of person to head the enterprise. It should also be a means of influencing the behavior of the incumbent. Normally, a board is reluctant to remove the CEO, except in a crisis. When disaster results from poor strategy, and the board acts, it is usually far too late. Directors are responsible for the well-being of the corporation, and, unless they are prepared to exercise their authority when the situation calls for it, they should not accept membership on a board.

Approving or Disapproving Major Financial Actions

In most companies, the board of directors has the authority to approve of or disapprove of major financial actions or policies, including: the size and timing of dividends, the sale or repurchase of securities, the purchase or sale of major fixed assets, and the annual operating budget.

The extent to which boards exercise this authority varies from company to company. Moreover, within companies, board authority varies from one financial area to another. For example, the board of directors almost always plays a significant role in determining dividend policy. It usually is active in decisions involving a sale or repurchase of corporate securities. Customarily, board approval is required for major capital expenditures, but, in many companies, such approval is perfunctory. Frequently, the board's consideration and approval of an annual operating budget is also more form than substance. To the extent that the directors actually exert their authority to approve or disapprove major financial moves, they can have a major impact on corporate strategy.

Acquisitions and Divestitures

Board approval is normally required for acquisitions or divestitures of operating units. Such moves often involve decisions on fundamental strategic issues, and they have long term effects on the company. The extent of actual board influence on such events varies widely from one company to the next.

Sale of the entire company in the case of public corporations is quite another matter. Here, partly because of potential personal liability, directors nearly always play a major role. However, a board frequently finds it difficult to initiate serious consideration of a sale if the management prefers that the company remain independent. Usually, it is after the question of sale arises that the board becomes active.

Other Strategic Issues

On a wide range of other matters affecting strategy, the authority of the board is exercised indirectly, if at all. Areas such as the scope of operations, basic operating policies, competitive positioning, development of corporate resources, allocation of capital among operations, and identification and evaluation of risks and opportunities are often discussed in board meetings before changes are made. However, the usual outcome is to approve management's proposals. As long as things are going well, the board is reluctant to force its will on the company and upset a successful management.

It is clear, then, that, at least in form, the board has the authority to have a decisive impact on strategy. In practice, however, the exercise of that authority varies widely from company to company and, within a specific firm, from area to area. Sometimes, the board of directors will assert itself and establish a policy in an area that is inconsistent with the strategy being pursued by management in other areas. For example, a board that insists upon a high level of dividends when management is pursuing a growth strategy could unnecessarily stifle the company's growth, to the detriment of the stockholders. Many companies would benefit by a clearer understanding on the part of both management and the board as to the responsibilities and authority of the directors. Both operating management and the board have a responsibility to develop a coherent strategy and consistent policies to further the interests of shareholders, employees, and other parties.

BASES FOR ACTIVE BOARD CONTRIBUTION

A properly constituted board can be an important resource for operating management in addressing strategic issues. Outside directors, in particular, can be expected to have a broad, objective point of view. Without the pressures associated with current operating problems, directors can more easily direct their attention toward longer-term issues.

A good board has members with expertise in key areas, some of which, such as corporate governance and control, may be quite outside the range of competence of the operating management. An important example is predicting the effects of major financial decisions on the price and marketability of corporate securities. This is an area in which operating management is frequently not well-qualified to deal. Directors with knowledge and experience about securities markets can be extremely useful in such circumstances, even if their contribution is no more than to voice serious warnings about assumptions of operating managers. Every board should have at least one member with a strong background in corporate finance. Accounting and legal skills can also be valuable in any boardroom, as can marketing, production, development, and industrial relations skills. Often, individual directors will have had experience with specific issues faced by the company. This experience and these skills are available to the top management that knows how to draw upon them.

The outside directors are usually less familiar with specific details of the business than operating management. However, by involving directors in the process of formulating and implementing corporate strategy, operating executives can usually come up with a more effective approach than by attempting to do the entire job themselves.

Operating management, by definition, must focus its primary attention on current operations. Finding the time to identify major risks is often very difficult. In contrast, outside directors are much freer to think broadly about the sources of major risks. In addition, they may have broader experience upon which to draw. Therefore, both the board and operating executives should expect directors regularly to scan the horizon and probe the company so that measures may be taken to counteract potential sources of trouble.

This involvement by outside directors might be seen as having four levels:

1 Offering functional advice on such matters as choosing an appropriate investment banker or management consultant for a given situation;

2 Reacting to the CEO's vision for the company's strategic direction (in many cases, if the board's reaction is anything less than enthusiastic, the CEO should take it as a warning signal);

3 Suggesting different approaches in the firm's strategy to improve its chances for success; and

4 Taking over and making radical changes in the company's strategic direction in cases of crisis or fundamental policy disagreements.

The appropriate level of involvement will, of course, depend on the circumstances of the individual firm. However, as noted earlier, there has been a generally positive trend toward greater involvement of the board, and particularly of outside directors, in the key strategic issues. The next section examines several of these key areas and looks at how the board might help a corporation to succeed.

KEY STRATEGIC ISSUES FOR BOARD CONTRIBUTION

A corporation's objectives are a fundamental basis for its strategy. A firm that is trying to grow at the rate of 20 percent per year will behave differently from one that is satisfied with the status quo. A company that focuses on sales growth will behave differently from one that looks first at return on investment. Many of the troubles that companies experience derive fundamentally from inappropriate objectives.

It is important that the board of directors and operating management agree on objectives. Normally, proposals as to what the objectives should be originate with operating management. The role of the board is to be certain that there are clearly defined objectives which are reasonable and appropriate for the corporation.

Effective competitive positioning requires that a firm define specific market segments and the particular capabilities required for success in those segments by developing competitive superiority. With the exception of money, nearly every corporate resource is more appropriate for one market segment than another. It is, therefore, almost always possible to find specific areas in which superiority can be achieved. Where a competing market leader takes advantage of economies of scale and has large plants geared to low-cost mass production, it is usually possible to identify smaller niches where flexibility, short runs, and specialized products can provide an advantage. Boards of directors are in a unique position to offer guidance on market positioning and to ensure that management has taken such factors into account.

To a large extent, this role is a cautionary one to ensure that the management is not taking on more than it can accomplish. An effort to serve all market segments almost invariably results in vulnerability to more specialized operations. The type of sales representative and sales compensation plan that is appropriate for stimulating demand for a new product is very different from what is most cost-effective in selling a well-established commodity. A cost system that would be critical to success in manufacturing a highly competitive mass-produced item would be entirely inappropriate in a high-fashion apparel plant. The board should satisfy itself that management has thought out such issues clearly and is implementing a plan of action that will develop the necessary resources.

Similarly, the board should make sure that the firm builds the capability of competing effectively in each business segment in which it elects to operate. Competitive success in an area depends largely on fundamental resources available to the entrants, such as management, money, technology, and physical assets. Pressure for current profits can divert the attention of operating management from the development of such resources, which are the key element in long-term success.

The heart of operating strategy is in positioning the company and its operating units in such a way that they enjoy a lasting competitive advantage. In this area, operating management has relatively more, and the board less, responsibility for initiatives than in financial planning and strategy. Nevertheless, the board is ultimately responsible, and it must assure itself that the approach being taken by operating management does, in fact, represent a basis for achieving corporate objectives.

The extent to which businesses try to emulate each other rather than developing distinctive differences for specific market segments is disappointing. It may represent a fear of failure in pursuing an independent course of action, or it may simply stem from a natural tendency to copy success. In any case, investment in approaches that are essentially the same as those of other firms rarely provides a superior return. The role of the board, therefore, is to assist operating management in developing business unit strategies that provide a reasonable basis for expecting superior results. This requires a clear definition of the specific markets to be served, and the careful and continuing development of the key resources and capabilities necessary to achieve a competitive advantage.

Another key strategic issue is the allocation of capital among the various business segments in which a company participates. Often, decisions on major capital investments are made individually, as a need or opportunity arises. Such haphazard investment usually results in suboptimal performance. Just as poor control of sales activity frequently leads to an unsatisfactory product mix, so uncoordinated investing leads to unsatisfactory returns.

Successful investing requires a deliberate program for channeling funds into those business segments that are likely to produce the best return over the long run. Even when operating management has developed a strategy for the allocation of resources, it is subject to pressures of various types to make contrary decisions. The manager of a weak division pleads for new equipment to become more competitive. The chief of the best division is satisfied with its performance and fails to go after additional opportunities. Again, an informed board can point to problem areas and suggest solutions.

Acquisitions are investments of special concern to the board of directors. As many companies have learned, to their dismay, acquisitions involve serious risks that are not often immediately apparent. Acquisitions are always strategically important, affecting, as they do, the allocation of capital and the direction of corporate diversification or concentration. Divestitures, which usually represent an effort to concentrate investment in more rewarding areas, are also inherently strategic in nature, and they demand the involvement of the board.

A common problem with acquisitions is that conversations with prospective sellers acquire a dynamic reality of their own, and strategic considerations are often forgotten in the effort to structure and conclude a deal. Under such circumstances, a board of directors may find it extremely difficult to restrain an ambitious and optimistic management. Through the eyes of the enthusiastic acquirer, the characteristics of the prospect often fall into two categories:

1 Strengths, which have obvious value, and
2 Weaknesses, which seem even more attractive, because they seem so easily correctable in a way that could add value to the acquisition.

Adverse observations by directors at this point are often most unwelcome.

To avoid such situations, getting the commitment of operating management to a strategy that is mutually agreed upon can be very helpful. Furthermore, an agreement that the board will be consulted *before* contacts are made with acquisition prospects that do not clearly conform to the strategy can allow discussion at a time when management is in a better position to be objective. The failure of boards to control overly acquisitive managements has been among the most common causes of loss of equity values in recent years. Companies from LTV to AM International have gotten into trouble—and, sometimes, into Chapter 11—by not pursuing a cautious and consistent acquisition strategy overseen by the board of directors. The board has a critical role to play both in determining the criteria that should govern the consideration of an acquisition as well as in passing judgment on each specific case.

If strategy is dealing with the issues that affect the long-term profitability of a corporation, then identifying and evaluating risks is an important part of strategy. The fortunes of many companies are more dependent on their ability to identify serious risks in a timely fashion and to provide for responding to unexpected reverses than any other factor. For example, LTV's heavy borrowing to acquire Jones & Laughlin Steel in 1971 during a period of increasing anti-trust regulation and higher interest rates almost caused the company to go under. Conversely, Genrad's decision not to grow in the 1940s and 1950s when the electronics industry began to boom left them in a weak position for almost 20 years. The board should provide the judgment and guidance necessary to keep the firm on an even keel through the shifting winds and rocky shoals of the marketplace.

Similarly, the board should provide the perspective needed for an appropriate balance between short-term and long-term performance. Numerous articles in the past several years have pointed to the enormous problems caused by excessive pressures for short-term performance in U.S. companies. Many observers have noted that Japanese companies, with job security, long management tenure, and a de-emphasis on stock performance have overcome this problem and obtained superior results over the long term. Although this situation is perhaps not as easy to achieve in the United States, given a different culture and the established patterns of managers, a far greater emphasis on long-term performance is clearly needed. In many ways, this is simply another way of saying that companies could benefit from a greater emphasis on strategy formulation and implementation.

Because it is not immersed in day-to-day operating minutiae, the board can often provide a longer-term perspective than operating management. Moreover, it has two essential powers that can help to foster such an approach:

- *Management compensation* can be structured to provide incentives for long-term performance by expanding at least part of the time frame for bonuses beyond the traditional one year. The board needs to concern itself only with such incentive compensation schemes for top managers. The message will reach into the ranks very quickly.

- *Resource allocation and development* by the board should explicitly take a long-term approach. The board can look to the future needs for everything from management talent to modern plants and equipment and make sure that they are provided for.

Usually, changing the relative allocation of capital among business segments cannot be accomplished easily or quickly. Decisions in this area have to be lived with over long periods. Therefore, such decisions should be made carefully and deliberately. The judgment capabilities of the board of directors render it uniquely qualified to make these decisions.

Perhaps the most basic strategic issue faced by any company is its long-term position with respect to investments. Companies with unique advantages or in a rapidly growing market tend to have more good investment opportunities than they have funds, while mature corporations usually generate more cash than they can invest attractively. One can envision an "investment opportunity spectrum," ranging from plentiful investment opportunities to a situation in which one cannot even get a return on replacing equipment that wears out. A company's dividend policy and basic financial positioning should depend on where a company is positioned on that spectrum.

A board of directors dominated by outside members is in a better position to make an objective determination as to where along that spectrum a company will lie over the foreseeable future. If it is likely to have many opportunities, the board may elect not to pay a cash dividend. Digital Equipment and Intel are two examples of firms that have been successful with such a policy. In addition, the board of directors will go to considerable lengths to ensure that the firm has ready access to capital markets, since it will be needing more money from time to time. In fact, when market conditions are favorable, the board may raise more money than necessary for its immediately defined needs, if it is confident that additional attractive investment opportunities will be generated before too long.

Because the usual orientation of operating management is toward growth, the board of directors has an even more important role to play in mature companies. The reinvestment of a high percentage of cash flow in operations may be counterproductive for shareholders, as the experience of companies such as U.S. Steel in recent years has clearly demonstrated. In such situations, the board of directors has a responsibility to recognize the position of a company on the investment opportunities spectrum, and to return most of the cash flow to shareholders, either as cash dividends or by reacquiring company shares in the market.

It appears that boards of directors frequently fail to discharge this responsibility well. A study of 1,700 companies in the Value Line Investment Survey in 1981 showed that more than half of the companies paid out between 10 percent and 40 percent of earnings as cash dividends. The percentage of total cash flow paid out as dividends was obviously much lower. Very few companies either paid no dividends or paid out 100 percent or more of earnings. These data suggest that boards feel that they need to pay out a small percentage of cash flow as dividends, but that they need to reinvest the great bulk or cash flow in operations, regardless of the company's position on the investment opportunity spectrum.

Like everyone else, executives are influenced by their own personal interests and motivations. They like to make economic progress, achieve recognition, and avoid risk. Despite the best efforts of everyone involved to make the interests of individual executives congruent with those of the shareholders and other interested parties, differences inevitably exist. For example, executives have a vested interest in growth per se. It affects their compensation, recognition, sense of achievement, and future opportunities. Thus, they may be motivated to make decisions other than those that are in the stockholders' best interests. Therefore, in addition to a strategy for allocation of resources, a control procedure is needed to keep management aware of the degree to which strategy is actually being followed in day-to-day investment decisions. The board should not only assure itself that such a control procedure exists and is being used by management, but it should also obtain summary information so that the directors, too, know that the strategy is actually being pursued. Such a system should be able to highlight the strategic implications of accounting changes, such as going from FIFO to LIFO for inventory valuation, and of the adequacy of inflation reserves and pension liability funding.

Normally, identifying the relationship between corporate capabilities and market opportunities requires the more intimate knowledge of operations that management is expected to have. However, emerging trends in the external environment and what they mean in terms of opportunity to the company may sometimes be more apparent to outside directors as a result of their other activities and experience. The board should evaluate the extent to which the company is aware of the environment in which it operates and alert the company to potential opportunities. It should call attention to shortcomings and suggest remedies. Moreover, the directors should individually try to assist management in this important activity.

Finance—and, in particular, the raising and allocating of funds—is generally regarded as one of the main areas for board activity. Presidents and other senior officers have typically risen through operations and, thus, they have been less familiar with finance than with functions such as production, marketing, and control. As a result, they tend to look for and accept more board input in finance than elsewhere.

The board should balance the need for financial flexibility and the cost of capital. Because debt is normally a cheaper source of capital than equity, companies are often tempted to borrow all of the money anyone will lend them. In a highly leveraged condition, corporations may lack the flexibility either to weather economic adversity or to finance additional investment opportunities that may come to their attention. The frequency with which companies get into financial trouble is testimony to the fact that insufficient attention is given to this need for financial flexibility. Some events that precipitate these problems, such as International Harvester's disastrous strike, are, to a considerable extent, under the control of management. It is essential to balance carefully the potential gains against the risks of such actions, and independent directors are often in a better position than management to exercise objective judgment.

External events over which management has very little control, such as a recession, have resulted in financial crises in companies such as the Chrysler Corporation. The timing and severity of such external events is often difficult or impossible to predict. An experienced board of directors will be sensitive to the fact that unexpected events are likely to occur. In structuring the corporation's balance sheet, the board must take such uncertainty into account and maintain enough financial flexibility to be able to deal with any but the most unusual situations.

In considering the strategic implications of additional debt, the board has an important role to play. It must deal with the question of how much debt it is prudent for the company to carry. It must see to it that the company carefully considers all of the various forms of debt that may be appropriate and that it considers enough sources to be confident that it is getting the most favorable available terms. Also important is the evaluation of the restrictive covenants in debt instruments, which sometimes prove to have a major effect on a company's financial flexibility. Quite often, the board can provide valuable counsel based on its knowledge of the past practices of specific lenders.

A decision to issue new shares of corporate stock, to invest in another company, or to make major dispositions of cash or other assets is usually one of great strategic importance. Because such decisions depend upon so many imponderables, they call for a high order of wisdom, objectivity, experience, and judgment to reach decisions in which one can be reasonably confident. For these characteristics, companies often rely on the board of directors.

Finally, investor relations is a highly specialized area that can have substantial strategic importance. The price of a company's stock, the availability and cost of debt, and the company's relationship with its lenders can be critically important, not only to the ability of the company to take advantage of opportunities, but also to its very survival.

In this area, directors can be invaluable not only as advisers, but also as active participants. The involvement of key directors in meetings with financial institutions and security analysts, especially if they have reputations or personal relationships that are relevant, can be enormously valuable to a corporation. Both operating management and directors should be alert to situations in which directors can assist in relationships with the financial community.

In a more routine way, the board should be expected to monitor the communications addressed to the financial community. Reports to stockholders, news releases, statements at annual meetings, and other pronouncements affect the credibility and image of a corporation in the financial community and, thus, they affect its access to capital. Leaving such communications entirely to the discretion of operating management can have very negative results. For example, the tendency of some managers to forecast either financial results or operating developments, such as new products, can badly damage a company's credibility, as the Polaroid Corporation, among others, has discovered. In addition, legal responsibilities to persons buying or selling stock require the utmost care that misleading information not be disseminated or private information used. The board members' experience can be invaluable in preventing serious problems.

A corporation's ability to adapt to changing internal and external circumstances has crucial implications for its strategy. A rapidly growing company must overcome successive crises as it evolves from a small entrepreneurial business to a large, multidivisional corporation. Mature companies must determine the most effective organizational structure for keeping managers efficient and well-motivated. Decisions such as whether and when to establish autonomous divisions, how to ensure adequate internal communication, how to develop management talent, and where to establish new facilities are all dependent on the particular organizational structure chosen. An experienced board of directors can assist in deciding what kind of organizational structure best suits a company's needs and objectives.

ORGANIZATION OF THE BOARD FOR STRATEGIC MANAGEMENT CONTRIBUTION

Organizing the board for an effective contribution to strategic management requires both operating managers and board members to make hard decisions concerning the board's size, composition, committee structure, access to information, coordination, and compensation. Without a carefully structured organization, the board, at best, is likely to flounder about uselessly and, at worst, is likely to be detrimental to corporate objectives. The following are some issues to address in planning for a strategically active board.

Determining the Size and Composition of the Board

Boards of directors vary considerably in size, from just a few members to over 25. A 1978 survey found the average number of directors was 13.[5] A more recent study found that the average number of directors has been increasing over the past several years, with the size of the board tending to be proportional to the size of the company.[6] Because a smaller board affords a better opportunity for its members to be fully utilized, it is often in a better position than a large one to play a strong role in representing the interests of stockholders. There are, of course, the practical constraints of having enough members to insure a quorum (fewer than five can create problems if two people are absent) and to handle the increasing workload of the typical board and its committees, especially in larger corporations. As a rule, however, the smaller-sized board will often prove to be more effective, and it is certainly less expensive.

For a company with annual sales in the range of $1 to $25 million, a five-to seven-member board is usually large enough. A seven- to ten-member board should be sufficient for most corporations with sales of less than $1 billion per year. Larger boards are often required for bigger or more diversified companies.

Directors should come from a wide range of backgrounds to ensure complementary skills and experience on the board. They should possess integrity and an ability to express and stand up for their convictions. They should also be able to view the company in its broad social context, as well as from the point of view of the shareholder. Finally, they should not have personal interests that could conflict with their responsibilities as board members.

Good prospects for board membership include senior executives from other businesses or nonprofit organizations, educators, representatives from the financial community, lawyers, accountants, consultants, investors, and retired persons. Some companies are now using executive recruiting firms to search for new directors, especially in order to help them make sure that both sexes and more than one ethnic group are represented on the board. Only one percent of directors in a 1981 survey suggested union representatives as a likely source of directors, yet 23 percent expected such representation on boards within the next five years.[7] One additional consideration might be to have at least one member who is well-versed in the formulation and implementation of corporate strategy. A business professor or a senior executive from a company known for its strategic planning capabilities might be ideal for such a role.

In general, there can be considerable variation in the most appropriate composition and size of the board. The key concerns are to recruit and retain enough strong people with sufficiently diverse backgrounds to undertake an active role in guiding the company.

---

[5] Edwin S. Mruk and James A. Giardina, Board of Directors, Fifth Annual Study (Korn Ferry International, Feb. 1978).

[6] *Organization and Compensation of Boards of Directors* 11 (N.Y.: Arthur Young & Co., 1981).

[7] *The New Director: Changing Views of the Board's Role,* op. cit. p. 22

Outside Vs. Inside Directors

Because a major part of the board's job is evaluating the performance of senior management, company employees who sit on the board, in effect, represent a special sort of conflict of interest. They are unlikely to be able to make objective contributions on key issues such as management succession, mergers and acquisitions, dividend policy, executive compensation, and other areas in which they may have a vested interest. The very presence of such employees at board meetings makes the discussion of many issues awkward. For these reasons, Harold M. Williams, a former chairman of the Securities and Exchange Commission, suggested that only the president be represented on the board.[8] One additional problem of having inside directors is that board membership can create an unhealthy executive caste system of those on and those off the board, while making it extremely difficult to remove an insider without losing his or her services to the company altogether.

Indeed, it is not necessary to have insiders as board members, since they are available as needed to contribute to board discussions and to make presentations. A growing number of companies seem to have made this realization: The 1981 survey of directors found that 72 percent of the respondents from publicly held corporations were nonmanagement directors, an increase of seven percentage points from the 1979 version of the study.[9] The company surely benefits in both the short run and in the long run by having at least the great majority of board members be outside directors.

Creating a Strategy Committee of the Board

There has been a great deal of discussion during the past few years in the business press on the advisability of creating a strategy or corporate objectives committee of the board. Despite this attention and a trend toward more board committees, few companies actually have taken the step of creating such a committee (it ranks behind the number having ethics committees and well behind those with public affairs committees).[10] One reason may be that, except in extremely large or complex corporations, a formal strategy committee is thought to be unnecessary *as long as* other committees and the full board make sure that strategic issues are fully considered.

Unfortunately, such consideration is not always the case. It is disturbing, but not surprising that less than three-quarters of the directors surveyed in 1981 reported that their boards approve of, or are even involved in, the company's long-range planning.[11] It might therefore be advisable to create a strategy committee, simply to ensure that the matter receives the attention it deserves. At a minimum, the board should reserve an entire meeting each year for discussion of strategic issues, preferably prior to the meeting that considers

[8] "The Role of the Director in Corporate Accountability," an address before the Fifth Annual Securities Regulation Institute, San Diego, Calif. (Jan. 18, 1978).

[9] *Organization and Compensation of Boards of Directors*, op. cit. p. 11.

[10] *The New Director: Changing Views of the Board's Role*, op. cit. p. 19.

[11] Ibid p. 32.

the annual budget. The board should also consider strategy and corporate objectives as they debate major decisions at other meetings throughout the year. For those boards whose members are unsure of the best way to go about discussing strategic issues, it is possible to engage a consultant who could help in tailoring an approach that meets their needs. The long-term direction and health of the corporation is too important to be left simply to operating managers or to chance.

Relating the Board to Operating Management

Most of the information received by directors comes from company personnel. In order to have meaningful results from the board's involvement in corporate and business strategy, it is important that the information provided be as clear, timely, and accurate as possible. Information generally should be presented in a long time frame, that is, in years rather than months or quarters. Such information should include measures of how well capital is being allocated (e.g., a measure of return on assets or of investments, with division, market, and product breakdowns), a forecast of the next year's projected sources and applications of funds, and summary budget versus actual earnings statements. In addition to such quantitative information, operating managers should provide information on the quality and depth of management personnel, competitors' moves, employee relations, technical developments and trends within the company and industry, the condition of fixed and other assets, and plans for marketing and manufacturing. Managers should keep in mind in compiling and presenting this information that an excess of material is almost as serious a problem for directors as an insufficiency.

In addition, presentations by various managers at board meetings can be helpful. A visit by board members to manufacturing sites, attendance at seminars or trade shows, and contacts with various parties that deal with the firm can also provide useful information that is often not even available to managers. It is especially useful for board members to meet occasionally with top executives, perhaps at an off-site conference where both formal and casual discussions can lead to more effective long-range planning.

Compensating Directors for Active Strategic Management Contribution

If a company expects a substantial strategic contribution from its directors, it should compensate them accordingly. In practice, director compensation tends to vary with the time commitment expected, the size of the company, and the role of the board.

One approach might be to pay directors, on an hourly basis, at least as much as the CEO, whom they are expected to select and oversee. Thus, in a company where the president's compensation package is worth $250,000 and he or she works approximately 2,500 hours, the directors would receive at least $14,400 if they were expected to devote 12 hours per month to their board duties.

The principal forms of director compensation are an annual retainer and a fee for each meeting attended. Most companies use a combination of the two. In addition, committee members receive additional payments, and committee chairpeople often are compensated at a higher rate than other members.

Most companies do not provide fringe benefits to directors, other than liability insurance. In particular, stock options are a benefit that very few firms offer to their outside directors.[12] However, stock options are one area where companies might change this policy to their long-term benefit. Stock options are provided by many public companies to offer key employees additional motivation to contribute, and to help them identify shareholder interests with their own. The same reasons are particularly applicable to directors, especially in smaller companies with substantial growth potential and a great need for the advice of seasoned outsiders to realize that potential not be overlooked.

CONCLUSION

A central role of the board is ensuring that the company has strategies that provide a sound basis for expecting attractive results. The concepts and techniques suggested above should allow corporations to reexamine the roles of their boards in formulating and monitoring the firm's strategic direction. The rewards for building a properly conceived and organized board of directors can be enormous for the firm, its shareholders, and society.

BIBLIOGRAPHY

"Accountability and the Corporate Board," The Journal of Accountancy 80 (Nov. 1980), excerpts from Williams, Harold M., Enterprise (journal of the National Association of Manufacturers, July 1980).

Andrews, Kenneth R., "Corporate Strategy as a Vital Function of the Board," Harvard Business Review 174 (Nov.–Dec. 1981).

Andrews, Kenneth R., "Replaying the Board's Role in Formulating Strategy," Harvard Business Review 18 (May–June 1981).

Andrews, Kenneth R., The Concept of Corporate Strategy (rev. ed.), Homewood, Ill.: Dow Jones-Irwin, 1980.

Andrews, Kenneth R., "Directors' Responsibility for Corporate Strategy," Harvard Business Review 30 (Nov.–Dec. 1980).

Carroll, Daniel T., "Boards and Managements: Ten Challenges and Responses," Harvard Business Review 62 (Sept.–Oct. 1980).

Clendenin, William D., "Company Presidents Look at the Board of Directors," California Management Review 60 (Spring 1972).

"Corporate Governance in the Courts," Harvard Business Review 50 (July–Aug. 1980).

---

[12] *Organization and Compensation of Boards of Directors*, op. cit. p. 28.

Cyert, R.M., and J.G. March, *A Behavioral Theory of the Firm*, Englewood Cliffs, N.J.: Prentice-Hall, Inc., 1963.

De Marco, Victor F., "The Triple Threat Against Fraud," Internal Auditor 39 (Aug. 1981).

Felton, Samuel M., "Case of the Board and the Strategic Process," Harvard Business Review 20 (July–Aug. 1979).

Heller, Jr., Milton F., "The Board of Directors: Legalistic Anachronism or Vital Force," California Management Review 24 (Spring 1972).

Quinn, James Brian, *Strategies for Change: Logical Incrementalism* 145, Homewood, Ill.: Richard D. Irwin, 1980.

Vagts, Detlev F., "Directors: Myth and Reality," 31 The Business Lawyer 1227 (March 1976).

Wrapp, H. Edward, "Good Managers Don't Make Policy Decisions," Harvard Business Review 91 (Sept.–Oct. 1967).

28

The Role of the Consultant

PETER CARROLL

Vice President, Hayes/Hill, Inc.

CHARACTERISTICS OF STRATEGY CONSULTING FIRMS

It has been estimated that the market for business consulting in the United States was $3 billion in 1980. It is probably only slightly higher in 1984 in real terms. This figure includes almost everything classified as a consulting service. Within this larger figure, between $300 million and $400 million could be described as strategy consulting. Much consulting that is not classified specifically as strategy consulting nevertheless is relevant to strategy within the firm for which it is performed. The vast majority of this money is spent by the largest corporations, with a smaller percentage spent by hospitals, universities, charities, and other organizations.

Some companies do not use consultants at all. Others spend millions of dollars each year on strategy consulting. Several companies spent over $5 million on such consulting in 1983.

There are probably fewer than 20 consulting companies, some of which perform services outside the strategy field, that account for 80 percent of the market for strategy consulting. Among these are

- Bain and Co.
- Booz Allen & Hamilton
- The Boston Consulting Group
- Braxton Associates
- Cresap McCormick & Paget (Towers, Perrin, Forster & Crosby)

- Hayes/Hill
- A. D. Little
- Marakon Systems
- McKinsey & Co.
- Stanford Research Institute
- Strategic Planning Associates

These firms range in the size of their annual U.S. strategy practice revenues from less than $5 million to over $50 million. In addition, many other firms turn their hand to strategy consulting and there are a variety of individuals who practice in the field, including business school professors and retired senior executives.

In discussing the role of consultants in strategic management, this chapter addresses the role played by the group of consulting companies listed previously and any others that act in a similar capacity. With their role thus defined quite narrowly, it is interesting that a wide range of approaches exists within the group. Some are mainly problem definers and solvers; others are more involved with strategy implementation. Some work mainly at the corporate level, some at the business unit level; others work at both levels. Some are very technically oriented, while others are less so. The focus of some is internal; others focus on the external environment.

WHY CONSULTANTS ARE HIRED

An Objective Outsider's Point of View

An outsider frequently can see a problem more clearly, or at least differently, than on-going management. An outside consultant's confirmation of an existing point of view also can be valuable to the management that hires him. This element of a consultant's value can never be an internal function of a corporation. Like a lawyer or an auditor, a consultant enjoys organizational independence and thus a greater degree of objectivity in judgment and evaluation. In addition, consultants often can put mundane things into an entirely new perspective. This does not necessarily happen in all studies, but often enough to be a significant advantage.

Expert Advice

Consultants usually specialize in particular kinds of problems, often in particular industries. Consequently, they bring state-of-the-art expertise to the client organization. However, they rarely have specialist knowledge greater than the leaders in the field.

Concentrated Manpower

Some firms staff for a base load of strategic planning activity and use consultants as an extension of management to cope with special work loads. For them, consultants represent a readily available pool of educated and experienced people.

Introduction of New Ideas

A consultant also might be retained to introduce new ideas. These ideas need not be factual elements concerning the business or technology associated with it, but general concepts concerning strategy as a whole. One way to introduce such concepts is by demonstrating their application to a particular issue or problem.

Problem Solving and Problem Definition

Sometimes a problem has been identified in a company but no solution can be found. This is precisely the sort of challenge that appeals most to a consultant. Consulting firms place a high value on problem-solving ability when they recruit staff.

As often as not the problem initially defined is actually only a manifestation of the real problem. Consultants are retained to recognize and define problems as much as to solve problems and implement solutions. More than anything else, this is the consultant's role. A consultant is constantly asked to recognize, define, and solve problems.

Stimulating Change

Consultants are often seen as, and deliberately used as, agents of change. Sometimes the direction of change, or at least the need for change of some kind, is obvious. The consultant acts as a catalyst of sorts to promote the change. Alternatively the consultant may stimulate change that was not foreseen. In many companies a particular problem or dissatisfaction with current performance may result in the retention of a consulting firm. To the management of the company the problem appears to be a combination of many specific areas of difficulty. To the consultant these areas of difficulty are all manifestations of a basic situation. It might have developed over years and be difficult for management to perceive. Such situations occur often in a single-product or single-process companies as well as in companies that outgrow the systems that served them for years.

Consultants help to stimulate change both by identifying or confirming the need for change and by acting as its focal point.

THE CONSULTANT'S ROLE IN PROVIDING DECISION-MAKING ADVANTAGES

The use of a consultant sometimes is seen as a variant of the make-or-buy decision. It is possible to view some consulting functions in this light. In the strategic management field, however, consulting firms increasingly are the generators of techniques and ideas. Consequently, the make-or-buy decision is less rele-

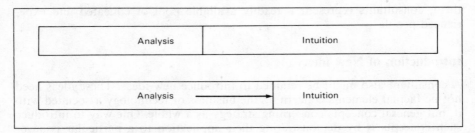

FIG. 28-1 Problem-Solving Models

vant. A consultant can bring new techniques and new ways of thinking, and can generate new insights.

Consulting services are used in three types of situations. In the first, the hiring company does not need, or is reluctant to admit the need for, a full range of consultant assistance. Such companies use consultants occasionally on a fill-in basis, often as experts in a narrow specialty. In the second situation, consultants are employed to extend the range and power of full-time management. In the third situation, the hiring company has a philosophy that views business as a stream of challenges and believes in the intellectual and practical value of applying resources to problems. Implicit in the third user's view is an acceptance of the need to make better decisions than its rivals, not necessarily on a point-by-point basis, but cumulatively as a stream of decisions. In particular, on issues that relate in some way to the structured basis of competition, a decision merits consideration in great depth. Every decision faced is a balance between analysis and intuition. The process of coming to a decision involves weighing these ingredients.

All decision making involves a level of intuition. A decision with no intuitive content is actually a calculation. As illustrated in Figure 28-1, moving the analytical boundary of a problem-solving model to the right produces a decision-making advantage over competitors. All firms are, or should be, attempting to reduce their dependence on intuition.

When attempting to shift the analytical/intuitive boundary, a firm should seek the highest incremental return on effort. Decisions of a broad strategic nature, which are of fundamental importance to the firm and of high intuitive content, represent the area of decision making in which such an attempt could and should be made. The incremental analysis that distinguishes one company from its competitors, through its effect upon that company's highest level of decision making, is strategic analysis. The strategy consultant's role is to provide the client with a significant advantage in decision making. He or she does this by conducting research and analysis relevant to the decisions that are made. He or she does not remove the necessity for judgment, but improves the validity of that judgment by focusing on the vital issues and by providing insights into those issues.

Consultants who specialize in strategic management problems think through and analyze several major problems every year. This represents more direct experience of its kind than most executives, even senior ones, see in their careers. Although such experience leaves untouched the hundreds of small practical steps by which the company must actually be managed, it does allow the consultant to develop valuable insights for the client. As a result, the required advantage in strategic decision making is transferred from consultant to client.

Whatever the field in which a consultant is retained, there is an expectation that a specific advantage will thereby be transferred to the client. It is in the area of strategic management that this advantage can be the most profound. Problems of strategic management have many characteristics that are different from those found in other areas of management. These characteristics include the following:

- They affect separate functional areas simultaneously.
- They are complex, not simple, and involve implicit trade-offs.
- They involve a time perspective that is not limited to a single quarter or a fiscal year.
- They often require either/or choices for the whole enterprise.
- They often disrupt the status quo.
- They often break with conventional ways of behaving in the business.
- They are risky and competitive.

HOW CONSULTANTS WORK

Modes of Consulting Services

Most consulting work is performed in the following general ways. Management perceives a problem within the organization. Through discussions between management and consultants, a broad understanding of the problem is developed. The consultants propose an approach to the problem that offers a solution. This approach usually includes a work program and an analytical or conceptual framework within which the problem will be treated. The proposal includes an estimate of the time and staffing required to complete the work program as well as a statement of who will work on the study. If accepted, this proposal serves as a study outline and budget.

Two other modes of consulting services are also in use. In the first, a consultant has a particular technique or computerized modeling approach and is called upon to apply it on behalf of a client for a relatively flat fee. These techniques are often applied to the various forms of portfolio analysis. In the second, the consultant does not sell a potential solution to a specific problem or offer a particular strategy technique. Instead, he or she sells the idea that problems of strategy need to be analyzed. A team of consultants is then put on a general retainer to identify and attack a range of critical issues. Although this approach has many advantages, it is also susceptible to abuse on the part of both the consultant (because it removes the competitive discipline of bidding on engagements) and the chief executive (because it invites hostility from line managers who feel they are being sidestepped and, worse, investigated). However, despite the trend to these two modes, the problem-proposal approach remains the dominant means of consultation.

Fees

A consultant's fee is usually expressed as an hourly billing rate. The billing rate within a firm ranges with seniority and level of expertise. The rates usually reflect varying salary rates within the client corporation. As a rule of thumb, a consultant's billing rate is 2.5 to 3.0 times his or her salary rate, in order to cover operating and maintenance costs as well as general and administrative costs.

In 1983 individual rates ranged from about $100 to $250 per hour. If these fees seem high, consider the economics of a consulting office. At year-end, for every million dollars of revenue, salaries eat up nearly 50 percent. Office and administrative expenses plus expenses to promote the firm's services account for nearly 25 percent. There may be a corporate charge, depending on the firm's structure. The rest goes to bonuses, taxes, and reinvestment.

Consider also that the alternative is not costless. Hiring internal personnel also involves high salaries for competent, experienced people; benefits, office maintenance, and overhead also must be considered. In-house consulting personnel must be trained and provided with an ongoing roster of studies and assignments. Given the fact that the consultant's analytical prowess and strategic management experience is his or her greatest asset, it is small wonder that firms often have a tendency to hire consistently from the same consulting service, often requesting the same team of consultants repeatedly.

What does the hiring company get for $100,000? In raw terms, it benefits from about half of one man-year. In practice, it gets three people working full time for six weeks; alternatively, it might get two people full-time for 10 weeks. The most expensive time in a study is the meeting time. Assuming the fully costed time of client and consultant alike is very similar, then a meeting that involves four consultants and six client personnel and that lasts three hours will cost $3,000. If the consultants' travel costs are included, the total might easily exceed $4,000. Because they work to definite cost budgets, consultants look at meetings this way. Because company employees do not, they are profligate with the value of people's time. One reason consultants' fees seem high is that people have a highly inaccurate concept of the value of people's time. When a value is calculated, it often focuses only on base pay and excludes other cash costs and experience value.

Staffing

A consulting firm sells its staff time. Its success is intimately connected with the quality, mix, and maturity of its staff. For a particular study a consulting firm selects a team of three or four individuals suited to the specific problem or industry. The team may contain a technical expert, an industry expert, someone who has experience with similar business problems, and someone familiar with the technique to be applied. Occasionally, the team builds on industry expertise, but the binding force is usually the ability to define and resolve a particular type of problem.

Many companies will specify the team of consultants to be employed once they have gained experience with that team. Most consulting firms provide details of the education and experience of prospective members of a study team. This is considered part of the selling features of the proposal.

Reports

Consultants have been defined as people who are 100 miles from home and show slides. The oral presentation of findings with visual aids has replaced the formal written report as the focal point of a consulting study. Most firms still provide a written record of the study, but it is frequently supplied, as a record, after the final presentation. The fee for the written report may be stated separately as an addition to the budget.

Conflicts of Interest

Clients sometimes require assurance that a prospective consultant or consulting team has relevant industry experience to minimize the amount of time needed to become familiar with the business. On the other hand, clients may be concerned about possible consulting conflicts of interest.

For the consultant, assignments with multibusiness corporations may present a problem. If a consultant has advised General Electric on some element of its strategy, he or she might not be eligible to work in 65 percent of U.S. business. In practice, consulting firms seem to employ two general rules. First, if a consultant has worked for one company on its basic strategy, he or she will not work for that company's competitors in the same business. That guideline permits a consultant to work for General Electric and United Technologies, but not for General Electric's aero engine division and for United Technologies' Pratt & Whitney. Second, if a consultant has performed a nonstrategy study for a client and has not been exposed to critical, confidential company data, then he or she is eligible to work subsequently for that company's direct rival. Thus, a consultant might review the world market for a particular turbine at General Electric and subsequently investigate the likely impact of airline deregulation on small-engine demand for Pratt & Whitney. But professional ethics always dictate that all company information remain confidential. Information from third parties may be relevant to both clients and can be used accordingly.

Implementation

Most consultants, responding to criticism from clients, claim to be very concerned with the implementation of their recommendations. When a study is proposed, however, it is a rare client that volunteers to increase the budget by 30 percent in order to enable the consultants to stay with the implementation phase. The economics of consulting dictate that individual consultants move on to another assignment once one is complete. It is very difficult to bring people together after two months to recreate the situation at the conclusion of the study. One way or another, implementation means peoples' time, and that has to be budgeted.

As a result, clients frequently do not invite consultants to help implement their solutions. This issue of implementation is less marked where consultant and client have a relationship in which many studies are performed over a two- or three-year period. In such a situation the consultants are on hand to assist with issues of implementation and have probably remained close enough to those issues to be able to help.

The question of implementation is a vexing one. When a consultant's role is bounded by the identification, analysis, and resolution of a specific problem, implementation is left hanging. There has been an increasing realization that reasonable strategic proposals have proven to be unimplementable in practice. To use the jargon, "The culture of the organization defeats the proposals for strategic change." Many clients believe that a problem has not been resolved successfully unless the solution has been implemented. The consultant's role is therefore not bounded by identification/analysis/resolution. The role includes "agent-of-change" for the process by which the solution is finally implemented. This aspect of a consultant's role is very different from the problem-defining and problem-solving aspects. It involves strong elements of negotiation, compromise, and teaching. The difference is analogous to that involved in giving a man fish or teaching him to fish. The consultant is no longer solving an isolated problem but is involved in a process of organizational development.

Nonetheless, an enormous volume of consulting recommendations that are accepted are not implemented. The fault lies only partly with the consulting firms. The primary responsibility for implementation of changes *must* lie with the company itself. In the long run a consulting study may prove to be a small step in a process that takes years: the process of moving a vast enterprise from one course to another.

WHAT CONSULTANTS DO

A consultant defines, analyzes, and solves problems, as described previously. To this end, he or she gathers relevant data and information, structures it, creates hypotheses, tests them, reaches conclusions, explores the logical implications of the conclusions, and tries to persuade others, notably the client, of the "correctness" of the implications.

The following description is typical. A consultant is approached by an old client. The firm has a problem: Sales growth has slowed and market data show a loss of market share—a major competitor has introduced a successful new product. The competitor has a different organizational structure. Is this the problem?

The consultant goes to the client to discuss the problem in general, but fairly detailed, terms. During the discussion, the consultant suggests that the competitor's product is only stealing share at the margin and that most of its success represents expansion of a new segment. The client has already considered that point but cannot be sure. One problem is the comparability of company data and market research data. Also, the client's corporate owner is focusing on the apparent share-loss data and is suspicious of excuses.

The response to the problem has involved two elements so far. First, data have been requested from the firm's distributors. Second, the distributors have been exhorted to redouble their efforts. The consultant suggests that the use of distributors in itself seems highly constricting. The client agrees, and wonders if the physical distribution should be brought in-house. When this option was last analyzed (sketchily) it appeared uneconomical and, since the company has a single product line, it seems unlikely this situation would have changed significantly. The competitor handles its own physical distribution but has four related product lines. It is one of these lines that is causing the problem.

The consultant suggests an analysis of physical distribution alternatives and a review of the market and its segmentation. Additionally, he suggests an examination of the joint economics of a multiproduct operation in all areas of the business from raw materials through manufacturing, physical distribution, sales, and overhead items. The reason for these avenues is both operational and strategic. The equation on physical distribution contains some calculable elements and some intangible ones. The number of trucks, drivers, calls per day, order quantities, and percentage of total demand within effective radius can all be calculated and compared with known costs of using distributors. In addition, there may be control, information, and flexibility advantages to an in-house distribution system. But over and above these considerations, tangible and intangible, is the strategic question: Is the competitor making inroads precisely because of its advantage (cost or otherwise) in physical distribution? This consideration raises the issue from the level of "make or buy" to "survive or die."

The suggestion to explore joint economics of a wider product line is a direct and logical extension of the possibility that physical distribution economics are strategically critical in this business. Has the client considered this? Yes, but not in the perspective of strategic necessity, only as a potential line extension to be viewed at the margin, on its own merits.

A proposal is requested, in this case without competing bids. The proposal relates the situation and outlines the issues contained within it. It is accepted and the study is performed.

The tasks are threefold. First, a detailed analysis of physical distribution reveals basic errors in previous analyses of this issue. Not only can 90 percent of current sales volume be distributed more cost effectively than through the existing system, but the analysis also reveals vastly different penetration by region. A prospective 30 to 50 percent volume gain should be realized when all distribution is managed by the company. This gain enhances the relative economic value of going direct.

Second, the company's single product is revealed to serve a narrow segment of the whole market. Introduction of new products is unlikely to steal sales from the existing product. On the contrary, there are many economic advantages affecting 70 percent of the costs of new and existing products. In particular, sales, sales administration, physical distribution, storage, raw materials purchasing, inventory holding costs, factory overhead, and general overhead all will show high levels of shared cost with new, related product lines.

Third, the competitor already has three of the five product categories that make up the market. The competitor's introduction of a fourth, and its success, has sparked the client's concern. The study reveals, partly from field research, the competitor's intention to enter the fifth segment (the client's only segment) directly within 12 to 18 months.

The conclusions? The competitor's new product is not a direct threat to the client's own product. The original problem is solved. Distribution should be taken away from independents and brought in-house. It will be cheaper. New products should be researched and brought into the line. A comforting note is that prices should be raised on the existing product, which is not fighting a competitive product. The rival is a serious strategic competitor despite the superficial irrelevance of its successful new product. The result? The competitor's parent, in a totally unrelated move, decides to trim its portfolio and offers the competitor company for sale. The client sees clearly the overwhelming strategic advantages of this and snaps up the rival. Six months before it would have sneered at the offer!

Of course, this is only one way in which a consulting firm can work with a company, but it remains the most common by far: direct involvement in strategy formulation for an operating business unit. The consultant has a role partly because no one in the business unit has time, partly because the consultant is expected to bring a strategic analysis to bear, and partly to arbitrate in a parent-subordinate relationship.

This example is most typical of a client-consultant relationship that poses no radical problems of implementation. The example is a real one. Some problems of organizational culture were evident. The operating unit had a strong, single-product mentality. The economic arguments for changing distribution and product line were resisted emotionally. Some managers identified with this position more than others, of course, and those at the parent company much less than those at the operating unit. Had the situation been more locked in the cultural and perceptual biases of the line managers, the role of the consultant would have been broader. A process of education might have been indicated, working with the management to see the problem more broadly and to effect the necessary change gradually in incremental steps.

Consultants rarely act in this broader role. The reasons are obvious: In order for the consultant to be retained as a problem-definer, problem-solver, *and* solution-implementer, the chief executive must perceive in advance the requirement for such a role to be played.

More often the original problem definition is narrow and presented to the consultant for analysis. Attempts by the consultant to broaden the scope of the study and allow for a period of learning and adjustment to facilitate implementation can be seen as self-interest because of the extra fees required. A great deal of the organizational development conducted by consultants occurs outside the scope (and budget) of specific assignments as part of a consultant-client relationship. In effect, the consultant is paid to solve a problem and then works for the implementation of its solution, more as a means of continuing the client relationship than as an explicit recognition of the importance of professionally managed change.

THE CONSULTANT'S ROLE IN STRATEGIC MANAGEMENT

Strategic management embraces four areas, in all of which consultants have a role to play:

- Corporate strategy formulation
- Business unit strategy formulation
- Strategic planning system design
- General education and transfer of experience

Corporate Strategy Formulation

Issues of corporate strategy are essentially allocation of resource issues. A multiunit corporation should be faced with scarce resource constraints. If not, its human resources will likely relocate and its financial resources should be returned to its shareholders. The pattern of scarce resource allocation can be dictated by two sets of forces. First and most important is the allocation of cash among existing units. A variety of systematic methods exists to guide the allocation of cash to alternative investments within the business units. Traditionally financial in orientation, these systematic methods attempt to channel cash to the specific projects with the highest apparent net present value. More generally, they attempt to favor some units' strategies over others, recognizing that a strategy implicitly contains a stream of investments.

Second, many firms face a "proportion of assets" dilemma. When most of a company's earnings derive from assets in the copper business, for example, it may establish asset mix targets designed to reduce this "dependence." Even very profitable firms are sometimes uncomfortable if too high a proportion of profit comes from a single field. There are theoretical arguments to show that concern over this issue is inappropriate for senior corporate executives. In practice, however, concern for balance, the absence of vulnerability, and avoidance of being acquired are powerful executive motives. Within this area, which relates to resource allocation, lie most major acquisition decisions.

The pattern of resource allocation in a large corporation, whether it is guided by the first set of forces or the second, can be established by consultants. This is in fact a major practice area for several large consulting firms. One firm in particular performs a portfolio analysis that says in essence, "Any unit that returns more than its cost of capital contributes to the value of the firm. Any unit that does not and that cannot be made to do so detracts from the value of the firm and should be sold or liquidated." This message is not profound, although it sometimes takes an outside agent to take a simple theory and apply it objectively to a real company and its operating units.

Consultants also get involved in resource allocation that is guided by the more subjective and often self-serving forces of "portfolio balance" and its first cousin, "major acquisition." Investment banks exert a powerful influence on this aspect of corporate strategy, often with the less-than-wholly objective eye of one who stands to make millions of dollars if a deal is made.

Overall, consultants can act at the corporate level directly to influence the setting of strategy, by establishing and performing a set of analyses relevant to the company's situation. This contrasts with work they may perform to enable a company to set its corporate strategy internally.

Business Unit Strategy Formulation

As with strategy at the corporate level, another role of consultants is to be directly and actively involved in the strategic analysis of the unit. This is still the largest part of the strategy consulting market and the one referred to most often throughout this chapter.

Strategic Planning System Design

A strategy consultant also may be involved in establishing or modifying the set of organizational procedures known as strategic planning. Most U.S. corporations now have implemented planning systems. Despite similarities, they are all quite different. Systems produce plans and thereby fulfill one of the goals set when the systems were created. As strategic planning moves into its second generation, it must cope with very real problems, such as the following:

- Are strategic plans, operating plans, and budgets coordinated?
- Does "planning" report to "finance," and does this limit its effectiveness?
- Does capital budgeting proceed independently of the strategic planning process and thus compromise it significantly?
- Do line managers sabotage and refuse to implement good strategies formulated by others?
- Do line managers formulate good strategies when asked to do so?
- Are strategies mainly based on market trends?
- Why is it so difficult to articulate clearly the basis of competitive differences in a business?

Some of these problems arise from the overselling of strategic planning in the past. If strategic planning is to avoid the fate of operations research and the total marketing concept, it must solve these problems. Consultants are trying to help by their work in redesigning planning systems. Their experience in working with firms of different sizes in different types of business is an essential ingredient in this type of work.

General Education and Transfer of Experience

Some consulting firms provide training as a primary service. There is no major firm in the strategy consulting field, however, for which training is a significant practice. Nevertheless, consultants are intimately involved in training.

Consultants provide help in this area in several ways. In the course of a study, analytical techniques and methods are often transferred from consultants to client personnel. More important, because consulting is not especially technique oriented, there is a transfer of attitudes. A consultant should project his or her generalized methodology: an open-minded pursuit of answers through the application of simple but relevant analyses.

An integral and essential role of consultants is to create the consensus necessary for the implementation of strategic management decisions. As specialists, consultants are in a position to keep up with the stream of developing techniques and philosophies of strategy. Indeed, many of these techniques have been formulated in the consulting arena during the last decade. The consultant must do more than simply "keep up." It is important to evaluate and compare alternative approaches. It is also important to contribute to such developments. The body of knowledge in the strategic management field is growing at such a pace that only specialists seem likely to keep abreast of it.

In addition to acting as educators-by-example, consultants also may offer training seminars. As strategic planning systems have developed, a tradition of annual planning meetings has emerged. A favorite format for such meetings involves one or more guest speakers, often on a topic related to strategy. Consultants are often approached to be involved in these meetings. They may do so as a way of becoming better known in the hope of consideration for future assignments. They may even promote a current approach quite openly. Alternatively, the consultant may prepare specific material for a specific client. Today, consultants are frequently key speakers at public conferences on strategic planning.

In these ways, strategy consultants may play a role not only in the active formulation of strategy at the corporate or business unit levels but also in providing assistance to a company's employees for the enhancement of internal skills that will reach the same end.

Index

[*Chapter numbers are boldface and are followed by a colon; lightface numbers after the colon refer to pages within the chapter.*]

[Chapter numbers are boldface and are followed by a colon; lightface numbers after the colon refer to pages within the chapter.]

*[Chapter numbers are boldface and are followed by a colon; lightface
numbers after the colon refer to pages within the chapter.]*

[Chapter numbers are boldface and are followed by a colon; lightface
numbers after the colon refer to pages within the chapter.]

*[Chapter numbers are boldface and are followed by a colon; lightface
numbers after the colon refer to pages within the chapter.]*

*[Chapter numbers are boldface and are followed by a colon; lightface
numbers after the colon refer to pages within the chapter.]*

[Chapter numbers are boldface and are followed by a colon; lightface numbers after the colon refer to pages within the chapter.]

*[Chapter numbers are boldface and are followed by a colon; lightface
numbers after the colon refer to pages within the chapter.]*

[Chapter numbers are boldface and are followed by a colon; lightface numbers after the colon refer to pages within the chapter.]

[Chapter numbers are boldface and are followed by a colon; lightface numbers after the colon refer to pages within the chapter.]

*[Chapter numbers are boldface and are followed by a colon; lightface
numbers after the colon refer to pages within the chapter.]*

*[Chapter numbers are boldface and are followed by a colon; lightface
numbers after the colon refer to pages within the chapter.]*

[Chapter numbers are boldface and are followed by a colon; lightface numbers after the colon refer to pages within the chapter.]

[*Chapter numbers are boldface and are followed by a colon; lightface
numbers after the colon refer to pages within the chapter.*]

[Chapter numbers are boldface and are followed by a colon; lightface numbers after the colon refer to pages within the chapter.]

[Chapter numbers are boldface and are followed by a colon; lightface numbers after the colon refer to pages within the chapter.]

*[Chapter numbers are boldface and are followed by a colon; lightface
numbers after the colon refer to pages within the chapter.]*

[Chapter numbers are boldface and are followed by a colon; lightface numbers after the colon refer to pages within the chapter.]

[Chapter numbers are boldface and are followed by a colon; lightface numbers after the colon refer to pages within the chapter.]

*[Chapter numbers are boldface and are followed by a colon; lightface
numbers after the colon refer to pages within the chapter.]*

*[Chapter numbers are boldface and are followed by a colon; lightface
numbers after the colon refer to pages within the chapter.]*

[Chapter numbers are boldface and are followed by a colon; lightface numbers after the colon refer to pages within the chapter.]

[*Chapter numbers are boldface and are followed by a colon; lightface
numbers after the colon refer to pages within the chapter.*]

[*Chapter numbers are boldface and are followed by a colon; lightface numbers after the colon refer to pages within the chapter.*]

[*Chapter numbers are boldface and are followed by a colon; lightface numbers after the colon refer to pages within the chapter.*]

[Chapter numbers are boldface and are followed by a colon; lightface numbers after the colon refer to pages within the chapter.]

[Chapter numbers are boldface and are followed by a colon; lightface numbers after the colon refer to pages within the chapter.]

*[Chapter numbers are boldface and are followed by a colon; lightface
numbers after the colon refer to pages within the chapter.]*

[*Chapter numbers are boldface and are followed by a colon; lightface numbers after the colon refer to pages within the chapter.*]

*[Chapter numbers are boldface and are followed by a colon; lightface
numbers after the colon refer to pages within the chapter.]*

*[Chapter numbers are boldface and are followed by a colon; lightface
numbers after the colon refer to pages within the chapter.]*

*[Chapter numbers are boldface and are followed by a colon; lightface
numbers after the colon refer to pages within the chapter.]*

*[Chapter numbers are boldface and are followed by a colon; lightface
numbers after the colon refer to pages within the chapter.]*

[*Chapter numbers are boldface and are followed by a colon; lightface numbers after the colon refer to pages within the chapter.*]

[Chapter numbers are boldface and are followed by a colon; lightface numbers after the colon refer to pages within the chapter.]

[*Chapter numbers are boldface and are followed by a colon; lightface numbers after the colon refer to pages within the chapter.*]

*[Chapter numbers are boldface and are followed by a colon; lightface
numbers after the colon refer to pages within the chapter.]*

[Chapter numbers are boldface and are followed by a colon; lightface numbers after the colon refer to pages within the chapter.]

[Chapter numbers are boldface and are followed by a colon; lightface numbers after the colon refer to pages within the chapter.]

[Chapter numbers are boldface and are followed by a colon; lightface numbers after the colon refer to pages within the chapter.]

[Chapter numbers are boldface and are followed by a colon; lightface numbers after the colon refer to pages within the chapter.]